STANLEY MORISON

STANLEY MORISON

NICOLAS BARKER

MACMILLAN

SBN boards: 333 13136
Library of Congress catalog card no.:76–189157

First published 1972 by
MACMILLAN LONDON LTD
London and Basingstoke
Associated companies in New York Toronto
Dublin Melbourne Johannesburg & Madras

Printed in Great Britain at
THE UNIVERSITY PRINTING HOUSE CAMBRIDGE

D. M.

TIMOTHEO

SIMON

LIST OF ILLUSTRATIONS

Between pages 512 and 513

PREFACE

THE invention of a completely mechanized system of making and composing printer's type at the end of the nineteenth century was an event of as far-reaching importance as Gutenberg's invention four and a half centuries earlier. In the fifty years that followed, the shape of letters was altered as drastically as in the first fifty years of printing. In the revolution, Stanley Morison's career was all-important. But this book is not a history of the typographic revolution, only an account of Morison's life. It touches on the larger story, just as it touches on the institutions with which Morison was connected, the Monotype Corporation, the Cambridge University Press, and *The Times*; but I have tried to set out the history of each only so far as is necessary for an understanding of Morison's part in it.

It has proved difficult enough to discover and assemble the facts of his career. When I told him that I wanted to try to write his life, he said, 'You will find it very difficult, because I have never looked back.' He was not a self-important person, and took little trouble to preserve any memorials of his past. Moreover, he led a very varied life, and tended to keep its different parts in separate compartments. As with his past, this was partly due to a natural secretiveness and partly to dislike of the irrelevant. To reconstruct his life has thus been a difficult task: even those who knew him well could only know the part that concerned them, and about his early days hardly anything was known at all. On the other hand, Morison's memory was, minor details apart, good: such remarks as he made about his youth that can be checked against contemporary documents are surprisingly accurate. When I began work, I was struck by the number of people who likened the pursuit of the details of Morison's life to *The Quest for Corvo*. But any temptation to imitate the model of A. J. A. Symons was easily resisted. With Morison, the quarry was much more important than the quest (he would have made a better pope than poor Rolfe): the need to build a convincing edifice out of the compartments counted more than the way in which the compartments themselves were constructed. I have learnt in the process how frail and unreliable human memory is, compared to documents contemporary with the events that they describe. If the result of this reconstruction too much resembles a Victorian 'Life and Letters' (a discredited form which nevertheless has merits, if properly handled), I can only say that I believe a true verdict on Morison, now and in the future, can only be based on contemporary documents.

I have been extremely fortunate in being able to examine a large amount of Morison's correspondence. My first and greatest debt is to his literary executors, Mr Brooke Crutchley and Mr Arthur Crook, who have let me use Morison's own papers and allowed me to quote from his correspondence and other writings, published and unpublished. Morison enjoyed writing letters, and wrote well, in both senses; his correspondents tended to keep his letters, both for their content and as examples of fine writing. Further, he owed a great deal to his successive secretaries, Mr Murton, Mrs Alexander and Miss Gaskin, who were often asked to do far more than an ordinary secretary would expect. His correspondence was thus large and various. It is unlikely that it will ever be collected, and so I have tried to include a representative collection of his letters. Considerations of space prevented this in the case of the two most extensive and important correspondences, those with D. B. Updike and E. A. Lowe, but I hope that one day they will both be printed in full. Since the invention of the telephone, a man only expresses himself fully to those he rarely sees because they are far away. To Updike and Lowe in America, to Jan van Krimpen in Holland and Hans Mardersteig in Italy, Morison wrote all his news, and I have been very dependent on these sources in constructing the narrative. To Graham Pollard, on the other hand, whom he saw often, Morison rarely wrote at length; but the correspondence lasted for over forty years, and it has been an invaluable source for dating as well as for the course of Morison's learned work.

Lastly, his association with Beatrice Warde, the closest of his life, is represented by a substantial but patchy correspondence (they only wrote to each other when separated by distance), and by Beatrice's vivid and lively letters home to her mother May Lamberton Becker and her grandmother Emma Lamberton. The chronology of this has presented some problems. She rarely dated letters, except by the day of the week; as she wrote to her mother on 4 February 1942,

If I ever year-date my letters, or had the foggiest idea what years things happened in, I should know when this enclosed was written and never finished.

Further, she had any number of private names for Morison: he figures as 'the Serpent', 'Lucifer', 'Mr Jackson', 'Aegidius', in her early letters; there is a brief patch when their circle takes on parts from *The Marriage of Figaro*; finally, they settle down on the old mnemonic for the forms of the Aristotelian syllogism:

Barbara celarent Darii ferioque prioris...

Ferioque is the *dictum de nullo* in its simplest form, and 'ferioque' they were to each other until Morison's sight failed, and he could read no more.

I am deeply grateful for permission to quote from all these letters: to the Huntington and Pierpont Morgan Libraries for those to Updike and Lowe, and to the Universiteits-Bibliotheek, Amsterdam, for van Krimpen's (all three libraries treated me with exceptional generosity, and I am particularly grateful to Mr Carey Bliss, Mr John Plummer and Mr Herman de la Fontaine Verwey for their part in this; I am also much indebted to Dr E. A. Lowe's daughter, Mrs P. L. Pitzele), to Dr Mardersteig, and to the executors of Mrs Warde.

I am further grateful to the following for allowing me to read, copy, and in some cases print letters and documents in their possession: Mrs G. E. Alexander, Greer Allen, Tony Appleton, the late Lord Astor of Hever, the Earl of Avon, Iain Bain, Mrs R. M.

Barrington-Ward, and Mark Barrington-Ward; the Beaver-brook Library, Senator William Benton, the Bodleian Library, Lord Bridges, the Cambridge University Library, and J. C. T. Oates; Martin Carr, C. E. Carrington, William Andrews Clark Memorial Library (whose magnificent Gill collection contains Morison's letters to him), William S. Conway and Miss Edna C. Davies; Dr Hugh Clegg, Douglas Cleverdon, Columbia University Library, New York (where the archives of the American Type Founders Corporation are, with Morison's letters to H. L. Bullen) and Kenneth A. Lohf; Fr Joseph Crehan, John Dreyfus, Mrs H. M. D. Fletcher, Professor M. R. D. Foot, Percy Freer, Sir William Haley, Anthony Heal, Philip Hofer, Ronald Horton, Laurence Irving, Frank Kacmarcik, Sir Geoffrey Keynes, Sir Francis Meynell, the Monotype Corporation, especially Alan Jones and John Goulding; the Metropolitan Museum, New York (the correspondence of F. Warde and H. W. Kent), Mrs Margot C. Munzer, Mr and Mrs Jan Naismith, Professor Ray Nash, The Newberry Library, Chicago, a second home to Morison for many years, where his letters to the library staff and other important modern typographic archives, such as Will Ransom's Frederic Warde collection, are preserved; Simon Nowell-Smith, Professor O. Hood Phillips, Sir James Pitman, A. P. Ryan, Hans Schmoller, Mrs Susan Simon (for letters to Oliver Simon), Paul Standard, Messrs Stephenson Blake and James Blake, Miss Joan Stevenson (for letters to Wickham Steed), Mr and Mrs Reynolds Stone, Mrs Evelyn Wardrop and Jacob Zeitlin.

The only other sort of original document I consulted were certificates of Birth, Baptism, Marriage and Death, and Borough and County Rate Books. I have no complaint about the latter, but facts derived from the former have (as will be seen) proved erroneous; I can only put this down to the general tendency not to feel on oath when filling in official forms. I am grateful to the General Probate Registry at Somerset House, the Greater London Council, Worcestershire and Essex County Record Offices, and the Archivists of the London Boroughs of Camden, Hendon, Highbury, and Haringey for their help.

Among printed sources, I owe a special debt to Mr James Moran; his *Monotype Recorder* on Morison was the first substantial biography, and I have been largely dependent on it, especially for the reminiscences which Mr Moran obtained from Canon Vance, Charles Hobson and Daniel Longwell, who died before I was able to get in touch with them. His *Stanley Morison: his typographic achievement* has appeared since, too late for me to make more than small use of it. I am also very grateful to the late Donald McLachlan, whose biography of R. M. Barrington-Ward, *In the Chair*, has recently appeared. I found it very useful, although I do not believe his estimate of Morison, who deeply admired Barrington-Ward, is correct. I owe to Mr McLachlan's generosity the references to Morison in Barrington-Ward's diary which he copied out for me. I have also leaned on the studies of Morison's typography and writing of John Dreyfus and James M. Wells, and the two exhibition catalogues *Stanley Morison et la tradition typographique* (1966) and *Stanley Morison: a portrait* (1971) compiled by Fernand Baudin and John Barr. The radio portrait of Morison, first broadcast on 2 February 1969, was Douglas Cleverdon's idea and a masterpiece of his art; it also provided me with invaluable material, and I am grateful to him and the contributors. I also owe a large debt to the late S. H. Steinberg, whom to my sorrow I cannot now thank, and to Mrs Christine Steinberg, who allowed me generous access to his papers.

Morison was much loved as well as admired, and it was to this, I feel sure, that I owe in part the always kindly and helpful answers that my many enquiries produced; but I am equally in debt to those, no less kind, for whom my question was the first time that they had heard of Morison. I should like to thank in particular: Frank Altschul, Marcus Arman, J. A. Armitage, R. Page Arnot, A. V. Austin, whose collection of material on the C.O. Work Centre at Wakefield Prison was especially valuable; Giles Barber, John Barr, Alan Bell, Daniel B. Bianchi, David Boulton, Norman Bratt, George Buday, T. F. Burns, Edward Burrett, Ronald Butler, E. H. Carr, Harry Carter, Matthew Carter, Roderick

Cave, William Clarke, whose wide knowledge and accurate memory saved me from many blunders in dealing with the history of *The Times* from 1951 onwards; Douglas A. Cole, Fr T. Corbishley, L. Deval, Lord Devlin, the Dominican Priory, Southampton Road, London; Alick Dru, A. A. Ettinghausen, M. L. Ettinghausen, H. P. R. Finberg, Sir Frank Francis, Miss Jean Fraser; Colonel Ivor Fraser, Rodney Fraser, Dr Funke, Miss Eleanor M. Garvey, M. H. B. Gilmour, A. W. Griffith, the Guildhall Library, City of London; Mr and Mrs R. Hague, Miss P. M. Handover, Sem Hartz, the Surveyor of Historic Buildings to the Greater London Council, Sir Herbert Bennett; Sir Rupert Hart-Davis, Sir Patrick Hennessy, Walter Holmes, Miss Dorothy Horman, Derek Hudson, G. Wren Howard, G. Allen Hutt, Peter Hutton, Ernest Ingham, whose recollection of the Cloister Press and Fanfare days was both accurate and vivid; Dr Hans Jessen, Fr Edward Kelly, St Peter-in-Chains, Hornsey; Professor Dr Horst Kunze, the Law Society, N. P. Lewis, Miss Winifred Lodge, the late H. C. Macro of the Westminster Press, Ronald Mansbridge, Mrs Francis Mathew and Thomas Mathew, Fr Gervase Mathew O.P., James Morris, Howard Nixon, the North London Homes for the Blind and Major W. F. Eyre, Richard Ormond Owen's (Boys) School, C. G. A. Parker, Mrs Esther Potter, Warren E. Preece, the late J. Holroyd Reece, Adam Roberts, Dr Julius Rodenberg, Miss J. Rosenberg, Professor Charles Ryskamp, R. Ruzicka, Dr Hugh J. Schonfield, Walter Shewring, Miss Muriel Silk, J. S. G. Simmons, Albert Sperisen, A. A. M. Stols, Sir Campbell Stuart, A. J. P. Taylor, Denis Tegetmeier, *The Times*, and in particular the late John Maywood, W. R. A. Easthope, Jack Lonsdale and J. A. Phillips; the Victoria and Albert Museum, and Miss Irene Whalley; Mr and Mrs John Walker, G. Wheatcroft, E. I. Watkin, Rev. Duncan M. Whyte and the staff of the London City Mission; Douglas Woodruff, Mrs Kurt Wolff, Miss Julia Wrightson and H. Youngman.

All or part of the text was read by John Barr, John Carter, Peter Clarke, Arthur Crook, Brooke Crutchley, John Dreyfus, Richard Garnett, Sir William Haley, James Moran, James Mosley,

A. P. Ryan, Donald Tyerman and James Wells, and I am very grateful for their criticism and advice; the proofs were read by John Barr and Edward Leeson, who saved me from many errors. Those that no doubt survive are all mine.

I have three special debts to acknowledge. I cannot sufficiently thank the London Library, and its staff. The library contains almost all the books I needed to consult – a remarkable holding, since typography is not one of its primary interests. Its open shelves led me to others of which I would not otherwise have known. I was able to take out many books, an inestimable advantage since most of the writing had to be done by night. To John Carter, whose long and close association with Morison must be inferred *ex silentio* (they saw each other too often to need much correspondence), I owe many insights while the work was in progress. My final debt is to Ellic Howe, who first suggested the idea of a biography of Morison to me, and with whom I have since been able to discuss its progress with pleasure and profit.

It is a convention to acknowledge help received in writing a book, and almost as much of a convention to give help. There was nothing conventional about the measure of help I was given, by those named above and countless others, and I am correspondingly grateful for it.

INTRODUCTION

THE letters in the formal inscriptions of Periclean Athens are square, monoline, sans-serif capitals. That is, the breadth of a full-sized letter is about the same as its height; the strokes of which each letter is composed are of unvarying thickness; the ends of the strokes are without terminal cross-strokes; and there is no variety in form, no 'large' and 'small' letters. The letters now before the reader are oblong, stressed, seriffed, and varied in form: taller than wide, the strokes varying in thickness and with cross-strokes at the end, a combination of capitals and minuscules. This transformation took 2000 years to achieve, and another 500 to refine to this particular form. Stanley Morison made a contribution of lasting importance to the history of this first period: his practical part in the latter process – the period dominated by the invention of printing – was even more considerable. The influence he had on the form of letters developed in the first half of this century is all-pervasive, and it is an influence inseparable from the history of letter-forms, which he did so much to organize.

The form of letters is inseparable from the means by which it is achieved. The Greek inscriptions took the shape they have because they were engraved on stone. The serif was added as the Greeks became more acquainted with the older civilizations of the Middle East; it probably derives from the wedges, made with a stylus in clay, of the cuneiform scripts used there. The Romans had a native script, called 'Rustic', narrow and painted with a brush, which gave it its stress, the thick and thin strokes which a brush naturally produces. Married with the Greek inscriptional letters, this produced the Roman capitals, such as those on the Trajan Column, which are universally familiar.

Below these formal letters were a diversity of informal, mostly pen-made, scripts which, with the decline of the Roman Empire, began to be promoted. One of the most successful of these, the uncial, perhaps originating in north Africa, took hold in Western Europe. It had a large part in forming the beautiful Irish scripts (it was in Ireland that the tradition of learning was preserved in the Dark Ages); these were brought by the Irish missionaries to the Continent, and there mingled with native cursives and the revived Roman capitals. Out of this, in the time of Charlemagne, came a new organized script, the so-called 'Carolingian minuscule'. In the Middle Ages, this developed into the various Gothic scripts, of which a round form, originating in the law-schools of Bologna, dominated the south, and an oblong form (which in England came to be called 'Black-letter') the north. At the end of the Middle Ages, the new influence of humanistic scholarship brought a revival of the simpler pre-Gothic forms, and this, mixed with the newly discovered Roman inscriptional capitals, became the roman letters as we know them today. The same movement also developed a sloped or cursive version, ancestor of the modern italic.

So far the forms of letters were all unique, the product of pen, brush or chisel on paper, vellum, metal, wood or stone; variation was due to the interaction of these means of production. The invention of printing brought a new dimension to the design of letters: the possibility of duplicating the same form. This (not the press itself, a piece of equipment common to several trades before Gutenberg's time) was the crucial part of the invention, and it depended on the mould in which metal type was cast, which could be varied according to the width of the character, from narrow i to wide m. In the mould the hollow matrix which produced the relief type was placed. The matrix itself was produced by striking into it a steel punch with a letter, engraved by hand, on the end of it. The art of engraving steel punches was a slow, difficult and skilled business; there have never been more than a few craftsmen fully competent to perform it.

Gutenberg (or his engraver) was one such, and his gothic types have never been equalled. Nicolas Jenson, the great fifteenth-century Venetian printer, had fine versions of both gothic and roman types. One of the first known punchcutters was Francesco Griffo, who worked for the other great Venetian printer, Aldus. He produced the roman letter (in Morison's judgement the finest ever cut) on which the type used here is based; he also produced the first italic type. He was the first to break away from the manuscript models used hitherto, and to let the act of engraving and his own judgement have their part in forming the letter. It was in his form that the roman letter finally overcame the rivalry of the gothic and other scripts. In the sixteenth century, dominance in the art of punchcutting passed to France, notably to Claude Garamond and Robert Granjon. Their work was preserved, enlarged and multiplied by other hands, notably the Antwerp printer Christophe Plantin and the typefounders (and also engravers) Guillaume Le Bé *père et fils* of Paris and Jacques Sabon, manager of the Egenolff-Berner foundry at Frankfurt. These types persisted all over Europe up to the end of the eighteenth century.

Christoffel van Dijck among others in Holland, and the German typefoundries at Leipzig and Frankfurt took over in the seventeenth century, with a taste for a narrower, thicker letter (William Caslon produced a native English version of it, less narrow, early in the eighteenth century). This had a perceptive influence on the printing type devised by Louis XIV's Académie des Sciences in 1692, although the new spirit of scientific enquiry called for letters constructed by pure geometry; it was, in fact, the first 'modern face'. The eighteenth century produced typographic reflections of the rococo and classic trends in the work of Simon-Pierre Fournier in France and John Baskerville in England. It was left to Giovanni Battista Bodoni in Parma to carry Louis XIV's *romain du roi* to its logical conclusion. Hitherto, 'old-face' types with a diagonal stress (such as the pen naturally produces) had predominated, following the example of Griffo. The vertically stressed modern face, popularized by Bodoni and the Didots, lasted through the nineteenth century, becoming more and more sharply cut till letters became almost painfully dazzling. The only relief was the first 'sans-serif' and 'Egyptian' types introduced with the vogue for neo-classicism.

At the end of the century came a reaction, which took two directions. Infinitely the slighter (if of much greater significance later) was the tendency to simplicity and the 'artistic' sans serif, pioneered by Stefan George and Melchior Lechter. Far more dominant was the example of the medievalists, especially William Morris. It is true that William Pickering, the first archaist in typography, revived Caslon's type about 1840, but it was William Morris and the Kelmscott Press, followed by T. J. Cobden-Sanderson and the Doves Press, who set the typographic style for the generation in which Morison grew up. Morris preferred ornament, Cobden-Sanderson the severer style of the earliest books printed in roman type; both acknowledged the example of Nicolas Jenson, and both set a high standard, in craftsmanship and materials, which put to shame those current in letter-design and printing generally.

But in the conditions then prevalent it was impossible for the commercial printer to do more than admire, from a respectful distance, what they achieved; the standard was too high to be imitated. (For other reasons, the Aesthetic and Art Nouveau movements, so influential in other applied arts, did not make any great or lasting impression either on the design or technique of printing.) There were exceptions. A. W. Pollard's articles on Geoffroy Tory and other famous printers in the *Century Guild Hobby Horse* in 1886–8 had shown how good printing had been in the past. Emery Walker, whose first lecture to the Arts and Crafts Society had been an inspiration to Morris, had both supported him and Cobden-Sanderson, and also formed a bridge between them and the ordinary printer. His influence was, however, more fruitfully exercised in two other directions.

He encouraged C. R. Ashbee to add the Essex House Press to his other craft activities, and when Ashbee moved his Guild to Chipping Camden he met (through Joseph Thorp) Bernard Newdigate, then struggling to revive an ailing printing business. Under his influence, and with the help of Paul Woodroffe, an artist member of the Chipping Camden community, Newdigate launched the Arden Press in 1904, the first ordinary printing house to interpret Morris's message at a commercial level.

More important than this was the first class in calligraphy, given by Edward Johnston at the Central School of Arts and Crafts on 21 September 1899. It was W. R. Lethaby, not Walker, who was the prime mover in this, and the revival of calligraphy, an art more totally lost than fine printing, owes everything to Johnston. His importance extends outside fine writing alone, since calligraphy lies at the root of lettering in all forms. In this, Johnston was as original and creative an influence as Morison himself. This was not missed by his contemporaries. Robert Bridges and his wife, already interested in calligraphy, were quick to see Johnston's unusual gifts; his work made the short-lived magazine *The Imprint* so influential; the sans-serif letter that he devised for the London Underground set that form on its successful way. It is only sad that nothing came of the book that he and Morison planned.

But none of this was to be seen in ordinary printing. The quality of the printing was generally poor, and types of poor and distorted design abounded. In America, at the Riverside and Merrymount presses at Boston, there were signs that new standards might be emerging, but from America too had just sprung the most distorted type-design of them all, the architect Bertram Goodhue's Cheltenham, later Morison's special *bête noire*. The contrary pressures of Aestheticism and technology, and the gradual disappearance of the craftsman as a mediating force between the artist and the machine, had reduced standards generally to a very low level.

But the knot was about to be cut, and, unexpectedly, not by the dominant artist but the despised machine. Throughout the nineteenth century art had withdrawn from printing, and the main influence on its development had been that of technical innovation. The increased speed of the mechanically powered printing press (and of communications generally) had concentrated attention on the means of speeding up composition – the art of assembling letters, not designing them. After many experiments, the break-through came with the invention, by Linn Boyd Benton of Milwaukee in 1885, of the mechanical engraving machine. This, harnessed by Tolbert Lanston to a machine for casting single type (Monotype) and by Ottmar Mergenthaler to a line-casting machine (Linotype), enabled steel punches to be made as easily as ordinary type hitherto. It was as decisive to letter-design as the invention of the variable type-mould in the fifteenth century. Like the first printers, however, the Monotype and Linotype companies were content to follow existing models. It was left to Stanley Morison to see, like Griffo in 1494, the new qualities immanent in the new process, and to revolutionize, more thoroughly than anyone since then, the design of letters for print.

1

STANLEY MORISON was born in 1889, on 6 May, the feast of St John *ante portam Latinam*, the patron saint of printers.* He was born at Kent Villa, Tavistock Road, Wanstead, one of two pairs of small semi-detached houses, into which his parents had moved a few months earlier. They had been living in London before, and their move out to Essex was probably the result of a number of considerations. First of all, with a second child on the way, they would have wanted something larger than rented lodgings. Again, it was a pleasant, still countrified part of the world, on the fringe of Epping Forest (where William Morris grew up). There were few houses, most of them old, a fine inn, the Eagle, with a large pond opposite, and trees in abundance. Wanstead itself was away to the south-east. But it was also an up-and-coming part of the world. A large part of Wanstead had been common land, the subject of a long Chancery action a few years earlier between the new Borough Council and a group of traditional proprietors which had gone in favour of the Borough. Rapid development was the result, and property – this was a last cogent reason for moving there – was cheap. The little development in Tavistock Road, off Woodford Road, is a typical speculative builder's development, its detail a debased version of the Venetian Gothic popularized by Ruskin; it was still new when the Morisons arrived. They stayed there until the middle of 1893, and then returned to London.* It was the longest period that Morison spent outside the metropolis in his life.

Morison was not inclined to look back at his own past, and only once did he turn his mind to his own forebears. After his mother's death in 1951, he received a little box in which she had kept family mementoes – certificates of marriages and birth, some old diaries of her own, photographs, the report of the 'Edith

Cole' Home for Dogs for 1918, a watercolour of a guinea-pig 'Topsy', and a clipping of fine fair hair wrapped up in half a leaf from *The Chemists' and Druggists' Diary* for 1884, inscribed 'Sunday, Feb. 15 1891. Stanley's hair. I cut it short like a boy for the first time. A.M.'. The contents of the box startled Morison into making a note or two: first of the date when his hair was first cut, then 'Parents of A. A. Morison . . . Morison & Marmorice Nash, Bedford House, Malvern', and finally 'Charles Saxon Orson? b. Marlborough Wilts, Charles Cole b. May 10 1778, Mary Cole b. Feb 13 1776'.

It is not clear what the source of these notes was; it was not among the material that his mother left. The note on his paternal grandparents is not correct, but the precise dates of the births of his maternal great-great-grandparents, Charles and Mary Cole, suggest that he was not drawing entirely on his memory. From then on the line is clear. Their son John was baptised at Kidderminster in Worcestershire on 24 March 1812. He married Jane Smith, a Shropshire girl, in 1833, and five years later they had a son called Charles. It is possible that the family moved to London; it was there on 9 June 1860, at St George's, Bloomsbury, that Charles married Julia Anne Jane, daughter of Charles Saxon Orson, 'artist' according to the marriage certificate (he was in fact a dancing-master). Both were living near by, Charles Cole at 19 Bury Street and Julia Orson at 9 Bloomsbury Market.

By 5 March 1863, when their daughter Alice Louisa was born, they had moved east to Whitechapel; Charles Cole was then a broker's clerk. Twenty years later he had changed his job to be a brewer's collector, and moved eastwards again: by 1880, the Coles were established at 7 Gore Road South, Hackney, a large and by then rather old-fashioned house on the edge of Victoria Park (it is now demolished). On 4 June 1887, Alice Louisa Cole married Arthur Andrew Morison, a commercial clerk, at the Clapton Park Congregational Chapel. She must have met her husband locally, for he was also living in Hackney at 13 Bodney Road, a new house not unlike Kent Villa.* This was the Morison's home until they moved to Wanstead, and it was here that their first child, Jessie Emma, was born on 29 March 1888.

It is significant that Arthur Morison gave his father's occupation as 'Solicitor', which he never was. By all accounts (but only the Cole side of the story survives) he was of a feckless and uncontrolled disposition, and it would be in character if, having so far lost contact with his family that he could risk a lie, he made them out to be grander than they were. Curiously enough, like the Coles, they came from Worcestershire, and seem to have been established in Malvern at least by the 1830s. A William Morison was living at Great Malvern in 1835, when he was described as 'brewer and coal merchant'. 'Andrew Morrison' (so spelt) was a 'lodging house keeper' there in 1842, and appears twice in the register of electors for 1843, once at Bredon House, and again at Holyrood and Newlie House. William Morrison, Arthur's father, regularly spelt his name with two r's. He lived first at Deveron House, moving to Trafalgar House in 1845 and to Link Farm in 1852. The last move may have been the result of his marriage, to a widow called Emma Bellers (*née* Mason). In 1854 he is described as 'farmer and tax-collector', and he seems to have been a coal-merchant as well. On 13 January 1856 Arthur Andrew Morison was born, and two years later the family left Link Farm; William, like Andrew, became a lodging-house keeper, and in 1860 and 1863 is so recorded at Bedford House in Great Malvern. By 1868 he had apparently gone.*

These fitful glimpses of Morison's ancestry provide very little scope for the student of heredity. Doubtless there is more to find out (who, for example, was the Marmorice Nash of Morison's note, after whom his younger sister was named?) but so far there is little to explain where any of Morison's extraordinary and diverse talents came from. A little more can be read in the photographs of his parents – his mother, plain but forceful; his father, handsome in a rather vapid way – but that is all. When the Morisons leave Wanstead, they disappear temporarily from view. It is probable that they returned to London; they may have gone to live with the Coles, who had moved to Cazenove Road,

Stamford Hill, to the north of their old house in Hackney.* At all events, they are next to be found near by, between Harringay and Hornsey, at 123 Fairfax Road, into which they moved late in 1896 or early in 1897.* It was in this neighbourhood that Morison lived for the next sixteen years, and in these unpromising surroundings that his passionate love of London was formed.

It was a poor area built up, like so much of London in the last quarter of the nineteenth century, along a railway artery. The railway that divides Hornsey and Harringay was the Great Northern Railway, to all who have been brought up on it the most romantic of all the main lines. The luxuries of the bright red Midland (the first to introduce Pullman coaches), the austere dignity of the black London and North Western, the royal blue Caledonian, the gay gold livery of the London, Brighton and South Coast, the solid splendour of the Great Western, with its gold and green locomotives and chocolate and cream stock – all these have their adherents. But the emerald green engines and plain varnished teak carriages of the Great Northern were irresistible. In Patrick Stirling the railway had a locomotive superintendent of genius, in whom daring technical experiment was allied with a keen aesthetic sensibility. He set a style which his successors Ivatt and Gresley, although distinguished in their own right, were content to follow. The austere cab, tall lipped funnel and domeless boiler of his locomotives were distinct from all other designs. The most beautiful of all was the famous '8-Foot single', with its one pair of huge driving wheels, which first pulled the 'Flying Scotchman' out of King's Cross, and which in the year before Morison was born had broken all records in the 'Race to Edinburgh' between the east-coast and west-coast routes.*

The railway ran along an embankment at the end of Fairfax Road, and the trains were easily visible between the houses of the road – Wightman Road – parallel with the railway that closed Fairfax Road at its western end. The temptation to dawdle on the way to and from school must have been considerable. Not only were there the outside-cylinder 'singles' that pulled the great northern expresses, but the inside-cylinder 'singles' that worked the Cambridge line, the first four-coupled locomotives that Ivatt introduced, 'saddle-back' tank-engines shunting in the new Harringay goods depot, and in 1898 the excitement of a novelty, Ivatt's first small 'Atlantic', almost as beautiful as the 'single' itself and as important a technical innovation.

All this splendour came back to Morison in vivid detail when many years later he achieved the summit of every boy's ambition – a ride on the footplate of the 'Flying Scotsman'.

At Liverpool Street I had learnt to love the rich blue livery of the Great Eastern Railway, holidays had revealed the dark green of the South Eastern, I had lost my heart to the dazzling orange of the London, Brighton and South Coast. But from the moment that my family settled in the suburb served by the G.N.R. and I saw, day after day, the splendour of a Patrick Stirling, the others lost all their interest to my eyes. The majesty of the eight-foot driving wheels, the elegance of the pistons at full speed – I needed no more to become besotted with the G.N.R. for life. At that time I loved its rails, signals, points, sidings, coaches, every kind of rolling stock, and above all its locomotives.

My daily journeys on the line, when I was still going to school, gave me the opportunity to make furtive visits to the engine sheds, to strike up acquaintance with a friendly fireman, a guard, or a signalman. That is how I learnt to pull a signal, grease an axle, and at night to wave a lantern. I worked so hard and so well that soon I got introduced to an engine-driver, and at six o'clock in the morning on a school holiday, I had my first ride on an engine, one of the small ones used for shunting the coal trains in the neighbourhood.*

But the railway was also the way to school. Morison was sent to Owen's school, a long-established grammar school with strong city connections, close to the Angel, on the border of Islington and Finsbury. He would go to Hornsey station and be whisked into King's Cross where the early-morning expresses would be waiting to depart. From there, it was either a stiff walk up the steep hill of Pentonville Road, or an 'inside' on the horse bus if the weather was bad (but it was slower than walking); the brand-new electric 'tube' railway was not yet ready – the extension of the City and South London through the Angel and King's Cross

27

to Euston was not built until 1906–7. No record of his career at Owen's survives, nor was Morison apt to recall his schooldays, except to say – perhaps unwarrantably – how little formal education he received: a glimpse of one master, kind and patient with a slow shy boy, and of another, less kindly remembered – but no more.

Excursions and amusements were rare enough to be better remembered. It was perhaps after a visit to the zoo that the six-year-old Morison first strayed south to the Nash terraces, which, as remotely beautiful as the Himalayas, must then have seemed beyond envy. Forty-six years later, by now living in those once-remote terraces, he was to recall that first sight, as he watched from the roof the bombs falling and the fires blazing, destroying all his possessions and much of the London in which he had grown up.*

There were other excitements besides railways and architecture. Chief of these was his aunt. Edith Cole was seven years younger than her sister Alice, and much prettier. On Boxing Day 1889 she made her theatrical début as the second housemaid in *Jack and the Beanstalk* at Drury Lane. Did her sister and brother-in-law leave their son to see it? If so, it was one of the few occasions that Morison missed a good pantomime; it was his favourite kind of dramatic entertainment. In 1891 she made her name by taking the principal boy's part at the Theatre Royal, Bradford, at only an hour's notice. She specialized from then on in travesty parts, touring as the Earl of Shrewsbury in *Joan of Arc* and Escamillo in *Carmen Up-to-Date*. She then switched to tragic and *femme fatale* roles, for which – her beautiful features were more than a little soulful – she was admirably cast. Her first great success came when she took the part of Josephine in *A Royal Divorce* at the Grand Theatre, Islington; and, if she lost Napoleon in the play, she gained a real husband in the imposing shape of W. W. Kelly, an American impresario seventeen years older than she, who had come to England in 1886 and was then lessee and manager of the Grand Theatre.

Edith went from triumph to triumph: as Frances Vere in *The*

28

Worst Woman in the World and Claire Forster in *A Woman in the Case*, she became famous. In 1910, the Kellys moved to Liverpool, where Edith's husband became the owner of his own theatre, later called the Shakespeare Theatre. Here Edith scored again, as Madge Thomas in *Strife*, and as Miladi in an adaptation of *The Three Musketeers*, which opened as the First World War broke out. What the Coles and the Morisons thought of this pyrotechnic career can only be guessed. In later life, when the Kellys had settled in Liverpool and Edith had thrown herself, as generously as histrionically, into the establishment and promotion of the National Canine Defence League, Mrs Morison found her whirlwind visits to London rather a trial. But that was hardly to be wondered at. In the meantime Aunt Edith's striking appearance and career were not without influence upon her nephew.*

My dear wife Carrie and I have just been a week in our new house, 'The Laurels', Brickfield Terrace, Holloway – a nice, six-roomed residence, not counting basement, with a front breakfast-parlour. . . . We have a nice little back-garden which runs down to the railway. We were rather afraid of the noise of the trains at first, but the landlord said we should not notice them after a bit, and took £2 off the rent. He was certainly right; and beyond the cracking of the garden wall at the bottom, we have suffered no inconvenience.*

The Pooters' house was a little older than the one into which the Morisons moved at the turn of the century – Harringay was developed later than Holloway – but that apart the situation was identical. By 1900 they were established at 107 Wightman Road, a very ordinary terrace villa with its stained-glass light over the front door and the garden running down to the main line at the back; it was Morison's home until he was twenty-three. The family had increased again: Edith Marmorice, her brother's favourite, was born on 9 August 1899. When, two months later, Mrs Morison registered the birth, she gave her place of residence as 123 Allison Road, which was probably a slip of the pen for '126'. There William Charles Cole, probably Mrs Morison's

29

brother, had come to live earlier in the year, and it seems likely that she had moved there with the baby at Michaelmas to be out of the way, while the rest of the family moved into Wightman Road.* It was, to all appearances, an ordinary family, amid very ordinary surroundings. They took their holidays on the Kent coast, like the Pooters, and no doubt had their troubles with tradesmen and neighbours. But all was far from well.

It was not a specially eventful period in Morison's life, but it was not on that account that he preferred not to remember it. He had much to trouble him. There was his father, the most immediate of his distresses. Arthur Morison was as unlike Mr Pooter as can be: not for him the small joys and miseries of a sedentary life in a city office and hum-drum suburban society, confided *in toto* to wife and diary. He was by now a commercial traveller, reputedly for a City firm of textile merchants, near St Paul's Churchyard. He was often away from home, and it is all too clear – to return to *The Diary of a Nobody* – that his evenings were not spent in the modest company of Cummins and Gowing, but with the likes of the odious Farmerson and Lupin's disreputable friends. He drank too much (Morison never touched whisky, recollecting what it had done to his father), and the mixture of drink and guilt made him violent at home. Eventually the strain became too much and he left his family. This was no doubt an immediate hardship for them, but it was also release from a nightmare. From 1905, 107 Wightman Road is recorded as the domicile of Mrs Morison only,* and so far as possible the family tried to forget that Arthur had ever existed; on the one or two occasions that he re-entered their lives, it was like the recurrence of a bad dream.

In 1903 Morison left school – perhaps already the family needed his earnings – and found his first job as an office boy at six shillings a week, in what he later called a 'shady mining syndicate'.* This classic phrase might have come straight out of his favourite Sherlock Holmes; but whatever the risks that beset his first steps in the world he escaped them. He kept a shilling of his wages for himself, which would not pay for much. But his pleasures were not expensive. Like any other boy, he waited impatiently through the week for Saturday afternoon to come, and with it the chance to visit the British Museum.

I first began regular Saturday attendance, with a note book, when I left school and went to work for my living. The rules excluded from The Reading Room students who were under the age of 21. I probably benefited from the rule, though I did not think so at the time. The fact was that in place of the multitude of books to which a Reading Room ticket would then have given me access, I was bound to give my attention to and take my notes from the objects displayed to the public by the keepers of the several departments of antiquities. Thus I became familiar with the Assyrian, Egyptian, Mediaeval, and other departments. I shall never forget those gigantic winged man-headed bulls that in those days guarded the entrance to the Assyrian Saloon. It must be something like 45 years since I first set eyes on the Rosetta Stone, and began to wonder why the several branches of the human family wrote in the funny ways they did.*

These visits were supplemented by reading, already catholic in its taste and scope. He was still only fourteen 'when the original two-volume edition of Frazer's *Golden Bough* reached the suburban public libraries'* – Morison learnt a lot in those public libraries and never ceased to give thanks for the benefactions of Andrew Carnegie. Besides libraries, bookshops also played an important part in his education.

In those days the most conspicuous edifice near the Museum devoted to books was situated at the corner of Museum Street and New Oxford Street. Here was Mudie's 'Select' Library. The word 'select' implied less a degree of specialisation than a correspondence with the taste of the 'select', but declining, number of people who preferred the atmosphere of the old 'Circulating Library' to that of the new sort of 'Public Library' that was being erected in the London Boroughs under the stimulus of Andrew Carnegie's benefactions. Mudie's was a place where the 'select' exchanged 2-volume biographies and 3-volume novels. Some of the members either gossiped there or crossed opposite to tea or coffee at the Vienna Cafe situated at the junction with Bloomsbury Street – on the corner now occupied by Barclay's Bank.

Crossing south over Oxford Street and bearing left, one stopped at the shop of David Nutt, a bookseller who specialised in French, German, Italian and Scandinavian literature, history, philosophy and economics. Many of these volumes were displayed in his large window. It was always worth studying. One who had not the means to purchase had thereby news of the latest arrivals from Paris, Rome, Milan, Berlin and Berne.

Crossing the Circus, avoiding Monmouth Street and passing the French Hospital on the left down Shaftesbury Avenue, one quickly arrived at the Charing Cross Road. Here, situated at No. 78, was another bookshop of 'specialist' interest before 1914 and after 1918. The shop was devoted to antiquarian and modern books principally on philosophy and linguistics. The proprietor, Mr Richard Jäschke, was a man of immense knowledge, depth and range of reading, who was specially interested in Slavonic languages.

Mr Jäschke was formidable in learning, but less remarkable for his commercial ability. Timid by nature, he disliked the increasing bustle of the street and the acceleration of business. He occupies a special place in the esteem of one who, as a Londoner and autodidact, was dependent on the Regent Street Polytechnic, the Tottenham Court Road Y.M.C.A. and the Charing Cross Road bookseller as his tutors. I was one of the lucky ones who as a boy was able, thanks to the Education Act of 1870, to leave school at fourteen, with an abundant sense of curiosity.

Mr Jäschke interested himself in my various questions, and at a time when means were slight, obtained for me specimen copies, free, gratis and for nothing, of the *Révue Historique*, *Historische Zeitschrift* and other learned journals. I have never ceased to be grateful to Mr Jäschke for opening to me the world of specialist criticism by specialists; also, for allowing me unlimited time to peruse the books that I could not afford to buy.*

For some reason – perhaps it was only the small rise involved, or it may have been the influence of the Coles reasserted after his father's disappearance – Morison did not stay long in his first job. In February 1905, he joined the London City Mission as a clerk, at a salary of £26 a year, increased at the end of the first year to £39.* The London City Mission may already have come into Morison's life. It was founded in 1835 with the object, like so many of the London missions, of bringing spiritual help to the vast new poor areas of London that grew throughout the nineteenth century. It maintained a field force of missionaries, working from the 'mission halls' built in the district in need of evangelization. Its special sphere was people at work, 'men in factories, on railways, in common lodging houses, and also theatrical employees'. It also provided holidays and days in the country for wives and children. It was from the start an inter-denominational movement, and is still run by a committee based upon an equal representation of Church of England and Non-conformist members.

The main office of the Mission when Morison joined was in Bridewell Place, close to Ludgate Circus and a stone's throw from the St Bride Foundation Institute which, then as now, contained the best collection of books on printing in the world. But this was before Morison's interest was aroused, and there is no sign that he visited the library so early. Nor does it seem likely that the work of the Mission ever engaged his attention: it was just a job that earned his living.

The family found it difficult to make both ends meet. After his father left – perhaps even before – Mrs Morison had had to look for the means to support her three children, to which the earnings of the second could have been no more than a contribution. Evidently her parents were unable to provide enough, and she became a shop-keeper, at a tobacconist's in Brecknock Road, Holloway, just off Camden Road. It was a convenient place, a short walk from the G.N.R. station at Holloway Road, itself only a few minutes' journey from Hornsey.* It is probable that she began to work there before Morison left school. In later life, he had vivid memories of buying the family supplies of fruit and vegetables in the Chapel Street market, on the other side of the Angel from Owen's. The heavy bag used to cut his hands on the long walk back to Brecknock Road to pick up his mother, a misery hardly relieved by the jellied eels, winkles and whelks to be bought at Manze's fish shop on the way.

But, if times were hard and work uninteresting, these were not the only problems that Morison had to meet. His mother was no ordinary person. Faced with the consequences of a disastrous marriage, she surmounted her difficulties with fortitude and independence of mind: she was not going to inflict her troubles on other people. Her parents were no doubt conventional in their life and beliefs: she was not. She had a keen and sceptical mind, with a natural if untaught tendency to philosophic and political thought, uncommon in a woman of her background at that time. Something of the strength of her personality can be seen in her face, and it must have been from her that Morison inherited some of his own strong character.

Her own beliefs were not so rare in the time and class into which she was born. They could be summed up as a militant agnosticism, a dogmatic free thought, linked with radical political opinions – a mixture that goes back to Thomas Paine. It is no coincidence that Paine's works were printed by the thousand in the last decades of the nineteenth century, and bought hungrily by the often uneducated but now literate working class. Mrs Morison was not 'working class', but her experiences had brought her to a very similar point of view. She could not, like others with the same opinions, refine them by the kind of education offered at the working-men's colleges that sprang up at this time; she was self-educated, with all the self-educated's strength and weaknesses.

On the evidence of Morison's account of his early reading, she must have been a member of the Rationalist Press Association (founded 1899). Besides publishing the works of the English pioneers of free thought, Conway, Clodd, McCabe, Gould and Holyoake, the Association also issued a cheap series of 'Sixpenny Publications', which included Huxley's *Lectures and Essays* and *Man's Place in Nature*, Sir Leslie Stephen's *An Agnostic's Apology*, Herbert Spencer's *Education: Intellectual, Moral and Physical* and his *Essays*, Renan and Hume, and the ubiquitous Ernst Haeckel, represented by *The Riddle of the Universe*, *Wonders of Life* and *The Evolution of Man* (a bargain, at one shilling for two large volumes). There were books on Spencer, Haeckel and Thomas Paine, and in 1909 the centenary of Paine's death was celebrated by a three-volume selection of his works.

No doubt Morison learnt her opinions early on. As far as Paine went, there was much in them that he liked and never left. He shared her distrust of all human authority, although he never ceased to be fascinated by its ways. Like her, he cultivated independence, and distrusted any form of convention or organization, traits that again never left him. He inherited from her an early socialist political opinion and a hatred of the capitalist system. But he came to differ from her when it came to rejecting all authority. If she had a strong personality, his was much stronger, and, perhaps instinctively and less rationally than he was later inclined to suppose, he came to look for authority, some framework in which to control his own strength of personality. He was convinced that, without such a framework, he would have been a very wicked man indeed. On the other hand, he had as well an almost uncontrollable longing and compassion, which contrasted so oddly with his strong rationality, and this must have been difficult to fit in with his mother's austere incredulity. A phrase from the psalms – 'Sicut cervus desiderat ad fontes aquarum – used often to recur to him in after life.*

But, with all these considerations, it is still difficult to imagine how he came to look for the solution – the complete solution for him – in the Roman Catholic Church. He made it sound so simple: 'bred a Victorian agnostic who found Huxley, Spencer and Haeckel insufficient guides to the kind of life he decided to live [he] submitted to the Roman Church in 1909. This act on the part of a man who was aware of his own constitutional lack of humility profoundly affected his subsequent thought and action.'* So indeed it did; but his 'constitutional lack of humility' was only part of the story.

What brought him to 'hang around Farm Street', to argue with a priest there, 'a complete stranger smelling faintly of port',* and to take up with the London Jesuit community at all? It was a long journey from Ludgate Circus – the Mayfair of those days abutted on a still almost rural Hyde Park. Perhaps the most likely cause is the simplest: Father Thurston, his first and closest friend at Farm Street, was the leading Catholic apologist of the time, and Morison may well have heard or read one of his many public utterances in defence of the Church. Herbert Thurston (1856–1939) was one of the few equipped to attract and hold Morison's exploring mind. He was at once a distinguished liturgiologist, a historian, an apologist (his historical learning deflated most of the rather naïve anti-Catholic arguments based on history), and investigator of psychic phenomena and bogus clergy; he had limitless curiosity and industry and wrote often, easily and well. He was also a sensitive and humane spiritual adviser. Altogether, he was a person of such calm resolution, such omniscient solidity, that he could well provide the answer to the problems that occupied Morison's mind.*

It is not to be supposed that the answer came at once, nor without long trial and argument. Chance and emotion had their part in the process. Before he was received, perhaps in the summer of 1907, Morison went on his first holiday abroad, to Belgium; these were the days when it was cheaper than England, even allowing for the fare. On the boat Morison met a clergyman who gave him a sovereign (did he say that he worked for the London City Mission?). This extended his range considerably and he found his way to Bruges. It is possible that Morison, like Sydney Cockerell and Eric Gill, went to Bruges in July 1907, and saw the Tournament and Exposition of the Toison d'Or held there in that year. He found his way to the Benedictine abbey of St André, recently built in an exotic mixture of Byzantine, Romanesque and Renaissance styles. There he first heard plain-song chanted. It was an experience for which he was quite unprepared by anything he had come across. It had an immediate influence on his spiritual indecision, and he remained addicted to it for the rest of his life – it was the only sort of music he really cared for. So, by such indirections, as well as the more direct path of argument, Morison came to accept religious belief and the Catholic Church. He was eventually baptised at the Church of Our Lady of the Assumption, Warwick Street, W.1 on 28 December 1908, by Fr Charles Nicholson, S.J. He took the name of Ignatius, instead of Arthur.*

It was not long before this that Morison first saw his name in print. It was nothing to do with his search for faith, but arose from an older passion which he never wholly lost – stamp-collecting. It happened earlier in 1908, and twenty-two years later he wrote:

I can still see the line and the place where it stood on the page of the philatelic journal which I had provided with a photograph of the French Morocco one centime grey, put out in 1908. I was then a rare connoisseur of the stamps of France and the French colonies, but now I have only the memory of my fine series of Nouvelle Calédonie surcharges 1881–1903 and those astonishing editorial words 'We are grateful to —', and then my name spelt without a printer's error.*

The passage from the *Postage Stamp* for 28 March 1908 actually reads:

Morocco. (French). Mr Stanley A. Morison informs us that the current 1c., 2c. and 4c. stamps of France have been surcharged in Spanish currency (centimos) for use in the French Post Offices in Morocco. The specimen of the 1 centimo which he sends is surcharged '1 Centimo' in red with the figure above the word centimo.

Morison's serious career as a stamp-collector came to an end fifteen years later, although he still retained a professional interest in their design and printing, an interest kept warm by his long friendship with the Dutch typographer and stamp-designer, Jan van Krimpen.

But soon something happened which threw all the preoccupations of his early years (all, that is, except his religious faith) into a twilight from which he could afterwards recall them only with difficulty, as if from the remote past.

He had perhaps been mildly interested in printing for some time. It was a special interest of Thurston who had published a series of three articles on 'The Printing Press in the Service of the Church' in an American theological journal as long ago as 1902–3. The articles were well printed and illustrated with fine facsimiles printed on buff backgrounds, in the style that Morison himself used with such effect for his own facsimile books.* There was also the British Museum. Despite his ineligibility for the Reading Room, there were books to be seen in show-cases.

In the Grenville Library and the King's Library, and from the low-priced guides that the Trustees publish, I found my attention turning to the form of books – manuscripts and printed; to the art of writing and printing; and to the technicalities of production.*

But none of this prepared him for the revelation which came to him, quite by chance, one autumn day in 1912. It was to project him suddenly, if not violently, into a new and quite unfamiliar path, whose course he was to change more radically than anyone for over a hundred years. Not immediately, but soon, he realized that he had found a vocation as well as a living. Just as four years earlier his spiritual indecisions had been resolved, so now a new sense of direction released him from the practical doubts and uncertainties of his life hitherto.

2

THERE was nothing to distinguish 10 September 1912 from any other day. Morison was, he said, on his way home when, on the station bookstall at King's Cross, his eye was caught by the Printing Supplement put out by *The Times* that day. It is not to be supposed that *The Times* (still threepence then – Lord Northcliffe's drastic cut to a penny was still in the future) was Morison's ordinary paper, nor was it any easier then than now to buy a morning paper in the evening. But the Printing Supplement was different. It had a striking outside page that would distinguish it on any bookstall; and its success was such that it was still being sold on the bookstalls for days after its publication.

The outside page was in fact an advertisement for W. H. Smith's printing, and the upper part of it bore the announcement 'Fine Books Printed at the Arden Press, Letchworth'. The advertisement was probably the work of Bernard Newdigate, for he was still at the Arden Press. The advertisement is in his style: clean, simple, set entirely in Caslon types, it takes you back, as compellingly as wood smoke, to the Good Old Days. When print was dominated by mechanical monstrosities and the sinuous complications consequent upon Art Nouveau, the 'squirminess and artiness' that Lethaby so much disliked, simplicity had an immediate power to attract, and no doubt Morison's eye was attracted.

The major advertisers had all risen to the occasion, and as he turned the pages the name and stock in trade of Thomas Nelson, William Clowes, David Allen and the Carlton Studios, both specialists in posters, W. H. Smith (the advertising side, this time), the Goss Machine Company, and the combined advertisement of the Medici Society and the Riccardi Press – all these lodged themselves in his mind. The last in particular must have struck him. The Medici Society belonged to Sam Gurney, whose cheerful iconoclastic Anglo-Catholicism later endeared him to Morison, and Philip Lee-Warner, who ran the Riccardi Press, one of the least known but not least distinguished of private presses, was publisher to the Medici Society. Their advertisement was distinguished by a vastly enlarged facsimile of a beautiful fifteenth-century Venetian wood-cut border, which stood comparison with the finest examples of the work of William Morris and others in the text pages.

With this notable example before him of what fine printing could achieve, Morison now turned to the text. Immediately, it was the pictures, especially the full-page illustrations of the Ashendene Press Dante and the Kelmscott Chaucer, that caught his eye, and they remained the most vivid memory afterwards. But the first article also excited him, a masterly survey of 'The Story of Printing since Gutenberg' by A. W. Pollard, ending with an acute summary of William Morris's achievement. Following this, there were articles on 'The Origin and Growth of the British Newspaper 1622–1714', a subject which probably interested Morison less now than in twenty years time, 'Early Printing in Scotland' and 'Fine Printing in Germany'. This last may have been written by Harry, Graf Kessler – the by-line is 'from a German correspondent' – since he himself is not mentioned, although the influence of Edward Johnston, notably in his work for the Insel Verlag in 1905–6, and of his calligraphic disciples, Graily Hewitt and Eric Gill in England, and Anna Simons in Germany itself, is stressed, particularly that of Gill. Kessler's latest production, *Die Odyssee*, with engravings by Maillol, lettering by Gill, and published by Insel, is singled out for mention.

After this came 'The History of Advertising to 1695' and 'Modern Advertising'; then 'The Oxford University Press "1468"–1912', which perhaps first directed Morison's attention to the types that Bishop Fell left to the University, a subject which he embarked on some ten years later and lasted the rest of his life. 'The United States: the Progress of Modern Printing', like the German article, contained many names soon to be

40

familiar, including that of its author, Bruce Rogers: it singled out for a special praise the work of D. B. Updike at the Merrymount Press, of Bruce Rogers himself at the Riverside, F. W. Goudy's Village Press, 'the decorative work of Mr Will A. Dwiggins' and that of 'Mr William Aspenwall Bradley', and noticed T. M. Cleland, who 'has developed from 18th century models a style which harmonizes well with type and gives him a medium for the expression of many charming fancies'. He is almost forgotten now, and it is difficult to understand the dominance of his *pastiche* style, a mixture of Boucher, Rowlandson and Sandby, on the advertising and graphic style of his hey-day, the years before the Depression; it may yet come back. Cleland soon became a life-long friend of Morison's, the subject of an article in the *Fleuron*; Goudy and Rogers, if both 'fellow-workers in the vineyard', exercised less attraction, although Morison and Rogers were to co-operate in several distinguished pieces of work. Morison came to admire, if he did not emulate, Dwiggins, and knew Will Bradley well. Updike, who shared the nascent preoccupations of Morison's mind, the liturgy, church history, printing and its history, was to become the closest of all his American friends.

After this came a long article on the techniques of colour printing, and on lithography and copper-plate printing, which provided an admirably clear introduction to the subject. Then, facing the leader page, came an article on 'Private Printing Presses', with the Kelmscott Chaucer illustrated in the middle, which concluded with some remarkably prophetic words.

We may borrow a phrase in daily use by printers, and urge that the hand printer or private printer shall 'set the style' for the machine printer in the printing of to-day and to-morrow. Let him strive after the finest type faces; for which purpose he shall either be a calligrapher himself, as Morris was, or at least in close association with a calligrapher; for, let us repeat, the designing of beautiful types can only come from the practice of calligraphy. The types from which he sets 'at case' shall in turn serve as models of good lettering for the dies and matrices of the composing machine. Let him show, too, how letters and words shall be grouped and spaced; and then his pages shall give measures and margins for those of the machine-set book.

41

The leader itself took a fine idealistic line about the benefits of the Press to mankind, which, it concluded,

exists to supply them with knowledge which they could not otherwise obtain, and without which they would play no active part in the political life of the country. . . . We have not made an end yet of social conflict; but it is now more conscious, more gradual, more capable of adjustment and compromise, than it has ever been in the past. It can be carried on without threatening the whole fabric of civilization; and we owe this great improvement in its process to the invention of printing and to the newspapers which printing has made possible.

Alas for ideals (and indeed for self-gratulation)! These pious hopes were so soon to be shattered, and it was in a more sober practical spirit that Morison, after the war, was to address himself to the same problem.

After this came two pages devoted to the printing of *The Times* itself, and 'the organization of a great newspaper', with a historical survey going back to the first John Walter and his 'Logographic Press', a faint precursor of Morison's work on *The History of The Times*. Two other things may have caught his attention: the six fine illustrations of the processes involved in producing *The Times*, and a short article on 'The Printing Trade Library' at the St Bride Institute, which may, only now, have told him what a wealth of reading was to be had so close to where he worked.

The rest of the number was given up to a series of solid articles on the technique and mechanics of printing. First, there was 'Typography', followed by articles on 'Printing Surfaces and their Preparation', on 'What Type Is' (it mentions the Benton punchcutting machine as the foundation of the mechanical typecasting machines – still a novelty – as well as the Wicks Pivotal Caster, which *The Times* who had pioneered it were reluctantly beginning to abandon), on 'Type Design' (this dealt only with sizes and legibility) and 'Type Faces' (still more perfunctory – it only mentions the Old Style and Modern faces, which admittedly still dominated the type-founders' catalogues and printers' cases). The last article under 'Typography' dealt with the Linotype and Monotype systems, the latter in more detail, no doubt because, as the article concluded, 'the Lanston Machine was installed in *The Times* Office for the printing of that journal in 1909; and this article has been composed and set up by it'.

After 'Typography' came the section on 'Printing Machinery', 'From Hand-press to Rotary', 'Book and General Presses', 'Lithographic Presses', 'Stereotyping', 'Electric Driving', and then the other technical articles on paper-making, ink and bookbinding, and some miscellaneous pieces on technical education, proof-correction, the printing of postage stamps (this may have got a more thorough reading) and so on. The number ended with more advertisements, including a fine full page for the Rembrandt Intaglio Printing Company, and another for the Monotype Company, which stands out in comparison with the rest by its poor design, or rather by the absence of any design whatever.

If Morison read on into the ordinary part of the paper, he would have found the world much as normal. The French were having trouble in Morocco, and Colonel Mangin had marched in and put to flight the pretender to the throne. Sir Clements Markham had thrilled the annual meeting of the British Association at Dundee with an account of the latest British Antarctic exploration. Sir Robert Pullar of Perth had died, there was a by-election in Midlothian and a fire at Islington Power Station. The South of England made 420 against the Australians at the Hastings Festival, although Hobbs hit wicket first ball (Morison enjoyed cricket). Major-General Allenby conducted a brilliant attack with four brigades on a masked enemy with artillery advancing on Cambridge – the last great cavalry exercise was in full swing. Lomond was favourite for the St Leger on 12 September, although the racing correspondent favoured Tagalie (Tracery won at 8–1, with Tagalie and Lomond unplaced). The exhibition of Gordon Craig's *Hamlet* designs had just opened, to great critical excitement, at the Leicester Galleries.

But, if the rest of the world went on its usual way, it was never the same again for Morison.

Looking back, there were perhaps three things in this kaleido-scopic vision of a new world that stuck in Morison's mind. First, there were the huge illustrations of the Ashendene Dante and the Kelmscott Chaucer, the most compelling visual proof of what fine printing could be. Secondly, there was the conclusion of the article on 'The Story of Printing'. Here it was pointed out that Herbert Horne and the *Century Guild Hobby Horse* had antici-pated William Morris by three years in calling for new types and that despite the enormous impetus of Morris

new founts were wanted, and are still wanted, that there may be a sufficient variety, each good of its kind for every sort of book. . . . Very real improvements have been made; but there are still problems to be solved in book-building, and they cannot all be solved by an appeal to the practice of Jenson.

It was to these problems that Morison was now to address himself, and, though never indifferent to the model of Jenson, he looked elsewhere for inspiration.

The other thing that Morison remembered about the Printing Number was a small advertisement (a quarter page) for a new journal called the *Imprint*. Its title was striking; it was not type-set but a reproduction of fine calligraphy – the unmistakable work of Edward Johnston. Beneath it appeared the names of the four editors, F. Ernest Jackson, Johnston himself, J. H. Mason and Gerard T. Meynell, and of an advisory committee of thirteen names, all distinguished in printing and publishing. The text, too, offered something new and different:

We take the opportunity, afforded by this special supplement to *The Times*, to make the public acquainted with the aim and objects of *The Imprint*. It will be an illustrated monthly magazine, price one shilling net, devoted to the printing and the allied trades, and the first number will be announced shortly. *The Imprint* will deal with every branch of the trade.

This claim was substantiated by a long list of the types of printing and publishing it proposed to deal with, and an even longer list of the processes involved. The magazine was directed at every member of the trade, from masters to workmen, and there was a special appeal to students specializing in the graphic arts. The editorial staff, it was claimed, would be 'the best in every department': Jackson was a master lithographer and founder of the Senefelder Club, Mason had worked under Cobden-Sanderson and Emery Walker before becoming Director of Printing at the London County Council Central School of Arts and Crafts, and Johnston was a master of lettering, 'acknowledged at home and abroad to have largely influenced its revival'; Meynell was not mentioned.

When it came to details, the manifesto contained some definite and unusual assertions:

No exclusive type will be used, and should a special face be cut for the magazine, it will be procurable from the makers at the usual rate. Mechanical means will be used to the same extent as they are used in houses turning out ordinary good work. . . . The chief aim is to benefit, and if possible elevate the printing and allied trades, and to show the place of the craftsman in the printing trade. It will endeavour in this connection to bring into the closest relation possible the artist, the author and the craftsman . . . in a word, to make an artist of the craftsman and a craftsman of the artist.

Finally, after noting the support and enthusiasm it had already aroused abroad, the *Imprint* had a request to make:

We ask that all those who are interested in *The Imprint* will write, giving their views and offering their advice and support . . . the communications should be addressed to Mr Gerard T. Meynell.

This document was all the more remarkable, since its programme pointed to, and indeed suggested a cure for, one or two of the problems referred to or implicit in *The Times* supplement text. Chief of these was the complete divorce between the aesthetic discrimination of types and the technical use of them. This artificial distinction must have been obvious even to a reader like Morison with no special knowledge. How was it possible to speak of typefaces without discussing their appearance and variety? Here the *Imprint* offered a way out, and it was this universality of approach which may have decided Morison to pursue the magazine.

A vision on the road to Damascus cannot be forgotten the next day, and Morison was unsettled (it may be that his conversion belatedly caused problems at the L.C.M.). He left his job on 2 November 1912, by which time his pay had risen to £65 a year,* and went to the London Branch of the Société Générale bank. Whether or not he had trouble with the figures in accounts, he was certainly unhappy. Life at the London City Mission had not prepared him for the coarseness of a commercial institution. He was, therefore, near desperation when the first number of the *Imprint* appeared, at the end of January 1913.

It did not fall short of the promises made in September. '*The Imprint* wishes to all its subscribers, supporters, and well-wishers, A Very Happy New Year: further, we will try and make them happy.' This course was largely charted. The *Imprint* would work for improved labour-relations, a better copyright law, the spread of technical knowledge. It would try 'to bring cheerfulness and gaiety into our pages', but 'be sure that our standards will be high, and our use of them severe'. Something of this high idealism was communicated by Johnston, in a note apologizing for the fact that his lettering, for the title, the caption to the reproduction of Blake's 'Glad Dawn' (symbolic of the enterprise) and the initial letters, were 'reproduced by zincography', of which he disapproved.

The text itself presented a fine variety. There were articles on 'the law of the imprint', on book illustration, paper and on printing in America (this by Richard Austen-Leigh, a printer who shared Morison's enthusiasm for the history of printing). Mason wrote on trade education, Jackson on the history of lithography and Johnston on 'Decoration and its Uses'. W. Howard Hazell, whom Morison was to encounter in very different circumstances in 1928, wrote on 'Cost Finding and Keeping'; there was an article on book-collecting, by Gerard's cousin Everard Meynell, and a reprint of Dibdin's *Bibliographical Decameron* – a rather half-hearted gesture to the bibliophile. And the text proper opened with a manifesto by W. R. Lethaby on 'Art and Workmanship'. Lethaby was very much the patron of the enterprise, and his clear call for the application of craft standards to machine-made things was the cause and the theme of the *Imprint*. 'It is a tremendous thing that whereas a century or so ago the great mass of the people exercised arts, such as boot-making, book-binding, smithing, chair-making and the rest, now a great wedge has been driven in between the craftsman of every kind and his customers by the method of large production by machinery.' 'Art is the humanity put into workmanship, the rest is slavery.' Yes, but ultimately 'Art is thoughtful workmanship'.

To Morison, all this came as a draught to one dying of thirst. There was, moreover, a paragraph at the end of the editorial 'Notes', which ran as follows:

Note. We require at the offices of *The Imprint* the services of a young man of good education and preferably of some experience in publishing and advertising. We prefer that applications should, in the first instance, be made by letter, addressed to the Business Editor, *The Imprint*, 11 Henrietta Street, Covent Garden, London.

Morison had none of the qualifications required, but he applied and soon found himself face to face with Gerard Meynell.

Meynell was then managing director of the Westminster Press, of which his uncle Wilfrid Meynell had been part-owner since 1887, when it was made over to him by Cardinal Manning. He had come to the Press from the family banking business in 1899, and a year later with Claude Gibson bought it from his uncle and his partner, J. G. Snead-Cox. The Press was at 411 Harrow Road, near Paddington, and had its London Office in Covent Garden, which provided the *Imprint*'s address. Meynell's role in the genesis of the *Imprint* and in the typographic renaissance has been curiously understated. This is partly because J. H. Mason, the last survivor of the four editors, was inclined in his note-books to ascribe to himself the major part. But it was part of Meynell's nature to avoid the limelight. He believed in getting things done, not in being talked about himself. The magazine grew out of conversations starting in 1911 between Mason, Jackson and Meynell over dinner at Meynell's house in Colville Square, near Paddington. But nothing still might have happened if Meynell had not met Johnston, earlier in 1912; it was this meeting that provided the final impetus. They were very different people. Johnston was tallish, with a noble head, an idealist who was never content with performance that was less than ideal. He brought the same standards to calligraphy (on which he lived) and to the manufacture of miniature shops for his children. He found it difficult to begin jobs, although once started he worked with miraculous certainty. It was a hazardous undertaking to commission work from him, but to know him was to love him. Gerard was the very opposite.

In appearance he was small and dark with a hooked nose, a blue chin and flashing spectacles. He resembled the popular idea of a newspaper man, cocking his head like a sparrow, his hat pushed back and – almost – his thumbs hooked into his waist-coat. He and Johnston together made a most improbable couple. Meynell was a master of the pregnant, unfinished phrase, eked out with a wink or a jerk of the head. Johnston, to whom this kind of shorthand dialogue was a foreign language, would watch him with the close attention of a boy at a conjuring display and having, after some unequivocal interrogation, guessed at his general drift, would say 'I'm not quite clear whom you intend by "*the boys*", but if, as I gather, the matter is confidential it might be best to say no more'.

Meynell acted upon impulse and with such energy as to force other people to fall in with his plans. He would burst in with the announcement: 'It's all arranged. . . . Nonsense, of course you're coming! We'll motor down to see him and discuss the whole idea. I've hired a motor, it's at the door now.' Even Johnston, under such pressure, would usually go.

Meynell saw the possibility of harnessing Johnston's gifts to his own energy and becoming a sort of business manager of him. Their association would not have been surprising had it been founded simply upon his business acumen and flair for spotting talent, but it was not. This incongruous pair was united by deep, mutual affection. One of the most surprising things about this surprising man was that behind his hail-fellow-well-met exterior, the reckless generosity and the

48

aggressiveness to which it could give place – for he made enemies as well as friends – was hidden an unimagined depth of sensitivity and understanding. Equally unexpectedly, he possessed psychic qualities which afforded him occasional flashes of foreknowledge or telepathy.

It was Meynell's generosity which first touched Johnston. About the time that they became acquainted, in the summer of 1912, Johnston was going through a difficult period. . . . It was at this juncture that Gerard Meynell, whom he hardly knew, sensing his difficulty, spontaneously offered him a sizeable loan. Johnston did not accept it but the incident made a lasting impression upon him.

The friendship ripened quickly, Johnston's diary becomes suddenly peppered with the initials G.M. – letters from or to him, wires, appointments, meetings in London, and then his visits to Ditchling. It was while Johnston was at Laurencekirk with the children in August 1912, that he received a wire from Meynell saying simply: 'Have chosen the simplest title – The Imprint.'*

Presumably by this time the contents of the journal were well under way, but there was the question of the type to be decided. This was still unsettled at the beginning of September, when *The Times* Supplement came out, although clearly under discussion. According to Mason,

I made a pencil layout for our new magazine *The Imprint*, and students in my classes set up the trial pages. However, I could not find a type that exactly met my conception of the way it should be set but I took the nearest I could get, this was 18-point Caslon Old Face. Now Meynell had a Monotype installed at the Westminster Press and wanted to use that machine, so he set up his own idea of a specimen page in a 'modern' face which he already had on his Monotype. This suggestion ran counter to all my ideas, and I expressed my disappointment and disagreement with his proposal to Jackson, who replied, 'You stick to your idea, Mason, and I'll back you.' This put heart into me and I took a firm stand. I had no objection whatever to using the Monotype machine but only to the 'modern' face which he had chosen. Meynell compromised by proposing that we should consult the Monotype people.*

By now it was the beginning of November, and when Meynell and Mason went to see Harold M. Duncan, then managing director of the Lanston Monotype Company, he told them that the 18-point size was too large to be fitted into the matrix die-case for the casting machine. They compromised on 14 point, and on 5 November Duncan sent down samples of the type to the Monotype Drawing Office. After some discussion, any attempt to reproduce the type as submitted on a smaller body was abandoned,* and on 26 November the matrices were ready; the whole design had been adapted in the Drawing Office. The proofs provoked a lengthy criticism from Meynell on 28 November, the substance being that it did not represent a 'true old face'. Further discussions took place, new matrices and proofs were submitted on 13 December and on 31 December the new 'Imprint Old Face' was ready. 'The entire journal (10,000 copies)', the editors noted, 'has been produced as part of the ordinary work of a small commercial printers – The Westminster Press – in about nine working days.'*

It was a remarkable achievement in the time, and the *Imprint* was proud of it:

The newly designed type in which our pages are presented to the reader was cut by the Lanston Monotype Company at our instance. We are exceedingly pleased with it, and congratulate the Monotype Company on having produced the finest face that has been put up on the general market in modern times. Its compeers among privately owned types – the very best of them – will find it bear any comparison. Mr Duncan has indeed added a fine feather to his cap in producing it. Though cut for *The Imprint*, it is on sale to the general public; we have made no attempt to tie it up; for our policy is sincerely to improve the craft of which we are so proud. The type has been christened IMPRINT OLD FACE.

The Imprint Old Face type was produced in an incredibly short space of time, and accents have not been made. Will readers kindly insert them for themselves, if they find their omission harsh? For ourselves we rather like the fine careless flavour, which their omission gives, after we have recovered from the shock inevitable to us typographical precisians [*sic*].

Gerard Meynell must have still been receiving the enthusiastic press comment and correspondence which the first number had stimulated, when Morison came to see him. The interview was short. Meynell asked Morison what had moved him to apply.

Morison said that he was tired of being a bank clerk, and Meynell just said: 'How right you are. I was once a bank clerk myself. The post is yours.'* No doubt there was more talk about the Printing Supplement and the *Imprint* itself, but the matter had been decided by one of those astonishing flashes of insight by Meynell, such as when he saw into Johnston's difficulties. Like Johnston, Morison never ceased to be grateful for it.

3

IN 1913, Morison was already a striking person to meet. Thick black brows, penetrating blue eyes, and a nervous trick of jerking his chin out, gave him an appearance of great determination. His real shyness, the lack of small talk which he never overcame, all increased this impression; the width of his reading, from W. W. Jacobs and Sherlock Holmes to the obscurest Catholic liturgiologists, and his self-sufficient manner must have been equally surprising in a young man not yet twenty-four. His mother was inclined to disparage his appearance – 'Stanley, they say we've sprung from apes,' she would say, 'but you haven't sprung very far.'* But despite his slightly simian jaw, he was good-looking if not handsome, and his physiognomy, his silences, and the originality of his mind when he spoke, all marked him as someone out of the ordinary.

It is unlikely that these characteristics appealed to all the editorial board of the *Imprint*, but for the time being he was happy enough. The next issue appeared on 17 February, just as Morison arrived. Its theme was children's books, and there were lots of illustrations in full colour. Walter Crane, Belloc and Alice Meynell wrote on the subject, and the original contributors, notably Johnston, maintained the quality of the rest of the number. But it was noticeable that the number of advertisers had dropped from 43 to 22. The March number, devoted to lithography, with an excellent article on Daumier by Frank Rinder, and another on 'The House of Macmillan' written by F. A. Mumby to accompany a lithograph portrait of Sir Frederick Macmillan, was perceptibly thinner. April and May dealt with wood-engraving and woodcuts, June and July with photogravure and offset lithography, with no apparent further loss, but the uncertain finances were already causing trouble.

Perhaps on this account, perhaps because he saw a better use for Morison's talents, Gerard Meynell had decided to get him another job. Meynell was always in and out of the Catholic publishing firm of Burns & Oates. His uncle Wilfrid had become managing director eight or nine years earlier, and although nephew and uncle were not particularly close they did a good deal of business together.* In 1911 Wilfrid had put his son Francis, then aged twenty, in charge of book production. He had already learnt a fair amount from Bernard Newdigate, to whom he was at once pupil and patron, and Gerard in his instinctive way realized that Francis and Morison had much to gain from each other. Wilfrid may not have been at first enthusiastic, Morison recalled.

But it was Gerard who made W.M. and you take me into the business – and you did so at the rate of the £2 a week forecast by Gerard. This was because Gerard, who despised all Catholics, had been astounded to discover that I, who even then was a Catholic, should know about Jeremy Taylor. By some obscure process of reasoning he thought that I would be of use to B. & O. When the expected demise of *The Imprint* occurred, and the finances of the Westminster Press could not support the burden of paying me 30/-d a week, he told me he thought he might be able to persuade B. & O. to give me £2 a week.*

In fact Morison left before the *Imprint* came to an end. It was in the summer of 1913 that he moved to Burns & Oates, nominally as a shorthand typist – 'feeble though I was in these two accomplishments'.* In the May *Imprint*, another advertisement appeared, for 'a young man of good education' as before, but this time 'a knowledge of shorthand, typewriting and book-keeping' were the qualifications, not 'some experience in publishing and advertising'. It is likely that there were no offers, for Morison was still there on 14 June when he wrote to apply for a Reader's Ticket for the British Museum, enclosing a recommendation from Fr Isidore O'Leary, Prior of the Austin Canons in Hornsey, near where he lived.

The next two numbers appeared punctually, but the August

number was ten days late. In it appeared the first of Morison's publications, 'Notes on some Liturgical Books' – a characteristic title and a characteristic subject. The article is not primarily bibliographic: it is more a description of the different types of service book used in the Middle Ages with a series of facsimiles, in two colours, of early printed examples. On the whole Morison seems more familiar with the liturgical than the typographic aspects of this subject. He quotes the three leading authorities on the breviary, Batiffol, Baudot and Baumer, Wordsworth and Littlehales' *Old Service Books of the English Church* and Gillow's *Origin and History of the Manual*. On the other hand, the typographic side was not neglected. The examples are 'only those most likely to be met with by visitors to the King's Library at the British Museum, or the book-production rooms at the Victoria and Albert Museum'; here no doubt Morison had begun his typographic education, and as he quotes from Gordon Duff's *Westminster and London Printers* it can be assumed that he had started reading up the subject too.

There was no *Imprint* in September or October, but on 27 November the final number appeared with no more apology and no notice that this was the end beyond a note: 'The Editors will be pleased to hear from all those interested in the future of *The Imprint*.' Significantly, Mason (who had contributed most of the editorial matter) dated his Notes 'Weimar, August 1913'. He had gone thither in July to work for Kessler's Cranach Press, and his departure may have taken some of the steam out of the enterprise. Still, the number contained a prophetic article on 'Poster Advertising on the Underground': it is anonymous but may well be by the vigorous and inventive Frank Pick, Advertising Manager of the London Underground who instituted the series of 'artistic' posters with their original drawings and the futuristic use of sans-serif type. It was Meynell who had persuaded Pick to mount these posters. 'February 2nd, 1914 will stand in printing history as the date on which the Art of the Poster was revived in Great Britain. On that day London was aglow with eight of the best posters that had been seen on the hoardings at one time.'* It was Meynell again who had persuaded Pick of the advantages of having a uniform lettering on all underground stations, trains, printed matter and so on, and had cajoled Johnston into designing it. He was then in the middle of the negotiations and discussions with the other two, which three years later produced the first logically planned 'block letter' – a sans serif based on classical Roman capital proportions, which was to have an extraordinary influence first in Germany and then here. By that time Morison himself, who cannot have failed to observe the first posters and their lettering, was directly involved in the work.

Johnston himself was not aware of the differences and recriminations that brought the *Imprint* to an end. Mason and Jackson on the one hand and Gerard Meynell on the other were very different characters. Hard words were said about money – for once Meynell's magic deserted him – and by the time the last number was out it was all over. On 3 December Meynell wrote to the editors officially announcing the winding-up of the *Imprint*. Matters dragged on: Meynell finally returned all the material that Johnston had produced the following June, and as late as March 1915 Mason was still writing to Johnston to make his position clear.* It was a sad end to an enterprise of great promise: like Meynell himself, the *Imprint* had tried to do too much too fast. Meynell and Morison continued on good terms; Morison did the Westminster Press a number of good turns, and they were enthusiastic customers for the new type-designs that he produced at the Monotype Corporation. This relationship was commemorated in an exhibition at Bumpus's bookshop in 1929 of books printed by the Westminster Press for the best London publishers, to which Morison contributed a special postscript. But not long after this, poor Gerard's magic left him completely: he took to drink, separated from his wife and finally ended his own life – he who had been so full of life, and once the inspiration of the two best minds in calligraphy and printing of this century. Morison had 'conceived an immense and lasting admiration for Meynell. He was a character. No man so invariably ignored personal credit for his own enterprises. For him it was the idea, not the individual, that counted. Meynell's contempt for personal publicity left a permanent impression upon Morison's mind; so, too, did his scrupulous care not to take credit for the ideas and achievements of others.'*

Morison, once rescued, now found himself thoroughly at home. As a professional Catholic (in 1910 he had considered trying his vocation as a Jesuit), he knew the Burns & Oates list well. Moreover, Wilfrid and his family had a knack of befriending people, and with Francis in particular Morison established a complete sympathy. Wilfrid left them much to their own devices, and for the time being Morison was content to watch Francis, two years younger than he was but with two years' more experience, and to try to make himself useful in any way that offered.

Typography was his first interest. He met Bernard Newdigate, and learnt to recognize the blue stationery of the Arden Press with Woodroffe's Stag and Tree device for what it was – 'the note-paper of printers who knew what printing ought to be'.* He got to know the equally distinguished Chiswick Press, and its manager Charles Jacobi. Later his long acquaintance with the Oxford University Press began. He learnt the limitations of the types then available, even of Caslon Old Face which all his mentors agreed was the best of them. He also began to learn about printers' flowers. The Caslon foundry still showed some of the first Caslon's work in this line, and in America Will Bradley had persuaded the American Type Founders Company to issue some of his own and some poor imitations of old flowers in 1890. Morison and Meynell knew little of this and made blocks of designs they liked in old books: one typefounder they asked said he had no sixteenth-century flowers because 'the books then were all written by monks'.* So little was known of the history of typography.

Looking back, Morison recollected that he 'still sought few opportunities to design books, and was more than content to offer occasional suggestions to Francis Meynell, whose talent as an inventor of interesting typographic display he increasingly admired'. He himself was 'interested more in publishing (i.e. in seeing that a certain book would be timely, and getting a suitable author to write it) than in any other activity'.* He wrote to Edmund Bishop, whose liturgical studies had already made a great impression on him, offering to publish his collected papers. This correspondence is now lost – 'There are a good many asides in [it] for the sake of which I should have preserved the file' – but his first surviving letter,* written perhaps late in 1913 or early in 1914, shows that he had quickly found his feet in the Catholic publishing world, in which Burns & Oates were making a name for lively up-to-the-minute books.

Burns and Oates Ltd
28 Orchard Street, London, W.

S.A.M. IN PARTIBVS INFIDELIUM (Archbishop's Ho)

Dear Mr Francis:

I saw Goodier yesterday. I like him very much. Like Moses, he seems meek above all men in the earth. He would very much like B & O to take over the Catholic Library altogether. And he would willingly relinquish the Editorship in favour of Hudleston (Downside) and Bede Jarrett. I don't recommend dropping his name altogether. Is Hudleston a 'docile' man? He does not want it to appear as a S.J. affair. I really hope you are keen about this because I feel that it is exactly the sort of thing we as Catholics do want. I mean that such books as Watkin's (which Mr Dewhurst tells me has sold well) and Joyce on MIRACLES are really valuable things. Not mere rubbish slung off by a Bernard Vaughan. There is nothing of that sort about the C.L. Amongst the books arranged for is FIRST PRINCIPLES OF MORAL THEOLOGY. A book with that title and for a shilling should pay well, very well indeed I think. The one Goodier is particularly anxious to have out soon is W. E. Campbell's LETTERS OF THOMAS MORE. Phillimore of Glasgow is doing another such volume. This will be really grand if we can get P. on to B & O's list of writers. I am fervently convinced that as Goodier has done so much in the way of breaking the ground, if we do not now take it up, we shall have lost a splendid opportunity. Remember the Quarterly Series, and how well it has paid the Jesuits. Goodier is coming to B & O at 3 on Tuesday in the hope that you will see him. He bears no illwill about the F.T. business so please see him. You know that there is a standing order of 1000 copies of each book from Herder U.S.A. That of itself should pay expenses of the printing almost.

Then DEVS FOR HOLY COMMUNION. Sales to date 5,500 sheets 3d. binding 4d. a net book 3/6. Neither Goodier nor Mother D'Arcy got any cash. Goodier 30 free copies and D'A 100. This seems 'inadequate' and the result was that Mother Stuart took THE EDUCATION OF CATHOLIC GIRLS (now in its 4th edition) to LONGMAN. I covet that book. Total number of Mercier sold 127,041.

Yours,
Stanley A. Morison.*

Besides the saleable little religious books and more substantial works of scholarship that Morison had gone to seek in the foreign land across the road, the firm had a good literary list. The most distinguished author in it, now – too late, for he had died in 1907 – selling in tens of thousands, was Francis Thompson, author of *The Hound of Heaven*. The Meynells had looked after him and promoted his work as best they could from 1888 when, half-starved and shirtless, he first encountered Wilfrid, to the day he died. He was Francis's godfather, but his elder brother Everard (author of the *Imprint* articles) was his special friend; the poet would come to Everard's Serendipity Shop in Westbourne Grove. In 1913 Burns & Oates produced *The Collected Works of Francis Thompson* in three volumes at six shillings each. Set in Caslon type, printed by the Arden Press, and bound in buckram, they are a very good example of the quality of Burns & Oates's production at this time. There was also Everard's life of the poet, which got respectful reviews when it came out with the *Collected Works*, and 'The Hound of Heaven Series' – 'each Booklet cost 1s. net in Japon vellum wrapper and 3s. net in limp velvet calf, stitched with ribbon'. The taste for such pretty little books has gone, but 50,000 of *The Hound of Heaven* itself were sold like this, and there were other successes, such as Alice Meynell's *The Shepherdess*. Alice, Francis's mother, was the firm's other great literary figure. Her collected poetry also appeared in 1913, and next year her collected essays – Morison kept a copy signed by her in 1916. There were the poems of Katharine Tynan and John

Banister Tabb, a long-forgotten poet with a small but quite distinct talent, Fr C. C. Martindale's *The Goddess of Ghosts*, the first book with a border of printers' flowers, which was to become the Morison–Meynell trademark, *Eyes of Youth*, a successful small anthology with poems by Padraic Colum and others (including most of the Meynell children) – altogether, it was an enterprising side to the business.

It was in this connection that Morison first got to know Eric Gill. Wilfrid Meynell had commissioned him to carve an altar-stone to commemorate Francis Thompson, and it was to Everard that he made the first approaches that led him in 1913 to the Catholic faith. Everard and Francis were quick to exploit his skill as a wood-engraver. His first work was an engraving of a chalice and host which Francis used first in 1914 for *The Spiritual Classics of English Devotional Literature* and *The Spirit of Father Faber Apostle of London*. Everard commissioned a Pegasus bookplate from him, and later on that year Gill engraved a device for Burns & Oates, with the arms of St Thomas Becket and the legend NOS NE CESSES THOMA TUERI,* which went on the title-page of the *Ordo Administrandi Sacramenta*, printed in 1915 by the Oxford University Press in the Fell types.

The *Ordo* was the first of a substantial programme of liturgical publishing. The style was very much inherited from Newdigate, but the decorations were something new. *The Missal for the Laity* was followed by *The Day Hours of the Church*, *The Layfolks' Ritual* and *The Prymer*. All of these had historical introductions by the Benedictine Abbot Fernand Cabrol except the last, to which Cabrol provided a preface and Fr Thurston the historical introduction. There were a number of lesser books – *The Order and Canon of the Mass*, *The Rite of Marriage*, *The Little Office* and *The Office for the Dead* – and the series was completed with *The Layfolks' Pontifical*, a *Vesperal* and a *Psalter*. In all this, Morison's hand can be seen, not least in the concluding note: 'The series has been placed humbly under the PATRONAGE OF ST THOMAS OF CANTERBURY, whose arms have been rendered as the Publishers' device by Mr. Eric Gill.'

There were also the Orchard Books. 'Can you reach back to 1913? and remember instructing me to write to Paul Woodroffe for a set of endpapers featuring an apple-tree with the text "Stipate me malis".' 'I don't think we got anywhere with Woodroffe, and E. Gill became our ambition. The apples came, I fear, not from the garden of the saints, but from Orchard Street, where we worked, and from the china shop of Mr Mortlock, whose window used to contain a bowl of "Blenheim oranges from Mr Mortlock's Somerset orchards".'* And besides the making of books, sacred and profane, serious and frivolous, Morison also learnt to write. When Wilfrid died in his nineties, Morison wrote to Francis:

It was good to know that, for so long, he was still at Greatham. It was knowledge that kept young the young man to whom he gave a publishing chance in the happiest conditions – now thirty-five years ago – and made him write whether the young man liked it, or not. So I wrote my first book review and discovered to the readers of The Tablet a new controversialist with a style of his own in the Rev. R. A. Knox, then a firebrand pamphleteer in the service of Sam Gurney's movement.*

One of the books by Knox that came to Morison this way was *Reunion All Round*, that perfect Swiftian *reductio ad absurdum* of ecumenism. 'I was tremendously excited at the time and read it walking down Regent Street, cackling as I went to my office where I wrote a review for our sectarian rag the *Tablet*.'* *Reunion All Round*, like its predecessor *Absolute and Abitofhell*, was published by the Society of St Peter and St Paul, a body whose main function was high jinks, literary and other, such as this, which might stick pins in the hierarchies on either side of the hyphen joining Anglo to Catholic.* Maurice Child and Samuel Gurney were its leading members, and Gurney gave them space at the Medici Society – he was later to befriend and help Morison. Besides this, there was the *Dublin Review*, published by Burns & Oates, to which Morison contributed minor reviews on archaeological subjects.*

But by this time more serious things were beginning to occupy

Meynell and Morison. In 1915, they produced G. K. Chesterton's *Poems*. It was one of the best things they ever did, with the plain Caslon setting by the Chiswick Press enlivened by the initials that Eric Gill cut especially for it, and a red buckram cover embroidered with printers' flowers. But in the advertisements appear *Aunt Sarah and the War* (fourteenth thousand) and Fr Thurston's *The War and the Prophets*, 'an examination of predictions now in circulation regarding this latter age'. If the war now intruded into the gentle affairs of Burns & Oates, it had disturbed both Meynell and Morison earlier.

A difference of opinion had grown up between Francis and his father. It had begun in March 1912. Francis, a keen supporter of 'Votes for Women', had gone to a large Anti-Suffrage meeting at the Queen's Hall and publicly opposed every 'resolution' proposed at it. In the altercation that followed he let slip that he was at Burns & Oates, who were not pleased by the consequent publicity. But next day Mary Dodge, an old if now distant friend of the Meynells, and a keen Suffragist, came to the firm with a cheque for £500 to show her appreciation. Mrs Dodge and Lady de la Warr, who came with her, were to become Francis's patrons. He shared their views on socialism as well as votes for women, and in 1913 Lady de la Warr introduced him to George Lansbury. This was a decisive meeting: Francis never lost his devotion to Lansbury, and plunged into active work for the Socialist movement. Lansbury's Herald League, like all the other socialist groups, bitterly opposed what they saw as a capitalist war and, like the Independent Labour Party (but unlike the parliamentary Labour Party), continued to oppose it after August 1914.

In 1915 Francis set up a press in his own house at 67 Romney Street, with no further plan than satisfying his passion for the Fell types (lent to him for this purpose by the Oxford University Press). Here with Morison's help he printed two books, *Ten Poems* by Alice Meynell, with hand-written initials by Edward Johnston, and *The Diary of Mary Cary*. It was the first time that either had handled type themselves, and in the Romney Street

Press they found the germ of an idea that later found fruition in the Pelican Press.

Throughout the year the pressure for conscription had grown, first industrial conscription and then military.* The I.L.P. had opposed it from the first: at the end of 1914, Fenner Brockway and Clifford Allen had founded the No-Conscription Fellowship, which went into action the following spring. In July 1915 a national register of manpower was authorized by Parliament, and in October the 'Derby Scheme', a personal canvass of all available men between the ages of eighteen and forty, was launched under the direction of the Earl of Derby, an active conscriptionist. The issues shrank: with Keir Hardie's death in the same month, what had been the opposition of an international workers' movement to a capitalist war became a strife between groups of activists, the N.C.F., the Young Men's Service Committee of the Society of Friends and the Fellowship of Reconciliation, and the conscriptionist movement in Parliament. The Prime Minister, Asquith, was by no means identified solely with the latter. He was not immune to the arguments, especially of the religious objectors. But, though the Derby Scheme might delay conscription, it also cut off hope for the objectors. If every inducement to volunteer was offered, it decreased sympathy for those who waited to be conscripted. In December, a Draft Bill to introduce conscription was authorized.

The end came on 27 January 1916, when the Military Service (No. 2) Bill became law. Its provisions were that all men who had been unmarried on 2 November 1915, and between the ages of eighteen and forty-one on 15 August 1915 (the date on which the manpower register was compiled), should be deemed to have enlisted. Exemption was allowed, 'absolute, conditional, or temporary' as the tribunals set up to administer the Act should judge, 'from combatant service only, or . . . conditional on the applicant being engaged in some work which in the opinion of the tribunal . . . is of national importance'. Morison and Meynell were both eligible: both determined to refuse conscription.

The immediate result of this was the foundation of the Guild of the Pope's Peace. With three other friends, J. F. L. Bray, Christopher St John and E. I. Watkin, they issued a 'Preliminary Notice'. Those who received it and wrote to the Secretary (Meynell) were sent another leaflet informing them that the Guild was 'an association of Catholics who wish to take literally and to heart the exhortations . . . of the Holy Father about the war; and who wish to work by prayer and propaganda for the making of the Pope's (that is, a spiritual) Peace'. The Guild was open to all Catholics prepared to pray daily for, and do all they could to promote, the Pope's Peace; the minimum subscription was one shilling, 'but all who can do so are prayed to give more, as funds are urgently needed both for Mass offerings and for the effective distribution of the Pope's utterances'.

To this last end Morison and Meynell gave all the expertise built up at Burns & Oates. The 'Preliminary Notice', with its fine calligraphic heading, prayer cards and leaflets with the text of Benedict XV's November 1914 Encyclical and other writings, even a broadside, were all designed and printed with the most loving care. Mr Watkin recalls that it was Morison who got one of the little books of prayers printed in Fell type at the Clarendon Press, and that he smuggled a copy to Rome for a Papal Blessing. The original four were now joined by two priests, W. H. Kent and H. S. Squirrell, and before long they were beginning to attract some attention. 'The hierarchy was doing all it could to prevent British Catholics from paying any attention to Pope Benedict's pleas for a negotiated peace, but only one bishop went so far as to pronounce a public condemnation of the Guild – not easy, one might suppose, since the Guild, whatever the private views of some members, did not preach pacifism but confined itself to the Pope's plea.'* It was at the end of April that the Bishop of Clifton, Ambrose Burton, attacked the Guild. He was reported in the *Catholic Times*, which provoked a response from the Guild on 2 May, and there was a correspondence in the *Universe*, mostly sympathetic to the Guild's aims.

This represents the high-water mark of the Guild's influence. Despite the attention they received, and the sympathy of Fr

Squirrell's diocesan, F. W. Keating, Bishop of Northampton, the Guild gradually faded away: the bulk of Catholic opinion took the 'patriotic' view of the war. From time to time, up to November 1917, subscriptions were expended on more well-printed pamphlets, but as Meynell and Morison were both engaged elsewhere the impetus was not kept up.

Meynell's own objections to the war were more political than religious. With Morison it was the other way round. True, he had now discovered Marx, and his political views, though nearer to the British Socialist Party than the Herald League, were certainly anti-war, but his argument was based on the Sermon on the Mount. He was soon to have an opportunity of testing it, but in the short interval he took another far-reaching step: like many of the young men going off to the war, he got married.

On 10 May 1911, Morison's grandfather, Charles Cole, had died. This was an event of some importance to the Morison family, not least because he left the largest share of his property to Mrs Morison, carefully tied up so that it could never pass to her husband. This converted near poverty to comfort, though hardly affluence. Still, Mrs Morison was able to give up the shop and the house in Harringay (her views on railways at the bottom of the garden no doubt differed from her son's), and move to a new half-timbered villa on the borders of Golders Green and Brent, 'Mon Abri', 14 Woodville Road. The move took place in the winter of 1912–13, just as Morison left the London City Mission for the Société Générale, and the bank for the *Imprint*. He was now forced to forsake the Great Northern for the Charing Cross, Euston and Hampstead (now Northern) underground line; it was at least more convenient both for Covent Garden and, when he went to Burns & Oates, Victoria. Mrs Morison continued to live at Woodville Road, with Edith, on a small income from rents and a mortgage on their old house in Wightman Road, until 1917. Morison helped to pay his way, and one Christmas

Eve (1915) the whole family went to the pantomime at the Golders Green Hippodrome.

Soon after his grandfather's death, Morison went on holiday abroad, perhaps for the first time since that critical holiday in Belgium. He went to France this time, and on his first day there he met his wife to be. 'It was', she wrote, 'on the Feast of the Assumption, August 15th 1911, the year of the great railway strike in England.'

As he came in the dining room of the convent he had little attraction for me then. Raw, awkward, long-limbed, with the growth of a two days' beard on him, he entered shyly into the long dining room in the picturesque village of Pont l'Abbé in Brittany. . . . Beautiful, graceful Sœur Thérèse placed him next to me, at my table, for we were at 8 o'clock breakfast. 'Miss Williamson will look after you and make you happy', she said. It appeared that he had had a bad night's crossing from Plymouth to Brest. Three days went by and little passed between us. He was so shy, so silent. We were a very jolly party at that table, and at one lunch time it was his laugh that made me first really look at him, a laugh that came from the heart.

Mabel Williamson was not the last to be captivated by that great gust of laughter, the more startling for being quite involuntary. She was herself an orphan: her father, a 'master art silversmith', had died at the age of forty-eight in 1891, and her mother four years later. She was a fresh-faced, comfortable-looking woman, several years older than Morison; at that time, as later, she was a schoolteacher at Gospel Oak. They kept in touch after the holiday, and Morison was to some extent responsible for her conversion to Catholicism not long after. So much can be guessed from a characteristically forthright letter from T. A. Lacey, the Anglican ecclesiologist.*

I am not surprised [he wrote on 25 March 1913] that the lady is dissatisfied with the teaching or lack of teaching which she finds in the Church of England. I should think ill of the spiritual state of anyone who was not dissatisfied with the teaching or lack of teaching found in any part of the Christian Church, since we should all desire to advance, as Newman put it, 'ex umbris et imaginibus ad veritatem'.

But if the differences between the churches were distressing, he went on, he could not persuade her that they did not exist; if she was convinced of the Pope's supremacy, there was nothing to discuss. Nor would he be drawn on the 'question of Anglican Orders'. There was no such question, except one of highly technical theology or ecclesiastical practice.

This long letter is doubly interesting, not only for the special problem with which it deals, but with the general nature of the theological problems which occupied Morison. These must have been uppermost when he wrote again to Lacey, eliciting another long letter on 1 April, giving the historical arguments from the early fathers for rejecting the papal supremacy. Morison kept the correspondence, and it may have occurred to him five years later when he was confronted by the problem of the validity of orders in a different form.

In the meantime, Mabel's doubts were finally resolved, and after instruction from Fr Thurston she was received into the Church in 1914.* In his only surviving letter to her, written one Saturday late in 1915 while the rest of the family had gone to watch the Golders Green Civic Guard 'clarum et venerabile nomen', he says he hopes to see her next day at St Dominic's – clearly the Priory in Southampton Road, near Gospel Oak. It is an interesting letter, too, for another reason: he has begun to take his own handwriting seriously, and the whole letter is written in a small and painful half-uncial, in imitation of the large and beautiful hand of Adrian Fortescue, a new friend.

Adrian Fortescue was a new addition to the Burns & Oates list of authors.* He was tall, handsome, strong, learned, childish both in a strong sense of fun and in moments of weakness, brave, charming, impatient with fools and severe in his judgement of them, austere yet with an overwhelming sense for the good things of life, overbearing yet diffident, subtle in thought yet simple and forthright in speech and writing – in all, to Morison, a friend and master of overwhelming attraction. He was perhaps the only man, certainly the only Catholic priest Morison had met, who could understand and meet Morison at every inch of the long hard road by which he had come to the Church. Like Morison he had a lonely youth (his parents both died when he was young, his father when he was only three). From 1891 to 1899 he studied at Rome and Innsbruck, finally obtaining his D.D. from the latter university: this gave him, like Morison, a sense of isolation from the majority of English Catholics. In December 1899, he began to study writing – he was a member of Johnston's first class at the London County Council School of Arts and Crafts only three months after it began; it was his normal hand, a perfect unhurried upright script very like the 'formal hand' that Johnston taught, that first compelled Morison to improve his own writing.

In 1906–7 Fortescue travelled all over the Near East, improving his knowledge of Semitic and Arabic languages and studying the Orthodox Churches on the spot. He then came home to be parish priest at Letchworth, in the same year that Newdigate moved the Arden Press there. They soon became friends. Newdigate's son Charles became Fortescue's curate; Fortescue in return gave Newdigate his lasting passion for calligraphy. In 1908 he built his own church dedicated to St Hugh; in September 1907 the Mass was first celebrated there according to the Roman and Byzantine rites. Since then he had published a series of books on the liturgy and the Eastern Church. In 1915 he was the obvious man for Burns & Oates to ask to revise the text of the English Missal. Francis Meynell and Morison had both been struck by him, and he had been further asked to write an introduction for *The Holy Week Book* in the Liturgy for Layfolk series, and an essay on hymns to accompany a translation of *Pange Lingua*, both published early in 1916.

'Morison was captivated – heart, mind and spirit – by Fortescue.'* He admired his learning and courage: his mannerism and habit of speech, even his rational but individualistic clothes, left an indelible impression on Morison. Already in 1915 when he wrote to Mabel, he was learning Greek, in trains, buses and trams, in humble imitation. Fortescue, on the other hand, disapproved of pacifism, and later in the year he wrote a tract against it and what he considered its confusion of moral and physical evil, but this did not alter Morison's admiration for him; moreover, in September, when *Pacifism* came out, he was in no position to provide a reasoned counter-argument.

But earlier in 1916 the future for the conscientious objector was wholly obscure.

The drafting of the provisions for C.O.'s was so unclear as to puzzle judges. It is no wonder that in these circumstances local tribunals were inconsistent in their decisions; nor that the military authorities, in the middle of a war, were uncertain how to deal with a problem of which they had no experience, and on which they received guidance all too slowly.*

The position of the C.O. himself was even more difficult. Faced with a variety of authorities, all in this state of confusion, he could never know from day to day whether he was, at one extreme, to continue his ordinary life, or, at the other, to be shot as a deserter. Between there was to lie every shade of compulsion from humane re-allocation of skilled workmen to sentences of hard labour in conditions worse than criminals got.

Morison already had some premonition of what lay in front of him. On 21 February he had applied for total exemption; on 16 March his case was heard by the Hendon Local Tribunal, and his application was refused after (by his account) a quite inadequate hearing. He was allowed to appeal to the Middlesex County Tribunal, which he did, and his appeal was heard on 5 April. Here the chairman was more sympathetic, and Morison was allowed to expand on the moral and religious reasons, in his view implicit in the Sermon on the Mount, for his objection. He was partially successful in establishing his case, and was granted exemption from combatant service only. This was not acceptable to him and, despite a further plea, he was not allowed to appeal to the Central Tribunal.* Apprehensively, he awaited the consequences.

In the middle of this process, its outcome uncertain, and perhaps feeling not unlike those about to be separated by the war itself, Stanley and Mabel were married on 18 March 1916, at the Church of St Peter in Vinculis, Stroud Green, by the Prior of the Austin Canons, Morison's old friend from Hornsey days, who was also rector of the church. According to the register, they were twenty-six and thirty-three; his occupation is given as 'publisher's reader'; he was then living at Golders Green and she at Parkhill Road, off Haverstock Hill. (Oddly enough, Morison's father's occupation is given as 'cigar merchant'; perhaps this was intended to cover both his disappearance and Mrs Morison's previous employment.) A little card, set in Caslon type with a flower border, was sent out, announcing their marriage and new address.

They had already found somewhere to live, at 9 Golden Square, Hampstead. They had got to hear of this through an unusual acquaintance, Ivy Low. Daughter of Sir Sidney Low, the famous editor of the *St James's Gazette*, she had been converted at the same time as Mabel by Fr Thurston. Shortly after, she lost her new faith and her heart to Maxim Litvinov, then a refugee in England. Ivy and Litvinov (they did not get married until 1918) had already moved out, because Litvinov disliked the low ceilings, before the Morisons arrived.* The house itself was a small plain eighteenth-century house, long since gone; it stood at the corner of what is now The Mount Square and Hampstead Grove, looking down Admiral's Walk. They had only two rooms, and had to climb a narrow staircase to reach them. Inside there were large open fireplaces, and outside a large old ash tree through which they would watch the sun setting. Morison christened the little house 'One Tree Cottage', and there despite their apprehensions they were very happy.

4

THIS comfortable state did not last long. Just as the Guild of the Pope's Peace was reaching its climax, Morison was arrested by his landlord, Sergeant Lambert of the Hampstead Police, on 7 May 1916. Mabel was away from home at the time and her anguish when she got back was only partly relieved by a letter from Stanley:

I was taken to Pentonville at 4 y'day and dressed in prison garments at 5. Then I pictured you getting back to One Tree Cottage tired and half-expecting me to be home. How disappointed you were! So I thought. When a hunk of coarse brown bread and a mug of porridge was handed in to me, I could not eat.*

In the end, Francis Meynell provided the £5 bail, and Morison was temporarily freed. This short patch of liberty enabled Morison to make some preparation for the future. Whatever it was to be, it was unlikely that he would be free to go on working at Burns & Oates. It was about this time that Francis finally left the firm, and again Mrs Dodge and Lady de la Warr came to the rescue. George Lansbury's pre-war *Daily Herald* was now appearing as a vigorous weekly, the *Herald*, largely financed by Mrs Dodge and Lady de la Warr. It suited both Lansbury and the ladies to have someone of Francis's opinions and printing experience in charge, so he was made Business Manager of the *Herald*. Both were anxious to exploit his typographic skill, Lansbury solely to promote Socialist aims, the ladies also thinking of the day – they were devoted theosophists – when Krishnamurti's gospel 'might be popularized in something better than Cheltenham Bold'.* Perhaps the arrest of Morison precipitated matters: it was, at any rate, 'in the early summer of 1916' that the Pelican Press was set up at 2 Gough Square, as an adjunct to the Victoria House Printing Co., which produced the *Herald* and much other socialist matter.

With this cause and these finances, Francis set out to produce the best typographic design for the purpose. The style was sixteenth century, French and Lyonnese rather than Italian, although the original 'pelican' device was adapted from the phoenix of the Venetian printer Hieronymus Blondus. Books of reproductions were ransacked and borders and initials taken from the work of Erhard Ratdolt, Jean de Tournes and Geoffroy Tory. In addition, the best available printer's flowers were added to the decorative equipment, and suitable types, Caslon and three recent American designs, Cloister, Kennerley and Forum capitals, were installed. With all this, Francis was able to realize his ambition.

The main source of all these typographic ideas was another friend, recently made, of Morison's. A. W. Pollard was a dominating figure in the Department of Printed Books at the British Museum, a bibliographer of great organizing power and catholic vision, with an equal taste for ancient and modern fine printing. He had written all the articles on the subject in the eleventh edition of the *Encyclopaedia Britannica*, as well as the article in *The Times* Supplement that first fired Morison's enthusiasm. As well as introducing Morison to the splendour of sixteenth-century printing, he also showed him the work of the American printers Bruce Rogers (whom he particularly admired) and D. B. Updike, and later sponsored Morison for the Bibliographical Society. Morison admired him profoundly. 'I have never forgotten', he once said, 'the sense of awe of being in that presence.'

With his head full of these new schemes and ideas, Morison awaited his summons. The outcome, since the failure of his appeal to the Middlesex Tribunal, could not be in any doubt. Trial was a formality, and the conscientious objector was immediately handed over to the Army. Morison was taken to Aldershot. Here he refused to obey orders, and found himself in the guardroom awaiting court-martial.

It was there that he met R. Palme Dutt, already an ardent Marxist, who was then, in his own words, 'the doyen of the guardroom, having successfully tripped up various preliminary stages of my court-martial on technical grounds'. He was delighted to have Morison's company, remembering afterwards his humour and intelligence, and the pleasure of matching his orthodox Communist opinions against Morison's equally strongly held Catholic views. For Morison, it was the beginning of a series of friendships with men whose views of society, its proper function and future, were as unorthodox as his, often formed like his in lonely isolation. Pacifism and prison, despite the miseries they entailed, provided Morison for the first time (apart from Francis) with friends of his own persuasion in social matters.

The number of conscientious objectors, the variety of their reasons and of the consequent degrees of unwillingness to help the war, had already embarrassed the Government, the Army and the Home Office, all equally anxious to pass the awkward problem on to the other. Guardrooms and detention centres filled up, the ordinary processes of military law were delayed, and before Morison was court-martialled Army Order X was issued on 25 May. This directed that objectors should be sentenced to imprisonment, not detention, and, after court-martial, transferred to the nearest civil prison. Morison's case came up at the beginning of July, and on 9 July he sent his mother a hurried postcard to tell her what had happened.

Aldershot, Sunday.
Today sentenced to two months hard labour for refusing to obey orders, to be served in H.M. Prison, Winchester, which will be my address for this 'stretch'. Hope all well. Will write again when able.

Stan

It is clear that Morison did not see his two months as the limit of his troubles, but he seems to have faced the prospect with some equanimity. Perhaps this came from his conversations with the Scots Guards Officer who represented him at the court-martial; to Morison, alternating between despair and defiance, he provided a common-sensical humanity at once deflating and comforting. He was equally fortunate in the Roman Catholic chaplain at Winchester, Fr Gunning, who brought comfort and smuggled messages from Mabel. It was he who warned her in advance of Stanley's transfer to Dyce, in Aberdeenshire.

The authorities had early recognized that C.O.s, however different their grounds of objection, could be divided into two main groups, alternativists and absolutists: those who were prepared to accept some sort of employment, provided that it made no direct contribution to the war, and those who refused alternative service as a condition of exemption. The authorities were naturally anxious that as many C.O.s as possible should accept alternative employment, and 'conditional exemption' was easily had. Nevertheless, about a thousand refused it; they presented a tiresome and never-ending problem. Matters were made more difficult by the ingenuity and persistence of the No-Conscription Fellowship, whose anxiety to present the absolutist case as forcefully as possible led some C.O.s to overstate their objection. In an attempt to solve the problem, the Home Secretary appointed a committee (the Brace Committee) to provide acceptable employment for objectors – acceptable at least to their principles, for the work involved was often disagreeable and sometimes painful. Work centres were set up, and two disused prisons, Warwick and Wakefield, were taken over, and those who would sign an undertaking to work and not escape were allowed out of prison.*

One of the first work centres was established at Dyce: it was then a fine summer, and the tents provided seemed reasonable quarters. Most of them were glad to be out of confinement and looking forward to open-air work. Fr Gunning told Mabel that Stanley would be arriving at Waterloo at 4.45 on 22 August. She was there, and hardly recognized him, for he had grown a red beard. He had got round the sergeant warder and persuaded him to allow Mabel to come with him to Scotland. She rushed back to the Meynells to borrow the fare: Francis was out, but his wife Hilda and her sister scraped together £5. She was just in time at the station, and then came the long hard journey (it was a compartment with wooden benches) north, in the distressing company of the other C.O.s. Mabel had only a cotton dress, and

73

the sergeant in compassion allowed Stanley to stay with her in a nearby farmer's house. The rest slept in the tents, without groundsheets. Next day Mabel had to start back. Stanley was allowed to go with her to Aberdeen; he was not well, and had a fever.

He was well enough on 30 August to send her a cheering telegram, but later in the autumn the weather broke, the camp was waterlogged and sickness broke out. Morison was fortunate in going down early, and he and some others were moved to farmhouses and barns. Here Morison read Chesterton's *Orthodoxy* with his companions, and as the discussion reached an apocalyptic point they were startled by a noise. They looked out and saw a white horse in the moonlight galloping down the deserted lane. But it was not the Second Coming: the next day dawned as drearily as before.* Before long, one of the prisoners died. Ramsay MacDonald asked in Parliament if C.O.s could not be better employed, and Dyce was closed at the end of October.

Morison was sent to Warwick, where he remained at least until the end of the year. Just before Christmas he wrote home:

The Settlement, Warwick
13 December 1916

Dear Mother

Many thanks for the somewhat remarkable 'assorted assortment of all sorts' which surprised me today. I need not say that it is a great pleasure once again to taste an apple pie (albeit sans top and sans dish) of your cooking, a steak too which I suppose is a joint I have not tasted since Woodville Road claimed me, an egg also is an old formula revived. I am very grateful for your thought and labour but if I conveyed the feeling that I was being starved here, I must plead guilty to having misled you. While it is undeniable that the food here is thoroughly bad it is equally true to record that of carrots, haricot beans and potatoes there is a generally congested abundance. The consequence is that apart from Oxo and Bovril I taste meat but rarely and so far as I can judge, with no bad results. . . .

About Christmas I can say little in this place. To begin with: I am not absolutely certain of being able to get to London for the Holidays. You will have seen that restrictions as to railway traffic have been imposed upon soldiers and munition makers. They have also

74

been applied to us. They have been lifted from the soldiers. It does not follow however that they will be lifted from us. For when soldiers are subjected to restrictions we are treated as soldiers: and when civilians are subjected to restrictions we are treated as civilians. We are so amorphous, anomalous, amphibious a lot of people. So there is a likelihood of our being kept here. And if I do come home I shall certainly come to No 14 for what will possibly be the last time. I do not know though that my spouse will come. I mentioned it but the creature contends that she is ill served in the matter of raiment and though quite innocent of any ambition to make a splash or be anything but neat in appearance would prefer I gather to postpone a visit until such time as she has come by some indispensables of dress. I rejoined that so far as I could see that this seemed likely to make the visit a *post bellum* one. What reply there will be to this I don't know but I will let you know in time. In either case there is no need to massacre fatted calves or to conduct a general offensive against Turkeys.

So der tag is January 29. It'll come quicker than you will desire no doubt. When I come I will arrange about the books. While I am about if I am about you might come to No. 9 Golden Square 'Pillbox Cottage'. It is very small but comfortable. I suppose you are rushing about getting Agents lists of 'Desirable Residences etc'. What about St John's Wood? or that part of Hampstead round about West End Lane? or Harrow?

I hope you continue to go to the Hampstead Garden Suburb Ethical Soc. and that you heard A. E. Zimmern. For a name like that he is very much more reasonable than one would have supposed. As a rule those with German names are jingo patriots of the worst and most blatant type.
December 16.

Since I wrote the foregoing I have eaten the steak and the eggs – both were really superb and most enjoyable. I forward an acknowledgement of your kindness and an earnest of Christmas wishes in the shape of the long deferred Oxford Dictionary which is as I said, authoritative and complete.

Renewed thanks and love to all,

Yours
Stan.

How Morison came to be released is something of a mystery. As subsequent events show, he had not altered his 'absolutist' point of view about the war. He may have been released, as other objectors were, under the 1913 Act granting temporary discharge to sick prisoners, the 'Cat and Mouse' Act that had been used to prevent Suffragettes from martyring themselves. He remained in London until the late summer of 1917. If he did not get away for Christmas, he arrived soon after, for on 5 February Adrian Fortescue wrote to him about his long-planned book on ceremonies and apologized for not writing earlier: 'It was pleasant to see you,' he wrote. 'I hope it will not be long before I do so again.'

On 20 February, Mrs Morison and the two girls visited 'Stan's Cottage'; 'small but comfy', she noted in her diary. It is odd that she had not been there before, but the letter suggests that Morison's filial solicitude had grown a little rusty. Still, throughout the spring and summer 'Stan and Mabel' appear regularly in the diary. Evidently, he was able to resume work of a sort at Burns & Oates; it was about this time that his friend William Andrew MacKenzie, author of *Rowton House Rhymes*, joined the firm. And Francis badly needed help at the Pelican Press. His appearance before the tribunal had been even more delayed and he was not arrested until 29 January. Unwilling to compromise or waste time in prison, he went on secret hunger-strike. When finally discovered, he was too far gone for forcible feeding, and was able to trade his discharge for a mouthful of milk. After his return on 11 February, he was still weak, but both he and Morison were active in the enthusiastic welcome given to the March Revolution in Russia. It was a busy year for the Pelican Press. As well as leaflets to print for the Guild of the Pope's Peace, there were Siegfried Sassoon's reasons for refusing to return to the front, H. G. Wells's *A Reasonable Man's Peace*, and *The C.O.'s Hansard*, in which Goudy's Forum capitals, a favourite of both Morison and Meynell, were used for the first time.* Another unexpected job this year was the privately printed memoir of Charles Fisher by George Lyttelton, 'printed by Stanley Morison'. Charles Fisher, killed in the war, was an irresistible and original character, and Lyttelton's memoir is a too-little-known classic. The job may have come to Morison through Adrian Fortescue's kinsman John Fortescue, a neighbour in Admiral's Walk.

But at the end of September Morison had to go back to prison, to the Work Centre at Wakefield. By this time, although conditions were no better, the surviving absolutists were more experienced prisoners. The *Tribunal*, the N.C.F. journal, was a great clearing-house of information on everything from legal matters to the smuggling of pencil leads. Morison found two old friends from Dyce, J. S. Toscenie, a pianist and like himself a Roman Catholic and Jan Mills Whitham, an 'ascetic atheist' and novelist. He also made some new ones, notably Walter Holmes and Robin Page Arnot, both Fabians and Guild Socialists: they set to work to convert Morison and he them. But as winter set in a general depression spread, and to counteract it the three of them, with George Smith, a Glasgow city councillor, got permission to put on plays. The old chapel was converted into a theatre; there were already concerts and lectures, but this was something new. *Fanny's First Play* was staged on 7 and 8 February 'in the Fifth Year of the Great War', with Morison in the part of Major Knox. Page Arnot played Lieutenant Duvallet and it was produced by George Smith; between them these two did the casting and rehearsing.

The programme was printed by the Pelican Press in its best style, as was that for a double bill *Snakes & Sleigh-Bells* and *Campbell of Kilgour* on 25 and 26 February. Morison acted again when *Major Barbara* was put on (24 and 25 April), this time taking the part, not of his namesake, but of Peter Shirley. Morison's only other recorded occupation at this time – apart from membership of the 'committees' through which the C.O.s ran the prison (the authorities had largely abandoned the internal administration) – was a study of the International Bible Students Fellowship, one of the many special sects who bombarded the objectors in prison with pamphlets.*

But it was a weary time; the war seemed endless, and as the casualty lists grew sympathy for the C.O.s became even less. Mrs Morison and the girls did their best to look after Mabel, but on the last day of 1917 Mrs Morison wrote in her diary, 'The last of this cruel year! I wonder what the next will bring. Stan is ill at

Wakefield.' This was more than a trifling ailment, and his spirits had clearly given way. On 26 January Fr Thurston wrote:

I am utterly ashamed of myself. Ever since your wife told me of the terrible time of illness and depression I have been meaning to write to you. . . . Barren sympathy is I fear a poor thing when you are brought face to face with the cruellest aspect of life . . . but I was truly glad to hear that . . . in health at least you are on the mend.

There was another blow to come. Len, son of Mrs Morison's brother Charlie, died as a result of a shooting accident, about which his aunt had misgivings. Morison wrote to his mother, in lodgings on the south coast, on 18 April:

So you think there was dirty work at Chatham? I wonder. Have you a local rag with the Report of the Inquest? If as you say what was the motive? Of course this sort of thing happens often at the Front but surely it is hardly likely to happen here. I am most sorry about it. Uncle Charlie must be frantic. . . .

Not much nearer home though several have come and told me of safe jobs – these however are situate at Manchester or Barrow in Furness or the like sort of provincial city. There isn't much gain from going there unless Mabel can come. There is the chance of my being let go home to find work and I imagine I could do this if I were not tied up here.

I suppose the more excited are leaving Eastbourne & the South Coast generally in view of the German offensive & their big gun. It is of course not at all outside the infinite possibilities of the war that the Germans may succeed in reaching Calais and Boulogne and the rest of the Channel Ports down to Dieppe or so and if they do it is only likely that they'll bomb the coast occasionally – but very little I think. Their big 80 mile gun will be trained on London and not upon coast resorts. Accordingly I desire to be in London and not at Manchester. It is highly likely that 'no small stir' will result if the gun does reach London and I mind guns less than I do air raids. However all this is speculation and it is not unlikely that the British Line may stand firm. I observe that Wytschaet is again in British hands and that without the bringing in of any of Foch's Army of Reserve. The Allies are playing a very desperate game and it may come off if Foch is the man Ll George & Clemenceau think. I see that George is riding for a fall over Home Rule and deliberately too. There is no doubt that we are in the decisive phase of the war. If the Line holds and Ll George fails there may be a chance of peace and a Lansdowne Govern[t].

But respite was near. On 29 April, Mrs Morison's diary reads 'sent Stan £5 for birthday (May 6), he being at H'pstd looking for employment of national importance'. Morison had finally accepted alternative employment. Then on his birthday itself comes 'About now I hear Stan to be employed at Finchley Tomato farm'. He saw the war out growing tomatoes, which provoked Page Arnot to send him a postcard with NOS NE CESSE TOMATOS TUERI on it. It had been a barren period in his life, apart from a fair amount of reading. Page Arnot was one of the few C.O. friends with whom he kept in touch, if sporadically. Whitham was another; he was even more immovable in the country than Morison in town. First at Parracombe, then at Combe Martin and Barnstaple, Morison used to spend week-ends with him and his wife Sylvia, protesting a little at the unfamiliar rigours of country life.

But before 1918 was out he had another job in hand. Fr Thurston was not the man to let Morison's despair pass by with a few consolatory words. He saw that the cause of the depression was a rusty mind, and he decided that work would be the best way to set it going again. In 1916 he had first become involved in the Church's attempts to deal with the 'episcopi vagantes', the bogus bishops 'consecrated' by an engaging charlatan called Arnold Mathew, whose creations had involved him – rather unwillingly – in the odder fringes of the Theosophical movement. For anyone interested in the more exotic forms of human credulity, this is a richly interesting episode. It is difficult, to say the least, to follow what is going on, as Mathew, Mrs Besant, 'Bishop' Leadbeater, James Ingall Wedgwood, and others pop up and down, now swearing allegiance to the Pope, now to Krishnamurti (*alias* Alcyone and the Lord Maitreya), joining and repudiating the Old Catholic Church, the Western Uniate Catholic Church, the Orders of the Rising Sun (later Star in the East) and the Rosy Cross, the Adyar and Theosophical societies, and the Universal Co-Freemasonic lodges, all with astonishing rapidity.

One can only wonder that ordinary Catholic apologists took it quite as seriously as they did. But Mathew was an agile and, worse, a litigious rogue: the editor of the *Month* had had to pay damages for a trifling mis-statement, and Thurston was cautious. His own contributions to the official attack on Mathew and his crew had been carefully moderate in tone, and Mathew had only responded by writing a dignified private letter of complaint to the Provincial of the English Jesuits.* But here was Morison, in need of mental exercise – Thurston saw an admirable opportunity of killing two birds with one stone.

The idea came originally from Morison who, knowing Thurston's concern, wrote on 15 May 1918 to say that he had received material including a photograph of the bishops in their regalia from 'the one and only (thanks be) "✠ Arnold Harris Mathew"'. As I have to return the photographs and cuttings, perhaps you'd care to call on Sunday next?' Thurston went, and left Morison full of enthusiasm for the chase.

My dear Fr. Thurston
Since your coming this morning I have secured a copy of a 56 pp. pamphlet THE OLD CATHOLIC MOVEMENT IN GREAT BRITAIN: published (?1918) by the Theosophical Book Concern, Krotona, Hollywood, Los Angeles. wherein it is made plain in the words of ∴ Sis. A.B. that 'it (the Old Catholic Church) is likely to become the future Church of Christendom when He comes'. The tykes! I will let you have this item in a few days as also some tripe & saw dust called MEDITATION for BEGINNERS by J. I. W'wood. I should dearly love a few days off the tomatoes in which to do a bit of research: I should love to get one in on the T.S.! I look to you to smite 'em.   S.M.
Hampstead Trinity Sunday 1918.

By 3 August, Morison was hard at work. He and Mabel were on holiday at Cherryford-in-Martinhoe, near Parracombe in Devon, where Whitham, also released, was now living. He wrote to Thurston:

About Arnoldus – I am alternately savage and sympathetic. He sends me all the enclosed wh. please keep & return to me some day. I think it well also to send what I have rewritten about the ordinations & consecrations.

Thurston thanked Morison on 8 August, adding, 'Mathew has again been writing to our Fr Provincial to denounce me. I do not think the Prov'l minds. . . .' Morison's letter was written on the back of a sheet of Burns & Oates paper, and in it he says he is going to see them on his return. Clearly old links were being kept up, and his next letter to Thurston is postmarked 'S.W.1'.

20 August 1918

My dear Fr Thurston

Many thanks for reading the M.S. & for sending me the proofs [of Thurston's *Month* article]. I am of course most interested in the Pastoral. Where did you get it? Could you let me see it? . . . It is odd that Mathew never mentioned this Pastoral to me. . . .

I wanted to ask you if you would kindly write me a 'Museum' letter. My ticket for the Reading Room is missing . . . so they say it would be easier to make a fresh start. . . .

Again many thanks for your kindness in reading my stuff & for your comments.

Yours
Stanley A. Morison.

By 8 September, the idea of collaboration had occurred:

I think if you do that part of the subject dealing with the history of the Old Catholic Church from 1872 to 1908 it will be most kind – it should be initialled by you, and if as an appendix we could have a summary of Mathew's career it would be most useful. . . . That 1000 copies rather excites my interest in the shekels & I must make some arrangement with Wareing, perhaps as a result I'll be able to get the price of a haircut out of the profits – but I question if my anti-Krishnamurtism will pay as a T.S. investment.

Morison filled in one or two details next day (written on the back of a Guild of the Pope's Peace hand-out), and then silence falls till *Some Fruits of Theosophy* was published early in 1919, by Harding & More, a small Catholic publishing firm in High Holborn. It is an unremarkable-looking piece of work, apart from the prelims where Morison's hand can be seen.* Although the text is divided in the way Morison suggested, Thurston's name only appears at the end of his preface, in which he speaks

81

warmly of Morison, who 'has taken great pains over the collecting and verifying the facts set down in this brochure, and I can only express a hope that his labours may be useful to many, Theosophists as well as Christians, who live without suspicion of the sinister elements latent in not a few of the religious movements fostered by this age of unrest'.

It seems unlikely that this hope was realized, although Morison's work deserves a place among the classics of fraud-exposure. He is at his best in charting the nefarious behaviour of the 'ecclesiastical free-lances who inhabit the clerical underworld', among them Anglicans who had come to grief like Mr Marsh Edwards, consecrated 'Bishop of Caerleon' over a shop in Barry, Glamorgan, on 14 June 1903.

His Lordship's flock, it is interesting to know, consist chiefly of goats (I am reminded of St Matthew xxv. 33) and nannies. I quote from *The Farm and Garden* (November 13th 1909). 'His Lordship the Bishop of Caerleon has a large flock of Nannies for sale, in milk and kid; very healthy and hardy. Apply Manager, Galatea, Chilworth, Surrey.' I have not space to tell the story of the Bishop of Caerleon's bankruptcy nor of the aged and milkless goats dumped on the unsuspecting purchasers.

Mathew makes his last appearance in May 1918, at a reception in Bayswater in honour of the Empress Eugénie as 'Mgr. l'Archevêque Marquis de Povoleri, Comte de Landaff' – shades of *Hadrian VII*. It was all good polemical stuff, but there is more fun than fury in it; as Adrian Fortescue later observed, 'What a comforting ass Mathew is.'*

The war was over: change was in the air. Morison, unlike some objectors, was released early. 'Hear of Stan's good prospects. Send him £5 (previous Xmas gift)', Mrs Morison wrote on 29 November. At Christmas dinner all the Morisons were united. Little Edith got a job at the Bank of England in February; her brother was still looking. Burns & Oates still went on as if nothing had happened, although Francis was now away full time at the *Herald* and the Pelican Press. Stanley and Mabel decided to try to find somewhere more permanent to live. They did not have to look far: down the hill from Golden Square, on the slopes of Mount Vernon, there is, as Pevsner justly puts it, 'a delicious secluded little C19 composition'.* The centre of this is the Catholic church of St Mary, Holly Place, one of the earliest in London. Founded in 1816, its stucco façade is pure Italian, with its Tuscan doorway, Virgin in niche above, topped off with an open bellcote. At right angles to Holly Place is the end of Holly-berry Lane, a cul de sac with two little cottages in it. The last of these, No. 11, was vacant, and the Morisons moved in before Lady Day 1919. Still quiet and shaded by trees, it must have been an ideal haven after the squalor and misery of the last three years.

Morison changed his signature: the 'A.' disappears, never to return. He also decided to take his handwriting seriously. The model of Fortescue's half-uncial had not withstood the turmoil of 1916, and Morison had begun to experiment with italic. He started with *The New Handwriting* by Mrs Robert Bridges, which he had bought in 1916, but finally chose the illustration of 'semi-formal writing' in Johnston's *Writing and Illuminating and Letter-ing*.* Now in 1919, he regularized the detail of the letters and set himself to achieve a greater degree of precision. The improvement can be seen already in the letter he wrote, the first of many, to D. B. Updike on Christmas Eve this year. Nearly thirty years later he wrote to his friend the palaeographer E. A. Lowe:

When I took my own script in hand I formed it on a certain, as I thought, rational basis and decided that, as far as capitals were concerned, I would stick to the *capitalis quadrata*. And for the lower case I stuck to humanistic pretty closely, but not absolutely. I abandoned humanistic which has a straight '*q*' in favour of the capital form which has the tailed 'Q'. I did this for the reason that the tail seemed to me to give the shape more dignity, and I got more fun out of it.*

But of all the changes of 1919, the most decisive came on 31 March, when the *Herald* became the *Daily Herald* again, and Francis, as Assistant Editor, was fully occupied there. He invited

Morison to take his place at the Pelican Press, as, in the words of his appointing letter, 'Designer of Printed Matter'. The title was rather grander than the job itself –

He later found himself described as 'our layout artist'. A 'layout', he discovered was a plan: 'artist' was added for the sake of impressing customers. The term 'typographer' had still to come, but 'layout' was in use in advertising agencies to describe the sketches made for the benefit of their clients, and later for their printers.*

But it made Morison think about the task expected of him. In Moxon's *Mechanick Exercises on Printing*, the first book ever written on all aspects of printing, there is a well-known definition: 'By a *Typographer*, I mean such a one, who by his own judgement, from solid reasoning within himself, can either perform, or direct others to perform from the beginning to the end, all the Handy-works and Physical Operations relating to *Typographie*.' Morison took this very seriously. He had learnt much from the Meynells: he had now to design 'by his own judgement, from solid reasoning within himself'. He was not himself a typographer since he could not himself 'perform . . . all the Handy-works and Physical Operations'. But 'direct others to perform' he could; and so, with their aid, Morison set about to define, in practice, what this new position should entail.

The Pelican Press now had Monotype machines and could therefore set type mechanically. Four Monotype designs were ordered – Old Face, Venetian, Plantin and Imprint – but some of the individual letters in each were unsatisfactory, and specially designed letters and ligatures were ordered.* In December 1918, too, Meynell had commissioned a poster type from Bruce Rogers, who had come to England in 1917 to work with Emery Walker and at the Cambridge University Press. This was completed the following June.* By then Meynell had left the Press, and it was Morison who dealt with the final stages of the cutting. There were four sets of decorative initials by Henry Ball; and there was the ever-growing collection of printers' flowers. Thus equipped, the Pelican could afford to look for more work among a wider range of customers. When Morison listed them in 1921, it made impressive reading: old friends, like Burns, Oates & Washbourne (as it now was), the *Daily Herald*, *Westminster Cathedral Gazette*, the Labour Party, Adrian Fortescue and Everard Meynell; friends of friends, like Cardinal Bourne, Percy Dearmer, Annie Besant and the Theosophical Society; publishers, Cape, Chatto & Windus, A. C. Fifield, Longmans, Putnam's and Sidgwick & Jackson; and big business, in the shape of Mac Fisheries, the Midland Bank, and – a name which was to mean more to Morison in the future – 'Heal & Son, Tottenham Court Road'.

The variety of the work, and of the customers who brought it, broadened Morison's horizon extensively in a very short time. The addition of capitalists, artists and publicity men to his acquaintance stimulated him, but did not cause him to alter his opinions or leave his old friends. He extended the already vigorous policy of self-promotion practised by the Press. Meynell had produced one broadside specimen of types in 1918, which had been praised by Bruce Rogers; together they produced another to celebrate the acquisition of the Cochin types from the Parisian foundry of Peignot in 1921. This, too, earned the delighted praise of Bruce Rogers.

Mount Vernon: New York
1 April 1921

Dear Mr Morison,

The gorgeous specimen sheets, which you so kindly sent me and which I have been so slow in acknowledging, came safely to hand and I am delighted to have them – I say 'them' – but they created such a stir amongst my printer friends that I have had difficulty in keeping even one of them for myself. I am hard pressed for it, also, so won't you please send me some more?

I can find no mention of price on them but you surely must make a charge of some sort for so elaborate and costly a piece of printing. You ought to, at any rate. A bookseller out here could do quite a bit of business in them. Perhaps I shall take them on as a side line. At any rate I want to pay you for further copies – and have hit upon the following ingenious (?) scheme.

I owe John Hogg 11/– as per enclosed bill. Would you be good enough to send him that amount out of the accompanying one-pound

note (a souvenir of my sojourn in England) and then send me 9/–
worth of the specimen sheets? – that is, if 9 shillings will cover its
cost – I have seen much smaller nine shillingsworths than that.

I congratulate you upon it, entirely. No printing office in this
country could show such an attractive collection of working materials
– or at any rate none has ever done so. The Merrymount Press *might*
possibly do so – but they couldn't display them to better advantage.

The Garamond type is not yet on the open market – but half a
dozen offices are using limited founts of it – we have perhaps as good
an assortment as any. I have set one or two little books in it – but I
am not wholly pleased with it for book-work. I think it will find its
widest use in commercial work. The italic is, in my opinion, distinctly
superior to the Roman. I am sending you several specimens under
separate cover of various sizes of it – I'm sorry they are so fragmentary,
but I keep almost nothing of my bits of printing by me for any length
of time.

I wish I could induce you to have a few characters of the Pelican
Poster type re-cut to better proportions. The cap H in particular is
too heavy for the rest – and then with minor improvements to be
made in other characters – but I haven't a proof of any of it here, as
I write, and can't specify them now. Will do so, however, if there is
any likelihood of their being made.

Wishing you all success

I am

faithfully yours

Bruce Rogers

The Garamond has the fault of most of the A. T. F. Co's. machine-
cut mats: a rather blunt and rounded bevel when it meets the face of
the type – which causes it to thicken rapidly when used on soft paper
or with much ink. (See Architectural League announcement.)

The new 'Garamond' type, produced by Morris Benton and
Henry Bullen for the American Type Founders Company, was
to become a matter of absorbing interest to Morison.

But if praise from America was encouraging, Morison was still
anxious to keep up old friendships, particularly with Burns &
Oates. Wilfrid had withdrawn from the daily running of the
firm, and most of Morison's dealings were with MacKenzie. It
was to Wilfrid, however, that he wrote on 24 June 1919, suggesting that his salary (then unfixed) should be £20 per quarter.

Above all, Morison was delighted to work with or for Adrian Fortescue. He had re-established contact at the beginning of 1919 by writing to Francis Meynell about his favourite project, which was to occupy the rest of his life.

I write this time to propose to you a plan that I have much at heart. I want you to print the Latin Text of Boethius: *de Consolatione Philosophiae*. First, it is really one of the most important books of later Latin. Perhaps you know already that it has an enormous influence through all the middle ages. St Thomas Aquinas and a score of other famous people wrote commentaries on it. In those days everyone read this book. It is one of the most important sources of Dante. Boethius was really the man who first introduced the philosophy of Aristotle to the West. He is one of the chief sources of the whole school, or schools, of Catholic philosophy. He is the original source of a crowd of sayings, proverbs, axioms, and so on, repeated from him by Dante, and then by everyone since. For instance: 'A sorrow's crown of sorrows is remembering happier things' was first said by Boethius in his Consol. Phil. It is also an exceedingly beautiful little book, alternately in prose and poetry, full of fine things and quite beautiful verses. I verified in the Museum catalogue the other day that this book was printed over and over again, with commentaries and without, from the XVth to the XVIIIth centuries. But now comes the incredible fact. There is not a single edition of the Latin text now in print, anywhere in the world. . . .

So I propose to you that you print it, with such beauty of type, and so on, as would make a really nice book (it will not be a large book, perhaps about 120 octavo pages). Could you not find a publisher to undertake the risk of this? What about Burns and Oates? A beautiful edition of so great a work (when there is no other) ought to bring great glory to the firm, and, I should think, ought at least to pay its way; even if it brings no great profit.

Morison took up the matter, and reported favourably. 'Your news is exuberantly good,' wrote Fortescue on 24 March.

So there will not be an end of all the good prospects that filled lots of us with hope, if you work for B. & O. Good luck to the plan; and may you take over more and more of their work. Perhaps after all we shall see the Missal done by them, and other liturgical things, and my hymn book. I am all eagerness for Boethius. . . .

Then I hope that you will be so kind as to look after the production of as pretty a book as possible. I have seen some work of the Pelican Press which I think beautiful. Would it be possible to have big versals [initial letters, he meant] and then to print some copies with the space for these left blank, so that one could fill them in by hand?

On 11 April, he sent Morison a copy of the text to work on, to which Morison replied with a long note. There is then a gap till 25 October, when Fortescue sent an advertisement for the Boethius, and commiserated on 'the evasion of the maid' – a rather unexpected sidelight on Morison's new prosperity. There was a meeting with Dr Orchard in the offing, to which Morison must have looked forward with some apprehension.

Before his conversion, Morison used to frequent the Congregationalist chapel at the King's Weigh House near Marble Arch.* The minister was a theologian of some ability and a popular preacher, W. E. Orchard by name. It is a tribute to his power that subsequently, with the agreement of his flock, he used to celebrate Mass and give Catholic teaching. Eventually he was 'ordained' into the Catholic church by Vernon Herford, a harmless crank who believed he had been consecrated bishop by a semi-mythical South Indian cleric, Mar Basilius. These dubious credentials did not prevent Orchard from acting as Catholic chaplain to the C.O.s in Wormwood Scrubs (it is likely that Morison met him again then), and he contributed to the N.C.F. commemorative history in 1919. As Morison feared, the meeting was not a success. Fortescue all too clearly thought Orchard muddle-headed, and Orchard told Morison that Fortescue was boisterous. In a mood of some irritation, Fortescue wrote a gigantic letter of explanation, taking as his text one of Orchard's more banal observations 'My heaven is being where God wants me to be'.

But in February he consented to lecture for Orchard:

St Hugh Letchworth Herts
17 February 1920

My dear Morison,

Thank you for your letter. Did Orchard really say that Logic is not everything? If he did, it is very funny; because that is exactly what I should have guessed he would say and the very words I should have put in his mouth for him. . . .

Please tell me any further criticisms of my performance you may hear. Has any report of it been published? There was nothing in the Tablet. Do not hesitate to tell me of any adverse criticism. To say truth, when I consider that meeting now, looking back calmly on it, I am not at all pleased with my part in it. First, I had prepared about four times as much matter as I could possibly get in in one hour. I had got comfortably through the preparatory matter, in a pleasant leisurely way, and was just setting down to the beginning of the subject itself, when I looked at Orchard's watch in front of me and saw that half an hour had gone already. From that moment on I was feeling driven at break-neck speed by inexhorable time. All the latter part was rushed in a wild hurry. I left out whole chunks of what I had meant to say (notably all about the Pope), I missed points and sewed up patches awkwardly. I think the latter part especially of my talk must have been a torrent of words, fragmentary, incomplete, disconnected. Afterwards I kept on remembering points that I had meant specially to make, important qualifications (to what exactly is a Catholic committed, how far is he bound to agree with the Pope, how far do we admit that the Church may really need reform, why the Reformation was a failure, the development of doctrine, are laws infallible, how far the Church has the right to make laws at all, and so on – heaps of points). All this I left out in my wild hurry towards the end. . . .

Now of other things. I send you the complete MS of our Report, that I want you please to print for me as nicely as you can. I also enclose the Report of two years ago, printed by some small local firm, to show about how it has been done so far. But you will do something much better than this. . . .

You settle what you think will look best in all questions of Caps italic and so on, also headlines and the whole set out of the thing. Funny thing. When first I heard of you I thought: 'Who is this ass, who has the cheek to talk to ME about writing or printing?' Now I have the most absolute, final whole-hearted trust in your judgement and taste in all such things, and I know that you know infinite streets more than I do about them. You see, at first you occurred to me only as a Burns and Oates person, whose ideal of fine printing would probably be the Granville series. Then I began to see the Fell type, and other things; and I began to understand that you and Francis Meynell were not exactly the sort of people I had imagined. . . .

Also, thank you very much for being so kind to me last Wednesday and for standing me that swagger dinner. I did not realize at the start that I was being your guest all the time, and it seemed rather a shame to mulct you of so much. But it was all the more kind of you to be so hospitable. The evening was fun on the whole; but I wish I had done it better. And I wish I could do it again, and that I had about three lectures of an hour each in which to expound my thesis.

Yours always
Adrian Fortescue.

This was high praise from a man who thought as deeply about lettering as Fortescue.

St Hugh Letchworth Herts
In Epiphania Dni, 1920

My dear Morison,

Here is a suggestion for the CRVX CHRISTI etc ornament. But consider this only a first suggestion. I can easily, and will, do it again with any modifications you may want. . . .

In the writing I have let myself go a bit in the direction of prettiness, thinking that the inscription is very short and could stand something of this kind. But, of course, I can write quite stern Roman capitals, if you like. I find myself now rather getting away again from my intolerant enthusiasm for pure Roman capitals, with no fancy lines at all. For years I have sworn by that principle, loathing Gothicky and all fancy letters. Now I begin to see another danger. If you write dead severe, and take great pains to get it all perfectly straight and true, you may end by making your writing look like type, quod nefas est agere. The worst of it is that printing is getting so infernally good and clever. The poor scribe has hard work now to do better than printing. Yet shame on us if we cannot write better than print. . . .

Let me know what you think about all this. . . .

Yours always Adrian Fortescue.

He also appreciated the special copy he was sent of *Living Temples* by Bede Jarrett, one of Morison's favourite Dominicans, later. It was printed by the Pelican Press, and – unusually – has Morison's name in the colophon. 'I am amused', wrote Fortescue, 'by the Revisers all Nihil-Obstating at each other at the beginning.' He was also prepared to take Morison's politics seriously: 'I will not write "Mr" nor "Esquire" on this. But should it not be "Citizen Stanley Morison"? This, I think, is the quite proper thing.'

By now, the Morisons were getting ready to go on a long journey and on 18 June Fortescue gave them some good advice.

Your big journey sounds very nice. I wish I could go abroad this year. I should go to Denmark, if I could. Nearly all the places you will go to are good and worth seeing, except Rome. Rome is a filthy hole, with nothing whatever to see. It is worse than ever now. Last time I was there was in 1913. I was struck by its general getting-worse since I was a student there. They have made it into a huge noisy cockneyfied modern town, with Cinemas and hideous vulgar new buildings all over it. The old Papal Rome (not yet quite extinct in my time) had at least a certain rather debased picturesqueness. All that has gone now. There never were more than three really good things to see there, S. Maria in Cosmedin, the tower of S. Giorgio in Vellabro (nothing else, the church is hideous), the plan and fragments of old work in S. Clemente. A catacomb may be worth looking at, and the inside of the Coliseum. There is nothing else to see in Rome at all. You can exhaust all worth notice in about three hours. Then take the train and go somewhere else. Above all do not go near either St Peter or St John Lateran; both are a repulsive nightmare. But there are a lot of very fine things in the little cities around, the Castelli romani, especially Frascati, Marino, Lariccia, Castel Gandolfo, Genzano, Grottaferrata. What is left of the old Roman life is to be found in these. They represent still, more or less, what Rome would be if generations of Popes had not destroyed it, systematically, expensively, thoroughly. Do not speak to any of the officials of the Curia, nor have any dealings with any of them. They are the lowest class of men that survives. If you go near them they will probably either pick your pocket or try to sell you an Indulgence. Remember me to the present Ordinary, if you see him. I am told he is a decent man. It was Leo XIII in my time. In Rome you can give a Cardinal five francs, one franc to anyone below a Cardinal. Do not offer more than this; it would be a waste of money. For five francs you can buy any sacred privilege you fancy – you can also get a very good dinner for that amount. They would sell the Holy Trinity for twenty francs. O Simon Mago, O miseri seguaci – that is Dante.

Anyhow, good luck to your travels. There are two things to see in Milan, nothing in Florence. Lots in Ravenna, nothing in Paris, Genf, one thing in Basel, plenty in Strassburg. By the way, will you give a message from me to the Roman Ordinary? Tell him to look after his own diocese and not to write any more Encyclicals, also that there were twelve apostles and that all bishops are their successors, also to read the works of St Paul, also to open his front door and walk out, also that the faith handed to our fathers is more important than either the Sacred Heart or certain alleged happenings at Lourdes.

Soon after they got back, there was another crisis. Throughout the summer Francis Meynell had been visiting Copenhagen, nominally to obtain paper supplies for the *Daily Herald*. There he met Litvinov, who had come to negotiate the return of Russians interned in England (including his wife Ivy). Between them they arranged for Russian support to the *Herald* – always short of money – in the form of precious stones which Francis smuggled into England, unbeknown to Lansbury, who denied all rumours with the headline 'Not a Franc, not a Note, not a Rouble'. But in September the story leaked out, and Francis was forced to resign from the *Herald*. It was a bitter moment for him, made more bearable by Morison's support; it was Morison who, on 15 September, wrote to beg Wilfrid to offer Francis shelter where he could 'think out first principles and then plans for the future'. Eventually Francis returned to the Pelican Press, and Morison in turn began to look for another job. Christmas came and went, but early in the new year, on 23 January, Mrs Morison 'met Stan and Mabel full of news. We go there evg. and hear it is that Stan has offer of good post Manchester but has not decided yet.' On 31 January Morison went up to Manchester to see, discussions followed, and by the end of February plans were all made for the move to Manchester in May.

Before Morison left, he produced for the Pelican Press a little twenty-page booklet called *The Craft of Printing*. The colophon is dated 'Ascension Day' (5 May), so it must have been almost the last thing he did before he left. Nominally, it is a piece of publicity for the Press, but its modest sub-title 'Notes on the History of Type-forms, etc.' gives a truer indication of its purpose. It is in fact the first draft of an enquiry which had already engaged Morison for over ten years and was to occupy him for the rest of his life. All this time Morison was trying to provide a co-ordinated history of the changes in the forms of the letters in the Graeco-Roman alphabet, from their first appearance, scratched on the Moabite stone, to what you read in today's paper. Not content with the genealogical task he thus set himself, he added to it that of ideological explanation. His quest for the inner springs of outward appearances was to him a passion – how many times did he hit the table with his fist (his wholly unconscious mode of releasing the vehemence he felt) and shout 'I want PROOF!'?

So here for the first time is Morison rehearsing, as he was to do so often, the connection of calligraphy with typography, the transition from the Roman inscriptional capital to the Carolingian book hand, and to black-letter:

Gutenberg's letters therefore reproduce in type the best formal writing of his time and place. His black-letter is undoubtedly an excellent specimen, and . . . there can be no question that it is beautiful when massed in a rubricated page.

In after years he would have regarded the condemnation of Plantin and his successors, who 'allowed the technical excellence of the craft to obscure the at least equally important matter of beauty in the final production', as too hasty. The characterization of the success of the Bodoni and Didot types as 'aided by their novelty and the degraded taste of the time' was also a prejudice taken over without due consideration from Morris. He would certainly not have found it in De Vinne's four-volume *The Practice of Typography*, although his enthusiasm for Pickering, as the first to revive interest in the fine printing of the past, comes from De Vinne, whose influence here and in the formation of his typographic style was considerable.*

But if *The Craft of Printing* is the first sign of the trend of Morison's main historical speculation, it is also the first example of his unequalled skill as a propagandist. As Morison concludes his 'Notes on the History' with commendation for the enterprise of Kippenberg's Insel Verlag and Bruce Rogers, it becomes apparent that all this is not just history.

England, however, has lacked a commercial press adequately equipped for the production of beautiful books in a variety of styles. Thanks to Wm. Pickering and the Whittinghams, it is nowadays easy to secure a plain book well printed in Caslon's letter. For work of a more decorative and versatile character, & to afford facilities for those who require their printing executed, not indeed with a pedantic straining after the *letter*, but the *spirit* of the ancient presses, the Pelican Press was founded in 1916. Equipped with the finest types allied to the most fitting ornaments – and what is more important, an understanding of the best traditions of their use – the Pelican Press offers its service to that increasing public which realises the difference between good and bad printing. Reference to the specimen sheet of types, borders and ornaments will show that in respect to material the Press is assuredly in a unique position. . . .

It is becoming increasingly evident that good material and good taste, sound design, good machining and rapid service command a ready welcome. For matter in fine type (and finely printed) attention is already bespoken. The commercial catalogue, the pamphlet (political, religious or what not), the leaflet, and newspaper advertisement setting alike secure this premium of interest at the Pelican Press.

And the message is rammed home with a final shoulder note 'The address: 2 Carmelite Street, E.C.' Time and again Morison was to use this technique. It was the basis of his talent 'for convincing powerful moneyed men that reasonable projects are practicable'.* First the reader's attention is caught by an original historical summary; this leads up to the statement of the problem; it is followed by Morison's solution which is thus shown to be historically inevitable. It was an instrument of immense power, which Morison came to use with an authority equally flexible and strong.

As Morison was packing up at Carmelite Street, another heartening letter from Bruce Rogers arrived.

Mount Vernon: New York
13 June 1921

Dear Mr Morison,

The posters and the two pamphlets arrived quite safely, each in its due time. I have sold eight of the ten specimen sheets and the others will be disposed of as soon as I can find time to let certain people know I have them. I enclose £3 (I hope the war-notes are still good in England – you must tell me if they are not) and for the additional 10/– you may send me either two more specimen sheets or whatever number of the pamphlet 'The Craft of Printing' that amount will pay for.

I think you are quite too modest about the pamphlet. It seems to me most admirably done, for its purpose. It is refreshing to read so well-written an exposition of a Press's capabilities – especially after so much of our own spread-eagle advertising and 'announcements'. Typographically I like best the pages in the smaller type. The 12 pt Cochin would gain, I think, by leading it a bit – but this is only a small quibble – the whole conception and arrangement of the pamphlet is a thing to congratulate you upon.

I can't help but regret that you are leaving the Pelican Press – I should say that it has flourished under your direction and that it was an interesting place to work – but I long ago learned that those outside generally know little of the real situation – and you doubtless have the best of reasons for making a change – which is more than I can claim for the many changes I have myself made in the past few years.

Wherever you go I predict success for you and certainly wish it with all my heart.

faithfully yours
Bruce Rogers

Curiously enough, just as I was about to seal this, I received the announcement of your new address – so send this letter there. I hope it is not going to burden you to get the specimen sheets or pamphlets – if it is, let them go. At least there is no hurry whatsoever.

5

THE proposal that Morison should move to Manchester had come about through Walter Lewis. He was ten years older than Morison, a printer with twenty-five years' experience of the trade. He was a West Country man by birth and apprenticeship, but from 1903 to 1916 he had been with Ballantyne & Co. in Tavistock Street, Covent Garden. Here he had got to know most of the London publishers and built up a goodwill that went with him when Ballantyne's was taken over. After resurrecting a small printing firm from bankruptcy, he was introduced in 1919 to Charles Hobson, who had recently set up a lively advertising agency in Manchester. Hobson wanted to start a press there to produce the sort of work his own business and other equally discerning customers demanded. A private company, the Cloister Press, was formed and through 1920 Lewis was occupied in planning the site at Heaton Mersey and choosing machinery.

Hobson decided that he needed a typographical expert, and Morison's name came up. Lewis had already met Morison: he had been impressed and had no hesitation in recommending him to Hobson as typographical adviser to the Cloister Press. Now he went to the Pelican Press, terms were discussed, and Morison and Hobson settled it over dinner at the National Liberal Club.* It was quite an adventure for Morison. He had never been away from London for any length of time before (except to prison), and he had never been far from professional advice and help from those he knew and trusted. He was now going to be entirely on his own. He was, however, fortified by a new friendship. Morison had been introduced by A. W. Pollard to the work of Daniel Berkeley Updike.* A year before Updike had written to Meynell at the suggestion of Bruce Rogers, enclosing some of his own work and asking for the Pelican broadside. With contact thus established, it was Morison who took the next initiative, sending Updike the *Ordo Administrandi Sacramenta*. This delighted Updike, himself a specialist in liturgical printing: 'I scarcely know any better,' he wrote. He was equally impressed by the broadside and a year later asked if he could procure some of the special Pelican initials. Morison replied on 14 March 1921 sending him a complete set, which he suggested Updike might have redrawn: 'Your own judgement and taste I am sure will also find room for improvement in several of the forms.' He also sent his own new broadside. Updike, in thanking him, observed:

I cannot help feeling that one of the chief results – perhaps the chief result – of the revival of better type-forms during the past fifteen years, is the reproduction of a certain mellowness felt in earlier fonts but which, until lately, too great mechanical perfection has successfully kept out of them. In this country some of Mr Goudy's types have this quality and the new Garamond type, brought out by the American Type Founders Company, in the italic, has been quite successful in this respect.* I am taking the liberty of sending you some specimen sheets of this, which you may not have seen.

Morison had not, and was grateful, as he wrote on 12 April:

I have recently been very much interested in this face. Last year, Mr Bruce Rogers showed me one or two advance pulls he was then considering, and last week I visited the Imprimerie Nationale, where the original punches cut by Garamond still remain. I was successful in purchasing some books printed for a Paris publisher in types made from these original punches. It is apparent to me that the American Type Founders' version, though in many ways excellent, has modernised the type, particularly in respect to refining the alignment. . . .

I am exceedingly interested to notice that you have a volume in preparation at the Harvard University Press. I am looking forward to this with enormous appetite.

He went on to ask Updike if he had come across 'a remarkably good Dutch letter rather of the "Fell" feeling' of which he enclosed a sample. Updike concurred with him about the A.T.F. Garamond, adding that he thought even the Imprimerie Nationale type 'somewhat refined'.

You must not expect too much from my book, which is only a kind of beginners' essay. If it furnishes a basis on which other people can build, I shall have done, perhaps, all that I can hope to do.

This characteristically diffident description of Updike's classic *Printing Types: their History, Forms and Use* did not prevent Morison from realizing that here was a master of his craft equal to De Vinne.

At Hampstead all was in turmoil. On 25 March, Stanley and Mabel left for a short holiday in Paris (where he visited the Imprimerie Nationale) and Rome, and Edith Cole arrived from Birkenhead for one of her whirlwind visits to the London theatres, and for what were known as 'animals' meetings'. This took up most of April, and then Morison's elder sister Jessie was taken ill with suspected appendicitis (she was still working at Eastbourne where Mrs Morison had gone for refuge in 1917). Worse was to come: it had been planned that Stanley and Mabel should leave at the beginning of May, and that Mrs Morison would move into 11 Hollyberry Lane on the fourteenth. But on 4 May, their departure was put off till the seventeenth, and then again to the thirty-first. Somehow, Mabel and Edith Morison both found time to sit for portrait drawings by Edward Hall Lacey. May 30 was spent packing, with a farewell dinner with Francis Meynell in the evening. Next day, 'Stan & M ready to start, when much wiring and phoning and postponement till tomorrow'. Stanley and Mabel went to *Man and Superman* at the Everyman in the evening; there was nothing else to do. On 1 June, 'they really start at 10.30', Mrs Morison noted thankfully.*

There was work to be done at once. A general prospectus of the Press, *The Distinguished Result in Printing*, with the object of 'introducing the Cloister Press to Publishers, Secretaries of Learned Societies, Schools, Churches, Universities, & all Kindred Bodies', was also produced; appropriately, it was set in the Cloister types. The A.T.F. Garamond was already on order: by July, a little specimen entitled 'The Garamond type: a first showing', was already printed. The text of the specimen was a brief and (as later appeared) erroneous account of the source of the type. It was an immediate success: Frank Sidgwick, of the publishers Sidgwick & Jackson, sent R. C. K. Ensor's *Catherine: a romantic poem* to the Cloister Press in consequence, and it was duly set in Garamond, with the same note on the source of the type.

But before the Garamond leaflet was out, Charles Hobson, Morison's new benefactor and boss, had impulsively swept Stanley and Mabel off to Italy to look for fine paper. They arrived back in London on 1 July and left the next day. They went to Varese, where they arrived on a sweltering afternoon.

The sun and the colours of the houses vied with each other in the strength of their glare. In our search for Signor Ricci's shop where we were going for nice papers, we suddenly collided with a cart drawn by two bullocks. We had never seen such steeds, if steeds could be applied to these sleepy large brown-eyed lazy beasts. I looked and looked and I have never forgotten the tawny animals lazily sweeping their long tails from side to side, as they were prodded with a thorn with two sharp points. Arrived at the little botega. We opened the door and entered. A heterogenous collection of china, glass of more or less value. Chiefly more, for we learned our host was a man of taste and knowledge. Here a vase from far China rested on a piece of rare French embroidery. An odd Florentine chair of the time of the Borgias stood in one corner. A Tuscan plate lay on the seat. But we had come to look at papers. End papers and papers of covers of books. Presently the owner appeared and with him his son who had had a severe injury to his ear in the Great War. His father explained that his son was deaf but the younger man soon understood what was the nature of our quest. With stately Italian courtesy we were soon looking at papers. But what papers! Such colours, such designs and textures. Hand made by a process invented by him. But they were poor and very glad that we had come to buy. Sheet after sheet we purchased. These papers were afterwards taken to Germany and France and England – where they were afterwards turned out by the dozens by machine.

They brought back to England a selection of these patterned papers, which had a considerable success. They were later imported by the Curwen Press, who produced their own famous papers, designed by Lovat Fraser, Paul Nash and others. Then they went on to Fabriano to the paper mill of Pietro Miliani. The austere countryside on the borders of Umbria and the Marche appealed to the Morisons, while Hobson brooded on its commercial possibilities. The mill itself impressed them all:

A great building full of light and air, and we were shown the presses where this lovely white paper was made. S. Scotti the head was most kind and we were afterwards entertained at a local restaurant by his managers.*

To Hobson, long afterwards, Fabriano was still 'the most lovely of all papers'.*

They got back at the end of the month to find a letter from Adrian Fortescue, grateful as always for the last lot of books that Morison had sent him and asking for help in preparing an armorial letter-head for the Archbishop of Liverpool, Morison's old friend Keating, who had befriended the Guild of the Pope's Peace. 'You see,' wrote Fortescue, 'he is already appointed and palliumed and recognised by his brother of Rome – and yet he cannot excommunicate a canon, till he has the proper note-paper on which to do it.' Morison gave him some advice, suggested the Cloister Press should produce what the Archbishop wanted, and enclosed what Fortescue, thanking him, called 'the interesting and most beautiful specimens of type etc'.

Morison was enjoying the new resources at his disposal. Hobson's agency had artists and copywriters, all of whom had skills which Morison could observe and, on occasion, use. Chief among the latter was W. Haslam Mills, a leader-writer on the *Manchester Guardian* and perhaps the best writer of advertising copy in the country, a man of obvious authority and charm. The artists included the fluent Horace Taylor, who could turn his hand as easily to imitate the Beggarstaff Brothers' style as to the two-dimensional line of the young George Morrow. All these skills and Morison's own considerable imaginative power were brought to bear on the series of large folio type-specimens – Morison's finest work in this line – that began to come out now (portfolios were available in October). These might have been enough alone to justify Morison to critical northern eyes (also on Hobson's staff was William Grimmond, a more inventive typographic designer than Morison, who laid out most of the Cloister Press publicity work), but he had a more strenuous standard to meet. The form of printed matter had come to occupy a less dominant position in his mind than the form of the letters with which it was made, and here he had only himself to satisfy. The limits of the existing range of types – the Cloister Press was provided with Goudy, Plantin and Caslon, as well as Garamond and Cloister – were still constricting. Morison wanted to extend the range. So he wrote to Sydney Caslon of H. W. Caslon, the oldest and most respected type-foundry in England, whose original Old Face he had done so much to promote:

Heaton Mersey, near Manchester
19 September 1921

Dear Mr Caslon: I have seen proofs of Mr. Menut's Garamond* and on the whole prefer the American version. For one thing, the original and the U.S. l.c. f has a beautiful kern but in the Peignot version there is a f like your Kennerley almost. Would it not be possible to recut some sorts if you had a concordat with Peignot? I very much want to have the cap J (this shd. be a descender as Caslon o.f.) both rom. and ital. cap Q , and original & ampersand for the italic.

I enclose for your interest a proof of the first job in which the American letter has been used. But if I were a typefounder (and I wish I were) I think that as the American Typefounders have a Garamond and Menut has one and Goudy is to cut one for the Lanston American Mono Company I should cut a face which was originated a little after Garamond's time by one of the Le Bé's who succeeded him. It is very like the Garamond in many ways, yet the R is more perfect (both rom. and ital.). Also I prefer Le Bé's M with the trifle-spreading legs in the smaller sizes, the general roundness of the italic as compared with that of Garamond (the original and the copy)

[a page or more is missing here]

I enclose two photographs for your interest. As I understand it, the American project (wh. is still in the 'talk' stage) is to fit up a foundry here for the casting of their Cloister, Garamond, etc.

About the Flowers, I enclose a paste-up of the varieties which I desire to possess. I shall be delighted to have any of them you hold.

In the event of the disappearance of one or two of the items I beg you to consider the possibility of recutting. If you do so I would willingly use my influence to secure orders from English and American presses.

Yours very truly
Stanley Morison

Having discovered the direction in which he wanted to go, Morison was in a hurry; in his haste, he made a mistake, and in writing to put it right made another friend of some consequence to his future, Henry Bullen of the American Type Founders Corporation (who did not, in the event, set up a foundry in Britain).

Heaton Mersey, near Manchester
9 November 1921

Dear Sir: I write to apologize for a serious error of fact into which I have unwittingly fallen. The accompanying circular attributes the initiation of the Garamond revival to Mr Bruce Rogers, to whom I sent a copy. He informs me today that the credit of this happy revival is wholly due to your Company and principally to you, Sir. I regret exceedingly to have given currency to a piece of mis-information. I am glad to say however that fewer than 100 of my circular have been issued and I shall of course seek every opportunity of placing the credit for this revival to your Company's name. In conclusion I should like to congratulate you most heartily upon the output of the American Type Foundry Co. and upon the Garamond in particular.

I am, Sir, with apologies & respect
Your faithful servant,
Stanley Morison

P.S. I should explain that mine is the first British house to use the Garamond and that I wrote the announcement before having seen any A.T.F. specimen. By separate post I send for your library a copy of the first book to be printed in the Garamond. To my knowledge the type is not yet in the possession of another British printer.

The Morisons had settled at Alderley Edge, a pleasant village still in the country, ten miles south of Manchester and over the Cheshire border. But Morison never did like the country, and apart from the John Rylands Library, a collection almost equal to the British Museum in early printed books, Manchester itself had little attraction for him; he did not find the sort of company he was used to in London. On the other hand, once a month he and Mabel came up to London for a few days' business, with a weekend added on. It was a time of much hope and concerted action. People who had not seen each other for years during the war now met; shortages, especially of paper, were a thing of the past; and there were high hopes for the trade, and the realization of the ideals of the *Imprint*.

It was to one of these joint meetings that Harold Curwen of the Curwen Press took his newly appointed traveller, Oliver Simon, who retained one clear recollection of them:

I remember little of the discussion except that it became both diffuse and heated. The man from the Cloister Press, however, spoke throughout with humour and good sense in a most compelling yet likeable voice which, coupled with what he had to say, compelled respect. He was dressed entirely in black with a white collar and shirt and appeared rather delicate and frail in physique. He had a keen, mobile face and in his eyes there was much sympathy, understanding and strength of purpose. After the meeting I followed him out and invited him to come with me to a nearby Lyons teashop for a cup of tea. My new acquaintance accepted and in a few minutes Stanley Morison was giving me some startling typographic opinions.*

Oliver, congenial and convivial, with a sense of quality in print as strong as Morison's and a passion for the graphic side of the business which Morison did not have, was the partner and co-adjutor of the most fertile period of his life. Morison owed much to his encouragement, and when Oliver died, thirty-five years later, he tried to sum up his debt:

Simon was an exceptional man. He may not have been impressive in appearance. His manner certainly was diffident. He attempted no brilliance in his writing; and never attempted to brighten his speech with would-be witticisms or attempted profundities. In a sense Simon was illiterate; he was not even well-read. His mind was totally un-speculative. . . . How came it, then, that this unimpressive, unintellec-tual, un-well-read, unargumentative man was regarded by so many of us as remarkable? In the first place he was endowed with an exceptional capacity to absorb wisdom from conversation and social intercourse and to bestow it upon others. The persons he found most attractive were those able to talk acceptably about the contribution that pictorial illustration makes to the typography of the printed book. He himself would listen attentively to the ideas of others; ready to give the generous word of praise which compelled them to continue talking; he himself insinuating the impression that he was a disciple rather than a master. . . .

Now, it could never have been said of Oliver Simon at any time in my experience, that he did most of the talking; but he did most of the inspiring. . . .

Many here have reason to be grateful to Oliver Simon. This is true of nobody more than of myself. While it would be silly for me to say that I am indebted to him for any of my ideas, I owe him, in the first instance, the place in which to express them. He was a creative, energetic and practical force.*

Oliver's sharp eye had distinguished Morison's remarkable qualities at first glance. The black suits came, as they did for the rest of his life, from a clerical outfitters. White shirt, black tie, black shoes and socks, black hat (the original slouch hat, which he and Francis first adopted as an act of rebellion among the sea of bowlers and top-hats, had a hole in the brim, to make it easier to hang on hat-stands), even a black cord watch-guard – it all indicated a careful, even studied, appearance of rational austerity. That unique voice, 'low-toned but loud, with a slight off-accent',* slightly nasal yet musical, with the incisive impulsive attack that he had adopted from Adrian Fortescue – this, too, struck Simon forcibly. And there was his enormous laugh, the violence – a slap on the thigh if amused, fist pounded on the table if serious – with which a feeling or opinion was put across. It was a personality in which strength was uppermost.

The meeting with Simon only increased Morison's longing to be back in London. Christmas 1921 was spent there – 'S and M early service' – and the Morisons sent out a fine card with the Holy Family drawn by Horace Taylor. At the beginning of 1922, the Cloister Press opened an office in London, in St Stephen's House, Westminster, and Haslam Mills's nephew 'Bingy',

G. H. Saxon Mills, was installed there as junior clerk. It was to be Morison's base for the next two years, although now only an excuse for more frequent visits. This event was announced with a fine leaflet, copper-engraved throughout. It was a dying process for which Morison had a passion, and a number of engravers, beginning now with G. T. Friend (always Morison's favourite), learned to produce what Morison thought letters engraved on metal should look like; his own hand had a powerful influence on the result.

In the meanwhile, a flood of books, brochures and pamphlets poured from the Cloister Press to astonish and delight the typographical *cognoscenti*. The mixture of Hobson, Lewis and Morison, if explosive, was both creative and fertile. 'We believe', said the *Fleuron* review of the Scott Moncrieff translation of Proust printed by the Press for Chatto & Windus, 'that the book under review has already, here and there, its influence on the everyday book published in England. . . . And yet each volume . . . does not cost one penny more than its ugly brothers.'

Morison found time to keep up his scholarly connections. He sent Updike a book, for which Updike thanked him on 4 April, adding:

What a pleasant sort of book 'The Daniel Press' is. I tried for a copy of the limited edition with extra illustrations but was too late to get it. I have a few of the Daniel books – in particular, the first one which was printed with the Fell type, which he was really the means of resuscitating. I met Dr Daniel a good many years ago in Oxford, but remember much more distinctly an extremely sarcastic Jesuit named Clark, who was at Mr Daniel's at the same time, and whose acerbity of manner entirely over-shadowed Mr Daniel's mellowness of disposition. So my only reminiscence of Mr Daniel is of someone else – to put it in rather an Irish fashion. I am wondering whether you have published a broadside specimen or other, of the types that you use at the Cloister Press? I collect such things. . . .

Morison replied rather firmly on 1 May:

Certainly the 'Daniel' book is a very delightful work. I possess but one of that Press's work, the Henry Patmore Poems. I am interested in your reference to the Jesuit Clarke (final 'e' please). He was a brilliant Anglican clergyman who became somewhat dull as a Jesuit. Yet he produced an amusing manual of Logic & wrote a number of biting papers on Mme Blavatsky, the founder of Theosophy. . . .

I have not yet completed a 'specimen' of the types in use at the Cloister Press. For some time I have been at work upon a number of sheets which when completed will form a small portfolio. So far I have done Cloister, Goudy, Forum, Black-letter, and Garamond. The latter is a failure and I must do it again. I will see that copies of all go to you. Recently I have had a sort of *Printing Supplement to the Manchester Guardian* upon my hands. This is a 16 pp folio advertisement of the Cloister Press and is not very interesting. I do not say this simply because much of my work has been interfered with though this is the fact. You will judge for yourself when copies arrive. There is a two page article by me upon the form of printing types.

The rest of the 'Supplement' was written by Holbrook Jackson, editor of the literary monthly *To-day*, author of *The Eighteen Nineties*, and a benevolent and articulate proponent of fine printing,* but the name of Charles Hobson appeared largely in it. Clearly the seeds of trouble were already sown, although allowance must be made for some self-protective apology on Morison's part in showing what he had done to such an expert as Updike. He was not so ashamed of the result that he did not send a copy to Bullen on 20 May, pointing out:

You will notice that the American Typefounders Company is by no means ignored. The type of the body is the so-called Plantin letter of the English Monotype Company. It is printed from type and not from plates, and is I hope not altogether a bad piece of work.

And to Oliver Simon he wrote a fine calligraphic letter to announce it, beginning 'dear fellow-worker in the vineyard' and ending '88°'; it was a fine summer.

Throughout the summer Morison worked on, although increasingly uneasy. Three more of his folio sheets appeared, *Typographical Decoration & Illustration*, in which initial letters are rather oddly mixed with some of Taylor's Beggarstaff-like illustrations, *Caslon Old Face*, where Morison's hand can be seen in the text, and *A Display of Fleurons*. This last is particularly interesting, since it shows how far Morison had come since those cheerfully empirical days at Burns & Oates, when printers' flowers of all sorts were used with some abandon. He had come across the work of Peter Jessen, the great custodian of the Berlin Kunstgewerbe-Museum library, whose *Der Ornamentstich*, published in 1920, had first shown Morison a coherent history of ornament. Jessen had been director since 1886, and had published a catalogue of his library's ornament collections as early as 1894; it was a work for which Morison developed a high regard.

On 5 April 1922 he had written to Jessen who had replied kindly from the Kunstgewerbe-Museum (the word 'Staatlichen' was rubber-stamped over 'Königlichen' in the letterhead):

> Berlin S.W.11, Prinz-Albrecht-Strasse 7a
> 8 April 1922
>
> Dear Sir
> I am delighted that you take an interest in the studies in which I am also engaged. My concern with engraved ornament as a whole is really limited to the forms that served as patterns. I have made no special researches into its use in books and bookbindings, except, as you will have read, and I can only repeat it, that there is work to be done on the subject. At present I have no further information about books with 'Mauresques' (that is the word we use instead of the more expressive 'Arabesque') published *before* 1540. After that I know of the borders in the book of hours of Geoffroy Tory (1543) and the composite pieces of Oronce Finé (1544). . . .
> I cannot add anything further about gilt arabesque bindings except that they appear in Venice, often under oriental influence at the beginning of the sixteenth century. As far as I know, no special study of this subject has been done, at least in Germany.
> I shall be very glad to try and answer any further questions and should be very interested to hear the outcome of your further researches.
>
> With distinguished greetings
> Dr Peter Jessen.

The result of Morison's researches is briefly summarized in 'Arabesque *or* Mauresque' (evidently Jessen's comment on

German usage had unsettled him), on the two inside pages of *A Display of Fleurons*. He deals quickly with the influence of the Levantine trade on Venice, lists the arabesque books of Pellegrini (1530), Jean de Gourmont (1546), Virgil Solis (1550), Flöttner (1549) and Balthasar Sylvius (1554), all of which he would have found in Jessen, and then moves on to the influence of Gourmont on Bernard Salomon, the wood-engraver of Lyon, and Bernard's on his son-in-law Robert Granjon, who, Morison rightly saw, popularized the type-cast ornament all over Europe. This was wholly new, and Morison's pursuit of the arabesque ornament persisted, finding its final expression in *Venice and the Arabesque* (1955) and his last great book on the Fell types (1967). Meanwhile he had equipped the Cloister Press with a small but well-chosen collection of flowers, including the Granjon flowers (perhaps obtained from the Oxford University Press), which were illustrated on the last page of the sheet.

The fine weather still continued, but Morison's unease grew. The informal meetings of those interested in fine printing went on, and towards the end of the summer five people – Oliver Simon, Morison, Francis Meynell, Holbrook Jackson, Bernard Newdigate – met in Morison's office to discuss Simon's proposal of 'a publishing society which should produce one book a year to demonstrate . . . that books set by machines could be as beautiful as the books of the Private Hand-presses'. Francis Meynell proposed the name 'The Fleuron Society', Jackson was elected secretary and some note-paper printed. But the two meetings that ensued were a failure. It became clear that Newdigate did not believe a machine-set book could look as well as one hand-set, and the final meeting ended in irreconcilable discord. Simon, however, was determined that the cause should not lapse.

Morison and I left last and we again had tea at Lyons. In this somewhat pedestrian surrounding, I suggested that we two at least might do something immediately tangible by launching a periodical devoted to typography.*

By now the fine weather of earlier in the year had turned sultry. Finally the storm broke.

St Stephen's House Westminster S.W.1.
7 September 1922.

Dear Simon,

I have just seen Victor Gollancz who has been persuaded by Albert Rutherston that I know a good deal about the history of printing. Gollancz has asked me to consider the project of issuing a portfolio of some two hundred collotype plates of typographical masterpieces from Renaissance to Rogers, including our little selves. He wants this to be a sort of five guinea affair, and to be accompanied by some ten thousand words of my sophisticated guff. Of course I feel very attracted to this. The two hundred collotypes fairly make my mouth water; but I told him that I had already promised to do something of the same sort, though of course much less magnificent, for you. What do you think about it? Would the issue of the Benn book bar or prepare the way for a smaller and more detailed work? Consider these things. Last night I spent with E. W. Humphries. I got on very well with him and we talked mostly about God. Such time as we gave to this world and to the typography thereof was hardly as satisfactory. Mr. Humphries is an admirable character and a very good head of his press. He would like me to join his staff as a canvasser. I should have the privilege of designing such work as I found, and would at all times have the right to approach Eric Humphries if the initials did not fit, or Cheltenham were thrust upon me. I have agreed to go to Bradford to see the press next week, but I do not feel that I should be happy if my work were primarily of the nature described. It is exceedingly kind of you to have so trumpeted my name in Bradford and elsewhere. I have a letter today from Phillips, asking me to meet him on Monday, and on Tuesday I go to Bradford. My fear is that Levers will worry after me again before I can come to any conclusion. But I am most excited about the Benn book. Gollancz showed me some of Lowinsky's astounding drawings for the forthcoming Shakespeare.

Yours
S.M.

His head full of Gollancz (then with Ernest Benn, publishing fine editions, art books and the first works of Dorothy Sayers), gratitude to Rutherston (one of Oliver's uncles), the prospects at Bradford with Lund Humphries, and Oliver's plans, Morison could not take the trouble seriously. Writing to Updike at Christmas to thank him for his *Printing Types*, he explained what had happened.

St Stephen's House Westminster S.W.1.
20 December 1922.

Dear Mr Updike:

I am sorry to have been unable until now to acknowledge the receipt of your last letter which was speedily followed by the two handsome volumes on Printing Types. I need not say that your work is unique – in its interest & its execution. The consistent high level of its erudition is amazing and the matter is, as A. W. Pollard said to me, remarkably well arranged. I have also found the volumes a source of consolation. Almost at the time of their arrival, the Cloister Press (wh. I am proud to see receives honourable mention in a footnote) went into liquidation; the troubles of this world were too much for it. Being therefore compulsorily retired from active printing I was pleased to have your work to take my mind off the subject of making ends meet. . . .

This was indeed a problem, even if it was more a question of choosing than finding a new job. Simon himself hoped that the new journal might provide a living. Morison had another idea: on 27 September he wrote:

Dear Simon:

You will call me a blasted nuisance. Hear why: I have written to yr brother [Herbert, then at the Kynoch Press, Birmingham] asking him to go further with me into the question of my representing him in London. After a good deal of thought I have come to the rather obvious conclusion that for fine printing at his low price there can hardly fail to be a market. If therefore it is at all possible I should like to make the venture.

Thus I should at least secure a reasonable freedom of movement & have leisure for the Fleuron. I have written the Press asking for the Suppt. copyright for nothing. Also I have asked for the transference of this office to myself. The Fleuron therefore will not fail to be housed here. . . .

And Oliver was thus able to realize his hopes for a London Office. For the immediate future, however, Morison had a long-standing plan, which he would not give up, to go abroad. It was for this, in all probability, that he sold his entire stamp-collection, breaking one of the few tangible links with his boyhood. In his Christmas letter to Updike he went on:

Having finished the books I went to Berlin & elsewhere in Germany and the neighbouring countries, visiting professors, printers & publishers. These abound in Germany & I found your name well known by the director of a library in Berlin where I studied for some four weeks. His name is Jessen of the Kunstgewerbe Museum. I was very pleased to find in the library a number of pieces of your printing. . . .

From there he wrote to Simon:

Hospiz in Zentrum
Holzgartenstrasse, Berlin
18 October 1922

Dear Simon:
   I should like you to consider re-naming our Typographical Annual. The name I recommend is *The Fleuron*. This would be an advantage I suggest. In the first place the title 'Typography' is very stiff and not absolutely free in the public mind from technical connections. The Fleuron possesses just that note of historical & romantic feeling which we need to express. I think too that the name of our publishing venture will be worthily sustained & provided with a happy inauguration from two points of view. *The Office of THE FLEURON* will possess double appropriateness.
   I work hard at the library here from 10 till 3 going sometimes without lunch. The custos, Dr Jessen is exceedingly good. He is thinking of my project that he should do a job for the Fleuron. I am sure he will do so. It is cold here & I often wish for Hollyberry Lane & its fireplace.

Yours
Stanley Morison

Jessen was absorbing. He told Morison more about the history of ornament; he gave him the run of the Grisebach collection, systematically arranged to illustrate the history of printing; he introduced him to what little writing there was on the history of writing, notably Servidori's *Reflexiones sobre la verdadera arte de escribir* (Madrid, 1789), which first gave Morison the idea, long worked on but never finished, of writing the history of Italian

writing-books; he provided photographs, and letters of introduction to printers.* But Morison still had time to think of the
Fleuron. More plans shot out a day or two later.

Berlin
22 October 1922

Dear Simon:

I have this morning discussed with Dr Jessen the publication by the
Fleuron of a monograph on the subject of Pattern books. The reason
that I have suggested this is because there at present exists nothing on
the subject whether in English or French. Even in German there is
only the chapter in Jessen's handbook, *Der Ornamentstich*. Jessen has
agreed to take the job in hand. It will be a substantial volume, a
royal quarto of 64 pp. text, 12 pp. bibliography & 250 plates by
collotype I suppose. Of course the work will appear in English only,
there must be no question of collectors waiting for the publication
of a German edn. which the exchange will make cheaper than our
own. I don't know whether you are familiar with Pattern Books or
if you share my enthusiasm for this publication but there can be no
doubt of its success because it will be the only work of its kind. And
this must be our programme, so far as possible to do unique books.
The *Tory* of Pollard & the *Johnston* book will be good from this
point of view. All these should be high priced books and elaborate
prospectuses should be issued. On the other hand we should do a
lower priced series to be printed at Oxford, Paris, Leipzig, New York
and elsewhere. I think these should be of the belletristic order. . . .

It will take a good deal of sacrifice of time & endeavour before we
achieve a reputation. I imagine Jessen's will be our first considerable
work and it should help us very much. . . .think about the belles
lettres & F.M.'s concurrence. I should like to secure his interest. Let
me have a note if you've time.   S.M.

By 29 October he was getting rather weary:

Dear Simon

I am glad to have a note from you. I wish I were back in London –
I feel at the moment like Nero fiddling at the burning of Rome. I
ought to be working hard getting a job and not wasting my time on
book-writing. Truth to tell I can't ever give my best to the Fleuron
until I am sure of my bread & butter, i.e. that I have some sort of
permanent job. It will be necessary for me to explore thoroughly all

possibilities on my return. But being here it is silly not to make the most of it. Nevertheless I shall try to return as soon as ever possible.

The next morning he was off at eight o'clock to Leipzig, then to the Klingspor foundry near Frankfürt. One further publishing idea had occurred to him, a facsimile of a Gravelot sketch-book at Berlin, but he was aching to get back: 'Congratulations on the excellent painting of the front door which Mills tells me of. I hope to turn the handle no later than Nov 15.' On 10 November came a postcard from Munich: 'I have visited two private presses to-day, the Bremer and the Rupprecht. I hope to see you not later than Nov 17.' And soon after that he was home, eager to set about the exciting business of planning a new life.

On his return, he found a long letter from Adrian Fortescue waiting for him. He had been away on a long holiday visiting the haunts of his youth in Bavaria and Tirol, and had got back in the middle of October to find letters from Morison. Boethius was almost finished, he wrote on 17 October:

Thank you very much for all the trouble you have taken and are taking in the interest of my Boethius. Yes, I got a letter from Burns and Oates that seemed as if they knew nothing at all about the Boethius, and did not even know what that word meant, a fabulously stupid letter, even for B.O. and W. I will gladly trust your judgement in the whole matter of publishing Boethius, if you will be so kind as to interest yourself still further in it. And I shall always be most grateful to you for this.

There followed detailed proposals for dealing with the book, which had grown considerably, some characteristically minute instructions for his church service-sheets followed, and the letter ended:

But I will write about this later. Meanwhile I hope all goes well with you; and thank you again very much.

Yours always
Adrian Fortescue.

Two months later Morison heard that he was incurably ill, and on 11 February 1923 he died, aged just forty-nine. With his death Morison lost the first and last person to understand fully what the Church meant to him. It was a devotion as profound as unorthodox: 'I wouldn't belong to this bunch of macaroni merchants for another second if it wasn't the way of laying hold on Christ,' he roared at T. F. Burns, consulting him, over lunch at the Holborn Restaurant, about his magazine, *Order*. It was a position that had been tempered in the aftermath of the modernist controversy.

My well tried friend Adrian Fortescue (R.I.P.) historian of the Eastern Churches & a man of amazing erudition . . . felt very uncomfortable at the practice of the present folk at Rome – but he had no doubt of the theory. Yes, the trouble about Modernism & Liberalism is that much of it is so true. This is borne in on me every time I hear the gospel for the last Sunday of Pentecost.*

Fortescue himself once set out the views that they shared in a letter thanking Morison for sending some works of biblical scholarship from Rome.

But I confess that I do not look to the Pontifical Biblical Commission for much light on the subject. I think that they are quite hopeless people, tied to Leo XIII's Encyclical and to decisions with which nothing can be done. Leo XIII commits himself to the historicity of every statement, not obviously a quotation, in the Old Testament. That is absolutely and finally hopeless. If we are really committed to that, there is nothing more to be done with the Bible but to let it alone & ignore it. I find in these days that some educated Catholics take this line & keep off any discussion of the Bible with terror. That is all one can do if one may not dispute the historicity of any statement. The Old Testament is full of statements that are not true, that are proved not true as certainly as you can prove anything in physical science or history. To maintain that the first eleven chapters of Genesis represent what really happened is to expose oneself to the derision of any educated modern person. You might as well uphold the Ptolemaic system of astronomy. When a man or Commission takes that line I know what it means, I do not want to hear any more of his views and I only hope that some intelligent Protestant will not get hold of what he writes. Do you know Loisy's six points, that he says are now so established that it is impossible to dispute them? They are that Moses did not, in any sense, write the Pentateuch, that the Pentateuch does not contain true history in the earlier chapters at any rate – and so on. I agree with him entirely. It is not that one wants to deny what the Pope has said. On the contrary one has the strongest reasons for wishing to justify him. But in such matters as this, one simply cannot refuse to be convinced by the evidence. The absurdity is that these Encyclicals and decisions of the Biblical Commission are not *ex cathedra*, they are admittedly not infallible, yet we are not allowed publicly to say anything contradicting them. I wish to goodness that the Pope would never speak at all except when he means to define ex cathedra. Then we should know where we are. Meanwhile the only way is to ignore what Rome says, as far as one's own convictions are concerned, and not to discuss the subjects publicly at all. It is a rotten situation.*

Rotten or not, the Catholic Church was for Morison the only one. He would argue and attack and abuse, but never doubt. In a strong man, his faith remained the strongest part.

6

Long before 1922 Meynell and Morison had taken in their stride the hurdle – if it ever was one to them – of machine-setting. While Morison was away, Francis had installed Monotype equipment at the Pelican Press. Consequently, when peace returned, and with it easier communication with the 'fellow-workers in the vineyard', they learned with surprise how widespread was the prejudice still existing against machines: the Monotype machine could *set* well enough, in their view; all it needed was better letters in its die-case. A few modest experiments at the Pelican had proved that the Monotype craftsmen could do what was required of them. The only difficulty was that they had very little idea themselves what letters ought to look like, or of the historical facts that underlay their forms.

The first indication that letters were more than a matter of accurate optics and engineering came with the irruption of Gerard Meynell in 1912. It is worth remembering, as an example both of the improvisation and the insouciance towards design then prevalent, that the Imprint type was originally considered both as an extension of the existing Monotype Caslon series *and* as a copy of Caslon Old Face. The inception of Monotype Plantin, the only other pre-war 'historical' design, is an even better example. About 1910, E. P. Prince, the last professional hand-punchcutter to work in this country, produced a new type for P. M. Shanks & Sons, type-founders in Bloomsbury. It was in essence an old-style type – like Imprint, the model was probably Caslon Old Face. But according to the Shanks catalogue, 'while closely following the old DESIGN the lines have been strengthened slightly to give additional colour'.* The object of this was to produce a type that would stand out on art paper printed on a machine-press as well as the original Caslon printed on a damp paper with a hand-press. It is not a very striking design, but for its special purpose it had some success, enough to worry the Monotype company into producing a competitor. Shanks had called their type Plantin Old Face, 'following the fashion of issuing new typefaces with names, however incongruous, reflecting the typefounders' own curious version of history'.* Monotype decided to inspect this alleged source.

In 1876 the ancient printing-house of the Plantin family in Antwerp, virtually untouched since the seventeenth century, became a museum.* Its first curator, Max Rooses, did much to publicize it, and in 1905 produced an *Index characterum Architypographiae Plantinianae*. It was probably in this book that Monotype looked to find out what 'Plantin' was: at any rate, the type used for the text was the model (even down to some wrong founts) for the Monotype Plantin which appeared in August 1913. The text type of the 1905 *Index* was not, in fact, one that Plantin ever used; it was acquired by his descendants after 1652, long after he was dead.* The Monotype version, however inadvertently, was a success.

The Monotype Corporation had been set up in this country in 1897 to exploit the 'Monotype' patent. Its technical adviser and, from 1900, managing director was Harold M. Duncan, who had been sales manager of the American company. He was a man of some stature, and to him was due the steady success of the Monotype in Europe. The addition of new type designs was a personal enthusiasm of his; in 1922 he was already ill, and had only two years to live.* His successor was to be William I. Burch, who had joined the company in 1898 as Secretary. He was then, one of the older Monotype directors recalled, 'a rosy-cheeked young man whom I thought extremely young for the job'.* He had not changed greatly in appearance, but in 1911 became 'Manager and Secretary' and since his election to the board in 1917 had become Duncan's right-hand man. Frank H. Pierpont, the Works Manager, was also an American, and an engineer of genius. He came to the company from Germany, where he had redesigned and promoted the Typograph machine, in 1899. Since 1908, when the new works at Salford were built, he had ruled over them with an iron hand, but, unexpectedly, the cutting of Plantin was his idea.* In 1899 he had brought with him Fritz Max Steltzer as head of the Type Drawing Office (which he remained until 1940). He was something more than a draughtsman; it was he who in April 1913 had provided Duncan with 'historical data' on Plantin. Finally there was R. C. Elliott, who had an equal gift for mechanical invention, writing and teaching.

In 1900, three years after its establishment, the Corporation put its first type-design on the market, an ordinary 'Modern' face; most of its successors were likewise what Morison, looking back in 1950, called 'bread-and-butter Albions, Clarendons, Grotesques, Old Faces and Moderns, currently used in the trade'. Exotic types were soon added, with an eye to markets overseas. The type-casting machinery was also improved. The 'Display Attachment' (1905) made it possible to cast single letters as large as 24pt; the 'D Keyboard' (1908) provided an infinitely flexible selection of characters; the size limit of text composition went up to 14pt in 1909 and to 24pt in 1914; from 1924 onwards it was possible to cast single letters in sizes up to 72pt or even larger for display work.

In 1911, the first original design was produced, for J. M. Dent, publishers of the Beardsley *Morte d'Arthur* and the Everyman series; this was Veronese, in which Morris's views on roman type were closely followed. Then came Plantin and Imprint. But the designs adopted thereafter were derivative: Caslon and 'Scotch Roman No. 2' were copied from the existing types of the H. W. Caslon and Miller & Richard foundries; the American Type Founders Company provided the models for Bodoni and some printers' flowers.

Morison had first come into regular contact with Monotype at the beginning of 1922. They had recently begun to have the *Monotype Recorder* 'arranged and printed' with their equipment by a different printer for each issue. No. 187, the issue for January and February 1922, was printed at the Cloister Press. Morison contributed two articles to it: an article on the Press itself and the other on 'Old Face'. The first was trenchant:

In all its work the Cloister Press seeks to be disciplined by principles of sound design and construction. These principles are based in great part upon the usages of early printers. This is not to say that the Cloister Press policy in this respect is a mere corrupt or even slavish following of the ancients. But it is demonstrable that the fewer types and greater leisure of the early craftsmen resulted in the elucidation of principles of page proportions, margins, etc., which have not been surpassed, though they have been largely discarded in our own generation.

And, if its principles were sound, so was its situation, which

while placing London at no disadvantage, brings the great industrial towns of the north within reach of what has long been for them an important desideratum, namely, a complete and intelligent printing service infused with a thorough-going modern spirit.

This was much firmer stuff than the mildly ruminative style adopted by Hobson's copywriters towards the customers of the Press. Nor was Morison's next piece less uncompromising. Written to commemorate the completion of the 'true' Monotype recutting of Caslon Old Face (series 128), exacted in 1916 by R. & R. Clark of Edinburgh as the price of installing Monotype equipment, he does recount the history of William Caslon, and his type, comparing it favourably with 'the old *style* letter, a rather savourless compromise between old and modern face'; he commends Imprint and Plantin as well. But he opens with a splendid diatribe against Cheltenham (which is not strictly to the point):

For long it was a faithful saying, and found great acceptance in advertising and other offices where they 'lay out' – *When in doubt, specify Cheltenham*. And as they were generally in doubt the magazine and newspaper advertisements, etc., were full of Cheltenham and its lusty offspring – the wide, the bold, the condensed, the shaded, and the outline. No face in recent years has had anything like the popularity of Cheltenham. Unhappily the letter carried the seeds of its own destruction. Cheltenham is what the advertising agents call a 'distinctive' letter – it has 'features'. Indeed it has. These very features are its undoing. Your good type cannot afford a trilled r or a stunt g. Your very good type avoids worrying the reader with its G's and A's. The devil of these distinctions is that they foul the type for use in books, and no type can live by job work alone. So the Cheltenhams are dying. In America you shall turn in vain the pages of the *Ladies' Home Journal* or the *Saturday Post* for a line of it. In the *Daily Mail* it has been largely supplanted by an admirable roman made in Hamburg by Genzsch and Heyse. For Cheltenham, however, let it be conceded that it is, at least, not a 'modern' letter, and that it has powerfully assisted the public taste to an appreciation of the old faces which are now succeeding it. Let there be no mistake, the future is with the old face. Nor is this matter for surprise. The mincing perfection of the modern faces renders them no match for the vigorous and free old faces.

And to prove it three-quarters of the illustration space is taken up with a page from Enschedé's *Proef van Letteren* (1768), the Fell types, and – Morison's new favourite – the A.T.F. Garamond.*

Morison had begun as he meant to go on – to educate these well-meaning barbarians. First of all, it was desirable to have the Garamond – a better Garamond – available for machine-setting in Britain. This was done, and next year Morison explained to Updike how it happened.

You ask whether the English Monotype Garamond is the same as the so called Goudy ('Garamont').

The English Monotype Garamond was cut at my suggestion. It was begun in January or February 1921 and at that time we were ignorant of any American Monotype intentions. I supplied a number of documents, old books printed in the early days of the Imp. Royale (I possess the first, the *Imit Xi*) and some of A. Christian's recent publications. Also I collated a number of volumes of Federic Morel, Vascosan, Colines, etc. The Monotype Corp^n went to great trouble & expense to get a good result and in the case of some of the sizes I am very pleased.*

The last page of the *Recorder* is taken up with the announcement – set in A.T.F. Garamond – that Monotype 'are cutting matrices on the model of the GARAMOND TYPE'. So it was that on

20 January the Type Drawing Office noted Duncan's wishes: 'Would like this face reproduced exactly as originals. Originals are inaccessible, being at Imprimerie Nationale in France, but Mr Duncan will try to get suitable print as a model.' Morison provided some books for this purpose, but nothing happened until 28 March, when Steltzer pointed out that the specimen books lacked a number of characters.* In April Morison went to Paris and saw the inaccessible originals, and bought some more books, printed in the Imprimerie Nationale 'Garamond'. Armed with these, Morison enlisted the support of his new friend Eric Humphries, who had commissioned him to design the next issue of the *Penrose Annual* of printing and the graphic arts. Carefully primed, Humphries with a deputation of other printers tackled Monotype again in May. They were seen by Burch who finally told them that Garamond would be cut, even if it ruined the Corporation.*

Some confusion was clearly caused by the difference between the French original and the A.T.F. rendering. Morison wrote detailed criticism in August to which Steltzer replied, but after several trials and proofs (toward the end of September Lund Humphries plaintively asked when the types would be ready for the *Penrose Annual* 'which should be commenced very soon') the difficulties were resolved. The 24pt was finished first, in September, and the other sizes from 12pt to 36pt next month.* A preliminary announcement was made in the September–October *Monotype Recorder*, and the November–December issue – printed by the Westminster Press – was given over to a complete showing. Morison himself contributed an introductory note, and no doubt the portrait (a contemporary woodcut) of Garamond and the layout as well. The fine decorative border and head- and tail-pieces may be by Macdonald Gill.

By December 1922 – no later – the *Penrose* was out and Newdigate, generously forgetting his prejudices, gave it a glowing review in the *London Mercury*. Morison had taken the opportunity the new type afforded to advocate Garamond against Jenson, and, wrote Newdigate,

It is at any rate nearer to the types of our own time, and if for only that reason is a better model for modern printing than Jenson's can be. Indeed, in weight and thickness of line, in the openness and generous width of the letters, and in the goodness of its design, this revived Garamond has advantages over any other letter which is within reach of the general printer of today.*

All had gone well, but there was throughout an unresolved misunderstanding between Morison and the works which typified their subsequent relations. Morison noticed 'the natural and good-tempered strife that underlies the relations between the branch and the head office', and added:

F. H. Pierpont, a forceful character indeed, strongly opposed to 'interference' from the head office, was, too, a notorious upholder of the sovereignty of staff engineers, of practical accomplishments and of accepted values. The ideas of outside experts with theoretical learning but of unproved utility were and always would be resisted. By the engineers such theorists, like the customers who were regarded as a necessary evil, would be kept in their place. And to the factory heads, as to many of the sales staff, a typographical adviser had no place at all.

In the case of the Monotype Garamond, it is surprising that there was not more trouble. The works were under the impression that they were producing a modified version of the 'caractères de l'université' as used by the Imprimerie Nationale from 1898 on, tidied up in the same manner, but not as drastically, as the A.T.F. Garamond. This last was irrelevant to Morison who, rightly seeing that Christian's italic founts were not pure, tried to improve on them, first by choosing as *his* model a very early use of the types, the *Imitatio Christi* of 1642, and secondly by correcting them against still older models. According to Beatrice Warde, H. L. Bullen was doubtful whether even the earliest Imprimerie Nationale types were by Garamond. He may have expressed his doubts to Morison, who later observed, 'Some slight knowledge of italic encouraged the Corporation's adviser in 1922 to regard the fount used at the Imprimerie Nationale in association with the "Garamond" as uncontemporary in appearance.' It was not until 1926 that he learnt the true sources of the roman and italic, which he now saw must be different. In 1922, the models pursued in the works of all those French printers that Morison lists to Updike were the sixteenth-century Robert Granjon's 'gros canon cursive', as used at the Imprimerie Royale from 1641 on, for the italic, and the 'gros canon' of the seventeenth-century 'caractères de l'université' for the roman, reduced from full size to 24pt. To this, Morison added a host of swash letters, including the terminal forms *nt e m* and so on, all derived from various sources.

Morison had in his mind's eye an *idea* of the true Garamond, which he was not to see clearly till 1926: the works had two modern printed examples, which they could see were different. It is remarkable, given the disparity of approach, that the type 'is, generally speaking and certainly in some sizes, successful'.*

It may be that initially Monotype had some misgiving about the danger and the difficulty of manufacturing new designs. Hitherto, they had been content to copy existing types. But any doubt they may have had about the risks of investing in the 'programme of typographical design, rational, systematic, and corresponding effectively with the foreseeable needs of modern printing' which he had broached to them, must have vanished in the warm reception that Garamond got when it appeared.

It is not clear when the casual association that had thus grown up during 1922 was put on a formal basis, but it was in the early part of 1923.* (It was a natural development, for the rival Linotype company had already, in September 1921, appointed a 'printing adviser', G. W. Jones.) Morison himself said it was Walter Lewis who 'convinced H. M. Duncan and W. I. Burch that Morison possessed commercial ability as well as typographical knowledge'.* Less, perhaps, than at any other critical point in Morison's life did those involved realize the far-reaching consequences of what they planned.

Lewis himself was on the point of taking an equally important step. He had hung on in Manchester after the financial crisis, acting as adviser on printing for Hobson while he looked for another job. It is very probable that this involved discussions with the Monotype people, known to Lewis since he went to Ballan-tyne's. It was at the end of January that J. B. Peace, the University Printer at Cambridge, unexpectedly died. There were a dozen applicants, but Lewis, although not a University man, impressed the Syndics with his good sense, experience and vitality, and it was he who was chosen. He went to Cambridge in May 1923.*

With Garamond safely out, Morison was free to pursue his programme with Monotype. In rapid succession there followed, historically speaking, a successor and a predecessor for Gara-mond. The types of John Baskerville had been much copied in and just after his lifetime, notably by Joseph Fry, but the revival of interest in them was due to Straus and Dent's biography of Baskerville, published in 1907. Stephenson Blake, the Sheffield typefounders, revived Fry's 'Baskerville' in 1910. While at Cambridge Bruce Rogers recommended the purchase of this version, but before he left he rediscovered the original matrices in France, and ordered a fount on his return to America. For Morison, learning from the confused progress of the recutting of Garamond, the question was which version to use. Duncan's first note to the works on 17 January 1923 ran:

Have sent for Life of Baskerville from which you can derive all the forms of types projected by Baskerville. One of the Caslons brought out a Baskerville face with improved italic. (18 Jan) Would like to examine Baskerville face brought out by Caslon in 1798. We agree it would be better to adhere to original type as far as possible. (19 Jan) Have asked Mr Morison to let you have the Caslon specimen.*

On 31 January, Duncan went down to the works and con-firmed the decision to use the 'original' Baskerville, but although by mid-February trial matrices were cut in 18pt a problem had arisen: there was a difference of design in the different sizes. Duncan's note of 25 March commented: 'Trial proofs of Rough & Smooth Baskerville. Cannot see any difference. Did you send 2 sets from the same designs?' Then follows the reply: 'Mr Pierpont will bring drawings of both series to F[etter] L[ane] tomorrow.' The problem was eventually solved by choosing the 'smooth' Baskerville. In answer to Duncan's query on 17 June 'Upon what interpretation was this face based?', the works answered: 'Baskerville type drawn from copy of Terence printed in Birmingham in 1772.' It was therefore Baskerville's great primer, the type of his famous quarto classics and folio bible, that was adapted for the Monotype 18pt, and the other sizes copied from that.

There were other problems, especially with the italic ligatures. On 14 September came the request to 'expedite delivery of face, which is required for Penrose Annual'. The 11pt text size was ready first, the roman about 29 September and the italic on 6 October. The 18pt italic ligatures were still giving trouble, but the last (*gg*) appears to have been settled by the middle of the month. No immediate publicity was produced, perhaps by agreement with the *Penrose Annual*, but a broadside specimen was produced with the January–February 1924 *Recorder*. Baskerville was Morison's first great commercial success. Its homogeneity, with all sizes based on the original great primer, was an advantage. 'The Monotype series judiciously produced on this model was to prove of greater utility to the trade than any of the other types named after Baskerville, introduced between 1925 and 1929.' The italic was, in Morison's view, less satisfactory. 'There is neatness, modesty and consistency in the design but it is lacking in nobility, picturesqueness and character. . . . But it is not to be denied that, all deficiencies apart, the design as a whole possesses a degree of efficiency well worthy of Birmingham.'

For his other design, Morison went to the fifteenth century. He had strong and then unorthodox views on the roman types of that period. The *Hypnerotomachia Poliphili* printed by Aldus in 1499 was already famous as the most beautiful of all fifteenth-century Italian illustrated books. Its type had been praised by Updike, although condemned by William Morris as 'artistically on a much lower level than Jenson's'.* The whole book had been reproduced in facsimile in 1904, and now Harry Lawrence, of the Medici Society, wanted to produce a translation in type-facsimile with the original illustrations. So Morison set to work. It must have already been under discussion before 5 May, when

Mr Duncan wishes us to consider face with view to reproduction. Only sample we have is process reproduction face of Poliphilo & 4 pages left by Mr Morison. Can you obtain loan of additional pages or complete volume?*

This proved impossible but by June the question of matching the new roman with an italic (non-existent in 1499) was under discussion. The design to be used was one originally produced by Ludovico degli Arrighi, the Roman calligrapher, in 1526, in the form used after his death by Antonio Blado, the papal printer. On 11 August the cutting of both roman and italic was to be complete 'next week'. 'When will these be ready?' asked Duncan on 20 September. 'Mr Morison wishes to use this face as a prospectus for "Four Centuries of Fine Printing".' On 6 November the works undertook a trial setting of 260 lines for Lawrence, and by the end of the month it was complete. Hitherto it had been known as 'Raibolini' (the Bolognese painter Francesco Raibolini was then thought to be the same as Aldus's punchcutter Francesco Griffo), but its name was now changed, after some argument about the merits of 'ph' and 'f', to Poliphilus.

The original was, moreover, copied as it stood, without allowance for the spread of ink which distorts the real shape of a letter as it is printed on the paper.

It was possible, in fact, to compose, according to the correct dimensions of the original, a page of the Monotype version, place it side by side with the original, and find no difference except in paper. This test was in fact made, and, naturally, it gave the greatest satisfaction to the works. Everybody was amazed and gratified at this demonstration of what could be achieved by conscientious photography, exact tracing and efficient engraving. It was no longer to be doubted that the technical resources available guaranteed a reproduction, faithful to the point of pedantry, of an original, the revival of which had never before been attempted.

Morison always regretted that care was not taken 'to find the best pages . . . instead of relying on the pages provided by Lawrence'. For this he blamed himself, in his hurry to get on with *Four Centuries*. The italic, on the other hand, 'may be ranked as a success':* it was based on Morison's own copy of *Vita Sfortiae*, printed in 1539 by Blado, whose press-work, unlike Aldus's, was consistently good.

Four Centuries was printed by the Cambridge University Press. Lewis's arrival there had been a matter of great satisfaction to Morison. He was finding the business of convincing Monotype of the desirability of his 'programme' uphill work. But Lewis and he were old friends and Lewis could help.

The custom of cutting faces in response to, not in anticipation of, trade demands, was, in 'works' and 'sales' opinion, not only the older but the wiser course. Accordingly the continuity of the plan hinged upon the possibility of counteracting the obstruction of the works by ensuring orders in advance for the matrices that were planned. It was, therefore, peculiarly fortunate that the typographical adviser to the Corporation should become associated in a similar capacity with the Cambridge Press, headed as it was by a Printer empowered to include or to exclude any typographical equipment that might be rendered available.*

Monotype could ask for no more influential customer than the Cambridge University Press, and the demand that Morison was thus able to create for his own wares had a large part in ensuring the success of his programme.

All this activity did not complete the work that Morison did for Monotype in 1923. He did the layout for the January–February *Recorder* (a fine example of his restrained style with flowers), and contributed a review of Updike's *Printing Types*, in which he is more severe (anonymously) than in his letters about Updike's distaste for Monotype setting. The next number must have been concealed from Morison, for it is set in Cheltenham: it contains, however, a note by Duncan on 'Recent Typographical Literature'; in it he praises Morison's work, and the piece itself is evidence of the enthusiasm that Morison had evoked.

There were two further articles by Morison, in the May–June and September–October issues. The first is a summary history of the development of 'modern' types (to introduce the Monotype Bodoni). The second, 'On Decoration in Printing', was laid out by Morison and set in Caslon; it was his farewell to a style of design he was now to abandon. Updike's *Printing Types* had an enormous influence on him, and helped him to formulate a style which was hardly to change for the rest of his life. It is best described in 'Mr Morison as Typographer', in words which are in part his own.

Morison, a rationalist born, and by deliberate choice interested in the *raison d'être* of things, was confirmed in his admiration for the Didots, to whose founts De Vinne's books had originally introduced him. Updike's masterly account of the great French dynasty, and his comparison of the styles of its most eminent representatives, sufficed to free Morison from the remaining vestiges of typographical dilettantism and eclecticism. He gave up all interest in bric-à-brac. He even gave up, when and where he could, Caslon in favour of modernized 'Old Styles', such as Mr. Goudy's design, brought out by the American Type Founders Company. He began the practice, and has never varied from it, of standardizing the running headline in spaced EVEN SMALL CAPS. Analysis will show that his style, at this time and since, is an anglicization of the style of François Ambroise Didot (1731–1804) and of Pierre François Didot (1732–1793). Apart from excursions into other styles made merely with the object of satisfying his curiosity, Morison has not changed his ideas regarding the printing of books intended to be read more than once. For twenty years, his method of dealing with text pages, appendices, titles, headlines, and chapter openings has remained constant. Morison's typographic style did not become unnaturally standardized to the extent of producing uniform books with uniform characteristics; rather what he produced was a number of books with a family likeness. The detail, like the format, was decided after a study of the means by which the particular text was to be made clear to the reader; but the underlying principles were not dissimilar. In his settled opinion, the typography of serious books needs to be serious: free, at least, from the beauty that is 'laid on'. His endeavour was to serve the intention of the author, and the purpose of the reader. The task of the designer was limited to establishing general conventions that could be applied by anybody to particular books. Typographic design, in this sense, was not so much one of the graphic arts as a branch of editing, in which order was an essential element in the construction.*

But at the end of 1922, it was the *Fleuron*, not new types, that preoccupied Morison's mind more than anything else. Articles for the first number began to come in. The first was to be Meynell and Morison on 'Printers' Flowers and Arabesques', the product of quest now ten years old. 'Morison supplied all the knowledge and I supplied the adjectives,' said Meynell modestly.* He had other plans himself. He had readily agreed to the use of the name he had thought of for Simon's new venture, since his own Nonesuch Press was already starting – its first publication, *The Book of Ruth*, came out a fortnight after the first *Fleuron*. In his Christmas letter to Updike, Morison set out these and his other plans.

I very much wish that you would kindly indicate to me the title and description of the book whose printing gave you most pleasure & with which you are most satisfied. I ask this because I am engaged upon a rather large volume to be devoted to printing. It will be printed with care & will survey the development of typographical style. There will be some 350 collotypes (in colour where necessary) and the whole will be introduced with some 100 pages of historical summary. The book is to be a super-royal quarto and will be sold at £5.5.0 in an edition limited to 500 copies. Naturally I want to show your works and those of Bruce Rogers & perhaps Nash of California. Perhaps you may be even kind enough to refer me to any piece of really first class work which I may be in danger of overlooking. Your own two volumes are of immense value to me.

I notice by the way that p. 134 of vol. 1 no mention is made of the specimen sheet issued at Frankfurt-a-M in 1592 by the firm of Egenolff. It is a valuable sheet as it contains ascriptions to Granjon & Garamond and mentions J. Sabon (see Rooses) who worked for Plantin. . . .

I observe that at p 205 vol 1 you 'know of no specimen of the Le Bé foundry' . . . but at the Bibl. Nat. there exists a specimen of hebrews, greeks, romans and music cut by Guillaume Le Bé.

and he referred Updike to Omont's monograph on it, ending 'I beg to wish you a happy & prosperous 1923 and am, yours Stanley Morison'.

Updike was both kind and interested:

You must let me know what your future plans are. I do not know anything more wearing than trying to do good work when one has anxieties as to making both ends meet. We have had such times and they are not easy to go through.

He thanked Morison for the references to Egenolff and Le Bé, adding:

I constantly feel how handicapped I am by not having ready access to collections like that in the British Museum. . . . The typographical collection of the American Type Founders Company, in Jersey City, is a very good one, but it has many lacunae; and there is in Chicago a collection in the Newberry Library, founded by a man named Wing, which has started out on very ambitious lines and which in a few years time will be probably the best typographical collection in this country.

I should be very glad to send you several [volumes typical of the work of this press], and you can see which you prefer to use. I shall have to think out a little more carefully what I shall send. . . . Rogers' work cannot be bettered.

Updike's sympathy brought all Morison's plans bubbling out.

14 January 1923.
Dear Mr Updike

Thank you for your letter of January 5. It is extremely kind of you to bear in mind my rather tall request as to the Merrymount Press books. I do not mean to put you to the trouble and expense of sending me the entire volumes. It occurred to me that you might be able (a) to be able to refer me to copies existing in England or (b) to give me a spare prospectus or specimen page. I am of course most anxious to see this projected volume as representative as it will be sumptuous. It will be rather fun to show a number of the productions of the Imprimerie Royale and of other illustrious but overlooked presses of the past.

At present I am concentrating on the work of selecting exhibits for this work. In addition I have engaged myself to do a monograph upon 16th century Italian handwriting. For this Edward Johnston has agreed to write some twelve panels to be reproduced by collotype. This I shall publish *at the Fleuron*. The 'Fleuron' is the name of a

130

journal of typography which will appear annually at least. The first issue will be ready in March and will be demy quarto 14pt (Garamond). There will be little of real interest or value to such an advanced student as yourself. Perhaps however you will be able to read a long article on the origins of printers' flowers written by Francis Meynell and myself. It is a subject in which we have been interested for several years & it is possible that one or two of our conclusions will be interesting to you. I hope also to publish a short ms. on Geoffroy Tory by A. W. Pollard who leaves the Museum this year.

So you see I am becoming a sort of publisher – and of bibliographical monographs. Whether these will be the means by which I shall lose the little I possess remains to be seen. Nevertheless I don't so much mind if it turns out so. I have another book too. The man Geoffrey Keynes (*not* the economist but the surgeon who did the recent Blake book for the Grolier Club) has in hand a work on William Pickering for whom I have a hearty regard. I will spend my all to get this last into print out of sheer piety. I wonder whether it would be possible to persuade you to do a sketch of another for whom I have enormous regard, I refer to Fournier-le-Jeune. Your lengthy treatment of him in *Printing Types* delighted me. I want to see a separate publication, not as bulky as Raffaello Bertieri's (by the way he is a splendid character and is at work upon a monograph of Marcolini), *L'Arte G. B. Bodoni*, but including that most interesting and delightful portrait by Bichu & full size reproductions of the titles etc. of his tracts (I love the title to his dissertation on Music Types). Also the Gando controversy could be treated a little more in detail. Did Fournier really steal Luce's ornaments? I fear Gando may be right!

I can understand that in America you sadly miss one or two things which have so far escaped the almighty dollar. The B.M. is I think rather weak in typographica. At St. Bride's there are one or two rare things and at Victoria & Albert Museum here rests the only copy of Pierres' specimen which exists to my knowledge in this country. I have written to Frankfurt about the Egenolff sheet and hope to get it for you. I don't know about the Berner Frankfurt 1622 specimen. I have written to Schramm's assistant at the Buchwesen Museum, Leipzig, one H. H. Bockwitz, a very zealous & kind person. I have asked him to make two or three pictures of interesting pages. I hope Champion will be able to send you the Omont paper on Le Bé. I can lend you mine if you like.

Do you know that Hebrew Commentary (I speak from memory, though I possess the book it is away from me at the moment) by

Quinquarboreus which Le Bé II printed and published in – 1630 or so. It is very well printed. The body is in Latin set in the Le Bé fount with its m n nt e et at and other italic ligatures which at my requisition are now to be had on the Monotype (English Corp^n) for use with their Garamond. In a day or two I hope to send you specimens. I invite your opinion of the face. I hope it is at least an improvement upon the A.T.C. [A.T.F.]'s version.

Yours faithfully
Stanley Morison

The Fleuron,
St Stephen's House Westminster.

It is a selfish, or at least egocentric, letter. It was to be Simon's patrimony that was lost on the *Fleuron*, and Simon is not once mentioned. Morison may have been as anxious to stake his all on its success, but he had not so much, if anything, to lose. Again, even Updike may have felt that its presumed uselessness 'to such an advanced a student as yourself' was a bit Heepish. But, if the idea crossed his mind, it must have been blown away by the passion to do so much and the longing, pent up for years, to communicate and discuss the minutiae of typographic history. Updike had just shown that they could be built up into a coherent view of one sort of letters: Morison's own grand design, of which *The Craft of Printing* was the first essay, was therefore practical. There was no mistaking his thirst for more facts and the means to publish them, and Updike, wisely or unconsciously, indulged it. Although thirty years his senior, Updike now treated Morison as an equal.

On 7 February he wrote and promised to send some books. He asked to be put down 'for your book on Sixteenth Century Italian Handwriting and also for the "Fleuron"', but gently refused to write more on the Fourniers. All he knew about them was in his book, and while appreciative of Morison's praise ('although I took more pains with that part of the book than with almost any other, you are the only person who has paid the slightest attention to it') and conscious that there was more to find out he had not the time to pursue the subject.

The books duly arrived, and on 23 February Morison wrote to

thank Updike, regretting that he could not fall in with his Fournier suggestion and begging for a note on the rare 1748 Caslon type specimen (of which he had just acquired a copy) 'should you have the time to dictate 100 words or so'. There was also the Monotype Garamond to show Updike, and yet another new project to broach.

Herewith I send an advanced proof sheet showing the English Monotype Garamond. It is not of course perfect, I think the italic cap. M is very bad and indeed there are several objectionable features still remaining, in spite of considerable pain and expense which was expended on it by your countrymen Duncan and Pierpont who direct the English organisation. Nevertheless I think that you may be inclined to agree with me if I claim that, as a whole, it is more tolerable than the American Typefounders version.

It occurs to me that you might care to possess some of the special ligatures and ornaments; I shall be very glad to arrange that you get any of these that you may like.

I should have said earlier in this letter that the book which you have kindly forwarded to me will serve another important purpose. It is the intention of the Medici Society to hold an exhibition of 20th century book production, and the arrangement and cataloguing of the exhibition has been placed in my hands. It is a great pleasure therefore for me to be able to display such excellent examples of Merrymount Press work. In addition it is proposed to print a volume of specimens of type available for good commercial work. The editing of this book has also been put into my hands and I would much like to show the Montallegro and Merrymount type. . . . I send you the measure of the page and would ask you to set a reasonable amount of matter in English or Latin, concluding with the alphabet in upper and lower case centred beneath the text.

Updike readily agreed to provide the specimens that Morison required, but there was no respite in the correspondence. Each was fascinated to plumb the depth of the other's knowledge. Le Bé's career and his specimen, the types of Jules Fick of Geneva, which Morison had pursued vainly in Geneva the year before, the relation of Blado's italic to that of Simon de Colines, the relation of the French Baskerville types, then with the Bertrand foundry, to the original, the 'Basel' italic, Fournier's music types, Talbot Baines Reed, the mystery of the Janson types, not finally solved till 1957 – even though every letter was answered by return, the post was too slow for the mass of question, answers and information from London to Boston and back. Then the correspondence was overtaken by the first major publishing event of Morison's career.

It was in the third week of April that the *Fleuron* came out. Besides 'Printers' Flowers and Arabesques', Simon's uncle Will Rothenstein produced the first of his 'Critical Appreciations' – one of his portrait drawings, with a page of text opposite, this time of Cobden-Sanderson in a typically pugnacious attitude. Percy Smith, one of the leading graphic artists of the time, wrote on initial letters, Simon himself on title-pages, and Holbrook Jackson a characteristic essay on Lovat Fraser, recently dead, whose illustrations had first fired Harold Curwen with the desire to print. There were reviews, including Morison on Updike's *Printing Types* and 'Examples of Contemporary Commercial Work' with some of Morison's Cloister Press pieces. All the text was set in the new Monotype Garamond: the large italic headings are, however, not the Monotype form, but are in the A.T.F. Garamond.

Morison still felt the need to disparage his own work to Updike, but gave Simon his due.

I hope you will not find it too bad. Everything was much rushed and there is plenty of room for criticism. The next issue will be more leisurely in its editing. Much of it will be in my hands I hope and I am a very slow worker. The credit for No 1 belongs entirely to my colleague who also sees to the bookwork of the Curwen Press. I want to make the next number a really fine achievement.

Again he tried to tempt Updike to an article, this time on 'the private presses of the French Rococo period'.

On 17 May, Updike had got his copy and was delighted with it.

I have looked over the articles of printer's flowers and arabesques, and I take off my hat to you, for the knowledge which it shows and the labour that is involved. That is 'going into the thing' in the way that it ought to be done, and I am sure I shall get a great deal out of it.

I may be able to make here and there some little additions, and, if so, I will send them to you. I suppose I should not have been human if I had not also read with avidity your excellent and most friendly review of my books; and I peruse with pleasure – if not with profit – my own communication on the lost Caslon specimen! Isn't it odd how we like to see ourselves in print, although we spend a *great deal of time* in somewhat unconvincingly denying it? (It is rather good fun to be honest, and it is sometimes taken for originality.)

The only thing which I do not like about The Fleuron is the shelf-back, which seems to me a little inadequate; and I possess so obvious a mind that I should have been tempted to put a fleuron on it! Perhaps it was because it was so obvious, that you didn't do it! But seriously, accept my congratulations on producing a piece of work which is the kind of thing that ought to be done and isn't done – that shows study and research and pains, and all the things that printing so much needs to make it better.

Although grateful for this high praise, Morison was still disposed to be critical of his own work, and he answered Updike in this vein. He had, however, something else to occupy his mind, another trip abroad. His correspondence with Updike and the research for his *Fleuron* article had revealed the importance of Lyon as a typographic centre. He had moreover been writing to Marius Audin, a printer there with very much the same interests as his own. 'If all goes well,' he told Updike, 'I hope to be in Lyons next month and will endeavour to make M. Audin's personal acquaintance. I judge from his *Architecture du Livre* that he is something of a wag.'

He was then going on to Geneva and Milan, to see Raffaello Bertieri, and then back to Berlin, perhaps stopping at Prague. The possibility that Rudolph Ruzicka, a Czech wood-engraver who had settled in America, might be there was an added draw: Updike had written to introduce him to Morison. He was off before the middle of June, and was soon able to report:

I have had an enjoyable & indeed uproarious time with Marius Audin, an exceedingly cheerful soul but very contemptuous of his own printing, and unlike most Frenchmen I met, very conscious of the defects of current French work. Unfortunately he cannot read

English, but he is very enthusiastic and takes a keen professional interest in his craft.

From Geneva he had to write to Simon, because he had had a letter from Gollancz, anxious to take over all the Fleuron publications. The matter, he thought, could wait till he got back, and nothing further seems to have come of it then. 'It is cheerful to hear of the continued success of the Fleuron,' he added, and that on no advertising. Geneva had produced an interesting find, which he thought might appear in the next *Fleuron*:

I have discovered some original Lyonnese 16th cent. woodcuts like that in the Fleuron p. 16 fig 17 (I mean the picture, not the arabesque border). . . . The blocks belong to a descendant of Jean de Tournes with whom I took tea y'day.*

From Geneva Morison went on to Milan and Rome,* and, missing Prague, by the middle of July he was back in Berlin: Gollancz had given him some commissions and there was Jessen to see (Gollancz had published Jessen's book *Rococo Engravings* at Benn the previous year, with a title-page designed by Morison entirely in the open type called Moreaule-jeune).

Hospiz-in-Zentrum
Holzgartenstrasse, Berlin
17 July [1923]

My dear Simon

It is extraordinary kind of even you to have thought of sending the £5. It was most welcome for a reason wh. I will tell you next Thursday July 26. The heat here has been simply terrific & I have been almost dead. Berlin is a terrible place at any time but these last days it has been diabolical. Yet I have been able to see Meier Graefe who says he thinks he can do the article but finds it difficult to name a date because Weiss is in Spain & is not expected back until the autumn, nor is his address known. This is rather unfortunate but M.G. promised to see about it at once.

I don't wonder at the Fleuron slumping during the heat of July. I am very eager to return, lots of interesting things must have happened. On Thursday I leave here for Zurich & then go to Paris (Hotel Louvois) for one night, returning to London by Thurs. I hope. I see no possibility of visiting Klingspor. They say here that Frankfurt is soon to be occupied. K's whereabouts are unknown to his friends here. I should like to get those ——————'s & have wired to Leipzig to see if I can see a man there. I have had no answer yet. Can we go to Lord's on Friday?

Yours
Stanley Morison

Morison had also to make arrangements for the plates of *Four Centuries of Fine Printing* to be printed in Berlin by Albert Frisch; and despite the heat he began a letter to Updike, who had written on 25 June to enquire whether the English Monotype Garamond was the same as 'the Goudy Garamont type' which the American Monotype Company had brought out.

I am now in the foulest of all places, Berlin. It is a dreadful hole and the heat is simply terrific, yesterday I thought I was dying. But I was galvanised to fresh life by your letter of 25 June quoting a trade magazine to the effect that the English Monotype Garamond is 'a version of the Goudy type'.

Now, I entertain very decided opinions about this latest of Mr. Goudy's achievements. I don't know why Mr. Goudy allows it (I know he has been ill and perhaps that accounts for it). But it appears to me that his press agent is disgracefully handling the ordinary proprieties of life when he gives Goudy's name the prominence he does. I very much detest the idea that this type was designed by Goudy. . . .

This sort of typographical nomenclature will only further confuse our present miserably anarchic terminology. But these fierce grumblings are not what you are interested in. You ask whether the English Monotype Garamond is the same as the so called Goudy.

He then went on to give the account of the genesis of the English Garamond already quoted, adding a letter-by-letter analysis of the differences, and ending apologetically, 'At least it is known as Monotype Garamond. I shudder to think of the terrible things that Mr Goudy now threatens to do. I suppose he too will do a Blado italic – and call it Goudy – I must get ahead first.' Before he finished the letter, he was back in London on 22 July. 'I am glad to have returned to some characteristic English weather,

137

i.e. rain in July – at least it encourages work, of which I have a considerable accumulation.'*

The chief of this was *Four Centuries of Fine Printing*, for which Gollancz was pressing him. He wrote to Bullen on 26 July for help with American examples, other than those of Updike and Rogers' 'peerless printing', particularly of T. M. Cleland and W. D. Teague's work.

My problem is this: first I do not know either of these men: secondly I don't know their address, 3rdly I am dreadfully afraid that they may have been so badly impressed by the misprints (& even errors of fact) in *The Survey of Printing* of which I was joint author that they will imagine me to be an entirely untrustworthy character. Also it occurs to me that I may appear as a mere specimen hunter. Of course I guarantee to return all pieces which anybody is kind enough to lend me. Do you think that it is possible that you may have any duplicates which it would be allowable for me to reproduce? This is an enormous favour to ask and I am conscious that it will be difficult to accede to. Nevertheless since I have no alternative may I beg you to help me if you can in the interest of a volume wh., in spite of shortcomings due to my own limited acquaintance with the subject, cannot fail to be taken fairly seriously by English students?

Gollancz, not content with *Four Centuries*, had other ideas; so had Morison.

11 Hollyberry Lane, Hampstead
London N.W.3.
27 August 1923.

Dear Mr. Updike,

A prominent firm of publishers here (who retain me as an adviser) have expressed a desire to do something in the typographical line. At first they thought they would like to issue a series of volumes in belles lettres printed at the world's fine presses such as yours. The firm in question asked my opinion on the matter and some discussion ensued as a result of which another scheme was voted for. This was a proposition of my own and I was (and am) empowered to proceed with it. The proposition is that you write a new printer's grammar covering the whole field of fine printing. It might be called a 'GRAMMAR OF FINE PRINTING'. The book would treat consecutively of paper, ink, type, impression of colour, every relevant detail would be noted butthese chapters would be prolegomena perhaps. The most important portion of the work would be the section on display. Here would be included a full length study of the conventions underlying book-construction; the various classes into which current literature falls; the special circumstances attaching to reprints in general and certain reprints in particular; the various uses and merits of 'period' printing would be adequately discussed and there would of course be abundant illustration. I need not go into further detail. The book required is the sort of volume you would bequeath to your successor at the Merry-mount Press. . . .

Such a book as that I have in mind is, I think, very much needed and you could make it fascinating to the printer and layman alike. I beg you to set your hand to it. No other possesses the competence, the authority, or the wit. I beg you to do it.

Yours,
Stanley Morison.

Updike answered him from his holiday house in Vermont. He wrote at length, saying he must decline. He did not write easily or quickly, and his efforts must be concentrated on the Press. But the idea of such a Grammar continued to occupy Morison for some years. Like the projected Writing Book (although lacking the extra delay caused by Edward Johnston's special gift for procrastination), it was never, in the event, to be realized. Before Updike's letter arrived, Morison had finally met Rudolph Ruzicka. This, and a previous enquiry of Updike's about book-sellers in London, prompted another long letter.

11 Hollyberry Lane, Hampstead
London N.W.3.
[c. 10 September 1923]

Dear Mr. Updike:
The Ruzickas (the plural includes their delightful children) came here yesterday afternoon and we all went for a romp on the Heath, a minute away from this house. . . . Ruzicka is a charming man and if you will permit an Englishman to say so, a little un-American in his modesty and general bearing. I like him very much and his coming to this house gave us great pleasure. . . . A talk with Ruzicka makes me wish to visit your country (not all of it!) and particularly to see you and your press. As you know, we have no such institution. Mr.

Hall at Oxford is a proficient printer and replies to most of his correspondents. Mr. C. T. Jacobi formerly of the Chiswick is the greatest bore in Christendom and very ignorant. The rest of the professionals are not worth mention. The amateurs, Emery Walker, Hornby, Newdigate & others are too arts & crafty for my taste, they feel it almost lèse majesté to admit that Morris was an anachronism. I must regret even that you share their tremendous regard for Jenson. Surely this goes too far – I notice in 'English Coloured Books' by Martin Hardie that Jenson invented old faced (*sic*) type. I harbour the wish to pull the mighty from his seat and to exalt the humble Aldus. This determination grew in me as the result of looking at the Golden Type. What a type! The tops of the l.c. ascenders range with the tops of the capitals. The Doves is in the same case. Walker has a suit pending against the executors of Sanderson (who was a queer mixture) and when this is over he intends printing in the Doves type. As far as I know Walker is only recutting the lower case 'y'. I am quite sure it is wrong to make the upper case the same height as the ascenders, it means that the caps are over-large and dominate where they appear. Even Jenson though he reduced his caps retained, as I think, too much strength. A better proportion is kept in the Aldine Poliphilus – so it seems to me. I admire, too, those early italics used by Colines and others. Here the caps are properly subordinated as in fine humanist MSS. This seems to me to be very important but I do not find anybody to agree with me that capitals should be reduced. I would much like to discuss it with you and hope that one of these days you will pay us a visit.

About buying books: I should recommend Maggs of Conduit Street who besides being important second-hand and rare booksellers (in importance only below Quaritch) secure new books to order and issue lists regularly. I think they are reliable. W. H. Smith & Son (of which firm St. John Hornby is a director) is too huge to give attention to individuals. For current literature Elkin Mathews' successor (trading under the same name at Cork Street, Bond Street) is good. But I imagined that Bawstn (isn't that how it's pronounced?) had several good shops, Dunster House and Goodspeed seemed intelligently run – of course I only speak from catalogues that I have seen by accident. Perhaps they are too bitten by this extraordinary 'first edition' craze which is all young collectors are keen on. I find this mania a nuisance. We have young Birrell (son of Augustine) and David Garnett starting a shop for these cranks. Perhaps it's just as well. Old books are getting more and more expensive. Any Barbou costs a guinea and a *Fournier Manuel* will run you into 15 guineas (I gave 30/- to

Sotheran for mine and exchanged it at Maggs for a large paper copy which included the Bichu portrait into the bargain). If new books are the rage perhaps the prices of the old will not gallop up quite as quickly. Did I tell you that I succeeded in getting a copy of Fick's album of *Anciens Bois*?

Yours,
Stanley Morison.

I am posting you a tract 'Reunion All Round' which may amuse you.

At the end of October, Morison wrote Updike a very long letter. It was partly an answer to his regretful rejection of the Grammar, and to a subsequent letter in which, following Knox's *Reunion All Round*, he had reflected on the differences between Morison's religion and his own Anglo-Catholic position. But in answering Updike he committed himself to a statement of where he stood, spiritually as well as professionally.

11 Hollyberry Lane,
N.W.3.
30 October 1923.

Dear Mr. Updike:

I am sorry that you cannot undertake the 'grammar'. Your reasons are conclusive although I cannot conceive that the Merrymount Printing can ever lack anything in the way of logic and distinction. Certainly, outside the two University Presses we have no printer capable of putting through the Carter Brown catalogue. I think this a truly remarkable work and worthy of great praise. We can muster one or two printers of pretty little books whose typography is their only reason for existence. I suppose old Newdigate (he seems old to us, he is above 55 and I am 34) to be our soundest printer. He is an educated man and a decent papist. I should like you to see his folio Aquinas done for Burns & Oates before I was born typographically. I wish Newdigate were a little less 'private pressy'. A few days ago we dined together at Emery Walker's house and talked most of the time about the late Mr. W. Morris of whose work I am by no means fond and whose Golden Type I think positively foul – but then I do not revere Jenson as much as Newdigate and Walker, not as much as you do even. The Doves type is alleged by Pollard to be the finest Roman fount in existence. I wish I could think so. Last week I protested to Pollard that respect for Jenson has degenerated into superstition and that there were other types. . . . His reply was that

141

he and Walker were septuagenarians and that when I was 70 I should still be chattering about Lyons flowers and borders! But Walker is a fine old boy all the same.

I am interested in your reference to one Rollins. I have a considerable respect for his work – what I have seen of it. I wish I knew more of him. All I possess is the very nice little book of Pollard on Rogers in which 11pt Caslon is used with 10pt upper case. This pleases me mightily and but for the fact that a man told me that the Montague Press had ceased I should have written to him. This week I have been visited by a lady from San Francisco who wished to warn me that there was a printer in that city who counted for a great deal, J. H. Nash. She was very enthusiastic and very troubled that San Francisco is so far away from New York – not to mention London. I had to promise to write and pay my respects to California. I hope my last letter did not leave you with the impression that I dislike the American visitors who come to see me. On the contrary I like them very much and am flattered that they search me out. I wish I had met Mr. Gress – I might have hinted perhaps that the Roman Forum hardly acquired its importance because Goudy had visited it and used it as a peg upon which to hang a type.

I am glad to know that Reunion-All-Round amused you. . . . It is curious that you should be an Anglo-Catholic. I should think that that position is more difficult to maintain than that of what you call the Roman Catholic Church (I don't really care about the word 'catholic' – if high churchmen call us the blue cockatoos it doesn't prove that theirs is the church of Christ). Your quotation from Acton is absolutely true in that the price for dogmatic certainty is excessive but you are the folk who have put up the cost. I suppose most intellectual papists feel themselves in a strait-waistcoat. From Froschammer to Tyrrell the case is the same but before your godly thorough reformation it was very different. We had then no tribe of people who thought that the Catholic Church was a sort of automatic machine into which you put a cent and pulled out a dollar's worth of infallible chocolate. The impact of modern knowledge upon ancient faith could have been differently dealt with had Xtendom been united. Your splitting up the unity of the west has occasioned centuries of rubbishy controversy which does not help us an atom today. The result is that we all suffer – you from disintegration and we from centralisation. Not that I mean to blame your theological forebears for the evils which lead them to break into schism. But at least they might have had the sense if not the grace to realise that their action led to religious disruption. . . .

142

At present I am in the most awful bondage to this Four Centuries of Fine Printing which is a terrible labour and the worst I have ever had. I work very hard at it with constant interruptions. I repent me that I took on the job. A much better man than I should have been offered it but I was seduced by the £100 which I badly needed. The most wretched thing is that the publisher keeps on worrying me for the finished MS. He gave me a year and I have been stupid enough to think I could get it done in about that time. Really I am a fool. And now comes your letter about that miserable Medici Type Face book. This was all that could be done in the time as the Society insisted on having it out while their exhibition was open. Work began in January and the thing came out in June while I was away. I was as angry as you when I discovered that they had printed your types from a line block. The explanation is (and I have verified the statement) that the electros you kindly made at your own expense did not arrive in time and have not arrived to this day. . . . Let me beg you to believe that I am sincerely distressed about the poor result. I am told that they used the very best block that Emery Walker could make.

But the whole book is rather fatuous isn't it? No Deberny *Ancien Romain*, only one of Goudy's! . . . reminds me. Yesterday I received from a man at the Princeton University Press (of whom I had not previously heard) a huge letter of four quarto pp in ten point. He is pro-Bullen and anti-Goudy and I must quote these lines to you: '. . . you would not have been quite at home at the recent celebrations, jubilee, medal-pinning orgy with which the more audible Bandarlog of this land indicated that they were proud of Mr. Goudy. It was very loud and very long and it may be that they chanted

"Goudyamus igitur: and rend air with cheers;
Iuvenes dum sumus: for discretion comes with years".'

This amused me very much and I must reply to the writer as soon as possible – Yours,

Stanley Morison

7

IN October 1923, Morison made two more contacts which were to influence his future considerably. On 12 October, a private press, the Officina Bodoni of Montagnola in Switzerland, wrote enclosing some prospectuses of its work, as requested by the advertisements which Benn put out on behalf of *Four Centuries*. Hans Mardersteig had moved to Montagnola a year before, and now had already printed three books, all in the original Bodoni type that gave its name to the Press. He was to become a close friend, and his home, first at Montagnola and then at Verona, a haven to Morison.

The second contact also came from *Four Centuries*, although this time the initiative was Morison's. Drawing a bow at a venture, he wrote to Robert Bridges.

11 Hollyberry Lane, Hampstead, N.W.3.
22 October

Sir: I am preparing a volume on typography which is to consist of some 250 large pages of collotypes & an introduction. In this connection I beg to ask a question of you. I have been interested to notice that your works are invariably executed by the Oxford University Press with a distinction remarkable even for that distinguished office & it has occurred to me that you may have designed the title-pages & perhaps other portions of some of the best volumes. I think the flowers on the title page of *Dolben* cannot have been arranged in the ordinary course of routine. In an early volume by you (Pickering circa 1870) I think I remember a border of flowers which struck me as having been a line-reproduction of the design you also employed for the *Yattendon Hymnal*. The 1914 Oxford ed. of yr Poetical Wks. has a title composed in a letter wh. does not appear to me to be Fell. These & other details in the typography of your books interest me exceedingly; May I ask whether you are responsible for the title page & headings to pp. 7, 11, 124 of the *Gerard Hopkins*, tail piece to index of the Spirit of Man? and further whether you would object to any attribution in print.

Asking your pardon for this intrusion upon your time

I am, Sir

Yours faithfully,

Stanley Morison.

The letter presumably arrived next day, which was Bridges' seventy-ninth birthday. A day later he answered with a postcard.

Chilswell, Oxford. 24 October

Dear Sir. You are right about those bks. but I am too busy to answer your letter fully, at least at present. If you sh^d happen to be visiting Oxford, I c^d show what there is to show – and I think it w^d interest you. Also I sh^d much like to talk with you on the subject wh: it seems interests us equally.

yrs truly

R Bridges

Morison had to come to Oxford a fortnight later, and Bridges invited him to stay the night. He came up to Boar's Hill after a day of work at the Oxford University Press on 8 November, and spent not one but two nights. There was much to talk about. Bridges explained that his interest in typography was indeed of long standing, going back to *Poems* 1873, which was printed by the Chiswick Press and published by Basil Pickering. In 1881, the year in which he was forced by illness to abandon medicine for poetry, he contributed to *The Garland of Rachel*, an anthology of poems printed by the Reverend C. H. O. Daniel at his private press in Worcester College, Oxford. This introduced Bridges to the Fell types, which were used thereafter for most of his books, whether printed by Daniel or the University Press. Morison, it is fair to guess, had known Bridges' works for some time. A number of the typographical instances in his letter are not quite right, and he sounds as if he is speaking from memory, rather than from notes made for *Four Centuries*. He may have bought Bridges' *Poetical Works* in 1914 (the book was first published in 1912); he certainly bought *An Address to the Swindon Branch of the Workers'*

Educational Ass^n (1916) soon after it came out. Morison did not read much other poetry, but he respected and admired what Bridges wrote, now and later.

They shared an enthusiasm for printers' flowers. Bridges had made ample and splendid use of the Fell ornaments. Morison had rightly observed the resemblance between *Poems* 1873 and the *Yattendon Hymnal* of 1896, 'a more sumptuous presentation of the ancient types than had ever been produced in Fell's day, or since'.* He had also sent Bridges, in advance of his coming, a copy of the *Fleuron*, with the article on printers' flowers which he had guessed might interest Bridges. Finally, they both had a passion for italic handwriting. Bridges was already planning a tract on handwriting to be published by his Society for Pure English, showing 'a series of cursive hands used, not by professional calligraphers but by mere human beings'.* Morison's hand in 1923 was as fine as it ever was, with some of the care and self-consciousness of novelty still on it: that first letter must have had an immediate appeal to both Bridges and his wife. It was her book *The New Handwriting* which Morison had bought in 1916 when he began to reform his own hand; after his visit he wrote to her about it, mentioning his own recent work on the sixteenth-century Italian writing-books.*

Although eighteen months elapsed before Morison resumed their acquaintance, he never forgot this first meeting. Bridges was thirty-five years older, naturally conservative, Anglican, a very professional poet: Morison was still a young man in a hurry, radical, Catholic, more interested now in the shapes of words than the words themselves. But these differences only bound them closer together.

As 1923 came to an end, Morison was remarkably busy. The Monotype Baskerville was now available and the second *Penrose Annual* that Morison designed came out in December, with a historical note by Morison on the type, ending with a word of gratitude to himself, under the name of the Monotype Corporation, for the use of the type. Poliphilus, now renamed ('I have spent more than a week reading up the wrong Francesco & have spent Sunday afternoon looking at the Bolognese School,' he complained to Updike*) was soon to be used for the prospectus of *Four Centuries* and a special *Monotype Recorder*.

The *Penrose* also contained an article by Morison on Benn's typographically adventurous publishing policy, sponsored by Gollancz. In it he praised their 'Players' Shakespeare' as one of Newdigate's finest productions. Nor did he spare himself: Julius Meier-Graefe's *Degas*, Jessen's *Rococo Engravings* – fine examples of Morison's design work for Gollancz – and others are described in laudatory detail, and their title-pages are judged 'outstanding successes reached by simplicity and an economy of means, and be it noted, in a remarkably short space of time'. Time was always short, but there is a richness about the 'simplicity' which belies any thought that it was enforced by speed.

Morison also found time to lay out the September–October *Recorder*, and contribute to it a short piece on 'Decoration in Printing'. This was to introduce Monotype recuttings of some of the flowers recommended in the *Fleuron* article, and the borders and head- and tail-pieces, perhaps prepared in conjunction with the Curwen Press who printed this number, are a fine fore-taste of *Monotype 'Flower' Decorations*, a separate specimen issued the next year by the Corporation, with a reprint of the text of Morison's Cloister Press *Arabesque or Mauresque*. Both are fine examples of Morison's doctrine of simplicity with virtuosity.

Earlier in the year, *A Survey of Printing* and *On Type Faces* had both appeared and, although Morison had reservations about both, they were original enough at the time. In the introductory essay to the second, Morison made a second attempt at the history of letter-forms, perfunctory perhaps, but interesting for its mention of humanistic manuscripts, particularly the Laurentian Library Aeneid written by Antonio Sinibaldi, which Morison must have seen the year before. This was to have some immediate influence on the next *Fleuron*, but it was an aspect of the history of letter-forms which long occupied Morison. The other interesting feature of *On Type Faces* is the specimen of 'Janson's Italic', the Dutch letter that so fascinated Morison: even the text of the specimen is different from the normal literary extracts or summary history of the type used for the others.* It begins with the largest size:

FROM Erasmus of Rotterdam to the Proctor and Collier Company of Cincinnati is indeed a far cry. In this instance the connection is intended to exhibit something of the peculiarities and eccentricities of the human mind in an attempt to trace to its beginnings the evolution of a type design. Next to his purely decorative designs, Holbein's portrait of Sir Thomas More has been always greatly admired by the writer.

There is more about Erasmus, More and Froben, till the specimen of 9pt:

IN 1910 the writer visited the South Kensington Museum (London), and purchased several sheets of photographic enlargements of early types; one in particular interested him because of peculiarities in the formation of certain letters: but who the printer was he did not know. A year or two ago, in looking through some old English art magazines, a reproduction of a few lines of type caught his eye and comparison disclosed at once that it had been made from this same photograph, a note furnishing the information that it was the type from Polydore Vergil's History of England, printed by Palma Isingrin.

This must be Morison speaking: he was always devoted to Thomas More, and who but he had so vivid a memory for typeforms? But '1910' can hardly be right, and most probably the passage should be taken for what it is – a parable rather than a memoir.

But by now Morison had moved on to other plans. A year earlier on 22 December he had written to 'the man Geoffrey Keynes' on the recommendation of 'my friend Mr Jacobi' to solicit a monograph on William Pickering to be published by the Fleuron. Punctually, a year later the manuscript was delivered (it was the only one of the series to come to fruition).

St Stephen's House Westminster S.W.1.
12 January 1924.

Dear Keynes,

Many thanks for the ms; it is without doubt a remarkably fine introduction and I read it with enormous pleasure. There is no need to have it typewritten.

There are one or two things about which I would like to make a remark, none of any importance. Perhaps the most serious is connected with the old face revival habitually dated 1844. I suppose this is correct. I have never set myself to verify my suspicion that Pickering used Caslon old face before 1844, but I do possess a copy of Jeremy Taylor, *Holy Dying*, whose title page with an architectural face [*sic* – border, he means] is composed in Caslon and is dated 1840. The body is in 'modern' but I have a notion that I have seen others of Pickering's books carrying Caslon at least in the prelims.

About the pictures I can only say at the moment that you shall have as many as we can possibly afford and certainly not fewer than 24. . . .

Yours,

Stanley Morison.

The explosion of the legend that had grown up about the reintroduction of the Caslon types was another example of Morison's keen and sceptical eye for typographic distinctions, and Keynes duly amplified the passage in his introduction.

There was the future of the *Fleuron* itself to be communicated to Updike. He wrote on 19 November from the British Museum:

We hope to do five numbers and close up. The next issue will have a portrait of Hornby and so finish with the private pressy people. In number three we should like to have a portrait of you and an appreciation (query by W. A. Dwiggins); No 4 should give Rogers and why not a critical summing up of Goudy and his work (sans portrait) in which the truth would be told? This cd go in No 5. After this we would take to the woods or otherwise flee from the wrath to come. I hear that Goudy's friends on the Grolier Club and other places where they sing are not prepared to let Bullen's sort of criticism go without a counter demonstration. No wonder Bullen is flying to Europe. But I fear that I shall myself be voted a thorough outsider when my article in the next Fleuron is read. I am quite sure

149

that nobody will like it and I am equally sure that I am right, or at least my method is.

Outside the *Fleuron*, there was Gollancz, still at Benn, anxious to follow up *Four Centuries*. 'It is intended to publish a similar volume devoted to the work of modern fine presses,' Morison wrote to the Officina Bodoni on 14 December; *Modern Fine Printing* was published in April 1925. Nor was Benn the only publisher in pursuit of Morison. The Cloister Press had printed William Heinemann's 1921 Autumn List, and subsequently Gerard Meynell had recommended Morison to Charles Evans, who had just become head of the firm, one of the most forward-looking and successful in London. Writing to Bridges on 28 December about the tract on handwriting, Morison sent some specimens of Adrian Fortescue's beautiful hand, and undertook, as Bridges had asked him, a letterhead for a friend.

I am very flattered that you should think my stuff good enough for yr friend's letter paper. I should very much like to do it & wd do so were there no question of a fee. The firm of Heinemann have just asked me to see to the typography of their limited editions & this means I shall have more money.

So 1923 ended, with more work and more money. Christmas found Morison scribbling away: his printed Christmas card had been a failure, 'but my wife insisted upon my writing up at least 30 greetings in a variety of English, Italian, French and Gothic and Batarde scripts – I went on strike when asked for civilité'. Updike was sympathetic; he had already written encouragingly on 7 January about the future plans for the *Fleuron*, and agreed 'to be the victim of an operation in its behalf'; he had seen the prospectus of *Four Centuries* 'one of the handsomest things that has ever been brought out, and your italic is delightful'. He was equally impressed by the special issue of the *Recorder*, got out by Morison to introduce Poliphilus and Blado. There were notes by Morison on each, and testimonials to the quality of Monotype setting from Bruce Rogers, S. C. Roberts (Secretary to the

Syndics of the Cambridge University Press) and Wren Howard of Jonathan Cape. The whole thing – Morison's design, Lewis's careful press-work, the special copies with a black case binding – put it (as Morison intended) in a class by itself.

Morison's other American pen-friend, Henry Bullen, was coming over on a sabbatical year from the American Founders Company 'to visit in a leisurely manner the best libraries and shrines commemorating the work of the early printers'.* Morison had struck up a warm friendship with him, undeterred (at least across the Atlantic) by what Updike called his 'all-overish' manner, and had cheerfully taken sides with him in his quarrel with Goudy, from which Updike had kept aloof. Like Updike, he was much older than Morison (he was now sixty-seven), but this did not inhibit Morison's friendly greeting (see Plate 4). They duly came to tea, and the meeting was a success.

> 11 Hollyberry Lane, Hampstead
> London N.W.3.
> 9 February 1924.

My dear Bullen (if I may drop the mistery!) May I suggest that you call up Harold M. Duncan of the Monotype? I happen to know that he wd. very much like to see you & as he isn't so well at the moment he plans to go away for a short time. It wd. be a pity if he missed you by accident. We very much enjoyed yr visit the other day and hope that you & Mrs Bullen will come again as soon as you feel disposed. If you came to dinner perhaps you and I cd. have a minute or two about printing books while the ladies are at literature proper.

> Our best regards to you & Mrs Bullen
> Yours always
> Stanley Morison.

Morison duly reported the meeting to Updike. He was making arrangements to have a fount of Poliphilus and Blado cast at the Cambridge University Press for him, since he had no expectation that the American Monotype Company, 'quite a separate affair', would take any interest in the face, especially since it was so large (16pt). Their exchange of views on religion continued.

We have several good Jesuits, one Herbert Thurston who comes here most Sundays is an all round scholar – and a thoroughly candid person which is quite a different thing. On the whole however we cut a pretty poor figure in comparison with the scholarship of the Anglican body. The truth is that we are mostly Irish too! Yet the Irish can boast of one or two very fine men. But I suppose the best papist theologians are to be found in France. The French Jesuit and Dominicans are excellent and there are many excellent seculars . . . Germany and Italy seem to breed reactionary people – at any rate I don't much care for the specimens I have met: one, a German Jesuit who teaches Accadian and Babylonian brick bats at Rome almost got me to join the S.J. when I met him in London fourteen years ago. It's a jolly good job that I broke my promise to him and didn't actually go forward!*

By this time the second *Fleuron* was out, all set in Baskerville, and with it Morison's 'Towards an Ideal Type'. It also contained Updike's practical article on 'The Planning of Printing' and Julius Meier-Graefe on E. R. Weiss, a similar portrait of Édouard Pelletan, and Newdigate on St John Hornby. 'Towards an Ideal Type' was the iconoclastic argument for capital letters shorter than the lower-case ascenders, of which Morison had forewarned Updike. Characteristically, the argument goes back to classical inscriptions and finds its solution in fifteenth-century Florentine manuscripts and the work of sixteenth-century calligraphers and the printers who copied them. The argument is closely reasoned, with a range of examples and quotation which shows how much hard work Morison had put in at the Museum in the last three years. Morison demonstrates with annihilating simplicity how ignorantly eclectic the arguments for the Golden and Doves type were: he concedes the calligraphic origins of all letters, but gently suggests that the mastery of Edward Johnston may have given the Carolingian minuscule too much authority. He ends with a slightly disingenuous bouquet to Goudy: 'Goudy Modern remains, however, an admirable letter. It is advertised as being based on a type by Bodoni, but Mr Goudy has left the Italian far behind.' The article is a fine original piece of work, and if its argument has had little effect on letter-design in general it did produce, five years later, Monotype Bembo, the type which

Morison preferred to all the others for which he had been responsible.

Both he and Updike were disposed to be pessimistic about their
contributions. Updike thought his piece better spoken than read:
Morison disliked rows.

I am rather a peace at any price person and wd. give my very trousers
to be on ordinary terms with people. Nevertheless 'suffering fools
gladly' is not my strong point and I easily get bored with our own
typographical worthies. That is one of the reasons why I wish to
remain in the background so far as the Fleuron is concerned. We
haven't many individuals here, beside Fra. Meynell, who are at all
competent to speak or write about printing.*

About the same time Morison started his fourth Monotype
design.

11 Hollyberry Lane
London N.W.3.
Candlemas 1924.

Dear Updike: I have succeeded in persuading our Monotype Corporation to put in hand the reproduction of the S. Augustin, œil
moyen, of Fournier. I hope this type will be ready in time for the third
number of the Fleuron but in any case I hope to make an interesting
little specimen of it. On Sunday last I re-read your pages devoted to
him and again enjoyed them very much. Do you happen to possess
that quarto tract, the last thing he ever did, on the printing of music?
It occurred to me that it might be possible to persuade the Grolier
Club to publish a translation of it. The whole is no more than 48 pp
& is full of interesting matter about Le Bé, Sanlecque – but you know
all about that. Cd you persuade them to allow you to edit the text? . . .

Yours Stanley Morison.

Updike was doubtful about this proposition: he was keener that
Morison should read and return the proofs of his edition of Rowe
Mores's *Dissertation Upon English Typographical Founders and
Founderies*, which he *had* persuaded the Grolier Club to publish.
But at this point Morison was diverted by the need to dash to
Berlin to supervise the printing of the plates of *Four Centuries*.
Berlin always depressed him, and stopping at the Hotel Louvois

in Paris on the way back he was in a black gloom about every-thing. 'All my stuff is filthy', he wrote, 'with this very hotellish pen', on 10 March, 'partly through sheer incompetence & in-attention but also through hurry. . . . You may well ask me why I undertake these things if I can't even satisfy myself, let alone the average buyer.' Still, he had been for a walk with Champion, the bookseller, 'who was saluted by an infinite number of professors, Bergson among them'. Finally, he added a cheerful p.s.

Robert Bridges our poet laureate (but quite a decent man n'theless) is in yᵣ country. Shd. he come to Boston please seek him out – I mentioned your name to him. He is an enormous character, brilliant creative erudite & a great wit & though a great poet is not conceited. Don't call him 'Dr' Bridges. Do you know that old humbug Hall Caine? He once called at Boar's Hill (where Bridges lives in a sup-remely charming house) to pay his respects to the poet & in his charac-teristic posturing way boomed forth a great polished & oleaginous greeting with abundant reference to, the great privilege, etc, this well-spring of English undefiled, immortal verse, perfection of form etc. etc. during wh. Bridges (who is 76 isn't it?) sat down, only rising at the conclusion of this volley to say, 'Sir, did you leave your Caine in the Hall?'
    R.B. is interested in printing & handwriting. We have agreed to do together a little work on writing illustrated by examples of current hands. Any contribution from you? First I beg you to take lessons from Yciar !*

'I will hunt him up if I happen to know he is in Boston,' answered Updike, although afraid he might miss him 'because I don't particularly frequent "Lions"'. And he tried to cheer Morison up:

I am afraid you are in the state of most people who are on the eve of marriage, – rather doubtful whether, on the whole, you have not made a frightful mistake, – but as soon as you get married, or rather, the book comes out, you will forget all about ever having hesitated.*

Morison's spirits were soon up again, and he could not resist sending Updike – with the comment 'The enclosed seems to me unique' – an advertisement for the Cochin types, which he had

154

imported from France for the Pelican Press and had recut by Monotype last year. It was put out by the New York Monotype Composition Co., and it ran

LES COCHINS

Early history records Les Cochins among the typographical designers though primarily he was a copper plate engraver. He interpreted some of the best types, which were afterwards remodeled in type and are found among some of the model books of that period.

And on 16 April he wrote again to announce a decision of great importance:

I have made up my mind to come to the U.S.A. towards the end of August and I shall be very glad if you will allow me to pay you a visit. I do not suppose that you will be at your office in August, but it is my intention to travel by steamer which goes to Boston, by this means I can hold off for a time one or two New York calls, the prospect of which rather frightens me. It occurs to me for instance that I may have to meet Mr. Goudy and Mr. Gress and Mr. McMurtrie. Perhaps you can tell me how to avoid these without upsetting the Anglo-American entente. I may add that I don't intend to advise anybody of my intentions because I want to work sufficiently well to be back here by the end of September. I shall be very glad however if you can kindly let me know whether you would allow me to visit you.

But before he set out for America there was still much to be done in Europe. After a brief holiday with the Whithams in Devon, the Morisons went off on another round-trip tour: first to Geneva to collect the manuscript of Cartier's bibliography of the De Tournes family;* then to Bertieri in Milan, who had 'a writing book by one Ruanus, Rome 1557 which is unknown to Manzoni, Blanco, Cotarelo & any other writer I know'; then to Frankfurt, to the Stempel foundry, where Morison met 'a strange man, Gustav Mori who . . . possesses an enormous typographical collection', and finally back via the libraries of Paris.*

Then Geoffrey Keynes's book on Pickering was published, which prompted a characteristic *arrière pensée*.

> The Fleuron
> 101 Great Russell Street W.C.
> 14 June 1924
>
> Dear Keynes: It might have been better – and worse. The background is too coffee coloured for my taste but better than dotted rules. I wish the point had been made that Pickering was the first to design books in an eclectico-antiquarian spirit: I mean that he was the first to go back to XVIth century Venice & Lyons for inspiration. Before his time the development of the book shows no instance of atavism. If I am right Pickering is the tribal chief of the Morris–Ricketts–Rogers school. This occurred to me only the other day or I would have submitted it to you in time for consideration in your most admirable introduction. The sales are not at all discouraging. The volume was published on Friday (y'day) & 150 were sold that day. I will see that duplicates or copies of reviews are sent.
>
> Note the new address: a respectable office where you will be welcome at any time.
>
> > Yours
> > Stanley Morison.

Finally, the Fleuron moved its office from St Stephen's House to 101 Great Russell Street on 1 June. It was a new part of London for Morison to work in, more convenient for publishers, booksellers and the British Museum than Westminster. There were new restaurants (the Holborn, at the top of Kingsway, was Morison's favourite) and new tea-shops (the Plane Tree became the point of typographical rendezvous). It was a move that marked a change in Morison's way of life. Leaving the old Cloister Press office, he gave up a direct interest in commercial printing (his last commission in this line was the design of some book catalogues for Maggs Brothers, an interest which he maintained after an uncertain start*). Morison's five years had a profound influence in this field. He could, on occasion, pour tremendous scorn on print for advertising, as he did on the young Ashley Havinden who had called on 'Bingy' Saxon Mills at St Stephen's House one evening. He would accuse the advertisers simultaneously of ignorance of history and failure to keep up to date, confronting them simultaneously with Garamond and the latest cubist designs from Germany or E. McKnight Kauffer. Havinden, at least, took the point: 'modern painting for inspiration for poster design but a return to the past – well before the horrid nineteenth-century period – for good typeface design, and fine standards of book printing for inspiration in advertisement design in newspapers and magazines'.*

It was a message that Meynell confirmed in *The Typography of Newspaper Advertisements*, for which Charles Hobson continued to set the style, and which Havinden himself rammed home in his work for Crawford's, notably in his Chrysler advertisements which so dominated advertising in the late twenties. Morison was to provide Havinden with Monotype versions of many of the letters he devised.

Nor did Morison desert even older friends. He remained very close to the far left, politically. The Morison Christmas card for 1920 was 'A Reminder to Prime Ministers, Tyrants, Red Revolutionaries, Big Men, Treaty-Makers, Hotheads, Journalists, Ex-Conchies, Nationalists, &c., &c.', set in Moreau-le-jeune and Cochin.* He was on close terms with most of the original members of the British Communist Party, including Page Arnot and Walter Holmes. The restarting celebration of the *Daily Herald* in the spring of 1919 was an opportunity for reunion to many who had been imprisoned together during the war; it brought new sympathizers into the circle, among them Dona Torr, librarian of the old *Herald*, who was to become Walter Holmes's wife and lecturer in English at University College. Morison and she were alike in their strongly empiricist scholarship, and she occasionally helped Morison, especially when his enquiries led into German, which he taught himself between 1918 and 1922.

Morison made serious overtures to be allowed to join the Party, after the reorganization effected by Palme Dutt's Committee in 1923, but never became a member. He discussed his position with many of the original members, but stimulating though they (and he) found his mixture of orthodox Marxism and Catholicism it is unlikely that either considered it a suitable basis for Party membership.* But despite its new traffic with capitalism, the Pelican Press continued to print for its original customers. When the *Labour Monthly* was started in 1921, Morison and Meynell designed and printed it, in Morison's new-found French Rococo style. It was Marxists as well as printers, publishers and priests, who made up Morison's evening company.

But Morison was now heading for the centre of capitalism. He was clearly anxious that either Updike or Bullen's A.T.F. Library, or both, should be a haven from whatever storms he might encounter. Bullen had been generous in smoothing the way:

28 April 1924
My dear Comrade. You are extremely kind to have done all this for me and I am intensely obliged. I do not go until August because I am hard up for time & must work. People tell me that if I go on the Aquitania second class August 16 and return by Scythia from Boston Sep 20 I shall do as well as I have any right to expect. It will be something of a rush no doubt – but why not? I am a rusher by nature & cut time with ease. I see this Aquitania goes to New York but I shall stick to my plan about going first to Boston in any case. I can kiss D. B. Updike's big toe with all the more appetite if I do it first thing!...

I appreciate yr. rubric about D.B.U.'s dislikes. His hand is against all men save Rogers – so it appears. Pray that I may be worthy to wipe my feet on his doormat.

Most of all, thanks to you for yr letter to Miss Becker. She will, as you say, write the dam book. I am most anxious to put in all my time at yr library & am only afraid I shall be weak in giving way to diver-

158

sion outside the museum. Lead me not into temptation. I am rather nervous of the whole business and feel that I must wear a very clean collar & a Sunday school smile when I get off the boat. . . .

Yours always
Stanley Morison

She was still Miss Becker, when she first, aged nineteen, 'made the tedious journey to Communipaw Avenue' in New Jersey, where the A.T.F. Library was, from Columbia University where she was an undergraduate. She was born on 20 September 1900, the daughter of May Lamberton Becker, an immensely popular literary critic and Gustave L. Becker, a composer and music critic. Her parents had parted before she went to Barnard College, and she was living with her mother. She was already interested in lettering, and when, two years later, Bullen advertised for an Assistant Librarian, she armed herself with a letter from Bruce Rogers and was given the job.* 'Miss Becker' she always remained to Bullen, although since 30 December 1922 she had become Mrs Frederic Warde.

Her husband was born in 1894 and educated at Harvard, from which he graduated in 1915. He first worked at the Mount Vernon Press of William E. Rudge, where Bruce Rogers also came to work on his return from England. Warde became fascinated by the task of achieving Rogers' rigorous standards of spacing on the Monotype Machine, and in June 1921 he left Rudge to work for a year at the Lanston Monotype Company in Philadelphia. In 1922 he went on to instal a Monotype plant at Princeton University Press and was hard at work there by August that year. His dilettante manner concealed a considerable technical expertise. It was he who had sent Morison the two doggerel lines about the Goudy celebrations; Updike had been tart:

The man that you heard from at the Princeton University Press is a gentleman called Warde, who, for some extraordinary reason, spells 'Frederique' as if he were a Frenchman and 'Warde' as if he were a Spaniard. He has lately married himself to an uncommonly silly person who was assistant librarian to Mr Bullen at the American Type Founders Company. I cannot make out how clever he is.*

159

Bullen no doubt gave the couple a different character (as indeed would Updike on another day). He wrote to Beatrice, and she to Morison, who wrote in turn to thank her.

> 11 Hollyberry Lane, Hampstead
> London N.W.3.
> 8 June 1924

Dear Miss Becker: My projected visit to your country rather appals me at times – nor does the man Mencken comfort me. On the other hand yr letter of 14 May is a great encouragement. I am not a particularly sociable person & tremble at any possibility of having to address gatherings of the Faithful. If, for example, I could effect insurance against being interviewed by the editor of the *American Printer* I should do so right away. Nor have I any Message to Soulful Typotects. Press-agenting and paragraphing I abhor. Naturally I want to see B.R., Ruzicka and F. Warde (I owe him a letter I think). The Metropolitan & the Grolier are very important to me. Also the Pierpont Morgan Library. The latter because I am the slave of a passion for manuscripts (cf fig 7 in the *Arts of the Book* with fig 25) which looks like defeating my interest in printing.

It is very delightful of you to offer me the hospitality of your house – but aren't you running a considerable risk? It will give me very great pleasure indeed to come out to you; my steamer leaves August 16 & I go to Boston first, then to wherever Updike will be. Having kissed hands I come to see the book collections in & around New York. I have the intention to return from Boston at about September 22 this means that my time in U.S. will be limited to 4 weeks.

> Please give my respects to your husband
> & believe me to be yours very gratefully
> Stanley Morison

The last few days were dreadfully full. *Four Centuries* came out at last on 23 July, without the great *éclat* that Morison had half-hoped. He replied with feeling to Keynes, who had complained of the paucity of reviews of his *William Pickering*.

> The Fleuron
> 101 Great Russell Street W.C.1.
> 7 August 1924

My dear Keynes,
I do not think 'The Times' or 'The Observer' or anybody else is seriously interested in printing. I have tried very hard to bring some

influence to bear upon the Literary Supplement and upon 'The Observer', without the slightest success. The Fleuron has never had any but the most miserable notices in the Times Supplement; they are only interested in 'Literature', whatever that may be.

I have, myself, got over my feelings of disappointment at the persistent silence, which is the reward of my efforts to secure even half a column on our publications. Were we to bring out a volume of bad poetry we could easily get it reviewed. This is my own experience but I do not know that it need be yours. Perhaps you could exert some influence.

Recently I noticed what I regarded as being a very sane review in Lit. Supp of some rather well printed books, and I actually got here the man who wrote it, showed him various things, spoke to him about Pickering, have sent him copies but it does not appear to have been of any use.

The most apparently we can hope for is an ignorant notice by the man who writes the 'Notes on Sales' column. That gentleman did give a couple of inches to Updike!

Yours,
Stanley Morison

Although Morison considered it 'a dull, pedagogic summary of typographical tendencies',* although the selection of the plates was too much governed by what was available in the short space of time allowed (there were no black-letter examples, because Morison said he had 'no accurate knowledge of the subject'), it was Morison's first substantial publication. The selection of the plates might be partial, but it was a stronger and more coherent view than could have been produced by anyone else in England.

On 16 August Morison set sail and arrived safely at Boston. Writing to Simon on 3 September, who had asked him to review *Four Centuries* for the *Fleuron*, Updike reported:

I had a pleasant visit from Mr Morison for two days at Heath [his holiday home], and two or three days here. He is now at New York ... I hope he won't get tired out, trying to do all the things that his friends are proposing.

This dry little note says nothing of an event even more important to Morison than meeting Updike for the first time. Beatrice

Warde, prompted perhaps by curiosity about the stranger Bullen had recommended, had come up to Cambridge herself. She arrived to be greeted by a shout of laughter, as Updike was telling his visitor a story about a bishop and a butler. 'I knew', she said, 'that the stranger must be Morison'; for he had been described to her by friends.

This visitor fitted their description as far as it went. 'He looks like a Jesuit', they had said. So he did, with his black looks, black suit and blue jaw. And when he turned to see who was coming into the room, his momentary frown of curiosity brought his heavy black eyebrows together with formidable effect. What I was not prepared for was the way in which that austere face, sombre in repose, could be instantly transfigured by a most captivating schoolboy grin that took at least 10 years off his apparent age. Behind his steel-rimmed glasses I saw grey-green eyes twinkling between thick black lashes, with their cool but somehow re-assuring stare of enquiry which is so characteristic of the man. Within five minutes of the general conversation that followed I knew that I was in the presence not only of a wit and a scholar, but of a personality more vivid and stimulating than that of anyone I'd ever before encountered.*

Morison also went to Princeton, presumably to see Frederic, just before he returned to Boston to meet Dwiggins and Winship.* He must also have met in New York Bruce Rogers, whose work he had shown generously in *Four Centuries*, and William M. Ivins and F. W. Kent at the Metropolitan Museum, both enthusiasts for printing and calligraphy. He came away exhausted, like most travellers after their first visit to America, and with mixed impressions. He had, he felt, wasted a good deal of time, though not at the Merrymount Press. 'You were tremendously kind to me and I shall never be grateful enough', the more so as Updike had been ill. 'I shall not easily forget my picture of you in bed, telling me of Mr Knopf's commissioning you to make a pretty book of Mr Mencken's ESSAY ON SEX!'

On the other hand he had found the dimmer members of the typographic confraternity no more appealing in the flesh than in print. 'I think on the whole that the only things worth seeing in

New York are the Pennsylvania and Grand Central Stations and the Morgan Library.' There, however, he had, not surprisingly, quarrelled with the formidable librarian, Belle Greene. And, he concluded:

The evening before I had been decoyed to a dinner party given by Frank Altschul – much champagne and female society. I was very tired and lay down on the parquet floor in my evening togs, much to the concern of the good Altschul. I was too tired & bored to do anything – the actual meal was over an hour & a half in progress! There were compensations in New York, the Grolier Club Library I found very restful and there were always the Wardes to whom I could go.*

He had a rough passage back, and was thankful when the *Aquitania* reached Southampton on 23 September. Before disembarking, he sent off two postcards. One was to Beatrice: it simply said 'Good riddance to the Aquitania', with the Q flourished in a triumphant way. The other was to Oliver Simon. It ran:

Must see you immediately but don't encourage anybody who wants to see me to imagine that I am back. Typographically there is little of importance in U.S. You knew that before, do you say? Well I know now. The only important typographical personages of the future are leaving U.S. for England in January. You will have something to publish besides my stuff. The two people I mention are after my own heart & will do the Fleuron no end of good turns. . . .

6-2

8

MORISON got back to a domestic crisis. 'I discovered my wife in a state of considerable nervous excitement', he told Updike, 'due to the rigour of the exercises of a retreat she had been attending. This was conducted by a somewhat heavy Jesuit, who apparently over-stimulated the imagination of one at least of his patients.' Matters were smoothed over, but with this as well as post-America exhaustion it was well into October before Morison was fit to start work again. He sent Updike a present, 'Joe Rickaby's translation of a minor work of St Thomas, printed in folio by Newdigate' and published by Burns & Oates before Morison went there. He also had another unexpected encounter with his past.

The first man I met on my return, and that by accident in the tube at Hampstead, was W. E. Orchard. I am going to see him again soon, but we had a little talk and I mentioned that I had been reading his latest book in your house – he was extremely surprised to find his things penetrating so far. I am going to talk to him very seriously about his intellectual position, which seems to me curiously unstable.*

There was another cause for sadness and alarm. On 9 October Duncan, Morison's patron and supporter at Monotype, died. He had been ill for some time, but his death left Morison wondering anxiously whether the policy that he had initiated and promoted would be continued.

It would have been in perfect accord with precedent and prudence if Duncan's successor had thought twice before authorizing the complete fulfilment of the plan accepted by his predecessor. It is not in the normal course of business for successive managing directors to be equally conscious of their business's rise to institutional status, with a responsibility to the public for the designs it may make and sell. Rather it was probable that the new managing director, facing the post-war depression, would more keenly feel his responsibility to the shareholders for the payment of dividends upon the capital they had risked in backing an invention of which many of them could have had no first-hand knowledge; and made in the interest of a trade which was indeed a 'mystery' to them. Moreover, any new managing director would be loath to seek a quarrel with the manager of the factory in which the machines were made and the matrices cut.

It was not until the end of the year that Morison's fears were assuaged, when Burch, Duncan's assistant, and for some time past managing director in all but name, was appointed his successor. Morison liked him then, and grew fonder of him year by year. He was, it is true, 'less imperative than his predecessor', an ally rather than a supreme power to be invoked in Morison's dealings with the works. Lewis again played a part in what followed, as Morison noted in paying tribute to Burch:

He was a man of outstanding force and suppleness of character, closely in touch with the printing trade; and had long enjoyed the confidence of its leaders. He knew and liked Lewis and had more than once discussed with him the matter of new type-faces. And he was prepared to listen to his argument that the plan agreed to by his predecessor was a practical one and not merely 'idealist'. Accordingly the position of typographical adviser to the Corporation was then confirmed and the holder given an office at the headquarters.*

Still, there was a new *Fleuron* to come back to, with much in it to cheer Morison: Dwiggins's portrait of Updike, with its fine photogravure portrait, 'The Chancery Types of France and Italy' written by himself and a new friend at the British Museum, A. F. Johnson, Method Kalab on the post-war Czech typographic renaissance (Morison was now in touch with Prague, which he had missed the year before), Updike's long review of *Four Centuries*, and notices of Morison's work at the Cloister Press, particularly of *On The Road*, written by Belloc at Hobson's behest for British Reinforced Concrete – the review began 'All lovers of printing will regret the slightness of the period during which the Cloister Press was controlled by Mr. C. W. Hobson, Mr Stanley

Morison, and Mr Walter Lewis.' Simon's interests were represented by Randolph Schwabe's article on Albert Rutherston and Hubert Foss on modern music-printing – a speciality of Curwen's. There was a characteristically graceful essay on 'The Amateur and Printing' by Harold Child, an actor turned journalist on *The Times*, and, like Holbrook Jackson, a keen follower of fine printing.

Time has dealt harder with 'Chancery Types' than most of Morison's scholarly typographic writing. The confusion which centred round the 'caractères de l'université' was to be cleared up only two years later, and original documents and specimens of the types and their designers have advanced knowledge far beyond Morison's first speculations. Even his eye – sharper at detecting typographic distinctions than any other – misled him (or was it caution?) into describing a type identical with another as a 'close copy'. But Morison's work was the foundation on which others – and he himself – built.

Any feeling of inadequacy must have been reassured by Updike's review of *Four Centuries*. He praised the 'sound sense' of the text; of the plates, 'I do not know where a better assemblage of examples of work typical of these interesting and neglected periods may be found'; of the typography, 'ample and noble – distinguished and sane – happy and unusual combination'. Morison must have been deeply content with this generous tribute from so senior an expert.

Ever since Lewis went there, Morison's connections with the Cambridge University Press had grown closer. They printed Morison's memorials for Adrian Fortescue, *Latin Hymns Sung at the Church of St Hugh Letchworth*, and the memoir by J. G. Vance and J. W. Fortescue (the long-planned Boethius was printed at Cambridge next year as was Siegfried Sassoon's *Lingual Exercises for Advanced Vocabularians*, also supervised by Morison). *Four Centuries*, an unusual book from any point of view, had made special demands on the Cambridge staff, and Morison had got to know them all, from S. C. Roberts at the top to F. G. Nobbs and J. A. Scott who ran the Monotype plant. For Nobbs in particular, quarrelsome and facetious but an unequalled master of his craft, Morison had a high regard; it was he who devised the title-page border of *Four Centuries* entirely out of lower-case italic *g*s (amplified with *z*s and ampersands on the jacket). Most of all, the respect which Lewis and Morison had for each other's ability had grown, and with it their friendship.

It was Lewis now who suggested to Roberts that Morison be given formal status as typographical adviser to the Press. Morison had lunch with Roberts at the Holborn Restaurant, soon after his return.* There was not much argument about it; Morison was the natural successor to the post left vacant when Bruce Rogers returned to America in 1920. Morison appeared formally before the Syndics. 'I understand that you would like to join us,' said the Chairman, Hugh Anderson. 'Yes, if you're interested in good printing' was the aggressive reply – Morison had come a long way in twelve years. Thus began – the date was fixed for 1 January next – a twenty years' partnership. Lewis and Morison could not have been more different. Lewis was short and square, with a permanent cigarette, warm-hearted and hot-tempered (he had a fine range of expletive), a rationalist and a practical man ('To Lewis printing was a job. To Morison, it was a link in the vital chain of communication'), as expert a judge of press-work as Morison of composition. If brought together by common adversity, they stayed together in increasing prosperity. Affection was added to respect, if veiled by the stream of argument and bantering abuse which was their usual means of communication. Despite their difference in appearance and character, both had an unselfconscious power of attraction – 'charm' is too weak a word for such strong characters – which captivated those who met them.*

So there were new prospects, and now Oliver Simon had another scheme to involve Morison in. With a group of familiar friends, Hubert Foss, Frank Sidgwick, Gerard Meynell, Wren Howard, S. C. Roberts and Holbrook Jackson, he planned a dining club for those interested in the arts of the book. It was to be called the Double Crown Club, partly after the paper size so called and partly from the soon-abandoned idea of 'crowning' two books a year. The inaugural dinner was held at the Florence Restaurant on 31 October 1924, and from the third dinner, early in 1925, when William Rothenstein addressed the Club on 'Book Illustration', a formal speech and discussion became part of the proceedings. Morison was a founder member, addressed it on several occasions, and regularly took part in the discussion which followed each address.

Morison would slowly unwind his figure as if every muscle in his body were in revolt and, while momentarily appearing hesitant and short of words, would soon have his audience especially attentive, imparting criticism, knowledge and original and unusual points of view with a slow, halting, yet concise delivery.*

A change was now blowing up in the affairs of the *Fleuron*. While Morison was away, it had acquired a 'charming and competent secretary book-keeper' in the shape of Ruth Ware. She looked after Simon and Morison (she used to wash his collars at the office when they looked as if they needed it), and quite soon she and Simon were to get married. While the *Fleuron* was a success, it had been expensive: the name of L. Simon, Oliver's father, had regularly appeared in the acknowledgements, and his financial subventions had been necessary to keep the *Fleuron* going. Oliver's debts and the expenses of the *Fleuron*, including the next number, were paid as part of his wedding present, but the *Fleuron* itself, now planned in seven not five volumes, was to be transferred to Morison, who was to become editor.*

The first four numbers had been a perfect apprenticeship for him. Simon, with his gregariousness and instinct for the best in modern printing, was better equipped to launch the new periodical than Morison. He had seen to it that each number appeared punctually (Morison's perfectionism was not to allow that to continue). The *Fleuron* had attained an established position and an international reputation. Morison, now, was ideally equipped to exploit it. It was remarkable how much he had crammed into the last five years.

He had absorbed and digested the styles of the English private presses, he now visited France and met Laboureur, Carlégle, Dufy and other artists: he travelled about Germany, talked to Anna Simons, Walter Tiemann, Anton Kippenberg, Rudolf Koch, Karl Klingspor, Emil Rudolf Weiss, F. H. Ehmcke and others; he filled notebooks in the libraries of Paris, Berlin, Milan, Florence and Rome. He gave detailed study to the works of important printers since the fifteenth century. It was fortunate for him that the office of the Pelican Press was a stone's throw from the St. Bride Foundation Library. He had begun there the reading and now mastered the whole literature of the subject from Moxon, Ernesti, Fertel, Smith, Luckombe, to De Vinne, Reed, Blades and Goudy. He also read Lepreux, Claudin and Faulmann. In 1916 he had formed a taste for humanistic calligraphy and based his personal hand upon a cursive commended and illustrated in Johnston's book. In 1923 he was initiated into fifteenth-century paleography by the Librarian of the Laurentian–Medicean Library in Florence. To the late Guido Biagi he owes his introduction to the scripts of Sinibaldi, di Mario and Poggio. Morison also began at this time to collect the books of the Italian writing-masters and began with Tagliente.*

But all the time, hammering away at the back of his mind was the memory of the Wardes and their coming *wanderjahr* in Europe. Morison, forewarned by his correspondence, had seen through Frederic's intellectual pretensions and cultural snobbism, and had recognized a craftsman in mechanical composition from whom he had much to learn and whose talents he could use. But nothing had prepared him for Beatrice. She was stunningly beautiful. With pretty brown hair, lovely face with a strong almost masculine profile, blue eyes, a body appealing in its contrasts – her waist was narrow, her hands large and thick-wristed (Eric Gill called it 'a fine American carcass'), and her fine, long legs, she was the sort of woman that men stop and stare at in the street. All this went with the most beguiling, open, warm-hearted, vivacious manner – any meeting with Beatrice left you feeling on top of the world and twice the man you thought you were. All this Morison had seen: he was also made aware of an obedient energy and a capacity for taking pains which made

Beatrice the best pupil – and later publicist of his work – that he ever had.

She in turn had been immensely struck by Morison – her first impression, recorded after he was dead, was as clear as the day she met him. His mastery of the field she was beginning to explore among the 14,000 books of the A.T.F. library, his dominant personality and compelling manner of speech startled and attracted her. Morison did not meet many women, had indeed an undeserved reputation for misogyny, but he had a natural gift for making each feel she was the only one. Beatrice was not so attached to Frederic that she was blind to Morison, and neither forgot the other when the *Aquitania* sailed. Morison had sent her a postcard and Beatrice had replied.

Unlike Gerard Meynell, Morison was less than normally acute in recognizing the inner springs of human behaviour: he enjoyed speculating about them, although averse to gossip, except with his closest friends. It was his ignorance that made him so fascinated by the motives and capacities of other human beings: he could never resist any chance to explore and manipulate, sometimes with a definite end in view, sometimes only to precipitate a change. He could thus hurt people, and they were not comforted by the realization that Morison was childishly innocent of malice: they called him scheming, when he was trying to achieve some object greater than the human beings, himself least of all, involved in it. On the other hand, one of the elements in his own great power of attraction was the high valuation he put on other people's motives, sometimes long after his trust had been let down. The bitter contempt which he could feel for a lazy or pretentious scholar or artist or a stupid man in a high position was intellectual contempt: it was none the less wounding for that, but it left untouched the charity and curiosity which he brought to bear on every person he came in contact with.

It is probable that his wife Mabel suffered from these strengths and weaknesses in him. If it was common loneliness that had first brought them together, if it was Morison who tried to bring about the resolution of her religious difficulties, it was she who had stood by him and comforted him during the war. She was clearly a much better-educated person than he, in the normal sense, and as much as he would accept of the ordinary social graces came from her. Furthermore, she had a not inconsiderable part in all the scholarly work he had done. She had helped with the *Fleuron*, a debt acknowledged in the second and third numbers. She had gone with him on his European travels (she disliked Berlin and liked Dr Jessen as much as he did).* She had investigated the Spanish scribe Ferdinando Ruano, tracing his manuscripts and translating his printed tract on writing, *Sette Alphabeti*, which Morison had found in Bertieri's collection. She had also translated long passages from Servidori's *Reflexiones* for him. Friends of those days still remember comfortable evenings spent at Hollyberry Lane.

Clearly she had none of Morison's blindness to the feelings of others. In the sudden flowering of his talent, Morison had overtaken her, intellectually and socially. He was perhaps too busy to notice – a bad sign in itself – but she was all too aware that he was receding from her. There is good reason to distrust what little Morison ever said on the subject, but it may be that it was her schoolmistressy explanations of the sights of Florence that first made him realize that all was not well.* His deep faith mixed with rough criticism of the Church may well have been too much for her. Now and later (as an over-assiduous assistant to the Catholic Chaplain of London University)* she took refuge in the sort of religious practices that irritated Morison so much. Already upset and nervous, she was quick – too quick – to sense danger.

Just now, Morison was full of the Officina Bodoni. The 'manager' of the press, Dr Hanna Kiel, had been in London in the autumn, and her account of the Press had captivated Morison. He had arranged with Bumpus to sell some of their books, and now learnt of their further plans, including a folio missal. He also had ideas for publicizing the Press in America. Dr Kiel forgot the details and had to write to Morison afterwards: what, she asked, was the name of the lady who would be so helpful?* Morison replied.

It was very kind of Dr Mardersteig to think of me – I wish very much to come to Lugano, and have the hope of doing so in a short time. I wish to buy some type in Frankfurt, and again to visit Munich perhaps – I will let you know more in a little time. . . . I am very interested in your projected edition of your MISSALE ROMANUM, and I should very much like to possess it. I think you gathered that I am a violent Papist in religion – but even I could hardly stagger to church with a Missal in folio size! If your book is intended for collectors it might be another matter, but I have usually found that book collectors are more interested if the text has some strictly literary – or porno-graphic – quality. I will answer the rest of the questions at Lugano.

'Dr Mardersteig charges me to tell you, that if you like, his little summerhouse 5 minutes from the press will be at your disposal,' she answered, and on 20 November he wrote again to say he was starting on the twenty-fourth, leaving his wife in Paris 'where she has friends', but on the twenty-fourth itself he wired that he was unable to come. They had got as far as Paris, had met the friends – the Bullens on their way home to America – and what had happened emerges clearly enough from a letter which Mabel wrote when they got back.

> 11 Hollyberry Lane, Hampstead N.W.3.
> 29 November 1924.
>
> My dear Mrs Bullen.
> I shall never forget your goodness to me in Paris, may God bless you and Mr Bullen for all your kindness to me. You both have greatly strengthened & heartened me & whatever happens (and I fear it is separation) I am now more able to stand alone. Come & see me when you come to London and I will show you Mrs Warde's letter (the part I have). With love and all good wishes for your happiness.
>
> > Yours gratefully
> > Mabel Morison.

From this one might suppose that all was over, but this would be to take far too melodramatic a view of the situation. Such may have been Mabel's view, but it was surely premature, since the pretext had not yet arrived. It can only have been instinct, but – for once – instinct was to be proved right. In the interval Morison did his best to prove it wrong, faced with hysterical outbursts, which he tried, within limits, to assuage or ignore. He was relieved from more embarrassment by the Wardes' tolerance and sympathy; marriage was not, they believed, to stop an independent choice of profession or way of life – they were, on principle, 'broad-minded'.

In the meantime, chance and Charles Hobson provided Morison with the means of solving the Warde problem. At the beginning of 1925 Hobson was to bring his agency from Manchester to London; although his connection with the Cloister Press had ceased – his shares had gone to pay its debts – he still wanted to have his own print workshop, to do his own advertising settings, and such things as specimen pages for publishers which trade printers would then set and print. It was the ideal opportunity for Morison. He explained Warde's peculiar abilities and convinced Hobson; and so 'the Fanfare' came into existence, as the imprint for the business Hobson had in mind.

When Morison next wrote to Mardersteig, it was to say that he would come at Christmas; 'as my wife is not well I shall be alone'. It was a memorable visit for both of them. The weather was mild that Christmas, which was just as well, since the 'little house' was unheated. Most of the time, however, they spent at Mardersteig's house, endlessly talking. Morison had discovered another friend with as keen an eye for typographic detail as for its history. They sat on the carpet, getting up from time to time to pull down a book. Morison talked about the earliest printed book on the construction of Roman capitals by Damianus Moyllus which he had just got to hear of, and Mardersteig told him about the similar manuscript by Felice Feliciano at Rome, which he had already seen. They talked of the mysterious Dutch 'Janson' type. Morison tried out the 'Grammar of Fine Printing' on Mardersteig; Mardersteig thought he might be able to interest his friend Kurt Wolff, making a name for himself as a publisher of art books, in a reprint of *Four Centuries*. They chose specimen pages of the Press's work to go in *Modern Fine Printing*, and they talked about the future and the Fanfare, which Morison hoped might become another Officina Bodoni.

After three days, all the books were off the shelves and in piles round them. It was an idyllic and exhilarating holiday. Morison went slowly back through Paris – 'no end of troublesome work awaited me, and I had to put in quite a lot of time at the printers of my book' – Jacomet, who did the plates of *Modern Fine Printing*. In London he looked back to Montagnola rather wistfully. 'I think often of you, the Bodoni Press, der Hund, und seine Platz, of your Christmas tree, and the happy days we spent.'*

On 7 January the Wardes landed at Cherbourg, and that evening Morison met them in Paris; the next few days were hardly 'troublesome work'.

We spent 4 gay and frivolous days there. Morison had a vast amount of typographical news, and we jabbered without intermission. Without doing any deliberate sightseeing we managed to get on friendly terms with the city; and oh what a city it is! My eyes kept bugging out until I thought they'd come loose. F. and Morison both abandoned all theories of diet, and we surrounded some memorable meals. . . . We heard Mass at Notre Dame, and snooped along the bookstores on the Seine, & thumbed our noses at the Eiffel Tower and had a hell of a grand time. Tuesday the 13th we started off for London, just missing a black fog. This is a most marvelous city, I think. There's a lot of it, but not too much at any one place, so that it's always lovable. You should have seen my first trip to the British Museum! The Reading Room! Morison got us readers' cards, and already I know the research ropes & have embarked on a few questions that may prove to be of typographical interest. We've visited all the important booksellers, and have met some interesting people. There seems to be a great deal to do, and F. especially will have his hands full with designing.

Morison took them to Cambridge on his next visit, and on 2 February there was more news to report.

'The Fleuron' has a charming office in Gt. Russell Street. Mr. Oliver Simon, its co-editor with Morison, is a delightful fellow who has dined us in style at Martinez's & expects us both to write articles for his learned and brilliant periodical. He is a nephew of Max Beerbohm [this was a slight exaggeration], and also of the artist William Rather-stone. By the way, you might do worse than to buy the last Fleuron (it is outrageously expensive) in order to appreciate my stage-fright at coming out in it.

Between us we are settling the typographic problems of the universe. It's rare fun.

She went to Westminster Cathedral, which she found 'gloomy and self-conscious', apart from 'the marvellous stations by Eric Gill'. She had a sharp eye and ear for novelties.

Last Sunday morning I'll never forget: the Basin at Kensington, with scores of wonderful little yachts tacking and scudding through tiny waves so demurely that the people at the water's edge seemed drolly out of scale. I've never seen such a nice assortment of babies: round, shiny ones with hair like pollen, and cheeks that seemed painted *and* varnished.

It's remarkable how hard it is for these Englanders to murmur. There's a marchioness across the room whose voice, low-pitched and charmingly tuned, comes whanging over to me like a temple gong, a great volume of soft sound.

and – joy of joys – 'Morison is teaching cockney, at which he is quite fluent.'

They stayed at the Hotel Rembrandt (handy for the V. & A. 'full of wonderful things in my line') while they looked for somewhere more permanent to live. Here Oliver Simon helped: there were rooms free beneath his at 115 Ebury Street, and to-wards the end of February the Wardes moved in; they were delighted with the tall eighteenth-century windows, the mould-ing on the ceiling, and above all the London-ness of it all. They went to Ditchling and fell in love with the country too. Frederic started work in the offices that Hobson had taken for the Fanfare.

You should see my offices in Bedford Square. They are so grand that the Duke of Bedford who owns the square sends his surveyor round every day or so to make sure everything is satisfactory – to the Duke – and that I have not absconded with one of his £1500 marble mantles designed by Robert Adam.

Morison and Warde were very busy, too busy for Morison to contemplate an Easter visit to Montagnola, although there was much he would have liked to discuss with Mardersteig. There was the 'Grammar of Fine Printing', which he had been discussing with Warde, and now Mardersteig's friend Kurt Wolff came to London with a new vast proposition: a six-volume history of the art of the book, to be published by Wolff's Pantheon-Verlag.* This did not prevent the Wardes and Morison from slipping over to Paris again in the middle of March ('I have occasion to be in Paris almost every month,' he told Updike – no doubt the plates for *Modern Fine Printing* were one reason). When he was there with the Wardes in January, he had made a discovery in the Anisson collection of documents on printing at the Bibliothèque Nationale.

A prospectus by Mr. John Bell of the British Library, Strand, London, announcing the completion, under his direction by William Coleman and Richard Austin, of a set of types which he claims to be superior to all other letters founded in England. The prospectus is set in the same type as the specimen, roman and italic, and the types are known to you as 'Brimmer'. The prospectus is dated May 1788.*

This had excited Updike, because it was the source of a type discovered languishing at the Riverside Press in Boston by Bruce Rogers in 1895 and by himself independently in England. There were other things he wanted Morison to look at for him – documents on the Fourniers, which introduced Morison to another part of his life-long study of eighteenth-century French typography and the transmission of the sixteenth-century French types.

Beatrice caught Morison's enthusiasm for Garamond, and began work on an 'essay' which was not to be finished for some time.* But meanwhile Morison found work for both of them on the current *Monotype Recorder*. Frederic designed it, with a bravura display of flowers on crisp matt art paper, and a pretty yellow on blue cover, and Beatrice wrote an article, humbly submitted in a careful imitation of the French *ronde* hand (see plate 4).

This must have been 'Calligraphy and Printing', an oddly disconnected account of the relation 'between the type forms of the early printers and the writing forms of contemporary calligraphers'. Black-letter, the transmission of swash letters from Arrighi, through Mercator and Garamond to Caslon (would they survive in a future dominated by 'old face' types?), the function of the colophon, the relation of geometrically constructed Roman capitals and humanistic script – it all suggests a not-quite-digested redaction of those conversations 'settling the typographic problems of the universe'. The illustrations too – 'The Coronation Book of Charles V', the Mainz Psalter, two pages of the writing-manual of Gerard Mercator, the Dutch sixteenth-century calligrapher and map-maker, a page from Arrighi's *Coryciana* 1524 – are equally heterogeneous; they may have picked up the first two on a visit to the Bibliothèque Nationale.*

It was the original of the last that Warde took back with him when, just after Easter, he went back to Paris. Morison had bought his copy of *Coryciana* some time before, and had illustrated a page of it in 'The Chancery Types of Italy and France' in *Fleuron 3*. Out of it, a new plan had been hatched – to produce a perfect modern version of Arrighi's elegant first italic. Morison was perhaps rather disheartened with Monotype: neither Garamond, nor Baskerville, nor Poliphilus and Blado had been produced exactly as he wished. Fournier had suffered a worse disaster: as with Baskerville, two versions had been produced, a 'rough' and a 'smooth'; while Morison was in America, there had been some doubt as to which version to pursue, and on 15 October, in the confusion after Duncan's death, the works decided to proceed with the one Morison did not prefer, the smooth. Matrices of 14pt and an 18pt italic were completed by March, but Morison had only just learnt what had happened. While he was away Burch and Pierpont argued, but it had gone too far for the 'rough' Fournier, later christened Barbou, to be reinstated; on his return at the end of May he succeeded in rescuing the matrices of one size.*

Morison was not going to be thwarted in producing his Arrighi type by what he saw as the stupidity, dilatoriness, and even opposition of the works: he was going to have punches cut by hand by one of the few surviving engravers capable of the task, who would then strike and dress the matrices. They would next be handed to a competent typefounder who would cast a fount of type. Ribadeau Dumas was the foundry chosen, and the punchcutter was to be Charles Plumet, an elderly but very experienced engraver. Warde and Morison, who was to follow him shortly, were at pains to impress on them the need for speed, because the Fanfare, where they planned to use the type, was just now going into business. Ernest Ingham, who had hitherto supervised the agency's dealings with printers, was deputed by Hobson to take charge of the day-to-day running of the press. He had come down from Manchester over the Easter week-end, and was now busy installing frames and cases of type, a proofing-press and other equipment.

Beatrice had been left behind in London. She was still enjoying herself. She 'refused a most tempting and munificent offer from a wealthy advertising man: he wanted to take me on full time beginning as soon as the Music Book was finished'.* She was filling a note-book, entitled 'Musicae Typographia' and neatly lettered BECQVER on the front cover, with notes on her researches at the British Museum, about which Morison made suggestions. She watched the Boat Race from the Emery Walkers' house at Hammersmith. She went to the office for Holy Saturday morning at Westminster Cathedral, where she 'saw the gang... finishing Lent up in style'. She was expecting her mother to arrive in the middle of May, and on 20 April, just in time to reach her before she started, she wrote:

On Thursday (F's absence having weighed on me) I did a bunk from London to Cambridge, walked 19 m. to Ely, roamed over the Cathedral, saw the market going on in the square, and a blind town-crier (bell, God Save the King, and all), stayed over at the 'Bull', then trekked south to the loveliest country in the world: that around

178

Bishop's Stortford (Little Hadham, Much Hadham, Braughing, Stanton . . . tiny villages of half-timbered, thatched cottages, ancient inns where the beer smells like thatch & acts like nectar, blacksmiths' forges where you'd hear the thin 'tink-tink' a hundred yards away; duck-ponds, pollard willows, crumbling mile-stones; churches with 10th century square towers, 14th century brasses, 16th century white-wash over the pious images on the walls, scars in the niches where saints had been ripped out, strange 17th cent. tombstones under the church-yard yews, war-memorial crosses just putting on a veil of green moss, and at their feet a bunch of daffodils in a little pail of water . . .) – the countryside was big with spring: there was always at least one lark throwing himself up at the sky & shouting about it: primroses, violets, cowslips, daisies; the 'unmatured green valleys cold', the 'green thorny bloomless hedge, and rivers new with spring-time sedge' . . . (and full of crisp cress and flanked with mint!) – The trees were all in green buds, not one out yet; the grass was virid; the sun blazed, and the wind pushed fat white clouds over it & then snatched them away. There was an apple-orchard in bloom, and under the trees, just matching the blossoms in color, were ten very young pigs, chasing each other and squeaking like puppies; each one had moist brown earth on his snout . . . I thought my heart would blow up with joy: I sang aloud all the ballads I knew. . . . April 17th (I write it fair as the happiest day of my life) I walked 28 miles, and wasn't even stiff.

She was jubilant, elated, as gay as one of the larks she saw. What she did not tell her mother was that she was soon going to Paris, and from there Morison and she were going on one of his long tours of printers, publishers and libraries in France and Germany. Frederic would not object; it was all part of their understanding that each should be free to choose their own way of life. Where did they go? It is not an easy question to answer. Mrs Becker was on the high seas, Updike was silent, there was a lull in the corre-spondence with Montagnola. There was no one to write to, and a lot to do.

They went to Lyon, and no doubt had a merry time with Audin. They went to Leipzig, where they surely met Anton Kippenberg of the Insel-Verlag, Julius Rodenberg at the Deutsche Bücherei, a friend of Simon's, who was writing on Karl Klings-por and his type foundry for the next *Fleuron*, and Carl Ernst

Poeschel with his American wife, a printer with a sense of clarity in plain type and decoration which closely resembled Morison's own, Oscar Brandstetter, Catholic and publisher, and in particular Jakob Hegner.* Hegner's career had its parallels with Morison. Seven years older, he launched Claudel in Germany and at the end of the war he had added a small printing-house to his publishing business. The books that he produced here provided more examples in *Modern Fine Printing* than any other German printer. His influence, more perhaps than any other, insured the victory of roman over fraktur; like Morison, he believed passionately in the superiority of the renaissance type-forms and of capitals for display. First the Depression and then the war (he was a Jewish Catholic) brought their troubles – Morison befriended him in unhappy exile in Britain – but he ended his career comfortable enough under the protection of Verlag Kösel. Just before he died, eighty and nearly blind, he was struck in the eye by the cork of a champagne bottle he was opening. From 1962, Morison opened bottles himself more carefully.

After Leipzig, Frankfurt: here there were excursions to the Rheingau, to the Hotel Au Müller at Rüdesheim,* and perhaps to the Klingspor foundry at Offenbach. But before Morison's tour was ended Beatrice left him to go to meet her mother, who landed at Cherbourg on 13 May. Frederic was to meet them at Paris, to which he came direct from London. He had returned from Paris on 19 April, just before Beatrice left, in a rather bad temper. Next day at the Fanfare, his first with all the staff there, he was altogether too inclined to lay down the law, and in the end Haslam Mills, who had come down with Hobson, had to point out to him that this was no way to go on. He had a fierce and pointless quarrel with Oliver Simon. It was a relief to go back to Paris for the reunion, and that not only with Beatrice and her mother. Morison, on his own, had been trying to catch up with undone work, in trying circumstances. He was behind with his article for *Fleuron 4*, due out in July, but on 18 May he wrote to Simon.

Baseler Hof, Frankfurt
18 May 1925.

My dear brother: Here at last in these nine dirty sides of copy is the completion of your script article – and may I never do another. I'm a terrible trial to you I know and have no excuse other than to say that I couldn't think how to end it. I have been knocking about between Lyon & Frankfurt for some time without accomplishing more than wasting my time & money. This is the last continental journey I take this year, I promise. In a few days I shall be back. My wife arrives in Paris on Thursday & we shall return on the Friday I suppose and I will give an account of myself then. In the meantime a tremendous thunderstorm is sweeping the town. It has been awfully hot – good for the Hagenback Circus which has been in procession through the town – big elephants & one baby, camels, coloured pagans of many races and what not who must have felt at home in the sweltering heat. . . .

I have discovered nothing in Frankfurt so far that I did not already know of.

S.M.

Back in London, there was too much work to do to think of anything else. With the ownership of the *Fleuron* now in Morison's hands, it was a question where to print it. Warde had ambitious ideas: in March he tried it out on Updike, who was cautious; France, Germany and Italy were all to be considered. In the middle of all this, *Fleuron 4* came out, with Morison's long article 'On Script Types', a further exploration of the later stages of the relation between calligraphy and type, Warde – even longer – on Bruce Rogers and Newdigate on Emery Walker, two pupils on their masters, Hanna Kiel on recent German book-printing, and an urbane piece by Holbrook Jackson on 'Robert Bridges, George Moore, Bernard Shaw and Printing'. Morison had been thinking a good deal about Bridges lately, for whom he had a plan in view; but whether plan begot article or vice versa, who can say?

His complete responsibility for *Fleuron 5* had begun to weigh on Morison. He needed help; relations with Mabel were such that he could not contemplate leaving London, and yet his journeys abroad had been very productive for the *Fleuron*. He

181

tried to set out what he needed, and how the Wardes could help to supply it.

F.W. & B.L.W.

Memorandum   10 July 1925

The degree of unity possible in the *Fleuron* is not very great because a certain amount of diversity seems essential in a journal. Nevertheless it is necessary for the Editor and contributors to share the same view point as far as possible. This is what makes it difficult to carry on the *Fleuron*. It is necessary not only to have contributions but contributions written from the same angle or the journal will degenerate into a bag of bones. Thus the editorial staff must be a very limited edition indeed. The advantage of the *Fleuron* lies in its being a periodical and it can and should give the reader more in the way of news than it has done. There ought to be at least two chronicles written in scientific fashion.

RECENT TYPOGRAPHICAL LITERATURE would inform the reader of all the books published since the previous issue of the *Fleuron*. Besides giving the bibliographical particulars it would give a paragraph summarising & criticising the author's thesis. Important books wd. of course be separately & more fully treated.

RECENT TYPEFOUNDING would chronicle the output of the type founders & machine composers of the world. The chronicle wd. present a specimen line or two of each face. When Cloister light face is issued we should criticise it in detail. The Mono. Baskerville shd. be compared diligently with the original & differences noted & remarked upon.

RECENT PRINTING would incorporate the present so called 'Typographical reviews' but wd. not be confined to English or American work. We shd give the bibliographical data & the typographical, type, measure, leaded, initials etc.

These three chronicles need to be accurate & scientific, they must be complete. We must not rely upon the stray review copy sent in for notice. D.B.U.'s *Rowe Mores* must be given a show in spite of appearances. There shd. be no regard to personalities whether German or American or English. It is obvious that if this work is done as it must be done if it is done at all there is a good deal of work. It shd. be tackled gradually. When a book comes in, it shd. be noticed in the same week & not left until the week of going to press.

The proper thing is for the editor to do this himself. Unfortunately this is not possible. As far as he can see the contents for no 5 are likely to be

Julius Rodenberg	:	The Work of Karl Klingspor (with portrait, many reproductions.)
B. L. Warde	:	The so-called Garamond Types.
R. Bertiers	:	Bookprinting & book illustration in Italy.
W. R. Lethaby	:	Edward Johnston & calligraphy in England.
S. Morison	:	The History & Use of Decorated Types or The Use and Abuse of Italic.

In addition there will be long reviews of Jessen: *Meisterwerk der Schreibkunst* and other things. Furthermore the Oxford *Fell* book and *Ephemerica* will tax my time. Very seriously therefore I need much help. Nor do I know where to get it save from the two Wardes. I wd. like the two to let me know exactly what in the way of assistance I can count on getting. Please don't be enthusiastic and promise all sorts of things. Remember I shall want the goods delivered & will pay at the covenanted rate at the covenanted time. I offer £1 a page for the Garamond article and more for expert reviews of certain books. The practice of working for nothing is hereby stopped. But what I want is the goods at the right time. I don't want to be told stories of Paris or Gollancz or Prunaire – or Montagnola.

S.M.

The last words refer to a new letter from Kiel, full of the Italian Government's competition for an edition of the complete works of D'Annunzio (which Mardersteig won and in consequence moved to Italy) and Francesco Pastonchi's scheme for a new series of Italian classics in a new type. Morison discussed it with the Wardes, and replied enthusiastically on the same day he wrote the 'Memorandum', promising Monotype matrices of the Pastonchi type in six weeks, and offering the assistance of Warde, who 'will be in France at the end of the month'. For himself, he said, 'at the moment I cannot leave London.'

9

IT was on 28 June 1925 that Morison went to tea at Chilswell again with the Bridges. The Wardes went too, and Morison broached the object of the visit. He explained about the new type, produced a copy of *Fleuron 3* to show what it would look like, and asked if they might have the honour of first printing Bridges' latest poems in it. Bridges was friendly, but there was a difficulty: he already had such a collection in hand with the Oxford Press, due out at the end of the year. But during the discussion a way round this emerged. Why should they not print a limited edition of some of the poems? Even if published before the Oxford edition (as would be desirable), a few copies at a high price could hardly damage the prospects of the latter. Bridges undertook to put this to Humphrey Milford, manager of the Oxford University Press in London.

Morison can hardly have been cast down by this outcome, nor apprehensive of Milford's decision. Since his first visit to Bridges in 1923, when he had also seen R. W. Chapman, Morison's links with the Oxford University Press had become closer. On 25 June 1925 the tercentenary of Bishop Fell's birth was celebrated by the publication of *Specimens of Books Printed at Oxford with the Types Given to the University by John Fell*, compiled by Chapman (then Secretary to the Delegates), no doubt with Morison's help. Morison also wrote an article that appeared in *The Times* on the anniversary day, the day after he wrote to Mrs Bridges. Chapman was anxious that there should be 'an historical investigation into the origins of the [Fell] types', and may already have asked Morison to undertake it. Morison later wrote that 'he accepted the commission with considerable reluctance, having some idea of what such a task would involve, knowing, also, that he would encounter obstacles of the kind usually classified as coming within the category of "pressure from other work"'.* Whether or not Chapman had made the proposal, he must have known that Oxford had much to gain from Morison, and that the Press would be foolish to obstruct the enterprise which he and Bridges had in mind. Even if he already knew the reasons for Morison's reluctance to undertake his task, he could hardly have guessed how many more 'obstacles' would delay publication of *John Fell: the University Press and the Fell Types* until the day after Morison's death.

Milford had no objection, and on 6 July Morison confirmed his proposal formally to Bridges:

Dear Mr Bridges

I am a little late in answering your letter because I needed to see Milford again about the question of copyright. From what he tells me I learn that you reserve the copyright in all cases so that I am in order in making money arrangements direct with you. My proposal is to print 125 or 150 copies of your new poems, using for the purpose a new type based upon that of Arrighi (see p. 24 of No. 3 of *The Fleuron* which I have caused to be sent you) and sold at some convenient price. I say 'convenient' as this business of cutting a new type is a very costly one and I should like, if possible, to recover a little of it. It is too early for me to be able to say definitely but I imagine the published price would be £2. 2. 0. Of this sum I would pay you a royalty on copies sold of 20% if you were agreeable. This cannot bring in a very large sum in the aggregate but perhaps you would be inclined to accept it as a help towards the venture.

The type is making better progress and I've seen the revised characters which are greatly improved. We should be able to make a start at the end of this month and publish at or about 15 September. . . .

Bridges agreed at once, and offered to provide the 'copy' as soon as they were ready; he added, 'I wish that in this book you as publisher would write (that is sign) the introductory note of description of contents & therein take all responsibility for format etc'. A week later he wrote suggesting that Morison use corrected proofs of the Oxford *New Verse* to set from, 'if you can wait for them – which will not be less than a month, I guess'.* But the delay was welcome.

Meanwhile Warde had been deep in laborious correspondence with punchcutter and founder. Plumet had sent 'smoke proofs' of the punches. Warde hastened to congratulate him ('avec un tâche bien difficile vous avez faites un très bon résultat') and to send some corrections:

Nous espérons qu'ils sont assez bon pour vous donner une idée suffisante pour les corrections. Malheureusement nous sommes un peu pressé par l'auteur qui a besoin de ces caractères et nous sommes très obligées si vous donnerez votre attention à ce travail et, après, voulez vous mettre les poinçons chez Ribadeau Dumas aussitôt que possible, avec l'ancien livre où vous avez trouvez vos modèles.

And to Ribadeau Dumas he wrote:

Je pense que vous avez besoin de ce livre pour gagner l'approchement exacte entre les caractères. Ça sera exactement comme dans le livre. Ci inclus nous vous donnons une table de caractères avec quantités.*

and he repeated the need for speed:

Et voulez-vous nous dire le temps nécessaire. Nous avons grand besoin de ces caractères et nous serons très obligés si vous avez le moyens de faire notre travail aussitôt que possible.

It is doubtful if either establishment understood quite what was expected of them. When Warde went to Paris at the end of July, he found that the size of fount was too small for Ribadeau Dumas to undertake; it would have to be at least doubled. With this settled, Warde went on to his first visit to Mardersteig. Morison had written to Mardersteig to introduce him: 'I believe Warde can answer a number of questions for you better than I can, as he is a practical man and I only an archaeologist.' On 5 August he added:

I hope you will be able to understand his English and that he may learn something from his inspection of the Officina Bodoni. I am full of ambition to do a like work here, but lack of knowledge is a great obstacle. Several of my plans have turned out either unworkable or less successful than I anticipated.

Morison was no doubt thinking of the Arrighi type. But both Warde and he had much to learn about the mechanics of the process they were now involved in; the final 'bill' for the fount was not made up till 20 August. Meanwhile Bridges, hearing nothing, wrote to enquire 'if you are still adherent to your intention of a de luxe volume'.* Morison hastened to reassure him, but it was Bridges who created the next problem. He was interested in every aspect of his craft – prosody, print, handwriting, and phonetics. Would it be possible, he asked Morison, to exploit the two alternative forms of g – *g* and *g* – which he had noticed in the *Fleuron* article, to distinguish the two 'g' sounds, as in 'language'? Morison agreed, but by 22 September, although all the punches were cut (bar the last), there was still no type, and it did not arrive until the beginning of October. Bridges was forced to enquire again. 'I have not heard from you since I sent you the proof sheets for "copy" of the poems,' he wrote on 6 October. 'I should be grieved to think that you were in any wise disappointed by the poems.'

Morison was repentant.

Sunday, 12 October

Dear Mr Bridges: I am so sorry to have appeared to be neglectful. Please be sure that I read all the poems the same night you gave them to me, being unable to put them down until the whole was once read. I am indeed very proud to be their first printer. Certainly I would not omit a single one. I like them all though I have questions to ask about two of them. In the meantime I am occupied with the type & setting. I expect the new g to arrive on Monday or Tuesday. With this I enclose a rough proof of the type wh. I do hope you won't too much dislike. It will take on more vigour when properly printed. There are one or two things to say. First: I have tentatively entitled the book *The Tapestry* as I liked that poem very much but you will of course give the collection any title you choose – not necessarily that of the Milford volume. Indeed I am of opinion that the titles of the two should be different: Secondly, I am still extremely short of type & would like you to initial this proof and return to me as soon as convenient. I will send you tomorrow another proof for you to retain. Thirdly, can you soon send me the copy for the statement about the first appearance of one or two of the poems elsewhere and the reference to Milford's book? I hope to see you again soon. I greatly enjoyed my last visit to you and Mrs Bridges. . . .

Yours
Stanley Morison

Bridges wrote by return:

My dear Morison

I am very much delighted by the appearance of your type: and am greatly excited by the promise of so beautiful a book.

But I am somewhat anxious about your prospect of getting it out in time.

In your letter this morning you speak of '*the 3 poems*' which you have already set up. As I wrote to you last night (a letter dictated to my wife) your printer has represented one of these poems by its first sections – and, in place of its proper continuation, has substituted the first half of another poem! and it seems by your letter of this morning that you had seen this and passed this.

It is plain that errors on this scale will much delay the printing – and I am aghast at the awkwardness and delay which such errors will cause if it takes two days post to correct every one of them.

Besides, as all the printing is to be done by you from printed copy one wd expect it to go pretty smoothly.

In the poem headed 'October' (which he shd not have printed at all) your printer prints *advance* for *adance*.

How are you going to get things printed in time?

I ought by this time to be receiving proof pages every day?

By the way, the narrowness of the page in the proof puzzles me. I suppose you are arranging for the imprint to take the full long lines of the later poems.

I hope you will be able to console me.

Yours sincerely
RB

Morison answered tactfully.

Dear Bridges: I am immensely relieved that you like the 'arrighi' type. The work of getting out the volume in the covenanted time is not so easy that I can afford to be cocksure about it – but I seriously think that we shall be able to send you the bulk of the proofs, carefully read and positively concordant with the original. I have rewritten the printers' note and send you a copy of it. . . .

Yours
Stanley Morison

Bridges was reassured: 'I do not wish Milford's book to be delayed – and I think that you might very well arrange with him that any slight discrepancy between the advertised and actual dates of publication should be ignored.'* This elastic view of publication was to be a blessing, for at the end of the month Morison was forced to confess:

I have failed you in the matter of the new g. The punch cutter, rather a harbitrary gent knowing his power, hasn't yet cut this solitary letter though I have done my uttermost to make him. I am most sorry for this real disappointment.

But the setting went on without it, and on 4 November Bridges was returning the proofs, pointing out that one poem 'The West Front' had been omitted. There was no reply, and Bridges became angry.

Dear Mr Morison, It being now the eleventh of November, and your book being due on the fifteenth it appears to me impossible that you can fulfil the terms of the agreement with Mr Milford. So that I hope you will see him and make a fresh agreement which will enable you to bring your book out *after* his. I do not see that his interests will suffer by this in any way, tho', no doubt the 'literary' value of *your* bk as a fine 'editio princeps' will lose whatever advantage it might possibly have on that account.

On the other hand a hastily edited and incorrect edition, at the price and with the pretensions of your book, wd be wholly undesirable and something of a fraud.

I always doubted your confidence in expecting to get your book out by the date required. The only hope for that was a very diligent editing and superintendence of the printers. But it appeared from the first sample of proofs that the printers did not know even what poems they had to print. And in the second batch of proofs one poem was omitted, which omission not only set all the numeration wrong: but

189

destroyed the claim of the bk to be a 'complete' collection of the poems written by me in the 'new verse'.

If by a miraculous reformation of procedure you shd actually present me with a full proof of the bk, such as can be passed without scruple, and be in time for the stipulated issue by the 15th, I will do my best to 'revise' it so as to secure its accuracy . . . but I think that you under-estimate the time and trouble that are involved in securing the immaculate correctness which such a book as yours shd have if it is to come up to its pretensions.

Considering the very elementary stage of the proofs hitherto sent to me, I very strongly urge tht you shd delay the publication until the printer's work shd be satisfactorily accomplished at leisure. Your book will be all the better for the delay – and will in any case be unique – especially if it shd include the new g.

Yours sincerely
Robert Bridges

But next day there was unexpected news from Oxford, and the excitement of the race dissipated his anger.

12 November

Dear Mr Morison,

I hear today that Milford's book is hung up by a strike of the binders. So it seems that it wd be worth your while to make that the basis of a rearrangement with Milford, & meanwhile *send me your proofs as fast as you can.*

Yours sincerely,
R. Bridges.

This crossed with Morison's distressed confession that it was too late to put 'The West Wind' in; he sent a revise which now included the new g. Next day Bridges wrote again comfortingly: 'Please understand that I am very much delighted with your book, and hope it may be the first of a future series.' But he begged him at least to alter the Printer's Note which contained the now inaccurate word 'complete'. It was too late; only three days later the book was all printed off and at the binder's.* It was to be a neck-and-neck finish with Oxford yet.

But no one can say who won the race. Oxford probably published *New Verse* on 10 December. By now, however, Morison was no longer interested – he had sold the entire edition to Bumpus's bookshop, where the great J. G. Wilson was then a great patron of new writers and private printers. On 19 December he was able to write in a more leisurely and dignified style to Bridges.

Dear Mr Bridges, I am sending you two copies of *The Tapestry* which you require for the King and Mr Asquith. I shall charge you for one of them at trade price less royalty. Bumpus has taken all the copies with the exception of one or two we had to set aside for presentation purposes, and they will account to me for them at the first quarter day in the New Year, whereupon I will send a cheque for the royalties due to you.

I must thank you once again for allowing us to use your splendid poems, and though the present book is by no means perfect typographically, I hope that on a future occasion, and given more time, we may make a greater success with a new work of yours should you be kind enough to entrust it to us.

I have asked Eric Gill to send you a piece of his writing, and I have not forgotten that I promised you some lines of my own. These I will send in a few days.

Yours
Stanley Morison

Bridges was collecting specimens for his tract on handwriting, and Morison, who had other reasons for writing to Gill, was anxious to help him. *The Tapestry* was finished. It is a handsome book, with the mannered grace of the Arrighi type, the Japanese vellum paper and elegant marbled paper binding. In its production, Morison came as near as he ever did to Moxon's definition of a 'Typographer' in performing 'all the Handy-works and Physical Operations relating to *Typographie*'. It was not very close. The Fanfare compositors set the type, Ingham and Warde shared the printing (on the Fanfare proofing-press) with some special black ink brought back by Warde from Paris, and Morison came in late at night to correct the proofs (all the copies have one final misprint, 'cretes' for 'certes', corrected in his hand).* He was not deft with his hands like Warde, and he lacked something of his thorough, even pernickety, attention to the detail of each letter. But he learnt one important thing from the trials of the autumn. Hitherto he had seen the transference of the design, the idea of the letter, to the surface of a type as a single operation; he had been resentful of what he saw as the mechanical inadequacy of the Monotype process in performing it. He now understood that the engraver of the punch has a crucial role in deciding the form of the letter; that Garamond, Granjon and his other heroes of the sixteenth century were supremely skilful artificers first, and artists in letter design after. Plumet had done what was required of him: to copy the original design. But being a good artificer he had done better than the original engraver, a famous goldsmith but an amateur in letter design. Plumet's skill emphasized the mannerism of the design; next time Morison determined that there should be equal partnership between designer and engraver.

Not content with all this activity, Morison was, during this time, writing hard as well: a double number of the *Monotype Recorder* (September–December 1925) on 'Type Designs of the Past and Present'. This is a much expanded reworking of *The Craft of Printing* (1921) and the *Brief Survey* (1923). It was Morison's first chance to return to his favourite theme since he had read Updike, and he had read much else, particularly on palaeography, since then. The development of roman, italic and black-letter from the Carolingian minuscule is much expanded, and recent discoveries like John Bell's type were included. The illustrations were generous in size and number. There are signs that it was put together under pressure (it was produced in answer to 'a request for "more history" expressed by several of our correspondents' after Beatrice's article in the spring – clearly she already had the knack of making interest among the trade in Morison's pre-occupations), but this is hardly to be wondered at.

Beatrice herself had been away for the last and worst part of the rush. At the end of September she went back to Paris to 'finish up my music title book and the Fournier treatise too'.* She was

to be joined a day or two later by Frederic, who was picking up
their older friend Tom Cleland at Le Havre. Frederic returned
after a week or so, but Beatrice stayed working during the day,
and doing her best to amuse Cleland, enraptured to be in France
but despairing over the language problem, in the evenings. Then
she was taken ill and had to come home. Frederic, however, was
pining to get back to Montagnola. Beatrice wrote to her mother:

7 November 1925
Dearest M.L.B.: I write from Bedford Square: it's half past four, and
getting sapphire-dark outside as only London can. F. is downstairs
superintending the prospectus for the Bridges book, the Serpent has
gone home somewhat spiritually frayed by an acrimonious appeal to
Scripture which nearly wrecked the large-folio Estienne Bible (1545)
in which it's so easy to find the wrong text; and I am stalling about
when I should be doing a review of several corpulent books which
have been stacked very pointedly in my corner of the room.
It looks as if we would be spending Christmas in Switzerland. . . .
F. W. and Mardersteig are very affectionate and can do each other a
good deal of good, I should say. . . .
This is an amusing place to come to. I have fallen into the habit of
dropping in for tea on weekdays after leaving the Museum, and by
the time I arrive there's always some provocative discussion going
on in which it's fun to join. If by any oversight they're still at work
when I arrive I throw off some aphorism calculated to annoy, and
all business ceases at once.

Kurt Wolff came over again, and excited Morison with another
fusillade of schemes, literary, artistic and typographical. Morison
half-undertook to write an 'Introduction to Modern Fine Printing 1900–1925' for him.* On 25 November (Beatrice had by
now recovered) they all went over to Paris again for a meeting with Mardersteig, at which all the plans for printing and
publishing were further discussed. Warde was clearly anxious
that everything, the typographical and calligraphic books that
Morison had in mind, the elegantly printed literary texts that he
wanted to produce, even the *Fleuron* itself, should be moved to
the magical Continent, and preferably to Montagnola. Marder-

steig, planning a move to Florence and the printing of D'Annunzio, was glad to welcome co-operation.

Morison, on the other hand, fond as he was of Mardersteig, contemplated the proposed migration with less enthusiasm. He was a Londoner, he had his work at Monotype and at Cambridge. 'I go to Cambridge once a week. I like the atmosphere and do very little more than take lunch with the Vice-Chancellor and an occasional title-page,' he told Updike playfully. There were commissions from Benn: the finely printed Julian Editions had just been launched, including the standard Shelley and *Comus* with Blake's illustrations; Morison and Warde had just collaborated in producing the first, Arthur Clutton-Brock's *The Miracle of Love* (printed at Cambridge, it was the first public showing of the Fournier design, in the Barbou form that Morison preferred). There was also Heinemann, now taken over by Doubleday. Morison had produced for them *The Devil in Love*, with engravings by J. E. Laboureur, a new enthusiasm of his; now Doubleday's were pressing him to go over and work at their new Country Life Press, at Garden City, New Jersey. The printing of the *Fleuron* might be a matter of doubt, but here again Heinemann would help; Charlie Evans would publish it. So Morison said good-bye to the Wardes as they set off to Montagnola on 20 December, reflecting on these and other matters.

His mind was in a state of turmoil: 'un peu paresseux . . . un peu déréglé, un peu – tumultuaire, agité, aussi préoccupé avec les questions philosophiques et religieuses', he told Mardersteig, and he wrote to Updike, 'My mind is full to bursting with theological difficulties'; he was reading Streeter's *Four Gospels*, 'an entirely marvellous book of serious importance', which had come out the year before. And he was behind with his work.

I am dreadfully in arrears with my work and my correspondence – all due to my fatal habit of 'saying yea to life' – I mean in the Nietzschean sense as I have no vocation to the rococo. But I can't say 'No' if I am asked to do any job of the slightest interest. This means that I am spreading myself very thin on the slice. But you can imagine how time flies and one puts off till tomorrow when one expects to have the time for the pleasanter tasks of correspondence. I don't need to remark on the obvious but the worm of conscience must make its obeisance and it is generally on its tail in my case.*

Last year had been fruitful as well as disturbing, and there was great promise for the future. Not only were there Warde's projects, which included a complete facsimile of Arrighi's woodcut writing-books, but other things were coming up. A bookseller called Douglas Cleverdon, a complete stranger to Morison, wrote to enquire about the *Fleuron*;* they quickly discovered a common interest in Laboureur. Morison wrote to a man at Johan Enschedé en Zonen, typefounders at Haarlem, founded in 1703 but owning matrices going back to the fifteenth century, who had reviewed the *Fleuron* in *Het Boek*, kindly but not uncritically. Would he write an article to remedy Morison's ignorance? The answer came in an elegant hand and vigorous English.

Tuinwijklaan 19, Haarlem
31 January 1926.

Dear Sir,
Your kind letter of the 21st January was received with thanks.

Concerning Rosart's script type, though I share your opinion that it is inferior to that of some other designers, I think you went too far using expressions like 'detestable script' and – speaking of Rosart's work as a whole – 'singularly ugly'. As a matter of fact some of this prolific punch-cutter & type-founder's work is fairly good.

I quite agree with you that van Dyck's & Voskens' types represent the classical Dutch period; (at least as far as the roman and italic types are concerned: during the fifteenth century our country has produced several black-letters – some of which are still in existence – which have never been surpassed). But I do not see that the indeniable superiority of the above mentioned craftsmen should substract the 18th century punch-cutter's, Fleischman & Rosart's, merits. Dr. Charles Enschedé's book is still purchasable; Messrs Enschedé however would be glad to exchange it for the backnumbers of the Fleuron, which they regret are missing in their library. One of these days they will send you a specimen of the 15th century black-letters from their typographical collection which has been finished just now and a few specimens of the roman type Lutetia designed by me.

I shall refer within short to your request concerning my writing an article for The Fleuron. I want to think this over for a while. Perhaps I have too close relations to some private presses as well as to commercial book-printing to speak about this subject with sufficient objectivity. . .

I am, Dear Sir, faithfully yours

J. Van Krimpen.*

Jan van Krimpen was to be a friend for life; a brisk correspondence sprang up, in which mutual interest and sympathy was tempered with long-lasting controversy.

You are quite right to object to the copying of old types which is a current characteristic of English typography. It is found at present impossible to secure a new design of any interest. On the other hand, it seems a pity that a number of fine classical types are out of reach of printers of to-day because they have been destroyed by careless printers of the past. I think, however, in two or three years it will be possible that the printing community in England will have been educated to the point of preferring a new work of art rather than a reproduction, and it may then be possible to persuade type founders to employ the services of an artist.*

When he wrote, Morison already had an artist in mind. He had known Eric Gill for years, since he first went to Burns & Oates. No one interested in lettering could ignore Gill's rapidly growing fame as an engraver of inscriptions. He knew of Gill's initial share in the design of Johnston's block letters for the Underground, and that Gill had since drawn an italic alphabet for Gerard Meynell to use at the Westminster Press. But it was not until 1924, when Gill and Hilary Pepler quarrelled, the Ditchling community broke up, and Gill retreated to Capel-y-ffin in the depths of Wales, that Morison began to consider what they might do together. He asked Gill to write an article for the Fleuron, but Gill refused politely, saying 'Typography is not my country.'* Another plan was to make a book of Gill's collected wood-engraving, but for the moment this was held in suspense by the lawsuit between Gill and Pepler.* But Morison, anxious to add 'a wholly new design corresponding with contemporary demands' to his Monotype programme, had yet another idea for Gill.

Profiting by the experience of *The Tapestry*, he planned to fuse the talents of a living designer of lettering with those of an expert engraver of punches and create a new type-design. Only when the type was in existence would he entrust it to the mechanical processes of Monotype. In November Plumet had been commissioned by Warde to cut alternative forms of b, d, h, k and l with serifs instead of looped tops for the Arrighi type, but his eyes were failing, and he was unable to undertake more work after this.* Instead, Morison got in touch with another engraver in Paris, Charles Malin, to whom he had been introduced by François Thibaudeau, who combined scholarly interests with practical work at the Peignot typefoundry. He began to persuade Gill to undertake the design; typography might not be his country, but Morison found it hard to take no for an answer. In the end Gill agreed, without much interest – yet – in what might become of his work: 'Drawing Alphabets for Stanley Morison in afternoon and evening,' he noted in his work-diary under 25 November 1925, and next day: 'Ditto, all day long'. The Perpetua type had begun.

Meanwhile the Wardes were back, Beatrice to stay, Frederic to return to Montagnola at the end of January. Beatrice wrote home.

Q. is trying nobly to pretend he's miserable at the thought of being away from me: but the thing is such a lark for him that he finds it hard to be sober. The Serpent has taken on so many jobs with adoring publishers who fight over him that he's in danger of being torn to pieces. I see him once a century & note that he gets gaunter every time. But I get fat.

Yours
B

F.Q.s' next books are to be in the Vicentino fount too: SM calls him the Head of the Holy Italic Empire.*

Morison was wrestling with the problem of supplying Bridges with a specimen of his writing: 'My hands and pens are palsied now I come to do something for publication.' Some of his theo-

197

logical preoccupations crept into the result. He was now reading Simkhovitch and R. H. Charles: 'The kind of argument with wh. the theologians supply me as an antidote . . . does not help me very much, but like the Scotsman who fried his bacon in Lux so that it shouldn't shrink – I'm doing my best.'* On 8 February he put another idea to Bridges, enclosing with it a specimen of van Krimpen's hand:

Do you think anybody wd. be interested to have a reprint of the twelve sonnets written by Mary Queen of Scots? I cannot remember that any of the private presses has made a book out of them & I think that an old Ronsardian type I have discovered might be suitable – but I must have a few words of introduction or how am I to work in a little italic?

Bridges answered in terse bibliographic detail:

The Poems of M Q of S were edited by Julian Sharman for Basil M. Pickering in 1873. A & B eights, C four, & D one. The poems beginning on last of A, that is on 15th page. . . . I hope that your italic may be used for some work of mine: & that you will enter into my plot to introduce some new letters.*

More was to come of this last suggestion (after protracted attempts by Morison to find an editor for Mary Queen of Scots, van Krimpen eventually printed the poems alone in 1930).

Meanwhile, Beatrice was lonely without Frederic, and Morison found work for her to do. Garamond and the *Traité* were laid aside. Morison had been forced to reconcile himself to the 'wrong' Fournier (he kept the only size of the 'right' Barbou, at Cambridge, where he used it for *The Miracle of Love*, and later for the *Fleuron*). The 14pt and 18pt were already cut, and now 12pt and 10pt were ready. The customary historical barrage on the trade must now be opened in a double number of the *Recorder*. Beatrice set to work and by 14 February 'Fournier swims off to the press this week'. Then she went off to Paris to meet Frederic (there was a slight coolness with Mardersteig – the new fount of Arrighi had still not arrived, nor had Monotype produced the Pastonchi type for him).

I've just had my hair so cut that both my shell-like (oyster-shell-like) ears are bared to the winds, and I've been scrubbing them frantically in consequence. The effect is very nice indeed. . . .

Q. has been distinguishing himself further: on the heels of the 'Julian' *Comus* triumph he's done a layout for the Fournier number of the Recorder that will make my undistinguished copy look like a million.

They went to the Imprimerie Nationale and looked reverently at the Garamond punches. They went to the Collection Doucet where the curator opened all doors when he heard that they knew Morison. They met old friends. Back alone in England, there was a reaction; but Morison cheered her up by taking her to a matinée of *Is Zat So*, the new American musical that was taking London by storm.*

The Vicentino book is going to be lovely, and quite important, I believe. My Fournier article is now in proof & looks rather dull to me. I have still to choose my pseudonym under which my Life Work will be done. Reputation made, etc. There can't be two bibliographic Wardes, now that every Rogers book is placed as 'WARDE 478' or something. Becker won't do in England or France or even the U.S., as, hang it, there is a bibliographic Becker too, cuss her. It won't be a woman's name anyway. Suggestions?*

'On XVIIIth century French Typography and Fournier le Jeune' appeared under the name of Paul Beaujon, a courtly, precise, even elderly gentleman of the *ancien régime*, an alias which served Beatrice well in the masculine world of typography and advertising, and when she needed to take refuge from her real self. It was an admirable piece of work, scholarly, well organized – all that her first little piece was not. It exonerated Fournier from his rivals' charge of plagiary, and first brought out his originality in the printing of music – eighteenth-century *chansons* and *bergerettes* were a special love of both Beatrice and Frederic. There were ample illustrations of 'the pagodas, trellises and formal gardens' which Fournier built from his ornaments, perfectly echoed by Frederic's lay-out. Beatrice had proved herself an ideal pupil. She was now 'installed at a desk at Heinemann's, where I

199

sub-edit the Fleuron', and, she added, 'Paul Beaujon stands to make £15 on the Fournier article, to my great joy. I was the first to congratulate him. He's a fine fellow really. . . .'*

Morison, after endless postponements, was bracing himself to go to America. After a long silence he wrote to Updike at some length:

It is now settled that I go at the beginning of April, and as the guest of Mr. F. N. Doubleday who wants to show me his bushes and flowers in the so called *Garden City*. I am very nervous about going, because I do not know how long I can stand being pampered by an American millionaire. Doubleday is a very decent sort, and I certainly should be very grateful to him for taking a fancy to me: I have a few private misgivings that I may not altogether justify myself. How does one act in these circumstances? You will know better than I whether I can break away from Doubleday for sufficient time to allow me to come to Boston. I need not say it will give me huge delight to be able to do this. In fact I have already told my host he must allow this. On my last journey I very nearly knocked myself up by doing too much running about, so I have made up my mind to take things a little more easily this time.

He went on to praise Warde's book on Rogers which 'succeeds better as a separate publication', but there was he felt 'too much of the auction room influence at work in Rogers' work itself'.

In the meantime, I hope you have not given up the habit of writing. Now that I am sole proprietor and editor of *The Fleuron* I am more than ever anxious to print you. May I beg you seriously to endeavour to give me something in the near future? For the next number I have an article on the work of Klingspor which you won't very much like (!), one on Garamond in which several new facts will appear, one on Bulmer and Bensley in which will be disclosed, for the first time, the origins of the *Brimmer* type, another on Laboureur, and, I hope, a series of typographical definitions by Ivins.

He ended with an apology for failing to extract the 'Janson' type which Updike wanted from Stempel; the conditions in Germany had made it impossible.

Just before Morison left, Bridges wrote to him again with more details of his new 'plot'.

My dear Morison

Milford was here yesterday. He wants to publish some volume or volumes of my prose. chiefly essays etc. & he is willing to use your new type, which I told him you were ready to lend him. My old interest in this project is in making Typographical innovations – The Clarendon Press consent to indulge my fancies. so that the practical question for me is whether you will join up with me. & get a few (one or two at most) new letters to add to the g.

I think I sh^d be able to embark on this business at once, but shall not consider details until I know what facilities you can provide.

First of all we sh^d have to consider the format. & Milford said that he wd negociate with you. Meanwhile I send you a sample of my notion of the size of the page. The *page* can be as large as the full margin shown, or might be smaller, corresponding to the pencil line. As to the imprint, I expect that *must* be very much as I have cut it. If it were narrower the lines w^d be inconveniently short. . . . But given the approximate measurements you can compose such a page as w^d best please you. . . .

Morison went to see him and talk about the problem of getting phonetic sorts cut; he came away with an answer to another problem – what he was to do at the Country Life Press. Bridges was already collecting his essays for Milford. The first was to be one on the influence of the audience on Shakespeare that he had written in 1906 for A. H. Bullen's Stratford Shakespeare. Morison asked if he might make another limited-edition book of it in America. Bridges agreed and, before Morison sailed on 7 April, corrected the copy, wrote an introductory letter, and settled the question of the copyright, a complicated problem involving three or four letters, a visit to Basil Blackwell, and a telegram.* All this in a week, at the age of eighty-one – it was quite a tribute to Morison's authority and gift of persuasion.

Morison spent a month and a half in America. He got *The Influence of the Audience* printed, a neat plain little book set in Caslon, with capitals two sizes smaller than the lower-case letters. He printed 100 copies which, he told Bridges, 'should yield a sum a little short of £50'. But he did not find out what he was expected to do. Doubleday wanted to be advised by Morison, but without thinking what he wanted advice on; it was a recurring problem for Morison. Still, he made some suggestions for improving the composing-room; he recommended the installation of Fournier.* He saw Updike; and he saw Beatrice's mother, May Lamberton Becker. Beatrice had seen little of him before he left; he was 'doing a month's work in advance (and three months behind) in the few days that remain'. But, she wrote, 'be nice to young Lucifer when you see him, because he really is the best man I know, and the kindest and in some ways the wisest'.*

Morison got back to find the Wardes over from Paris (Beatrice had gone to meet Frederic on his way back from Montagnola). He also found a letter from Malin. He had given Gill's drawings to him before he left, and Malin had already sent him smoke proofs of the 14pt punches. Now he sent a smoke of some new 12pt punches:

I have followed the indications you gave me and I think you will be entirely pleased with the result. I have given the fount a slightly darker tone . . . I think it much better than the first attempt – it has a solider look and is more legible.*

Morison did not reply immediately. The General Strike was on. Mardersteig was coming over at the end of the month, anxious to hear about America. Morison wanted to talk to him about his third great folio for Benn, an *amende* to black-letter (excluded from *Four Centuries*), on German incunabula. There was much to discuss with the Wardes. Hobson was selling the Fanfare to the London Press Exchange, although he still retained 41 Bedford Square as a base for Warde and Morison. *The Calligraphic Models of Ludovico degli Arrighi surnamed Vicentino* was out, and looked very handsome; Morison's introduction was the first monograph on Arrighi, the most influential of the sixteenth-century Italian calligraphers in this century. The translation of Plato's *Crito*, also in the Arrighi type but with the new serifed ascenders, was out as well, the first of Warde's books published with Harper's in New York under the imprint of 'The Pleiad'.

But Warde was to leave before the end of the month, for Paris, 'my headquarters from now on'.* There were also Gill's engravings to worry about: Morison had charge of a fair number and was anxious to use them and to pay the owner (the lawyers were still arguing about this). He also wanted Gill to illustrate the Synoptic text of the Gospels (this came of reading Streeter). Gill was reluctant, but he was setting to work on the blocks for *The Passion of St Perpetua and St Felicitas*, which they were both agreed should be the first specimen of the new type.*

Above all, there was the *Fleuron* 5, already late by Simon's standards. The programme outlined to Updike was exacting, the more so as Morison was expanding the number of reviews (mostly written by himself) and writing the third and last of his long articles on italic. The Garamond story had taken a new dramatic turn. At work in the Museum one afternoon, Beatrice had discovered a title-page with the familiar types and the imprint of Jean Jannon of Sedan. Pausing only to look up Jannon in the reference books, she caught the night boat to Paris, went first thing to the Mazarine Library, and there made a discovery which solved a problem that had been nagging Morison for the last four years.* A telegram came on 23 July.

JANNON SPECIMEN SIMPLY GORGEOUS SHOWS ALL SIZES HIS TYPES WERE APPROPRIATED BY RAPACIOUS PAPIST GOVERNMENT HOORAY FERIOQUE. MONTSOURIS.

Jannon was a typefounder and 'imprimeur de l'Académie à Sedan'. In 1621 he published the specimen that Beatrice had just discovered, showing types that were close copies of the earlier designs of Garamond and Granjon. Leaving Sedan in 1639, he was printing in Caen in contravention of Richelieu's new restrictions on the press. His goods were seized and transferred to the newly founded Imprimerie Royale. Here they became inextricably confused with the older types, and so it came about that the 'caractères de l'université' (the Protestant academy of Sedan, not the Sorbonne) were thought to be by Garamond. It was a notable tribute to the sharpness of Morison's eye, his 'feel' for the design, that as early as 1922 he had realized that there was something wrong, something un-sixteenth-century, about the big 'Garamond' italic.

Morison came to terms with Pepler about the book of Gill's engravings, and had high hopes of the type for the *Passion* book. He had written at midsummer to Malin to proceed and on 27 July he told Gill:

I hope in a few days to have smokes of the majority of the characters, and it should take about a month to have matrices made and type cast. So I can promise you a couple of pages in about six weeks from now if this would be satisfactory.*

Next day Malin wrote enclosing smokes of the 12pt capitals and figures; these were now cut, and he was at work on the lower case: 'I hope that the work will give you satisfaction – you will have a beautiful letter there.' After Malin's holiday he had to remind Morison to give his verdict on the capitals and sent a laboriously made up specimen of text, each letter a separate smoke proof. Morison wrote, full of praise and suggestions. Malin replied, pleased with Morison's reaction, and full of comment on the minutest details. It was clear that the design had aroused his enthusiasm too. 'I take pleasure in working for you. The work you are asking me for has an artistic side to it, which cannot be said of what I do for other clients, replacing broken punches or cutting special signs for various directories or letters I am not acquainted with &c.'* All this was passed on to Gill, who also had his comments to make: 'It is difficult to judge the effect at present but it is, I think, a decent and legible type.'* The co-operation of designer and engraver had come about, just as Morison had hoped.

The Wardes were back. Frederic was busy: Beatrice settled down patiently to rewrite her *Fleuron* article on Garamond in the new light of Jannon. Gill was engraving a profile portrait of her – ought he to charge £25 for it, he asked.* Morison was delighted by her discovery and anxious to do justice to Garamond and Granjon, even though it meant resetting all Beatrice's article.

He was also anxious to do something about Gill's new interest in what he called 'block letters' (following Johnston, with whom he had been at first involved in the Underground lettering). Gill had done some lettering of this sort first for notices for the occasional trippers who came to Capel-y-ffin, and then for the Army and Navy Stores in Spring 1926. The idea had caught his imagination: it needed '1, good letters, 2, absolutely legible-to-the-last-degree letters, 3 letters which any fool can copy accurately and easily'.* The problem had continued to occupy him since. Morison wrote to his friend Robert Blake of Stephenson, Blake, typefounders of Sheffield. Like Thibaudeau, Blake was a scholar as well as a typefounder. First he dealt with Morison's Garamond question: he was not, however, encouraging about Gill's new letter.

The Letter Foundry, Sheffield.
24 August 1926.

Dear Mr. Morison,

You have the faculty of writing very interesting letters. I shall look forward to your article on Garamond in the 'Fleuron' and will promise you that this shall not be passed on by me to Charles Peignot!!

The photograph which you enclose of the (?) Garamond is very attractive indeed; I am not surprised that you are in love with this face, but it would be very difficult to reproduce it as part of its charm is the inequality, the *same* letters showing considerable variation one from another.

I am very much afraid that we shall not be able to adapt the Dumas Garamond and will have to engrave one – I shall be seeing you again before long and shall await further news of you through the 'Fleuron'.

As regards the new Grotesque which you send impressions of, we might produce this in a few sizes – I presume you would not engrave it less than 14 or 18 Point? What price would you want for these drawings? As a matter of fact, we are very full up at the moment with one type face and another, some of which are being engraved specially for special customers. . . .

With kindest regards,

Believe me,
Yours sincerely
Robert G. Blake.

They were soon deep in Morison's quest for the types of John Bell, he was becoming increasingly convinced of its importance: the new Perpetua was to be its twentieth-century equal.*

Everything seemed to be going on as before. But it was not. For months, clouds had been mounting. Everyone tried to pretend that there was no storm in the offing, with such success that the bolt, when it came, surprised as well as terrified them. Morison now had a room near the Étoile restaurant in Charlotte Street and no distance from Bedford Square. He saw less and less of his wife, whose view remained explicit: he had never come back to her from America. 'A woman stole his real personality, or did the real Stanley, glimpses of whom I saw in the early days of our acquaintance, the Stanley his mother knew, return? I do not know. A changed man returned – rough, cruel, indifferent.'* Perhaps Mabel's hysteria made them reluctant to believe what had happened. The independence of action that the Wardes believed in implies trust. Trust there was, but no longer in each other – only trust that nothing would disturb the mirage of Paradise. Change they would have had to admit. Beatrice tried to prepare her mother, over again in the summer, what to expect:

You will find me considerably older in the world, but otherwise not awfully altered. The past year seems like a very crowded lifetime. I have lived with an emotional intensity so new to me that I really do feel reborn. I have found out more things about the human heart and its potentialities for joy & suffering than I dreamed of. Gosh, my whole system of mensuration is altered from yards to miles.*

Well, Frederic might reflect bitterly, had she nicknamed Morison 'the Serpent': that new knowledge had stolen his simple girl away from him. Morison, all that intensity of feeling aroused which he had tried to curb by 'submitting' to the church, read and read the Gospels like a man repeating a charm against the evil eye. Poor Beatrice, did she know what had happened to her on that long day's walk in Hertfordshire? Or when did she find out

206

that she was in love, head over heels in love, with a man who could never marry her? To be independent is to be free, but she had no choice – she was not free. Frederic's anguish and rage grew, the more so as, despite gossip,* there was nothing to vent it on. But at the end of the summer the storm broke. Powerless to attack the main cause of his misery, Frederic chose a different target. Beatrice wrote to her mother

I feel like the last stanza of a pre-Raphaelite poem: the last few weeks have been given over to readjustments, securing working arrangements, and settling the matter of income at the Fanfare; and you cannot imagine what a racking thing it is to listen in on both sides alternately, as it were, and be constantly and consistently the apologist for one who, speaking impersonally, has very little case. W. is showing a curious petulant rapacity which is very difficult to condone; while M. is doing very little better by a policy of complete and Quixotic self-abnegation which only makes things worse. Poor little Murton (who was thought so efficient only a month ago) is now being scolded unmercifully, and is hanging on to the job in the teeth of the gale simply because he adores M. and has some obscure idea of championing him. M. says nothing, devotes himself to business, has cut up his personal income so that W. is guaranteed more than half of it – and on those rare occasions when we have tea together at the BM asks me to find out for him what W. wants and how he can be made happier. I really think W. has a mild form of persecution mania. Heaven knows I'm bad enough at taking criticism, but with him anything but praise is an attempt to 'discourage' or 'belittle' him – even from me, mind you!

If my loyalty to W. weren't paramount, I would still be prevented from raising my finger to defend or support M., for the not very lucid reason that my sympathies are on that ground. Glücklich wär' ich wenn ich für ihn sterben könnte; also muss ich niemals im wenigsten für ihn kampfen.*

They had finally bitten the apple, and it was an apple of discord. The world went on as before. Malin was about to start work on the 24pt punches for Perpetua, and wanted to know if he would be required to cut the italic. He added:

J'ai beaucoup aimé l'humour avec lequel vous me parlez du caractère catholique romain et italique de Monsieur Gill. Il doit 'créver' sérieusement du haut, d'après ce que je comprends, ce qui est très gênant en typographie et même pour monter dans une couchette de sleeping.*

So indeed Morison found it. Mardersteig, too, wrote cheerfully. He apologized for not writing before, 'but, I think, you have a feeling heart and understand that sometimes the bad life chokes our best feelings and intentions'. All was well with him; the lengthy negotiations with the Italian government had come to fruition, and he was to move, not to Florence but to Verona, at the beginning of next year; he would order Poliphilus, Gara-mond, Fournier and 'Janson', and 'realize all the ideas I had for Florence'.* Other friends, Gill, Cleverdon beguiling Morison to accept a late advertisement for the *Fleuron* with 'the swank of having a Laboureur cut', went their ways cheerfully too.

On scraps of Thomist philosophy, Catholic liturgy, typo-graphic history and modern letter design, on Horace, Du Bellay, eighteenth-century French songs, *The Marriage of Figaro*, and other bits and pieces, literary, spiritual and professional, Morison and Beatrice began to build up something of their old relation-ship, some fabric to shield them against the cold, cold future. Paul Beaujon, with the rigid code of manners he inherited from the past, found it easier to talk to Morison than Beatrice Warde did. Immediately, brought face to face with reality, there was nothing for it but flight. Beatrice went off obediently with Frederic, to interpret for *him* on a visit to printers and publishers in Germany and Austria. She left him 'chumming with a Russian prince in Prague' and returned to London.* As she arrived, Morison left for another visit to America.

The *Fleuron* 5 was out now, with Rodenberg's fine article on Karl Klingspor, typefounder and printer at Offenbach and patron of Tiemann and Rudolf Koch, and others on Laboureur and William Bulmer (the last rather a disappointment – there was nothing about the origin of Bell's types in it). There was Paul Beaujon's decisive and final account of the Garamond and Jannon types, as good a piece of work as ever appeared in the

Fleuron. In 'Towards an Ideal Italic', Morison summed up his views. It was a fine sustained argument, tauter than the previous two articles: taking the letters devised by Louis XIV's commission for the Imprimerie Royale as his text, he pointed to the trend away from a separate form for italic and prophesied that 'typography will have to come to terms with modernism' – in the shape of a sloped roman. Experiment has, on the whole, proved him wrong; upright shapes do not look right when bent, and the italic forms (Morison was sceptical of the evangelization of Robert Bridges and Roger Fry) have been more resilient.

In every way, the new number was a big one. There were reviews of Jessen's last book, of Warde on Rogers, of Beatrice's Fournier *Recorder* and Bridges' tract on handwriting; there were specimens of the Fournier, the elegant *Eulogy of Pierre Simon Fournier* with a cut by Gill, and the new Granjon cut by the Linotype Company, belatedly catching up with the Morisonian revolution (George Jones, who printed it, a congenial character if of doubtful scholarship, was cast by Linotype to play opposite Morison). To look at, the *Fleuron* was even more striking than before. The Cambridge Press (despite hesitations about expense, the lure of his old friends was too much) had set it beautifully in the Barbou type, and the *Fleuron* now had a publisher in America – Doubleday.

It was this that had brought Morison over. He also visited Updike again, and collected an article for the next *Fleuron* from him.* He visited the Lanston Monotype Company at Philadelphia ambassadorially. He did a cover for the *Saturday Review of Literature* which was a great success.* About 23 November Beatrice arrived for a long stay. Next day Morison left; they only glimpsed each other. At the same time Frederic, back in London, beside himself with rage and misery, was packing up. On 25 November, he left for Paris, never to return, typing as his train sped to the coast a long diatribe against historicism in modern typography to his friend William Kittredge.

Morison got back. He had sold his calligraphic books to Graham Pollard of Birrell & Garnett, a new friend who combined orthodox communism with a passion for the intricacies of typographic and calligraphic history.* He had sold his Laboureur collection to Douglas Cleverdon, and the invoice for Cleverdon's *Fleuron* advertisement was noted 'Please send at once if you can – very hard up here'. He settled £500 a year and the house in Hollyberry Lane on Mabel, and began to look for somewhere else to live. Long letters started arriving from Paul Beaujon, whose affected bewilderment at the unfamiliar wonders of New York concealed an aching misery that sometimes crept out. 'You are more, and I am less, In Bad than you perhaps realise. I feel very humble and unhappy about this business, and only my consciousness of recent heroism on my part fortifies me in examining my position. . . . Avoid trouble straitly. Be all sorts of a conservative, and as kind as only you can be.'* It was a bleak Christmas.

10

THE threads were there waiting to be picked up. Malin had finished the 24pt Perpetua capitals, and was grateful for Morison's recommendation to Mardersteig. Gill was now depressed about the result, and said so bluntly.

> Capel-y-ffin, Abergavenny
> 31 December 1926
>
> Dear Morison,
> Thank you for yours of Dec. 29.
> I look forward to seeing the Fleuron.
> Re smoke proof (returned herewith): looking at these dispassionately as the work of someone else, I think the letters as such are very decent but very dull. I think they would be an excellent model for *shop sign writers*. I think when the *thin* strokes are so *thick* the thick strokes should be thinner – i.e. for *type* – or if the thick strokes are right then the thin strokes shd. be thinner.
>
> AAA if you follow me?
>
> In sum: I think the letters on the smoke proof are in themselves good letters (tho. dully executed – mechanical & insensitive) but bad type.
> Yours sincerely
> Eric G. T.S.D.

Nothing seemed to be going right. For the moment Morison let the Perpetua proceed without pressure. The Monotype works began its own long series of trials from prints of the fount cast by Ribadeau Dumas.* But Cleverdon was cheering: he had published Gill's *Art and Love,* and was anxious to help Morison with the book of Gill's engravings. Morison was glad to let him.

If you are going to make a name for yourself as Gill's accredited agent and publisher, and this agency includes publishing and selling books by him as well as his prints, there appears to me a very good reason why you should have the big Gill book also, especially since you are always seeing Gill and know what he is doing. When you next come up perhaps we can discuss it.*

Morison began to rework his notes on Blado and Arrighi for the first *Recorder* of the year. He had also to go to Oxford again. Bridges wanted to talk to him about another matter besides the phonotypes. Since last March he had been at work on a long new poem, at present nameless but eventually to be called *The Testament of Beauty*: by the end of the year he had written some 800 lines. He was, however, in some difficulty: being old, the labour of writing and rewriting was painful; further, he wished to have copies to work on and to send to a number of friends for their criticism. To make this easier, the Clarendon Press had the draft set in the Fell english roman, a fine large letter, with ample margins; twenty-five copies were printed and sent to Bridges at the beginning of the year. On 17 January Bridges wrote, 'Come as soon as you can. . . . My poem is in type so that you will be able to take it away with you – & you will be interested in it if nobody else shd be.'

Bridges was right: Morison was not only interested but deeply moved by the new poem. Over the next two and a half years his criticism was constant and valuable; some traces of it still survive. Bridges also had Morison's practical gifts in mind: even now he was thinking 'of letting Morison publish 100 copies in America', without any corresponding English edition. Before the poem was published, there were already signs that the American passion for limited editions might not be inexhaustible, but Bridges had been impressed by *The Tapestry*, and he was not going to give up the idea of Morison printing an edition of the great work of his old age.*

But this was all in the future. Now Morison decided to go abroad and console himself among his old friends there. February found him in Berlin. His old friend Jessen retired in 1924 and had recently died, but Hans Loubier and Arthur Lotz welcomed him. He also arranged with Hegner to publish a German translation of *Type Designs Past and Present* by Hanna Kiel.* He then moved on to Frankfurt where he went to see Klingspor at Offenbach. Rudolf Koch gave him a copy of *Schrift und Handwerk* inscribed with his name (mis-spelt as usual). At the end of the month he reported progress to Walter Lewis at Cambridge:

> Hospitz Baseler Hof,
> Wiesenhüttenplatz, Frankfurt
> 27 February 1927

Dear Lewis:

When I was in Berlin I did a rather silly-ass thing (I think I can overhear your somewhat stronger characterisation) which landed me there for a long time. I had done all I was keen about when I ran across a capitalist who is a great amateur of calligraphy since as one of his activities he is head of the biggest firm of pen makers in the world. This man has a sort of museum of calligraphy ancient & modern, Latin & Oriental. Unfortunately he had no specimen of the writing of a man named Tschichold (don't bother!) & when I asked why this really fine scribe was [not] represented in his collection, Mr Blanckertz said that T. was a communist. So of course I had to knock him down, hadn't I? After a statement like that I oughtn't to have permitted him to live, but I spared his life unfortunately and we had a long argument about the services of capitalism to Kultur. But, dear brother, I was ass enough to challenge him – and in this way. Having proved that he was under-paying his manager (who was standing by) I said that if he really had the good of civilisation at heart he would establish & finance a first class Review of Calligraphic Studies to do for Writing what the *Fleuron* does for Printing. HE IMMEDIATELY OFFERED TO DO IT NO MATTER WHAT IT COST as long as I would edit it. Now I had already bought my ticket & was most anxious to leave Berlin but I couldn't drop the argument at that point could I? So we argued for exactly 8 days, with all sorts of people who could help and because I insisted on having a hun collaborator I had to go to Leipzig and bring him to Berlin. So the

Jahrbuch
zur
Kunst der Schreiber
in
Vergangenheit & Gegenwart

Herausgegeben
von

STANLEY MORISON & JULIUS RODENBERG

BERLIN
Heintze und Blanckertz
1927

was founded at Potsdam last Friday at 4.30 p.m. after a Crown Council lasting 8 hours. This means a certain amount of work in the future but I expect it can be done.

I have accomplished a little for the *Fleuron*. Klingspor is very much pleased with the show he gets and in order to illustrate adequately an article on Rudolf Koch whose work was only touched on in the present number Klingspor has offered to make the blocks & print all the plates, some 12 or so in varying colours. Two Berlin collotypers are making me really superb colour plates of manuscripts to illustrate an article and the typefounders here are anxious to print some insets of an extraordinary fine appearance. With this help and that of others I can make the next number bigger than the present issue. I have also sold several pages of advertisements and a number of copies. This is the advantage of publishing huge books – people here think I'm correspondingly a big man! It is literally true that I can get almost anything I like here – except a fried sole and a copy of *Punch* neither of which has come my way for a long time. I'm sorry to have been away so long – but it's all for the good of the cause and I shall be back next week. I will come to Cambridge instantly. . . .

Yours
SM

The *Jahrbuch*, like Audin's *Livrets Typographiques des Fondeurs Français*, Cartier's *De Tournes* and Johnson's *Bibliography of Italian Writing Books of the XVI Century* (all announced for early publication under Morison's aegis in the *Fleuron 5*), was put off, in this case to the Greek Kalends. At the moment, however, it was very much in the forefront of his mind, for he repeated this account of its foundation in equally long letters to Mrs Bridges and, on his return, to Hans Mardersteig. For once, he found himself wondering what to do next: he rarely had time to repeat himself before or after. He wrote to Mrs Bridges from Paris, adding the detail that the *Jahrbuch*'s foundation took place in a wood. He had gone, hoping that peace might be made, to see Warde, but found him unrelenting. They still had business to do: Warde had arranged to publish Morison's Damiamus Moyllus facsimile, printed at Montagnola in January, with John Holroyd Reece who had just joined him and started the Pegasus Press at 37 rue Boulard, Warde's address.

It is probable that no life of this strange man will ever be written: it is 'a story for which the world is not yet prepared'. A creature of grandiose schemes, he flashed across the typographic world like a comet. He caught up Warde, Morison, Mardersteig, Simon (101 Great Russell Street was his London office), Kurt Wolff, van Krimpen, and dropped each one of them, breathless, exhilarated, and sometimes very much the poorer. He had a gift for hurting even those of whom he was fond, and forgetting it the next minute. After the Pegasus Press, he made a fortune out of Albatross Books, paperbacks in English for sale outside England (Mardersteig designed the covers). They were the successful rival of the ageing Tauchnitz series, and the prototype of Penguin books. Later, he bought up Tauchnitz itself, but the war and the destruction of Tauchnitz's massive plant brought an end to his schemes, and despite attempts at revival the comet finally burnt out in 1969.

Now he was planning to publish a French translation of Morison's *Fleuron* article on script types (it appeared as *Caractères de l'Écriture* later in the year, the title reproduced from Morison's writing, with fine flourishes), and had many other plans to discuss.

But Morison was anxious to get away; his mind kept reverting to Chilswell. He mentioned none of these things to Mrs Bridges:

Grand Hotel, Paris
10 March 1927

. . . But I didnt mean this letter to be any more an account of my own doings than is required to explain the absence of my report on the new characters for R.B.'s Shakespeare Essay. These new types have been cut, but with only moderate success – at least the g is in need of revision. Before I approach the Monotype Company about that letter I'd like you to tell me what you think of the ẓ & ṫ. The ẓ is very difficult to improve because it is such a thin letter & is necessarily cast upon a very narrow body. In the accompanying proof they've forgotten to include the normal *g* (as distinct from the new *g*) therefore pl. explain to RB that both forms will be available. If you will send me a piece of the text duly marked for the Compositor I will have a specimen page set in order that you may see precisely what the effect of these new forms will be.

I found the new poem intensely interesting. I read it as a testament and I have derived much religious consolation from it. I do not easily 'Ask what is reasonable' though I hope I have a humble mind. But such piled up horrors as that mining accident set me to re[ad] the poem again and I seemed to feel that the conclusion was a little abrupt and the acceptance of Christianity – even of private interpretation – a little unexpected, as scarcely being implicit in the body of the text. I half expected something like a more explicit reference to the determinist tone of certain earlier passages.

But I write fast, almost fiercely to catch the post with this belated letter. I hope to leave here on Monday or Tuesday. If you think well enough of the new characters & will send me a postcard to 41, Bedford Square my Secretary will ask the Monotype Co to make a specimen page. This may save time. I am most glad that Milford has finally arranged the copyright business. As soon as may be after I return I should like to come to Chilswell for a night. On the last occasion I left to see those Dominicans & I was misinformed by one of them as to the train & I had to remain the night – but we argued until morning.

Yours
Stanley Morison.*

Was Morison repeating Bridges when he described the poem as a 'testament' or did he sow the seed of the final title here?

When, finally, he got back there was a new and inviting job waiting. He had found somewhere to live at 27 Fitzroy Square: it was on the west side of the square (post-Adam, *c.* 1827–35), and a stone's throw from Roger Fry's Omega Workshops. The rooms were fitted up in the most modern style, and Morison extended his sartorial colour-scheme to the decoration. Walls, windows and doors were white; tables, chairs, book-cases, black. Ambrose Heal, then making 'The Four Poster' in Tottenham Court Road a world name for good furnishing design, was a great help here. Morison had met him just before Christmas, and discovered a common passion for English writing-books. All the smart new furniture came from Heal's, and Morison was still very hard up.

No 27 Fitzroy Square W
21 July 1927

Dear Heal,

I owe your admirable Mr A. R. Moore the sum of £75 which I am sorry to say I cannot pay until the end of August. Do you think it a great imposition that I should force our conversations 'de re calligraphica' into domestically economic channels? I'll be bound that you are as afraid of Mr A. R. Moore as I am so I shall understand it if you tell me I must make my peace with him directly. Most of my hard-uppedness is due to my last visit to the U.S. and to my having to pay for the printing of the *Fleuron* but I spent £65 in buying two manuscripts which I shd like to show you. I paid for these on the nail (don't tell Mr A. R. Moore that) and that completed my undoing. But I shall be all in order by the end of August.

Yours
Stanley Morison

This next trip to Doubleday's was now beginning to absorb his attention again. He was not going to kick his heels this time if he could help it. While talking to Cleverdon about the Gill books another idea had come up, an edition of Farquhar's *The Beaux' Stratagem*, illustrated by Laboureur. Farquhar led to Marston, and soon Morison was writing:

27 Fitzroy Square, W.1.
6 April 1927.

Dear Cleverdon,

I think that it would be a good idea if you had another book to follow the Farquhar. It might be that Doubleday would feel encouraged to launch out well into the deep, if he thought that there could be a set of six volumes printed in the course of time. There need not be any elaborate preliminary beating of the tom-tom, but if things go well there and new types are made for my use the books would gain considerably. There would be more prospect of this if I could assure them that Farquhar is not an isolated publisher [publication]. English is a subject, about which I know nothing whatever, though I have 'done' it at one time. I believe, however that I am right in saying that the plays of Marston are extremely difficult to procure, and when they are all got together we can choose a printer. I had Vernant's address. I think that it should be possible for you to have the copy with one of the original drawings, but I am not sure that it would be necessary to put this in the colophon.

I will make a heroic attempt to come to Bristol. I demand very little in the matter of what I believe you Non-Conformists term 'hospitality', a couple of sacks on a not too mousey floor will do.

Yours,
S.M.

The visit took place over Palm Sunday week-end, and Morison enjoyed himself. Cleverdon's 'new book and print shop' was 'in an old building near Bristol University, one which boasted two different well-authenticated ghosts and a large comfortably furnished living-room adjoining the photographic studio of the late G. Methven Brownlee'; Miss Brownlee – 'Brownie' – was another welcoming character.* Cleverdon's shop now had its sign-board in Gill's sans-serif lettering. Gill had been ill there in October last, and had done it to while away the time. He had also done a book of alphabets, which Morison looked at and pondered.

Morison sounded Doubleday, but had not heard when he left about the middle of May. He went off in better spirits. He had got to know Daniel Longwell, who did the production and advertising of Doubleday's books.

Morison convinced Longwell of the desirability of standardisation in book production, particularly with regard to the lettering on bindings and to the layout of title-pages. According to Morison, standardisation of these two items would make it possible for the work to be entrusted to an office boy. And after Morison had helped Longwell to devise a standard format for a 'Crime Club' series, the saving on production costs was found to leave a bigger margin for advertising.*

There was congenial company on the design side too: Wilhelm Klingspor, Karl's son, had come to America to get experience, about the time of Morison's last visit. Beatrice had taken him to see Rudge at Mount Vernon, and shown him round. He was now at Garden City: 'You should see the amount of sweat he put into the title-page for the important Wilson letters that's coming out next fall – used your little decorative slug.'*

The Life and Letters of Woodrow Wilson also came Morison's way: for it he designed his first typographic jacket combining a displayed title and 'selling copy' – the prototype of the 'Gollancz jacket'. But the idea did not catch on: salesmen and booksellers clung to the 'picture jacket' to which they were used. By the time he left, he was prepared to regard the place with a certain grim affection, even the Long Island line, his favourite anathema: 'Floral Park ... Nassau Boulevard ... Stewart Manor ... Country Life Press! ... and HEMPSTEAD!!!'

Morison also found his way on this trip to the two great American collectors of calligraphica, George A. Plimpton and C. L. Ricketts. The first was rich and not much interested in the books or Morison, who, despairing of listing all the titles, hired a stenographer to dictate to. Caught in the act, he was brazen:

'Who's that?' 'A Remington man' 'Who's paying for him?'
'You are.' Ricketts, on the other hand, was learned and no mean
calligrapher himself. Ricketts lived near Chicago, and through
him Morison got to know the Newberry Library, especially the
Wing Collection of which Updike had spoken to him in 1923.
Since then, Morison had met Pierce Butler, its Librarian, who
stayed in London on his visits to Europe to buy books. Morison
became fond of Chicago, 'Shicorger' as he spelt it to Ricketts,
and was to grow fonder. He saw Updike again en route for
Chicago; on 15 June he caught the *Mauretania* home.*

Back in England it was a cold bleak summer. There was
enough to do: the agreement with Doubleday to discuss with
Cleverdon, the continuing squabbles of Gill and Pepler, in which
David Jones and Desmond Chute were now involved.

THE FLEURON
27 Fitzroy Square, W
27 July 1927

Dʳ C. I am three quarters dead this morning because Gill & Jones
came at 10.30 (without warning) and we argued. Chute came at 12.30
and we adjourned to the Etoile (you know how its spelt) and argued
until 2.45. Chute came back here and left at 3.45 or 4 – and I'm hanged
if Pepler didn't walk in at 4.30. I had a 'date' at 7 & so couldn't get
any work done the entire day. . . .

S.M.

The slow progress of the Perpetua type had taken a new turn.
Before he left for America, Morison had borrowed the italic
drawings that Gill had made for Gerard Meynell, and sent them
to the works. Nothing had happened while he was away, but
now at the beginning of August the works learnt what was in
his mind: 'Mr Meynell's drawings to be discussed with Mr
Morison in endeavour to make one face represent both types.'*
This Delphic remark refers to Morison's ambition to achieve the
'ideal italic' which would be a sloped version of the roman it
went with. In September, Meynell and Morison concluded that
such a match was possible, except for the italic capitals. Meynell

sent more drawings, Gill made some more for Morison, and the works was asked for specimens from all three sources: Meynell's drawings, Morison's drawings and Malin's type. The works protested that it was not worth the expense and suggested tracings of the three instead. On 25 October there was a meeting: the new drawings were pronounced too narrow to match with the original material, and the design was now to be based on matrices made from Malin's punches, with some alternative characters based on Gill's original drawings.*

There were other problems to sort out as well. Updike was at long last installing Monotype equipment and having difficulties, complicated by the differences between the English and American companies. Morison did his best to help. He also helped Francis Meynell with the elaborate flower head-pieces for the Nonesuch edition of Thomson's *Seasons*.* Beatrice was back to help with the *Fleuron* and to take charge of the *Recorder*. 'Running the *Fleuron* is a most exacting labour', Morison had protested to Updike, 'since, being associated with it from the first number, I have contributed to it both with articles and ideas, so I am now almost entirely used up in both departments.'* Beatrice set to work with a will. She took an article for *The Times Literary Supplement* off his hands, wrote most of the September–October *Recorder* on Baskerville using Morison's original 1924 piece as the basis, and, entirely on her own, produced a leader and a lively account of the process of manufacturing Monotype matrices, 'What Accuracy Means', for the next number. Morison, who had persuaded Burch that she was essential to the *Recorder*, was delighted, and so was Burch. In addition to all this, her facsimile of the Jannon Specimen, with an introduction written in New York, but printed in her absence at the Chiswick Press, was selling well at Maggs. 'Mr Beaujon's activities are bringing him in great fame,' she wrote; 'he pays Mrs B. Warde's rent (by his literary exertions) and even occasionally buys her some fluffy underwear'.*

In August Longwell came over for a return visit. Morison was much preoccupied in entertaining him, and got Cleverdon up to

London to meet him. When he left, Morison was exhausted and empty; Beatrice was away.

THE FLEURON
27 Fitzroy Square, W
[26 August 1927]

Dearest friend. Longwell came and left – me with a headache wh. I can't shift with aspirin. It is the first bad headache I've had for several months and as I didnt feel up to work I went to see Ingham & thence to Elkin Mathews. Driven by rain rather than appetite I made for an omelet (is that the American spelling?) and have returned here short of 8 oclock to write this & then I shall hit the sheets. I don't feel lonely yet but I shall tomorrow morning so I shall clear off to the Museum. The stormy air in the square makes these rooms very close & sends my mind off to Wales. It seems a wild place. I wonder what you'll make of the Taffies. D.L. is quite taken with London, thinks 'we' get more out of life here but that America has a lot more than soda fountains it can give us, that 'we' only consider quality, waste much effort on books intended by nature for a very limited circulation instead of going in for big numbers, wants to ginger up Chatto & Windus, hates the dirt and sloth and food of Brown's Hotel, liked the staff at the Etoile (he had minestrone, sole & mixed salad & 2 lagers) believes that there is something about London wh. gets him, is vastly amused at the toy LNER express wh. brought him to Kings Cross from Edinburgh & had a sleeper & was delighted at the roominess and quietude, is tickled to death at the 12p = 1s 20s = £1 of our coinage, thinks our £5 notes worth framing alongside his graduation certificate, considers London much less noisy than N.Y.C., that we eat & drink too much & so do infinitely less work than Americans, that to see 150 people watching the mending of Piccadilly was an utterly strange sight, considers . . . and so on for a long time, all very interesting and charming. He enjoys it very gratefully and wants to live here for a time, is most struck with this office and is ordering a table etc. from Heal. Pianos are going in the Square – giving me Fitz. this shall go to the post with all my hurrying [?] and infinite affection.

S.M.

September found Morison coping with a crisis in the printing of *The Beaux' Stratagem*, and seeing *German Incunabula* through the last stages. Gollancz had broken away from Benn to start up on his own, and this was to be one of his first publications. Morison had agreed to be one of the directors of the new firm and he started laying plans, as he had at Doubleday, for plain but good, and above all fool-proof book-design, which was to become the trade mark of the new firm. He was also collecting ideas, to take advantage of Reece's Midas touch at the Pegasus Press. In one of these, a facsimile of the two unique fragments of the Spanish writing-master Andres Brun, he conscripted his new friend Henry Thomas, who, now that Pollard was retired, came to be Morison's principal friend at the British Museum.

There was, indeed, small difficulty in establishing contact with Dr. Thomas as he was in the mid 1920's, when he was in daily charge of the North Library. To attract his attention in those days it was only necessary to commit some minor misdemeanour. At that time (circa 1923) he occupied a high desk, from which he could with a glance from an eye that a golden eagle might envy, observe any barbarian who should turn down the corner of a page, or lick his forefinger for the purpose of speeding through a book. Detection in an offence of this sort immediately brought Dr. Thomas down from his high desk to the side of the astonished delinquent. Such an incident provided my first opportunity for speech with him. Was the book I was spitting on my own property or that of the Trustees?

The chiding was unforgettable, like the occasion, years later, when Sir George Hill, then Director and Principal Librarian of the Museum, seeing me seated in the Reading Room gave me a message from Sir Frederick Kenyon about the Codex Sinaiticus. Immediately, there rose from M12, no less a figure (in every sense) than Dom Henri Leclercq, who proceeded to rebuke Sir George and me for talking, thereby breaking the rules of the Reading Room.

But my transgression in the North Library was a *felix culpa*. I now had the personal acquaintance of Dr. Thomas whom hitherto I had known by sight as five and a half feet of the finest Anglo-Spanish bibliographical learning, and by gossip as an official of the strictest sort. He was then fortyfive and I thirtyfive. From my answer and the books I had in hand, he judged me to be what I was, a native Londoner, less efficient indeed than himself, but more philistine; with whom however, something could be done. My word, on the honour of a Cockney, that the 'spitting' offence would not be repeated, was accepted. Thus began a friendship that endured for nearly 30 years. Our interests overlapped. Work on the *Short Title Catalogue of French Books of the XVI Century* fitted him to join in such an enterprise as a

223

bibliography of the books printed by Denys Janot. This we began together. I was a rank outsider in Cervantes studies, but we came together over Spanish calligraphy, and other general subjects.

A year or two later we met not only frequently, but weekly. Desiring to order his movements to suit colleagues with greater domestic responsibilities than his own, he put in more than his share of the attendances at week-ends and high festivals in the official 'Residence' in which routine by turn immures the Keepers and Assistant-Keepers. Christmas, Easter and Whitsun regularly found us together in Bloomsbury. The 'Residence' while not exactly an elegant apartment in which to study, had slightly more amenity than the average hostel. There were two comfortable beds, one of which I occupied on many occasions – either because, before the war, our talk lasted overlong; or, during the war, the state of the skies and the streets discouraged the walk home. Bombs were of no personal concern to him, but he never ignored his duties to patrol the Museum. I vastly enjoyed these evenings. The 'Residence' in Thomas's days embodied a capable and competent cook. Thomas much loved a cut off the joint and 2 veg, – and still better to display his high craftsmanship as a carver on the round of beef or the shoulder of lamb, which were procurable before the war. I generally contributed the Valdepenas or the Rioja. Thomas was not remarkable as a bibber (nor was I a chain-drinker), but he could be tempted by wines from Spain. As the 'Residence' was a precinct of the Museum, books could be brought over from the Reading Room for our purpose. Dinner over (there was no fingering of the Trustees' property until the table was cleared), he would describe a recent visit to Montserrat and his conversations with Dom Anselm Albareda, Librarian of the Abbey (and now Prefect of the Vatican Library), or make a running oral translation of Don Domingo Servidor's *Reflexiones*, or some other Spanish work. We collaborated on plans for numerous publications, some of which were actually achieved.

In these evenings he made himself my preceptor in bibliographical method, and raised me above the raw autodidact level at which I must otherwise have rested.*

In November, November 1926 seemed a century ago. Beatrice wrote home:

11 November 1927
Dearest family: Just now as I was writing I got a hunch to go and look out the window – for no particular reason. My watch had

224

stopped. When I looked out I understood: it was as if someone were signalling in a quiet room, but it was only a horse-drawn cart rounding Fitzroy Square. The odd thing was that it sounded like gunfire because there was none of that continuous background of noise – that great soft murmur of London – it was as if it were the only sound in the world. And then, far off, a siren sounded, and the horse stopped, and the silence became so *solid* that you would think it couldn't be broken. Not even in the country have I heard *absolute* silence before: it was a staggering experience. The air was full of frosty sunlight – it was bitter cold – but most of the inhabitants of the Square were standing on their doorsteps. A man came out of a cellar area just before the siren, and stood with a lighted cigarette in his fingers: overhead the leafless trees were speckled with sunlight, and not a twig fluttered. It was not so much a deathly silence as a *prenatal* one: full of intentions, living, an enormous Rapture.

And then, miles off, a gun sounded like thunder; far down Tottenham Ct. Road a bus started its engine: motor-horns sounded: and slowly the sea-shell roar of London began again. (And I thought this was a quiet town! I can hear the basic hum of it, now that I've *heard* that silence.) The old woman trudged on: the man in the area took a great puff of his cigarette: people went back to work. The two minutes were over.

All goes well here, the Fleuron will be a fine one; my Baskerville number is in the printer's hands, and various other things are moving rapidly, including the Times leader. Murton presented a very fine green parrot to S.M., and because of its 'low wicked eye' we named it Grimes. It used to eat out of Morison's plate at tea and follow him around. But alas! It fell off a table and must have broken a leg, for it died. I had little chance to see it, for between Fetter Lane & Chelsea I only have 2 mornings a week now for Fleuron work: but SM was heartbroken, for although the bird had never spoken a word it was a charming little fellow. We were all very husky about it for some days. Anyway, Grimes had a wonderful ten days. But – no more parrots. What sore hearts these little creatures leave behind them! SM said 'I know how your mother felt about Henry now'.

My letter – writing time is invariably stolen from weightier tasks, which explains the shortness of my missives. But they are full of affection. Give my best love to Q: I'm writing by this mail. Most loving greetings from your

B

It had been a quiet year.

In January Morison's spirits were beginning to pick up again. Graham Pollard, tempting him to sell his copy of Fournier's *Modèles* 1742, was told 'my muscles are hardening on it with the slight improvement in my financial situation'.* The Monotype works got a brisk answer to the first proof of the complete Perpetua:

Pulls from type appear satisfactory but l'case p would be better if narrower . . . and if new l'case g is cut after Mr Gill's original design it will perhaps be better.*

Gill himself was becoming interested in the process, and made his own suggestion for pushing on with the block letters.

[50A] Glebe Pl[ace S.W.3.]
31 January 1928.

Dear Morison:
    Enclosed speaks for itself. I have nought to send but it occurs to me that if you and Lanston M. Co. thought well you might send an opening, broadsheet (or what you will) using my 'sans serif' letters. What d'you say. If it be possible I wd. suggest a broadsheet using the largest size & the 2 smallest. Size must be 40^{cm} by 50^{cm} (which way up?) Matter? Genesis *they* suggest but what do you? Don't worry if this is a nuisance.
                                                        Yours   E.G.*

Relations with the works were becoming easier, and Morison no longer felt it necessary to get punches cut by hand for his next design, although it was one he set even more store by than the Perpetua, namely the 'perfect' version of the Aldine roman, unblemished by the errors of ignorance that had spoiled Poliphilus for him. He set to work on 11 January.

The book 'Bembus de Aetna ad Chabrielem' given to Mr Pierpont yesterday for 3rd line of Page indicated to be reproduced – we can then decide whether we shall make an addition to Poliphilus – Book will be bought back, if we wish to sell, in 6 months' time.

A month later the news was promising:

Mr Morison very pleased with few experimental characters for general design & finish but the face is too heavy – Please recut keeping as much difference as possible between light and dark strokes. (10 February)

The works acted promptly:

Making sufficient matrices to print a small paragraph . . . – face is being cut lighter than sample letters already cut. (11 February)

This was delivered only three days later.

Mr Morison satisfied with specimen left – he says they will be successful with a few modifications.*

These he proceeded to give in detail. When he wrote to Updike next he was cautiously optimistic about the new type. It was the first real letter he had written for some time, apart from one apologizing and explaining the lack of liaison between the two Monotype companies. The American company had thought that they were losing the valuable prestige order from the Merrymount Press because Updike told them he was waiting for news from Morison: 'Can you not speed up Mr Morison?' the President, Mr Best, wrote to Burch. This, as Morison said, 'tickled him "some"'. The delay was, in fact, due to a huge order from the Imprimerie Nationale at Paris. Now he wrote on other matters.

There is a little Monotype news which I would like to communicate to you in confidence. Mr. Bruce Rogers, it seems, has made an arrangement with Mr. Best by which the Centaur is to be cut as a Monotype face; but Mr. Rogers would not allow this to be done in the United States, having insisted that it is to be cut here. This has been arranged and I believe Mr. Rogers is about to leave the United States for this and such other countries as Europe has to offer. I gather that Warde is accompanying him on some sort of typographical wanderjahre. I am rather nervous about the arrival of this constellation, because I think that the Monotype Company will feel over awed and possibly make a less good job of it than they would if left to themselves; but there would be no fees going in that case! Secondly (and this is not confidential) I was visited recently by some very decent people from the Enschedé foundry, who desired my advice about one or two things, and as a result of several conversations a concordat between our Monotype Company and Enschedé has been arrived at. This means that the Lutetia, roman and italics, will be reproduced for use on the English machines. . . . Just for your examination I am sending you also the first proof of a few letters which have been cut from the type of the Bembo De Aetna (Ald. 1495). I think it has possibly a trifle too much colour, but I am rather pleased with the general aspect of it. . . .

I am most anxious to wind up The Fleuron in the most satisfactory way possible and I would love to have something from you. I have in hand a somewhat lengthy article on contemporary Dutch printing by Mr van Krimpen the MS of which is almost ready; an article on the lettering and typographical work of Eric Gill, which will show his new type and some new decorations especially made for the article; there will be an article by me, either on the use of U and V or a treatise on serif construction; an article on the notion of Modernism will come from Mrs. Warde; an article on the work of Hans Mardersteig of the Officina Bodoni; and I am hoping to publish this number some time towards the end of this year, I hope before Christmas, and thus to get myself free from the sort of pleasant enslavement in which I have been involved for some time.*

At this moment, the *Fleuron 6* was not yet out. At the end of March, Morison was still expecting the sheets daily. He had been to Gill's exhibition at the Goupil Gallery and had been much impressed. 'I congratulate you on a truly superb achievement, and hope that you feel rewarded for the very arduous labour of the past several months.'* He wrote to Cleverdon in the same terms, recommending him to buy some copies of the special poster done for the exhibition. Other matters were less well: the Gill–Pepler affair *still* dragged on (at the last minute Howell, who used to sell separate prints of Gill's engravings at the St George's Gallery, threatened to sue), and Doubleday, despite

Longwell's friendly help, had contrived to foul up *The Beaux'*
Stratagem. Morison was busy again:

The fact is that during the last three weeks or so I have been exceptionally occupied and now that the Encyclopaedia Britannica has
demanded a couple of articles which it wants in record time – one of
them by April 1st – I have my nose pretty constantly to the grindstone.*

The articles in question were on 'Calligraphy' and 'Printing
Type', both made up from previously published work. A third,
on 'Typography', which Morison had to write later in the year,
required some original thought. To be on the safe side, he sent the
article on 'Calligraphy' to an expert palaeographer at Oxford,
a pupil of the great Traube and a specialist in South Italian Script.
Morison had only just met E. A. Lowe and he must have been
agreeably surprised by the answer he got.

Dear Mr. Morison,
    It was a pleasure to read your Enc. Brit. article. It would be imper-
tinent of me to praise it. All I can say is that the Editors may consider
themselves lucky to have got you to write it.
    I have no criticism to offer. I am delighted to see that you do not
follow the methods of the dry as dust bibliographers. I wish you would
make a remark or two next to each item. That is the value of a bibliography. If you will accept *quid quid in buccam venit*, here are a few
suggestions. . . .
    I did not forget you in Rome. I asked the officials in charge of the
Archives to show me a very ancient example of 'corsiva cancelleresca', but they could find none without research. The Briefs must
be looked for elsewhere. I'd like to see one that is dated from the
Pontificate of Eugenius IV.
    If you are particularly interested in the rise of the humanistic scripts
you may care to see a few photographs I had made for me at the
Vatican Library.
    You did not say whether I am to keep your article or not. I am, as
usual, giving myself the benefit of the doubt. Of course I am fully
aware that it is not yet *iuris publici*.
    Very sincerely yours,
                                        E. A. Lowe.

In addition to these scholarly extras, there was also Gill's other type, the sans-serif design. This had been presented to the works in the form of tracings, suggested for 'Titlings for advertising' in 24pt and 48pt, on 8 July 1927. The works at once found a defect: 'Designer has overlooked the fact that descenders are impossible – J and Q need modifying.' They were firmly told to make the rest high enough to accommodate the short tails of the two letters, and work proceeded smoothly from then on. The design was going to be a success, and on 8 September it was decided to make it in every size from 14pt to 36pt. On 3 November, proofs were ready, but, apart from a little work on O and a momentary hesitation about the width of M, there were no corrections. By March 1928 the figures and points were ready and Gill added a fist, with which Morison was delighted: 'this shall be produced 2 ways, hor. and diag., right and left hand of each'. Gill, becoming fascinated by the mechanics of type design, continued to play with details until late in the year, but by 1928 matrices were officially made available.* By now Morison had plans for launching it, but the *Fleuron* still hung round his neck, more like an albatross than a millstone.

'God only knows when the *Fleuron* will come out,' he wrote to Cleverdon. It was now 24 April: 'I have had an incredible series of reverses in conjunction with it during the last fortnight and am entirely sick to death of it and its printers.' Notwithstanding, he was busy trying to round up articles for the last number. He wrote to Mardersteig for an article on the Officina Bodoni;* to A. J. A. Symons, the personification of the Nineties, for an article on the books of the period, and he sent him a copy of the Mrs John Lane Sale Catalogue, 'which contains a number of books likely to find a place in the article'.*

On top of all this, he had promised to address the Publicity and Selling Congress of the British Federation of Master Printers at Blackpool on 21 May. It was an unfamiliar scenario for Morison. If there had been any single identifiable source of opposition to the programme that Morison was putting through (and the opposition, if mute, had not been inconsiderable), the Federation might have stood for it. Many printers took the line that they had enough expenses – always rising, at that – without having to change their composing-room equipment every other year. It was with the expectation of a row that Alfred Langley, president of the Federation that year, invited Morison to speak on 'Robbing the Printer'.

Never averse to controversy, Morison seized the opportunity, not only to explain what he was doing but also to introduce Gill Sans: the titling was now ready, and there could be no better way of drawing attention to it than to launch it into enemy territory. As he hoped, the programme, circulated before the meeting, aroused violent opposition with its eccentric design and 'Gollancz' yellow cover: one critic described it as 'an abomination that ought not to have seen the light of day'. Morison was delighted, and made a preliminary counter-attack in a leaflet 'The 2 Kinds of Effectiveness', which the audience found waiting for them on their seats. 'Competition for attention', it said, 'has reached a point where the explosive, arresting force of *novelty* must be used as never before.' The master printers, tweed-suited in the main, regarded the black-suited, short-cropped, almost Mephistophelian figure with some apprehension.

His message was simple:

The influence of power presses has shifted the centre of gravity from the composing-room to the machine-room, and instead of printers being interested in a job as it strikes the eye, they are interested in the job as it has struck the charging-out clerk. . . .

The notion of craftsmanship has completely disappeared, and if anybody in the whole house has any pride in his work it is the boy who lays a clean sheet of blotting-paper in the fumed oak board-room where the directors come in and decide upon their dividends. . . .

It has meant that as a result of it people in publishing and in publicity have lost faith in the printer. They do not believe that he has either intelligence enough or resourcefulness enough, or brains, types or anything of any value to them. Printers, they say, have the machines, and all the risk of labour troubles . . . but we will show them how to do the stuff. Printers have become the hewers of wood and the drawers of water. That is robbing the printer.

He ended up:

We have got to revive not the styles in which the great printers
worked, but the spirit in which they worked. We have to revive not
this or that antique style, but revive the use of our intelligence.

The discussion began with a bang: he was immediately accused
of 'teaching your grandmother to suck eggs', and Mr W.
Howard Hazell wanted to know where lay the beauty in 'the
programme with the red hand'. Had Morison met Mr Hazell
since the days of the *Imprint*, when his views on costing were a
breath of fresh air to the trade? They were both older now.
Morison was bland: he thought it 'perfectly ordinary, perfectly
natural and rather obvious'; he had 'rather liked' the new sans-
serif letter, that was all. Besides, he added, 'I think my programme has its uses. I saw Mr Hazell kill a fly with his copy.' In
the end it was left to Richard Austen-Leigh, 'a link between the
art of printing and the organizing bodies of the printing trade',
to smooth over the dispute and bring the meeting to an end.*
    But the row continued. J. R. Riddell, head of the London
School of Printing, until recently an adjunct of the St Bride
Institute, had always been suspicious of Morison, and had
blocked his election as a governor of the Institute.* He believed
that artists should be kept in their place, and he had all the tech-
nician's resentment when they (in the form of 'typographical
consultants') strayed into the printer's preserve.* He demanded
the withdrawal and substitution of Morison's programme before
the congress, and continued his opposition after it. It was a long
time before Gill Sans was taught in schools, but it throve despite
opposition.
    Gill was now getting into his stride. Typography was no longer
'not my line of country'. At the beginning of June he was put
on a regular retainer:

I'm now a salaried official at the Lanston Monotype Corpn. What ho!
This means advice in 'type faces'. Salary v. handsome too & I like
typography don't you know.*

Although heavily committed to the Golden Cockerel Press, for illustrations and type design, he tackled Perpetua now with a new enthusiasm; the 'y' – tail straight or curved? If curved, with ball at the end? – was a great difficulty.

Capel-y-ffin
16 June 1928

Dear Morison

Thank you for yours of the 14th. The proof of the new Roman type is certainly a great improvement on previous proofs and the type wd. I think look better still when there's a bit of *impression*. The space between letters wants alteration, but, as you say, that can be done independently of me.

Re the l.c. y: No, I can't bear it as it stands. I won't say that the ball end is absolutely barred (I can imagine a good form is possible) but the form you have at present is v. bad. But I certainly do think of the alphabet as a whole as being without balls tho. not without guts so to say. E.g. the l.c. a & the l.c. f and I'm thinking that in order to preserve the character we'd better try and make the y do as the a & f do. I will try and make sketches to send herewith. Also I will draw sorts for fi & ffi.

Re Italic: Yes, I agree & I think the right step wd. be to make an italic fount which, while being an improvement on existing forms, would not jump out at the reader as a novelty. This must be done & 'England' shd. do it. But my agreement with G.C.P. specially bars me from designing new founts of type except for the G.C.P. and they are particularly anxious that I shd. do a new italic to go with the Caslon l.c. & yet be an improvement on the existing Caslon italic. My agreement with the Monotype Corpn. does not touch the designing of new types by *me* – it relates simply to advice & criticism of types brought out by them & of which other people are the designers. (n.b. the Sans Serif & this new Roman l.c. are not an infringement as they were designed before the G.C.P. agreement.)

You'll see the point of all this. I think it's all fair and square. G.C.P. wants me to do for them various types. I agree. So they say well give us the bloody things then & don't go spreading yourself on other people till you've done ours. So I agree. I don't quite see why the Monotype shd.nt come into it & make the type & give G.C.P. exclusive rights for say 5 years – but that's not feasible perhaps. Thing to do wd. be for you to design the italic to go with the '*new Roman*' & then I could criticise it. Would this be wangling? I don't think so.

It wd. be in the ordinary way of business in accordance with my agreement with Monotype Corpn. & G.C.P. knows of & approves of that agreement.

Yours
Eric G.

Could you possibly come and see us here this Summer. I wish you could – we may not be here another summer. You ought to see the place before dying.

EG

This was followed up immediately.

Capel-y-ffin
23 June 1928

Dear Morison:

Further to yours of 18th & 20th (as they say)

1. I take it that you are acceding to my request . . . to let me have photo enlargement of the 'Gill Roman' so that I may do the balled & non balled y. I await this before proceeding. Is that correct?
2. *The Italics.* Yes, I think it can certainly be held that the Italic drawings I made some time ago were intended for you to turn into a type. I only doubted whether in view of the fact that you, for good reasons, have turned the Italic drawings down, [you] can call upon me to make a new set of drawings seeing that in the interval I have entered into the agreement with the G.C.P. I doubt it – that's all. But I do not doubt that it can be got over – either by agreement with Gibbings or otherwise.

But you will remember that when I made you these drawings of alphabets I expressly disclaimed the suggestion that I was type designing. I did not & do not even now profess to know enough about it – (i.e. typographical exigencies). The same applied to the Sans Serif alphabet I drew. You remember my surprise when you showed me the pages of the Sans-Serif. I was v. pleased because I thought such a good thing had been made & it was an honour to me. . . . The same applies to the drawings I made for Gerard Meynell. (By the bye: I recognize an Italic cap B, on an advert. of a *Reader's Guide* which I have received from *Cape*, as being one of the letters I did for Gerard M.! It is I think a photo-zinco reproduction – actual size of my drawing.)

All this is simply matter for conversation & discussion betwixt you and me & the Monotype & the G.C.P. We are all I think friends in need. So I am hoping that you will be able to come to Gibbings' when I am there next week. Can you?

If what you want me to do in the matter of the Italic is simply to redesign certain letters – no doubt I can do this without qualms. But then, dear man, I'm doing what I did not bargain to do – viz: to design type – ad hoc & as such & so forth. . . . The £5 extra you paid me – yes, and I took that to be for just the kind of thing I've had to do in the matter of the Caps. & l.c.

However I am coming round by degrees to consider myself capable of designing a fount of type, so its all right & all difficulties can be got over. . . .

Yours   Eric G.

Then there was a new design, which Morison had in mind. He had borrowed Cleverdon's alphabet book again (see plate 7). Gill was amused by Morison's use of the word 'blonde', and followed up his marginalia with some suitable suggestions for a name for the new design: 'Cleverdon Blond', 'The Charlotte', 'The Gent's Preference'.*

Morison persuaded Gill to go and visit the works, and the visit was a great success. He told Gill so: they were already planning the first showing of Perpetua, a new text of the *Passion* by Walter Shewring with engravings by Gill for the last *Fleuron*.

. . . I am much pleased by what you say re my visit to Horley. I enjoyed it very much indeed. I want to go again & spend longer in the 'pattern' shop – i.e. where they photograph & enlarge & draw & trace & cut wax. It wd. certainly be an admirable thing if I had an 'experimental station' there. We shall see. Meanwhile I have about 16½ tons of work on hand. . . .

You'll have got the Walter ms. when you get this. Re what you say about further illustrations: – I don't know what you have got or what you have chosen. I wd. like a list if you could send one. I only feel that to balance the rather large portion devoted to Inselverlag I shd. like as much of *later* things as possible. I suppose you are putting in reproductions of the drawings for the Sans & Roman types – i.e. as well as the types themselves.

As soon as poss. you must send me – no, my mistake, you said that page of the *Perpetua & Felicitas* which you have already set up is correct for size – didn't you? So I will make my wood engravings the same.

Despite his oddities, Gill was very popular. Burch, as well as Morison and Beatrice, enjoyed his company, and so did everyone else in the Monotype organization.

To have met or spoken with Gill, or even to have caught a glimpse of that bearded figure striding up Fetter Lane in his leather-belted work frock, is not an experience that anyone is likely to have forgotten. . . . But where Gill capped and crowned his own unexpectedness was by making it clear at first glance that he was as far removed from mental likeness to any crank as he was from sartorial likeness to any bowler-hatted business man.

Witness to that fact can come most convincingly from the recollections of those who were serving the Monotype Corporation in relatively humble capacities in 1927, when Gill, already a renowned sculptor, first visited Fetter Lane to discuss with his friend Stanley Morison the possibilities of a new sans-serif type face. A mechanical engineer says: 'What surprises me most when I look back to that first impression of him is just the fact that there didn't seem to be anything "peculiar" about the man. You'd never have put him down as a famous Artist. You'd sooner have said he was a good mechanic – or anyway some good workman who knew his job.'*

The *Fleuron 6* was now finally out. It was an even more impressive tome than its predecessor, with a spectacular black, gold and green binding. There was the promised article on Koch; A. F. Johnson had finally done Tory (Pollard was now old and ailing); M. Beaujon had a lively piece 'On Decorative Printing in America' with appreciations of Cleland, Rogers and Warde (poor Frederic was now back in New York, miserably contemplating divorce and wondering whether to join Rogers), ending with a long account of Dwiggins's new experiments with stencil patterns. Morison himself had produced one of his most impressive articles, on 'Decorated Types'. He had recently discovered G. B. de Rossi's *Roma Sotteranea*, and with it the fourth-century inscriptions in decorated letters of Damasus I. That a pope should be responsible for such a significant advance in letter design delighted him. His style, a touch laborious hitherto, was blossoming:

Philocalus was a calligrapher as well as a mathematician, and Damasus was something of a poet as well as an administrator. The pope, finding that the freedom of the church from persecution had been followed by a lessening of Christian zeal, determined to recall his flock to their first fervour by commemorating the virtues of the martyrs in a series of new inscriptions worded and lettered with originality.*

It was, in sum, yet another pilgrimage along a familiar route. With a brief pause at the Golden Psalter, the tale was picked up with the exotic letters of French sixteenth- and seventeenth-century calligraphers, before moving to the Union Pearl, the seventeenth-century English decorated type (Morison had not yet discovered Ichabod Dawks, for whom it was cut), the Fournier, Gillé and Didot ornamental letters, and the more modern designs, French and German, that Morison and Meynell had together done so much to popularize. Updike contributed the translation of the Report of Citizen Sobry on the types of Citizen Gillé, a Revolutionary document which made a suitable appendage to Morison's article.

The book reviews as such were few (they included one on the massive *festschrift* for E. R. Weiss, to which Morison had contributed a brief article on eighteenth-century flowers as a compliment to Weiss's own work of this sort). But there was a massive series of type specimens and facsimiles to review, many of them published directly or indirectly through Morison's work. He could (if he had wished) have surveyed them with some complacence. There was a mellow and even retrospective tinge to his notice of a book on Goudy.

One of these days this book will be enjoyed as 'period printing', the period being that ante-bellum time when we were all a little more noble and complacent than we dare be now; and some time there will be a Goudy Revival; but before that day it is to be hoped that some-one will compile a tribute to this sincere craftsman, seriously documented. . . .*

The *Fleuron 6* ended with a splendid collection of specimens of new type. Morison was not content to take what came, but demanded a high standard from those who submitted designs for review. Van Krimpen's Lutetia was shown as a broadside and in an eight-page poem by Malherbe; Weiss's new roman with an elegant little book of *Bergerettes* paraphrased in English by Paul Beaujon, with a vignette by Eric Ravilious; the Stempel Baskerville had a text by Shewring and an engraving by David Jones; the same two co-operated (on a text from Aesop's fables) for the Monotype 'New Hellenic' Greek, for which Morison had gone to another Museum friend, Victor Scholderer (it was based, like Robert Proctor's 'Otter' type, on the Greek of Cardinal Ximenez' Complutensian Polyglot); Pastonchi was shown in a story by Sylvia Townsend Warner with two colour prints by Ceri Richards. In all this Morison's hand can be seen, as in the eight pages of elegant advertisements for Cleverdon's publications.

But Morison was past all this now. Gollancz was demanding more of his time. The celebrated yellow jackets (with green for fiction, magenta for non-fiction) were devised; McKnight Kauffer did the original square 'V.G.' device. They were the result of a council of war between Gollancz, Morison and Ingham (still at the Fanfare, now under the wing of the London Press Exchange). The cause was the admitted failure of the first jackets, done by Gollancz himself in his best *Sunday Times* advertisement style, for two Dorothy Sayers novels. As at Doubleday's, the salesmen preferred picture jackets, but Gollancz was prepared to risk 'the only test – of experience'.* It was a startling success. The formula appealed strongly to Morison's sense of rhetoric, and had the advantage of being easily and quickly done; it was a style that Ingham quickly picked up. But Morison was often about, producing new books – he brought in Ceri Richards' *The Flying Horse*, picking up a new book and running his eye down the page an inch from the print and ejaculating, 'Foul, foul', delighted when Miss Horsman lost patience with Gollancz in a bad mood and threw the order books brought in for signature at him, one by one. But the odd row only added to the fun; when Susan Glaspell's *Brook Evans* came out in March, Morison was delighted to get a copy inscribed 'Stanleio Morison, insigni librorum adumbratori, optimus omnium editor, non sine amicitia, V.G. d.d. Kal. Apr. 1928'.

Mardersteig and Reece were now in active collaboration, and they too wanted Morison's help. Mardersteig had safely made the move to Verona at the end of the spring, and it was from there that he now wrote.

Via S. Nazaro 1, Verona
9 June 1928

Dear Morison

I do not know whether Reece told you that the Collection published under your direction, namely 'Typographische Bücher' is to be published by us jointly. Since Vicentino and the Moyllus have been printed by the Officina, I should like to continue on these lines, more particularly as I should be delighted if the work of the Officina Bodoni could be built up on an historical basis as well.

In the near future three publications are planned, and I should like to ask you for a few explanatory words. . . .

The three publications were the little 1525 writing-book of Eustachio Celebrino, which Morison had discovered in Manzoni's *Studi di Bibliografia Analitica*, Andres Brun, and Johnson's ill-fated bibliography of Italian writing-books. Mardersteig was anxious to know what typographic ideas Morison had for them, and also anxious to hear about Perpetua, and the new Bembo – they had discovered a common passion for the original type when they first met. He ended:

I would like to repeat: please do not take into consideration, in choosing characters, which types are at present in my possession. It is of course understood that I wish to augment my material from year to year, and if I can follow any suggestion of yours, I shall be only too glad to do so.

Please accept my best thanks beforehand for your kind reply,
And believe me
Yours sincerely Hans Mardersteig

Morison replied:

27 Fitzroy Square, W.
9th July, 1928.

Dear Mardersteig,

I shall be very happy indeed if the Brun can be set in Janson, and I look forward to receiving proofs in due course. The smaller size would equally serve me for the Cellebrino.

239

Most certainly I am only too pleased that you should assist with your advice in the production of the Bembo roman. Reece did inform me, in a recent letter, that he would like the Company to send a certain amount of the type to you at once. I replied saying that I knew the Company sufficiently well to think that they would prefer to postpone doing this, until they had made the type as good as they themselves could. I have not mentioned the matter to Mr. Burch, but there is not the least objection to your doing so. On the contrary, I would recommend it.

I have acted in the matter of the italic, but without following any historical precedents. It is true that I very much like the Marcolini and others, but I have preferred to get a new italic drawn, which I hope will mate satisfactorily with the roman. As only about 4 characters have been cut, it is too early to say. I agree with you that the general question of roman capitals is most difficult. A set of capitals has been made here, and they are, in my opinion, an utter failure, since they did not follow the original sufficiently. Of course it is not possible to follow Aldus literally; indeed, considerable departure seems to me to be a necessity; but these capitals which have already been made, depart in the wrong direction.

You are quite right about the Gill type. The smoke proof that I showed you a couple of years ago is the basis for the new 'Monotype' version. The latter is a decided improvement, but even now is weak in certain sorts. However, you shall have a proof as soon as possible.

Yours,
S.M.

In September, the proofs of *Brun* and *Celebrino* arrived, to find Morison in difficulties over Bembo.

27 Fitzroy Square, W.
3rd October, 1928.

Dear Mardersteig,

I have today received the proofs of the Brun and Celebrino, both of which are admirably composed. I think the Janson type was well worth waiting for. I hope not to keep you waiting, but it happens that Dr. Thomas, who is partly responsible for the introduction, is away from the Museum with illness. However, I believe he returns on Friday, so that you could expect to have the revised proof, with any corrections (I do not think there will be more than one or two very slight changes), on Monday.

In the matter of the Celebrino: I have sent two zincos which were made by Emery Walker some time ago, before I was persuaded by Reece to give up the idea of publishing and distributing the book gratis. Perhaps I may have told you that I started with the idea of making this a Christmas card to a number of friends who, like yourself, I have treated shabbily in the matter of correspondence. These zincos have now been forwarded to you, and in addition I had a number of photographs made as a result of Reece's encouragement. I would rather leave the making of these blocks to you, and also the arrangement, because the amount of matter put into the book depends upon the conditions of publication. I do not know how much you intend to charge for the book. I think it will make some 32 pages altogether. It could make more if you were to put in all the blocks that I could procure, allow them a page each, and avoid printing on the verso. I am quite content with the format of 16.5 × 25 cm., but this, I think, makes it desirable that the blocks of the Tagliente be printed lengthwise, and facing. The blueprint which I enclose, with my maquette, is the exact size to which my collotype folds. I don't know how you will elect to fix it in the book, but as you will see from my new paste-up, I think it might well be preceded by a half-title.

The Bembo type makes very slow progress. From what I can see of it, the whole of the work which the Monotype Company has so far done has been pure waste of time, because they have not hit on the right conformation of serif. I don't in the least know how it occurred, but I have the suspicion that between Mr. Burch and the Works, an idea of departing from the original was imported into the work. Whatever the cause, the effect has been to depart from the original. I have seen no more than a page, which I sent Reece some time ago, and half-a-dozen capitals. I wrote to Burch about it at the time, but nothing has been shown me for some months. I am rather pleased with the italic, but I have yet to see proofs of it. Mr. Burch has gone to the States, and will be gone some little time, but I have the authorisation to visit the Works to see what progress is being made, and this I intend to do as soon as I have any time. I will then report to you about it.

Would you kindly let me know if any progress has been made on the article on Officina Bodoni for the 'Fleuron'? I am making rapid headway with the next number, and would be most indebted to you if you could let me know how the text stands, or will stand. The matter of the inset is not urgent, but I do need to have the text within a short time.

I still have the ambition to come to Verona before very long. I do not quite know when, but I promised to visit some people in Basle before the weather entirely breaks up, and if I could run over the Alps to see you, I should enjoy it very much. If you are likely to be away at all during the next month, will you kindly drop me a note?

Yours,
Stanley Morison

P.S. I will correct the proofs over the weekend and post on Sunday night.

The works' note on the design is perhaps significant 'copied from the book "Bembus de Ætna ad Chabrielem" printed in 16pt. Drawings have been thinned and made smoother.'*

Shortly after Morison went to the works. As a result nine characters were recut, and on 10 October the order to proceed was given, both with roman and italic. Morison liked the latter, an independent design by Alfred Fairbank based on the same Arrighi model as Blado, but there was a good deal of opposition to it; the works' view was that it was 'ungainly in comparison with the roman'. At the end of October Morison went to Paris to discuss plans with Mardersteig and Reece; they also talked about the Bembo type. It was their first meeting for two years. By 7 November Burch was back, and Morison talked to him; twelve more characters were now redesigned (a, c, e, g, p, q, and C, G, H, L, R, S). Pressure grew for an alternative italic, and on 7 December Morison went to the works again.* On 11 December he wrote again to Mardersteig.

27 Fitzroy Square, W.
11th December 1928

Dear Mardersteig,

Very many thanks for kindly returning the Gill alphabet. There is still some trouble with the Bembo type, but I assure you that it is not my fault. I have done every conceivable thing to speed the production, but the authorities have now decided that the italic which I suggested is a trifle too condensed in comparison with the width of the Bembo. Though I am not as positive on this point as they seem to be, I am bound to say that I think their view has some foundation; and as this italic has already been cut, and they are prepared to cut another, I have acquiesced in the making of an experimental fount, based on the more open and somewhat more free italic of Tagliente. This has been put in hand and I hope that it will be ready so that we can show you a proof before Christmas.

Yours,

Stanley Morison

The new italic was based on a chancery script adapted to type, like Arrighi's, by another writing-master, Giovanantonio Tagliente, and used by him at Venice from 1524. What was sought was a design with 'less personality', and for this purpose the original design had to be 'severely revised'. Morison later observed, 'While not disagreeable, it is insipid: though it may serve the Bembo roman in some slavish sort its absence of character unfits it for textual use.'* Now, he tried to preserve the first italic, despite Mardersteig's opposition.

What a pity that the completion of the Bembo type takes such a long time. But at the same time I am glad to hear that the Italic is to be replaced by a new cut.

I have frequently and with pleasure looked at the tests which you gave me in Paris, and the impression I had at first has been confirmed that the Italic is too thin in comparison with the Roman. I have also the impression as though the more severe Italic does not go quite happily with the Roman. As the Roman had a much more 'lively' effect than the too severe Italic it seems to me that your decision to base the new Italic upon a more free and easy Italic of Tagliente has much to recommend it.

I really had intended to write you a few lines about this Italic but I did not wish to act as a mischief-maker and retard your painful labours. All the better that you yourself have come to the same conclusion after divers deliberation, to change the Italic type.*

Early in the new year, an impasse was reached on the italic. The works reported, 'Italic characters quite impossible – suggest visiting works with Mr Morison and discussing fount.' Burch and Morison went immediately. It is not clear what the trouble was; but it must have been connected with the difference in width and weight. At any rate, Morison came back convinced that

Mardersteig was right, leaving only Burch obstinate and, as Morison told Mardersteig, 'despondent'.

But the roman was now going ahead at full speed, urgently wanted 'for setting important book for Italian customer', and was ready by the first week in February. Work continued on the Tagliente italic. A first trial on 6 February was pronounced unsatisfactory; even then the first italic seemed preferable. Six characters were redesigned, 'l' remaining obstinate, but by 19 March complete layouts for roman and italic were despatched to Mardersteig.*

Morison never really reconciled himself to the new italic, and preferred the old where feasible. But when the smaller sizes were cut it was essential to have an italic that would combine with the roman in the same die-case, and for this the Tagliente italic was essential. The roman, on the other hand, was his favourite, and with reason. 'It was inspired not by writing but by engraving; not script but sculpture. It rendered all previous romans archaic . . . and the design as a whole ranks as . . . one of the major typographical "watersheds".'*

'I am sorry', Morison wrote to Updike on 3 December 1928, 'that I have not been able to visit you in Vermont.'

I had the intention of joining my partner, Mr. Victor Gollancz, in a business visit to see New York publishers, and I had hoped that he would be able to leave at a reasonable time; but after one postponement and another, he hit upon December as a convenient time; and I must say that it is not the first time that I have found one man's convenience my poison. In any case, I am very busy just now with a number of dated things which I should find it difficult to leave at the present time. I suppose, therefore, that my next visit to the United States cannot take place until the early Spring. I am ashamed to say that I am conscious of having treated you, and many others, badly in the manner of correspondence. As you see, I have turned out a volume on gothic Incunabula – a job which I was given on condition that the whole work (the writing of the introduction, the selection of plates and the manufacture of the book), was done between January and September 1928. There were other things which I was also committed to, to say nothing of the business of earning a living; and this means that I have left undone many things which I ought to have done, nor is there any health in me at the moment. I had to lay aside a great deal of the work on the new edition of Reed, and so many things had accrued which I had to do the moment I was able to get free from the gothic book, that I was, and am, prevented from completing that job.

With the sudden surge of type-design work, and the several demands of Mardersteig, Cleverdon, Gollancz, and the *Encyclopaedia Britannica*, Morison's output fell a little below the astonishing level of the last five years. He still contributed one of his best articles to the *Recorder*, for the March–April number, on 'The French National Printing Office'. He had begun in 1927 to study Richelieu's plans to place all printing under government control, and the influence of the *romain du roi* design never ceased to fascinate him. The article also contained a notable prophecy:

Once in a century comes the greatest festivity of the printing world. This time it will be particularly impressive; for in 1940 the whole of civilisation will honour the five hundredth birthday of the Mother of Arts. We shall all, let us hope, live to see that historic Jubilee and to help in making it memorable.

Some of the illustrations in the article came from Graham Pollard's Birrell & Garnett *Catalogue of Type Specimens*, printed at Cambridge under Morison's direction and issued in December. It contained an extraordinary number of unknown pieces (for which Pollard had a magnetic attraction) and influenced Morison's historical researches in typography considerably. He wrote to Pollard on 21 February:

> 27 Fitzroy Square, W.
> 21st February 1929
>
> Dear Comrade,
> I hope that by a permissible extension, bibliography may be included as a qualification. At any rate, if I am not technically a comrade, you are, and may be addressed as such, even by one not of the true fold.

The catalogue is very interesting, and – looked at as a bookseller's catalogue – not too bad. Looked at as a piece of printing, it is of course abominable. The title-page is very attractive, and is, I think, good advertising.

I don't think I could have an account of George Bickham in *The Fleuron*. A certain amount of liberty has been given already to those who think I lay the axe of calligraphy to the tree of typography. There is too much talk about striking and sprig'ed letters, and not enough about poor printing. I should like to see an account of George Bickham, and I believe this, that if you wrote it, the thing could be produced in a limited edition and could be bought by the interested, provided there were some pictures in it.

Yours,
S.M.

P.S. The will of John Bell is now being copied for me at Somerset House. Why didn't you recommend me to get this done before?

Beatrice continued to keep the *Recorder* lively, and Morison must have been particularly pleased by No. 223, celebrating the Monotype cutting of the Cochin series. Life was blooming again for her. She was living in Chelsea, and the susceptible Eric Gill had fallen for her. He made a series of profile drawings of her in his best style, and she was later to model extensively for him. Meanwhile she lived a comfortable 'artistic' life with the Shuffreys. 'They never go to bed until about two in the morning, so there's no trouble about playing the gramophone late. . . . At my last party we all adjourned to the basement and made pots on the wheel. Mr Burch made a beauty, and they baked and glazed it for him.'*

In the middle of January Beatrice went to visit her family in New York, returning a month later. During her absence Gill, disconsolate, wrote to her.

I saw S.M. this morning. He seemed well & cheerful. He wants to engineer some arrangement whereby a more definite & extensive connection is established between me and the Monotype. He talks of a press, for books etc., independent of Fetter Lane but financed & supported by the Corp[n]*

It would be fascinating to know what Morison had in mind for himself and Gill. Beatrice was enthusiastic to join them: 'What could we do,' she wrote back.* As a question, it was never answered.

For Cleverdon, 1929 opened badly. Doubleday had finally made a completely unacceptable job of *The Beaux' Stratagem*. There was nothing for it but to start again, and where else but at Cambridge. Morison set about the job.

27 Fitzroy Square, W.
26th January 1929

Dear Cleverdon,

Thanks very much for the copy of *The Beaux Stratagem*. I have forwarded it to Lewis, with the particulars which you enclosed, and have asked him to quote a very low price. I am quite sure he will. I don't know what the size of Lewis's paper will be, but it might make it advisable to make the book wider and not quite so long. From what I can see of it, we could do with more space on each side of the engravings. This means a wider book, but the length of line of the type is very comfortable at present. Before the job is actually tapped, however, we shall of course see a couple of specimen pages, so that what happened last time shall not happen again.

You did not enclose the prospectus, but I think that the same paper for the plates and for the text is undoubtedly indicated. It is astonishing how good Doubleday's paper is, and yet how rotten it looks.

I have read your manifesto to Doubleday, and I think it a very moderate and decent statement, which cannot fail to be effective.

I think I shall be at the Double Crown Club on January 31st, but at the present moment I am so bored and busy that the bustle and bunk of the Double Crown Club may be too much for me. On the other hand, it would interest me to take, as it were, a clinical observation of their attitude towards Mr Rogers, about whom a number of them must be excessively ignorant.

Yours,
S.M.

Morison had been more kindly disposed towards Rogers since he came over, even though the Monotype recutting of Centaur with Warde's Arrighi took exactly a year – February 1928 to February 1929 – to complete, with an infinity of minor changes and re-changes. He was anxious that his waning popularity should be restored.

The kind of thing people are tired of is the *Silver Cat*, but the Grolier Club's *Champfleury* is a very different thing. So that it remains for him to regain any lost position by producing a book of some size – I mean more than 32 pages.*

The Oxford Lectern Bible was to vindicate this judgement.

Morison's circle was broadening. 'Literary' people besides Bridges were coming his way. He met Vita Sackville-West, 'the most handsome and accomplished female that I have ever clapped eyes on'.* Cleverdon and Gollancz had brought a fresh breeze into the dead air. Morison would have liked to spend Christmas in Bristol in the cheerful Bohemian company of Cleverdon and Brownie, but family piety prevailed ('I was able last year to back out of it'). The year had been mixed, but he ventured a speculation for 1929. His letters to Cleverdon, like Gill's to him, were apt to take the form of marginalia. On 7 September, text and comment ran as follows:

By the way, could you come down next week for two or three days? *No, more enslaved than ever until 25 of this month & then I hope to slack off.* Brownie sends her love; we're all rather depressed at the moment. None of us have any money, and the cat has just scratched Wilfred, and Brownie has a headache. What a life!
Most sorry. I also am pretty penniless now that the inc tax has conquered my little reserve. 1929 will see us flourishing perhaps. The Ency. Britanᶜᵃ has now had abᵗ £75 worth of my work – payable on publication of the entire damb work.

A LETTER TO BEATRICE WARDE

YOUR question asking me to tell you if anything is clever enough to be better than anything good and kind, and to tell you what I would tell a stranger calls out what there is in me by way of answer.

I have suffered a good deal from people's kindness, and I have caused suffering to others when motived by the same feeling. If I analyse this feeling, I think it seems to consist in the regard for the good estate of others, but of late years I have been very sensible of the difficulties of living a life of charity. I have worked by a kind of formula such as always giving to a beggar in the street, always doing what I am asked if it is possible: in other words, attempting to carry out a whole-hearted service to others in my private life. It is this feeling which leads me to Communism and other activities for the greatest good of the greatest number. I seem to find this position unsatisfactory because it is undiscriminating. For years I have never prayed for any particular good or immediate need – only have I said *da mihi intellectum*.

The life of charity needs to be ruled by intelligence. Though my reason is not equal to God's, it is good enough to prevent me from prompting His – suggesting that this or that would be to my ultimate good. Here at the word 'ultimate' we have the greatest of our difficulties. It is plain that it is not good for every individual to have that without which he is unhappy. The kindly person who will come along and give it to him because he asks for it and because he is miserable without it, is not kindly. In my own life I have drawn away from doing good by habitually acting in accordance with my own formula – rather I have altered the formula. There are people I know who would like me to visit them often.

X, for example, is a person I respect and like, he respects and likes me and is always asking me to visit him. If I do not go it is not because I think I have any right to live entirely for myself, but because my experience has shown me that my going there lacks reality, and that there must come a time when I could no longer physically support the effort of continuing. So to save X from a disappointment which would increase in accordance with the frequency of my visits, I find it 'kinder' to appear unkind. But this solution has only been arrived at after considerable thinking and the exercise of my best intelligence.

My real kindness consists in the exercise of my intelligence for X's ultimate good – that he knows nothing of it, and thinks me cold and standoffish (as your mother would say, 'self-centred'), argues on his part a certain rashness of judgement. This is what I find all round. Some time ago my mind determined that unless human relationships were founded upon reality there could not be any permanence in them. And, where reality exists, a certain fire bursts forth – spontaneous combustion if you like. It is something of its nature to be revelatory, free, strange, unexpected and triumphant.

This divine thing, reality, when it enters into human relationships gives them greater or less permanence according to the degree in which it is present. By 'permanence' I mean the even and uninterrupted satisfaction of the intelligent mind contemplating an intelligible object. There is nothing in the world comparable to the ecstasy with which one intelligent mind contemplates another intelligent mind – all love, all friendship, all happiness depends upon this principle insofar as permanence is desired. With reality there is spontaneity and freedom – there is neither service, duty, nor even kindness. Kindness is that pathetic effort of the will to create reality; unfortunately this is not possible to any human being. The spirit of reality bloweth where it listeth; we can but pray for it for ourselves and for others. I am sure that this is the best thing we can ever do, and then to wait upon the finger of God, controlling pity, disciplining charity, refining kindness by that same principle of intelligence which hides behind reality. It is not a question whether anything is clever enough to be better than anything good and kind. There is no virtue in cleverness – there is no more disgusting word in the language. We do not need sufficient cleverness to be good at parlour games and to shine at tea-tables, but we do need intelligence and we do need to exercise it: without it, no matter how keen our pity for the tortured heart of humanity, we shall only spread the plague of sentiment. It is less difficult to talk or to write, to sympathise and to sob, than to do none of these things but to sit with the door shut and to plan permanently, because intelligently, a life so secure that in those hours, days, and years of your own weakness and failure you shall not be the cause of other people's stumbling and falling. It may be that the supremest act of any individual is a humble confession of failure. This is a much more searching act than the giving up of all we have to the poor. Possessions mean nothing to the man who truly loves God, and God is the sum of reality. We can only help a man by helping him towards God. Very often it is wise not to use the word 'God' – I should never use the word in New York, if I could avoid it, unless I was talking to a very carefully screened and hand picked society. I certainly should never mention the word to F.Q. because I think I could put it over better by avoiding an association-word. Even 'reality' is a mouldy word – I don't know another word to use – and so employ it here. In you, there is a specific real nature (this sounds like Freud & the rest of whom I've never read one word I swear) and that is real which helps that nature to ascend from the implicit to the explicit, which helps you to be yourself. No matter how much you might with your intelligence admire the life of a Carthusian, & you might try your vocation with them it is not the life for you because it cd. never be spontaneous, it would be against the analogy of your character. If while you were considering the subject another admirer of the Carthusians made you understand this would he not be neighbour to you rather than if he had pressed you in the other direction – because your own desires lay there? But this is too elementary – I mention the illustration to show that intelligent kindness is a very different thing from helping forward some immediate desire. Let us hold fast to the principle of intelligence and be as scrupulously intelligent as we are kind. This is what I would say to a stranger.

Draft of a note written by Morison
for Beatrice Warde, c. 1927–8.

11

MORISON had not lost touch with Robert Bridges since March 1927. Later that year 'The Influence of the Audience' appeared as the first volume in Milford's edition of *Collected Essays Papers &c*, with the first four of Bridges' planned series of phonotypes. It was a most elegant little book, its design embodying most of Morison's favourite theories as well as those of Bridges: it was set throughout in Blado italic, 13pt for text and 10pt for footnotes, with Poliphilus 16pt small capitals, instead of the normal italic capitals, in the best Aldine manner. Four more phonotypes followed in the next volume, published in 1928. These had just been finished when Bridges wrote to Morison on 15 November 1927. He had received the Oxford print of Book II of the new poem in September, and was now at work on Book III.

The letters seem quite as we wished; the only doubt I had was whether they might not be a little thicker than the rest of the italic.

As soon as these letters are approved and cast for the printer to use we shall be at work with them.

I am getting on with my long poem, but I often wish that I saw you oftener for I usually get some advantage from hearing your 'aspect' of the difficulties. I am longing to get to the end of this section so that I may be dealing with morals & religion.

Is there any chance of your paying us another visit soon?

This and other visits probably followed, but there are no further letters till next year. The Oxford Press printed Book III for Bridges in May 1928. In September he wrote again, recommending George Gordon, professor of English Literature at Oxford, as one who would 'do your new version well' (Morison may have been asking him about *The Passion of St Perpetua and St Felicitas*). 'Meanwhile,' he ended, 'my Bk IV is going on all right but is slow.'

By the beginning of 1929 another volume of the *Collected Essays* was in hand, for which another three phonotypes were required. Bridges wrote to Morison about this, and told him that he was expecting the first 1135 lines of Book IV from Oxford shortly.

27 Fitzroy Square, W.
23 February 1929.

Dear Robert Bridges. I am delighted to have a letter from Chilswell; your news about the 4th Book of the Poem is most exciting to me. I read and re-read the parts already printed and have gained enormously from it. I look forward to seeing what you have done with a most urgent appetite for the questions you are tackling give my mind little rest and it is a very great consolation to be able to turn to your poem.

I am ashamed to say that I have forgotten the l's. Since I saw you last I have worked with great speed and concentration first upon Incunabula and then upon a technical question and now upon the 18th century, scarcely resting, except to work at something else. I am glad to report that the severe weather left me unscathed but I must apologise for my bad memory. I know we discussed some letters on my last visit and I think these were made.

I have sent a memorandum to the Monotype Co. about the fount and have asked the Oxford Press for proofs of any revised or new characters which they may have had during the past few months. If, in the meantime, you or M.M.B. will send me a sketch of the desired new sorts I will unfailingly see that they are made instantaneously.

I have to give a lecture to Fairbank's Society of Calligraphers on Wednesday at 8 p.m. & hope to catch the 10.20 to Paris – returning on Friday. If your drawing came on Wednesday morning I think I could promise that the matrix or matrices (if no more than 3) would be ready within a week.

I am very sorry to have to put you to this trouble and hope to be forgiven. In a month I hope to be free from the present pressure and would very much like to come to Chilswell. At the moment I have so many promises to keep that I must postpone the excursion. The preparation of this lecture now exercises me: I fear that the lantern slides will not be in time and that I shall have to make up for their absence by inventing samples of that most depressing of all compounds – lecture-room humour.

Yours
Stanley Morison

For four years Morison had been working on John Bell (1745–1831), newspaper proprietor, publisher and originator of the transitional type of which he thought so highly. Bell's vigorous, unorthodox and slightly raffish personality appealed strongly to Morison. Politically, it was an attraction of opposites, but Morison must have seen parallels with himself in Bell's refusal to accept the customary standards book in typefounding and publishing. He and Lewis had hit on the idea of printing a small book – sixteen pages or so – as a Christmas present for friends of the press, and Bell was to be the subject. When Morison wrote to Bridges it was already clear that ten times that extent was not going to be enough (it was not until Christmas 1930 that *John Dunton's Sketches* appeared instead).

What with this and other preoccupations, Morison evidently failed to respond promptly when the print of Book IV was sent to him. Bridges wrote to remonstrate:

Chilswell
12 April 1929

My dear Morison.

I hope you hav not been ill, as most other people – I have expected to hear from you before now – . I am back again working at my poem hoping to finish it up, and correct the whole during this summer if there be any summer. I am getting on with this, but I sh^d be sorry to miss the advantage of any criticism – and attach great importance to matters in which you w^d find obscurity or offence. Perhaps you have not been able to come to any definite judgment – but there is no point on which I sh^d not value your animadversions. – what I most want is to have faults pointed out, or difficulties in diction or meaning – But most of all of course the impression on yr general 'feeling' –

But do not trouble to write a long letter. My present section is on the relation of Religion to Ethic.

yours sincerely
Robert Bridges

Morison wrote on 16 April to excuse himself. When he wrote, he was wrestling with the Monotype preparations for the Printing and Allied Trades Exhibition at Olympia in April. The Stand there was a conspicuous success;* it was designed by Gill and he and Burch were photographed there demonstrating the progress of letter-design (see Plate 7). With Henry Thomas, Morison had organized a simultaneous exhibition of modern fine printing at the British Museum. The catalogue, printed at Cambridge, was all set in the one available size (16pt) of Bembo (with Fairbank's narrow italic). In its absolute simplicity, it is one of the finest things that Morison ever designed. With all this to see to, and a chapter of petty accidents at Monotype, 'I have been exhausted at the end of the day', he wrote, 'when I looked forward to being able to write'.

16 April 1929

... I much enjoyed the Poem, I am greatly helped by several portions of it (the section dealing with Pleasure, for example, though I have more sympathy with that Jesuit than you feel; wasn't he just in training? Remember that celibacy may necessitate a greater discipline of the appetites in some than in others) but I found difficulties in the lines which treat of Good Disposition. I suspect my mind is still affected by touches of Pauline theology – but it was precisely a distrust of my own natural 'Disposition' which turned my attention to Christianity with its doctrine of a human nature warped by concupiscence.

But I will write again – I hope to-morrow. I rejoice that you are at work again. My own health has been poor of late but I am thankful to have the health to continue at work. Enclosed is the title page of my latest enthusiasm. I look forward to seeing you & Mrs Bridges soon. At least I am in Oxford next month for the opening of the new Dominican Priory Church & will come to Chilswell then if not before. I beg yʳ indulgence for this, my rapidest-ever cursive.

It is not surprising that Morison, himself early drawn to the Society of Jesus, should feel sympathy with Gerard Manley Hopkins in the early days of novitiate, 'tried' by a hurt and contemptuous Bridges.

And so,

When the young poet my companion in study
and friend of my heart refused a peach at my hands
he being then a housecarl in Loyola's menie,
'twas that he fear'd the savor of it, and when he waived
his scruple to my banter, 'twas to avoid offence.

But I, upon thatt day which after fifty years
is near as yesterday, was no stranger to fear
of pleasure, but had grown fearful of thatt fear; yet since
the sublimation of life where to the Saints aspire
is a self-holocaust, their sheer asceticism
is justified in them. . . .
Wherefor they fly God's garden, whose forbidden fruit
(seemeth to them) was sweeten'd by a fiend's desire
to make them fond and foolish. Nature ne'ertheless
singeth loud in her prison. . . .*

Three days later Friday brought peace and leisure, and Morison
sat down to write his considered criticism of Book IV.

27 Fitzroy Square, W
19 April 1929

My dear Bridges

Is it possible to distinguish in the sense of Duty: between the *I Must*
of the Individual and the *I Must* of Society? You dramatically challenge the inflexibility with which the Church outfaces the Prophet
and Poet, but have we not to deal with a sharper struggle than merely
that of the Bureaucrat with the Individual i.e. the People against the
Man whose sense of Duty is at variance, as they think, with the comfort of the State.

The lines dealing with the development of conscience which trans-
figureth the instincts are good; and I have found y^r treatment of
Pleasure most suggestive and valuable. At line 225–9 you well say
that 'Duty instill'd with order . . . and elsewhere that Virtue is a
matter of conduct rather than of doctrine. But I suppose Virtue can
be subjective only and the lover of the beauty of social order demands
objective Virtue – hence the prayer of the psalmist *Da mihi intellectum*.
I note that y^r acc^t of the development of Conscience stresses the view
that it is Reason functioning in Morals & isn't a sense *in se* – the
truth as it seems to me, a concomitant of that *habitus* of Virtue in the
reflective and well-disposed man. Line 700 sqq are admirable and
when at 780 you tackle the mystery of Knowledge your words are
most penetrating; y^r contention that *Reason* is a means towards, &
not the *Creator* of the Idea of Beauty is squarely and beautifully expressed. But, throughout, the passage of yr thought is superbly easy
to follow and your argument though condensed is so happily wrought
as to win its way into the understanding. I very much like the down-
right forcefulness of lines like 910 & 949–50 and you come at 1099 to
the only answer possible.

Bonitatem et disciplinam et scientiam doce me!

I think your conclusion has great verity and grandeur . . . and I turn, as I have turned before, to re-read the Poem. It is easy to read yet it is not easy to read more than three or four pages at a time – so, at least, is my experience, as the subject and y^r solemn treatment of it are the matter and form almost of a sacrament. I am most grateful for your having done this work; those tens of thousands of perplexed souls in this and future generations who ponder the tremendous problems you tackle will be unspeakably grateful for your teaching, for your courage & for your poetry. I look forward with enormous interest (and necessity) for your concluding § – and then it must be printed in an appropriate form.

Don't think I have forgotten that final character for the Chilswell phonetic type. It is the most difficult of all. A design has been made – but it turned out to be useless when reduced as you will see from the attached print and we have another in hand. I was delighted that you knew *Bell's Life*, though this was not my Bell but a nephew who, however, used the name in his title because his uncle had made it famous with his *Bell's Weekly Messenger*. Unfortunately I haven't been able to touch that Memoir for a long time. I hope the present sunny days are not merely favour for London but extend to Chilswell,

Yours,

Stanley Morison.

P.S. I think the criticism of Socialism is harsh; wd. B^d Shaw allow that he preached Class hatred as the enlightened gospel of Love? Marx does not desire Class hatred – he only points out that A will hate B if B's wealth is accumulated at A's expense or by the organisation of a number of men like A who will starve if they don't enter B's service at the wage profitable to *him*.

That postscript was elicited by Bridges's too easy contempt for Marx as well as Jesuits.

> Thus 'tis that levellers, deeming all ethick one,
> and for being Socialists thinking themselves Teachers,
> can preach class-hatred as the enlighten'd gospel of love;
> but should they look to find firm scientific ground,
> Whereon to found their creed in the true history
> of social virtue and of its progress hitherto,
> 'twil be with them in their research, as 'twas with him
> who yesteryear sat down in Mesopotamy
> to dig out Abram's birthplace in the lorn graveyard
> of Asian monarchies. . . .*

The magnificent analogy with Sir Leonard Woolley's excavations at Ur really proves nothing, as Morison pointed out. He had come a long way now since that first formal diffident letter in October 1923.

Bridges was touched and delighted.

Chilswell
29 April '1926' [1929]

My dear Morison

What a shame, said my wife when she saw your letter, to hav made the man write all that! Well, I told you that I did not wish you to put yourself out. My gratitude is none the less; it will all be useful. Though when I say that I don't know what *objected* and *subjected* mean, you will despair of me. Please sir! I used to know once: and I suppose managed to handle the terms when I was in for Greats. They must find it hard to find their way about my poem. I am getting on well enough with it & have got in the continuation as far as the finale or epilogue, which will have to wait for a favourable moment also I have almost completed the correction for press of Bks I and II. Your general appreciation is very encouraging. As for publication I don't like to consider that before the thing is ready. Oxf Univ Press & Milford will no doubt do the main edition, but there must be a luxurious format – and nothing w^d please my taste better than a volume like the one you did for me wh you called The Tapestry. If there is any chance of your being able to do that, it might be arranged with Milford. – Meanwhile, thank you very much for your letter. We shall look forward to seeing you when you come to the Dominican gala

yr sin   R Bridges

Bridges was still keen that Morison should produce the 'luxurious format' in America. Morison himself was anxious – remembering *The Tapestry* – that there should be a decent interval between the limited and the ordinary edition. Bridges disagreed and, with gentle pressure from the Oxford Press who wanted to be sure of publishing these and any other editions, it was finally decided that there should be three editions, luxe, ordinary and American (the last to be separately printed by Rudge), all published simultaneously. The poem still had no title; Bridges had two in mind, was reluctant to abandon either, and was inclined to publish it under a different title in each country. At the beginning of July he capitulated: it was to be *The Testament of Beauty*.

Morison's first plan was to set it in 13 pt Bembo roman, the next size to become available.* He still wanted to be allowed priority if only, as before, by a few days. When he next wrote, it was to relate a familiar difficulty.

> 27 Fitzroy Square, W
> 23 July 1929

Dear Mrs Bridges. I send you rough proofs of the 13 pt Bembo type which I propose to use for The Testament of Beauty, an idea of the size of the page and two proofs of a suggested title-page. The type is now at Oxford and is being composed; and I can only hope that you and RB will approve when you see the poem in a decent proof. I send these as an indication of progress, having feared that your patience might have given way under the strain of repeated post-ponements of the delivery of the type.

I hope it is not too late to effect the issue of this edition first. In this connection it is important that there be a dated preface or colophon. . . .

It seems to me that the type of the ordinary edition looks very small and mean – I wish the Testament cd. have gone out to do its work without handicap. For short poems like those in New Verse the type was much less objectionable but here I feel strongly that it is inconveniently small.

I hope you are withstanding the continued heat – I find it almost intolerable. My duty to R.B. & to yourself.

> Stanley Morison

His attempts to change the format of the ordinary edition (the type was deliberately small, so as not to break the long lines of *The Testament of Beauty*) were fruitless. Rather anxiously, he wrote again on 26 July.

It is a pity that the small type must be adhered to. I should think from what Milford said today that he would agree to use my type but if uniformity of size with the other volumes is required now this, as you say, is impracticable.

I am very anxious that if the ordinary edition goes out in the small type, reviewers should be sent 'my' edition – at least the *Times*, *New Statesman* & *Observer* (possibly others). It seems to me that as the poem is so important & requires such careful estimation no handicap should be placed on its legibility.

The change in the weather is an immense relief to me.

Bridges himself wrote a day or two later to explain his reasons for keeping the small type, and Morison replied at the beginning of August. He had evidently been told that the poem was to be dedicated to the King, which Oxford did not discover until mid-September – Bridges seems almost to have enjoyed tantalizing the Press. The first page of his letter is missing, but the drift of his argument is clear. All his life he had known what it was to be reading against time in uncomfortable conditions. So he could tell Bridges

that besides myself being a victim of lack of due time for reading, I have witnessed the effort of many men to read, mark and inwardly digest in the tiny intervals which journeying to and from their work allows them. Many of us have to read in the bus and tube.

While, therefore, realising the point of your remark that this edition's 'incompetence' – a stronger word than I would myself have used – is a graceful modesty, I would answer that this is a virtue here out of place as being against the nature of the work. In other words, here, if ever, you have written a poem which, being ecumenical in its—but I will not dispute any longer; humanity will force its way to the heart of your teaching even though the type be black and blue and upside down.

I note your wishes as to the dedication. It has struck me that it might be possible to engrave it in white on a solid ground which could be printed in a royal red – that is, if you care for the idea. It would not take long to arrange and would afford that differentiation from the text which a dedication should not merely possess but display.

I very much look forward to reading the conclusion of the poem. If you should have a spare proof I should be greatly delighted to have it. I think you may take it for granted that I shall like it as you say it is the 'most decidedly Christian part of the whole poem'. All I should think of doing, with your hope that I shall not in consequence 'dislike' it, would be to put double quotes to the word "Christian"!

And he added a postscript:

I have written to Oxford and I am sure Johnson will put the job through at once. You will receive your proof from him. 𝕿𝖍𝖊 𝕿𝖎𝖒𝖊𝖘 has offered me – and I have accepted – the job of revising the typography of the daily paper.

In these few words Morison announced the last of the three major appointments of his life, and the one which held his loyalty deepest and longest. He had a clear idea of what he wanted to do. He went to see the manager of *The Times*, William Lints Smith, on 1 August, and writing next day to accept the job of 'typographical adviser' he defined his task as 'to begin at once that gradual revision of minor detail which shall, in time, bring us to the important matters of text type and headings. . . . If things proceed satisfactorily . . . it will not be too optimistic to hope to make *The Times* the finest piece of printing, without exception, in the world.'*

Meanwhile *The Times* offered new opportunities for seeing that *The Testament of Beauty* had the success it deserved. The editor, Geoffrey Dawson, already knew Bridges.

> 27 Fitzroy Square, W
> 17 August 1929
>
> My dear Bridges. I think I can get *The Times* to move in the matter of the spelling and will report next week after a meeting which is to decide several points and may even deal with the S.P.E.
>
> If the agreed (i.e. between you & G. Dawson) spellings have been forgotten or mislaid, *The Times* will write to you about it – I am sure the authorities are now in the humour to do what you tell them however neglectful in the past.
>
> In the meantime I have heard from Mr. Batey the recently appointed Assistant Printer at Oxford that the composition of the Testament of Beauty in the large Bembo is to begin at once. I enclose his letter (which please destroy).
>
> The weather keeps fine. I am glad you are in the sun.
> Yours
> Stanley Morison

261

Bridges had not been satisfied with Morison's first page in 13pt Bembo; nor had the second, entirely set in the first 16pt italic, Fairbank's narrow design, met with greater success. In the end they settled for a large, demy quarto book, using the original 16pt Bembo roman. By this time it was already late, and Morison must have contemplated the history of *The Tapestry* and wondered if history was going to repeat itself.

It is characteristic of both men that they should give so much trouble and thought to the dedication. Evidently no luxury was to be spared, and Gill was commissioned to do the inscription.

27 Fitzroy Square, W.

27 September 1929

Dear Bridges. This is one idea. The colour, at present far too crude, spoils it but there is a chance that properly cut it would look at least decent. I cannot make a tolerable vesica form and believe that the parallelogram is the only shape I can get; it has the merit of suiting my title-page I think.

An alternative I am considering is to engrave the

on copper and print that in a subdued red. I send this glazed and unhappily crude proof to show that I am not wasting time. If you should have a better idea than the ⚬ which after much barren flourishing appears to me to be the most tolerable form I can invent, please send me a card. Remember that the proof is only an interim one. The motto will not be broken and the spacing of the title page will be revised.

I very much wish I could see you with the final proofs but I am not sure that I can take the time. If I can rush away one afternoon to get your imprimatur I will.

Yours

Stanley Morison

Finally, *The Testament of Beauty* came out on 24 October, one day after Bridges' eighty-fifth birthday. Its success was enormous and immediate: 25,000 copies sold in the next six months. Morison achieved what he set out to do, both at *The Times* and on *The Testament*. A month later he was apologetic, although he had little to apologize for; he had quickly found his way about Printing House Square.

THE FLEURON
18 Woburn Square, W.C.
5 November 1929

My dear Bridges,

I am delighted that you liked the look of the 4to edition of *The Testament*. I knew that the sales of both editions would be satisfactory, but the rapidity of sale is, I think, a record.

I am glad you noticed the leader in *The Times*. I take some little satisfaction to myself on account of it because on telephoning to Sisam I found that, while Oxford had seen that the *Literary Supplement* received advance proofs for the purpose of its leader, nothing had been done for *The Times* itself. I took it upon myself, therefore, to collar the first copy of the 4to edition released by the binder, and with it I interviewed the man, immediately under the editor, who has charge of these matters. I could have wished that the leader had been better written, but as I did not succeed in getting a copy of *The Testament* until late in the evening of Monday, to get the poem read in time for the publication of a leader in Thursday morning's paper was, therefore, rather quick work for Printing House Square.

I am sure you must be very, very gratified at the reception of the poem by the literary people. As to the theologians, these are, as you know, slow-moving folk. I spent a weekend with the Benedictines at Downside who had just received their copy. The Abbot (a man named Chapman) who is, I think, respected in Oxford as a patristic scholar, intends to read it; but I do not know the reactions of the more formidable theological folk such as the Jesuits and Dominicans. We shall probably have to wait for a long article in *The Dublin Review*. You will know better than I shall what the Anglican folk think. I should particularly like to know the opinion of Streeter and W. Temple.

I do not understand those who find the verse form difficult, though I do think it is not the poem to be read when the mind is tired. If it is possible to do another edition, I should have several recommendations in the way of typographical apparatus. One of the difficulties about a poem of this length and concentrated matter is that of finding this or that passage. It would, I think, be a great help to a pious reader if he were given something in the way of shoulder notes or an argument for each of the books. This, perhaps, we could discuss when the time comes, if ever. I imagine that no publishers desire to multiply editions.

For the past fortnight or more a rather serious disturbance of the focus of my eyes has upset my normal activities, amongst them the writing of letters. This is why I was not able to send you a birthday greeting in time for the day – but I see by the calendar that I am in time for your octave, so this letter can carry my best salutations without my being completely behind the market, as they say.

I should like to repeat what I said before, that I derived an enormous benefit from the reading of the poem when you sent me the fasciculi, and now that it is complete I turn to it as to another scripture. I am sure it will rank as one of the greatest works of the century.

It has been the utmost pleasure for me to have been connected with the publication of the work, and the generosity of your recognition of my slight typographical talent gives me great happiness. Now that it is finished, and the public reception has been what it has, I hope you will enjoy a good rest. I hope also that you will not have a foggy winter at Boar's Hill.

With all affectionate regards to you and to M.M.B.

Yours
pp Stanley Morison
GEA.

On the last day of December, Morison wrote again. His eyes were still giving trouble; it was the result of too much work over the last eight years, and he never wholly got rid of it.

THE FLEURON
18 Woburn Square, W.C.
31 December 1929

My dear Bridges,

I must ask you to accept a typewritten receipt for your very kind letter of Christmas. I only wish that, in addition to your generous good wishes, it had conveyed better news of your daughter. I pray that things may mend and that the skill of the specialist will avail.

I have been too much occupied with urgent work to have much time for frequenting ecclesiastical society. I know that the Unitarian minister at Bristol has been preaching a course of sermons on the *Testament*, and I am sure that this is by no means a singular occurrence. The papistical camp always say 'non tali auxilio' to every outsider. I have not seen a review in any of our denominational papers; and, in view of our small number and lack of thinkers, I do not hope for any adequate, let alone favourable, estimate of the book's importance.

I congratulate you very heartily on the production of your old play. I shall be very surprised if, after all, the box office report is not eminently satisfactory.

I shall be quite pleased if Fairbank can design any new letters that you may require, so please have no scruple whatever in asking him to undertake any draughtsmanship you may feel disposed to commit to him. I would like him to do more in the way of type designing, and intend to ask him to do some further work for the Monotype, but am unfortunately prevented by the necessity to execute long standing promises to do quite different and less agreeable labour.

My work has been put in still further arrear by a trouble of the eyes which lasted for several weeks and had a paralysing effect on my activities, but I think I can safely say that all the trouble is now over – except the mass of accumulated correspondence and overdue printers' proofs. You must not understand this to be an indication that I have no time to do anything for you if there should be a need for the little services that I can render. I hope in a week or two to be abreast of my commitments, and if you should have any work, big or little, that needs to be printed, I shall be very happy to give it attention.

With all best wishes for the New Year to you and your household.

Yours
Stanley Morison

'To be abreast of my commitments' was a lifelong, yet never fulfilled, ambition. But there was to be no more work of Bridges to add to them. He died on 21 April, and so ended a relationship as close as it was unexpected. Throughout, Bridges had been in his eighties; it is a remarkable proof of his vitality that he kept pace, and more, with Morison in the sudden flowering of his talent. First *The Tapestry* and then *The Testament of Beauty* had come, both at critical points in Morison's life: both had had a marked influence on him. Despite their differences of opinion and outlook, there was a common magnanimity in Bridges and in Morison: it was this, and their recognition of it in each other that had made their friendship so mutually rewarding.

Morison had begun the year feeling rather unsettled. The last items in his Monotype programme – Bembo, Perpetua, Gill Sans – were all but finished. What next? He felt that Monotype should acknowledge and establish his position, with a seat on the board. (Burch gave him gently to understand that he would be happier and have more influence off the board than on it.) He was planning a new edition of Talbot Baines Reed's *The Old English Letter Foundries* (a pioneering work first published in 1887), but could not get started. C. G. G. Dandridge, the newly appointed Publicity Manager of the London & North Eastern Railway (successor to Morison's old favourite the Great Northern), was examining Gill Sans, with a view to establishing it for use as the railway's standard lettering, not least among the ninety or more printers who produced its timetables and other printed matter.* Morison had given up the £100 retainer he still received from Hobson. Beatrice was full of ideas for publicizing Monotype. She devised floats at the Lord Mayor's show with the 'twenty-five soldiers of lead' in full armour, life size, or showing the history of lettering from Roman inscription (cut on a real stone by Gill's pupil, Lawrence Cribb, on the journey) to Monotype caster. She had just produced a mock newspaper, the *Adverteaser*, with the date line '29 February 1929'. It was full of esoteric nonsense, like the romantic serial whose heroine, Aphasia, was depicted in post-Harlow style. Morison wrote to tell her how things were going when, just before it came out, she went back to America for a quick visit.

29 January 1929

E.G. has made a portrait of Aphasia for the 'Teaser. Today W.I.B. lunched with Mr Woodruff – with useful repercussions, each thinks the other intelligent & both think you remarkable. I have written some ads. in the staccato Plantin style in between my work on the Talbot Reed – one or two minor discoveries of interest wh. will make the book of value to those who already possess the old edition. The Dandridge posters have turned up in your room. So I'm having the place scrubbed out against y^r return. Any dead bodies shall be pickled for y^r inspection, all else will be filed. The Home Office promise Westover your permit within the next 2–3 days and then we'll cable. I enjoyed your NLT received this morning giving news of rousing reception at Boston. I am most glad y^{re} not knocked up by that frightful storm. Wish I cd. be in Boston with you. The Reed wd. be the gainer. No more news. I observed to W. I. B. y'day that it would be untrue, or at least an exaggeration to say that the delivery of my memorandum (re status) had led to an outbreak of unaccustomed verbosity on his part. He smiled hugely and said his breath had almost left his body. Not permanently I trusted since not a word in my memo. can be altered. We agreed to talk about it in the near future. . . . I'm saving cash at present and need to. Finance has been causing me some thought lately but today I'm most cheerful. . . . I don't expect any letter from you but a NLT is always a great help to me. It has been cold but is now warm and rainy. Fleet St today is a clean and beautifully drenched street agog with Goddard case wh. is anything but clean. Fitzroy Sq. is noisy as ever & Mr & Mrs Rossi barely keep the peace. I have hooked to La Renommée with an occasional Baby Chianti. On the whole I am pretty dry these days – I hope you also. BR just arrived.

S.M.*

It was not all solitary evenings at La Renommeé. Despite protestations to the contrary, Morison enjoyed the Double Crown dinners. 'Thank you', he wrote to Holbrook Jackson, 'for letting me insert my guest at the last minute. I enclose a cheque.'

I look forward to hearing your paper on the 'Anatomy of Melancholy'. I am glad the subject is in your hands and not mine – imagine what I should do with a real melancholy subject!

Kettners would have to supply tear bowls, relays of pocket handkerchiefs, wielded by ample-bosomed comforters!*

In May Henry Thomas addressed the Club on the newly opened exhibition at the British Museum. Francis Meynell tried on this occasion to sabotage the club's conventional misogyny, but Beatrice would not play, as she told Gill.

I hope you'll come Weds. F.M. has suggested I appear at the Double Crown Dinner that night disguised as a man, as they don't admit ladies. I replied that Mr Beaujon considered modern male dress indecent, that he wore a perruque and had contempt for 'chevaliers sans peur et sans culottes,' and if he suggests I come *culottée* I shall say that I have a more important engagement elsewhere.*

Mrs Morison sent her son a present for his birthday. 'All thanx yr fine parcel. Some sox too striking as you say,' he wrote on a fine picture postcard of S.R. 'King Arthur' class No. 797 *Sir Blamor de Granis*, adding 'This day have voted "Socialist" to use Ld Rothermere's word.'*

On 16 July 1929, Morison's boyhood dream was realized: he went to Edinburgh on the footplate of the Gresley A1 Pacific 2566 *Ladas*, hauling the Flying Scotsman. To Graham Pollard he was terse: 'I went to Edinburgh on Tuesday, on the footplate ... but I found nothing about John Bell.'* The article which subsequently appeared in *Arts et Métiers Graphiques*,* on the other hand, is flowery in the extreme: 'extrait de notes inédites de Stanley MORISSON' it is called, but more change has taken place than that. It is a fine piece of French English spelling (the driver and fireman's names are given as Topkins and Coflon – what would the record-breaking Tompkins and Coffin have said?) and the descriptions of the English countryside are improbable, to say the least. But there are some fine photographs (see Plate 9), no doubt provided (like the trip itself) by Dandridge. The link between the L.N.E.R. and Monotype had grown closer.

The Times job did not come entirely out of the blue, nor was Morison unprepared for it at the start. It all began when Edmund Hopkinson, acting advertising manager of the paper, called on Burch to ask Monotype to take a page in a new Printing Supplement due to appear later in the year. He found Morison with Burch. In 1912, it was the advertisements and the pictures that had caught Morison's eye. He now knew why the text had not: it was set in a poor thin letter, drably laid out on the page. The revolution since in the design of books and advertising had passed by *The Times*, which in 1929 looked much as it did in 1912. Moreover, his researches into the life of John Bell had shown Morison how well a paper could look: the original *Daily Universal Register*, later *The Times*, had been as attractive to the eye as Bell's own *The World* and *The Oracle*. When Hopkinson said that not only would *The Times* make itself responsible for the text of the advertisement, but also for the type-setting, he was interrupted. Morison hit the table with his fist and said vehemently: 'We'd do much better to pay them a thousand to keep their comps off it.'

The strength and violence of Morison's expression was unforgettable. Hopkinson told Lints Smith how he had been received at Monotype, and the result was the meeting that took place on 1 August. The progress that followed towards making *The Times* 'the finest piece of printing, without exception, in the world' was gradual.

Shortly after his meeting with Morison, Lints Smith arranged a small lunch-party at the Devonshire Club for members of the senior staff to meet him. On this occasion he repeated his strictures on the existing appearance of *The Times* with a vehemence that impressed and even alarmed those present. It was then that he demanded, both as an earnest of the serious intent of *The Times*'s wish for a change in appearance and as an example of the attention to minor detail that was an integral part of his gospel, the omission of the full point after the paper's name in the headlines. It is reported that after the lunch Lints Smith said to him, 'Well, Morison, I hope that when you come to know us better, you will like us a little more.' The paper, at any rate, was anxious to conciliate Morison, and on 13 August 1929 the full point was duly removed (although its final universal extinction took years). He was fairly under way with his programme.

Morison had begun to read up the subject in March, when Graham Pollard sent him a three-page list of works on the history of newspapers.* His first steps at *The Times* itself were of a more immediately practical nature. He prepared a report on the 'Types used in *The Times* Office'; this was the equipment used for advertisement settings and jobbing, about which Morison had been so scornful. He now proceeded to substantiate his view. The text types he carefully ignored, but he was caustic about the regular use of Caslon with it in advertisements, 'as if a Chippendale table were the invariable display piece in a modernist drawing room'. He distinguished between the demands of 'the L.P.E. school' (the style that Hobson had given to the London Press Exchange) and those for whom anything 'of sufficient novelty' would do. He was not enthusiastic about what new faces he saw: 'Not every new face is monstrous but there are many faces which have nothing but their novelty to recommend them!' Cheltenham collected a new epithet, 'that note of gratuitous swagger which a publicity type must have in order to please the advertiser'. Cushing, Bulfinch and Merion were consigned to the melting-pot. He recommended 'the new fount designed by Eric Gill', which 'redeems the sans serif from the stigma which has been put upon it by the production of the very coarse varieties which *The Times* at present holds'. He generally recommended the new homogeneous Monotype series, in place of the hotch-potch of founders' types acquired over the years. All through, he emphasized his view of the function of type in *The Times*:

The chance reader of the paper is a negligible reader: *The Times* is edited, printed and published for a reader of unique fastidiousness and deliberation to whom the mere idea of another newspaper which shall be 'good enough' is inconceivable. To such a reader the typography of the advertisements has its importance no less than the typography of the news itself. It follows that the selection of the types of both advertisement and news columns has to be in some sort of relation, and that the wise advertiser will adapt this setting to the known fastidiousness of *The Times* reader.

The report is not addressed, but it was carefully prepared by Morison with pasted-in samples of the types discussed and marginal notes in his own hand: it presupposes technical knowledge in the reader, and was probably intended for Lints Smith himself.* Morison had begun as he meant to go on.

Next came the Printing Supplement itself, on 29 October. It was an impressive number, if not so excitingly original as the 1912 Supplement. Morison contributed an article on 'Newspaper Types' to it. He had clearly spent a lot of time investigating the types and design used by *The Times* and other newspapers, in the past and present. He had also begun to make some practical tests of likely types. He did not describe these tests in his article, only concluding 'the question of an ideal type is, indeed, one of the greatest difficulty, complexity and risk for any newspaper, and whatever the final result of recently conducted experiments, the type of *The Times* Printing Number of 1929 remains that of its predecessor of 1912'.

The text of the Supplement was elegantly printed as a book next year. Morison clearly had a hand in the layout, even down to the almost ironic 𝕿𝖍𝖊 𝕿𝖎𝖒𝖊𝖘 on the spine. His own article ended with an extra note to explain that the text of the book was set in Monotype Baskerville, 'a round, open and therefore legible type': the significance of this note will be seen shortly. The book was produced in the private Printing Office of *The Times*, and was, perhaps, a trial run for the more arduous task Morison now imposed. *The Typography of The Times* was a huge folio, whose dimensions were dictated not so much by *folie de grandeur* as by the need to reproduce full pages from the paper, life size. There were forty-two of these, from 1 January 1785 to 16 June 1930. Morison wrote a general introduction as well as the historical notes for each plate. This text was set in a new large size of Bembo, 24pt (the largest ever cut for machine composition), for which matrices were specially cut for this book. It was intended to inform the Chief Proprietor, the Hon. J. J. Astor, of the previous changes in the appearance of *The Times*, in preparation for the presentation of a new text face and a new title, which would be seen to be the inevitable outcome of the progress thus depicted. A single copy was printed, for presentation to the Chief Proprietor.* As a piece of typographic homage, it has no equal except in *Médailles sur les Principaux Événements du Regne de Louis le Grand*, printed at the Imprimerie Royale in 1702.*

All this time the contents of the seventh and – Morison was determined – last *Fleuron* grew and grew. Specimens of Bembo and Perpetua had to go in, but as their final completion was postponed by the re-design of detail after detail, so publication was delayed. Christmas 1928 came and went. Every month that followed brought more work to do, more new books and types to be reviewed. The situation threatened to get out of hand. What was more, John Holroyd Reece was agitating to continue the *Fleuron*, or to start a new *Fleuron*, if Morison was adamant that the *Fleuron* proper must be ended. His first approach Morison brushed off firmly. Reece had enquired about the costs; on 10 September 1929 he replied, enclosing a copy of the accounts for *Fleuron 6*, which showed an adverse balance of £476 at the end of 1928 – a state of affairs which, in Morison's view, spoke for itself. He concluded:

. . . I do not see how I can possibly remain editor of the Fleuron. For two reasons; first that I have exhausted all my own ideas and have no list of articles to go in future numbers. When I say that I am exhausted, I mean that all the individuals who could be of service in writing articles of the kind that I would consider possible form an excessively small group. I have had incredible difficulty in getting articles even from these. I do not believe that any secretary would have equal, let alone better, chance with the same individuals; nor do I think that the group could be extended by the inclusion of new recruits. I do not believe there are any new recruits.

My plan has been a perfectly straightforward, and, I think, practicable one – it has been to improve the quality of printing, not by improving the printer, but by improving that much more important man, the printer's customer. Nearly every article from the very beginning of the Fleuron has been written to my specification; there has been no sending out a letter to a man asking him to write me an article. You can imagine what this means in editing – very often that I write out a skeleton of the article to start with, and, in the case of one or two, have re-written them. Secondly, I have a very strong desire to devote my little energies to something entirely different. I know, without the slightest possible doubt, that you cannot continue the Fleuron and pay me anything more than a mere bagatelle, and, having worked so hard already, I see no reason why I should not have a complete rest from this sort of job, particularly as I am absolutely certain that there is no possible chance of any new writers coming forward.

Therefore, if you are able to invent a scheme for taking over the Fleuron, you must find a new editor. Why not make an entirely new thing 'incorporating' the Fleuron, only have it more widely bibliographic and bibliophilic. . . . You could get an instantaneous public far wider than my very specialised Fleuron, a publication indeed in which it would be absolutely necessary for every antiquarian bookseller and important publisher to be represented, and one in which authors would compete to appear.

My answer, therefore, is that I am quite sure that it will be impracticable for the Pegasus or any other Press outside the Garden of Eden to pay me sufficiently well to continue through the everlasting grind which I have been at for more than seven years. If you do not mind my saying so, I have had more experience with this sort of thing than you have, and when I say that I feel sure you cannot put up a practicable scheme for taking over the Fleuron, for paying me, for paying a secretary and so on, I am not indulging in any oblique references to your publishing ability. There is only one way in which this thing can be done, and that is by your being able to sell 1,000 copies to America at half price and by your having 50 pages of advertisements at £20 a page. And then you would have to get the authors.

Reece next tackled Jan van Krimpen, who came to Paris, on the subject. Meanwhile Morison was desperately trying to get the *Fleuron* 7 safely out. On 30 October, he wrote to ask Updike to review a book on Cleland's work that had just come out, and added

After a succession of very serious postponements, due to defaulting contributors, progress is now being made, and I am going to press within a fortnight or so. I will put the reviews at the end of the book, so that the last possible date shall remain open for receipt of your copy. I do not think it will be possible for me to send you a proof, but I will make every endeavour to do so.

In addition to these problems, he had to move out of Fitzroy Square at Michaelmas, although no further than to 18 Woburn Square (it was still not quite Nash, but a pleasant building by Sim, 1829). Another Christmas came and went, and still the

Fleuron dragged on. Morison was also trying to finish off two other books, the Mercator writing-book that Mardersteig was printing for Reece, and *John Bell*. He had become more and more fascinated with Bell's type. At the end of October he wrote to Updike to try to sort out the tangled tale of its survival in America, and in England (Morison had duly got a fount from Stephenson Blake for Cambridge).

I have written what I thought was a footnote to *Reed* on the subject of Bell, and it has extended to a book of some 128 pages or so which will be printed at Cambridge and published some time this autumn. I am sending you a proof of one of the sheets of it, from which you will see the scale I have been working on.

I had the occasion to show some proofs to Mr. W. I. Burch, managing director of the Monotype Company here, which is, as you know, quite independent from the Philadelphia concern, and he expressed the wish to recut the face in facsimile, and, if I agreed, to speak to Mr. Blake of Sheffield about it. Mr. Blake on behalf of his firm has agreed to the recutting.*

This was an unexpected addition to the Monotype programme, and it was one of which Morison was particularly fond. But the book was not finished that autumn. Just after Christmas, he wrote to Cleverdon:

I consumed a good deal of that excellent Bristol Milk which came at a most opportune time – my non-existent cellar having been bone dry ever since I thought of putting it in; I was able to finish off the Bell book with greater ease, content and perhaps intelligence on Christmas and Boxing Day thanks to your bottle. . . .

I wish you every good thing for 1930. I hope we shall meet soon. If I could come to Bristol I would – I ought because I feel very grateful indeed to Brownie for attending to my neck and for lending me her scarf. The scarf is very important, and if I am able to earn a good deal more money this year than last, it will be entirely due to the terrific effect of the scarf upon the capitalistic classes.*

Jan van Krimpen wrote anxiously to enquire about the binding design he was to do for the *Fleuron*. Was it too late? 'No, Sir,' replied Morison on 22 January, 'the *Fleuron* has not gone to press, but it will this week.' A week later he wrote again.

As you know, there has been a great deal of conversation lately about the future of the *Fleuron*. The one point I have made is that under no circumstances whatever will I go on editing it. The next thing was that Reece thought he could edit it and produce it. Now Reece is a very delightful phenomenon but he is not in my opinion a good editor. If he did it, there would be too much of the English which you will find in the description of the Brun book printed in a very agreeable prospectus composed in Lutetia type which I have just received. Nor, in fact, does Reece know enough about the subject. I told him that I would agree to your editing it. There are several reasons for it. First of all, your English is better than his and of course your knowledge leaves him nowhere. Now he promised me that he would speak to you about it. Whether he has or not, I do not know. I don't want to ask him about it now for several reasons, the chief of which is that I am, on the whole, very nervous about his having anything to do with it. Would you mind letting me know what the situation is more or less, as far as you yourself are concerned?

In my opinion, there is a great deal to be said for Reece's suggestion to me that it would be a good thing to have the *New Fleuron* printed at Enschedé's. On the other hand, there are many reasons why, if it is in English, it should be printed in England.

A proposal of some financial support has recently been made to me on the condition that it is printed here. Suppose you tell me exactly what you think? Do not trouble to write a long reasoned letter but just make statements – as though you were a bishop!

Given financial backing, Morison would rather have kept the *Fleuron* in England, with Pollard, perhaps, as editor. But he had a high respect for Enschedé's printing. Van Krimpen told him that Reece had made approaches to him in September and November. He agreed (modestly) with Morison's assessment of his chances as editor.

The Fleuron, or the New Fleuron, must go on, I think – some day again under your sole editorship, I hope – and when I don't do it, somebody else will; and most probably somebody as bad as I am, and still more probably with less good intentions for the future. And that is all or nearly all.

I do not quite agree with you that the Fleuron, being an English paper printed in English, ought to be printed in England too. The Cambridge University Press did not do it bad, or even good, but I think we can do it better. A journal like the Fleuron should be printed somewhere where there is daily a more or less foolish or maniacal man like one of us. It need not be somebody of the kind of Van Royen or Porter Garnett, but just a tempered or practical maniac.*

He was, moreover, alarmed by what Morison said about Reece. Morison replied with a five-page letter. 'If any *New Fleuron* should be done', he wrote, 'you should do it, and if you do it you should have maximum freedom.' He was anxious that Enschedés should offer van Krimpen all the help he would need, and that no publisher should constrict his editorial freedom.

The question of a publisher brings me to my remarks about Reece. I like Reece as an individual quite a good deal. I am not at all a sociable individual myself and the only reason I avoid Reece is the same reason I have for avoiding almost everybody. I am by practice rather than by conviction an individualist and perhaps that is the reason why I am giving you the advice to keep everything so far as possible in your own hands. I think you might find Reece occasionally rather a nuisance, though he would never mean to be. He has as high a standard of production and conscientiousness in every detail of it as anybody could ever have. He has all those good qualities of the artist without the bad ones. I know that he has not the bad qualities of the business man, but neither am I so sure that he has his good qualities. . . .*

On the other hand, Reece reported good sales of the calligraphic books and was anxious to add Yciar and Tagliente to them. Why not, said Morison, employ Reece as a publisher on commission, 'as I employ the Cambridge University Press'.

At the end of June, he went over to Paris to negotiate further with Reece, and on the way had an unexpected encounter.

On the deck of the steamer I noted a splendid figure in a white suit with a black bowler as headgear; and seeing him alone and travelling alone I went up to him and said 'You are Mr George Moore'. He invited me to sit down and to talk to him (he meant *listen* to him talk) and so we sat until debarking time. Amongst other of his dicta were one to the effect that his *Daphnis & Chloe* was the best narrative English ever written; another that the monotype was a machine & all machines were bad methods of securing an inferior (to handwork) result; that the only remedy for the present economic troubles was more and better birth control; that Newman was feeble-minded; that the modern interest in good printing was due to him; that nobody knows two languages 'perfectly' and he can only write one well at intervals; that Brentano's bankruptcy was a great blow; that he wasn't going to Paris for anything in particular – 'only because that long lack-lustre street of Ebury drives me mad' &c.*

In Paris the weather was sultry, and Morison found it heavy going. 'From 1 to 7 I was with Reece. There will be a further session today and then I am finished; we could have finished y'day but 729 for six wickets cast a gloom over the proceedings and anyway the weather exhausts me.'

It may have been Reece; it may have been the weather; it may have been Bradman's all too faultless 254 in the Lord's Test Match; whatever the reason, all these schemes to prolong the *Fleuron* came to nothing. Enschedé were unwilling to take a risk on Reece (rightly, for the Depression was fast overtaking the limited-edition maker). Perhaps, in the event, Morison and van Krimpen were both a little thankful to turn from a task which would certainly be laborious and possibly dangerous to the more congenial business of type-design.

It was August when Morison wrote once more, again about the binding design, and November before the matter was settled. The *Fleuron* 7 finally came out at the end of November,* and was soon out of print. It was the largest, most various and most splendid of them all; no one could possibly complain that it had not been worth waiting for. For a start, it contained Morison's 'First Principles of Typography', an essay that grew out of his *Encyclopaedia Britannica* article, a statement of the basic facts so simple yet so compelling that it quickly became a classic. There was also Rudolf Koch's portrait of Heinrich Holz, a sad little tale, told without a spare or extravagant word, of a man who lived only for his art and died young. There was the long article by van

Krimpen on 'Typography in Holland', and Paul Beaujon on Gill, the result of long, affectionate and acrimonious correspondence between subject and author.

This last provided the occasion, at long last, for launching Perpetua. Beatrice's article gave a detailed analysis of the type, praising equally the contribution of Gill and Malin. The first Monotype cutting (December 1927) based on Gill's criticism of Malin's smoke proofs was illustrated, as well as the final version. Of the italic, only a first proof was shown, but it was presented as the outcome of 'Towards an Ideal Italic': it had 'become frankly the italic *of* a given roman, with only slope . . . to distinguish it from the upright version'. But this claim could not long be made for Perpetua: only a month after the *Fleuron* was published, it was further revised, and the sloped f was replaced by 'the gracefully descending italic f' whose passing Beatrice had prematurely regretted. At the end of the article came the finest type specimen ever to appear in the *Fleuron*, the final version of *The Passion of Perpetua and Felicity*, printed the previous year as the first showing of the Perpetua type; after it there was Cleverdon's catalogue of Gill's engravings.

In the specimen, the y problem was unresolved. Two versions (Gill's, tail flared and straight; Morison's, curved with a ball at the end) were scattered indiscriminately. The problem, already in dispute in June 1928, remained unsettled until 15 April when Gill sent Morison a postcard: 'I still intuish & think that the dotty y is out of keeping with the fount in spite of the round punctuation points.' He proceeded to draw six alternatives: 'What about No 6?' This was a y with a curved and flared tail, and it was this form that was finally accepted. But not immediately: both it and Gill's original y appear in the July–August 1931 *Monotype Recorder*, and it was not until 17 March 1932 that it was finally approved. It was perhaps the longest recorded argument about a single letter; it might have been decided earlier if Gill and Morison had not so enjoyed arguing with each other.

If the celebration of Gill was the most striking thing in the *Fleuron*, there was other matter of great diversity. A. J. A. Symons had written on the typography of the Nineties, a choice of subject far ahead of the time it was published, with grace and with knowledge; the long-planned article on the Officina Bodoni appeared, and so did Updike's appreciation of Cleland. There were notes by A. F. Johnson, Beaujon and Pollard; and two by Morison, one on the Reverend Dr Trusler and his script types, used *c.* 1771–96 for printing Trusler's sermons to look like real writing (for the use of less industrious preachers), and the other on Arrighi's first printed book of 1510.

The types reviewed were the new Monotype cutting of Centaur, Bembo, Hewitt's Treyford (a type, like Bertieri's, too closely based on humanistic script), van Krimpen's Antigone greek and Romanée roman, Bernhard and Goudy Modern. Again each was illustrated with a separate inserted booklet, again by Sylvia Townsend Warner, Rose Macaulay and other hands. Morison reviewed them all, producing a long apologia for Bembo, with the familiar theme that calligraphy and Jenson were not so satisfactory a recipe for a printed letter as engraving and Aldus. He notes most of its features approvingly, while noting that e, c and r need to be redrawn. (He does not mention the M with the right hand upright unserifed used in the British Museum Exhibition Catalogue, *The Testament of Beauty*, and in the Rose Macaulay story here; Monotype clearly preferred the more normal variety used in all the Monotype Specimens.) 'We predict', Morison concluded, 'for this letter a permanent future.' The future has proved him right.

The Goudy specimen was also warmly welcomed, in an expansive notice (Monotype had just recut it); again Morison predicted its success. The book reviews were also extensive, and all by Morison except for his own *German Incunabula*, which was reviewed by Victor Scholderer. Particular but not unstinting praise was given to the Birrell & Garnett *Type Specimen Catalogue*. The advertisements were as extensive as ever; four pages were taken by R. R. Donnelley of Chicago to advertise their beautiful new series of American classics, and Morison himself designed a calligraphic page for Birrell & Garnett's 'catalogue of some 200

Writing Books'. But this never appeared; they were sold *en bloc* to Ivins for the Metropolitan Museum, before the catalogue was even set up in type.

But before the advertisements came Morison's 'Postscript', part history, part *mémoire justificatif.*

It has taken nearly eight years to bring THE FLEURON to its scheduled end. Nobody ever made a penny profit from it. The staff has not at any time been more than two and a secretary; and, as the one member who has contributed an article and reviews to every number, I may be pardoned for congratulating myself upon release from a task which, originally light, made during the last five years heavy demands upon the editorial leisure and means. The increased bulk of numbers 5, 6 and 7, to some extent due to an acceptance of such moral discipline as was necessary to accomplish the job decently, had another cause in the increase of typographical material and activity both here and abroad. New types were being cut; new presses being established; printing became 'fine' printing; and printers, publishers and booksellers, between them, made typography fashionable. It would be unprofitable to enquire what responsibility, if any, attaches to THE FLEURON for this development – but some expansion in its pages necessarily resulted. There are signs that, due allowance being made for the speculative section of the book-buying classes, the residue of readers able to distinguish good from bad typography is now sufficiently large to exert an influence upon publishers who may consequently be expected to encourage their printers in maintaining a normally high standard of craftsmanship.

In all the variety and novelty recorded, even generated, by the *Fleuron*, Morison looked for – stood for – simplicity and unobtrusiveness.

To this end, there is need for obedience to the simplest possible conventions. Standardisation of display seems an ugly phrase, but uniformity has its value and the printer has no direct call to make his books objects of 'variety'. Such business as letter-press has with the eye should be discharged purely in the rôle of trained servant – the greatest of whose virtues is self-effacement. The body is more than the raiment; it is not the business of the printer to costume his text. It is not for a printer to assess the literary value of a text and to apply himself with more or less 'enthusiasm' to the task of printing it, but to exercise the craft as an efficient master of tools for the removal of any physical impediment to the understanding of the text by the reader. If printing is a combination of the work of a writer with that of a printer for the purpose of serving the community, the reader's interest is in the writer *qua* writer; and as he requires the writer to make his writing clear, he requires the printer to make his printing equally clear since he is only interested in the printer *qua* printer – demanding clearness of writing and clearness of printing for the sake of clearness of meaning. Clearness in printing makes demands upon the printer's intelligence rather than upon his emotions, upon conscientiousness rather than enthusiasm. A number of books – and the printer, least of all, can prophesy which – have a future, requiring in their printing the exercise not merely of intelligence but of foresight. Hence the supreme requirement, in a book which may circulate in the future as well as in the present, is intelligibility.

Beauty is desirable – and beauty will come if unsought. There is nothing so disastrous to typography as beauty for the sake of beauty or change for the sake of change. Mannerisms designed to reflect current philosophical tendencies are only tolerable where they are appropriate – as the waving of a signal. Such novelty as is required by reasonable exercise of the appetite for individuality should be reserved to pages whose decipherment is optional, *i.e.* display pages and the like. The apostles of the 'machine-age' will be wise to address their disciples in a standard old face – they can flourish their concrete banner in sans-serif on title-pages and perhaps in a running headline. For the rest, deliberate experiments aside, we are all, whether we like it or not, in absolute dependence upon ocular law and national custom.

The justification for the 1500 pages in which THE FLEURON has discussed typography – that admittedly minor technicality of civilised life – is not the elaboration therein of any body of typographical doctrine, any simplification of the elements of arrangement, any precising of the lessons of history, though these may have been attempted; but rather its disposition to enquire and its conviction that the teaching and example of its predecessors of the English private press movement left typography, as THE FLEURON leaves it, matter for further argument.

The Postscript concluded with an engraving of a hand shutting *Fleuron 7* firmly. It was by Gill ('What did SM say about the

Fleuron tailpiece?' he asked Beatrice, 'did he turn it down?'*).
Above it in Gill's fine capitals was the word EXPLICIT.

It was in a sense the end of the first decade of Morison's life-work.
Finishing the *Fleuron*, like editing it, was something that grew
out of the contents; it was not the long-planned *comble* that
Morison and Simon had assumed to exist. Its end came partly
because Morison had run out of ideas, partly because his official
programme at Monotype was complete, and partly because the
battle for the international recognition of fine printing was
won.* It was time to take stock of his position, and this could
best be done without the constant pressure of the *Fleuron*. So,
amid the protests of its readers, Morison put Gill's EXPLICIT on
the last page.

12

In the transition from the *Fleuron* to *The Times*, Morison had been obliged to procrastinate other commitments, like Ambrose Heal's book on the English writing masters.

Dear Heal,

I will make the W.M. the very next job. My present situation is that five weeks ago I was asked to write a treatise on the typography of The Times 1785–1930 and print and bind by end of June. This has meant working Day & night almost for several weeks & that is why you and Mr A. R. Moore (you can tell him I will fill up a chq as soon as I can find the book – For once I have the money but no cheques) have heard nothing. In fact you're lucky to 'hear' this because I don't open letters unless I recognise the hand of the writers on the env. – all typewritten letters are held up until 30 June. If I'm not too fagged then I will complete the W.M. job. In the meantime I am glad to know Cambridge is making progress. Thanx for asking me to lunch but I can't manage this week because I have to cut my lunch time very short in order to get this job done by the time; and anyhow I simply don't at the moment remember so much as the name of a single perishing writing master. If I can come another day soon I shall be a much more intelligible vis-a-vis. Don't think I'm spurning your spaghetti.

S.M.

2 June 1930

The Typography of The Times had indeed been an exacting labour, and its speed of execution impressive even given the resources of the Private Printing Office. But it was merely a prelude to the serious business of transforming the appearance of *The Times*, to which Morison now began to devote himself.

In 1930 *The Times* had begun to feel solid ground under its feet after the tempest of Lord Northcliffe. The career of Alfred

Harmsworth, 'the greatest figure who ever strode down Fleet Street' in the judgment of Lord Beaverbrook, later became a matter of absorbing interest to Morison. Northcliffe bought the controlling interest in *The Times*, at the instigation of C. F. Moberly Bell, the Managing Director, in 1908. The paper had suffered a steady decline since the death of John Walter III in 1894. The ownership was divided among the Walter descendants, and management suffered. The link with Horace Hooper (another character who fascinated Morison) only delayed the decline. His 'Century Dictionary' and *Encyclopaedia Britannica* promotions had introduced *The Times* to modern advertising techniques, but had precipitated the 'Book War' with the publishers over *The Times*'s offer to sell books direct to the public at a discount below published price.

Northcliffe began quietly. He put an end to the Book War. He did not alter the editorial character of the paper, but concentrated on its mechanics. It was he who in 1909 replaced the Kastenbein composing machines with Monotype machines, and he who instigated the series of Special Numbers of which the 1912 Printing Supplement was the most spectacular. Moberly Bell's sudden death in 1911 removed the restraints on Northcliffe. Buckle, who had been editor since 1884, retired. The price of the paper was cut from threepence to a penny, and the gamble succeeded: the circulation shot up. With the war, Northcliffe's energy was diverted to other ends: propaganda, securing finance for the war from America, to run the Government without being part of it, but at the end of the war the pace at *The Times* grew hotter. The new editor, Dawson, resigned to be replaced by Wickham Steed in 1919. The crescendo came to an abrupt end when Northcliffe went mad and died in 1922. Steed left; Dawson returned; life went back to its normal pace.

The new proprietors were John Walter IV, who used the family option to defeat a counterbid from Lord Rothermere, and Major the Hon. John J. Astor, who put up the money for the purchase of Northcliffe's shares and became Chief Proprietor. The independence of the paper was guaranteed by an *ex officio* committee of notables who must approve any sale of the controlling interest. There was a general reversion to the earlier traditions of *The Times*, and, although the layout and heading style had been brought up to date during the Northcliffe era, it was not inappropriate, in Morison's words, that the typography of *The Times* in 1930 should 'recall the early Victorian manner'.*

Morison himself never wrote a complete account of the year's work that followed the publication of the Printing Supplement, but the general drift is clear from *Printing The Times*. There had already been a considerable revolution in newspaper typography when, in 1926, Ionic first appeared. This was a face specially adapted by the American Linotype Company to withstand hard use in newspapers, particularly the pressures of stereotyping to make plates for modern rotary presses. It was basically a sort of modern face like *The Times*'s, but with all the thin strokes thickened and slab instead of hairline serifs. It was already in use by the *New York Times* and *Herald-Tribune*, and spread rapidly in England and elsewhere. Morison implies that there were already objections to it in the house, on the grounds that it was uneconomical (it has a 'wide set': that is, it is wide in relation to its height) and vulgar.* He may or may not have shared these views: if so, he was shrewd enough to suppress them. The two types used for the early experiments that he referred to in his article in the Printing Supplement were Intertype 'Ideal' and Linotype 'Excelsior', both closely resembling Ionic.*

It is impossible to say whether these were chosen out of a spirit of open-minded enquiry, or as an ingenious foil to better and different types – whether indeed they were chosen by Morison at all. But, with his connection with Monotype, it is not to be supposed that he did not hope it would be possible to adopt or adapt one of the designs he had promoted there. It is unlikely that he found much opposition to the idea. So, after experiments with two types, not as yet used in England, but made specifically for newspapers, three book faces were tried out, Plantin, Baskerville, and Perpetua, and a third newspaper face, Ionic itself.* The scope of the investigation was thus considerably widened.

All these faces were subjected to the same tests. A specimen setting of each in the current style of *The Times* was moulded and stereotyped, and the plates printed in the normal way. This stage was probably reached not later than mid-October 1930. By this time Morison was ready. At an office conference on 24 October he formally proposed 'that the type faces used in the editorial and advertising columns of *The Times* be redesigned and brought up to the standard obtaining in the average book as brought out by London publishers'.* At this meeting, the Manager appointed a committee to consider the proposal, under the chairmanship of R. M. Barrington-Ward, consisting of Harold Child, Colonel J. A. Jenkins, F. P. Bishop, Dr R. M. Wilson, A. A. Barnes and F. G. Easto.

Of these, Harold Child was an old friend. Actor turned Shakespearean scholar, leader-writer and critic, his connection with *The Times* went back to 1902 when he helped Bruce Richmond to start *The Times Literary Supplement*. He was also a founder member of the Double Crown Club and a contributor to the *Fleuron*. The others were more directly involved in the organizational changes involved by a change of type, except for the chairman of the Committee.

R. M. Barrington-Ward was now thirty-nine to Morison's forty-one. He had originally come to *The Times* straight from Oxford in 1913, had left after the war for a period as assistant editor of the *Observer*, and rejoined *The Times* in 1927 as an assistant editor to Dawson. The editor's original intention had been that he would deal with home affairs, but the unexpected retirement of two of the foreign staff gave him an extra opening, and Dawson came quickly to rely on his judgement. A man of rapid decision and great energy, he still found time on his hands, at any rate until 1934 when on the retirement of Murray Brumwell he became Deputy Editor. He was to be the most powerful and energetic supporter of Morison's proposals, and became his closest friend on the staff of the paper.

But before the Committee met, Morison summarized his remarks at the meeting in a note to Lints Smith on 29 October.

My proposal, therefore, is that to the very best mechanical skill, already available in *The Times'* office, there shall be added, in place of the early Victorian founts which *The Times* has used for so many years, a new body of text and heading types.

These new types, or type, since with minute variations they would all be of the same root design, would be selected *not* with a view to their being of striking, but rather of subtle allure. The face would be chosen for its effectiveness as much as for its 'beauty'; the criteria of effectiveness being a maximum of clearness in impression and a maximum of legibility to the reader who neither knows nor cares, one way or the other, for the mysteries of typographical minutiae.

This statement of the problem, he went on, was unlikely to be found objectionable, but there would be considerable discussion of the design itself. 'I am going to suggest, therefore, to you, Sir, that authority be given for the compilation by me of what I will call an Articulation of the Problem.' Morison had clearly developed a rather Early Victorian manner with Lints Smith: what he wanted was 'a dozen proofs of a memorandum' printed at the Private Printing Office.

The contents of this memorandum were to be divided into two parts: historical and practical. The first would indicate the 'ideal typography' in a survey of typographical changes from 1480 to 1880, the 'date' in Morison's view of *The Times*'s existing typography. He would then show how much change there had been elsewhere in the last fifty years and how little at *The Times*. The practical section promises a text type in four sizes (small pica, bourgeois, minion and ruby); types for headings, with variation in colour; strengthening for the departmental headings (Law Report, etc); and an argument for the romanization of the main heading on the front page. To this Morison was to attach specimens of the existing types, alphabets of the new text and headings types and a suggestion for the front page heading.

It will, I hope, be found that my proposals are simple, in that they are all based on one, and not several, root type forms (capitals and lower-case); that that simple design, being of maximum elasticity, permits the necessary variation in strength to support the desirability of freeing the important pages from monotony; and finally that the design will accommodate itself, to the greatest possible extent, to the moulds and existing mechanical equipment in the office.

As, in my experience, even exhaustive discussion fails to remove a certain hesitancy to put a revised typography into action, the committee might like to call for the opinion of the printers to the universities of Oxford and Cambridge.

I perhaps ought to say that I do not think the compilation of this memorandum will take more than three weeks, so that the first meeting of the committee could take place, let us say, on Wednesday, the 26th November. (i.e. a week after the circulation of the Memorandum.)

This private note to Lints Smith is particularly interesting because it is much more specific than the *Memorandum on a Proposal to Revise the Typography of* The Times *1930* itself. The *Memorandum* is a substantial quarto of thirty-eight pages. Its layout is interesting: Baskerville for the text, with eye-catching shoulder headings in the wide margins set in Plantin capitals; lettering and types are illustrated in mass and in detail.

Its aim was to provide 'some sort of background against which any new fount may be placed – and judged'. It dealt largely with the history of the 'roman' letter from Alcuin, and the history, nature and structure of printing type. The experiments of John Walter I were respectfully mentioned, and the new type of his contemporary John Bell. The last century of newspaper typography was sketched, the defects of *The Times*'s present types contrasted with those used in contemporary books, and current developments in type-design were related to medical research on legibility. (The Medical Research Council had published its 'Report on the Legibility of Print' in 1926, and its findings were used to support Morison's argument.)

Centuries earlier, when forms were less established, it might have been possible to alter the shapes of letters: now, Morison argues, it is only possible to play with the serifs (an essential feature of the legibility, as well as the 'character', of a letter).

It is in this manipulation of serif that the human appetite for variety finds its satisfaction. For reasons already made clear no alteration in essential form stands the slightest chance of acceptance by any printer of books or newspapers. There remains the serif, in the designing of which the typefounders swing from one extreme to the other – from the coarseness of a blunt Venetian to the sharpness of ultra-Bodoni. At the moment the pendulum is moving in the direction of old-face.

It may be prophesied that the pendulum will swing back to the 'modern' serif in another twenty years. The new types proposed for *The Times* will tend towards the 'modern', though the body of the letter will be more or less old-face in appearance. . . .

It is hoped that the experimental fount now in preparation for scrutiny by the Committee will have at least the merit of being free from all that is academic or 'arty'. Type should not ape calligraphy; it should, first and last, look like type, but good type – *i.e.*, good for its purpose. It follows that in all this welter of thicks and thins, slab-serifs and bracketed serifs, &c., a knowledge of the purpose of the type affords a valid criterion of its suitability. Most types have all sorts of uses, whereas the fount now being considered has only one. It is proposed to use it for the text of the editorial portion of the paper and, if approved, to revise the headings according to the same design.*

The tone is impartial, detached, even Olympian. The new design itself is not described in detail, and it is possible to trace signs of two possible proposals. When Morison began to write the *Memorandum*, it seems as if – however careful he was to suppress his own view – Baskerville was his choice. It leads the table of type-faces used in the 'Fifty Best Books' of 1929, and Morison is at pains to point out that its popularity is due not to 'any artistic, stylistic or archaistic association', but 'its broad legibility, liberality and John Bullish poise'. Only one newspaper face had been 'adapted' since *The Times*'s current types, the American Ionic. 'The Ionic', Morison noted, 'is also used outside America – the *Brisbane Courier* and other Antipodean newspapers employ it. It is also used increasingly for the composition of certain French newspapers.' Since Morison's purpose in writing the *Memorandum* was 'to assist the Committee towards the adoption of a fount which shall be in English in its basic tradition, new, though free from conscious archaism or conscious art', it cannot be doubted what his preference was.* Confirmation is to be found in the article he wrote subsequently for *The Times House Journal*, in which he acknowledges that 'at one stage Baskerville was highly favoured'.*

On the other hand, in the only place where Morison approaches a technical description of the new type, it is clear that he was not thinking of Baskerville. In discussing legibility he had distinguished between the bracketed 'old face' serif, and the unbracketed 'modern' serif: 'The new types proposed for *The Times* will tend towards the "modern", though the body of the letter will be more or less old-face in appearance.' This cannot apply to Baskerville, and of the types so far considered would be most applicable to Perpetua.* The cutting of Perpetua had occupied Morison for the last five years, and it was the first original design that he had sponsored; it was, moreover, completely English in inspiration and execution.

It was on 10 November, after Morison's note to Lints Smith but before the first meeting of the Committee, that the Monotype works at Salford received instructions about a modified Perpetua: '10 pt to be made to go on 9 pt body. Large and wide as poss: reducing ascenders and descenders. Urgent.'* It may seem curious that there is no mention of this, or any other specific type, in the *Memorandum*. But this would be to misconstrue its purpose. The *Memorandum* was Morison's artillery barrage: the battle was decided by the infantry attack. No note survives of the proofs and specimens or of the informal discussions that went with them. Twenty-five copies of the *Memorandum* were printed on 21 November, but, faced with this massive document, the Committee's first meeting, due on 26 November, was postponed.

This delay may have been to suit Morison's convenience. The programme he had set himself at the end of October had been tight, even at his normal speed. At all events, experiments were still continuing with Perpetua, 'when Plantin and Baskerville, Ideal and Excelsior had been rejected'. On 8 December, further modifications were requested, but the disadvantage of Perpetua as it stood was that it needed too much space above and below the line. The attempt to fit a large face on a small body resulted in painful constriction: 'The Perpetua stared at the reader.' Morison was forced to admit that, like Ionic, it was 'too basically circular', too wide, to be economic for newspaper use.* The altered Perpetua may have been a final expedient to make use of an existing face, produced perhaps after the *Memorandum* but before the first meeting of the Committee, now fixed for 28 January. By then, however, Morison had moved on to the idea from which the Times New Roman was finally developed. He probably went to the meeting armed not only with the arguments against the existing types, but also with two ideas, not one, for a new type.

Morison did not believe in surprises at meetings: he brought no new design on 28 January, only a number of settings in 'recognized founts'. After discussion, six conclusions were reached: a new headings type would be necessary; a new text type must appear to be larger; it must not, however, take up more space; in consequence, it must be either taller (more condensed) or have more colour; it must have the 'squareness' traditional to *The Times* (i.e. it must fill the body, which none of the types hitherto tried had done), and it must be the exclusive property of *The Times*. Barrington-Ward's minutes, succinct and to the point, concluded with a brief for Morison, based (no doubt) on what he had told the Committee of his new experiments:

The Committee therefore asked Mr Morison to prepare
   (a) A specimen of 'modernised Plantin', i.e. Plantin approximated to present *Times* practice, with sharper serifs
   (b) A specimen of thickened Perpetua.
The Committee, on the whole, preferred Plantin as a basis as being nearer *The Times* tradition. The Committee understood that it would take Mr Morison about two months to procure the modified types.*

As will be seen, Morison dropped the idea of further modifying Perpetua, and concentrated on the 'modernised Plantin'. From his own account of this, his intention was to sharpen up the even lines and blunt serifs of the normal Plantin, which stereotyped badly, to give greater contrast of line and sharper serifs, as in Perpetua.* He did not, as might be thought, use 'Monotype' Plantin as the basis for the new letter. He said himself that he 'pencilled the original set of drawings, and handed them to Victor Lardent, a draughtsman in the Publicity Department whom he considered capable of producing an unusually firm and clean line'.* According to Lardent,* Morison handed him 'a photographic copy of a page of a book printed by Plantin to use as a basis', from which Lardent drew a series of alphabets, each successively amended by Morison till he got the effect he wanted.

What was 'the page of the book printed by Plantin'? This poses a very interesting problem. The type on which the Monotype Plantin was based was the text type of the *Index Characterum* of 1905. This is the 'Gros Cicero' of the famous French punch-cutter Robert Granjon, originally cut *c.* 1568 and much used for two centuries after. It is a type that fits the Committee's prescription exactly, being large for its body with the long letters correspondingly shortened, but economical in horizontal space. But Plantin himself never used it in its entirety: he took the shortened extenders only to adapt his existing Garamond face ('St Augustin') for the smaller body. The whole fount was only acquired by Plantin's successors, the Moretus family, after 1652. Even then, the fount was contaminated with some wrong letters of later date, which were reproduced in Monotype Plantin. The final form of the Times New Roman corresponds very closely with the pristine form of Granjon's 'Gros Cicero', which is first to be seen in use by a number of printers in Cologne, Basle and Frankfurt about 1570. It was probably a book printed by one of these, rather than by Plantin or his successors that Morison used as the basis for Lardent to work on.*

The process of drawing, correcting and redrawing must have been a long one, even for so skilful a draughtsman as Lardent. It was not until 8 April that the bourgeois (9pt) was put in hand with Monotype; the minion (7pt) and ruby (5½pt) followed on 27 April. Modifications and adjustments followed, but by the end of May, specimens of all three sizes were ready.* On 4 June, the next meeting of the Committee on Typography was held.

Morison explained that he had only proceeded with one of the two designs, the 'modernised Plantin' that the Committee had preferred. He had had a leader page and a bill page set, showing all three sizes, with specimens of the new titling. The Committee approved them all. They preferred the 9pt to be cast on a size larger body (long primer), but 'this can be done the more easily because the new type occupies less space than the type now in use'. The minion and ruby sizes were unreservedly approved, the headings were 'on the right lines', and Barrington-Ward's minutes concluded with a general approval: 'The design of the new types generally is dignified and not precious and offers a simpler form of letter than we now use.' There was no need to invoke the Printers to the universities of Oxford and Cambridge. The Committee adjourned *sine die*, submitting their conclusions to the Manager and Editor for consideration. 'It will be a big change if we make it,' Barrington-Ward noted in his diary.*

There was, however, a problem yet to be solved. It was outside the Committee's terms of reference, and it was to prove more intractable than the type itself. Implicit, in Morison's view, in the change of the text type was the change from gothic to roman for the title on the front page. He had said as much in his note to Lints Smith. He now set about it, as he had with the text type, by writing and printing an impressive document, *Supplement to the Memorandum on a Proposal to Revise the Typography of* 𝕿𝔥𝔢 𝕿𝔦𝔪𝔢𝔰 *1931*. There was a strong opinion in the paper that the black-letter title was *The Times*'s trademark: to substitute roman would be to destroy not only good will but an essential part of the paper's character. The issue was an emotional one, and it was further clouded by controversy about the inaccuracy of the royal device, and the double rules enclosing the issue number, date and price. It was not likely that Morison's reasoned arguments, set forth on 12 June 1931, would be eagerly accepted.

Morison, over-confident, was not disposed to take the problem seriously. The conservative were not soothed to have their prejudices taken back to Strawberry Hill, to the time 'when the mid-century taste for sham medieval ruins, so evocative of the mood of poetic pensiveness, had developed, at its best, into a cheerful relish for turrets, pinnacles and such fripperies; and, at its worst, into a stale mixed grill of overdone gothick, underdone chinoiserie with a garnish of Louis Quatorze'. In 1788, when the *Daily Universal Register* became *The Times*, the title was in decent roman capitals. But within three months John Walter changed it to imitate a rival. Morison enjoyed John Bell's colleague Captain Topham as a character, but he deplored the *World*'s taste in titling. 'For the first time a piece of gothic text was tricked out with an utterly damnable white line which turned the traditional, masculine black-letters into a set of beastly soft characters only too consistent with a degenerate background of paste-board pinnacles and bogus battlements.' He pursued *The Times*'s imitation of the *World* to the present, ending that if a redrawing of it were now required 'it is unlikely that the desire could be satisfied by any living English artist, architect, or scribe'; it would have to be a joint work. 'The result would probably be mid-way between the *bondieuserie* of the church furnisher, the heading of the *Berliner Tageblatt*, and the label of *Châteauneuf du Pape*.'

Morison also asserted, more dubiously, that the removal of one of the double rules would strike the reader more than the change of title lettering. On top of all this, the heraldry of the Royal Arms was all wrong, and there was only one solution: 'to range a well-cut, correctly drawn Royal Device between the title set in disciplined roman capitals of the utmost simplicity'. Morison had injudiciously shown a sample device (one of five commissioned – another was forced out of a young art student called Ronald Horton whom Morison had recently got to know) by Harold Stabler, designed on correct heraldic principles. This was pilloried at once. He had not shown a sample of the title lettering he recommended, and on this argument continued.

Beatrice had gone to visit her family in New York, and Morison reported to her.

Dear P,

There is nothing to report except that all things are going satisfactory here and at P.H.S. The Roman Head Mystery is not yet
solved but a full conventual lunch is to be held next Fri. with the
Major in the chair and – so I am 'tipped off' – the change is to be
aired before the whole house. The l.c. italic & small caps are due.
Lints S. visits Horley on Monday. W.I.B. will be in attendance. . . .
Since you left I have not seen much of life and nothing of engines
or theologians only type specimens. When The Times job is finished
I shall go in for an older enthusiasm than them all – Chemistry or
something unconnected with type.

On 14 July, the Tuesday before the meeting, he wrote again. Lints
Smith's visit to the works with Burch had been a great success.
But he was apprehensive about Friday. W. H. Smith who had
promised to recommend the roman heading had done the
reverse: 'I am unlikely to get it through'. But on Friday evening
itself he was jubilant.

Dear P

The meeting at P.H.S. in the presence of J.J.A. lasted from 1.30
to 3.45 today and occupied itself with the question of the heading on
the front page. S.M. spoke . . . and . . . I'm told that mine was a
brilliant, enjoyable and convincing effort, witty and final, etc. . . .
Bruce Richmond whom I saw at ice hadn't read my memo but did
so at once and spoke after me, dotting my i's & [crossing] my
t's . . . next Barrington Ward. It is the consensus ecclesiae that Lints
S was converted. The matter of the device of the royal arms was
decided in favour of allowing me to do what I wished in the matter.
That delivered them all into my hand.

I have to rush this in a steam of perspiration and suppressed excitement. I am glad to have the device settled . . . the rest will follow.

He was still elated three days later.

I went to King's X to see the Flying Scotsman off on the first trip
of the Non Stop schedule commencing 20 July. Completely fresh
painted train, all with mint new destination boards & the 4472
brilliantly cleaned up, sparkling in the sun, pressmen all around like
flies & a cop on the platform to keep the likes o' me off the metals.

But all was not over; on 27 July Barrington-Ward addressed a powerful note to the Editor and Manager, advocating a change in the main title on general not typographic grounds. The public, he said, would be shocked, but the shock would be good for *The Times* both internally and externally. And, however shocked they were, it was highly improbable that readers would cancel their orders on an issue like this. It would liberate *The Times* from the plagiary of the *Sunday Times*, the Times Furnishing Company and so on. Altogether it would give the paper a valuable reputation for modernity, taste and efficiency. Further ammunition for the change came from the favourable report on the legibility of the new type from Sir William Lister (30 June), which Morison communicated to Lints Smith and Barrington-Ward to Dawson.

On 29 July there was what Barrington-Ward called 'a strange lunch' at *The Times*. Besides most of the Board and the staff concerned, there were present Lord Crawford, Lord Lee of Fareham, Sir Malcolm Robertson, John Buchan and St John Hornby. 'They mostly approved the type. But they divided on the title. Buchan and Hornby were for it; Lee and Robertson were vehemently but not very intelligently against it. It all helped to clear our own mind.'* Next day there was a board meeting, at which Morison and Barrington-Ward (to whom Morison gave the credit for the accepted solution of the title problem*) were called in. The conclusions of the Committee on Typography were unanimously approved, although the alteration of the heading was only 'on the whole favoured in principle by those present'. Morison undertook 'to prepare sketches based upon the original title lettering'. A decision was held over until September for further soundings to be taken, especially among the staff.* Morison was jubilant again, and cabled Beatrice: 'BOARD DIRECTORS AND ALL EDITORIAL EMINENTISSIMI UNANIMOUS ROMAN HEADING.'

On 10 August, Barrington-Ward, forcing the issue a little, sent a detailed programme for the change to the Chairman, Editor, Manager, Kent (Deputy Manager), Brumwell, Morison and Child. This involved a regular programme of announcement in the paper, advertisements, and, following the change, special arrangements for dealing with correspondence pro and contra. Finally, Barrington-Ward sent to the same seven a copy of a long and enthusiastic critique of the new design by Sir John Fortescue, the former Royal Librarian. It ended: 'The first or title page will be a difficulty but not insuperable. Oh, that my kinsman, Adrian Fortescue, were alive to take it in hand. He was the finest calligraphist and one of the best heraldic designers in England.' It might – may – be Morison speaking.

But when September came there were further delays. 'It was decided to postpone our circulation campaign and new type until after the Election – probably until January,' Barrington-Ward noted on 16 September. No further progress was made at the board meetings on 24 September and 8 October. Morison was depressed and ill. He went to Tangier to write and recover. It brought back one long-forgotten memory: 'This is a sort of John the Baptist place – without the water. Note the two types of 1^d red surcharge – about the only luxury I've observed here.'*

During the rest of 1931, the new equipment necessary was laid in. An order was placed with Monotype for matrices and new keyboard equipment, amounting to nearly £2000.* This was delivered over the next four months, ending with the smallest sizes of bold type in December. A similar order went to the Linotype and Intertype companies for a total of seventeen founts of each size in September costing about £4000. These, too, were delivered by the end of the year. But then argument about the title flared up again. The board meeting on 7 December reached an impasse, and directors were asked to state their opinions to the secretary in writing before the next meeting. The most eloquent of the opponents was John Walter, who felt very strongly that 'the Gothic letter *means The Times*', and that good will would be sacrificed with it. In any case he preferred it to 'the unadorned plainness of the resurrected form'. Dawson put in a moderately phrased but cogent approval of all the new forms, but urged the importance of unanimity. On 7 January, the board minuted its approval of the changes in type, but still deferred decision on the heading, noting John Walter's dissent from the majority view.

Then followed another long pause. On 3 May, Morison's *The English Newspaper* was published, and it received an enthusiastic review in *The Times*, which ended by pointing to the recent revolution in book typography and added 'similar forces could be brought to bear on newspapers'. In a leader, Barrington-Ward put the point even more forcefully. 'Everybody must be affected', he wrote, 'by the physical appearance of the papers he reads.'

Though the aesthetic problem changes, it is always in the self-respecting craftsman's mind; and however exacting are its standards, the better kind of typographer tries to live up to them. To a large extent it rests with the reader to back him when he experiments conscientiously and *secundum artem*; but the reader, curiously enough, as Mr Morison shows, is not always the best judge of his own interests.

But the board were not to be hurried.

John Walter's hereditary position gave his opinion great influence, and Astor was plainly anxious to avoid hurting him. At the end of June, the change was still not settled, and Astor wrote privately to Robert Brand at Lazard's and Sir Guy Granet, chairman of the L.M.S. Railway, both directors of *The Times*, asking for their advice in his dilemma.* Both replied urging him not to stand in the way of progress. At the June board meeting, the Manager reminded directors that the changes, if made, must be made together, and a final decision was held over for the next meeting. Meanwhile plans were being laid for the change on 3 October. The final board meeting was held on 22 July and the decision to change was finally made. One of those absent on this occasion, Ralph Walter, declared his views in a long letter which summarizes the cross-currents and feelings very well. While approving the change, he sympathized with the dissentients, and rebukes as 'special pleading' the advocates who claimed publicity as one of the by-products of the change – a reflection on the point made by Barrington-Ward.

But the decision was now final, and Barrington-Ward hastened, on 3 August, to confirm and elaborate the plans he had sketched a year earlier, working out in detail the plans for announcing the change in the paper and elsewhere, to the trade and to the public. A pamphlet was to be printed, which appeared as *Printing The Times: A Record of the Changes Introduced in the Issue for October 3, 1932*, in which Morison's views were summarized in magisterial style. Finally, £7500 was to be expended on press advertising.

At the beginning of September, Morison sent Barrington-Ward a complete trial paper, on which he commented in detail. These suggestions were adopted but as the day grew closer, Morison clearly became apprehensive. In a note to Lints Smith on 13 September, he expresses his concern about that morning's dummy run and wonders whether the foundry is at fault. There was a last-minute order for two more sizes of titling from Monotype. But these and other misadventures were dealt with and on Tuesday, 27 September, six days before the change, Easto was able to report that all was ready. The last matrices came in the day before, and the final specimens were to be ready on Thursday. A poster press was reserved until Monday. Special ink for the new paper had been supplied and the presses were to be cleaned and reclothed over the weekend before the change. Any number up to 265,000 could be printed.*

On that Tuesday also Barrington-Ward stayed all day at the office, writing a leader about the change for the following Monday. On Friday night all the Monotype and eight Intertype machines were changed over, the other Intertypes following by stages. By Saturday morning, the signboard on the roof, the glass panels on the clock in Queen Victoria Street, the circular plates on the front door, the small plates on each side of the main entrance, the headings for the four notice boards for small advertisements, and the enamelled signs in Printing House Square, Ireland Yard and Playhouse Yard, were all taken down or changed.* That evening, Barrington-Ward, annoyed by a report in 'a dirty little Fleet St rag, called the World's Press News' that he had engineered and fought for the change for a year, went down to watch more of the Intertypes changed over.* And on Sunday night, 'all the office hierarchy' were there to see the machines start. Major Astor pressed the button (see Plate 11).

It's too early to be confident yet, but it does look as if The Times change were going to be a huge success. It happened Monday, after the most feverish week of my life. Lots to do about it here, and hanging over all that sense of irrevocability, enormousness, earth-quake. Short and very intensive preparation of the public's mind. Prayers (the B. Thomas More, whom I love, was tipped off very early) and sweatings.

And today's paper – well, read what the readers say. And it really represents the majority reaction.

In as few days from now as he can manage, Morison is going abroad for just about the well-est earned holiday that a man ever had. He is as thin as a knife, but has been as cool as a lily all through it. I really think the man is a saint, complete with Invisible Means of Support. The only thing that worries him is getting his name suppressed in connection with the affair. But that isn't saint, that's *Times*.

So Beatrice wrote home on the Tuesday after. St John Hornby and Walter Lewis both had long letters of praise in the paper she sent, and there was only one complaint from a retired army officer. Gordon Selfridge joined in the praise, and Humphrey Milford, Roger Fry and Enid Moberly Bell, daughter of the last managing director, all wrote privately to the Editor. Oliver Simon and Mardersteig sent their congratulations to Morison: both guessed that it had not been the design but 'getting the thing actually carried out' that was the triumph; 'you must have had some thrilling days while it was being done', said Mardersteig.* Nobody noticed (despite Morison's predictions) that one of the rules on the front page had been removed.

When Morison got back, there was a celebration banquet at the Dorchester to celebrate the change ('Types Change') and the tenth year of Astor's Chief Proprietorship ('Companionship

Stands'). Some 200 people were there, including all the members of the Committee, and Burch among the visitors. Morison was among those who spoke. 'Speeches on a high level, brief and witty,' noted Barrington-Ward, who enjoyed himself.*

One letter arrived at *The Times* very late, being written on 2 November. It was from Paul Standard, then unknown to Morison, who wrote perceptively: 'The design itself looks like the result of collaboration between Stanley Morison and Eric Gill.' Morison drafted the reply sent by Kent. It was formal and not communicative: 'it remains only to repeat that the design was made in Printing House Square without outside assistance'. The preference for anonymity that Morison had learnt from Gerard Meynell was now already fortified by identification with *The Times*.

But 1932 was not the end of the reform of *The Times*'s typography. There were countless details still to be put right, and new problems to be met and put right. The last of these concerned the middle size of text type. Morison had privately felt that the minion was too small, and in 1934 began to press for the size to be increased from 7pt to 7½pt. Easto expostulated that the new matrices would cost £3000,* but Morison persisted. The estimate was found to be only £1800, and on 30 March 1936 Barrington-Ward, always warm in support, wrote to Lints Smith giving the Editor's approval of the change. The change was approved on 2 April* and when the new size was introduced Morison wrote to Lints Smith.

THE TIMES
15 June 1936

Dear Lints Smith

This day witnesses the incorporation into *The Times* of the 7½pt. which finally completes the typographical reformation of P.H.S.

It has taken exactly seven years to do this job. All this time I have had your constant guidance & support. It is proper for me to send a word of thanks.

Perhaps I am better able now than formerly to estimate the difficulties – or some of them. At any rate I realize that I owe you a great debt of gratitude for the generosity with which you, all the time, treated our scheme; and not the scheme only – but also me personally.

I take this occasion therefore to thank you most cordially for the unstinted cooperation you have given me.

Yours
Stanley Morison

Since then, 'The Times' New Roman has become the most universally used of all Morison's types. The qualities that dictated its form, its economy and legibility in small sizes, have found for it markets, notably in complex technical books and magazines, far beyond the demands of *The Times* which it was originally designed to meet. Its popularity never ceased to astonish and delight its creator.

13

'MORISON is still in the land of the living, and I understand very busy, which probably may be the reason why you have not heard from him recently. Whilst at times his head may be in the clouds, I am glad to say that his feet still rest on terra firma.' So Burch wrote to Robert Blake on 12 December 1929, to explain a pause in the fascinating quest for the original matrices for the types made by Richard Austin for John Bell, and the even earlier script types of Ichabod Dawks, Bell's seventeenth-century predecessor. (Morison owed this discovery to Harold Child; he had also just bought a notebook used by Ichabod's father Thomas Dawks and Ichabod himself, and was in consequence planning another book.)

The last three years at *The Times* had at times distracted Morison from his old friends and haunts. But he still largely maintained the diversity of acquaintance that he had accumulated in the last ten years. He kept up with his political friends. Asked for 'something that is in the Proletarian tradition of the Nineties' for the Marxist Library series published by Martin Lawrence, he undertook to 'put up a Jacket from which you can copy for henceforth' at the Fanfare. His old friend from Wakefield Prison days, Walter Holmes, had moved from the *Daily Herald* to the *Daily Worker* when it was started in 1926; there he produced the 'Worker's Diary' with a heading in the fine italic hand that he had learnt from Morison in prison. Morison kept in touch with the *Worker*, sending such useful cannon fodder as a 'catalogue of furs' which 'might be reviewed' in suitable terms.* He was the natural person to ask for a new titlepiece for the paper. The *Worker* had become a tabloid on 1 January 1930, with an unsatisfactory shaded title. Morison now chose a version of Gill Sans Bold, which he had engraved on wood by T. N. Lawrence with the hammer and sickle superimposed on it. He was soon able to report to Pollard:

This is the first state of the block for the *Daily Worker*. You will notice that the capitals are shorter than those at present in use. This will allow more space over the headings where you can put in more and more slogans as well as late London edition.*

Pollard himself called at *The Times* to collect the final version, which he delivered by hand to the *Worker*. The new title was introduced on 1 May, appropriately, when the paper became a broadsheet again; it was used for two years.*

Beatrice was making a new life for herself. Her talents as a teacher and publicist were blossoming; Dandridge had commissioned her to write a book for the L.N.E.R. on England for American visitors. She was modelling for Gill who had used her for the 'Belle Sauvage' engravings he did as a device for Cassell's the publishers. She had also met Cleverdon and Miss Brownlee – this conjunction had suggested a new enterprise. After spending Christmas 1929 at Bristol, she wrote to Gill:

I enclose some proofs of Brownie's work. There was not enough light to take instantaneous snaps, so we tried a few poses involving contortions which couldn't be held for more than a few seconds, or positions which, held upside down, might give an idea of flight. The ones you particularly want must await a bright day, and I ought to see you before trying to get them with a camera. I've written to ask Brownie for a set of darker proofs to show every shadow.

I've just got my big L.N.E.R. job finished, with some loss of sleep. I long to reach the haven of Pigott's and sanity, with time to soak off the grime of publicity in the Well of Truth.*

She kept her family posted of Morison's doings. 'It's beginning to be wintery here now, just in time to discourage the crocuses,' she wrote on 20 March. 'Morison is addressing the Double Crown Club tonight on one Ichabod Dawks, an early newspaper proprietor. His John Bell Book is going to be a sensation.'*

So indeed it was, when it came out in June. *The Times* gave it the lead review, clearly written by a friendly hand, who, after noting that it was 'printed in a fount new cast' from the original matrices of Bell's type, added: 'And, though the book is characteristic of Mr Morison in the mingling of text and illustrations, collotypes, and what not, the whole is as informative as it is beautiful.' The *Literary Supplement* acclaimed its 'significance beyond that of its highly competent specialisation'.

It was indeed Morison's first excursion outside the confines of printing and calligraphy, and he handled the new themes of publishing and politics, clubs and clergy, newspapers and the theatre, easily and well. The book itself, with its engravings, colour prints and facsimiles, and the high standard of composition and presswork at Cambridge, was 'a revelation'.* A. J. A. Symons was among those impressed by it, and he arranged for 100 of the 300 copies printed to be reserved for his First Edition Club. These were issued to members, and a celebratory exhibition was held at the Club's rooms in Bedford Square, at which many of the newspapers and books that Morison and Pollard had discovered were exhibited. It was opened in April 1931 by a new friend, Lord Riddell, chairman of the *News of the World*, who was very impressed by Morison.*

The First Edition Club also helped to publish (and Cambridge printed) Ambrose Heal's *The English Writing-Masters and their Copy Books 1570–1800*, a majestic folio of nearly 300 pages amply illustrated, which finally appeared in August 1931. After repeated delays, Morison had completed the introduction, his first comprehensive account of post-renaissance calligraphy. Heal had been a little clumsy in the matter of payment for what he regarded as six years' hard work; Morison looked at it differently:

November 10, 1930

Dear Heal,

You are not so much businesslike as business-man-like in your letter today. There was nothing perverse about my answer to your very decent suggestion. The reason I take the line I do about these things is because I am not a literary gent. In other words, I do not depend upon writing for my living. If I did, I should get as much out of you as I possibly could – that would be business. There is nothing a business man hates more than to be under an obligation; he thinks money was invented in order to give him the right to rationalise and to mechanise personal relations. That is why it comes about that a man can paint a picture which can be 'bought' from the artist [for] X and sold by business men to each other for 500 X. When I take money from business men, I feel that I am supporting this sort of system. However, I should be very sorry if you felt that the world was going wrong because I had principles different from those which are not only ruling but ruining the world. I know you make a point of 'paying' for what you have. I am quite sure that you think, that all these arrangements are the fairest possible in view of market conditions for which you are not responsible. Don't think for a single second that I have any snobbery about money. I need and will get more than you will ever think of giving me, but I prefer to get it in my own way. As far as I know, I have never made a penny by selling books that have been presented to me; I have never made any money out of the books that I have written or shall write.

As far as your book is concerned, there are two points which are important. The first is that not only are you not publishing the book in order to make a profit, but in all probability there will be none. Secondly, my liking to write an Introduction to your or anybody else's book entirely depends upon whether I like the idea or not, and if I do I will write the Introduction whether I am paid or not. I have incurred expenses to the extent of £9. 10. 0 on this business, and if you feel that you would like to pay these, I should be quite happy to allow you to do so, and to consider the whole affair satisfactorily settled.

I think Hewitt's book is certainly deserving of shelf room in your library.

Yours
Stanley Morison

Morison's retort may have been sharpened by his sense of guilt at not finishing his part earlier. When the book came out, he was generous, although fearful that it would not be appreciated by modern devotees of the italic hand, who would have none of the old copper-plate masters. 'It is a true and worthy monument to them,' he wrote, 'and by shouldering all that labour and expense you have earned more gratitude and respect than you'll ever receive from this generation. On the contrary, I can envisage a severe-but-more-in-sorrow-than-in-anger attack on the book being made by Graily H[ewitt].'*

Next day he got a letter from Heal to enquire if the book had come, and he wrote again to apologize – 'wanted to write with a pen instead of through G.E.A. and her Royal Typewriter'.

Dawks will not be out until Oct 1 – my delay in passing an appendix I decided to go in for. I will send you a copy when it is available but you will find it all excruciatingly dull. . . . I am in the thick of a nauseating job, of immense detail, analysing the London Newspaper 1520 to 1920 . . . also a dull job, and I am knee-high in cuttings. I wish I had an electric filing system wh. wd produce a *Morning Post* of Nov 1772 and a *London Diurnale* of 1642 at a moment's notice!*

The 'nauseating job' was the Sandars Lectures in Bibliography at Cambridge, which Morison had been invited to give in 1932. At the end of 1930, Graham Pollard had enquired what his subject was to be. 'The effect which epigraphic lettering has had upon modern calligraphy, and both upon typography, in medieval and modern times,' Morison told him.* But this was not to be: that massive topic was to be reserved for another thirty years and the Lyell lectures, the sister foundation at Oxford. The history of newspapers, what with Bell, Dawks and *The Times*, came now more easily to hand.

So Morison set to work. He enlisted the help of Ronald Horton, then an assistant at Birrell & Garnett, who, having studied as an art student, could do rapid facsimile drawings of type and cuts. Morison asked him to examine the Burney collection of newspapers at the British Museum for him, and the instructions he provided illuminate his own technique:

My purpose is to isolate as far as possible the physical elements of journalistic typography between 1620 and 1920. I may not reach the latter terminus, but if you will be good enough to undertake the period from 1700–1800, I think I may be able to manage the rest, as well as check your findings.

Your search should cover a very great deal of the most interesting period of all, so that I look forward with great interest to your report.

The most conspicuous feature, the heading, is of course of great though not maximum importance. It is essential for me to be made aware of the development of the headings of long-established papers, and, in this connection, I should like to ask you to be sure to use the usual printers' indications for caps, small caps, italics and so forth. The only indication missing from the usual table supplied in the trade handbooks is for black-letter. I always use a wavy underline for this.

It is important also for me to know the main variations in the use of the transverse rules enclosing the serial number and date and place of publication etc. Sometimes these are single and sometimes double rules, and sometimes the double rules are equal and sometimes they are thick and thin. I shall be glad if you will indicate the column measure from rule to rule in inches. It is not necessary to measure the type area of every journal, only those in which the variation would be obvious to the general reader.

I would be glad to have a note taken of the use of factotum initials at the end of column (1) and in the case where their design is good, I should like a record to be made. It is still more important that the size of these things should be noted when they are more than four lines in depth. You will find cases of 'facs' 14 lines deep.

One of the most important details of which I should like a note to be taken is the position of the mast-head. By mast-head I mean the name of the paper, generally printed in slightly larger roman capitals than the body, and set over 'Answers to Correspondents', 'Notices to Subscribers', articles of a certain sort of importance which gradually develop into the leader.

Also please be careful to note the place and use of material headed 'Postscript'. Of course, anything like display in the news columns would be interesting, and this, of course, extends also to the advertising. I am not going to make much of advertising, but whenever a size of type larger than that of the largest type of the body of the paper is used in any advertising, I think a note might be made. I don't mean every time it is made, but when the practice has become a practice. When it is established there is no need to note anything more than the fact that the practice obtains. This general rule is good for most of the details which you will be covering.

You will, of course, find any number of similarities in typography and makeup. If you could make a rough and ready analysis of these into three or four general types, it would be convenient. I daresay you will find that the papers from 1700–1750 or 1760 and the papers from 1760–1790 require two very different treatments.

I shall be glad if you will make a note of the Burney number on your slips so that I may quite easily get the same volumes out when I go over the ground which you are clearing for me.

I think the foregoing notes may be of some service to you, but you will, of course, have a hundred and one points to ask about, which I have not mentioned. I suggest, therefore, that we meet after you have had two or three days in the Newspaper Room.*

The text was largely written that winter, while Morison was convalescing at Tangier, and the six lectures were given between 20 January and 4 February, culminating with a typically Morisonian *tour-de-force*. *The Times*, which had reported each lecture at length, described it: 'At the end of his lecture Mr Morison showed a slide of the actual day's Evening Standard (special edition), portraying the latest stage reached in the development of the newspaper after 300 years of evolution.' It was a trick he was to repeat with equal success thirty-five years later.

No later than May, the printed text, another folio with over 150 illustrations, was published by the Cambridge University Press as *The English Newspaper: some account of the physical development of journals printed in London between 1622 & the present day*. The preface is dated 19 April, and Morison, converting it (it was a trick of his) into a letter of presentation to Lord Riddell, only had to alter 19 to 27. He had a wonderful gift for persuading printers to work fast. Morison and Pollard had reason to be grateful to Lord Riddell, whose help, as Treasurer of the Friends of the National Libraries, they had asked in placing two collections of seventeenth-century newsletters, including that of Ichabod Dawks.*

The English Newspaper was the occasion of another example of Morisonian speed. Although Blake had given his permission two years earlier, it was not until November 1931, when the text of the lectures was virtually complete, that Morison decided to put in hand the Monotype recutting of Bell's type, to be first used in his book. By 17 December Cambridge were already alarmed that it would be late, but the next day a set of 14pt matrices was sent to them; another followed on 1 January, and the 12pt a week later. It was not a moment too soon for Cambridge, but all was well, although the Monotype version, perhaps due to this lightning speed, is not a perfect rendering of the original design.*

309

In addition to this, there had been *Ichabod Dawks and his Newsletter,* and a host of minor works, many of them printed by Lewis as Christmas or New Year presents for friends of the Press, in which Morison had a part. *The Tribute of a London Publisher to his Printers,* a reprint of John Dunton's sketches of his contemporaries, came at Christmas 1930; *The Art of Carving* by Dr John Trusler, that unusual cleric, in 1931; *Captain Edward Topham,* first produced for *The Colophon,* a New York typographic journal, in the same year, became the 1932 Cambridge book; and *G.D.'s Directions for Writing,* a copy-book of 1656, came out at Christmas 1933. As well as these, Morison found time to interest himself in the ordinary Cambridge publications. In 1932, when the Press published E. E. Reynolds's *Junior Exercises in English,* an elementary textbook for schools, Morison provided a sample letter for reproduction in the book, in which, unvexed by the self-consciousness that had beset him when he tried to do the same for Bridges, he took the opportunity to set out his own views

To my mind handwriting must be 'natural' because it must be fast. I like to see an obviously speedy piece of script. I hate a letter which exhales the scent of some calligraphic cosmetic. Give me a true cursive, let it run as fast as one can make it and at the same time keep it sufficiently regular.

With *The Times* on top of all this, Morison was in arrears again. At Christmas 1932 he wrote to apologize to his old friend Whitham, a more punctual reviewer than himself in *The Times Literary Supplement.* All his life Morison was apt to get fits of depression when the burden of work, promised and unfinished, grew too great; often, as now, depression was banished by a trip abroad.

In Paris I had some bad food wh. made me really ill & miserable for more than three weks. I supported the toast to *The Times* at a celebration of Astor's proprietorship, & of the new type but I cd. scarcely stand up. And I haven't been really recovered for more than a week.

Even so I have had to keep promises, as for instance to do 10, or 15,000 words on [Lucia de Pacioli] by Nov. 15; to lecture on Newspaper History last Thursday; to write an article for a German *festschrift*; and on Jan 2 I go to New York to deliver two lectures on the history of handwriting – neither lecture being started. I have all the lantern slides to make . . . and with the Christmas hols intervening there is hardly any time. . .

I have no choice – if I had I wd. drop all and go on with my History of the English Post Office Vol. 1 1482–1840. Is there any chance? No! I have to earn a living. Item: reply on behalf of the Firm to a toast at a Banquet celebrating the Vth anniversary of Vic: Gollcz Ltd – easy enough in itself but just one more of those things which have to be done & wh. make it difficult to do other things, such as writing to you, and other things I would do if I could. I kick at it as you might, having some nauseating nonsense to review for the Literary Suppl[t], or having to go a journey, coming to London maybe, or write some rot for a advertising agent. You won't believe me I know – you think I do as I like; but it isn't so actually. Since I last saw you I have not stopped working except to sleep (was at *The Times* until 12.30a.m. & 9.15p. this last week) with the single interval of the wasted continental trip. . . .

I read yr piece on Abbé Gregoire with much acceptance. We cd do with some such clerks today. The catholic church is becoming an enemy of communism and nothing more. At the Gollancz celebration I sat between Viola Garvin (who, at one point, said I had insulted her . . . & rose to leave the table – fact!) and Mrs. Gould who said that communism was worse than the worst form of capitalism – fact! Miss Garvin is not interested in politics – hence her irritation with me. Altogether the catholic church is probably taking a very useful line. From what I hear things in Unholy Russia are getting into an unholy mess and very largely thought to be a crisis of town bred intellectuals forcing agrarian policies down the throats of the people that grow the food.

. . . Hence this is my Christmas letter & it carries my wish that you should spend a pious time. I imagine you will turn on the Beethoven records. I shall probably read a few Post Office Reports and gnash my teeth at the prospect of going to America. But I shall consume a mince pie or two & I will munch one in honour of you and Sylvia, to whom all blessing & peace. As for prosperity – it is too much to ask or to wish. I believe this years end will see me absolutely free from all forms of debt. This is GRAND. The *Fleuron* cost me in solid sterling £2000 and I shall have paid all off by Dec 31.*

The trip to America on the *Aquitania* was no better than he expected. His arrival was saddened by the news of the death of Beatrice's grandmother, Emma Lamberton, of whom he was very fond. He was met by Bruce Rogers, who was designing the book on Pacioli, whose manual on the construction of capitals, printed in 1509, had engaged Morison after Moyllus. Morison was appalled by his appearance.

Rogers has a beard – or a sort of collection of hairs, thickly spaced as if they were Ludlow set; & not in any sort of alignment and with no standard of height. Pierpont would condemn the whole lot.*

Despite this initial shock, Morison got on well with Rogers, and *Fra Luca de Pacioli*, printed at Cambridge and published by the Grolier Club of New York, was a successful combination of their talents. The Club was to entertain Morison on his last day in New York: 'I go down to the ship from the Meet of the Grolier Grandees on the 26th,' he told Beatrice.

When I've gone thro' Geo Plimpton's Collection again on this occasion and read my lectures & done my book for Cambridge I apprehend that – with this *Hist of the Times* on hand – I shall do no more work on the history & practice of handwriting. My time will be spent in reading the lives of Grenville, Eldon, Wellington, Peel, Pitt and all the rest of the statesmen & memoir writers of the period 1785–1841. Curiously enough there is a print of Hickel's portrait of Pitt in the smoking room of the *Aqui*: He is reading the True Paper – I wish to heaven we could get a copy of today's!*

The idea of a history of *The Times* had grown out of the work of G. E. Buckle, editor of the paper 1884–1912, first on the life of Disraeli and then on Queen Victoria's letters. It was resting with Buckle, then seventy-eight, when Morison's Sandars Lectures suggested to Harold Child and Dawson (and perhaps Barrington-Ward also) that Morison might be the man to set the History moving.* Just before Christmas, there had been a meeting at *The Times* about it. 'Conference at the office on the great Times history,' Barrington-Ward wrote in his diary on 22 December

1932, 'G.D., Buckle, Morison, [Dermot] Morrah and I. We succeeded pretty well in our object of getting Buckle to focus the work into a definite programme.' It was not to be expected that Buckle, old and tired but thoroughly versed in nineteenth-century political history would find much in common with Morison, at the height of his powers, well read in newspaper history, especially of the eighteenth century, but conspicuously ignorant of the detail of politics. But his ability to assimilate a great deal of information quickly was remarkable. All through 1933 he worked away, fed by Pollard with books on the Press and stacks of contemporary newspapers, and at the beginning of the New Year he had something to produce to Barrington-Ward, who noted:

I have begun reading the first instalment of the History of TT – Morison's draft of the Barnes period. He has had to dig Barnes out almost completely, from the substratum of anonymity and oblivion, and he promises to succeed brilliantly in establishing the identity of the real formula of TT and of independent, professional journalism. It has been a task of huge labour in research. Still loose-ended, of course, and wants compression in places.*

It was a remarkable achievement, and not merely as a piece of historical research, for in clearing away the undergrowth and rubble from the early days of *The Times* Morison had discovered – as Barrington-Ward was quick to recognize – its *genius loci*. Barnes, with his preference for anonymity, was far more a man after Morison's heart than the self-assertive Delane. As well as Barnes, he had discovered Barrington-Ward: one to share his ideal of *The Times* as a greater force than the words in any issue, greater than the men who staffed it at any time. It was a vision of the paper that now drew them closer together, and to which they held through the difficult days of the war. It was the same vision that Morison sought to preserve after Barrington-Ward had gone.

Throughout 1934 further instalments were finished. In April it was decided to print the *History* at the Private Printing Office.*

Morison was anxious to build up the P.P.O.; he had already discovered its uses during the campaign for the new type, and he had used it to produce a special four-page dummy paper when he addressed the Double Crown Club on 'The Old English Newspaper and *The Times* New Roman' on 8 December 1932. Now, as later, he preferred to work directly with the printer, regarding galley proofs as copy to be worked on (not for nothing was he known as 'the printer's friend').

In May, Keith Feiling and Harold Temperley were asked to vet the work, which, as Barrington-Ward put it, 'lacks form'.* They read the proofs, made suggestions, but were unanimous in their praise of it, 'an important piece of work from every point of view'.* The Walter family were inclined to feel that Barnes had been promoted (to the distinction of the coloured frontispiece) at the expense of John Walter II, but were consoled by Geoffrey Dawson with the offer of the frontispiece to the next volume. Finally, the book went to press. On 20 November, Morison wrote to Barrington-Ward promising a revise of the last two sheets.

They go on the machine (we are now using both the Miehles) tomorrow morning. I share your excitement that this point has been reached. The house owes you a huge debt not to be liquidated by the Octavo. I don't know anybody else who would have consecrated himself so freely and fully to the dreariest form of all drudgery – the heeling & soleing of my thousands of leaky paragraphs. You have made a flowing narrative out of a set of smudgy blue-prints.

Pollard, too, had been generous with the criticism of the *History*, and together with Morison was planning the establishment of some provision for the study of newspaper history at London University.* Morison hoped *The Times* might contribute to the cost.

8 July 1934

Dear Pollard

I enclose the early draft of the account of the foundries making the new broken eff.

The Manager of The T. tells me that the Major mentioned that business to the Board the other evening (they must have had a short agenda) and that they talked sympathetically about the idea. G.D. (it was pure guesswork on my part when I mentioned the detail to you) named me as the incumbent of the Readership (their word) but the Major explained that I was much more ambitious than that etc.

S.M.

That cryptic first sentence refers to another of Morison's achievements: the discovery of the typographic part of the evidence that convicted T. J. Wise of forging first editions. It was in July 1934 that John Carter and Graham Pollard published *An Enquiry into the Nature of Certain XIXth Century Pamphlets*. On 9 January 1933, Morison was *en route* for New York, primed as to the suspect nature of Elizabeth Browning's *Sonnets from the Portuguese*, '1847'; 'I will do my best with the Bronte (or is it Shelley?) dossier,' he wrote. 'Any startling but really dependable discovery shall be cabled.'* Soon it came; the cable was sent,* and Morison followed it up with a letter to Pollard.

The Morgan copy of the E.B.B. Sonnets was acquired from Quaritch and it has 47 numbered pages all set out much as they might have been if the book were what it purports to be. The sheets appear to me to have been printed dry; not wet as one might have expected from an office in such a time and place. The point taken by itself is inconclusive.

A close examination of the type used for the composition reveals two characteristic sorts which are of some significance in yr. enquiry. There is a l.c. rom **f**. I have distorted the false kern as indicated but in the original (wh. is printed in about 10 point) it is quite clearly visible.

Secondly the query mark to the fount is not as expected, i.e.

not ? but ?

In other respects the fount is an ordinary slightly condensed modern. Now these two sorts ought to enable a positive identification of the fount to be made, whether S.B. & Co Caslon or whose; and it is possible that a local directory anno 1846 or 7 giving lists of trades would also list names of printers, these names may still be traceable in, e.g. S.B. & Co's ledgers. I should hunt up local printing of the time for even if the two sorts appeared in London it would be highly

315

unlikely that Reading would have them at all promptly, after their first appearance in town.

On the other hand it may well be that the fount with **f** & **?** originated in the early 40's. If so I shall be surprised. Secondly I shall be driven to the conclusion that prima facie the thing is what it purports to be. This is as far as I can carry the matter at present but I think I have made it plain that an examn from the typographical side might yield something. I may be all wrong but I have not noticed the broken backed f as early as 1850 and if I had been asked I should have said that it was evolved in order to prevent broken kerns occurring on high speed presses, of which there cd. have been few in Reading or anywhere else in 1847. . . . Had you asked me before this enquiry I should have given you a guess that it first appeared during the 90's.

Nothing more to report. . . . My second lecture satisfied me; it attempted to show the points at wh. common U.S. handwriting developed a movement away from the inherited English Round Hand of the Snell type. . . . I came right down thro' the early New York masters to Dunton, Spencer & Porter to a mid Victorian survival of Engl. Round Hand in Indiana. This was considered a good effort.

S.M.

The product of the New York lectures was an article on 'American Penmanship' in the *Colophon*. The last stages in the history of writing, acted out in the Middle West, had a particular interest, even pathos, for Morison; the tradition was so soon to be overtaken by the typewriter. Morison returned to the subject in *American Copybooks* in 1951, and Ray Nash has since enlarged and expanded on the foundation that Morison laid.

When he returned to London, he pursued the suspect fount of the 'Reading' *Sonnets*, and wrote to Blake at Sheffield.

My friend will be very interested if you can turn up the Reed bourgeois. If you will notice, the lower case **f** is slightly bent back. If you should happen to have any note as to the earliest appearance of this kind of thing, I should like you to tell me. My opinion is that it does not go back before 1870 or so.*

It did not. The 'button-hook' 'f' and 'j' and the suspect question mark were traced to the initiative of Richard Clay, the innocent printer employed by Wise. Neither Clay nor any of the founders listed by Morison showed these shapes before 1883. It was one of the most telling pieces of the evidence that Carter and Pollard built up against Wise, to which, despite the public furore, he made no reply.

In the first half of 1933, Morison had been persuaded to write an introduction to W. Turner Berry and A. F. Johnson's *Catalogue of Specimens of Printing Types, English and Scottish, 1665–1830*. Anxious to see the work publicized, he at first hoped it would be 'written by some elder saint, the discipline of whose learning has already condensed upon his head a shining bright bibliographical nimbus'. But as one of the editors of the Oxford Bibliography series, in which the book appeared, he could not refuse the task himself. He wrote to his co-editor Pollard.

24 Fitzroy Square W.1.
11 April 1933

Dear P:

Unless one looks upon the Typefounders' specimens as documents of evidential value one can't prevent people taking them up as objects of aesthetic value. If they are valued for their evidential value to the record of the mutations in the form of the types used for English books only a small group of technicians can be interested. If the appeal is made to collectors of 'fine books' the observation of typographical minutiae is degraded into a pastime and a pastime practised by those incapable of making fine distinctions. Moreover these people follow a lead. In this country the professional bibliographers have dictated the line taken by collectors – cf A.W.P.'s *Fine Books*. There was no Bruce Rogers cult until A.W.P. placed the nimbus in position. Proctor was a great influence also. If any serious understanding of the formative influences in English printing is to penetrate to the 'collector' it will be done by one of the High Priests of Bibliogry. who will be influenced by a motive of his own – dating – solving an anonymous attribution – detecting a fraud. Such a High P. will pick up several ideas from Berry & J's book if they can be wheedled into giving it some attention. My intro. is calculated to meet such people on their own ground. The reason why this is reasonable is that there are more of such people than any other – & they are organised. Finally if they buy the book, the aestheticians and the beauticians will follow. The technicians amount to half a dozen . . . and they will buy the book anyway. Robert Blake will probably buy two copies.

S.M.

Few scholars achieve such striking confirmation of the validity of their methods. In the aftermath of the publication of *An Enquiry*, no amount of bluster on Wise's part could shake the evidence, and it soon became clear that no defence was possible. Morison also had an important part in another national excitement. 'The Codex Sinaiticus has come to London,' Beatrice wrote home on 12 January 1934. 'S.M. acted as the pivotal point of that most amazing book-deal of our generation.' Maurice Ettinghausen, then with Morison's old friends Maggs Brothers, was (like many dealers at the time) in touch with the Russian government, who were cautiously trying to sell off relics of the past. From them he learnt that the Codex might be for sale, and it was Morison who got in touch with Sir Frederic Kenyon, then just retired from the British Museum and chairman of the Friends of the National Libraries.* In the negotiations that followed, it is small wonder that Dom Henri Leclercq had to complain of raised voices in the Reading Room, but eventually it was bought for £100,000. Morison's hand could be seen again in the posters on the underground: all along the Central Line there were posters in Gill Sans with a picture of the codex and directions to the British Museum. Ramsay MacDonald offered him a knighthood, which he declined.

Another stroke of detective work, not unlike the affair of Wise and the button-hook 'f' and 'j', had occurred in the progress of Morison's preparatory work on the Fell types. Just before Christmas 1930, Bumpus put on an exhibition of the work of the Oxford University Press, organized by the Printer to the university, John Johnson (a great admirer of Morison).* Five large folio broadsides were produced for the occasion, on one of which Morison, who had been assisted by the Press typefounder, Sidney Squires,* was able 'to separate the Fell pica italic from its larger capitals, to combine them with a set of smaller capitals without lower case, and so to reconstitute the "litera currens Ciceroniana", originally cut by Robert Granjon for Chr. Plantin and first used in 1566'.* Other identifications followed. This discovery was too important to wait. On 3 November, Morison

wrote a long letter (all but a column) to *The Times*, to announce
it, with a line illustration of the newly amalgamated type. He
concluded with a politely worded command. 'In its authentic
seventeenth century form it will no doubt receive the compliment of use,' in the fine printed books for which the Oxford Press
is celebrated. He did not wait to tell van Krimpen: 'I have been
able to identify some of the small Fell types with the Garamond
and Granjon faces in the 1592 specimen published by Mori.'*

Van Krimpen was still wrestling with Reece. Morison wrote
to try to help him on 20 February next.

43 Fetter Lane E.C.4.
20 February 1931

Dear van Krimpen,

The situation about our friend in Paris is, I think, exactly that his
wealthy and friendly supporter here, who might have been expected
to remember him in his legacies, died suddenly without doing so;
further, that the winding up of the estate probably means the repay-
ment by the Lord High Romantick of considerable sums of capital
lent for various enterprises; further that some of these enterprises,
notably one acquired from Wolff, have been found to be encumbered
with complications not suspected when their purchase was made by
J.H.R.; that the complete collapse of the United States has had a very
serious effect upon all books, including those from the rue Boulard.
There is not the slightest justification for anybody at any time ever
thinking that there is any shadow of intent to deceive, or to impose
upon anybody. I think that Reece's mind is so saturated with Romance
that he often fails to realise that for the execution of his plans a prosperous world is a necessary condition.

I, personally, would hestitate very much before committing myself
to anything but a modest scheme. As you know, I did not believe,
and do not believe, that he could organise, publish and produce
The Fleuron. I think this: that if you were to keep everything entirely
in your own hands, using him as a distributing agent and paying him
on the sales effected by his organisation, he would be very glad of the
arrangement, feeling that the books were a credit to him, and you
would have the satisfaction that you knew where every penny of the
proceeds went.

I have been publishing now with Reece for several years, and when
from time to time I have been very hard up, I have asked him for any

money to which I was entitled. I think on one occasion he sent me a cheque for £50, and another cheque for some other smaller sum; but I have never received any formal account, or, indeed, any account of any sort; nor, in fact, do I know how many copies of these books have been sold. I have no knowledge, therefore, of the state of such a book as [the] *Brun* or the translation which he made of my *Caractères de l'Écriture.*

All this happened before any financial shock had been given to his organisation. I cannot but think, therefore, that the hard times we are all passing through will make him even less inclined to take an interest in dull subjects such as figures.

A man at the Limited Editions Club made a suggestion to me that I should continue *The Fleuron*, even going so far as to promise to return what various sums of money I have lost since 1922, and offering to take 1500 copies of any further affair. My answer to him is contained in the accompanying cut. I am not so sure that the man who sends that offer is possessed of the means to carry it out. Certainly I should not desire to see the thing take any notice whatever of books printed and made in the United States unless they were up to European standards, as very few of them are.

I am now at work on an affair at *The Times*. Immediately afterwards, I will come to see you in Haarlem – probably about the middle of March or so.

Yours
Stanley Morison

But George Macy of the Limited Editions Club was no more successful than Reece in refloating the *Fleuron*. Morison subsequently contemplated with some amusement the prospect of their meeting (van Krimpen was expecting Macy).

That is very good news. I have here also at the present time the Commendatore, John Holroyd-Reece. I only wish I could be present at an interview between Messrs Reece and Macy. In fact, I would give a great deal to see these two paladins endeavour to get the best of each other. I have written today to Reece asking him to remain here until Mr Macy lands.*

It is not clear if this carefully staged encounter took place. Reece was in any case about to abandon fine for mass printing. Albatross books were launched in March 1932, and in May Mardersteig was writing to order a special 9½pt size of Baskerville for them (he was also printing a Dante for Macy).*

The new Fell discoveries made Morison keen to explore the equal wealth of old types at Enschedé, and in March he agreed to write an introduction to the translation of *Fonderies de Caractères* on which Beatrice had been working two years before. He was also hoping to revive the types of Christoffel van Dijck, owned by Enschedé. On 3 August he wrote van Krimpen an eight-page letter on these topics, and another of three pages on van Krimpen's own current designs. These included the beautiful italic script, later called by the name that Morison now gave it, Cancelleresca Bastarda.

I don't want to interfere with your ideas, but I have, naturally, a great curiosity about the script type. To my mind the scriptorial quality ought properly to manifest itself in the first and last letters of the word and still more in the capitals. What has never been done is to make a capital which could be set as a line of capitals. Here is the fundamental difference between gothic and roman; that roman is not a script type, whereas gothic is a script type, and, like all script types, its capitals cannot be set as a title line. This is why, in the superb books of Estienne, Morel and the other fine printers of the French Renaissance, a very large upper- and lower-case roman is used. They did not use lines of capitals on their title-pages because they had not grown out of the conventions which had been inherited from gothic typography.

Roman type is not a script type, hence it is heresy to make a roman type from the hand of a scribe working in the formal Johnston manner. It follows that, to cut a script type seems (to me, as one humble individual) to necessitate the creation of a script whose nature shall partake of cursive and of formal qualities – in a word, your new script will have to be a *cancellerescha bastarda*.*

In September 1934, Morison wrote a little wistfully to van Krimpen. He had been to dinner with Oliver Simon and

learnt a little gossip about the world of 'fine printing' with which I do not now seem to have much connection. Gill was in here during the week and seemed to me more disposed, for the future, to keep to his business of sculpture rather than writing or type designing.

We all seem to have worked our way through the 'art of printing'. I suppose this is due to our all having become over forty.*

But there were compensations. There was Beatrice, who had got a sculptured Belle Sauvage from Gill. 'I have a slightly un-Christian, and certainly very un-Mosaic regard for that graven image,' she told him; she was, none the less, going to part with it.

I am going to give her to Morison, and I think you will be glad that it's not to anyone else. S.M. is my complete idea of a saint, sense of humour and all, and with all that he's done for me, all the sympathy and help, all the toleration of stupidity and all the faith and encouragement, I've never had a chance to do one thing in return. No, I don't mean that exactly, because there's a kind of 'not-doing' which may count as 'doing'. I really mean I've never been able to give him anything. My house is full of his books, and a lot of his ideas are earning me money under my name, and when I say 'quid retribuam?' I haven't a blessed thing. But it occurred to me that the Belle Sauvage has in it that 'otherness', that unreasonable beauty, which would be not so much a foil as a complement to his reasoned and ordered mind. So when I found that he appreciated the thing, it sort of automatically became his as far as I am concerned.*

There was Beatrice gay, as well as Beatrice grave. *Enjoying England*, her L.N.E.R. book had come out in February 1932, full of her fresh and vivid view of the English countryside. London, the Dickensian Christmas London, was an enthusiasm she had inherited from her mother. Beatrice and Morison had a high old time together at Christmas.

Mr George Jackley is performing at the Lyceum panto. Which I have not yet seen, but the Boss and I are going this week. I must tell you what a grand party we had just before Christmas. Murton and I were taken by S.M. up Ludgate Hill and off to the right and through no end of small twisty streets, with queer old courtyards, any one of which might contain Cheeryble Bros. house, and past funny thumbnail sweetshops – one was also a barber-shop – until we came to Knightrider Street and Sermon-Lane, where is the Horn Tavern, where Mr C. Dickens used to drop in for a quick one. The neat eighteenth, no, seventeenth-century façade looks enchanting under the greenish gas street-lamp. We pushed through the swing-doors and found ourselves in a capacious bar. The bar itself swept round in a wide curve, and above it were the ancient kegs and casks, polished with generations of dusting. The letters of FINE OLD SHERRY and the rest are not yet too dim. There were spigots and taps, two blonde barmaids, and an occasional short partition branched off from the bar – not enough to form booths, but so that we could occupy one section without seeing or being seen by our neighbors. There was a warm smell of spirits, tobacco and sawdust. A certain amount of pre-Christmas jollity was in the air. A barrel-organ stopped outside and played, a great many times, a tune called 'All Good Pals and Jolly Good Comp-an-ee', and as often as it began again, the people behind us at the other bar would join in with the words, part of which run:

Never mind the weath-er, Never mind the rain,
Now we're all together, WHOOPS she goes again;
La-de-da-de-dah, La-de-da-de-dee:
All – Good – Pals – and – jollygood companee!

(The La-de-da part is in the original lyric, and I think it is an inspiration. So did our singers, for they came out very strong on the line and ever stronger on the WHOOPS-she-goes, which is the climax.) Then one of the celebrants would shout 'Where's old Stanley?' which caused Mr Morison immense joy. He explained that most of these people would be late home for dinner, it being understood that there was a great deal to finish up just before the holidays. . . . Well, we finished up another round of sherry ourselves, and came away in very high spirits. . . .

On Christmas Eve itself the Boss and I dined at Pagani's and went on to see Nervo and Knox – do you remember their 'troupe of acrobats?' They also revealed a 'fairy ballet' of corpulent gentlemen in gauze skirts, wands, and black socks with sock-suspenders. It was fine.*

At Christmas 1933 they went to *Babes in the Wood* at the Scala, and next year it was an 'Old Fashioned Music Hall (complete with Chairman's Table) where SM and I have been roaring all evening'. They went to a Bach concert at the Queen's Hall: 'Unfortunately we arrived in time to hear an aria in which any one word was likely to be stretched through ten or twenty melodic syllables, and then repeated; which is an anathema to SM's direct mind. The first Brandenburg Concerto restored peace.'*

Nor was *The Times* all history and typography. Hopkinson continued to regard Morison with kindly patronage, despite the fact that he came from the wrong place. 'We're all Hoxford 'ere,' he would say in his rich voice, and enquire whether Morison had enjoyed his jaunt to 'the Mediterraneum'. In 1931 Tom Casson, who had a great reputation for press advertising, came to *The Times* as publicity manager.

Casson and Morison quickly became friends and engaged in discussion on how *The Times* could be sold by publicity that neither cheapened nor distorted. In the 1930s there was a wine shop under the railway arches near Ludgate Circus which Casson, who like many gifted people had to create his own working conditions and found those at P.H.S. uncongenial, used as an annexe. He and Morison and F. P. Bishop, the assistant manager, there talked 'shop', planned campaigns, wrote copy, drafted illustrations and laid out advertisements and booklets. The result of this lively collaboration was a series of posters and pamphlets of a quality unknown in Fleet Street and still unsurpassed. The effort was justified by the steady rise in circulation until the second world war.*

At Christmas 1933, Morison renewed his old friendship with Francis Meynell when Monotype gave a Christmas lunch at the Savoy to celebrate the work of the Nonesuch Press. While Morison was out of the country in October 1932, he got a less agreeable reminder of the remote past. He learnt that his father had died at the North London Home for Blind Christian Men and Women in Highgate.* They had only met once since Mr and Mrs Morison parted. His father had sought him out. There had been a cautious meeting in an A.B.C. teashop, but – 'I didn't feel inclined to repeat the experience'.*

With the pressure of all these new events and people, Morison's own attitudes and opinions had been changing. The decisive change in his political beliefs came – as it came to many who shared his views – on 27 October 1931, when the Labour Party was annihilated at the election that led to Ramsay MacDonald's second National Government.

Morison was ill at the time, and went to Tangier to recover. He wrote a diary-letter to Beatrice, beginning at Algeciras on 5 November.

This is a shabby part of the bay opposite Gibraltar. There is a dock with many flies and still more touts acting on behalf of the bus companies who maintain the only serious connexion with Malaga Seville & Cadiz, – for Algeciras has no more exciting form of locomotive transport than a contractor's engine wh shifts trucks of stones for a embankment repairing job. The place is echt Spanish; there is nothing English or Moorish or Jewish about it – and Gibraltar is all that, with policemen & firemen all constructed on the London standard. The officials in Algeciras all have rather fine uniforms – all having that rather comic-opera-cum-cinema-attendant effect which anything you're not used to seems to produce when it is a question of ceremonial dress. But when the Moor dresses & walks he 'knows how' – and the effect is not that of these chaps who hawk carpets along the Paris boulevards. The female moor is a stately creature.

Yesterday in Gib. I sat beside a moorish mother – beshrouded in mahomet knows how many yards of stuff – with her little son, about 7, equally enwrapped & topped off with a fez. Next were two Spanish children of 5 & 6 perhaps who endeavoured to entice young Mr Moor with conversation and in play. He was very standoffish, upon which the Spanish christian infants sent up cries of 'Allah' and pushed and poked Mr Moor until his mother took him off into an off-street. I couldn't help thinking that the young mahound ought to have read the aggressor a lecture on the history of Spain in general & Gibraltar in particular. Apparently in Gib the khakifolk run into clink anybody who now makes the slightest sort of trouble, industrial or religious. The unions don't burn up any property in Gibraltar! Anti-aircraft gunnery practice is carried on regularly and the place run generally as if it were Aldershot: no sort of irregularity, no tendencious postcards. No Spaniards allowed from neighbouring towns to stay in Gib. after 10. Barriers drawn at that time. Algeciras like Gibraltar (& like Oxford) must be seen as a whole. . . . In neither can anything like a decent meal be had though both probably surpass Tilbury or Plymouth, the analogous places. But who wants much food this mid-summer weather! Fancy, all blinds drawn to keep out the sun!, no paint given to the outsides of any houses becos the sun burns it up so quickly! And in November the sun is still burning! It's doing me great good & though I cannot pretend to be much interested in Algeciras I am looking forward with enormous curiosity to arriving at Tangier this afternoon at 4.30. In the evening I shall send you a telegram. There are indications that I may stay at Tangier some time. The strike there is over but there is a more serious one in Andalusia which makes Seville unreachable from Cadiz by train. Here at Algeciras the houses are chalked with Viva the strike of the railway workers . . . and there is no railway here. I may have to give up my notions about visiting Lisbon. In the meantime I am thinking of two things one that I miss you secondly that I [am] most renewed in health. This letter is the most energetic thing I've done since catching that train at Tilbury. Thirdly I am thinking about the utter rout of the poor old Labour Party, now put back for thirty years. This means that for a generation nobody of mature years will bother with the Party. It looks to me as if the new Liberal Party will gradually draw off much of the anti-conservative vote. The essence of politics is expedience. As far as I can see from the miserable Gibraltar Chronicle it is little use to vote Labour. The end of an . . . epoch . . . because the capitalist system is still strong, too strong for the idealists who have been for so long the support of the socialist.

Save the surcharged stamps – first I've seen, *used* it will be rarissima.

As ever, for ever,

S.M.

TANGER November 5 [1931]

My dear Friend

The pencil thou gavest me is wore out and this scratch is all that's left of a successor – like the first, exhausted on the Sandars. But no pencil ever made could do any justice to this extraordinary and pulverisingly 'different' place. Apart from working on Sandars which has taken all my mornings the reason I have not written is more than anything the extreme difficulty of giving any sort of aperçu of the place, or of the spiritual reactions which have seized me as I have prowled observantly through the lanes of this old, oriental city which until 20 years ago, and even less was the centre of lawless tribes led by particularly resourceful brigand leaders. The place was conquered by the Portuguese in the 10th century and when Charles II married Catherine of Braganza it came to England as part of her *dot* but 'England' found the cost of maintaining it too much for its

326

finances and simply let it go, only returning some few years ago, for the purpose of protecting the lives of English subjects who were either kidnapped or knifed otherwise – or even so! To cut the history, apart from the 'pacification' of the natives the place is exactly the same, with Europeanising only slightly present and not enough to affect the colour or life of the place. It is a hard place, on a hill of stone on a slate base. The hills are most uncovered with soil, no trees, no sort of decent vegetation. If the Arab found trees he cut 'em down either for immediate fuel or because his enemy might shoot from its branches. The place looks distinctly unfriendly from the sea. There are no cliffs, stone hills slope in a surly fashion to the waters edge. But the people are quite friendly and mostly handsome. They are very mixed. Arabs, Negroes, Berbers, Senegalese and Turks, Spaniards and Jews. All except the Spaniards wear the most complicating and enveloping clothing on the hottest days and doing no matter what heavy work. There is a minimum of exposure of the body to the sun whether by women or men Arab. Some modernists do without the enveloping thing called jellaba which normally goes over the jacket and knickers. Legs alone are allowed to be uncovered and often the feet. The women do an enormous amount of exceedingly heavy work which would break the back of any English man, let alone woman. One sees them fast and barefoot with a huge load of firewood not worth sixpence but very heavy strapped to her back, the weight calculated to fall upon the end of the vertebrae *and* a baby on her shoulders. Often also you see the moke overloaded just ahead, carrying an enormous mass of vegetables balanced each side of him and the peasant himself sitting in the middle singing what I imagine to be a prayer since it is a miserable drone composed of about three notes – all they seem ever to get to. The market here is a fascinating sight, yet an appalling sight, impossible to describe the mass of men women donkeys, mules [two pages missing here] but nothing more in the way of transport except a railway with two trains a day. There is no berth for a ship. When you arrive you are debarked first into a tiny motor boat holding 15 persons. The port is shallow so this debarkment takes place well out. This motor boat with much pitching gets you to a rickety wooden pier where, if the thing isn't capsized you are met by 500 of the indigenes who are paid by the hotels to shout out the name and address of three principal places in Tanger. The row is terrific. My own method was to treat the situation as a public meeting and shout 'Quiet, I'll deliver my decision after the customs inspection'. The sea of bobbing fezes and jellabas subsided, but only for a moment – sufficient for me to get

327

my bags under my own control. I had to make up my mind – and quickly in order to pacify a fresh outburst and announced 'Hotel Continental' upon which a tall ebony fez-topped figure in khaki jacket and purple breeches stepped forward and took everything in charge. I chose the Continental because I could see it and because it faced the sea and had gardens. It has turned out a satisfactory choice. There are two cats, one European, one African in type with a head stuck on its neck like the head of a nail. It is impossible to sleep after 5.15 which being about an hour before sunrise is the muezzin. This chant, the total sense of which is (I am told) 'Rise, it is better to pray than to sleep' takes 15 minutes or so it seems and as it is sung from the minaret of every mosque and that without synchronisation the function takes anything from half to three quarters or one hour perhaps – it seems a terrific time. When this drone – it is on about three notes – is over some five thousand cocks salute the dawn already heralded by the chant. It goes on, as I found out, from 6 to 7.30 and seems to acquire a kind of rhythm by means of some obscure self-drilling. You hear this every morning, windows shut or open. The muezzin sung again at 12.30 but by some casuistry no interruption of business takes place and you can hardly hear it. It occurs again in the evening at 7 or so – and then again you can hear little else. At 7 too there is often a religious procession with acetylene gas lamps carried on the heads of boys and accompanied by men with torches, drums and fifes, the whole lot drumming, fifing and whining a monotonous chant of the same three notes and repeated infinitely as the procession goes up the main street to the market place. There is a Catholic church, conducted by Franciscans principally in the interest of the spiritual life, if any, of the Spaniards. The high mass is unbelievably noisy, a sort of organ, a sort of raucous choir and much violin work deliber- ately calculated to delay the action of the mass and consisting of the highly decorative and saccharinous sort apparently well regarded in Spanish cafes. The congregation consists only of Europeans. Yet the church is a great benefit to the musulman since it is the only building in the busiest street which has outside railings – upon which the musulman can hang his carpets exposed for sale. From the enquiries I have made no sort or kind of Christian propaganda makes the slightest effect upon Islam hereabouts. We have three sanctified days here every week. Friday is the sacred day of Islam and one notices it although it is not by any means absolutely kept. Business is greatly reduced at any rate. Saturday is the day which the Jews choose to keep sacred. They being the money changers it is next to impossible to get half-a-sovereign's worth of silver on Saturday. On Sunday the Christians shut shop. Four days a week therefore are the only normal days. From my observations Sunday is the most abnormal day. The Jews are very conspicuous however for, tho' not very numerous, they own the money changers' and other streets. There is a money changer every other door in the main street. We use £ sterling; Frs. francais, Frs. Hassan ie. Maroccan frank; Pesetas and you never know what your change is going to be, or whether it is right or not. So the Jews are very necessary. They do not seem to be regarded with any favour by the indigenes. The Arab looks upon the Jews not as European and with some reason since there are tribes which are Arabs Judaised, i.e. converted to Jewish practices but not being Jews in race. They were here before the Arabs seemingly. The one point which struck me most of all as I walked through the narrow streets of the town was that it was as near medievalism as was possible. There are boot-makers altogether in one series of huts or houses with no windows. You lean in or you drive up on your mule and shove his head inside through where the window isn't. Next door to the morgue a moment away from the hotel is a little collection of six shops, three facing three and each containing a calligrapher who squats before a desk and inkpot writing at the dictation of a Arab up from the outskirts who is getting his correspondence through after having sold his skins, or hens or goats. Secondly I realised that, for the first time I was living in touch with a community which had never been through the discipline of the roman empire or the roman church and possessed a completely separate set of 'values'. Whatever they are they do not seem to admit of any sort of 'ambition' as occidentals would understand it. I have said they work very hard – on the understanding that this is the will of Allah, rather than having, by experiment, found there is no sort of possible alternative. A religious fatalism seems to prevent experiment. Hence the most enterprising Maroccan relies upon pillage and abduction as a means of 'getting there' and, so far as I can see you have to be able to get away with a claim to be of kinship with the Prophet to be immune from pursuit by even stronger brigands. I believe the modernist Islam attitude to marriage teaches the maximum of four wives – to those who can afford it! I see no visible signs here of any who can afford one but let alone four. For such reasons the polygamous doctrine of Islam is likely to be ignored in the future, the more so as Moustapha Kamal, the Mussolini of Turkey has forbidden it. On the other hand I've observed none of that flood of 'art studies' of French or U.S.A. manufacture. There is no solicitation in streets or cafes so far as I have been able to see. The town is reasonably well cleaned by a staff of Arabs who have a water skin strapped to their back. The skin is a goat's and has a small hole where the head of the animal used to be. When this is unstopped the running dribble is flicked by the operator across the road and a follower with a besom brushes the dust into the faces of the passers by. The water skin is filled at a fountain and at such a place there may be seen many from the country with similar skins being filled, placed on the back of a donkey or a woman for transport, a sight held to be pleasing to Allah no doubt (and perhaps Eric Gill) but which almost makes me mad to think of. From there, and similar observations I am driven to the opinion that life in any modern factory, inspected as they are and governed by trade unions, is infinitely preferable to the slavery entailed in the effort to live in this country and climate without the aid of scientific agriculture and labour saving machinery. They have a rudimentary machine in use on road repairs which is even more inefficient than a true hand labourer's foot would be. I can't quite make out how the town governs itself. The north of Africa from Tunis to Algiers and Oran is a French protectorate. The French nation became 'interested' in Marocco and when the anarchic conditions in the country became intolerable they 'stepped in' to punish a tribe which had bumped off certain Frenchmen. The Spaniards also were 'interested', for they still smarted from the Moors now as in the 11th century. Spain secured the seacoast of the mediterranean and France the Atlantic and interior. Tanger, for some obscure reason is British French and Spanish, isolated by customs barriers from the French and Spanish zones. Hence all these currencies. I imagine that the British desire to have Tanger and will ultimately do a deal with the French and ignore the Spaniards and all the rest of the [two pages missing here] fortunately there is an airline Tanger–Gib. I have now entirely recovered – you mustn't judge by the writing of this dispatch – and how tiring is this writing with a stub of pencil – if you write at speed as I seem naturally to do! The sun here has done me all the good in the world and though I regret the expenditure of time I must confess it hasn't been wasted. I have not felt as well for a very long time. I am, though, full of impatience to be back and see you, having thought of you daily almost hourly. I don't suppose I have spoken 250 words since I parted from you on St. Pancras Station. Such converse as I've had has been with the indigenous able to speak French. If you ever go back to America I shall confine myself to myself, repeating your cracks, your observations and your 'methods' my dear Holmes. I look forward with inexpressible excitement to arriving back. I hope you'll find me less 'dumb' than I have been many months before I took the plunge and sailed for these furrin parts. I wish with all my heart it were possible, had been possible for you to 'be along'. You would enjoy this place a great deal and could have opened my eyes to much more than they will ever, of their own strength, observe.

Note

The election, as far as I can see, wipes out Socialism for 50 years.

That I shall then be 92!

That given a leader the Liberal Party will return to the second position and that, with a financial genius it could hope to govern in 20 years or less.

That a young man with political ambitions would do well to join the Liberal Party since the Conservatives have too many possible office-bearers as it is.

That unless the 'National Govt' makes a wholesale muck of things it will re-stabilise capitalism for generations. That this should be done by McD. and Snowden!

That I shall have to take serious thought as to my own political position as a lower middle-aged man.

That this will probably mean the adoption of expediency to the exclusion of principle as a political motive.

In other words I may vote according to my ideas of what is immediately the desirable thing for the country. This means believing in the statesmen and their power to tell the truth. We've seen little enough of that in the last campaign so I shall probably end by abstaining from any sort of action or interest in domestic politics.

So much for that. For you, all my mind and everything.

S.M.

Saturday.

14

THE first volume of the *History of The Times* was published on New Year's Day 1935. J. L. Garvin filled the first two pages of the *Literary Supplement* (under his own name) with a warm review: 'The candour, grip and glow of this volume reveal the real life behind the anonymity through the creative decades, and replace the vague pomposities of mid-Victorian homage by an epic of flesh and blood.' Morison had sent Pollard a review copy ('No prizes or salvage money is offered for misprints, reversed pages, missing accents or any other pieces of the flotsam and jetsam of our illiteracy'); Pollard was trying to negotiate a review of it in the *Labour Monthly* by Palme Dutt, but the threatened terms were steep, £5 to the journal and a printed statement that the review was paid for – 'he would like to know why on earth you want it.' The review when it came in the May issue was a splendid denunciation of the capitalist system, as typified by *The Times*, with a vision of its early doom. On 27 January the Barrington-Wards invited Morison to supper.

He has a good mind yet it is an odd jumble of beliefs and prejudices continually in contradiction. He has betaken himself to traditionalism in religion and resents it everywhere else in life. His politics reflect his own life and environment . . . with their insistence on class. Much talk of TT, which he loves and disapproves almost equally, and of how it must meet the future.

But for once Morison was looking forward to a future less strenuous than hitherto. He had rashly said as much to Lewis, who had a triumph of his own to recount, over William Maxwell of R. & R. Clark, the Edinburgh printers.

I think you would like to know – even if Maxwell would not – that I have got the Greville Memoirs. I am putting it in hand at once but there are one or two points I would like to discuss with you, and I think Nobbs has one or two things he would like to see you about. So can you come down on Monday or Tuesday of next week? For God's sake don't come down on Saturdays. Now that you have nothing to do it should be an easy matter for you to get down.*

Morison was impressed.

I congratulate you immensely. It is one of the most important things that any printer could have brought off – I don't mean the subject matter of the books but the bringing back to the fold of an ancient customer who now has such strong dynastic connections with Edinburgh and Glasgow. According to precedent, you ought to marry into the Macmillan family!

Your suggestion about Monday or Tuesday is quite agreeable. I will come down on Monday.*

Lewis and Morison respected Maxwell, who had the same instinctive feeling for fine printing that they both had. To have taken a large order from his main customer – Macmillan's links with their Scottish printers were strong, and Clark's rivals at Glasgow, the MacLehoses, were related by marriage to the Macmillans – was a triumph indeed. The eight substantial volumes of Lytton Strachey and Roger Fulford's edition of Greville are one of the finest pieces of work produced by Cambridge between the wars, and occupied Morison and Lewis for many a day.

It was an agreeable diversion from the rigours of London to take the 'kipper express' to Cambridge in the morning. Usually Morison would go to see Lewis first, entering his room noiselessly. Lewis would be working at his tall desk by the window and sometimes ignored Morison quietly working over copy or proofs, even when he slipped out again and up the stairs to the comps, where Nobbs would be waiting for him. Sometimes Morison would go to see S. C. Roberts first, but this was time wasted for Lewis.

After ten minutes I would hear Lewis's voice on the house-telephone: 'You got a chap called Morison with you?'

'Yes.'

'Well, ask him who pays his fare.'

Then, with a burst of Homeric laughter, Morison would slap his thigh and hurry off to Lewis's room, to be greeted with 'Well, old tin-ribs, how many cancels are you going to want for this job?'*

And so work would go on until lunch, usually taken at the University Arms, with Morison tucking into 'a growing lad's portion' – then back for more work in the afternoon, Morison drafting layouts with personal instructions to Nobbs or 'covering the margins of proofs with corrections – and corrections to corrections', to the alarm of Roberts's assistant, G. V. Carey, as well as Lewis.

Around four o'clock the two men would walk through to the Syndicate room for a stand-up tea with the officers of the publishing business. Like everyone else, they found Morison interested in anything and usually with his views well formed. He seldom expressed opinions as such but spoke *ex cathedra*: not 'I think', but 'According to me . . .'. It might be politics or religion, history or palaeography or (more lightly) the Sherlock Holmes canon, in which both Roberts and Carey's successor, Charles Carrington, were expert but Morison hardly less so. Discussion – argument, rather – could continue for an hour; then back to the Printer's room where Nobbs might be waiting with a proof or a query. By half-past six or so it was time to walk or take a bus to the station, where Morison would remember that he had no money for his fare back to London and Lewis would fork out (duly entering the amount in his petty cash book next morning); a parting glass of sherry, and Morison would finally sink back in a corner seat, not without first surveying the locomotive, his chin thrust out pugnaciously as was his manner when judging any object larger than himself.*

One job that Morison brought to the Press was even more impressive than *The Greville Memoirs*. King Manoel of Portugal was an enthusiastic collector of early books relating to his country, and his appointed booksellers were Maggs Brothers. It was as natural that they should turn to Morison as he to the Press to produce the great catalogue of the King's library, *Early Portuguese Books, 1489–1600*. This occupied the Press from 1927 to 1935; in the end it ran to over 2000 pages of royal quarto. It was a master-piece, both of composition and press-work, but the five years that it took to produce did not pass without strain on both sides. Morison and Lewis, both radicals, found the idea of a royal author hard to bear: the deference with which Ernest Maggs treated him only stimulated their feelings. Lewis would tell him bluntly to put out his cigar before entering the works; the King would respond with equally firm remarks about unauthorized corrections. To Morison, admiring both his learning and his typographic skill, he was more polite. In the end, all three were immensely proud of the book, and a specially illuminated copy was made for the King to present to the Pope.

Another customer, the new publishing firm of Faber & Faber, brought Lewis and Morison up against doctrinaire German typography. Herbert Read had demanded that Herbert Bayer should lay out his *Art and Industry*, and Richard de la Mare had unwillingly consented. Morison did his best to console Lewis.

If you see Mr. de la Mare you ought, I think, to assure him on one consideration. You should tell him that this business of going to a German for typographical intelligence is most unreasonable. Owing to the fact that Germans use blackletter and fraktur so extensively they have become quite incapable of understanding typography in roman. If Mr. de la Mare wants to employ a German he should bring out the book in a so-called gothic fount. That no German understands roman typography is proved beyond all question by the fact that they do not use small caps, do not use italics for the purpose of articulating the text. They do at times set some of the prelims in italics, but they have never rationalised their use as we have. The reason for this is that there are no small caps or italics in black-letter so that, as far as modern typography is concerned, the Germans are in precisely the same position as William Morris was forty years ago. You will find no italics or small caps in any of his founts; nor in Cobden Sanderson's.

This Mr. Bayer, not content with being ignorant of the function of italics, deepens his ignorance by wilfully shutting his eyes to the utility of capitals. Of course he did not invent. Like most of the modern tricks which the German Jews have elaborated into an intellectual theory tied on to contemporary architectural customs, it

335

was invented in Paris. (By German Jews I really mean Jews in Germany.) The effect of it is to make typography a romantic thing instead of a rational thing.*

At the same time as this ordeal, Morison's thoughts were turning to the next Christmas book, and he wrote to Lewis with a new scheme.

I think it likely that I could produce a little book on the same subject as the Pacioli but about a different person, one Felix Felicianus or Felice Feliciano who produced the first known MS. giving the proportions of the roman capitals according to the classical invention. By the use of your name I have got put in hand here a set of 72 point capitals based on the designs of this man, and if they could be printed with some explanatory text and a facsimile of one of the pages of the original book existing at the Vatican, and which I have had photographed, you might care to send it out.*

Sadly, nothing (except the still extant if seldom used Monotype Felix capitals) came of this scheme, which was only brought to fruition by Mardersteig in 1961. Perhaps the last stages of *The History of the Times* diverted Morison's attention; whatever the cause, it was not Feliciano but Thomas Barnes who was the subject of the Christmas book. The material came easily to hand from the *History*, but the book was very much Morison's own tribute to the man he had so largely discovered.

Altogether, Morison enjoyed his weekly excursions to Cambridge. As well as his friends at the Press, there was A. F. Scholfield at the University Library and other friends, theologians especially, outside the book world. In particular, there was Sydney Cockerell, once William Morris's successor and co-adjutor, now Director of the Fitzwilliam Museum, who had as fine an eye as Morison for manuscripts and lettering; Morison acknowledged his critical gift with half-amused awe. All this he enjoyed, and was flattered as well as delighted when Cambridge later made him an honorary Doctor of Letters.

But Cambridge, although vastly congenial, was always something of a holiday; business, for Morison, meant London. After a brief return to Fitzroy Square, Morison had finally achieved his childhood dream: in June 1933 he moved into 22 Park Crescent (Nash, 1812). He deluded his friends by saying that he was going to live in the country. 'Where?' they would say, stunned – 'REGENT'S PARK' (this with a slap on the thigh like a starting-pistol). On the rare occasions when he ventured into the real country, he did not enjoy it. London drew him like a magnet: homesick in New York, he wrote to Lewis, 'But oh, for a sight of the Balls Pond Road'. In Regent's Park he remained till the war, and those last few years were, in the main, happy.

In 1935 Morison redesigned the Post Office Telegram forms, rather on the lines of the L.N.E.R. restyling. The confusion of the old form was put right in Morison's common-sense way, and the result was one of the more conspicuous examples of his skill in this direction. Most of March and April that year he spent abroad. He found his friends Pereire and Vox in Paris boringly enthusiastic about the Ludlow, a more expensive display setting machine than the Monotype Supercaster. 'As the orders are given by the man who takes a rake-off he automatically gives the order for the highest price machine – simple!' At Cologne he was surprised by the Hitler Youth. At Leipzig he found it necessary to explain modern British democracy. At Haarlem, visiting van Krimpen, he was overwhelmed by the Enschedé collection of type-specimen books. He came home to find the new Silver Jubilee Stamps, and the offer of a Knighthood. He was un-enthusiastic about both. The stamps, it is true, were 'not as bad as I expected – a little Curwenpressish'.* He wrote to Lewis:

Very many thanks for your admirably wise letter. I think, however, that what is happening is that the authorities desire to make some splash on account of the Jubilee, and are looking about to find a few respectable names to leaven the lump of careerists and pushers.

I excuse your shewing that letter to S.C. and other friends. Don't, however, put it about. I don't enjoy being chattered about.

As to the turning down, I honestly think there would be no com-mensurate economic advantage.*

Shortly afterwards, he was taken ill with jaundice. It was the first time he had had a serious illness (apart from an occasional collapse due to overwork) for nearly twenty years, and he resented inaction. 'Whatever you do,' wrote Lewis, 'do get a good rest and don't rush things. It may seem a long time to be inactive, but when you look back on it, how short it will seem. I do want to see your beard though, so don't get it shaved off.'* In July Morison could bear it no longer and in consequence had a relapse. He had to postpone a convalescent trip to Vichy: 'I am still yellow,' he wrote plaintively to van Krimpen on 25 July. He did not get away till the end of August. By 4 September he was at Vichy,* and from there he wrote to Barrington-Ward:

It is just over a fortnight since I returned to the world. A few days after finding my feet in Regents Park I was counselled to stretch my legs a little more before undertaking the journey hither and went to Eastbourne where I arrived at the same hotel on the same day as Ralph Walter and a relative, Catherine Walter, lineal descendant (so I was informed) of J.W. 1., cause of all our troubles. *The Times* in one sort of personification or other, seems to cross my path with curious persistency. . . . Here at Vichy on the occasion of taking my first bath I was surprised out of my wits by running into a man whose job it was until lately at P.H.S. to keep the linotypes & intertypes up to concert pitch. Every evening found him dickering about with the moulds & matrix channels. A Frenchman by the name of Fleuriet ('Floo-ory' to the comps & the canteen) he has now retired to Paris and comes annually to Vichy. We refreshed each other with technical gabble and I shall look him up again.

The bath business is rather an experience. Water as hot as can be borne rushes out of a hose held by an artist who aims first at your middle and then covers the entire front. Next you turn round, receiving the concentrated force on your backbone & again at your feet. The rite is performed twice or three times in 3 or 4 minutes. Thus you who go in looking human in colour come out as a red mullet to be dried. In addition you go to one of the springs four times daily. The whole is performed under the authority of one of the many specialists. My Docteur Mathieu de Fossy has given me quite a long schedule of what I mayn't eat, and a short one of what I may. To my surprise red bordeaux is commanded, to be taken with Vichy-Celestins.

The doctor's reports were encouraging.

Now these being the findings – & such the consensus – I have proposed an excursion to myself – with the approval of Drs Crimp and De Fossy. This is the excursion: next week Arthur Upham Pope is leading a pilgrimage of students of ancient Iranian Art to Leningrad & Moscow. It is a short affair which will allow me to return here to report to De Fossy on Sept 25. I should not think of going if Crimp were not of the party. Cases of Vichy water are being sent to the steamer which I shall join at Hamburg. . . .

I have not mentioned this excursion to any but my secretary & a close friend. There is a chance that some would regard it as a wanton piece of levity on my part. My judgement though, is that it is time I did something that interested me. . . . This means that I ought to return to work in the second week of October. Thus I shall be here when the *Lit Suppl* appears in its revised layout. You will, by the time this reaches you, have seen my suggestions. . . . We can make further changes later. If you care to send me any proofs here I can reply by Sept 27 – too late I am afraid. But I feel I ought to go about a little, and this Russian trip with 4 or 5 days sea journey each way may benefit me. My brains are extraordinarily sluggish at present & my memory very poor. The world strikes me as odd (I am not thinking of the 'foul wallowing & boisterous' Mussolini) and I haven't yet become used to the smell of tobacco. I have wished that the Anti-Noise Society had a branch here. The loud-speaker is a frequent offender & also the lap dogs belonging to the chic females make a terrific yapping. . . . For the present I beg your blessing upon the journey. . . .

Yours most gratefully
Stanley Morison*

Apart from an uncomfortable evening in Hamburg trying to find the Sovtorgflot steamer, his further excursion was a success. Morison was fascinated to see the Russia he had so often discussed with fellow-comrades.

I can't begin to tell you my impressions, but that they are infinite in number, & in confusion like the country if this hotel is any real example. On top of the general confusion due to general dilapidation there is a mental dilapidation on the part of the older people & an enormous keenness on the part of the younger generation. The trend is towards culture with a huge C. I go down badly because I can't recognise Shelley like the husband in the Five foot shelf ad. A working day of 7 hours with a 5 day week leaves a whale of leisure for culture. All this as we [ ] the visit is of tremendous curiosity value to me & I thrive on it. It takes hours to do anything or get anywhere. The workers of this world unite & they fairly love uniting rather than anything else. They unite outside my bedroom door of a night but they cannot get together on producing any sort of meal under a minimum of $\frac{1}{2}$ hr. This is good even for cold dishes – & they're all cold whether hot *or* cold – if you get me. You can understand therefore why it is that bells ring not, lights don't switch on, basins have no stoppers but as they're tied on loosely to taps one can be got by raiding an unoccupied room and there is no paper where above all places paper ought to be. But the people are trying their best – & could probably do much better if not distracted by all this music &c . . . very noisy. In the restaurant, as one piece by the orchestra finished I roared at my loudest 'No Crimp I cannot hear a word you say while this infernal noise is being made by the orchestra'. The maitre d'hotel, one of the few people here who understand a European language acted . . . & the noise was abated. Triumph of Philistines over art. Long live the Philistines.*

He saw the great eighth-century Anglo-Saxon manuscripts of Bede in the Leningrad Public Library; he went on to Moscow, 'an animated and lively city'.* Then he returned to Vichy, where the doctors passed him fit.

I am now passed by the doctor here as having a perfect heart, perfect liver, perfect kidney – & so on. In fact a perfect die-case.

This means that I hope to come to Cambridge on Monday or Tuesday next week. I propose leaving here very soon & having a day or two in Paris. Am now feeling *very* well.*

He got back to find that the Reece bubble had burst. Van Krimpen had warned him earlier that the transfer of shares in Albatross Verlag G.m.b.H. from the Charterland & General Exploration & Finance Company to the Fanti Consolidated Investment Company Ltd did not bode well.* He was right: the whole situation now became painfully clear.

It was entirely because of my illness that I did not reply to your revelation about Reece. Heaven knows where he will eventually get to. I did not know that your firm was so concerned in him. I should be very pleased, even pleased for his sake, if Enschedé determined to press Reece to face the facts. My situation is this; that for seven years I have had no account of the sales of books upon which I was supposed to have some royalty. It is not the question of the royalty which interests me. I am quite prepared to believe that very few of the books were sold, and anyway it was my understanding that the royalties on those calligraphical books should accrue in order to make it possible for me to carry out my ambition of getting printed the bibliography of Jean de Tournes. This was started a tremendous long time ago and I feel very nervous that I have an infinitely unlimited liability on this. Further, I commissioned Reece to publish at the Pegasus Press Audin's bibliography of French typefounders' specimens. I agreed to have this printed here at Cambridge on the understanding that Lewis would grant me the credit (he refuses to give any credit to Reece), and that the Pegasus should publish the book at such time as would enable me to make a substantial payment from the sales to Lewis. In spite of the fact that the edition was printed and sent to Paris more than eighteen months ago, I can get no word of publication. Of course I have had to pay Lewis. I do owe money, but, at the end of this month I shall have paid Lewis £200 on this book. Such a sum is to me very serious, and of course I have no sort of idea whether Reece will publish the book or, if he does, whether he will return me a penny. You will understand, therefore, that I am really at the end of my enthusiasm for publishing books on the noble subject of typography, and shall save up my last copper for the work of publishing a chapter from my memoirs dealing with Hermann Riess, formerly of Munich, now known as John Holroyd-Reece.*

To Mardersteig, who wrote 'I am getting more and more worried about our friend JHR. I cannot get any answer from him even in urgent matters', Morison was even more apologetic. 'He was here in London last week, and although I telephoned, knowing for certain he was in the office, I was put to the humiliation of an answer that he was not at home.' He told him of Enschedé's plight, and ended 'I cannot tell you how much I regret your situation, knowing as I do that it is more than a merely directly personal liability'.* That was the trouble: they all three had been – were, despite themselves – fond of Reece. Even now, cheated and neglected, they could wonder if his ebullient charm might not still prove irresistible, if he were to reappear with another infallible scheme.

Reece has turned up in London. I had him out and gave him a good talking to. Whether it will have the slightest effect I do not know. He took it so humbly that I think something must be more than a little wrong. He has invented a new company. . . .*

They watched his progress. Could they recover their books? Would he (it was now 1937) pay? No, was the answer, but in 1939, before the war put a sudden stop to European communications, Morison was able to tell Mardersteig almost sympathetically that 'the Commendatore's affairs are in better order'.

Meanwhile Morison and van Krimpen got back to the serious business of type-design. It was an easy relationship: they had both been practising the art for over ten years, seeing and thinking about letters in every form from stamps and coins to newspapers, books and posters. Van Krimpen had as sharp and critical an eye for the detail of letter design as Morison, although he lacked the generous width of vision based on thorough historical knowledge which marked all Morison's work. But this limitation had the advantage of giving his work a recognizable personal style. He had the gift required by Moxon of 'solid reasoning within himself'; a fine draughtsman, he could convey this idea to the skilled engravers at Enschedé; he also knew and studied the history of his own distinguished firm and of typefounding in the Netherlands generally. This mixture of skills gave his work a professional touch which the Monotype craftsmen could only admire; when his first design was produced for mechanical setting, it produced a notable *Pierpontianum* (as Morison called Pierpont's *obiter dicta*): 'I knew, when I first saw Lutetia that it was a copy of one of my founts.'*

In 1935, Morison and van Krimpen were at work or about to start on three designs: Van Dijck, Romulus, and that old Dutch letter which Morison had once called Janson.

I very much rejoice to hear about the Van Dyck italic. This ought to be a very famous addition to our faces and help us very much at

Cambridge and other places where a really fine historical face of that period is required for certain literary purposes. I am very much afraid that our cutting is not calculated to please our brethren at Oxford; but we shall have to do our best to placate Johnson by some means or other.

So Morison wrote when Enschedé agreed to release this ancient and famous italic, of which they still had the original matrices. The roman was a problem: no original material survived:

As for the roman, which is, of course, a supremely important matter, I hold the tentative opinion that examination of the Van Dyck specimen sheet might yield a design which you would work over and of which you would prepare new drawings.*

This latter task proved to be exceptionally difficult. The model eventually selected was a book printed in the genuine Van Dijck 'augustijn Romein',* but the conversion of the design to a modern body involved endless complications. Remembering Perpetua, Morison asked for six specimen punches, which were cut by hand under van Krimpen's supervision by P. H. Rädisch. A first specimen appeared at the beginning of 1937, but the first two sizes were not officially released for another year.*

Work began on Romulus in 1932, before the long-drawn-out work on the Perpetua italic was finished. Morison wrote to van Krimpen:

I do not think I can say anything useful until I see a photograph of your first drawings reduced to 18 point. If you could do this, I would, as they say in Germany, study it, and let you have my opinion immediately. I may say that the sloped roman idea does not go down so well in this office as it does outside. The reason of this is that when the doctrine was applied to Perpetua, we did not give enough slope to it. When we added more slope, it seemed that the fount required a little more cursive in it. The result is the enclosed latest trial. This is rather a compromise, but I propose to pass it as possessing that transitional nature which could prepare the way for a more logical and thorough-going production by you. The reason I was against having much slope on the letter was because I desired to retain the old two-piece lower-case a. You cannot make a success of this if the

343

slope is at all serious. The cursive single piece was a necessity and you will see it in the new proof.*

Van Krimpen began work on the not-too-sloped roman that autumn. Next March he finished his drawings which Morison proceeded to criticize in detail.* Again the long process of drawing, trial, proof and correction was repeated, and the design was finally completed at the end of 1936.

The last design arose from van Krimpen's own historical interests. At the end of November 1935 Morison wrote to van Krimpen to enquire – under protest, but German printers were pressing him – if Enschedé would release the eighteenth-century Fleischmann designs. Van Krimpen agreed, and four days later Morison sent him a German specimen which purported to show the types.* This stirred memories in van Krimpen.

I would like to keep Zanker's Fleischmann specimen. I am almost sure that the type faces shewn are not by Fleischmann. The firm of Zanker seems just an inch too clever by mentioning a year, 1732. Zanker shows at least eight sizes and dates them all 1732. . . . I would like to see the punchcutter able to cut at least twelve hundred punches within ten months of time, and to justify at least as many matrices. Anyone would need at least some three or four years for that!

I don't know what Zanker's 'aus dem sechzehnten Jahrhundert Stammende' typefoundry exactly is like. But I know that about 1870 there has been a German, called Zanker, with Enschedé as foreman. He was sacked because of his misbehaviour; he passed more hours and even whole days in a small public house than in the foundry, and at last even flatly refused to come when he was sent for, saying that it was better in a 'kleine reine boel' (the pub) than in a 'grosse Schweineboel' with which he meant the typefoundry. He may have been of the Nuremberg family, and he may have stolen some type; but this seems rather unlikely since about 1870 nobody thought of old type as people did about 1900 and later. His christian name was Adalbert I think. There are more reasons to believe that Zanker's Fleischman are not 'Originalschnitte', but the one that they could not have been cut within one single year is conclusive.*

Morison was amused. 'You will have to write us a short article for the *Monotype Recorder* a little later – of course bowdlerising the

344

account of Mr Zanker's fondness for what, in England, is called "pub crawling".'* And from Zanker's types his mind went back to the vastly preferable idea of recutting the 'Janson' types (also in demand from Germany) whose style Fleischmann adapted for his own types.

A question about the Janson type. I think I told you that some German customers have been agitating the Monotype Corporation to cut all the sizes of roman and italic, and that we have agreed to cut them if we can get hold of the original material. I said this because I was under the impression that some of the sizes in Stempel's list are modern re-cuttings, and by no means facsimiles.

Following up the matter, I discovered that Haag-Drugulin seems to have lent the original punches or matrices to Updike, and, for some reason or another, are unable to secure their return. Updike is a very tight-fisted little bantam, and I may have to get on to him, but, before doing so, I want to ask whether there is any foundation for the statement made to me that the successors of Anton Janson sold the material to Amsterdam about the year 1700; if so, whether any trace of it remains?*

The consequence was that Morison was led to explore again the winding paths of late seventeenth-century typographic history that he had first set foot in twelve years earlier. He thought to borrow Francis Meynell's fount of the Stempel Janson, and to make a start with that; but the Stempel cutting was too heavy, and he had not enough to go on. In May 1936, Morison dropped the idea and the punches so far cut were destroyed. But he did not stop work, and with the help of Gustav Mori he traced the types to the Ehrhardt foundry at Leipzig, *c.* 1710. There was no connection with Janson, whose name Stempel had given to the type, a mis-ascription followed by Morison in *On Type Faces* in 1923.

Cheered by this discovery, Morison took up the idea of re-cutting it, and – uniquely – his instructions for it survive. On 26 January 1937, armed with photographs of Mori's original Ehrhardt specimens, he wrote to Mr Steltzer in the Type Drawing Office.

Last Spring we put in hand with you the initial work of re-creating the old Dutch Face for which more than one of our customers were asking.

Through paucity of material however, we were unable to satisfy them and the several characters in Series 453 were abandoned.

We are now sending you:–

A. A photograph of the Ehrhardt Series, which amongst other sizes shows a portion in Tertia, both Roman and Italic.

B. Five photographic prints showing the same fount with a small amount of Italic.

We now ask you to put in hand the work of a few Roman and Italic characters.

The ultimate completion of the Roman alphabet would not seem to be a matter of much difficulty but in the matter of the Italic, some obstacles may be encountered as in the capitals several are missing.

We think, however, that for the present the accompanying photographs will supply you with sufficient data for the making of the specimen characters.

We should like the Face to be as big on the body as the 14pt. in Series 101 [Imprint].

We imagine that the weight will be between Series 101 and Series 110 [Plantin].

Finally, we shall be glad if you will regularise the fount as regards alignment.

For the time being, the Face should be called 'Ehrhardt'.

By 20 February, he already had proofs.

I am very interested in the proof of the Ehrhardt series 453 14pt. roman and italic, but I am prevented from making up my mind definitely in favour of these specimen characters owing to the fact that the set appears to me to be so wide. I should like to see a specimen on a narrower set if you could have this made.

At first glance the fount appears to me to be a little more condensed than I expected. Also I do not recognise the capitals. Having no copy of the photographs of the Ehrhardt specimen, I do not dogmatise, but my distinct impression is that the capital G. though correct in colour, proportions and general form, is not correctly seriffed at the top or at the bottom. There is a serif, I think, at the bottom of the capital G. where the thin curve joins the thick perpendicular. I should have said, too, that the horizontal at the foot is a trifle too short.

346

I am speaking now only from memory, but I feel sufficiently confident to ask you to look into it.

The lower-case roman letters appear to me to be sound.

With the italic I am not quite so pleased. I should have imagined, for example (and here again I am now only speaking from memory) that the italic lower-case g. would have had much more sweep to it.

After that, all went smoothly; the design was approved in August, and matrices were made available in November 1937.* There was a full showing in the Summer 1938 *Monotype Recorder*, and Morison himself set out the history of the type in the March 1939 issue of *Signature*, the 'quadrimestrial of typography and graphic arts' which Oliver Simon had started in November 1935; the article was set in the new type. Morison had discovered most of the story; the last part, the discovery of the identity of the punchcutter, a Hungarian called Miklós Kis, had to wait till 1957.*

Morison had welcomed *Signature* when it first came out,* and it now provided the perfect instrument for the exposition of Ehrhardt. So Morison's first design, Garamond, and his last, Ehrhardt, were both described and displayed in periodicals edited by Oliver Simon.

The cutting of Ehrhardt was the end of an era in Morison's relations with Monotype; another came with the death, on 11 February 1937, of Frank Hinman Pierpont. While he had sometimes thwarted Morison, his genius as an optical engineer and the iron discipline with which he ran the works had provided Morison with the quality of engraving which, as well as the designs themselves, had made his programme such a success. A tribute to him appeared in the Spring 1937 *Recorder*, to which Morison contributed his first article for some time, on 'Black letter: its Origin & Current Use'. This was produced to celebrate the cutting of 'Sachsenwald', a handsome elongated black-letter designed by Berthold Wolpe, whom Morison had known in Germany as a pupil of Koch. He had been forced to fly to this country in 1932, and Morison had immediately commissioned an inscriptional display type from him, which had been issued as 'Albertus' the previous year. Now came Sachsenwald, and reflecting on it Morison took up another aspect of the great theme, an aspect he had neglected in his early days, when he skipped from the Carolingian minuscule to the humanistic hand. It had now come to occupy him more and more, and, since this occasion found him unprepared (Beatrice had gone to America for a longer-than-usual stay and Morison had to fill the gap), he continued to work on it the harder. He wrote to Updike in some embarrassment.

My dear Updike
    I lately had a message from Mrs. Warde who read me an extract from a letter of yours which decidedly put me to the blush. I was at once flattered and confused, for I entertained a mean opinion of the article on Black letter which I wrote to fill a space in her Recorder while she was in America. The Recorder is not exactly intended for your eyes and had I known it was likely to get to your office I would have revised the proof. It went through without any sort of reading by me and there are paragraphs in it that I wish could have been altered.
    I do very little nowadays of that sort of writing. For one thing I consider that Mrs. W. does it all a very great deal better, more gracefully, more humanely and more informingly because less donnish and 'scientific' than I find it possible to avoid. In fact I get more and more scholastic, narrow and specialist. It is one of the real merits of *Printing Types* that it can be enjoyed by people who have a humane, and not a trade reason, for studying the book. So also with Mrs. Warde's writing. I supported therefore your suggestion of reprinting some of her pieces. It ought to be done.
    Mrs. Warde also tells me of your interest in the Times Roman. For your curiosity I send you a few sheets of the folio edition of the History of the Times set in the larger sizes of the fount. It is my one effort at designing a fount. I wish it could be re-designed, but it seems to be doing its job day by day in *The Times*. It has the merit of not looking as if it had been designed by somebody in particular – Mr. Goudy for instance, who has designed a whole century of very particular looking types. . . .
    Do pardon my incivility in not replying in reasonable time to your letter. I have been so occupied with the Life of Delane that I have not been able to permit myself to return to other interests. . . .

My being general editor leaves me very little time for typographical work, which, however, I cannot completely drop. I feel very wicked though when I find myself indulging in it and I am looking forward to a positive debauch when *P.T.* ed. 2 comes forth from the Oxford Univ. Press.*

Earlier, Updike had delighted him by writing to announce a second edition of his own book, which prompted him to put down some long and deeply held thoughts on the purpose of typography.

That you are projecting a new edition of *Printing Types* is most exciting news. I can well imagine that you are finding the work a considerable labour. The original edition of 1922 was at once a revelation and inspiration. I do not believe that any of the work since done by others would even have been attempted otherwise. I am sure that you are not able yourself to realise the immense effect the book made fifteen years ago. Moreover, in spite of what has been done by others, the book holds its position. It is no denigration of its scientific value to say that its style and sagacity would maintain it even if half the dates and names were wrong – and they are not. As the original book did not claim to be an encyclopaedia, I see no reason why a revised edition should be allowed to grow into a completely different book. In many ways your work is very personal, and ought to remain so. As you know, the Germans consider that you seldom miss an opportunity of laughing at them. At the present stage of the European situation, I should not be willing to make any concessions to Teutonic pride, but I suppose a strictly scientific historian would not have admitted certain of your lines directed against them. . . .

It would be very useful if you could give us a few words towards clearing our minds of some of the current typographical cant. Owing to the European situation and the consequent immigration, we are suffering to a greater extent to idle chatter about art. One or two fluent Teutons are setting about to blow up the whole of English typographical tradition. They do not see that typographical tradition is the embodiment of the common sense of generations. They wish to substitute style for sense. You have similar tendencies in America, and I imagine you are referring to them when you mention in your last paragraph the changes for the worse. You are quite right in diagnosing 'sloppy exhibitionism'. There is too much egoism.*

The denial of 'egoism' was, to Morison's mind, essential in an art whose purpose was to attract and hold, without compulsion, every eye it met. Robert Blake had written to praise Gill Sans (Stephenson Blake were now making a wood-letter version under licence from Monotype). Morison replied:

I agree that it is difficult to assess the degree to which the success of a type face is the consequence of 'the beauty of its design'. In the matter of the L.N.E.R., however, it was the commonsense quality and absence of trickiness which led to its choice. If the Gill Sans had been as romantic as Futura or Cable this could not have happened.*

The day after he wrote, on 4 May 1936, the L.N.E.R. used the letter in a new and strikingly beautiful way, for the 'Silver Jubilee', the first streamline train to run in England. It was all silvery-grey from the new streamline locomotive, No. 2509 *Silver Link*, to the last of its six articulated coaches. It ran between London and Newcastle in four hours. Gill and Morison were lost in admiration of the new use to which their work had been put. Everything, the name plate of the engine, the stainless steel lettering on the coaches, the notepaper and envelopes provided for the use of passengers 'free of charge', all bore the trademark of Gill Sans. 'The novel arrangement of lighting using tubular lights', the restaurant 'veneered in quartered Australian maple', Table d'Hôte first-class Luncheon 3/6, Dinner 5/0 – it was a wonder of clean modern design and elegant luxury, a worthy successor of the Stirling Single and its smart teak coaches of Morison's boyhood.

The 'Silver Jubilee' and its even more elegant successor the 'Coronation' of 1938 (blue and silver with maroon wheels, it went all the way to Edinburgh in six hours, and had the added luxury of an Observation Car) were the last beautiful manifestations of the Machine Age. All too soon now it was to come to an end.

15

POSTAGE stamps, like railway trains, had long had a romantic attraction for Morison. But for some time past he had taken a directly practical interest in their design. He had taken part in arranging the exhibits at the Double Crown Club meeting in March 1933, at which Guy Harrison spoke on 'The Design of Postage Stamps'. He maintained a keen, though critical, interest in Harrisons' stamp-printing, and on the accession of Edward VIII he had a considerable part in determining the plain but distinguished design of the new issue. An amateur design had been submitted by a seventeen-year-old enthusiast called A. S. Brown, and Harrisons were experimenting with it as well as other designs submitted, photographs by Bertram Park and Hugh Cecil, and a whole series of matchless ugliness, showing the monarch in plain clothes and in naval and Highland uniform, prepared at the G.P.O.* It is possible that Morison was responsible for the selection of Brown's basic design, and its combination with Hugh Cecil's photograph. He can certainly be credited with the simplicity of the final design. On 29 August 1936, he told Graham Pollard:

I had yesterday an agreeable letter from Guy (that is his fore-name) Harrison thanking me for assistance with the new stamp. Layout (omission of REVENUE & value (THREEHALFPENCE) in words, all festoons of tripe) seems to be approved. I did *not* suggest the use, direct use, of a photograph for the Monarch's head; nor do I agree with it – at least, if you do that, you can't use the conventional cut through the neck. If you have the photo you must have the Fifty shilling tailored neck & shoulders.

Today's *Times* contains a rational leader on Spain. I see that the F.A.I. people have already shot 3 of yr brethren for suggesting the disarming of the masses. In the meantime while the 'liberal' element here is backing up the Spanish 'Reds' & the Russian Trotskyists, and attacking *The Times* for being too 'Right', a couple of advertisers (I've seen the correspondence) have cancelled their contracts because the paper is too 'Left'. These are not inch ads. or smalls, but £36-ers.*

The Spanish Civil War had just begun. To Morison, no longer drawn to any political party of the left, the confrontation of Church and Communism was a new moral crisis, requiring stringent self-examination and determination. Gill was in a similar position. Their point of view on the Church, and the distressing 'solidarity of the ecclesiastical class with the banking class', was identical.

I do know that we are at one on the subject of church and money. One satisfactory feature of the worst scandal of the day – that the church militant should be militant in favour of the creditor class – is that the church militant in this respect does not know what it is talking about.*

In politics, however, Gill had thought Morison too contemptuous of organization, and Morison felt obliged to explain.

There is a type of person who takes up any modish piece of intellectualist or economic 'thought' and makes it his own until something fresh catches his eye. There is another type sincerely convinced that something 'ought to be done' and joins anybody who is actively engaged in intellectual or political or economic agitation. Others simply hate to be left out of anything which they think is part of the general movement of their own sort. But I have no recollection of making any harsh remarks about any of them.*

But his own attitude was different: 'I take more seriously the expression of the worker than of the worker's representatives, particularly the self-elected representatives of Rome and Moscow.' From a Marxist point of view, neither had any, or at least enough, influence on the economic base of modern society.

For the last thousand years, the means of production, distribution and exchange (i.e. 'wealth') has been passing into the hands of groups specializing in the exploitation of human needs, so that we have come, during the last hundred years, to the creation by these groups of the notion of a 'standard of living', the king, the army, the church, the universities etc are not outside but inside the production system. . . . Production must exercise the ruling power as long as there is a 'standard of living'. So it has, for years, been my opinion that the Reformation was the creation of the bourgeoisie and that the intellectuals only butted in.*

When the Spanish War broke out, Gill wrote to Morison to complain that the Republican cause was being misrepresented in *The Times*, notably because no distinction was made between the Communist and Anarchist positions. Morison answered.

August 22, 1936

Dear Gill,

The main cause of the ignorance of the Press is that the Press correspondent's job is arduous, ill-paid and encyclopaedic. As he has to deal with events which may be anything from a boxing match to a currency question, he must necessarily fail to do justice except to those subjects in which he takes a personal interest. That being the case, how can it be expected that the Reuter Havas Exchange and A.P. correspondents, all of them respectable products of middle-class educational institutions, distinguish the essential from the accidental; distinguish the fabric from the furniture of a revolutionary philosophy, distinguish, as must be done here, Marx from Bakunin. These correspondents supply the entire world with news, with the exception of one or two journals like *The Times* which maintain their own correspondents.

In the case of *The Times*, the Madrid correspondent is a Catholic, perhaps Right Centre. The Barcelona man is a free thinker well to the Left. The prejudices of proprietors of newspapers are shown in their leading articles. But it is not difficult to distinguish views from news. Hence, it does not appear to me to be accurate to say that the whole of the Press is so corrupt as to remove the basis for a reasonable judgement on the situation. As it seems to me, there are two points of view possible. One is that of an observer whose experience has, he thinks, compelled him to distrust intellectual contraptions. He always wants to know just precisely what is the next step. There is the other man concerned, like you, with first principles. Either the social philosophy of this second man will 'work' when the 'next step' has been taken by people acting on the advice of the first man, or it will work later if at all. Marx and Engels were efficient because they not only possessed an intellectual contraption, but gave up their lives to organisation. But it was not so much the creation of an organisation as the guidance of it.

They did not invent the revolutionary impulse, but gave it a theory. The importance of theory in revolution is that only it can create unity. There can be no consistency without theory, no revolutionary consistency without revolutionary theory. Now, as I understand it, all the Left parties are theoretical parties separated by varying interpretations of Marx and Engels. You, I take it, do not include the Anarchists in the Left, but it is they who are the strongest single power in the Spanish peninsula, and they are overwhelmingly in the majority in Catalonia, and have been for two generations. Their 'first principles' came into collision with those of Marx and Engels in the 1860's. Whether your first principles are those of Bakunin or of Marx, I do not know. It is only the state of emergency which has been brought about by the suddenness of the declaration of war by the army that has brought the Marxists and the Bakuninists and others into some sort of purely temporary 'front'. When the emergency passes away, it will then be found that in a revolutionary situation the word 'Left' means absolutely and precisely nothing. It is only in a state of Liberal muddleheaded compromise, as here, that the word 'Left' can signify anything. At the moment the Marxist or the Bakuninist Party comes to effective power here, they will decide, presumably with your consent, that you are a counter-revolutionary.

Gill's answer moved the debate on to the question of the temporal power of the Church. Here Morison was more hopeful.

But the issues in Spain are not as simple as the Stalinists try to believe. I agree with your view that the Church as at present 'led' is a subject for the most serious disquiet, but I cannot think of any period of history, since at least the Reformation, when this was not so.

The supersession of a decadent religious Imperialism (was it not that admirable Dominican, Saint Pius V, who presented the whole of the American continent to His Most Catholic Majesty, the King of Spain?) by secular and mutually destructive Imperialisms has taken pretty nearly half a millennium. 'Spain' is the last 'Catholic' country to come into the modern world; and from Feudalism at one jump without the slow-moving industrial development of England, Germany and America. Vatican City is still feudal. The present Pope two years ago passed a law giving every bishop the title of 'Excellency'. You and I may be living at an awkward junction of time, but

354

we do at least witness the church being forced out of its Imperialist position, compelled, slowly it may be, to drop 'Catholicism' in favour of the gospel of Jesus Christ.*

This did not, however, mean giving encouragement to the cause of world Communism.

I do not see any advantage to the anti-totalitarian or the anti-Fascist cause by giving statements or interviews to the Stalinists. The Third International is such a blundering contraption that it cannot prevent itself from doing more harm than good. It is quite true that it does good, but its leadership, conducted by a most conceited set of jacka-napes, is an affront to any reflecting worker. In my judgement, our people, i.e. the papists taken as a European group, hold a pretty good hand of cards; they could do a great deal for spiritual liberty if they would stick closely together on spiritual issues.

To my mind, the value of the smash-up in Spain is that it forces the most grasping and reactionary element in the Roman Curia (the Spanish Cardinals have been obstructive for years: compare the record of the late Cardinal Vives) into the confessional box. It is bound to do a great deal of good, and as the whole rickety institution necessarily progresses at the pace of the slowest, and as crisis tremen-dously accelerates the process of movement, I add my rejoicings to yours that so much of the trumpery has been destroyed. But I am not prepared to take Stalinists into my confidence. I look forward to a little punishment fitting their little crime. I see already that in Barce-lona the attempt on the Stalinists' part to disarm the Bakuninists has resulted in the shooting down of those who think that enough shoot-ing has been done.*

Gill and Morison were now thoroughly warmed up, when Gill diverted the subject into a different channel. He sent Morison a copy of a pamphlet, of which he disapproved, appealing for funds for Blackfriars, the Oxford Dominican house. Morison seized on Gill's argument 'that the endowment of Mass stipends automatically tends to create and extend the parasite class which lives on interest which has to be provided out of somebody's labour'; he felt some classes, 'the priests and the professors', were necessarily dependent on rent. Gill retorted with some sharp observation about the degree to which Morison's own position in life depended on interest. This provoked a massive counter-blast.

About taking interest: I have never taken a penny of interest or rent. On the other hand, I do not condemn those who do, although I avoid their society. I do not condemn them because I think the church is irrevocably committed to the principle of giving and taking interest on certain money transferred to certain people for certain purposes. How long I personally may be able to survive in this world as it has been developed by, amongst others, Catholic philosophers and theologians without myself taking interest, I do not know. The reason I put the question to you in my last letter was because you told me that you had declined to subscribe to the Blackfriars Fund since the administrators were going to invest your gift in Government securities. Now, inasmuch as I hold that the church is committed to allowing the taking of interest, above all by an individual or society which places its funds at the disposition of the community, e.g. through its own Government, I wished to know whether you considered the Blackfriars object itself so inconsistent with the communal interests as represented by the Government that you considered it unbecoming of Blackfriars to do what would otherwise be allowable with these subscriptions.

As to war, I do not take part in it, and have spent a certain amount of time in Pentonville and similar places in consequence. Nevertheless, I do not condemn those who do take part in it. Hence, my attitude both on interest and war is identical with your own. On the other hand, unlike you, I don't make a principle of taking no interest or a principle of not taking arms. I would be prepared, and am prepared, to give a Christianist–Rationalist justification for my attitude both towards interest and war. When it is perfectly clear that by reason of past endowments, investments, accumulations and what not, 75 per cent of the money wealth of a country is owned by 7.5 per cent of the population, it is perfectly clear that the population as a whole is, in the event of war, fighting for the 7.5 per cent, just as in the event of peace they are working for these 7.5 per cent. It is these 7.5 per cent who maintain everything because it pays, including the Church of England or the Church of Rome as the case may be. They pay all the theologians, professors, artists just as they pay the engineers and the labourers. The whole of the western world is under this system which, as far as historical enquiry can discover, originated somewhere in the 10th or 11th century. Nevertheless, and this is where I differ from you, I am not prepared to suggest that the present world should go back to the 9th century, behind the middle-class system described above, back to feudalism and serfdom, primitive simplicity, with every physically weak man at the mercy of every physically stronger. In other words, if you ask me to make the choice between what I may shortly call factory ideas and peasant ideas I choose – and without the slightest hesitation – factory ideas. This is in part helped by the fact that I am born a Londoner, and will never live anywhere else, so that my native heath is a concrete flagstone, and I prefer the No: 11 bus to the sight of a horse or cow. However, I am not, as far as I know, sentimental about such things. I only mention it because it is fair to admit such a bias. Allowing all other people a similar degree of bias in the contrary direction, I still cannot believe that the greatest material good of the greatest number of all sorts of men – Christian and non-Christian and anti-Christian – can be assisted, let alone achieved, by the destruction of the machine. No programme, yours or mine, could be put into operation by a single stroke. At this moment, people of your sort (the Anarchists) and people of my sort (the Socialists) are arguing out these matters in the face of an aerial and artillery bombardment by the military and their mercenaries. 'Spain' as a whole is underfed materially, hence it is comparatively indifferent to me that your people have bombed the churches. It is important that they spare the factories. From what I can see of it, humanity stands in need of more and better churches, and more and better factories, not fewer. I say that we need a more thorough and efficient exploitation of the industrial machine. I wish it to change hands. And the same with the Catholic Church. This super-exploitation of industry can take place if interest is turned into wages.*

Gill, still rejecting Morison's view of the necessity of rent and interest as a stabilizing factor in a machine-made world, must have equated the creative craftsman with the anarchist in not requiring rent as an automatic part of their reward. Morison again replied trenchantly. Gill, he argued, with his eyes on the Second Coming, was ignoring the facts of the human condition as it was, and considering only the artist, a man who by definition does what he likes doing. Human responsibility was more complicated than that, especially for those who were not doing what they liked. To obtain social justice, it was necessary, if not to compromise, then to be more patient with the forces of this world than Gill was prepared to be. At the moment, Gill was enjoying the benefits of being a famous man, a 'West End artist', but satisfying his own conscience by living simply, without admitting the responsibilities of his position.

When the Anarchists took over the biggest cinema in Barcelona and found there was a contract with a certain famous tenor who filled the house, they pointed out to him that he was receiving something like three hundred times more than the weekly wages of the charwoman who swept up the cigarette ends from beneath the seats of the patrons who provided the reservoir from which the salaries were paid. The charwoman was paid 15 pesetas a week (about 16/8) and nowadays the stalls accommodate each evening half a dozen Anarchists whose revolvers cover the tenor while he is singing – (also for 15 pesetas a week.) Now, this tenor's responsibility is for his song. I do not doubt that with the revolvers pointing towards him he sings better than he ever sang in his life. Thus, the Anarchists enforce what they regard as social justice – that is their idea of human responsibility. It is their duty to secure social equality, and this is what they are 'making' – to use your favourite word. Now the one common bond between you and the tenor, i.e. distinguished persons, and those who have no capacities which leave them distinct, is the physical one, the desire for food, shelter and women etc. Because all these in themselves are more immediate and urgent to the greatest number of mankind, the style of the optional things to be made is of correspondingly less importance today. And I say that social justice is the 'thing' which, as members of a given geographical constituency, we each have to feel and to take responsibility for. I do not see, therefore, how you advance social justice now by drawing attention to the 'right' making of chairs and tables, as chairs and tables.*

Gill was more gentle in his answer.

I imagine all decent people are ultimately anarchists – certainly all Christians must be. The only problem is how to bridge the intermediate stage.

It seems to me common sense to suppose that the ultimate anarchy to which Christianity leads is not to be achieved here below. Nevertheless, a Christian politic should always be one which leads in the heavenly direction, looks to anarchy as its guiding star.

Meanwhile I agree with you that patience is all-important. Surely in this connection, verse 2 of the 4th. chapter of 2nd. Timothy, and all that follows is to the point. And I do think that one does exhibit patience by arguing, in season and out of season, that while we live in an industrial machine-using world we must make the *best* of it and not the worst, and that this best, as regards things made, means such things as GILL SANS (begging your pardon), the new Daily Express building (except the sculpture inside), plain furniture and utensils etc. As regards politics, I entirely agree with you [about] the transference of ownership of the means of production to the workers. . . .

But of course I cannot submit to your definition of 'Artist' – 'A man who earns his living by doing what he likes doing', unless you include in the word, doctors, lawyers, many priests, many soldiers, yourself and all those many hundreds of still remaining bricklayers, carpenters, masons who regard their jobs as their vocations. If you do include all these, then of course I agree with you. But I should prefer to say not that the artist earns his living by doing what he likes doing but by doing what it is his vocation to do – he acts according to his nature (Aristotelian sense of the word), not according to his whim. Moreover I think it is somewhat unfair or at least undiscerning of you to regard me primarily from the point of view of the French Gallery and the art critics rather than from the point of view of Fetter Lane, and that of the weary widows who want tombstones and of the architects who sometimes, for quite good reasons, want stone carvings on their buildings. A man is what he tries to be and intends to be rather than what foolish people advertise him as being. . . .

So you see we really agree entirely. I only ask that you cease to regard me as a West End artist, and to believe that my efforts to reach the truth about human work and property do not prevent me from taking a practical line in relation to the present situation. And in that matter I value your judgment exceedingly.*

Before it arrived Morison added another note on 16 September, in a rather depressed key, about the growth of pro-Fascism in the hierarchy and laity, and the problems of the individual dissenter.

What is happening is the organisation of an authoritarian block comprising Italy, Austria and Germany with punctual railways, good regional cookery, but no sort of intellectual freedom.

By 26 September, Morison had received Gill's letter, with which he mostly agreed; he now defined where they differed.

359

I am glad that business about the 'West End' artist has been cleared up. I have been so busy with business lately as to have no time for anything serious. I have one or two things to say about Anarchism. As soon as I can, I will get them off my chest. I now think we are getting somewhere near the point at which we diverge. I readily agree with you that a Christian world is one of vocations; as readily that a vocation for everyone is impossible in these times. Where you and I differ, it seems to me, is that you regard these times as peculiar, whereas I regard them as being characteristic – in this vital respect. To my notion, the *New Testament* makes it perfectly clear that 'not all are called'. So far from it that the 'world' will always be in opposition. Hence, I regard your insistence upon, and expectation of, universal vocational content of work done for wages as Utopian. It is consistent enough with your theory that Christians should be Anarchists, but it is not consistent, to my mind, with the doctrine of the 'Prince of the World'.

Whether we like it or not, there is something in this doctrine of original sin.*

This correspondence is the only relic of an occupation to which both devoted a great deal of time. When Gill came up to London from Pigotts, he would often stay the night with Morison, and the disputation that followed often went on well into the small hours. On essentials they were not opposed, but because they were both committed to their beliefs (Morison gave up Italian food and wine at the time of the invasion of Abyssinia), it was necessary to define them, down to the last detail. In much they agreed: their differences gave each a more exact definition of what he believed.

At the beginning of 1936, Morison went to Germany again. This time he was more disturbed by what he found there.

I arrived in the thick of the celebrations of the III Anniversary of the 'Revolution' i.e. 30 January & as this hotel is bang opposite the Chancellery where the local Haile Selassie has his dugout there was much to be seen & heard. For instance incessant Heil-ing all day & half the night; a huge torchlight procession with bands & flags, banners & all sorts of childishly romantic 'glamour'; splendid uniforms & a very great deal of singing, well-drilled cheering &c.*

Moving on to Munich, he found more to worry him than the childish posturing of the Berlin processions. He wrote to Barrington-Ward.

I have been bustling about in these parts, talking to palaeographers and professors of one thing or another. I imagine you still in the Isle of Wight – a long way it seems from this city & this country where I never meet with a Nazi – or only one, a waiter in a railway station. Curious thing, the academic body here which bulk so large in the life of the country (not to mention the cartoons & caricatures) has no influence. The professors ran like rabbits when the Nazis began their pressure. I cannot imagine such an – almost automatic – crumpling-up of the people at Oxford & Cambridge. I am almost persuaded that the learning of Germany is literally, book-learning; ignored or forgotten at the bidding of uniformed, even if self-constituted 'authority'. Today I have been through all the University with a friend: a splendid series of reading-rooms and private rooms for professors, seminars, privat-dozenten & whatnot all dedicated to the study of LAW, yet it is acknowledged that many persons are arrested, get taken to concentration camps without their relatives being informed for a month or more. The study of law in this University reminds me of the meetings in the Café Royal (Regent Street) of Freemasons who have never used any except a ritualistic trowel.*

Soon after he got back, there was further cause for alarm. During the weekend of 7–8 March, Hitler occupied the Rhineland. Both Dawson and Barrington-Ward were out of town, and came back to Printing House Square on Sunday. There was not much opportunity for consultation between them, nor was it necessary. The stance of *The Times* grew naturally out of the closeness of their working relationship. Barrington-Ward expressed it in a series of leaders – six in six days – which argued forcefully for consideration of Germany's demands for a revision of the Treaty of Locarno, and pointed out the dangers of a too rapid reaction against Hitler. 'Appeasement' is the great perhaps of the first half of this century. It is, however, indisputable that ' *The Times* was accurately anticipating and preparing the way for the official view, as well as reflecting majority opinion'.*

Like most other readers of *The Times*, Morison was deeply

impressed by Barrington-Ward's performance. He had, however, a special reason for writing to him about it: it was one thing,
he had discovered, to redesign a paper, and another to see that
the design was intelligently used.

Without doubt, this must have been a week of exceptional activity
and anxiety for you. The way in which the first leaders brought out
the significance and implication of the day's events made the whole
series most memorable. I, for one, have cut them out. After all
recollection of the eventualities themselves has passed away, the
sentences and paragraphs will remain worthy of re-reading, and by
others than mere students of the art of presentation of opinion.
Though it seems paradoxical to say so, several of these leaders possess
one merit they alone should not have been allowed to possess. On
several days, in my judgement at least, the news of the League's proceedings was more easily obtained by reading the leading article
than by reading the accounts on the Bill page. Only on those days
when there was a double-column heading did the Paper present the
reader with a summary before going on with the solid detail. I am
writing now from memory, but I can only recall one issue in which
a single-column heading to the Bill page was provided with a few
lines of italic summary. . . .

I do not think it an exaggeration to say that one almost needed a
pneumatic drill to get the real news out of some of the Bill pages this
week. I recollect a headline, FLANDIN'S THREE POINTS, and finding them
stowed away in the second column under sub-head, THE BELGIUM
POSITION.

For a score of similar reasons, I am led to ask that the efficiency (it
may well be too much to expect the artistry) of the leader page may
be extended to the Bill page.

I have often felt critical before, but never so much as this week.
It seems to me that the art of presentation of news has not been
studied as it deserves, and as the serious nature of world events
justifies readers in demanding. I do not urge that *The Times*, of all
papers, should dramatize the news; but I do suggest, with all respect,
that it should be so presented as to be comprehensible at a glance.

He was having similar trouble with the *T.L.S.* The reforms
which he had described to Barrington-Ward had gone through
more smoothly than those to the main paper, since Richmond
approved of the principles involved in Morison's new line. When

it came to detail, however, Richmond's natural conservatism created difficulties. Simon Nowell-Smith acted as buffer between Morison and Richmond in these matters, as when Morison removed the vertical rules between columns in the last trial but one:

'You can't do that. Richmond will have a fit.'
'You must see that he doesn't.'
'Anyhow, you can't scrap the vertical rules and leave in the horizontal one under the date-line.'
'No' (writing *dele* in the margin), 'I can't. But I am making your task the harder.'

The first *T.L.S.* to appear without any rules was the issue of 2 November 1935. 'Looks well,' Barrington-Ward noted. 'Morison will still have to keep Richmond up to scratch in some things.'* This was not altogether easy, as he confessed to Pollard ('My powers of self-repetition are limited') next year,* but by then he was deep in the next volume of the *History*. He had to refuse Porter Garnett, who had written to him from America to ask for an introduction to a book on type-design.

If you had asked me to write you an Introduction to a book on Peel, Brougham, or some other politicians or journalists of the nineteenth century, I could have turned it out without asking you – as I did in my last letter – to do half my job for me. You are, dare I say, too incredulous; I am not so good at holding so many faces in my memory. I have, indeed, a very good visual memory, but I have been overloading it, and a lot of stuff has been pressed out to make room for other material.*

By the middle of 1937 Morison had thoroughly established himself on the *History*: 'Early official use of this title,' he scribbled triumphantly in the margin of a letter from Barrington-Ward describing him as 'in charge'.* By the beginning of next year, the next volume was in proof; John Walter, to Morison's relief, was 'genuinely pleased' with the new work. Barrington-Ward was staying up late over the proofs, and providing a host of useful suggestions, as he had on the first volume. Morison was correspondingly grateful.

The whole house ought to be very grateful to you for this by no means the least of the services you have rendered it. Dragging that mass of proof about with you must have been highly exasperating – or would be to me. Your report is an immense relief to my mind, oppressed as it has been with a very keen sense of the shortcomings, repetitions, dislocations, and, what is to be most regretted, the failure to reveal significance.

I agree with you that the political history, British and foreign, is well done – as Morrah wrote the original chapters, it could hardly be otherwise, and under compression by Tomlinson it has gained. Although these chapters require a good deal of knowledge of European politics, they are, I think, perhaps easier to read than the rest. It is the material that is not in the files that is so difficult to deal with. I have this week very much revised the chapters dealing with the repeal of the taxes on knowledge, and the price of the Paper. I hope, in the attempt to point out the significance of these trade events, I have improved them. I re-worked these chapters because, having submitted myself to the task of a consecutive reading of the proofs, I came to the conclusion which underlies your own letter, namely, that there does not appear to be any 'story'. It is like an excellent piece of butter before the cow has been stamped on it by the grocer, which ought to be done at least when mother has company. This book at least has a chronological sequence which it will be difficult to improve, but, although the material is fairly consistent (though it can certainly be improved), it has no pattern. This, however, was only to be expected since you have got to order your half-a-pound of fresh butter before your grocer will stamp it for you. We now have the butter, and, as for the pattern, I have come to the conclusion that if, in the inevitable rewriting of 'The New Regime', care is taken to insert carefully drafted forecasts of the new material I have put into the trade–price–circulation chapters, and other paragraphs are inserted as echoes at certain dramatically justifiable points, the book would read, in the whole, as a study in the development of 'the tradition of *The Times*'.

And this, I am tempted to think might not be a bad title for this second volume. Volume III would deal with the reconciliation of tradition with truth, sketch the profound benefit which *The Times* derived from the 'tradition'; prove that without this 'tradition' *The Times* would not have survived to be worth reviving; that the continued vitality of institutions and traditions is dependent upon the self-criticism of their subjects. I also wish to point out the significance of the growing centralization which was a marked element in John Walter III's regime; that, while this benefited *The Times*, it was also responsible for a gradual reduction in editorial power and therefore editorial vigour. If the editor of *The Times* is not in paramount command of all the columns of the Paper, he ceases to be an editor and becomes a glorified sub-editor. The editor of *The Times* is either a strong editor or he is not an editor. These are some of the things that will have to be let out in the third volume – and this is to anticipate.

He added a postscript. Richmond had retired from the *Literary Supplement* on 31 December 1937, to be succeeded by D. L. Murray.

This week Murray, S[imon]. N[owell]. Smith and the Adv^t man of the *Lit. Supp.* met in my room for what turned out to be a very important confab. Evidently Murray means business. I fancy he will make a literary & a commercial success of the thing.*

The second volume appeared in February 1939, four years after the first, and with equal éclat. A minor disaster overtook the special folio limited edition, printed at Cambridge. Lewis wrote:

With regard to the inverted line, this is a blasted nuisance. I am quite prepared to set and print a cancel for your copy if you wish. I have traced it to the confounded machine-minder. (I am probably saying worse than this). It looks as if the block was too high and he took it out, rubbed it down, and put it back upside down. This is proved by the fact that both the press proof and the machine proof are correct. I leave you to guess what I have said on the matter. . . .

Nobbs, of course, is highly elated that it is not the comps. and with the usual printer's flair for finding excuses, he points out that although the line is inverted it is followed by (*sic*). This is quite a new one on me!*

Morison replied:

I quite understand. In fact I imagined it was something of that kind. What aggravates the matter, of course, is the fact that the photographic facsimile faces it. I don't mind telling you that when I came back on Monday night, having left you, and I took the book down to glance at it for a certain purpose, the volume fell open on that page and the inverted line jumped out as though it were printed in phosphorescent ink, embossed and somehow it appeared to be set in 24 point. I can well imagine Nobbs' whoop of triumph.*

But by now he was already pondering the implications of the continuation, then planned as a third and final volume. This, Morison thought, might take another two and a half years, and his other work would suffer. Six months after volume II came out, Morison had extended the finishing date to 1942 or 1943. 'By then I shall have given more than ten years to it, and I shall stand in need of a complete change of interest.'

In the event, Morison had no need to look for a change. War still seemed remote. There were excursions with Henry Thomas.

Every other week during the summer months we customarily caught at London Bridge the cheap mid-day excursion to Brighton, where we took in at five miles an hour the whole of the sea front from Hove to the Brighton end. This feat entitled us to an *hors-d'œuvre* of whelks and cockles (floating in vinegar) from a stall on the beach level, and a good dinner at the Ship or the Albion. A swift walk up the hill to the station took us to the train. We shared an interest in railways and collected pictures of them, while not making a cult of ferroviarianism. Inevitably Thomas was all for the L.N.W.R. and the Webb compounds, with a respect, of course, for the great Junction at Clapham through which more trains pass in an hour than through any other station in the country. . . .

During the Spanish Civil War, when strangers of all sorts from the Peninsula were about London I invited him to one of the many new Spanish restaurants ('English Spoken') that were then being started up by and for these refugees. The place had been open only a week and we were given marvellously ample refreshments, the whole having been ordered by me in English. We were both fully satisfied and while waiting for the bill, I reposed with a lofty conceit of myself for discovering the place. The bill, when it came, was modesty itself. But I couldn't meet it – I had come without cash. Worse still, Thomas had enough for himself only. The black-jowled proprietor who looked like an anarchist (and probably was) expressed in the best English he could (and for his purpose it was more than sufficiently clear), that he was not impressed by promises to pay, I must fetch the money now. Only then did Thomas prove that he had something worth more than money. He looked discriminatingly at the proprietor and spoke to him in Catalan. We were saved. Our new-made friend showed us photographs of his children in first communion dress and a villainously coloured picture of the Pope.*

Morison went abroad again, to Rome in May 1937, only to find the Vatican library shut. He felt the absence of *The Times*, which had been banned by the Fascists, and he sent Lewis a postcard of the relief maps which now plastered the Colosseum with new Italian ambitions of expansion indicated: 'this is what the modern Roman is thinking about', he wrote apprehensively. In March 1938, he went to Germany. The year before Dr Ruppel, the Director of the Gutenberg Museum at Mainz, had written to the Vice-Chancellor of Cambridge (beginning 'Your Magnificence') to announce plans for the commemoration of the quincentenary of Gutenberg's invention. Lewis had passed the letter on to Morison, who replied:

In the matter of the Gutenberg Celebration, the proper thing, I suppose, is first of all to ask His Magnificence of Oxford what he would like to do. As I assume the academies of the world are being invited to manifest their gratitude to the inventor of the art by which you and I make our living, I certainly think that it would not do for Cambridge to be omitted. My only anxiety is that anything done should not be twisted into Nazi propaganda.

You might perhaps tell S.C. that I am meditating on the matter and we shall have to have what Printing House Square would call a 'conference' on the subject.*

By now Morison was already forming his own plans for the anniversary. He went to Frankfurt, and learnt that Mori was expecting to publish a two-volume book to celebrate the event. He also learnt that his fears about the Mainz celebrations were groundless. Goebbels, with the 'official' celebration in Leipzig, did not look kindly on them. Morison also went to arrange for his latest work on writing, *Latin Script since the Renaissance*

Printed at Cambridge, it was to be included in an anthology edited by Klaus Blanckertz, with whose father Morison had planned the journal of calligraphy in 1927. This short piece, like the *Monotype Recorder* article on Black Letter, was the seed of much more substantial work. This time Morison took a lot of trouble to make sure it was accurate with the result that the correction bill was twice as great as the original cost of composition (a not infrequent occurrence with him).*

Gill and Morison continued to correspond, a casual remark by either provoking in the other a display of argumentative pyrotechnics. Gill said that design existed 'independent of the tools used to do it with'. 'But are you not thus committed', Morison rejoined, 'to the view that "design" is less a matter of hands and tools than a matter of pure mental conception?' Ought this to be extended to the Monotype works? 'Should we not also do our best to render the girls themselves, with their hands and all that belongs to them, capable of complete self-effacement in the service of the mental conception?' Beatrice also kept up with Gill, who had been working intermittently on the photographs that Brownie had taken. He told her:

For a long time I have been intending to make a book of Nudes, and at last I have done it. It will be published in a month or two, by Dents or Fabers, I think, and will contain 25 engravings. As a few of them are from drawings I made of you, it is only fair that you have prints, and I send them herewith, hoping that you will not mind their inclusion in the book, and will not think them too intrinsically bad.*

On 24 August 1938, Morison and his friend the railway enthusiast Canon Fellows went on a 'special' from King's Cross to Cambridge, to celebrate the fiftieth anniversary of the 'Flying Scotchman' of 1888. A train entirely made up from rolling-stock of the period, hauled by Patrick Stirling Single No 1, was used for the excursion, and Lewis met the train as it pulled in. On the return journey, he saw them off and Morison and he were photographed together as they looked at the engine. Another photograph, showing the train at full speed, was used as the frontispiece of the next Press Christmas book, written by Fellows, entitled *London to Cambridge by Train, 1845–1938*. Morison sent a copy to King's Cross, as a small thank-offering.*

But a month later came Munich, and all thoughts of railways were forgotten. Like the vast majority, Morison himself was in favour of any diplomatic action that might avert war. He may have been critical of the *Times* leader of 7 September (whose construction he described in such dramatic detail in the last volume of the *History*), in which the cession of the Sudetenland to Germany was first suggested.* But Barrington-Ward was away then, and on his return Morison shared his anxiety to avoid 'the peril of war upon a confused issue fastened upon an unconvinced and disunited people'.* At the end of the week in which Czecho-slovakia finally gave way, Chamberlain flew back to Germany for further talks with Hitler. Barrington-Ward was firm but not without hope: on 23 September, writing on 'Mr Chamberlain's Mission', his words summed up the general view. 'The conversations now in train at Bad Godesberg will do more than any gifted speculation to give democracy its line for the future – whether it is to be the line of concerted resistance, or, as we must still all hope, the way of progress by mutual concession'. But next day Goebbels published an inflammatory communiqué and Barring-ton-Ward took a stronger line in a leader headed 'Facing the Issue'.

Is Germany now to insist, or to try to insist, upon taking by force what, in so far as her claims are legitimate, is already and admittedly within her grasp by agreement? . . . No one will look gladly or willingly for the alternative, but no one will flinch from it. If the German Press has faithfully stated German policy, then here is an issue on which every British citizen without exception knows where he stands.

Morison was delighted. Here was the voice of *The Times* speaking, as it had spoken in the years after the Reform Bill, independently of politicians and parties with the authentic voice of the country. He wrote the same day to Barrington-Ward.

I have resisted the impulse to telephone a word of admiration for the line and language of the first leaders of Friday's and today's dates. Their sturdiness and clarity of statement, their dialectical power, and – equally supreme virtue at such a crisis – their up to the moment factual basis, place them on a level, at least, with the very finest that have ever appeared in the journal. They are Barnes-worthy.*

There was no higher praise. But on the final issue of the talks he had misgivings. At Cambridge, Lewis was vitriolic: 'Somebody seems to have suggested to W.L. that the Pitt Press should be renamed the "Chamberlain" Press in honour of the Prime Minister's Peace effort – hence the row this afternoon.'* Next week the trenches were being dug in Regent's Park, and Morison, promising Pollard to return some books the week after 'wh. I suppose will be as "peaceful" as the present time', added:

The Reading Room very vacant today; I fear that not a few of our scholars have already done a bunk; but N. H. Baynes & H. Leclercq O.S.B. gave a good example. A. F. Johnson told me privately that the B. Mus. will close on the Declaration – reading room and all.*

By now Morison's views on war had changed from the extreme pacifism he had maintained in 1916. Gill, however, was resolutely against war. He wrote in some dejection to Morison, after an unsuccessful attempt to sell pacifist pamphlets in High Wycombe. Morison replied in his most trenchant style.

I am not surprised at what you tell me about the lack of response to the Peace Booklet in Wycombe market. The truth is that since January 1933 the world situation has completely altered. So much so that no man who rightly values his personal intellectual and moral integrity could subscribe to Point 2 in the 'Basis' of 'Pacts' as printed in the leaflet enclosed with your letter. This is my judgement.

Furthermore, it is my opinion that the current of post-Boer War anti-imperialism and pacifist idealism which still flowed during the years 1914–18 and broke up to the surface after the Armistice is almost completely dried up under the shocks of 1925, 1933, 1935 and 1938. The accumulative effects of the events of these years has been to deprive non-resisters of all influence.*

370

He was not prepared, however, to go as far as Henry Wickham Steed. Steed had been editor of *The Times* briefly, from 1919 to 1922, at the height of Northcliffe's power; when Northcliffe went, Steed went too. Morison, thinking of the *Times* history to come, had got to know him, and had helped him with his book on *The Press*, published by Penguin Books in November 1938. Morison had helped him with the historical and technical passages, but cannot have been unaware that Steed contrasted *The Times*'s independent line in February 1852 over Louis Napoleon's *coup d'état* with its current obedience to the government line. He probably did not know that Steed had added a post-script, written after Munich, accusing the 'leading journals' of suppressing the country's rage at the instigation of 'certain large advertising agents'. Barrington-Ward was angry at this false accusation, which, in consultation with Morison, he rebutted in the paper.*

Next March, after the second volume of the *History* had come out in London, Morison went to New York for its publication there by the Macmillan Company. He was beset by demands for 'explanation' of the European situation, to which he replied with Barrington-Ward's 'geographical necessity' theory about the Axis policy, and with strong criticism of the American abandonment of the League of Nations, and the encouragement it gave to 'reactionary elements in Europe'. He was glad to get away from a depressed New York. He had another ride on a locomotive, this time on the Chesapeake and Ohio. He went to Chicago, and R. Hunter Middleton of the rival Ludlow company gave a 'do' in his honour: 'I hope to behave in the presence of Mr McMurtrie,' Morison wrote to Beatrice.*

He also went to see Updike at Boston, who was interested in the Monotype recutting for the Limited Editions Club of the 1792 Bulmer type. The design had been thickened up at George Macy's request ('I can't think why,' Morison wrote to Updike*). Updike was anxious to have a true recutting, which Morison was glad to offer at no more than the normal cost. But this was not to be. As the correspondence stretched on into the summer,

Morison grew more and more apprehensive: thanking Updike for a list of his type specimens, he added:

It is not easy to give one's mind to archeological matters when the state of Europe is what it is – and it may well be a great deal worse by the time this letter arrives at 339 Marlborough Street.*

The outbreak of war disrupted Morison's life completely. The Monotype Office in Fetter Lane was immediately evacuated to Salfords, and Morison had to go too; his secretary, Mrs Alexander, who knew his work so well that he used to leave her to sign all his letters, was forced to go to Basingstoke, where she got a job in Barclays Bank. He wrote to her:

For my part I still feel very unsettled but my conclusion is that I was much more affected by the war-declaration than was really necessary. In the second place it is possible to get the war in better perspective here than in London & tho' I hate being here & still more hate being at Clemsfold where the smalltalk is so terribly minute. I go to London tomorrow Thursday & hope to spend the evening with Steed. I miss you very much but there is little to do and now that I have no secretary I don't seem to have the external stimulus which would set my teeth for work.*

The Times, too, was in difficulties. The young men went off to the forces and others were enrolled as experts in Government departments. Morison wrote to Wickham Steed to thank him for sending his account of Northcliffe's last months, 'one of the most exciting narratives I have read for a very long time'.

As you can imagine the office is very upset. There has been a complete cessation of advert^g and I suppose *T.T.* is worse hit than any other paper. Among other economies I have had to close the History Dept wh. consisted of three assistants. Astor, Dawson, Kent & B-Ward spoke words about me wh. were very gratifying and I shall doubtless maintain some sort of connexion. . . .

The most urgent thing seems to be a declaration of our War aims. None seems to know what to do with 80 million Teutons; where to put 'em; what to punish 'em with. They mustn't be rewarded for attacking Poland – & that's the only clear point we seem to have made. It's time you had a letter in *The Times*.*

Other friends found unfamiliar jobs and uniforms. To Ellic Howe Morison wrote while he was still wondering about the implications of war.

It may or may not be over soon. That depends upon the number of Germans behind Hitler; behind Hitler – not necessarily behind the Nazis. Bad as they are & have been there was a certain dumm idealism in certain sections of the support which Hitler used to rely upon. Today I received a letter from Poeschel of Leipzig sent off on Aug 31 in answer to mine 'Yes, you are right; we understand each other perfectly & shall go on doing so ... for ever yours ... &c'. Now that is only one expression but it is the sentiment of all my numerous friends in Lpz and elsewhere. I don't see how the thing can go on for years & years. However The Sacred MS. is safe here looking, in its box, like a Holy Cow or something.*

This was Morison's long-planned 'Collected Papers' now almost ready to be sent to the Harvard University Press. But this and his other work on humanistic and black-letter script was now much impeded. There was unfamiliar work to be done as well. George Barnes, a Cambridge friend, once at the Press and now at the B.B.C., enlisted Morison's help in fighting the German propaganda machine, and he undertook to write a memorandum, 'a scientific study of "News Communication by Press, Radio & Film" as practised in Germany and elsewhere'.*

The worst immediate casualty was the Special Lectureship in the History of the Newspaper, which Morison had worked so hard to establish. Early in the year the University of London had finally accepted his proposals (circulated in a printed fly-sheet the year before) and the position had been established on guarantees of annual payments of £500 from Astor and £100 from Morison. Pollard was to be the first lecturer, and all through the summer he had been packing up at Birrell & Garnett, whence he had sent Morison a present of writing-books from time to time: 'For years I have longed sicut cervus desiderat ad fontes aquarum for any sort of copy of Lucas . . . and now this superb copy has come.'* They had had elaborate plans for a Cambridge *History of Journalism* and a journal of newspaper history called *Mercurius* to be printed at *The Times* and published by Cambridge. But now University College migrated abruptly to Wales, and were quick to point out, both to Morison and Astor, the difficulties involved in combining research in London with lectures in Aberystwyth. Morison wrote to Pollard:

It isn't any business of the subscribers whether the teaching is done in this that or the other place; it isn't necessary that the 'volume' (or extent) of the teaching should now be what was hoped in peace-time. As long as the University or party of the first part is actively fulfilling its part as far as circumstances allow the other parties of the second part will fulfil their promise. . . . There is an appalling fog of vagueness over everything at present. The atmosphere of stagnation is noticeable in every direction and the present peace talk increases it. Nobody is getting down to anything. I am leaving here on Thurs. & shall not return to stay in the country until some of this vagueness & stagnation is dissipated. It is absurd to regard this situation as a state of war except in the pre-1914 sense. The Univ. most certainly ought to plan a colony in London & occupy the place gradually. There are empty houses all over London. Ring up on Thurs or Fri. There are several people talking round about me & I can't write properly.*

Once back in London, he found it easier to concentrate. 'I am labouring at a paper on the beginnings of humanistic script and roman type,' he told S. H. Steinberg, a German historian who had come to England as a refugee in 1937, bringing a letter of introduction to Morison from Julius Rodenberg. Morison had done his best to find a job for Steinberg, who in turn provided Morison with criticism and help both on the 'Collected Papers' and his new work. About this time Morison had bought from his old friend E. P. Goldschmidt, the learned antiquarian book-seller, a fifteenth-century writing manual which he had dis-covered in the Abbey of Melk in Czechoslovakia. Morison first persuaded Carl Poeschel to print it as a tribute to Klingspor in

1938 with an introduction by Bernhard Bischoff, whose palaeographical skill Morison was quick to appreciate. Now Steinberg and he were also at work on a complete facsimile and edition, to be printed at Cambridge.

Shortly before the war broke out, on 24 June, Morison had moved out of Park Crescent to 10 Cambridge Gate. This was rather a come-down after the elegance of Nash (it was built in 1875 by Archer & Green on the site of the old Coliseum), but it offered Morison and his housekeeper, Mrs Rowe, more space and greater convenience. It was, moreover, closer to the Barrington-Wards in Chester Terrace. In the general change and unrest, Morison in self-protection wrote hard to finish the work he had in hand, grudging the still frequent journeys to Salfords.

We ourselves have been pretty exhausted with taking the 8.20 from L'pl St–Cambridge; 12.57 Camb–Lpl St; and then to Mono office & then to *Times* & then to Mono Wks all in the same day – and at Our Age. This leaves us little time for food or spiritual refreshment. We bought Fr D'Arcy on St Thos. Aq. but haven't had any chance to look into the book. In order to clear our minds of the subject we have written a hefty piece on the beginnings of humanistic script which embodies all the notes on the subject we have made since the end of the first German war. It may or may not be one of our better studies. This morning we received from Fkft ªM via Bale some types cut from our designs. The metal is now being analysed in order that we should know whether the Hun is hard up for lead or antimony or tin. For the rest there is no news. There are still folk who believe that the fuss will be over this Christmas. But there are others who believe it will be a long business.*

Morison was convinced that it would be a 'long business', although he did not foresee more than a passive war. Monotype had been warned to prepare for a change in production, but

There's nothing moving in the munition world as far as guns are concerned because there is no wastage – no wastage because there are no battles. Business in the printing world is 'picking up'. I go to Basel in a few days.*

375

The purpose of this visit was a secret conference with three representatives from the German Monotype company (then the most successful European satellite of the English Company), to try to concert action during the isolation of war. Morison, chosen for his long familiarity with the German industry, went reluctantly, wrenching himself from the more agreeable prospect of a visit to Roger Mynors at Oxford to examine the early humanistic manuscripts given to Balliol College by Bishop William Gray. He stayed for a week or more but returned before Christmas.

By February, he was able to re-establish himself in Fetter Lane in something like the state that he and Mrs Alexander had enjoyed in peacetime.

For prudential reasons connected with the structure of the building (i.e. the top floor & the façade fronting F-Lane) I have been moved into Westover's room & now have everything down. A tremendous cleaning took place and I am here, on the whole, permanently & go to Wks once a week. I have all my locomotives on the walls & the place is 'satisfactory' to use the Master's word. We now have a private line to Wks but somehow the main Redhill cable is bust & so nothing goes through until it is mended. Yours is a very long deprivation & must be very inconvenient.

I didn't hear K[ingsley]. Wood and don't know why you care to lend him your ears. But don't forget that in my opinion you are a very severe judge. Personally I have found that just as Religion is not effectively presented by Bishops so Patriotism is not accredited by the utterances of Politicians.*

Morison learnt with delight that Pollard had succeeded in giving two lectures in Aberystwyth. Morison himself, now more settled and undeterred by the war, joined in the plans which Brooke Crutchley was now making to commemorate the Gutenberg quincentenary with an exhibition at the Fitzwilliam Museum. At the beginning of March a prospectus was circulated to librarians, members of the Bibliographical Society, the Roxburghe Club, and others.

Though more than half Europe is at present too tragically absorbed in the future of its civilisation to be able to pay much thought to its past, the five-hundredth anniversary of Gutenberg's invention none the less demands to be recognized. The conditions which make it impractical to hold a worthy exhibition in London are happily absent in Cambridge; and plans for staging here a modest tribute to Gutenberg's memory have developed into a resolution to make good the general deficiency with a major exhibition.

The theme of the exhibition was then set out; a full representation of every aspect of human thought and action served by Gutenberg's invention; 'wherever civilization has called upon the craft of printing from movable type to promote its ends, there is subject matter for this exhibition'.

The response for the request for loans was conspicuously prompt and generous. Nearly 100 lenders produced over 600 exhibits, and the exhibition opened for six weeks on 6 May, 'the feast of *St John ante Portam Latinam*' and Morison's fifty-first birthday. It was a remarkable display ranging from the earliest fragments of Gutenberg's printing to one of the Identity Cards that everyone in Britain now carried. Most of the world's great works of literature, philosophy, religion and every other art and subject were there, including a special exhibit for the year 1859, the year of *The Origin of Species*, *Idylls of the King*, *The Ordeal of Richard Feverel*, *Self-Help* by Samuel Smiles, *A Tale of Two Cities*, Fitzgerald's *Rubá'iyát*, *Adam Bede*, *Beeton's Book of Household Management* and *Mill On Liberty*. There were also special displays to illustrate the history of journalism, music and printing.

But only days after the exhibition opened, the German offensive in the west began. Holland, Belgium and Luxemburg fell, and the French front was penetrated. The exhibition closed after only ten days, although the catalogue was printed and reprinted again in July, as a defiant testimony of faith in the exhibition's purpose. At the beginning of June came Dunkirk, and the future was as dark as the great clouds of oily black smoke from the burning refineries on the French coast which blotted out the afternoon sun as far away as Cambridge. Morison's *A Fifteenth-Century Modus Scribendi from the Abbey of Melk* came out: 'I thank you ever so much for thinking of us in these days of distress,' wrote

377

Updike when he received his copy. In July Steinberg, who had just finished an article for a Gutenberg Commemoration number of the *Recorder*, was interned. Morison wrote to Mrs Steinberg: 'Not for the first time in the history of the world the innocent simply must suffer for the guilty.'

Morison went back to *The History of The Times*. On 26 August he wrote to Barrington-Ward, convalescent from shingles, and begged him not to come back before he had to.

I rejoice that you like the draft of the third vol. It must be a financial success whatever else. For my own part I shall go on thinking that Vol 1 was a good original and critical contribution but it hasn't (except to one or two) the exciting quality of the Pearson–Northcliffe duel. It should be possible to print most of the details of that episode. The gentle reader would be glad to be spared all that chartered accountancy & litigation business. I found it fatiguing enough. You are very conscientious to have fought your way through it.

Don't think of expediting the return of the thing. By way of having a holiday I am, for a week, giving my mind to the thorough revision & rewriting of papers chosen out of the articles on the history of calligraphy and typography I have written in the course of time. They are being brought up to date at the request of the Syndics of Harvard and will be published at their cost in a handsome form next year, Oxford issuing it over here. As I seem pretty well fixed in the history of journalism I may as well drop my older interests and this Harvard offer gives me the opportunity to clear my mind of the subject.

I shall be glad indeed to come round to 19 Chester Terrace. If the cuisine is any difficulty (as it even ought to be) we could eat at the Garrick Club or the Athenaeum & then go on to your place, events permitting.

There has been a certain amount of exercise on the part of our Albany Street 'sirene' as the whole town calls it. The officers in charge let her go with vast gusto. This wakes up the whole neighbourhood, the lions & bears in the zoo and all. The only time I heard the guns was on Thurs a.m. at 3, i.e. half an hour before the lads at Albany Street let the siren go. They had cause to sound her on Sunday–Monday night twice. On Saturday I was caught & took refuge in one of the public places off Tottm Ct Rd. This was in the afternoon soon after I had left the Museum. I enjoyed the experience. The thing is taken as a mere matter of course. Newspaper-sellers come down with the *Star News* & *Standard*, choc. bars etc. I picked up, down there, that a family having had a baby in the middle of a raid christened the girl 'Sireen'. Adolph will find it difficult to tread down those folk.

But worse was to come. On 8 September, Madame Tussaud's was bombed and all the windows in Cambridge Gate blown in. Morison's new secretary, Miss Meinhardt, was 'axed' in the economy drive. On 26 September he told Mrs Alexander:

Since I wrote a land mine blew inside out all Camb. Gate & much more. I have abandoned the place (temporarily I hope), particularly as it was afterwards incendiarised. . . . Awful fag. *The Times* front in Q. Vict. Street was visited by the bombs on Tues night and scored a direct hit on the building wh. was wrecked but so strong was J.W.III's Bearwood brickwork that it stood up & only the ceilings, windows & all furniture, partitions &c were destroyed. The glass in the private house is out but my place is relatively unscathed.

It isn't any use my trying to go on with the 'Business as Usual' sort of thing & I may as well make up my mind to look after myself and my sleep. I may go to Mrs Warde's place (in Surrey) for a week or two. At present I stay at the Waldorf Hotel, or rather half stay there as I go in to P.H.S. & stay there all night once or twice.

He was rescued from this plight by Barrington-Ward. His family had retreated to the country: 'Why not join forces?' he suggested to Morison, who was thankful to accept, bringing Mrs Rowe with him to look after them. In the evenings, with the threat of destruction so close, they got to know each other. They exchanged their life-stories, and Barrington-Ward's admiration for Morison grew. He saw parallels with J. L. Garvin, who had been a much loved chief to him at the *Observer*. Morison,

like Garvin, exhibits all the advantages of a successful self-development without the sometimes dubious blessings of a formal education. His mother, to whom he owes all, is, he says, a strong rationalist. He – by the exercise of his reason, as he puts it – joined the R.C. Church as a young man. He has little tolerance for other communions . . . [but] we differ with amenity.*

379

They talked of religion (Morison showed Barrington-Ward his plain-song books) and of what would have to be done to make the world safe against Germany after the war. (This was a subject which preoccupied Morison a great deal; he had long discussions on it with refugee Germans like Egbert Munzer and Dieter Mende.) They were bombed again on 9 and 15 October. This last depressed Morison. Next day he began a letter to Pollard

I simply can't do any work even at weekends which I spend out of town. Then I sleep all the time. . . . Last night (i.e. Tues) we were badly blasted, losing ceiling windows & doors. This at 3 a.m. in the course of a night such as I had not been thro before. I think we shall have to sleep here at PHS for the future since there is a pair of un-exploded things in Albany St back of us & the prospect of an enforced evacuation of the whole Terrace. . . . Thanx for yr offer to house some of my junk. If I ever get enough energy I will select the things I should like least to lose. All I have done is to pack up my best writing books & put them in the Monotype safe. This came through their blast quite well although 24 people were killed. This was last week – Wednesday. Half a ton of earth bricks & what not buried my table & books but the cleaning up has restored most of what I am interested in. Unhappily we can't restore the lives of the 24 victims. As a result of there being no water, no heat, no gas & no windows on my side of the Fetter Lane building I am making PHS my headquarters, pigging it in the jobbing Composing Rooms of a night with J.J.A., G.D., B-W. We go back to 19 Chester Terr when the O.K. or Orlklear toots forth, G.D. letting us take his office car for the purpose.

Christmas was bleak, but Morison grew more cheerful as the spirit of the emergency took hold of him. He invited Pollard, now living near Oxford, to supper at *The Times*, but he did not come.

The Major laid a knife & fork & wineglass without attracting you. Did I think of the wrong Monday? I reckoned it would be the first Monday after Dec 31. Has the Headington Rite a special local Use? Going back to 1690?*

Morison made little further progress with the *History*, but had the eleven chapters he had written already set up at *The Times*. He sent proofs to Steed.

Before I die I want to do a book about God, please Steed, from the Papist position. But before giving God his due I must be just to Steed and Dawson & Northcliffe, a Trinity that will probably be the death of me. I do my best to be thorough and the method I adopt is to rely upon the documents for the draft and not till then to ask for reminiscences. Except that I incorporated one or two things that G. Sutton explained to me orally there is nothing in the draft which is not my own guess based upon letters and documents. I shall have to ask other people to look at portions but so far only yourself, G.D. (rather horrified at so *much* intrigue), J.W. ('I read your novel') and Kent. All criticised my English. One of J.W.'s remarks was that it was unwise to dissent from Steed: 'He has an awkward habit of being right after all'.

Steed replied in detail, to Morison's delight. His notes were 'full of supplementary matter. I could do a volume on him.' Fetter Lane was bombed again. 'It is a miserable thing to see the wreck of the Gough Square, Fleet St (back of) district, where once was all bustle with the rattle of Monotype machines dominating the noise of the typographic trades.'*

His new intimacy with Barrington-Ward grew. They lunched together with Tom Jones, and discovered a common taste for wine. Morison had to go north.

I ordered claret to my lunch in the LMS diner. I had a superb bottle (*not* ½ bottle) of Medoc price 4s. 6d. . . . I feel like travelling up & down from Euston to Crewe in order to have more of that excellent drink, in its way, almost the equal of your Haut-Brion.*

Morison grew more familiar with the sources of power, and with familiarity came the occasional chance to exercise it himself, sometimes with apparently very rapid effect. His old Cambridge friend Charles Carrington, an enthusiastic disputant at the tea-time debates, was now acting as liaison between the War Office and Bomber Command. It had been a hard winter and there was much talk of reprisal raids. With the coming of spring and clearer nights, R.A.F. Intelligence turned to the possibility, suggested by a recent Air Ministry Directive, of bombing Italy.* Out came the target-maps, and jokes were made about making 'Musso' jump for the dug-out. Carrington became increasingly perturbed: had they forgotten the many Irish-American priests in Rome, that the Vatican was a neutral state, that the United States was still neutral, that the Irish-American lobby was powerful at Washington? When the maps passed from Intelligence on to the table in the Ops Room, he decided that it was time to act.

He rang *The Times* on the secret telephone right out of the Ops Room and arranged to meet Morison for lunch that day, 7 April 1941, ostensibly to discuss a broadcast that he was due to give on C. K. Ogden's 'Basic English'. Morison knew its inventor well, supported (within limits) the invention, and delighted in the conversation and the quirks of that philosophic and bibliophilic polymath. When Carrington arrived in Fleet Street, he explained that his friends might bomb Rome, pleading the Air Ministry Directive after the event. Could he find someone to warn the Government at the very highest level? Morison arched his eyebrows, stuck out his chin, and said yes, he thought he could. Two or three days later, the target-maps of Rome were bundled out of the Ops Room back into the secret cupboards of intelligence. The subject was dropped, but on 18 April, the Government issued a truculent statement about reprisals. We would not hesitate to bomb Rome if provoked enough. But provocation did not come. Had Morison done the trick, Carrington asked.

You were quite right. What I did was to communicate your intelligence to the Cardinal's right-hand man, a Bishop who, having done well at Balliol, thought fit to join the British Navy and become a midshipman before tumbling to it that he had a vocation. At any rate he is quite smart and promised to act instantly. Apparently he has kept his promise. He said that he would be very glad to be of any further assistance at any time when action is required.

You might care to look at the enclosed which came to me yesterday. Of course . . . the reprisal nonsense is not only the merest but the most transparent humbug. But I am not sure that both sides don't welcome it. At any rate I am morally certain that the time will come when the Hun will be very pleased to give up night bombing.*

The last of the pre-Christmas sorrows had been particularly bitter. 'Gill is being operated for lung trouble this week. Very hard up. All those people living on him,' he told Mrs Alexander on 14 November. But the operation failed, and three days later Gill died. He had not been forgotten in all the diverse tasks that the war had brought. In his last letter, on 6 April 1940, Morison had written to Gill: 'Turn in when there is an opportunity. I had a job of work that might have been in your line.' Now he was dead, and there were to be no more jobs in Gill's line, no more type-design, no more happy controversy over the interaction of religion and politics. The six months that followed Gill's death were another climacteric period in Morison's life. He gave up his direct interest in the design of new letters, and turned to their history as if to convince himself, as he had convinced others before, of the historical inevitability of what he had done. Many other matters engaged his active mind, but history, of letters, the liturgy, *The Times*, was his preoccupation; and history to him was the art, not of recording, but of explaining the past.

'BLACK LETTER' DAY

In the leisure hours of recent years I have been revising papers on historical aspects of calligraphy and typography, originally published by me in various places during the last twenty years. They were to accompany some new studies and form a volume which the Harvard University Press several years ago honoured me by offering to print, in a form to be designed by Mr. B. R. By the beginning of the war most of these papers had been entirely rewritten, their references checked and brought up to date; work had been done upon new studies of humanistic script and of the origin of black-letter. There were interruptions. Regent's Park, where I live, is a district favoured by the enemy. On September 20th, 1940, towards midnight, a very heavy bomb floated down on to the border of the Park, opposite Cambridge Gate, the terrace in which my flat is situated. The tremendous detonation blew in all the doors and windows and brought down all the ceilings within a wide radius. I was, luckily, fifty yards from that explosion, and got off with bruises on the legs and wrists, but the flat was badly damaged by blast.

That night, R. M. B.-W., a friend and colleague, living in one of the finest of the Regency terraces that surround the Park and a stone's half-throw to the north and on the fringe of the damaged area, took me in. Later my housekeeper, Mrs R. (and her husband) were accommodated, and I remained with R. M. B.-W. while Cambridge Gate was being repaired. During these six months there were many raids. Some score of high-explosive bombs fell close to No. 19, some within a hundred yards, others within closer range, one within six yards of the front door. In November, windows were blown in, ceilings brought down and doors blown off their hinges. Something similar occurred at intervals. It was not an uneventful winter that we spent in the basement, but on the book progress was made.

During the spring of 1941 I was occupied in the task of selecting the pictorial illustrations to the revised papers, and to the completion of the new. In April I was able to send the humanistic paper to Harvard, and it was determined to send other material at short intervals. It was a good plan. But it was not carried out.

Early in May it pleased the Luftwaffe to effect the most spectacular and destructive of all the air raids that had taken place over London since the war began. There had been little peace in the spring, yet at the beginning of May my own flat was repaired. Removal was due to take effect on Monday, May 12th. It was forestalled by the Luftwaffe's great attack on May 10th. I spent the night in and about 19 Chester Terrace. Mr and Mrs R. were there, but R. M. B.-W. had gone to the country on Friday to visit his evacuated family, thus missing an experience that he, as a Major in the last war, and a D.S.O., M.C., was more competent than I to enjoy.

The raid began at 11 p.m. on Saturday; hundreds of planes were in it. It lasted until dawn on Sunday morning. Dozens, counting the d.a.'s, of high-explosives, and scores of fire-bombs swished over the house before, at 1.45 a.m., it shook violently. I was half in bed, trying to read, at the time. I knew well enough what was the matter. A furious banging on the front door confirmed that the place was on fire. I opened the door to a group of three volunteer fire fighters; Mr R. and I, joining them, charged up the five flights of pitch black stairs to the very top of the house. A magnificent glow from the huge fires to the right and left met us; and, at close range, as fierce a belch of flame as I have encountered. With pumps and pail the five of us managed to put the flames out. The volunteers went off to other fires. But our fire, the cunning enemy, was not out as it pretended, and we thought. Fresh smoke gave its game away. Twice again was the bath filled, and twice again the pump and pail brought back; twice again the burnt rafters we had saturated to soft pulp were dried into brittle crust; twice again it burst into new flame, helped by the wind, at new places. Tearing some of the slates off the roof we discovered where the third fire was hiding. Raking its recesses with a tablespoon, Mr R. and I were able to soak the surrounding charcoal. We had to make a precision job of this, by tipping, with every care, doses of water from a breakfast cup into the gleaming vestiges.

Straddled thus on the roof, at a good height, and facing the Park directly, we had a fine view of the spectacle to the north, south and west. It was a sight of the greatest splendour, but unspeakably and unforgettably grim and sickening to one whose whole life had been spent in London, and who had been familiar with this very district since his earliest years; and, from the age of six, had admired Nash's terraces. Several had already been ruined. It was our turn. A couple of houses next-door-but-two were in full flame, another house at the back also. Great beacons, too, lit Marylebone Road and Baker Street; ablaze were Oxford Street and Gt Portland Street. Illumination from dozens of incendiaries that had fallen in the grounds of the Park flood-lit Chester Terrace. A few yards south of us was a smaller fire, no more than a point of interrogation; possibly, I wondered, in

Cambridge Gate. The vast crescendo of noise offered little opportunity for thought. Our great A.A. guns booming with but the shortest of intervals, the incessant drone of the bombers, the tearing shriek of the bombs as they hurtled through the air; the thud and tremor of their explosions, the crackle of collapsing timber and the crash of masonry, combined, with the bells of fire engines and the shouts of firemen, to challenge at the same moment all one's senses of sight and hearing with a deafening and continuous roar and a dull acrid smell in the midst of the blazing surroundings. The moment Mr R. and I had satisfied ourselves that we should be justified in clambering down from the roof to the ground floor, the noise seemed even more unbearable.

It was, I calculate, about 2.30 a.m. when, still in pyjamas, I went back to the basement to get into trousers. Mrs R. informed me that, while her husband and I had been on the roof attending to the fire, our garage had been struck by a fire-bomb. She had succeeded in getting in the A.F.S. – 'another lot that didn't know how to wipe their feet when coming into a gentleman's 'ouse' but, with her, had disposed of the garage fire.

Now, more or less dressed, I was ready to make a move towards Cambridge Gate. The small blaze to the south that I had seen from the roof had become larger. It might be No. 10. It was. The blazing top floor was a fine sight against the contrasting masses of black smoke blowing out of the windows of the suite below. The London Fire Brigade (from Belsize Park Station) were mounted high, at several points, on a side building, and were hosing the place for all they were worth. When I got into my flat on the mezzanine floor, I found it full of choking smoke, with water pouring through the kitchen ceiling. The rest was untouched as far as I could see in the almost pitch black. Before obeying the Fire Chief's orders to leave within two minutes, I managed to turn a few things into the hall and to grab from my work-table an armful of papers. I could do no more in the darkness and smoke. Though the place was dangerous I was assured that it was likely that the building would be substantially saved. I left No. 10 at about 3.30 a.m.

The raid was still in progress, the neighbouring streets peopled with aimless folk burnt out of their houses, or busy turning out their furniture on to the street; firemen pumping and hosing; some taking refreshment from the mobile canteens operated by the women's branch of the A.F.S. Sightseers and hardened connoisseurs of raids were coolly comparing notes on previous disasters and other scenes of devastation, discussing the comparative nauseousness of smells.

The loathsome stink of burnt and soaked and then dried-out houses would, it was agreed, last for ten days.

Returning to No. 10 at about 4 a.m. I saw that a new fire had broken out at the back, and that there was little hope for the inside of the building. During a lull of half-an-hour I sought sleep in the basement of No. 19. The enemy returned in force at 5 a.m. Pandemonium was renewed and the raid only terminated at 6 a.m. All told we had had a good seven hours of it.

I slept for a couple of hours. Going to No. 10, I found that my flat was still burning. The draught let in by my opening the door fanned an excellent pair of curtains into a beautiful flame. The illumination opened to my view a confused mass of burnt carpet, broken glass, lime and plaster from the ceilings, upturned book cases; the whole sodden with torrents of water still descending from the roof and upper floors. Three rooms of my flat, with all their contents, had disappeared as if they had never been. Everything had fallen into a vast cavity burnt out in the back basement, some thirty feet below. I was able to distinguish metal bookcases which, until then, had accommodated a large number of political and other books. These had all gone. My run (to the last *livraison*) of Leclercq and Cabrol's *Dictionnaire*, Hastings' *Encyclopedia of Religion and Ethics*, a set of liturgical books, together with collections on the History of Printing and of Journalism had been destroyed, and much else, not to mention pictures and a decent striking clock. Works larger than folio which were not in these rooms I was able to save. In the torrent still streaming from the firemen's hoses, I was able to shift Chatelain, *P.C.L.*; Lowe, *C.L.A.*; Rand, *Survey of Tours*; Zimmerman, *Vorkarolingische Miniaturen*. Other portfolios I kicked into shelter under my large dining table. Dozens of octavos and quartos had already been badly scorched and then soaked; the vellum leaves of the Canon of the Mass in Stuchs' *Benedictine Missal* (Leipzig, 1501) were congealed; the leather binding of Louis XIV's folio *Médailles* of 1702 was ruined. Much good stuff was done for. Outside, the borough authorities were nailing up the official warnings to passers-by: CAUTION UNEVEN ROAD SURFACE and CAUTION UNEXPLODED BOMBS, &c.

The finished chapters and all the illustrations and material for the 'Harvard' book went in another fire at the same time in another place, thought safe, a mile or two away. That, too, must have been a fine fire. I was not able to get there until the afternoon of Sunday when it was still burning. I managed to rescue some good things, including copies of Yciar, Lucas, and a fine *De Aetna*.

From the preface to '*Black Letter*' *Text*.

16

BEATRICE spent the Sunday after the big raid in some apprehension. Morison usually had Sunday lunch with her, but this time he did not come. The damage to London had been easily seen and heard in Horley. The telephone lines were all down, so there was no way of finding out what had happened.

The wireless reports led me to spend the day burying and digging-out all my friends in London. At 9.30 that night there was a knock on my front door and in walked S.M. in the flesh. He had to be at the Works the following day and so had accepted a lift in a colleague's car to Redhill. I've never been so glad to see anybody in my born days, and Mrs Ellis and I plied him with refreshment, heard the grim tale, and packed him off to get some sleep.*

Well on into July Morison was still trying to count his losses. Ellic Howe was an immediate support; he produced a cheque to finance the printing of the 'armful of papers' at once (for fear of further calamities), and arranged for the rebinding of the salvaged books by T. Harrison. Some of these were needed for 'Black Letter' Text. 'Inform me when you can if the vieux Harrisssson has my Kruitwagen on Schepel's Musterblaat,' Morison would write. 'If he hasn't I've lost that too.' It had gone. 'Sorry about poor Kruitwagen – a loss on my scientific side but an ugly piece in itself.'* In particular, Howe provided a new missal. The text was ordinary, but the binding was not.

I never saw sow's ear so beautifully turned into silk purse. I feel much honoured, for, without any exaggeration, I can say that I never have had anything so comfortable in my hands as this book. The one I had used for 32 years went up on May 10 & really I was v. attached to it. But with this in hand I am at last reconciled to that loss.*

Morison kept his missal in an inside pocket wherever he went. He kept his ready money in it, and cheques too until they were removed by his secretary (sometimes he used them as bookmarks, and then they proved harder to find); more than once he left it behind in a church, from which it had to be recovered.

All Morison's friends heard of the disaster, like Updike, 'with mixed feelings – of relief that you were safe, and sorrow that your belongings were gone. You are very cool and philosophic about it, which is the way to be. But it fills me with fury that useful work and the accumulation of material that it has taken a life-time to collect have perished.'* If Morison was philosophic, he was also dazed.

Since May I have been living the life of a vagabond. But I am glad to report that yesterday I took a flat which promises some relief from my present condition of fretfulness and disintegration. It is a poor thing to say, yet, notwithstanding the number, ardent character and sympathetic understanding of my friends, I find the continued living in houses not my own, to be something of a vexation. I never thought to have it demonstrated to me in this particular fashion, that the stability and continuity of tenure, even of a measure of private property – over and above the umbrella and tooth brush – is necessary to the integration of one's personality. This long-winded statement really means that I have become very lazy and inefficient, through the destruction of habits which were made possible, to a greater degree than I realised, by the power of association with particular rooms and the particular tasks I had already discharged in those rooms.*

Updike would have none of this self-reproach. 'The effect *you* call laziness and inefficiency . . . is really the result of being uprooted and being a deeper-rooted person than you suspected.'* Gradually, Morison began to recover, and to pick up the interrupted threads of his work.

At *The Times* Barrington-Ward was about to take over from Dawson as Editor. Morison was delighted by this, although he and Dawson had always been friendly (Dawson's impartial approval of the type-change had perhaps counted more with the board than Barrington-Ward's more active support). Morison regretted Dawson's lack of the 'Barnes' touch, and he disliked the gentleman-amateur style that he adopted. There was too much of the 'Establishment' about it: it would not do for *The Times* to be pro-Government, pro-Conservative or pro any other clique or interest. Barnes was the opposite: not a gentleman, a complete professional, he spoke for no party but the country. Barrington-Ward, who could see in Dawson and Morison what neither saw in each other, told Morison that he underrated Dawson and his editorship.* But the first volume of the *History of The Times* had left its mark on Barrington-Ward as well as Morison.* Just as Barnes after the Reform Bill had struck away from the Whig Establishment to support the Duke of Wellington, Lyndhurst and Peel, so now *The Times*, having supported the Government up to the war, should give a stronger voice to the social discontent that had grown since the depression. If there was something a little selfconscious in this deliberate imitation of the past, it is unlikely that either Morison or Barrington-Ward pursued the historical analogy to the full. Barnes had paved the way for Peel and modern Conservatism – would a new line at *The Times* do the same for Socialism? As Barnes had kept aloof from party, so should his successor.

Dawson had been due to retire at the end of 1939, and had only stayed on when *The Times* lost so many of its staff. As the war went on, Morison felt more and more strongly that Barrington-Ward should not wait any longer. But Dawson was ready to stay on and Barrington-Ward felt that he must have more support. At this point Lord Reith solved their problems. For some time, Barrington-Ward had had his eye on E. H. Carr, up to the outbreak of war Professor of International Relations at the University of Wales at Aberystwyth. Dawson was not so enthusiastic, but Carr had written several leaders in a style both readable and rather more *parti pris* than was usual in *The Times*. Barrington-Ward wrote to him on the first day of war, just too late to prevent him going to the Ministry of Information. A year later Reith dismissed him, and Barrington-Ward did not miss the second chance. Carr joined the staff on 1 January 1941.

But before he arrived the new line was announced in a leader which Carr wrote in *The Times* of 13 November. Morison set great store by this. The day before it appeared he wrote to Steed:

You may find this week a long leader dealing with the general philosophy of democracy. If it appears I beg you to study it as it is likely to be our Credo. I think you will approve the stand I believe it will take against party, or at any rate the Conservative party machine.

'Vital Democracy' was the heading. Carr took as his text Roosevelt's third inauguration speech of 11 November 1940, in which he set America's task as the creation and maintenance of a 'New Order', a new deal for the world, to counterbalance the new 'World Order' with which Hitler was trying to tempt Molotov at the same time. This the leader construed to be the regaining of the confidence of ordinary people in politics. Politicians, by their inability to control the economy during the Depression, had lost that confidence: they could only get it back by economic and social measures that would appeal to the 'little man'.

The only way to surmount the crisis of democracy is to restore to the 'little man' his waning faith that representative institutions really do play a role in his life, and do not leave him the helpless plaything of the vast impersonal machines of organized capital and organized labour.

Morison summed it up succinctly to Steed. 'Economics should come before politics. Whereas the modern state does recognize the existence of external (i.e. foreign) menaces to security it declines to shoulder the responsibility of protecting society against internal menaces such as the abuse of power by capital.' He sent Mrs Alexander a cutting of the leader with the comment: 'V. important I think. Written by E. H. Carr whom I am so mad on. If you are interested in Russia get his lives of Marx and Bakunin.'

Carr's impact was considerable. As an 'amateur' he might have immediately aroused the dislike of his professional colleagues; this did not happen. But he quickly got across Dawson.

Barrington-Ward generously hoped that his prejudice might disappear, but at the end of March Carr wrote him a note pointing out that it was impossible for him to put forward the policy they shared while Dawson was still there. With Morison's help, Barrington-Ward composed a soothing answer,* but the impasse remained. Meantime, Barrington-Ward's regard for Morison grew. His admiration of Morison's progress was simple and unqualified.

All these hardships and vicissitudes have left, amazingly, no scars, no grudges. He seems to have profited by all. And there, with only part-time education, he is – a man of great erudition and balance and taste. Like Garvin he has the original qualities of a man who has given himself the education which circumstances denied him, though he maintains he is the poorer for it.*

In the end, it was neither Morison, Carr, Barrington-Ward, nor Dawson who precipitated the situation, but the Chief Proprietor of *The Times* himself. On 5 May Astor, unprompted, spoke quickly and kindly to both the last two: the time had come, he said, for the change. Barrington-Ward spoke of the need 'to prepare for the great social changes after the war'. Astor agreed and praised Carr's articles of last year. Afterwards, Barrington-Ward walked home with Morison.

I imparted all this to Stanley Morison, my sole confidant, as we walked through burnt-out Holborn and battered Gray's Inn to a little Italian restaurant, the 'Casa Prada' in (of all places) the Euston Road. It was a delicious meal and his company was particularly well-timed.*

Next day Barrington-Ward discussed the matter with Dawson. After a little bargaining (Dawson suggested 31 July, Barrington-Ward the end of the year) they settled on 30 September.* In the meantime, Morison spent a week-end with the Carrs and came away as impressed by Mrs Carr as by her husband.* On 17 July the news leaked out in the last edition of the evening *Star*, to be confirmed next day in *The Times*. At the end of the month, Mrs

Carr found Morison a flat, which he could move into at the beginning of September, which the Carrs (then at Woking) could share when in London. Morison thanked her and added:

There is little to report except that B.W. is now much better, having recovered nearly completely from writer's cramp contracted by acknowledging his fan-mail. Serves him and his hexametrical name right. He ought to be in good shape to shake hands with the Prof. on Thurs.*

September 30 was an emotional day for everyone at *The Times*, for C. W. Brodribb who made a little speech at the daily conference, for W. F. Casey, now to be Deputy Editor, and for Barrington-Ward himself. The next day Dawson came in again to tidy up; although he had managed to keep up an appearance of indifference,* he was melancholy now at leaving. Morison did his best to cheer him up.

A most excellent lunch with Stanley Morison at Scott's (oysters, partridge and savoury) followed by a visit to the new film of the original Reuter (introducing Delane) which we thought we must see.*

Barrington-Ward's parting present to Dawson, who was retiring to his native West Riding, had been bought by Morison. It was well chosen: a colour-plate book, *The Costumes of Yorkshire*. It was 'completed with a Latin inscription which Morison caused to be engraved by Reynolds Stone, an Etonian (appropriately)'. Stone, Barrington-Ward further noted, 'is said to be the best letterer in the country since Eric Gill died'.*

Morison must have said it: when later asked what he thought of Stone's work, he simply said, 'The World'.* Reynolds Stone, after taking his degree at Cambridge, went to the University Press, where Nobbs divined his skill in engraving. By this time, he had already made a name as an engraver, both of lettering, in the sixteenth-century style that Morison loved, and of landscape scenes and decorations in the manner of Bewick and his followers. Morison had just started him on the blocks for a new breviary for Burns, Oates & Washbourne, a task which he took

393

with him into the trying conditions of Air Force life. Cambridge were setting up the text, a task which grew harder and slower as skilled men left to go to the war. Stone and Cambridge were also conscripted for *Lapidaria*, a collection of Latin inscriptions by John Sparrow, to which Morison gave the most minute care.

Morison did his best to cheer them on in their difficult circumstances. MOST SPLENDID DO NOT WISH ANY SLIGHTEST ALTERATION YOURS MOST GRATEFULLY MORISON came the telegram when the colophon block for *Lapidaria* was completed, followed by IPSISSIMUS SPARROW DELIGHTED.* Stone had trouble with his blocks, which split 'when I light the stove in this hut and sit too near it. . . . They go off like a minute pistol shot.' 'Like bottles of champagne,' replied Morison, comforting him.*

At Cambridge, life was enlivened by the irruption of the Dean of Liverpool, Dr F. W. Dwelly. Liverpool Cathedral was due to be opened in 1941, and, having a special interest in the liturgy and its presentation, he was anxious to have the service sheet as well printed as possible. He enquired if Lewis knew a man called Morison who had written on the subject. 'Know him,' cried Lewis, 'I've got him in the next room.' Morison was indeed working next door, and was soon introduced. 'I am not of your persuasion,' he said firmly to the Dean. Dwelly was delighted, and soon he and Morison were fast friends. The result was to be *The Order of Solemn Entrance in Time of War*, 'a demy folio, correctly printed in red and black, and employing magnificent large initials to distinguish the several most solemn portions of the service'.* But in the meantime Dwelly persuaded Morison into another service. Morison wrote to Howe, busy with the rescue work on the books saved from Cambridge Gate.

The missals may be of use to a new projected publication by me on the printing of liturgical books, undertaken for the benefit of the Protestant Cathedral at Liverpool & to be done at the request of the Dean. We are rising in the world.*

Morison had it set up and sent a proof to Dwelly. He was just in time to send it also to Updike – 'What do you think of the matter from the point of view of a conservative liturgist' – and to beg a copy of an article by Updike on liturgical printing. Updike sent it, and Morison thanked him for it two days after Pearl Harbor.

To-day comes the news that your country is now explicitly involved in the task of restraining the aggressor. No one knows when the task will be finished: I am sure America has set its teeth and that the result is not in doubt. In the course of it you will find yourself doing more and different printing. There will be the same problem, but you will do it from still another 'aspect'.*

But Updike died on 29 December. So much had happened since Morison had first heard his name, twenty-five years before. It was an irreplaceable loss. To Ray Nash, writing about it and about the qualities of the Times New Roman (which Updike had put in at the Merrymount Press), Morison summed it up.

He had an immense accumulation of wisdom, but it never seems to have got in his way. He was not one of those who cannot see the wood for the tree. It is not for me to say whether you are right or wrong about The Times New Roman, but I did think it a compliment that he should discern its practical and utilitarian virtues. He was, in many respects, hard, though not hard-boiled, and though he had as good an eye for the aesthetic value of a type face as anybody ever will have, he did not see 'beauty' as something stuck on to the essential forms of lettering, but rather as something that grew out of the practical cunning with which the various lines had been treated.*

On the whole, Morison and Updike had ceased to discuss professional matters. They had come to talk more about religion: 'both felt keenly the intellectual and moral difficulties in institutional religion', as Morison put it in the memoir he wrote of their association.* Despite the differences of background which had seemed so large in the twenties, Updike would go with Morison 'to Mass in a rather poky, not to say dirty, Catholic Church in Boston of his own choice'; Morison found it easier to talk to him about religious matters than to some of his own persuasion. It was a gap in his life that he always felt.

Now Beatrice was shortly going over to America, partly on Monotype business, and partly to promote, as only she could, Anglo-American relations, especially the Books Across the Sea exchange service. 'As having stuck it out here, voluntarily, and as having acted as an American at the Outpost throughout the Neutrality period, she is entitled to talk to the natives of her native country,' Morison wrote to her mother.* She set off in February. It was a long voyage from Lisbon to Montreal.

As day after day went by, my anxiety mounted to a nearly unbearable degree. You can imagine my delight when the long desired cable came. . . . I cannot begin to tell you how empty the town is now you have temporarily vacated it, but that feeling of loss is swallowed up in the joy that you have got safely across.*

Dwelly did not allow Morison to pine. His natural ebullience poured over the paper when he wrote (his hand was consequently all but illegible). 'My Dear Magnanimous', 'My dear M', 'Dwelly the Dean to the Incomparable M' or just 'Hi?', he would begin.

It is thrilling. I could not put it down until I had read it right through. . . . I think the way you have made each section grow with spice and piped it with punch will inevitably arouse discussion. It far exceeds the hopes I had – and they were high enough after reading your article in *Imprint*.*

Morison was delighted.

To my mind these books are of great interest and, if the present squabble between Christians is to give way to something better, the Liturgy, which seems to attract the belated admiration of Wesleyans, Congregationalists and others, may win ever wider recognition as one of the 'Diversities of operation'. I attach some importance to this consideration. It seems to me to entitle the Radcliffe Liturgical Library to a much greater degree of respect than is deserved by a considerable collection of religious books.

For the rest; if any passage in what I wrote seemed offensive to you and your colleagues, I ought to apologise. In order to get a job of this kind done in the time available and against the obstacles presented by present day circumstances, it is necessary to get up a certain amount of steam. You might therefore explain to one of your eminent colleagues who has annotated the paper at several points that it was not part of my endeavour to take a rise out of him. Do what you can to get him to forgive my exuberance.*

It had first been Dwelly's plan to publish it under the name of the library given to Liverpool by Sir Frederick Radcliffe, but even the Dean's ecumenical enthusiasm could not suppress some criticism of Morison's 'pro-popery', and it was transferred to the Cambridge University Press. Morison remained calm: his own interest, he told the Dean, was a small one.

If, when we get to this point, you see your way to authorizing the payment to me of some author's fee for sweeping together all that liturgical sawdust, I shall be very happy; rather more than happy. I have urgent need of an easy chair in which to flop on Saturday and Sunday afternoons when worn out with the debauches of the week.*

Morison seized the opportunity to rewrite and enlarge the text, and by August the new version was ready. As before the Dean ('Thine with a profound sense of unworthiness of the interest and care you have taken in perfecting our schismatic tongue!!!') was delighted. At the end of the month, Lewis and Morison went up to be entertained by the Dean and his housekeeper Christine Wagstaffe, a devoted ally of the pair. The Dean persuaded Morison to include mention of the vocational services of which he was an energetic advocate. Morison wrote:

Accordingly, I have thought it well to mix up in the account of your special Services, a lot of irrelevant references to the Roman ritual, in an attempt to prove that your Services are really no novelty at all. You may permit this. My experience in this country leads me to the conviction that, in order to get an Englishman to do something new, you have to prove to him that he has already been doing it for 20 years.*

Morison sent a proof of the new version to his friend J. H. Arnold, who was delighted with it and asked for 200 copies for the Alcuin Club of which he was secretary; and also to his old

friend Sam Gurney, with whom he had a cheerful correspondence about the Society of St Peter and St Paul, Papal Infallibility
and the ecclesiastical events of the sixteenth century.

What a tragedy it all was. Do you really think that the difference
between your theological position and ours, justifies the destruction
of Christian unity? Would you take the same stand all over again,
or would you, had you been Queen Elizabeth, have sent representatives to the Council of Trent?
 You are very kind and patient with me. I must not plague you.
I was never a member of the Church of England, and have no particular interest or animus concerning it. I have no temptation to join
it. The difficulties of the Christian life which beset me are those of an
entirely different order, most of them were with me when I was
received into the Church 34 years ago to-day, and will be, I suppose,
until the end.*

 Christmas came with a present of shirts from the Dean and the
good news that Archbishop Lang had written an enthusiastic
letter about the book, which Dwelly was now going to try on
Temple at Lambeth. Soon after the text part of the *editio maior*
of *The Solemn Entrance* was ready. Dwelly sent a telegram:
SWAGGER INDEED YOU MAKE ME VERY HAPPY AT LAST WE HAVE A
WORTHY PIECE OF LITURGICAL PRINTING THANKS TO YOU. 'Fizz is
indicated', he added, writing later. 'I look forward to breaking
open that bottle of fizz that you have in your mind's eye,' replied
Morison. 'There are several matters outstanding but I think it
would be better to delay their discussion until news comes out of
Lambeth.' Eventually they decided to try it on both archbishops.
New proofs were pulled at Morison's suggestion: YES I AGREE
NEW PULLS ONE FOR EACH ARCHBISHOP WOULD BE A STIMULANT
AND A COUPLE ALSO FOR GRATEFUL. DWELLY. Morison replied:
ONE ARCHBISHOP IS ENOUGH AND OUGHT TO KNOCK THE ALCUIN
CLUB CROSSEYED. Temple produced the foreword on 19 Febru-
ary; it was not quite what they wanted, being mainly about the
vocational services, but they pressed on.
 Then a blow fell. Temple had seen an advertisement of the
series with his name as author of the preface, and protested that

what he had written was only intended for the vocational services. In vain Dwelly pleaded that he had been given, had seen the proof of Morison's book; the Archbishop was adamant. Morison was comforting. Temple's attitude might seem to them shabby (Morison had been specially proud of the 'war-economy' layout he had done for Temple's *The Resources and Influence of English Literature* early in the year, even – rare for him – putting his name in the colophon). But perhaps it was better without any archbishop. The first edition was suppressed, there was a quick rearrangement of the prelims, and the book was published in November 1943. Radcliffe, once critical, was now full of discriminating praise.

It was a remarkable little book in many ways. It was a miracle of 'war-economy' production, legible but without a wasted inch of paper. It was learned – who but Morison would have noticed the reappearance of the type of the Emperor Maximilian's *Liber Horarum* (1513) in a 1555 Sarum *Prymer*. It was even prophetic. 'If we are right in thinking that the liturgy has a future as well as a past, we have reason to count ourselves fortunate that the elasticity of the responsoral element in the liturgy makes it easy for public worship of that kind to participate more and more closely in the general social impulse so characteristic of our time.' Morison was not so enthusiastic about that participation in the form in which it finally came. Now he spent the next few months delightedly reading the reviews, good, bad and controversial, that appeared in the *Journal of Theological Studies*, the *Church Times*, and elsewhere. He had made a name for himself in a new field, and *English Prayer Books* realized Dwelly's hopes by running to three editions by 1949.

Beatrice had enjoyed the success that Morison predicted in America. Her speeches were a wild success, support for 'Books Across the Sea' poured in, and she embarked on an extensive tour of the whole country. Morison's news was less elating. A young man called Fries, who had been working on the *History*, was called up. Morison had had hopes of him, and was deeply distressed when he died suddenly of food-poisoning. He wrote a note for Barrington-Ward explaining his plight. The *History* could not be left abruptly in 1922; it must go on to the 150th anniversary in 1935. He was without help, except for the generous efforts of Miss Winifred Lodge, who normally worked on the Court Page, in sorting the material now deposited in the strong room because of the blitz (it was thus in no sort of order). Barrington-Ward was reassuring. He saw to it that the companionship of the blitz did not lapse, and lunched with Morison once a week.

I am more than pleased with the way the journal is now being conducted. Last night I went to Steed's (where I had a fine piece of salmon and sauce, made by the hand of Mrs W.S.) who said that the journal was a good 75% better today than it was in the previous regime.*

Nor was *The Times* the only paper to demand Morison's services.

Another piece of work just finished has been the redesigning of the main title of the *Daily Express*, the *Sunday Express* and other members of that family. The Beaver suddenly decided that his conscience was wrong and had been ever since *The Times* had changed from Gothic to Roman. His paper should have been the first to do that, his paper should at least have been the next; his paper had done nothing. If his staff had not the brains to do the job, let them send over to *The Times* and borrow the brains. The change took place on the night of last Sunday, for Monday's issue, July 13th. A cutting is enclosed. As you will see it is a super-fatted and extended Perpetua.*

If the impetus came from Lord Beaverbrook, Morison did not on this occasion meet him, but dealt with L. A. Plummer. He drafted an admirable short memorandum of twenty paragraphs on the layout of the *Express*, the gist of which was that 'it must always be lively and look lively'. It was written in a simple style, calculated to appeal to those to whom it was directed ('The new title should be heavier though not much larger than anything else on the front-page. It should be black. And Simple. White lettering on a stippled ground; shaded, shadowed, interlined or anything "featuresome" should be avoided.'), and was immediately effective. Monotype cut the new title lettering, and Morison was put on a retainer for three years. He proceeded to tackle the *Evening Citizen* with equal success; the *Standard* was left as it was.

'*Black-Letter*' *Text* was printed off and circulated in May. Morison wrote cheerfully to Steinberg, now released and teaching at Sedbergh: 'Should you happen to be writing a review of *Black Letter* you might reprove the writer for his negligence, culpable blindness, or what not, in not noticing those charters written at St Gall in the eighth century.'* He was delighted to get a letter from E. K. Rand at Harvard, whose great work on Alcuin and the Carolingian minuscule he had long admired.

The calm reserve with which you tell the story of the fate of the magnum opus only heightens the heroism with which you met it – as well as the indignation of him who reads.

This is one of those works that sheds real light on a subject. No palaeographer and no student of art can neglect it. It opens up for me new and pleasant highways in 'darkest Gothic'. I still am enamoured of the free if careless grace of the script of Tours – only that I had not known that it was careless.*

Morison was delighted too when E. A. Lowe begged a copy and was equally impressed.

My education has been sadly neglected. A palaeographer should also be a scribe. He should be a master of the technique of the craft. To tell you the truth, what has really attracted me to the subject was the artisan side of it – the fact that it was a craft. I like people who work with their hands. I have come to the conclusion that you & I ought to get together that I may sit at the feet of a master.*

The only cloud in all this was the continuing ill-health of Burch. Morison was first inclined to make light of it, but by the end of July he was worried. He took Burch down to Bognor for a long week-end, but it only produced a brief improvement; on 3 September Burch died. Morison was desperately sad; it was the end of an era, in which Burch had run Monotype single-handed. Morison was also more than a little worried about his own position, but this was soon cleared up in conversation with the chairman, Sir Geoffrey Ellis. All this was reported to Beatrice in New York.

I explained that, as far as I was concerned, I was not and never had been in the employment of the Monotype Corporation; but that I employed the Corporation as a vehicle of my ideas. Hence, if he, as Chairman, was prepared to authorize a statement to the effect that there would be a continuity of Monotype publicity in respect of type faces, publicity and our educational programme; I should be quite happy to continue my association with the Monotype. He agreed and I later confirmed this with Buckle. . . . I do not want to hurry you back from New York, but I would beseech you not to forget the Monotype when you are considering the disposition of your time. Buckle will write confirming your present position.*

H. L. Buckle had been Works Manager; he now became General Manager. He quickly confirmed Beatrice's position, but Morison was disappointed in his hope of seeing her home soon. In May next year he went up to Edinburgh at William Maxwell's request to give away the prizes at Heriot Watt College. Coming back on the 'Flying Scotsman', he wrote and told Beatrice all that he had been doing. He told her about Monotype. He told her about Dwelly and *English Prayer Books*. He told her, in boastful detail, about his success at *The Times*.

For the rest I have been hard at work on the final vol. of the *History of T. Times* which I have put myself under bond to finish by the end of this year. I have already done the home & foreign part down to 1908, unearthing a fascinating amount of stuff about Britain & Germany & Britain & Russia between 1896 and 1908. A certain amount of new material regarding U.S. relations has also turned up. The mass of correspondence is immense, whereas the old problem was shortage. I now have too much in the way of files of *The Times*, letters, telegrams, &c, for the modern period. I hope to complete the political part to 1912 in a few weeks & then to give the summer & autumn to Northcliffe & so wind up. In the meantime I give plenty of attention to the present day. What I regard as a worthwhile contribution to the war effort was the change from Dawson to B^n-Ward, with

E. H. Carr as Assist. Ed. The change has brought others & inevitably almost, meant my being invested with much 'occult' influence so that little is done without prior knowledge. Hence I am dining regularly & weekly with B-W & the others to discuss the policy of the paper & the re-arrangement of the staff. With all this I have little time to spare on my hands.*

He wrote about the state of the world, the imminence of the invasion of Europe. Anglo-American relations (on which he was insistent at *The Times* – he had a reference to the Pacific war inserted in a leader by Carr on the three-power talks), and he talked about Beatrice herself, all her news and news of her friends in England. 'Gosh I do miss you. The place is different as chalk and cheese, as Ferioque and yours faithfully.'*

At the end of the year, Beatrice came back to find Morison looking forward to the New Year. He had been much involved in the Publishers' Association Technical Advisory Committee, and the formula of the Economy Agreement ('All books to be no larger than 11pt; composition to be 50% more words on all Cr 8vo; La Cr; Royal 8vo; v.sm. margins; v. thin boards')* was largely of his devising. He had explained these principles of economy to Francis Meynell, now at the Ministry of Supply, and was enthusiastic about them. It would mean 'thinner books and handier books. This will be regarded by many of us who cannot, for love or money, buy bookcases at the present times, a permanent gain.'* He had had a happy weekend with the Barrington-Wards. They had walked in the woods and talked about the future, with an increased role for Morison in the *Literary Supplement*.* Now there was a real hope of being allowed to finish the *History* without more interruption, and 'be free for his life's work',* the resumption of the studies interrupted on 10–11 May 1941. He talked to Barrington-Ward again about the terminal date for the *History*, which he now thought could hardly be earlier than 1939.* By May, they were convinced that it would be four volumes not three, and at the end of July Morison put in a long memorandum 'with a plan covering the first four vols' which he now hoped to complete in 1947.

Matters were now further complicated by difficulties with Carr. Morison had warned Barrington-Ward not to expect Carr to have a principal part in *The Times*'s staff after the war. He was, Morison thought, incapable of distinguishing his own views from those of *The Times*.* In the spring of 1944, Carr was near breakdown, and Morison had an idea for a possible support and successor in Donald Tyerman, the assistant editor of the *Economist*. He had lunch with him, and Tyerman was interested. Carr had his own views on how the office should be run, and wrote a vigorous memorandum expounding them. Barrington-Ward was decidedly taken aback by this; it revealed, he thought, very little sense of the practical details of editing the paper. On 27 March, he, Casey and Morison had a conference on the staff problem, and resolved to make recruitment a matter of urgency. By May, Tyerman had been approached; he joined in October and by the end of the year was at work as assistant editor. Peter Utley (another Morison protégé) and other new hands had also come in, and Carr was able to revert to part-time working.*

Morison's anxiety to help Barrington-Ward was endless. He took him to lunch with John Sparrow, now a major in the Coldstream Guards, who, he thought, might be a future editor of the *T.L.S.*; 'and so he might', agreed Barrington-Ward.* He talked to him about the management problem, now that Kent, Lints Smith's successor, was coming up to retirement. He arranged with George Barnes for a B.B.C. broadcast on the history of *The Times* to celebrate its 50,000th number, which delighted the Editor, on 24 November. Two days later there was a generous profile of Barrington-Ward in the *Observer*, concocted by Morison with Ivor Brown and Tom Jones. He spent more week-ends with the family, and as a result of one wet walk had to borrow a pair of trousers – the first time, as he said, that he had worn anything but black for twenty-five years.

One problem, however, remained unsolved – the *T.L.S.* Morison had said in 1936 that it needed cheering up: Murray's editorship had only succeeded in lightening it. He and Barrington-Ward had fallen out over the Beveridge Report. The crisis came when Charles Morgan, to whom Morison had made approaches, talked to Murray. Murray was furious that this should have been done without his knowledge and without thought for his own nominee, Simon Nowell-Smith; he would only stay until a successor could be found. On 26 October, Barrington-Ward dined with Astor and told him that he proposed to offer the job to Morison himself, which he did next day. Morison asked time to think, but, hoist on his own petard, he accepted, only asking that he should have, as Richmond had, the status of 'assistant editor in charge of the supplement', and the right of reconsideration in a year's time, and a secretary; 'all these seem tolerable conditions', Barrington-Ward noted.*

Morison was not so enthusiastic. In his note to Barrington-Ward, he had made six points, which (paradoxically) were almost the exact opposite of his recipe in 1936.

1) That I should act as an assistant of yours, placed in charge of the editorship. Thus I should continue to keep in intimate touch with *The Times*.
2) That the *Literary Supplement* should be made relatively more scholarly, more inclusive, and less solemn than at present. Any worth-while book published in the country should be at least mentioned, remembering that unless the author is established as a writer, his work will hardly get mentioned at all if he does not get it in the *Supplement*.
3) That the weekly chronicle of books be restored, thus affording mention automatically. Even if it extends only to the author's name, title of the work, publisher and price, it is covetable. This list was proved in times past to be of national value and consulted by librarians all over the world.
4) That the reviews and other contents of the *Supplement* be arranged on a generous basis that takes into account political consistency. Reviewers should not contradict one another on points upon which the policy of *The Times* is known. Where it is known the *Supplement* should adopt it. Literary matters also come under this ruling. Whether the *Supplement* should side for or against such a controversial subject as 'Basic English' should depend upon the policy adopted by *The Times*.
5) That there should be adopted a policy towards religion similarly consistent with *The Times*. The *Supplement* is not a religious paper

and I should distinguish between devotional books and religious books, giving the latter fuller treatment when they consider the social and therefore political aspects of religion.

6) To do all possible to increase the usefulness of the *Supplement* to authors, publishers, librarians and the general public and to bring to bear the best critical pens available to deal with the output of philosophical, religious, political and historical works, while giving poetry, biography, memoirs, art and art history, and fiction their due. It should thus be possible to render the *Supplement* a critical and constructive medium of thought which would deserve recognition, in due time, as a literary institution.

While he hoped to put this programme into effect within twelve months, he could not let the *History* drop, and there was his twenty-two-year connection with Cambridge to be considered. He had just designed the permanent edition of the text of the Thanksgiving Service for Victory in Europe and had thoroughly enjoyed it.

I am quite at your disposal in the whole matter and if you judge that in all the circumstances of gossips being what they are my connexion had better be relinquished I will readily acquiesce. It remains that after a score of years' super-teutonic study I possess a unique knowledge of certain aspects of the printing art, and it might be that *The Times* would not find it easy to refuse advice to the King's Printers, Oxford and Cambridge, regarding the form of the Crown books.

I have been associated with Cambridge for 22 years. They gave me encouragement at a time when I had no reputation and, for that reason alone, I do not relish breaking the link. The feeling has no financial basis, and I would be quite happy, if *The Times* thought it a solution, to answer the typographical and liturgical queries of Cambridge on a voluntary basis, i.e. I would remain the Honorary Typographical Adviser of the Press.*

This was the solution finally adopted, but the tenor of Morison's working life had been sufficiently disturbed for him to complain to Mrs Carr.

9th March 1945.

I am very glad to have your letter, even if it does refer to *The Literary Supplement*. You send me no sympathy that I can notice, – much as I deserve it. Would you like to attempt a weekly literary rag with three debilitated assistants, a secretary in hospital with pneumonia, and an arrears list of reviews dating back nine months?

There are two sorts of reviewers I find. First there are the hacks. These I shall probably be taught by experience to prefer. They can always be relied upon to give a summary of the book and leave the reader without any particular taste in his mouth. Secondly, there are the non-hacks. These can always be relied upon to rise superior to the author they are reviewing, and show off their own knowledge. Both sorts send their reviews in late, and both sorts, when something in their review is questioned, can't answer it because they have already sold the books. The best reviewer of the book is the author. I asked an author the other day whether he could suggest anybody who would review his book, – thus giving him the chance to do it himself. Unfortunately he was such an English gentleman that he did not even like such a question being put to him. So of course I had all the trouble of finding an alternative, one of these people who was so superior that he wrote an essay on the subject rather than a review of the book.*

In the last few months of the war, there were other signs that 'business as usual' was about to return. In 1942, as well as the *Express*, Morison had redesigned all the forms and stationery for the Cable and Wireless Company, for his friend Ivor Fraser, a director of the *Morning Post* and old friend of Lints Smith, who had also given him valuable inside information about the Pearson–Northcliffe duel for *The Times* in 1907. VIA IMPERIAL now appeared in a much more striking and rational form, with a device for which Morison had enlisted Reynolds Stone's help.* Morison was officially thanked by the board for his work on 1 May 1945.

In March 1944 Eyre & Spottiswoode were turning towards post-war problems and the effect that shortage of paper would have on their responsibility, as King's Printers, to produce bibles. Morison's old friend Douglas Jerrold wrote to beg for his advice, offering a directorship of the company. Morison was tempted, but it would clash with his commitment to Cambridge, where Lewis was anxious to have more, not less, of this time, and he felt obliged to refuse the offer. He was rather less enthusiastic next month about Jerrold's plans to re-start the *Dublin Review* with T. S. Gregory as editor, but was willing to contribute in any way, for the sake of old loyalties.*

In September, the *Daily Herald* asked Monotype for help in changing the heading. 'I have advised them that we will be only too pleased to help them, and that you will go round to see them as soon as possible,' Buckle told Morison.* Morison was un-enthusiastic, both about the job and the manner of asking. The paper, as the journal of organized labour, was not the *Herald* of his youth, nor was this the way he had worked with Burch. He acquiesced in a form of bold Plantin capitals. He took more cheer-fully to the task of designing the new *Chambers' Encyclopaedia*, about which he had been approached by Mrs Margaret Law, the new editor.* 'There is no doubt in my mind', wrote Morison hopefully, 'that, given the possibilities of peace-time, a special fount should be cut for the Encyclopaedia. The cost is trifling in comparison with that of the composition as a whole.'* He had a variety of specimens set up at Cambridge, which formed the basis of the page finally adopted in May 1945.

Cambridge was in a depressed state, and Lewis, nearing seventy, felt the strain. 'Am just getting over a cold, so am not in too good a humour,' he wrote to Morison when he sent the specimens for Chambers'. 'I have been getting rid of the cold for the last three months and if I don't get rid of it, it will get rid of me.'* Morison tried to cheer him up with the recollection of past glories.

All I can do therefore is to suggest that you tell Nobbs to set up a page in Bell to the measure he knows best. If S.C. passes the page I shd like to do the chapter heads & prelims. I like handling old John Bell. What a lark that book was! My opinion = one of the least bad jobs by you and me that I can call to mind. Topham also was a fair piece. The handmade ed. of poor Dom Manuel's 3 vol work was something in the way of machining &c &c which was notable. I wish I had kept, or you had kept for me, a few sheets. Do you remem-ber that illuminating we had done for the Pope? The book is now safe thanx to Alexander's strategy. My impression is that the II Front will start tonight or Wed night.*

Eventually peace came, and with it the promise of better things. John Dreyfus, recruited to the Press just before the war and now a captain in the Army in Holland, wrote to tell Morison that van Krimpen was still alive and well.* Soon Morison got a letter from him, full of enquiries about conditions in England and in particular about the progress of his own Romulus type. Morison was not unhopeful.

No doubt the Corporation will revive. What is wanted is labour and materials. With only three punch cutting females who are exclusively engaged in cutting the odds and ends of special sorts required by the international trade, there is not much hope of immediate typographical progress. But I do not myself despair of an eventual return to past standards, in both quality and quantity of output.*

Before Christmas was over, van Krimpen was over for a long visit. His shrewd eye saw that the future at Monotype was bleak for him if Morison was wholly committed to *The Times*. He put the point to Morison who tried to reassure him.

It is not that I feel that journalism is a wider or more useful form of activity than that which the Corporation might offer; rather my feeling is that the Corporation, under the present management, does not hold out to me the same degree of satisfaction that I felt under W.I.B. Nothing, however, is settled, and I am in no hurry to see it settled. If I continue at Printing House Square for another twelve months I do not think it will affect the situation one way or the other. In other words, I do not think another twelve months journalism would necessarily reduce my interest in typographical problems.*

But he was soon forced to admit that van Krimpen's apprehensions were all too real.

The changes in the Corporation have been profound. First of all there are the circumstances of the total destruction of Fetter Lane, which carried with them the subordination of the whole Head Office to the Works. Secondly, there was the death of Burch, which brought into power certain influences that had remained submerged for so long. Next, the labour difficulties, more extreme today than even twelve months ago – restrict to the barest minimum any engraving;

409

with the necessary consequence that the whole type face department, once so conspicuous, has virtually ceased to exist. Finally, my own preoccupation with other matters has necessarily withdrawn me from the counsels of the Corporation, with the result that I, who exerted a very powerful influence, have now been excluded, and have excluded myself, from the inner circles.*

It was a sign of his changed position that his presence was no longer considered necessary in Queen's House, the building that Monotype occupied after the destruction of Fetter Lane. He had been given an office in a dingy building near where the old Monotype House had been. 'Now that I have been put in this siding at Fetter Lane, I might as well be in Patagonia,' he told van Krimpen bitterly.

I should add in fairness that any new man working in the difficult circumstances of today would inevitably take a 'low' view of the importance of typographic design; & until the Corporation can attract labour (of the right kind) to the Type-designing and Punch-cutting depts. my services are largely superfluous.*

But in the meantime *The Times* had provided compensation. The new *T.L.S.* was a success. Namier, who had ostentatiously given up reviewing for it, now came back. He entertained Morison at Manchester in May, only a few months after he had started, and even then was prepared to admit that, though it had sunk very low, it was already greatly improved.* In July, Edmund Blunden joined the staff, an occasion for a celebration lunch with Barrington-Ward.* Morison continued to provide the Editor with invaluable information, as, for example, on the use made in Washington of *The Times*'s leaders on Greece to put pressure on the Government, which prompted Churchill's bitter attack on the paper. Equally, Barrington-Ward was a support to the Editor of the *T.L.S.* 'There goes', he had once said as Morison left the room, 'one of the most intelligent men in England',* and he never wavered in his high opinion of Morison. There were those who, knowing Morison, were prepared to see pro-Catholic bias in his editing, without much justification. True, he expected his readers to share his interest in the less conventional aspects of Continental Catholicism, such as the philosophy of Maritain.

I have always been one of his admirers, and used to meet him regularly, even ten years ago or more. He was brought into the church by that curious Jew, Léon Bloy, who wrote that curious work *Salut pour les Juifs*.*

Léon Bloy became something of a King Charles's Head to Morison. There was, too, the business of the article commemorating the centenary of Newman's conversion. The article was unprompted by any book, and from the beginning – 'Newman Decides: into Port after a Rough Sea' – to the end, it expressed the warmest sympathy for Newman's predicament as he prepared to leave the Oxford Movement. The reader's eye was caught by a photograph on the second page, showing Newman's surplice and other *personalia* at the Birmingham Oratory ingeniously disposed not as *nature morte* but *nature vive* (this was specially arranged by Arthur Crook – its effect was carefully calculated by Morison). The last words were: 'After having rendered signal and lasting service to the Church of England, he still had the second half of a long life to devote with unfaltering loyalty to the service of a greater Church.'*

Morison's critics saw their worst forebodings justified. Nor were they amused when *The Times*'s compositors hung the photograph up with the caption 'Next, please' (it did look rather like a barber's shop). But Morison had a characteristically dramatic answer: the article was by Canon Hutchinson, a faithful (if High Church) member of the Church of England. Barrington-Ward stood firmly by him.

I assured Morison once more of my confidence that he wd see fair play done to all religions. Felt sure he was making a great thing out of the Suppt. and did not want him to prejudice himself with some suspicious readers by the kind of inexpediency produced last week. Naturally Morison and I were able to talk without any heat or strong feeling.*

On 10 January 1946 Morison was able to report a resounding success to Barrington-Ward. The net sale of the *T.L.S.* was up from 22,000 to 30,000 and was only restrained from further increase by the paper shortage. The amount of reading matter had gone up by twenty-two per cent, advertising was up and profits trebled. On the other hand, he had made no progress with the *History*. He now contemplated finishing volume III in 1946; volume IV, even with more staff, would occupy him until 1950 'by which time, I calculate, I shall have devoted 20 years to this task, and I certainly do not enjoy the prospect of its prolongation'. He hoped that he would be allowed to take on a deputy who would relieve him on the *T.L.S.* and allow him to get back to the horrific but agreeable intricacies of the Northcliffe era. Barrington-Ward promised the necessary support as soon as it could be found.

Meanwhile Morison was preparing for his first post-war visit to America. He was to receive the Gold Medal of the American Institute of Graphic Arts, and to take delicate soundings among *The Times*'s American correspondents; he also hoped to meet some old friends, in New York and also in Chicago. The presentation of the medal took place on 5 June. Christopher Morley, once a colleague at Doubleday's, gave it to him. Morison in his reply was unusually warm: after the war years, his visit had revived many memories, particularly of Updike, no longer there. He tried to sum up all that America had meant to him, and justice to his old friend did not prevent him from acknowledging his greatest debt to De Vinne; if Updike had better taste, De Vinne was the more influential thinker. He had had another memento of the past: a pathetic pencil-scrawl from Goudy, too ill to come.

It is a great disappointment not to see you receive this deserved honor. I also wish I could have presented you with a copy of my latest (and probably last) literary (?) effort – 'A half century of type design and typography'. I wish you might find it possible to visit me here at Deepdene. A chat with you after 16 years would be wonderful.*

Morison had a more invigorating meeting with Lowe. There was more to tell and hear than could be crammed into one day at Princeton. They talked and talked, ending up with a simple supper in a roadside diner. He was also able to transact his *Times* business satisfactorily, and returned with the welcome news that Willmott Lewis, the Washington correspondent, was still fit and willing to carry on.* Apart from this, he was impressed by the lack of confidence in post-war America; it was different from the determination with which Barrington-Ward was to face the new challenge of austerity, utility and equality in Britain.

But Morison, to his distress, began to see that all was not well with Barrington-Ward. Carr left at the end of August. A month before he went Barrington-Ward, with Morison and Tyerman, gave him a farewell lunch. He was full of gratitude for all that Carr had done: 'No one can take his place, and yet "the same arts that did gain a power must it maintain".'* Early in the new year, the *T.L.S.* succession problem was solved over lunch at the Ritz with Alan Pryce-Jones, who was to become assistant editor in June and succeed Morison on 1 February 1948.* They had a happy week-end together at the end of April; the Barrington-Wards had rented a house at St Margaret's Bay, and Morison was 'enchanted with this place', and approved of the liturgical practices of the Convent of the Annonciades there.* In June, another question had to be solved. Pryce-Jones had come, and had settled in well; his succession as assistant editor had been approved. But in May, Blunden asked for, and could not be refused, a year's leave to take up a visiting professorship in Japan, and Pryce-Jones received a tempting offer from the *Observer*. 'What Price Jones?' Morison asked:* the answer was satisfactory, and Morison was relieved. But in July Barrington-Ward was ordered three weeks in bed and he spent the summer at St Margaret's Bay. At the end of August Morison went to see him, and was full of concern for what he saw. He had, he wrote to Astor, been prepared to believe that Barrington-Ward was suffering only from overwork, that nothing was seriously wrong.

When I met B.W., however, I saw at once that there was more to it than I had thought, or had been said. His voice was flat, he had that difficulty in speaking that marks the over-tired man. His silences were

413

longer and more numerous, and his walking even slower than when I saw him a month before. His shaving exhibited a very uncharacteristic lack of precision; the whole of his processes had decelerated. Most certainly I felt I was in the presence of an exceptionally worn out man.

At once I announced myself as feeling overworked, and as having no will or capacity to set up any new records for long cross-country tramps. In March last B.-W. had taken me a fast up-and-down 12-mile walk that completely fagged me out. Now, six months later, he himself promptly ruled out any such activity. Throughout the afternoon, we both reclined on a chaise-longue, and walked only for ten minutes or a quarter of an hour. This became the routine for the rest of the week-end.

. . . B.-W. will need very severely to ration his energy. He will never again be able to work the always inhuman hours that his theory of conscientious editorship has so long imposed upon him. A fourteen-hour day will never be possible again. His theory that a week-end in the country would restore the balance may have had some justification years ago, but his use of this device meant that what he gained at the week-end he overspent the following week. He has, therefore, run through his capital, and the present month or six weeks will be nothing like sufficient for his restoration to health. I doubt, in fact, whether a rest of any length whatever will ever bring back the B.-W. of ten years ago. But, if he had a longer rest than he now plans, he might return to the office in a state of health fully equal to the task of editorship. But he certainly must not be allowed to reestablish the old fourteen-hour day. In fact, a reorganization of the editorial department should make such a thing impossible for B.-W. or any other editor. B.-W. has, in fact, carried departmental responsibilities which have greatly increased the burden of actual editing.

That burden is very great. The constant interruption, the switching of the mind, at less than a moment's notice, from one topic to another; the innumerable decisions that have to be taken; the multitude of people to be seen and listened to, the many telephone calls, exact a fearful price from the editor.

I conclude that either B.-W. will stop the old routine, – or the old routine will stop him.*

In the autumn he seemed to be better, and Morison took the opportunity to straighten out his own future. Anthony Powell had succeeded R. D. Charques as reviewer of novels for the

T.L.S., and Morison was satisfied that his work there was done. It had not been an easy task.

It was necessary to reorganize the whole staff and change its methods. In addition, it was necessary to revise the entire panel of reviewers and increase the pay of such as deserved it; to change the layout of the paper in order to accommodate more text and more advertisements; and to raise the advertising rates. By this programme of rehabilitation, and controlling every detail of the work, I made *The Supplement* not only a better three-pennyworth than it was in 1944, but a more remunerative property. The circulation has steadily increased from the time the paper came under my control. To-day *The Supplement* is, once again, a member of the family that The Times Publishing Co. Ltd. might be happy to own.

But this state of affairs had been achieved by 'the hardest work I have ever placed at anybody's service'.

I am not afraid of work; I am fortunate in possessing the physique necessary to the discharge of the task involved in the editorship of both *The Supplement* and *The History*. Except for one leave of absence of three weeks in America, I have had no holidays in thirty consecutive months. Were I unaware of the value, in terms of money, of these two jobs of work, I should be worthy of neither. During the twenty years that I have worked for The Times my market value outside P.H.S. has increased. In consequence, the rate I receive from The Times Publishing Company Limited, is low compared with that I used to receive from other sources. If, when it is known that I am resigning the *Supplement*, the Cambridge Press should think fit to offer to revive my appointment, I am sure it will be at an increased figure. Twice, recently, I have postponed consideration of a half-time offer from a large book publishing house, with a very considerable export business. For this half-time work I was offered a salary of £3,000 a year. In addition, I have had offers of temporary appointments from three American Universities. I have an interest in finishing *The History* and it is probable that book-publishing, even on a half-time basis, would be too much of a distraction. I do not care to put myself into any position that would prejudice the punctuality, completeness and quality of the fourth and final volume of *The History*.*

In short, he proposed that his present combined salary of £2500 (his Monotype salary was then, as for many years past,

£1000) for the two jobs should be maintained while he concentrated on the *History*, and, as in the past he had been 'of service to the House', so, 'as long as it should suit the convenience of the Editor and the Manager, I should propose to take, in the future, as much interest in the prosperity of *The Times* as in the past'.

Two days later, Barrington-Ward saw Astor, and they talked it over. 'Agreed on Morison's future – historian, typographer-in-chief, and "Special duties for the Editor". Same pay as now.'*

But all too soon Barrington-Ward's illness took a turn for the worse. Astor begged him to take a long rest; Campbell Stuart, a director of *The Times*, provided passages on a liner to South Africa. It was too late. Barrington-Ward died at Dar-es-Salaam on 29 February 1948.

It was a tragedy to Morison: 'tragic that he was not given the time in which to continue to expound rationally and persuasively the novel and necessary social and economic changes that the effort and expense of two world wars in one generation rendered inevitable';* tragic even more to Morison himself, who had lost the one man he had admired unreservedly, who had returned his admiration in the same degree.

17

WHILE in Chicago in the summer of 1946, Morison had made the acquaintance of the new (since 1942) librarian of the Newberry Library. The Wing Foundation, the special collection on the history of printing and writing, of which Updike had written hopefully long ago in 1923, had grown in scope and importance, and had come to mean more and more to Morison, since he met Pierce Butler, twenty-five years before. This time, he had gone to the Newberry just to see how it had got on since his last visit, but in Pargellis he found someone after his own heart, a man of large vision and great energy, who positively enjoyed meeting and overcoming the difficulties that came in the way. Moreover, he had sound views on both burgundy and champagne. Morison wrote to him on his return: 'I rank my chance, so to speak, acquaintance with you as one of the two most pleasant and fruitful passages in my American visit; the other being the day I spent at Princeton with E. A. Lowe. . . . I thoroughly enjoyed every moment at Chicago and it was an extra treat that you came back with me to New York on the 20th Century.'*

Pargellis had co-operated with another American friend, Philip Hofer, in the publication of A. F. Johnson's translation of Verini's *Luminario*, which Morison wrote an introduction for and had printed at *The Times* Private Printing Office in 1947. With Morison he had also discussed the future of the Wing Foundation since the librarian, Ernst Detterer, was getting old. On 9 November 1947, Detterer suddenly died, and, in response to his request for advice, Morison wrote Pargellis a long letter on 27 November.

It is a great loss to this branch of study which, as far as America is concerned, he had made his own. There was nobody to touch him for depth and range of knowledge of calligraphical literature. The people at the Metropolitan Museum, N.Y. who were trained by Ivins knew a good deal about the 16th and early 17th Century calligraphical manuals but they did not enjoy the benefit which access to the Ricketts collection gave Detterer. More recently he had access to the Hamill collection and these two, with the Wing resources, amount to a mass of material far greater than the sum of the Metropolitan Museum and Plimpton collections. It is certain, therefore, that you have there in Chicago the finest and the greatest collection of books on the art of writing that exists in one city and most of it under your own roof. It is reassuring to me, personally, that your letter indicates that this aspect of the situation is recognised. I suppose that, by a series of accidents on the one hand and an abundance of curiosity on the other, I know as much as anybody about the subject and, in more favourable times, took the trouble to inspect every note-worthy collection west and south of Leningrad. When I say that the Ricketts and Hamill collections are noteworthy, you may believe it.

The choice of a successor to Detterer has proportionate significance. If I can be of any help I need hardly say that I shall be delighted to have the privilege.

He suggested either James Wardrop of the Victoria and Albert Museum, or else some potentially useful if at present untrained graduate of the University of Chicago, as a successor to Detterer. He had known Wardrop for years; they shared a common enthusiasm for the sixteenth-century Italian calligraphers, and Morison could see great advantage in having his friend so placed. On the other hand, his health was uncertain. Of the two possibilities Morison inclined to the second. Of himself he said:

My position amounts to this. Since that night when I left you to go back to Chicago and I went on to Washington, I have not had more than three or four days holiday, or even leave of absence. In other words I have a good deal of leave due to me. Last week I sent you a copy of the History of *The Times* Volume III which I think you, as the historian of industry and commerce, will be interested to look into. I have a fourth volume to do in order to complete the narrative but I do not intend to do very much on it in the early part of the year, i.e. next year. In order to free myself for this concluding instalment of the History of *The Times* I am being liberated from the *Literary Supplement* and from February 1st shall have what I have not had for three years, namely a reasonable working day and working week.

It is the heavy and continual pressure of all this work, combined with the innumerable frustrations caused by this highly industrialised country being subject to an indefinitely long shortage economy, that has made the *Verini* so late.

It occurs to me that I might take time off to come to America to do one or two odd jobs. Allan Nevins, for instance, pressed me, at one time, to give a few talks at Columbia. If it turns out to be possible to get the necessary currency (and this holds good for Wardrop) I do not see why I should not make a short trip. In this case, supposing you are so good, I could go out to Chicago and give some time to the man you may, by that time, have selected.

Pargellis was delighted, not least by the news that Morison was coming to Chicago. Expressing interest in Wardrop, he cast a delicate fly in Morison's direction:

Would it be at all possible for you to come to Chicago, not for a few days only, but for two or three months? If you could so plan your work and the trip that you could spend that much time with us, I should like to offer you a temporary post as Visiting Fellow in the Wing Foundation.*

Morison took some time to answer Pargellis's letter. He was spending Christmas with the Astors at Hever Castle, and there the question was successfully resolved. He wrote from Hever:

I cannot imagine a more agreeable proposal than yours. I should feel at home in your collection, with Mr. Hamill, and with you. I have many friends in Chicago and I like the city. There is much for me to learn from the Library. When, therefore, Colonel Astor asked me if I really wanted to go I had no hesitation in answering 'Decidedly yes'. 'Then by all means go', he then said, 'but I would be glad if you would stay to help me with ... (there are internal problems at Printing House Square that need solving) and go off, say, in March or April'. I think, therefore, I can rely on being able to give you a hand in the late Spring if, in the circumstances, your Institution could make use of me.*

These plans were interrupted but not upset by the news of Barrington-Ward's death. Its suddenness gave no chance for the lengthy process of consultation and sounding that must precede the appointment of a new editor from outside. Morison was able to put the view of the editorial staff that someone within the office – and Casey was the obvious man – should be appointed Editor. Casey had been virtually editing the paper for over six months; on the staff since 1913, Deputy Editor since 1941, he could bridge the gap admirably until a successor of the right calibre could be found. Casey himself had other views, as Morison confided in Wickham Steed:

When, about March 14th 1948, Casey asked me to take the job in his stead, and offered to remain as my deputy, I told him that I thought it was easier to find another solution to the Editorship of *The Times* than it was to find another solution to the Editorship of the History; and that, even if I wanted the Editorship of *The Times*, I should still regard it as unfair to the House if I did not finish the History.*

Casey's offer may have been half-serious, but Morison had no doubts. His loyalty to 'the House', an ideal vision of *The Times* as the sum of its parts, 'past, present and future', came to have all the solidity of faith. It was thus easy to answer Casey: harder to decide what the future would ask of *The Times*. To Morison at Barrington-Ward's memorial service on 31 March, there was a certain inevitability, almost rightness, about his career. 'Geoffrey Dawson is 58 to-day and has shown no sign of retirement; Barnes died at 58; Delane went mad at 58; I resigned at 58; and no man can edit *The Times* after 58 and live.'* So Buckle had told Dermot Morrah in 1932. Here now was Barrington-Ward's name to add to the list. The trouble with Dawson was that he did not fit. Immune from that total devotion to 'the House', immune (as it were) from the family curse, he was an anomaly. With Morison, building, as with the history of lettering so with that of *The Times*, a pattern of events that came to have the force of dogma in his mind, evidence that did not fit could not exist; or, if it did exist, must be shown to be of little importance.

On 31 March, Morison himself was fifty-eight. He, too, had spent his strength with as little thought for the consequences to his physique as Barrington-Ward. He, too, had begun to feel warnings that he could not go on as he had. Whatever might happen to him, the *History* must be finished. But first he must have a rest. So it was easy to answer Casey, easy to answer T. S. Eliot, reproaching him for leaving the *T.L.S.*, easy to leave the *T.L.S.* itself and to welcome Pryce-Jones at a dinner at the Garrick Club on 6 April (a month before his birthday, when he would be gone), easy to leave Monotype for the moment. He sat impatiently through the Pilgrims' dinner after the unveiling of the Roosevelt memorial, said good-bye to Dwelly, to Stuart, to Casey, and was off to welcoming Chicago.

He went to America with Gavin Astor, his old friend's son, now preparing himself for future responsibility. They looked at the newspapers, struggling with a strike of compositors, and met a defiant Arthur Sulzberger at the *New York Times*. But Morison was anxious to get to Chicago. He took a roomette on the Commodore on the night of 27 April.

I arrived on Apl 28 and have not had a meal or a minute to myself since 8.40 a.m. on that day until this evening. Most of the time it has rained, as a rule heavily, sometimes thunderously. I am installed on a ground floor, 1002 N. State Street, five minutes from the Drake hotel and three from the Library. The flat consists of a bedroom, bathroom, kitchen with gas-stove that lights itself on & off, & sitting-room, all newly painted & well, though senselessly, furnished. I am expected to put the calligraphical collections in order & I work away at this from 9.30 until 5.30 with interruptions for lunch and cocktails. There is always someday [body] to be lunched or dined with. The Librarian and his trustees are generous. . . . I am, therefore, getting fat in every sense, for my cheeks are rounded out and I have not felt so chubby for many years – & that in spite of my not caring for the meat they have here unless it is tinned, which they know well how to do. All told everything has been most happy and successful. The Library keeps me busy and the time races away, I am as eager to remain as I am to be back – if you take my meaning. This *is* a beneficial change and the Library a great relief from the constant chat of P.H.Sq. A successful holiday in fact.*

Living this eremitical (if far from ascetic) life, walking, hunched against the wind off Lake Michigan, between his cell at 1002 North State Street and the uncompromising romanesque façade of the Newberry, greeted there with warmth and admiration by all the staff from Pargellis downwards, Morison began to feel the rigours of the long winter softening, and new hopes, ideas and prospects beginning to form. There had been little relaxation since the first days after the outbreak of war, when the whole pattern of life, at Monotype, Cambridge, *The Times*, seemingly immutable, had suddenly dissolved. The austere discipline that took its place had surmounted the calamities and the hard work, the destruction of Cambridge Gate, the reorganization of the *T.L.S.* with paper short and staff hard to get, the death of Barrington-Ward. Morison could now afford to relax the bonds; among new friends, without the need to maintain austerity or authority, his natural gaiety began to assert itself more and more. He had a high old time in Chicago, now and every time he came back.

He could also afford to think about his own future. At *The Times* there was and would be for some time the *History* to finish, Casey, as warm if not as stimulating a companion as Barrington-Ward, to help, and the friendship, closer after the trials of the war, of Astor. What would become of his other preoccupations, letter design and the typography of books? Very little, Morison decided. The new men at Monotype were busy trying to replace equipment damaged or destroyed all over Europe, with all materials in short supply. At Cambridge Lewis, who had stayed on all through the war, had retired two years ago, aged sixty-seven. His successor, Brooke Crutchley, a warm friend for nearly twenty years, was wrestling with the same problems that confronted Monotype.

So Morison said farewell to publishing. He said it on 26 July 1946, in company with Beatrice. She wrote home after the party to launch the Penguin 'Shaw Million', the first sign that publishing was returning to normal.

I must tell you how my high-flying week ended up with the Lane dinner-party, which was simply marvellous. I got away from the Works, along with the 25 art teachers to whom I'd had to make a speech, & arrived in London in time to join William Maxwell and

Ella at Brown's Hotel. I just had time to repair my complexion when the car arrived with Morison and Wendy Hiller (who created the screen role of Eliza in the Pygmalion film: you remember her in 'Love on the Dole'.) We drove out along the Gt West Rd. to the Lanes' charming house out near Harmondsworth, where another car had just arrived with John Wilson and Dame Sybil Thorndike and Feliks Topolski and his very beautiful wife who is an actresss. Allen Lane and his batchelor brother Richard and his pretty wife met us and we had sherry on a smooth lawn that sloped down to a little weir, and a Siamese cat came and conversed with us. The dinner was superb – Scotch salmon and chicken and a compote of raspberries which Richard L. had canned himself, and home-grown peaches: iced Hock, and no end of Champagne. A.L. proposed the toast of Bernard Shaw – who, by the way, had that afternoon startled everyone by turning up unexpectedly at the opening of the National Book League Shaw Exhibition looking full of beans. You'll see a photograph of him with Maxwell in today's *Times*. He popped in after the speeches, made the round of the party and on his departure addressed the goggling multitude: 'Well, now you've seen the animal.'

We were presented with sets, in specially inscribed cases, of the ten volumes of the new Penguin 'Shaw Million', and each of us autographed each person's Pygmalion fly-leaf, so my copy will be quite a nice Association item, as everyone present had something to do with the edition or with Shaw. I hadn't realized it, but the notion of bringing out a million copies of his works at a price which would enable the poorest clerk to secure them was Morison's: Lane realized that it would be an infinitely more gratifying tribute to Shaw than any gorgeous limited edition, so he put the whole thing in hand as lately as last Feb., since when William has been straining every nerve (and turning down all other orders) to complete that colossal job. Shaw has now given Lane the copyright of the plays, and the Major Barbara volume is a Shaw First because it's the new film version with a lot of new material written specially for the film.

S.M. made a brilliant little speech toasting the Shaw Million as the most significant event in publishing in our time; and then there was more Champagne, and then William suggested that one of the ladies should say a word & A.L. called on me; I proposed the health of 'a corporate entity known to us all, and important to us for the same reason that the gospel of Democracy is important to us: because it takes its strength from the assumption that the Many matter more than the Few,' and with not many more words than that I gave them

'Penguin Books', and everybody said it was a very felicitous speech. We had a lovely time: everyone was in good fettle. Morison at a dinner-party is almost a revelation to me, for we are such old friends, and have so many serious things to talk about in the way of business when we meet, that I don't think of him at all as a person setting the table in a roar, capping epigrams etc.

When we were finally motored back it was so late that I stayed over with Peggy, and this morning I met S.M. & the Maxwell's and saw the Shaw Exhibition, then lunched with S.M. at Dorset House and walked in Regent's Park and Murton joined us for tea. Now I am having a nice quiet evening at home.*

He said farewell to printing. It was not at all final (he resumed his connection with Cambridge when he gave up the *T.L.S.*), but he had now reached a point when he felt he had no more need to take on more than interested him. The breviary that he had begun before the war at Cambridge for Burns & Oates was now finished, although the printing had had to be shared out among a number of firms. A disaster befell one of the many blocks, and Morison wrote to apologize to Stone, who had laboured on them throughout the war.

You are quite right about that block of the Alpha and Omega. The caricature of your design arises from my having forbidden Cambridge to part with the wood. Hence the 'thing' that you see is a bad print from an indifferent electro, made by some misbegotten knave.

On the whole, however, taking the four volumes in red and black, upon India paper of varying quality, substance and thickness; printed in wartime by, as it became necessary, 12 or 13 hacks in the trade, the edition is not too contemptible. I assure you that the second edition, printed respectably by one house, on the sort of India paper we may hope to have in peace-time, will do the printers, the publishers, you and the Holy Ghost no discredit.

When I think of six years agony, difficulty and battle; the deaths of bishops; changes in the hierarchy of Burns and Oates, and my own troubles, I think pretty well of the achievement. It was a vast satisfaction to me that you were prevailed upon, rather late in the day, to provide new frontispieces. The book that you have done so much for is not the work of one author, it is the culmination of the effort of a committee, not of poor figures like Cranmer, Latimer or

Ridley (I assure you they were not at all the characters that are presented in the English mythology taught to scholars in non Catholic Schools like Eton) but it is a presentation of the poetry of worship distilled by 70 centuries of God-fearing, resolute, intelligent and sensitive souls.

It is the greatest work, after the Bible, that mere man can set his hand to, either in the way of doctrine, or printing. I hope that you will read some of it, and I am certain that, in the course of time, you will not regard your trouble as having been wasted.

Last autumn I had a long talk with the Bishop of Nanking: Monsignor Yu Pin. He is a first rate theologian and liturgist, a member of the Nanking Legislature and, as you know, learned his theology and later lectured on the subject in the Nanking Seminary in the Latin language. I shall send him a copy of 'your' Breviary. I don't doubt also, that other bishops in Chile, Basutoland, Gozo and God knows where will take delight in the frontispieces and decorations that you, at great inconvenience at the time, cut for their edification and pleasure.

I hope that sometime early in the New Year the Archbishop of Westminster, who says Mass daily according to the rite brought into England by St. Augustine 1400 years ago, and used by St. Bede, St. Aidan, St. Eleutherius and everybody else down to 1547, will preside, or at any rate be invited by the publishers to preside over a little repast one evening to celebrate the accomplishment of this historic enterprise, to which you have made so notable a contribution. You have, in fact, made the edition. When I think of those other cuts I had secured, and your own willingness literally to have a 'cut' at a new set, and the publishers' desire to raise the highest standards, I am really delighted that, notwithstanding the deficiencies due to the multiplicity of hands at work, and the inequality of the paper, the present result is so good.*

With the return of peace, if not of plenty, it became easier for Morison to work with Stone. In 1949 he commissioned a new device for the Bill Page of *The Times*. As always, this was a matter for attention to the most minute detail.

I approve the block for *The Times*, past, present and future. The clock, the oak leaves and the olive leaves are all excellent; so is the scythe. The only point of criticism is the lettering. I do not know how you are going to get out of it, but, according to my eye, you have too much space between H and E in THE. As time goes on, I get more and

425

more interested in the spacing of the letters than in the letters themselves. Try it on your own eye and see whether you think THE is well spaced. You have also rather overdone the serifs on the cross-bar of the T. These perpendicular serifs on a capital T look very well when lower-case letters follow but they do not quite harmonise when, as in this case, there are caps. There would be no particular point in bothering about all this if it were not part of our scheme to use the block every day, and I can tell you that, whatever we do, our readers are very harsh judges.*

By 1951, the shortage of newsprint was presenting acute problems of space, and every inch that could be saved was valuable. This was an emergency which overrode other demands on Monotype, and they produced the smallest version yet cut of *The Times* New Roman, for the front page, the Stock Exchange prices and other parts of the paper where hitherto the $5\frac{1}{4}$-point size had been used. The new size was $4\frac{3}{4}$ point, and it was justly named 'Claritas': Morison called it 'a triumph of typefounding'. At the same time, Morison finally had his way with the heading, thus reversing the minor defeat of 1932.

23 April 51

Dear Stone: A new device is required for the title of the Paper. It must save the space indicated on the attached. Hence there must be a new design. Can you do it for us pretty quickly? While you are at it you had better do the lettering as well; so as to get an evenness of colour.

As to the device, you can lengthen the bodies of the supporters, if you choose. You will have trouble with them. One thing: don't copy the old centre arms with the lilies of France. Make them as they now are. If you want to send a sketch first you are at liberty.

'Your print looks well,' wrote Morison when the block arrived. 'I am very pleased with the engraving.' On 18 June 1951, the new Claritas and Stone's heading were introduced simultaneously, and from that date until the news was put on the front page in May 1966, the lettering in *The Times* was entirely inspired or originated by Morison.

On 16 March 1948, a month before he left for Chicago, Morison received the Gold Medal of the Bibliographical Society. His mind went back to those early visits to the British Museum, before he was old enough to enter the Reading Room, to A. W. Pollard who had first introduced him to the work of Bruce Rogers and Updike, and had proposed him for membership of the Society in 1921. This occasion, too, was a partial farewell. Morison's interest in letter-forms was turning away from printing-types (with the notable exception of those acquired by Bishop Fell) to consider Greek and Latin inscriptions, Byzantine coins, medieval and pre-medieval manuscripts. His life had hitherto been mainly occupied with the forms of letters of the last 500 years: there was not much time left to explore the preceding 2000.

From *The Craft of Printing* in 1921, in his early plans for the Sandars Lectures of 1932, Morison had been pondering the task of a co-ordinated history of the subject, dealing with the interrelation of one form with another, the reaction of engraved on drawn letters and vice versa. For as long or longer, two other ideas had filled his mind; the nature of power and the nature of religious faith. He had been brought to consider both seriously; the first by the ever-increasing fascination he felt for the titanic, daemonic figure of Lord Northcliffe, the second by the writing of *English Prayer Books* and the dialogue with Dean Dwelly that had accompanied it. Gradually, the paths of scholarship, which had till now gone uphill and through separate ravines, began to broaden out, to join; the gradient disappeared, and a long and wide prospect took its place, in which all these themes merged. Power, letters, faith: a pattern began to build up in Morison's mind, and working it out filled the last twenty years of his life.

As parts of this large theme took, or began to take, coherent shape in Morison's mind, he would publish them, or at least set them up in type. *Latin Script since the Renaissance* was finished in 1938, although the composite work *Die Schrift und ihre Werkzeuge* for which it was intended never came out, due to the war. 'Humanistic Script and the first Roman type' was published in the *Library* in 1944, and '*Black-Letter*' *Text* had been circulated in 1942; and, since the war, 'The Adoption of Latin Uncial: a suggestion', published in *Miscellany composed for H. W. Meikle* (Edinburgh, 1946), had taken the story further back. The standardization of the Carolingian minuscule, and the theological position as 'Son of David' adopted first by Pepin and then by Charlemagne in relation to the papacy, seemed to Morison to occupy a cardinal point in the threefold pattern. Just after the war, too, an event took place which led Morison to reconsider radically the part of Alcuin at this point. He wrote to Steinberg:

Enclosed I send you on loan photographs I recently got out of Monsieur Philippe Lauer of Maurdramnus, his Bible. To my mind this is an even finer piece of writing than anything that Alcuin caused to be produced, and I simply do not understand how it comes about that no worthy appreciation of this script has been offered to the memory of this great abbot. No doubt Alcuin was a far better organiser, but I am inclined to think that he did not possess the artistry of Maurdramnus.*

The pursuit of the Maurdramnus script, its relation to the scripts used at the abbey of Corbie before Maurdramnus became abbot in 768 and to those developed after his removal by Alcuin at the Palace School from 781 and later at Tours, came to have a dominating part in Morison's quest. The great bible of Maurdramnus, split in two parts, one at Amiens and the other at Paris, was (he became convinced) 'the greatest achievement of Pepin's reign';* its script was one of the most noble and powerful expressions ever given to the Roman alphabet.

Lowe shared this passion. He was now in Paris working to complete his own great work, *Codices Latinae Antiquiores*, an – the – illustrated catalogue of all pieces of writing in Latin before 800. It was a work as long preparing as Morison's – the first volume came out in 1932, the last (like Morison's) is yet to come. This common interest now drew them closer. They were both getting older, and already some of their still older friends had gone; there was no time to lose.

People are getting older and the mortality among paleographers is depressing. Don't overwork your eyes. I try to act on this advice myself . . . and resolve to study only a fine large and handsome script like the Maurdramnus – but there is nothing *like* the Maurdramnus script. I want – how I want – to see every leaf of that Bible and choose out the most perfect of each character; then I should like to write a piece of purely aesthetic criticism and demonstration of my conviction that here we have the finest piece of Latin script ever contrived.*

Too soon Morison's time in Chicago came to an end. He left behind an article on the Newberry *calligraphica* for the *Library Bulletin*, and on 24 June set sail on the *Queen Mary*. His mind began to turn back to the tasks waiting for him, and in particular to the *History of The Times*. Sea voyages bored Morison to distraction (later he preferred to fly the Atlantic), but on this occasion, looking down the passenger list, he saw that there was a chance that his time might not be wasted. There was the name of Lord Beaverbrook. As with Bridges, twenty-five years before, Morison decided on a frontal assault.

27 June 1948

My Lord

If you aren't too occupied in telephoning, writing, dictating &c &c would you consider answering a question regarding the circumstances of your early proprietorial connexion with the Daily Express?

I need certain of these details for the chapter on the London daily newspaper press that forms part of IV (& final) volume of the *History of 'The Times'* – & I should prefer, with your assistance, to be accurate.

I am, My Lord, Yours
Stanley Morison

They met next day at twelve o'clock on the sun deck. Each was delighted with the other. Morison discovered that Beaverbrook knew a lot, not merely about the London newspaper world before the First World War, but also about his great hero Lord Northcliffe – like Morison, he was fascinated with that flawed genius. Beaverbrook, on his own side, found Morison equally stimulating. His pungent conversation, his black clothes ('Bring the bishop another chop,' Beaverbrook told the waiter as they lunched together), his own appearance, always commanding and now, since his hair had gone white, immensely distinguished, his knowledge of Calvin and John Knox, the twin roots of Beaverbrook's obsession with Presbyterianism – all this made an indelible impression. Their friendship slowly grew.

Back in London, Morison found a number of things demanding his attention. Buckle had been succeeded by E. Silcock as general manager of Monotype, but the situation was still unpromising. In the autumn, van Krimpen and Mardersteig decided to make a concerted assault. Mardersteig had survived the war, although his beloved Verona had been badly damaged in the German retreat, despite his personal appeal to the German commander. Both were anxious that typography should not be neglected in the reconstruction of their war-torn countries. Morison promised them his support, but was not optimistic.

One thing I can say is, that Silcock himself has now a personal interest in the production of fine founts. He has been about the world a little during the past six months, and has been so placed that he could not fail to notice the great importance to the past, as well as to the present, of the sort of things you and I are interested in.*

Morison was disposed to look back and remember past achievements. When van Krimpen sent him the Enschedé Christmas book, he touched an unexpected chord: 'I once was very keen on du Bellay, Ronsard and people of that period, and have lately been reading Marot. Your keepsake, therefore, arrived when I was just in the mood.'* Van Krimpen was, however, determined to get something done now. Silcock was now apt to take Morison with him on his journeys abroad to pacify Monotype's European customers. After a visit to Amsterdam, Morison wrote:

I do not look forward with great pleasure to discussing Emergo, for the simple reason that I do not see how the Corporation can tackle it. I find myself turning down designs every week, some of them meritorious. What cannot be turned down, however, are pressing requests from the University Presses for new Bible faces. You already know of one! Another has now been put forward . . . very difficult to resist, though I have done my best. This seems to mean that the Corporation can possibly resist a talented artist, but not an historic Press.*

To Mardersteig, he explained the whole situation.

The old Corporation is not in the position it was when you and I, as young men, managed to make it do what we wanted. The war was bad enough, but the political consequences flowing from it have had a worse effect. Thus, the rise of nationalism, beginning in Ireland in 1916, has been followed by all sorts of small countries, and some large ones, who have abandoned the Latin character in favour of exotic alphabets.

India, having dispensed with British rule, has given up English courses in the universities; the departmental (formerly governmental) printing offices have gone back from roman and italic to the native languages. In consequence the Corporation is faced with demands for Tamil, Telugu, Devanagari and whatnot. Also from Pakistan and Egypt there are demands for Arabic. Finally, from France and Germany come demands for Didots and other bread-and-butter material. Mercifully, not yet for Fraktur.

As you can imagine, a matrix cutting programme of this kind is of no interest to me, and I have very radically abbreviated my attendance at the office. I can recall nothing done by the Corporation during or since the war that has afforded me any pleasure or satisfaction. Indeed, in many ways I am out of touch with the Corporation. So many people have died or retired: Mr. Burch, Mr. Westover, that the face of the Institution has changed.

Much of this I have explained to van Krimpen. He, too, has found his patience greatly tried by promises being made and then not fulfilled. I do not myself believe that it is possible for the Corporation, or any other type founding or machine composing Company in England, to cut a new design of roman or italic. I wish with all my heart that the opposite was true. Contrasting the past with the present, it looks as if the time when you and I first met in Montagnola was a golden age.

The only consolation I can report is that the present heads of the Corporation have convinced me that they are truly appreciative of the virtues of the matrix policy of the past, and that they truly desire to follow it up in the present. I know they have applied for permission to extend the matrix department by erecting a new building to supplement the existing facilities. The official answer was, that if the Corporation desired to increase their canteen facilities they would receive the licence. Fresh attempts are being made to get this decision reversed. There are reasons for believing that this new attempt might be successful. But even so it must be sometime before we begin to reap the fruits of any such success – and in consequence I am afraid that the only thing we can do is to muster up our patience.*

Better times were to come, but there was little comfort in the situation then.

The Times, too, abounded with problems. Long before Barrington-Ward died, 'the management problem' had been troubling both Morison and him, as well as the Chief Proprietor and Board. There was no obvious successor for C. S. Kent, who had succeeded Lints Smith. In October 1944, Barrington-Ward had dined with Sir Harold Hartley, a distinguished scientist and director of The Times (he was also a railwayman, but, in Morison's view, on the wrong railway – the L.M.S., for whom he pioneered the 'Coronation Scot'). They discussed a letter from Geoffrey Faber the publisher, listing possible candidates, which Morison had annotated. In May 1947, Hartley suggested that Gavin Astor should succeed Kent.* Barrington-Ward was against this: his role should be that of deputy and successor to his father, though he might be assistant manager for a bit.* The meeting was inconclusive. Lord Astor discussed the matter with Sir John Anderson, hoping that in the general post in the armed and civil services, some sufficiently able person might be free. Other candidates were recommended by Sir Ronald Weeks, Sir William Haley and Lord Burnham. Over a dozen were interviewed; none seemed right. It began to look as though they would have to look outside the industry. Morison dissented; the risks of alienating the staff were great, and the problems of re-equipping The Times and meeting all the other problems that would vex the trade in the post-war era would need experience, not just administrative ability. Campbell Stuart wanted Morison to become assistant manager, and train a new successor, but who would then finish the History?

Morison had his own view of the situation. He had long had his eye on Francis Mathew, then managing director of St Clement's Press. He had first come across him towards the end of the war. Mathew had had a varied career, selling machinery round the world and then, in the war, involved in secret printing. This had made him (like Lewis) both ingenious and self-reliant. Morison had liked him, and when in 1946 he had direct dealings with him in tidying up the *Pharmaceutical Journal* he had been impressed. When he got back from America, he found the problem still unsettled, and a few days after he got back he went to dine with Mathew, with satisfactory results. He introduced Mathew to Astor, who was very impressed, took him out to dinner with Campbell Stuart, and saw to it that he met everyone who mattered. The reaction was universally favourable. The problem had been solved, and in June 1949 Kent retired and Mathew took over. Thus began a long and happy association which only ended with Mathew's sudden and early death, a catastrophe from which Morison never recovered.

With Mathew settled in, there only remained the problem of finding a new editor. He wrote a long note for Astor on the climate in which they were now looking, and the qualities they must find. There were, he wrote, three principles involved.

For these principles of independence, impersonality and anonymity *The Times* has in the past sacrificed commercial advantages and the proprietors social privileges. As long as these principles of conduct are maintained *The Times* will attract to its service men of ability, breeding, education and character, who perceive in the paper an organ essential to the welfare of the nation, and wish to be associated with it. The health of *The Times* is dependent upon its power to attract this type of man. . . .

The paper cannot rest upon its prestige. If it does not press forward it must lapse backward. By accepting the present day implications of its historic role of leadership *The Times* commits itself to a forward policy. By so doing it must design the means as well as will the end. The means, put simply, are the old means: the attraction of men able to write vigorously. The task remains today of recruiting and training the type of man required if the organisation and staffing of the office

433

is to be adequate to the production of *The Times* in a fashion worthy of its past, unique in newspaper history, and equipped to perform a similar service in a future that cannot but offer the whole free world a challenge it has never before faced.*

Morison had strong views himself on the sort of man who would measure up to this challenge. He wrote to Wickham Steed, discussing the possible candidates; he had no regrets for his own rejection of the job.

Obviously there would then have been, just as there would now, be a lot of sectarian opposition to the nomination, but unless I made a spectacular fool of myself and a laughing stock of the paper it would soon die down (except in Cliveden, where the antagonism is intense). The real objection undoubtedly was, and still more is, my age. Casey was about six years older than I when he took on the job, and has tolerated abuses that a younger man would have dealt with promptly and effectively. There will be much to clear up after this editorship. It is a paradox that we should both have to tell him that he must remain as long as he possibly can. Only so shall we gain the time to consider the situation properly.

I am not in favour of the name (G[eoffrey]. C[rowther].) you mention, good journalist that he is. I don't think he is the right sort, or has the right experience, or the right convictions. Moreover he wants to be a national figure, a city man, a broadcaster. He is a nice egoist, but an egoist. I have known him reasonably well for years.

It is the convictions of the candidate that seem to me to matter most at this stage of the world's history, or at least the present phase in Western Europe. I hold the opinion (I don't say conviction) that if you cannot have both in the same man, you had better choose the right convictions rather than newspaper experience. In other words, it might be well to look outside journalism altogether.

There is something in your wife's P[eter]. F[leming]. idea, and I once put it squarely to J.J.A. I was much in favour of it, as I have also told Casey. P.F. is a part-time contributor; he was in Dawson's time an Assistant Editor under B.W.; he knows the Far East, which I think to be important. He knows the office and has its goodwill; indeed he has all the gifts; but, according to J.J.A. and others, he is disinclined to settle down to a regular job involving the entailed drudgery and grind, day and night. Casey went to stay with him not many weeks ago, and threw a fly over him, with no result. If a bit of a war came near, P.F. would be after it within hours.

434

I am inclined to think that if P.F. won't take it, and I don't think he will, you should now consider the problem in terms of a person with the right convictions, a practical mind, one who knows the world, has the art of getting on with journalists, though not one himself. Or do you think it imperative to have a man with newspaper, as distinct from writing, experience? What did Haley know of broadcasting when he went to the B.B.C.? J.J.A. asked me what I thought of Haley as a candidate, and whether I thought he would come. I answered that I thought he would come if the Television were taken out of the hands of the B.B.C. He was probably at P.H.S. in your time and you have subsequent knowledge to draw upon. I like him greatly, but I think it would be difficult to make an Editor out of him. If we had not succeeded over Francis Mathew (who is getting on very well) I would have been delighted to have Haley as Manager. It seems to me that the place does need a sort of Editorial Manager.*

The hunt continued. Meanwhile, Morison worked away at the *History*. He now had assistants: Miss P. M. Handover at *The Times*, and M. R. D. Foot, a young historian who specialized in the twentieth century. He got in touch with Lord Beaverbrook again.

September 15, 1949

Dear Lord Beaverbrook,

I am the 'clergyman' with whom you discussed very various and amusing matters on the deck of the Queen Mary last year. On that, for me, pleasant occasion, you told me that you had in your possession a number of letters from Lord Northcliffe and that, if I asked you for the sight of them when I got to the appropriate point in writing the HISTORY OF THE TIMES, you would lend me them.

I am now busy with the period 1912–22, and have written an unconscionable number of words. Your name crops up several times but, as yet, vaguely.

Do you now feel like letting me have a look at those letters? I need not say that if, in addition, you have any memoranda which would enable me to have a clearer idea than I possess at present of the Northcliffe–Lloyd George squabble, I should welcome them. In those days you seem to have had a lot of private information about our goings-on in Printing House Square.

Yours,
Stanley Morison

'I too enjoyed your company on the journey across the Atlantic,' replied Beaverbrook. 'I think of you everytime I meditate on the *Times*. . . . I send you particulars of letters etc which may be of use to you in the writing of the History of the *Times*. A biography of Northcliffe would be more interesting.'* Soon they were deep in the details of Northcliffe's life, Beaverbrook's part in the dropping of the anti-Kitchener campaign, the events at Evian on 26 August 1922. Morison re-read *Politicians and the Press*. Did Northcliffe really want to join the Cabinet 'at the end of 1918' after his previous snubs to Lloyd George?

From the historian's point of view you are a tantalizing writer. What the historian wants is dates! d a t e s !! DATES!!! D A T E S !!!!... I would be very grateful if, when you are shaving on Sunday morning, or while in the kirk during the sermon, you would scratch about in the recesses of your memory and dig up the dates and particulars of any conversation you may have had with Northcliffe, at this precise time.*

Beaverbrook's replies, on the other hand, had all the authenticity of experience.

I think you put the best construction you can on Wickham Steed's activities. Northcliffe was engaged at that time in an anti-Lloyd George propaganda expedition, and when the boss is on the warpath, the editors certainly do not smoke pipes of peace.*

As Morison proceeded with his narrative, Beaverbrook seemed to be reliving his past, and each new instalment produced a detailed letter of comment and (generally) praise.

In January 1951, Morison's mother died at the age of eighty-nine. He had found the visits to Eastbourne something of a trial, but his devotion for all she had done for him never slackened. His friends wrote to condole with him, and among them Beaverbrook. 'I am terribly sorry to hear about your mother,' he wrote. 'This is the first word I have had and I do send you my deep sympathy. It is an occasion when the parting, even though anticipated for long, is painful indeed.'*

He then moved on to another subject. On the boat Morison had rashly told Beaverbrook that the Lloyd George papers were for sale and that he hoped to be able to buy them for *The Times*. Beaverbrook, who had his own archival plans, had anticipated him, and Morison was now anxious to make use of the papers. He had sent Beaverbrook the galleys. 'I am fascinated by your story,' Beaverbrook wrote, acknowledging them. 'It is of course familiar ground to me, but it is stated with such vigour and such nervous energy that I read it with deeper interest than you can imagine.' He went on now:

I will get Blackburn to speak to you about the Lloyd George papers.

If there is anything more you wish from the Lloyd George papers, or if you want to have a look at Bonar Law on Northcliffe, or if you care to delve further into my file, you are welcome indeed to any information we can supply.*

Over the next month, he sent Morison a flood of detailed comment and explanation. Morison was delighted and thanked Beaverbrook in his own hand, each N for Northcliffe sprouting a Napoleonic crown as he wrote.

31 May 1951

Dear Beaverbrook

Good & fast work. I rejoice that you find nothing to quarrel with in those chapters; and that some passages are not, altogether, bad reading.

You enjoin me to publish 'soon'. The date aimed at is April 15 next year. Speedy help like yours is encouraging. I get nothing from 'the' family. And, after twenty years on this task with manifold interruptions I lust to touch the binding of the finished, fourth, and final volume of the History of this newspaper. As you say, nothing like the N story has ever appeared. After doing dreary Delane I am lucky to have N fall into my hands. You will see my summary of him. I hope to improve upon it in the revise. I now send you Chapters XVII–XX, which four chapters cover a mere eighteen months; but catastrophic months. If you care to glance at the galleys you will see recurrent references to Cherkley, surely at the time (& since?) as notable a focus of practical political talk (intrigues as outsiders call it) as English life has seen since Lady Palmerston's parties!

Yours,

Stanley Morison

On 13 July Morison formally asked permission to quote from the Lloyd George papers. He thanked Beaverbrook for sending him the new edition of *Politicians and the Press*, and sent him in return *English Prayer Books*, 'an effusion of my own that has closer connexions with Presbyterians and Papists than the other two P's'. On 20 July, he wrote 'at 4.25 p.m., having passed for press sheets up to p. 400 – in fact a third of this walloping great book', to thank Beaverbrook for all he had done. He was quite unprepared for the letter from Blackburn, sent to him on the same day, objecting to the use made of the Lloyd George papers, in view of the forthcoming biography of him. Morison was thunderstruck.

24 July 1951

Dear Beaverbrook

   I simply CANNOT believe that you mean what Blackburn writes. . . .

Assuming that Beaverbrook had failed to brief Blackburn, he begged him to be reasonable. Peripheral material he would give up,

But you really must let me have the letters that refer to Northcliffe and *The Times*. You saw all these last year too. What was the point of my asking you for, or your giving me, the photograph of the entry in your visitors' book for August 26, 1922, if you were going to 'ban' the letters, your own included, bringing Lloyd George, Birkenhead and Churchill together? Come now: let us be reasonable. I will not ask for everything. Cut out your own letters. Cut out every one that that does not refer to Northcliffe, and *The Times*.

But Beaverbrook was adamant. It pleased his sense of mischief to see Morison groaning over the pages that had to be reprinted because of his refusal. Morison wrote to Barnes, who had invited him to holiday with them in France.

What an age it is since I had your letter about Beauvais! I was too fascinated with that prospect to be able to reject it, & too overloaded with work to accept it; so I hope for some interposition of Providence to make the second possible. But the Deus ex machina has not intervened; rather the Diabolus. His name – Beaverbrook. He has caused me 36 pp of cancels, after he had seen the proof & the troubles are not over. I cannot come, alas! I cannot.*

However, Barnes's letter gave Morison an idea which might enable him to get his own back. Why should not Barnes, now at the B.B.C., arrange for Beaverbrook to review the last volume of the *History* on television. Writing to him to congratulate Beaverbrook on surviving the reading of 'so many words and paragraphs', he told him the book should be about by the beginning of April.

This is how things now stand: the lawyers, with eminent counsel, having read the book twice (thus earning their fees for once) have caused me to reprint certain pages, thereby again delaying publication. They have now signed a memorandum saying that all reasonable precautions against libel having been taken (thereby protecting this House and me against the charge of negligence) there still remain pages which, on the grounds of 'taste' cannot be said, they think, to correspond with the past and present pretensions of Printing House Square! I have no doubt that John Walter will give me the green light, but I must wait for him to switch it on. The proprietors of newspapers dislike being ignored, don't they?*

The broadcast was finally fixed for 14 May, a fortnight after the book had come out, to great acclaim. For once, Morison, still anonymous, had more than his fair share of praise (the reviewers tended to forget the other hands who had helped over the last twenty years). The praise was mixed with surprise (and, in the house, some sense of injury) at the critical confidence with which *The Times*'s recent history was despatched – Morison had grown impatient. Just before the broadcast Beaverbrook had another mischievous idea, to take Morison up to Highgate Cemetery and begin it at the tomb of his political master.

9 May 1952.

My dear Beaverbrook,

I AM MOST ALARMED.

About the Karl Marx idea.

Brilliant for you, but death for me.

The Times people tell me that it would do them and me a lot of damage. As you know they don't like personal publicity of any kind. And this is a very bad kind.

I think they are right.

Anyhow, though George Barnes did not know what *The Times* people felt, he told me the same thing late last night.

No words, however well chosen, will prevent a large proportion of viewers connecting me with Marxism; thereby doing me, and *The Times* irrevocable harm, – quoth Barnes.

Fortunately, your camerman took pictures of me getting into and out of a car. These ought to serve the purpose.

I expect to see the 'rushes' this afternoon, and will confer with Blackburn who understands that the selected pictures are to be cleared with me before processing.

I know you will accept this and not get me fired from Printing House Square; upon which I forthwith would die of a broken heart – only to be buried at Highgate Cemetery in company with Karl Marx, Herbert Spencer and other philosophers.

If only it were another occasion I could be filmed meditating on the grave of this great sociologist, and you could have great fun with Woolworth's competitors!

Yours,
Stanley Morison

And we meet, praise God, on Monday.

But again, Beaverbrook was not to be dissuaded, and Morison, invited to watch the performance with John Walter, clearly felt some kind of forewarning desirable.

13 May 1952.

My dear John Walter
I am delighted to be your guest on the night of Ld B's television appearance. You will have to keep a very straight face in the preliminary part of the script – where I, who have never been photographed except for a passport, am made to visit the grave of Karl Marx to oblige his Lordship. I am terrified that the general public will run away with the idea the PHS is under the domination of Marxists, Calvinists and Jesuits. Whatever would J.W.III think!
S.M.

As he sat, watching himself on the screen peering at Herbert Spencer's grave, he listened to Beaverbrook's rasping Canadian accent.

The responsible writer is Mr Stanley Morison. He is 63 years of age. He is an authority on Karl Marx, on John Calvin, and he thinks he knows something about John Knox, but he does not. I asked him to show me the grave of Karl Marx, in Highgate Cemetery. I took the precaution, of course, of having a cameraman there. And here is the picture. But he is not a hero worshipper of Marx or Calvin or Knox. He was converted to the Roman Catholic faith at the age of 22. From Atheism not Presbyterianism. He likes to be called a Papist. He dresses like a Jesuit; always in black and wears a black clerical hat half a size too small for his head. You would like Morison. His laugh is infectious. Ringing out loudly at his neighbour's jokes, and also his own. He does not make the mistake of pouring old wine into new bottles. If the wine is old and really good, he has another use for it. Morison's fame will grow.

The minute it was over he dashed off a note to the protagonist (see Plate 14).

It was thirty years since *The Times* changed its type, and brought Morison fame for the first time. Then Walter had viewed Morison and his innovations with some suspicion. Now, firm friends after the trying days of the war, here they sat watching one of the most recent of *The Times*'s competitors paying tribute to the paper, through a new medium which was already radically changing the traditional role of the newspaper. How little could such a scene have been imagined in 1932! Least of all could he have supposed that he would help *The Times* to find its seventeenth editor.

Morison, as he had indicated pretty clearly to Wickham Steed, knew the man he wanted: William Haley, Director-General of the B.B.C. since 1944. He had known Haley since 1945. In April that year George Barnes, torn between returning to Cambridge and taking a new job at the B.B.C. after the war, had chosen the latter, and had found on arrival that Haley was as keen as he was that the B.B.C.'s publications should live up to the high standard set for broadcasting. They had all three dined together in December that year to discuss the problem. The matter was shelved for the time being, until the economic conditions were better. Morison, however, was impressed, and in November 1947 brought Astor and Haley together at dinner. In 1949 Barnes revived the B.B.C.'s problems with Morison, and wrote 'to seek your advice as to the possibility of acquiring a distinctive house style without lessening the appeal of each paper to its own public and the need for each supplementary publication to be designed for its own particular purpose'. Morison wrote him a long reply.

It is obvious that an institution with your broadcasting ideals should have an appropriate typographical style; and the appropriate typographical style should be one that reflected your broadcasting ideals. . . .

It was also my opinion that no standardization of style should be applied to the whole range of publications, – though possibly to those which fall into groups. You are quite right in saying that the Editor's personal views of layout are strongly held. This was always my experience, and I have no objection it. He would be a poor Editor who had no views about layout. Nevertheless, it does not follow that all editors should always have what they want, or think they want.

Hence, if the B.B.C. were to decide that it could not permanently shelve the question of style, it would have, at the same time, to consider the appointment of an official whose business it should be to draft certain orders relating to layout, and to see that these were respected to a reasonable degree. He would also consult with the editors on any changes that might seem desirable.*

Whether or not such a man might be found on the Corporation's staff, he left it to Barnes to consider. These recommendations were put into practice, and Morison saw Haley in action again. The more he thought about it, the more he liked the idea of Haley at *The Times*, either as Editor or in the role he had suggested to Steed.

At Easter next year, Casey and Morison went on holiday to France. They had a happy time, eating and drinking well, for a fortnight. They visited Beauvais on Good Friday.

I was there long enough merely to sing four verses of the Stabat Mater; but the wonder of the place, in full use, made me tingle, so thrilling was the sublime unity of purpose & procedure amid that marvellous mingling of line, colour & shadow as we sang, choir & people, *Fac ut ardeat cor meum in amando Christum Deum ut sibi complaceam*, according to the custom of the Universal Church.*

They talked over the office problems, and, when they got back, dined with Mathew and talked more. Next day Morison saw Laurence Irving, an artist and friend of Astor's, who had become a director of *The Times* just after the war. Morison had known him since Heinemann days, and was delighted when Irving joined the paper: 'Ah,' he said, 'the Flight from Capital'. Gradually, Morison's ideas began to carry conviction. There was a lull in the winter: Morison himself was seriously ill with pleurisy after his mother's funeral. With the spring came the siren voice of Lowe from Princeton:

It was a joy to get your letter this morning. I didn't just read it: I swallowed it, I was that hungry for news of you. If I had the wings of a bird that could cross the Atlantic I'd be with you to-morrow, for I have faith in the curative effect of affection and admiration. But you are well on the mend, I am sure, to judge by the fine, bold, clean-cut Morisonian strokes. Script is a mighty trustworthy register of physical condition, like gait or sound of one's voice. I feel cheered by yours. But you've had a devil of a time, et ça explique tout, and my one regret is that I wasn't in London to help & perhaps cheer you once in a while. Reports of your sunless spring have reached me and your resistance to banishment to Madeira was as concise as it was characteristic of you. I have a brilliant suggestion: pack your grip (& pairs of pyjamas ditto underwear socks & 3 shirts – nylon if possible since they are easily washed –) hail a taxi, say 'Northolt air-port', leap into the next plane for N.Y., cable hour of arrival at La Guardia field, I'll be there to meet you with a bouquet of lilacs, dogwood & a photo or two of Maurdramnus. The next day sunshine will embrace you & warm you, & before May turns into June you'll be yourself & ready for Vol. IV, and Casey and hoc genus omne. What do you say?*

Morison replied:

Would that I could take the plane, as you suggest, and leave everything here to some stalwart. Alas, he does not exist. I need a Bischoff, yea, and more than a Bischoff.

My situation is that I have finished *The History of The Times*, but I have not finished it *off*. This is the most boring of all the stages of the work, and must last for some weeks – 12 at the most, I hope.

443

In addition, a solution to our Editorial troubles which, it had been hoped, was found at last, has now broken down; and I am wanted at headquarters until some other solution has been tried.*

By now Lord Brand had put the question to Haley, without immediate success, and in January 1952 Morison himself took a hand and went to see him at the B.B.C. Haley was impressed ('To be visited by a prophet is a moving and disturbing experience,' he wrote, thanking Morison for his visit). But he did not accept at once. The problems of commercial television were presenting a crisis in the organization of the B.B.C., and he did not want to leave before the debate in Parliament on the B.B.C. Charter. He begged for, and read, the last volume of the *History of The Times*. The Chief Proprietors waited anxiously. But in the end all went well, and on 6 June, just after the new Editor's name was announced, Barnes wrote to Morison:

This is great news. It had to be released because of the barrage of enquiry & speculation, but I think it is a pity not to have waited until after the Charter debate on the 11th.

I had two long talks with Haley before he accepted. I am sure he is right. Your visit to B.H. had its effect.

A week later Morison, with the Editorship settled, revised his note to Astor of 1949 about the future of *The Times*: 'if it does not press forward it must lapse backward'. He pointed out again that 'no systematic investigation into the efficiency of the organisation had been made for more than a quarter of a century. Its [*The Times*'s] adequacy in the contemporary world depends upon this being taken in hand.' But the time was not judged ripe, and when (too late) it was, he reminded Mathew, 'I then had in mind the appointment of a Proprietorial–Managerial–Editorial committee to get to work before H[aley] arrived.' He had sensed the dangers in retaining the pact of mutual non-interference between Editor and Manager, which Dawson had demanded on his return after Northcliffe's death. Morison felt that in the new conditions after the war difficulties might ensue, without some controlled method of communication between the two. For

444

the time being, however, he awaited Haley's arrival (or rather return – his first job had been at *The Times*) on 1 October with every hope that a new spirit would be breathed into *The Times*.

More honours came to Morison. Honorary degrees at Cambridge and Birmingham, a Fellowship of the Royal College of Art and of the British Academy. He had at long last seen the publication of A. F. Johnson's catalogue of sixteenth-century Italian writing-books, announced by the Pegasus Press in 1927 and now published by Simon in *Signature* in 1950. He wrote to Johnson:

> I do not forget that our collaboration has extended over a period that goes back to the first number of *The Fleuron*, – something like 25 years ago. During this long time I don't suppose I have ever thanked you properly for all the kindness you have shown me, not to mention the generosity with which you have shared your knowledge and discoveries.

Pre-war pleasures returned. He went to the theatre with Beatrice, while convalescing at Brighton. On his sixtieth birthday, his friends gathered to give him a dinner, on 6 May 1949 at Brown's Hotel. Each guest had a menu cunningly got up to look like a board from one of John Bell's bindings, and an eight-page pamphlet printed at Cambridge, with a frivolous account of Morison's life compiled by S. C. Roberts in his best style, under the title *Prolegomena ad curriculum vitae*. Morison had become an institution.

After the war, he moved rather more frequently than before; the gradual re-acquisition of books made larger and larger flats a necessity. In October 1946 he had moved from Dorset House (passing on the flat to Casey) to 7 Cleveland Square. There he remained for three years, but when he got the opportunity to move back to Regent's Park he was glad to take it. He stayed at Freeling House in Cumberland Terrace from just before Christmas 1949 until September 1953, when, now that Mrs Rowe was getting old, he moved to a modern flat with service, 130 Marsham Court, in Tufton Street, Westminster.

King George VI died and Queen Elizabeth II succeeded. Morison's views on the monarchy did not change. He sent the first stamps of the new reign to van Krimpen, with the message 'The temptation to hear your comments is greater than the disgust we feel over the new Elizabethan stamp.'* Van Krimpen answered: 'In one word: trash. In two words: a pity.' Morison agreed: 'I believe that they may be better when enlarged but this is not saying very much.' In 1935 Morison had criticized the Silver Jubilee stamps and was offered a knighthood in the next honours. On 12 May 1953 he found himself writing 'Properly sensible as I am of the high honour which the Prime Minister thinks of recommending for me on the occasion of the Coronation Honours I regret to say that personal reasons make it impracticable for me to accept'; and at the head of the letter he carefully wrote, 'obediently I quote your reference KT'.

Since 1948, he had kept his connection with Chicago warm. After his visit, he had written Pargellis a long letter, and sent the *History of The Times* to the Newberry as a thank-offering, ending

It is hoped that the Newberry Library will accept these with the compliments of The Times and that you will give accommodation to the concluding two volumes. Volume 3 has already been set aside for you and will reach the Library by some secure but time consuming means of transport. The set, as a whole, will be a poor compliment in recognition of all the friendship lavished on this stranger as he was to begin with.

I say no more but that I expect you to consider me in the future as some sort of candidate for a second term as visiting fellow in 1002. Believe me, I was much more than content with the decor and have nothing but grateful memories of the wallpaper, the rugs, the bathroom, the tea and the self-igniting gas stove. May I soon test it again.*

In 1949, Pargellis had come over, to find a letter in that striking hand waiting for him: 'My dear Pargellis, Exspectans exspectavi!' it began. When Pargellis returned, Morison went with him and spent another happy six weeks in Chicago in June and July. Returning, he saw at Pargellis's request an American graduate student, James Wells, studying the literary aspects of the Arts and Crafts Movement. Morison liked him and reported to Pargellis that he should take him on, which he did, and Wells became Curator of the Wing Foundation.

Morison was delighted. He now kept up a double correspondence. He told Wells all the news: the move, the new gigantic folio *Printing The Times* which he had produced in record time, partly to meet the criticism that the technicalities he knew so well had been omitted from the *History*, and partly for *The Times*'s contribution to the British Industries Fair (the Korean War had revived memories of what nuclear war now meant, and *The Times* must come out, even if London was in ruins).

This year a curious contraption, amounting to a miniature Printing House Square on wheels, will be exhibited. About two years ago there was a panic in Fleet Street which resulted in an enormous amount of money being spent on this aforesaid contraption, so as to permit the paper, in the event of what is here always politely called 'an emergency', to be produced in any hole or corner of the surviving country. Hence, it was decided to have a book to commemorate all the mechanical inventions pioneered in Printing House Square, many of which are now part of the routine of newspaper production on both sides of the Atlantic and elsewhere.*

He had been down to Edward Johnston's house at Ditchling to help with the publishing of Johnston's *reliquiae*, as he had helped with money while he was alive.

Years ago I had a talk with Johnston about a new book on handwriting that he had in mind. It was a volume to be made up of the Lectures that he gave at the Royal College of Arts, illustrated with the drawings and diagrams relevant thereto. I told him that Cambridge would be interested in the publication, and as he thoroughly disliked the existing edition of *Writing, Illuminating and Lettering* put out by Isaac Pitman (who had bought the rights from the Estate of John Hogg, the old publisher) Johnston was quite willing to consider Cambridge as the place to print and publish the new book. I had not much hope that he would ever finish the book in his lifetime. Nor did he. . . .

I was summoned to go to Ditchling, where I have not been since the Master's death. A very fatiguing interview it was. Not for the first time have I thought that there was something morbid about the

447

cult of calligraphy as practised in Johnstonian circles, although not in Johnston himself. . . . I understood that any additional drawings that were required would have to be done by a first-class person, and that they would consider themselves very lucky if they could persuade Mrs Wellington to do them. It would be a fatiguing undertaking for Mrs Wellington, but she will probably regard it, as I regard my expedition, as all in a good cause. I looked at the typescript, at such intervals as I could procure, and at once saw that it was a book worth suffering for.*

Among these memories of the past, Morison was settling down to the prospect of old age. He was prepared to meet the changes that would come, provided that he was left with the time and the means to finish the work he had in mind. He told Pargellis:

You are too young to appreciate exactly the significance of attaining Sixty Five, and the attendant necessity to architect a New Way of Life; very new in this new epoch in which two wars have made saving, in the Victorian manner, utterly impossible. Yet somehow I've managed to save, but only a mere matter of £10,000. But I have sisters to support, my mother having left the small Family hoard to Our Dumb Friends League. I am helped a little by my maternal grand-father's will which was a strictly family will – only the family was so large that the shares are small. I am not the least anxious about all these things; but I want to clear it up, all of it, and find the level at which I can pursue my chosen studies.*

18

Removed to Westminster ('Just the kind of situation I, as a born North Londoner, dislike. I fear it will be very stuffy down there'), Morison found himself, for once, disposed to look back. It was the autumn of 1954. Oliver Simon had revived old memories in a series of autobiographical articles in *Signature*, which he had brought to an end the previous year. A little incident suddenly brought the early days of the *Fleuron* welling back to Morison.

130 Marsham Court

My Dear Simon,

I thought of you particularly (of course I often do, generally) yesterday, when rummaging over a large collection of printing specimens got together by one Hyett, a traveller for Waterlow's. It surprised me to find that they had anybody but what's his name Vivian (or Victor?) Goodman capable of reading and writing. Anyhow it's quite a mass of stuff of the 20's and 30's, 'early' Simon catalogues for the Bibliographical Society when A.J.A.S[ymons]. had succeeded in persuading A. W. Pollard of his respectability. Such things brought up all sorts of Great Russell Street memories. G. W. Jones recollections and early Monotype ideas. You have set down much amusing-cum-useful details of this curious period, vanished for ever. Has anybody the idea of going any further with it? You? Now that you have put the razor to the throat of *Signature*; and, as I'm told, put your feet to the mantelpiece can't you dictate something about Percy Smith? I ought to do a piece about Graham Pollard I suppose. But A.J.A.S. really should be done; and who but you, a tolerant philosopher, could essay the task with justice & mercy. You would be an admirable biographer of that unadmirable man. Where is Marrot nowadays? Forgive my rambling on in this way. Blame Hyett, the travelling salesman for Waterlow. Don't think of doing anything. Too much is being done. And I'm one of the worst offenders.

At present I work like a dynamo at the 'Fell' book promised to John Johnson 28 years ago. I've done a lot, a vast lot of stuff, all couched in a kind of Warburg Institute sort of style; unreadable I shd say. After this I tackle nothing more, and will take the advice I give you now, if only because my sight is in a bad way and I am feeling terribly senior. Also my housekeeper (confessing to being 79) has fallen down and broken her hip, thus complicating things at the above address. I broke my own right arm at Christmas, sprained my right leg at Easter and have no reserve of health to boast of. In other words am in an unusually passive condition, possibly becoming even tolerant. Time will tell. I go about very little but did step out to visit R. Stone at Something Cheney where he lives happily next a church wholly ruined by the Protestants but certainly planted in a very pleasing paysage. The sun actually came out and we quite enjoyed ourselves. Laurence Whistler came in, a mild mannered man, and good talk was had – Mrs. R.S. is interested in food so that all went well. What I always notice on these occasions is that folk who live in the country have much more news of what goes on in town than I ever hear, Tate Gallery news included.

I had news of you also. R.S. told me he thought you weren't aggressively well to which I replied that Simon's health had always been a topic of conversation ever since I first met O.S. he had always given himself the airs of being immensely my senior and how he would make me his literary executor next week & so forth. And the joke had lasted. But, I said, I didn't want the joke carried too far and it finally turned out that rickety as S.M. is O.S. is more so. Of course we can't always go on as we did, guffawing over George W. Jones & the other heroes and plagues we come across in the Hyett collection. But there's something to be done yet I suppose. I never have any ideas of my own. You were the active man in spite of your age & bad health in the 20's and you had the Fleuron idea.

I owe you a great debt, (the greatest after F. Meynell who first took me up at Burns & Oates & again at the Pelican). You immeasureably helped me with that Lund and Humphries connection & in many other ways, which I never forget. You took all the responsibility for St. Stephen's House when the Cloister broke up (or down) and gave me a fine example of capacity, sense & stability. It was a very fortunate day for me when you desired my presence in your office. And on hundreds of occasions since our ways necessarily parted you & your wife have manifested the utmost generosity to me. Though I swear not to do anything more & urge you to take a similar vow I sh not fail to succumb to the temptation of 'doing' something in collaboration with O.S. But let it not be. We shall never get it out. There seems to be a permanent jam in the trade: shortage of . . . or at the final end, the 'readers'. No doubt Herbert S.

does some miracle, but if I 'do' anything it will have Greek in it, that being the latest fad; and that won't do in London E 12. Cambridge seems fairly stuck with the work I put in hand weeks ago. So we will do little more than keep going. I go to the oculist tomorrow for the Nth time.

Meanwhile my writing (shades of Arrighi; what would J. Wardrop say of my present style?) is out of alignment and fast growing illegible; not at all like Will Rothenstein's which was, and is, and will be the most elegant & the most speedy of all personal autographs. But the script, such as it is, may suffice to be the medium of the assurance to you that I although I'm not exactly demonstrative I have it in me to be grateful for all your example and counsel have meant to me over the long span of thirty and more years. If, therefore, you should occasionally feel that weariness of the body that comes, and the fatigue of the spirit that accompanies it, I hope you will, in the course of the illness & convalescence, take a measure of invigoration from the thoughts, expressed in one form or another, of those who, like myself, have benefited from your unselfishness and large heartedness. And don't, to be sure, think of acknowledging receipt of this screed, but believe me to be, as ever,

Yours
Stanley Morison

But at the beginning of 1956 Simon died. Morison, paying tribute to him at the Double Crown Club which he had founded, repeated his gratitude, and added, 'If it is sad that we shall not, in this life, see him again, we need not make a sad occasion of this evening's proceedings, as he himself would be quick to agree.' E. P. Goldschmidt, too, had died, early in 1954. He had been ill for some time (Morison used to visit him at Brighton), but it left an irreparable gap in his life. He gave the address at Goldschmidt's funeral, reflecting how rare was the combination of knowledge of old books with a lively understanding of their texts. More and more often, Morison was reminded that there was not much time left, and a great deal still to do. As he had written to Pargellis:

I shall be 65 next May; and you know what a significant anniversary that is. And I can't make up my mind what to do about it. I know what I want to do. I want to drop out of Printing House Square so far, at least, as to permit me greater freedom of movement. Can I get myself pensioned off at such a figure as will enable me to reserve my remaining energy for myself, and any writing I, myself, choose?? And be, at last, my own master??? And come & go whither & when I choose???? These are questions I ought to get decided this autumn. I would keep the Mono connexion but lessen all the rest. The reasons for settling with The T—s now are that Astor is older than I, John Walter is 80, new people are coming on, people who know not Joseph & if my past efforts are to be 'recognized' it can only be done by those who were there at the time, & saw for themselves. Otherwise I shall find myself treated on an actuarial basis . . . & this will neither be just, nor satisfactory. I think I must settle this matter this summer, as soon as the holidays are over I should like to start these tedious, & sure to be delayed, arguments.*

He now turned his attention to this neglected but vital question of how he was going to support his old age. He wrote to Silcock at Monotype:

The Corporation can speak for itself about the increase of business which has resulted from the following up of my typographical programme begun in 1922. Remember in this connection, that these were not ideas I worked out on the instructions of the Corporation: they were ideas worked out by the Corporation on my instructions. For thirty years this work has gone on, not without difficulties created by departmental opposition, of which I propose to say nothing. Throughout the whole of this time I have subordinated my personality to the Corporation, and refused such titles as 'Artistic Director' etc. which would have gained for me the kind of notoriety I do not desire.*

He had made it a principle in the past not to ask for more money, and he asked Monotype to be generous now, which they were. His salary of £1350 was continued after his official retirement, and he retained his office and secretary there.

His life at *The Times* was very different now. When the *History* was finished, Morison wrote a note to Mathew summarizing what he had done and what he had received for it, ending:

A man who has been treated by the Proprietors in the manner I have described, cannot but feel content to leave the figure, the medium and time of payment in their hands. I say the same of any arrangement about salary that they may propose.

Equally, as to the future, I leave myself in their and your hands. I know I have written myself out of a job, and it was pleasant to be assured last week by the Chairman that I have not necessarily sacked myself from the staff. I hope that you, as Manager, agree.

I need to add that having three times this week forgotten to wind up my watch, I also know that I am seriously in need of a good rest before I can face any fresh job in the office. When, however, I have had this rest, I hope I may be permitted in future to serve in some practical capacity the institution upon whose past and present I have spent upwards of twenty years.*

The Times too maintained his salary (£3000) unchanged, nor was he due to retire formally until he was seventy. But, money apart, Morison was extremely dissatisfied. For more than ten years now he had been the Editor's close friend and confidant (nothing had changed in this respect when Casey succeeded Barrington-Ward). He was liked and trusted by the Proprietors, equally old friends. Recently, the coming of Mathew had added a new dimension to Morison's sphere of influence at Printing House Square. Haley, like Mathew, owed his coming to Morison, but he saw no reason to continue the connection on which Morison's authority rested. As it was unwritten, resting merely on a habit of consultation and a degree of confidence, it might have merely lapsed: but Haley, acknowledging its existence and considering it an administrative anomaly, brought it sharply and deliberately to an end. Morison felt lonely and isolated, although Mathew and his other friends kept him posted of what went on. Haley, on the other hand, was generous in his praise of Morison's work in what he regarded as his proper field. On St George's Day in 1953, the year after he became Editor, the final version of the title, engraved by Stone, was introduced, and Haley wrote:

23 April 1953

My dear Morison
On this auspicious date and day I would like to send you a note of unreserved congratulations. 'The Times' is in front of me as I write.

453

It looks most handsome. The new title, to my mind, conveys all you said it would. It sits well on the page, has force and dignity, and proclaims the paper to be no mean, inconsiderable, or stereotyped organ.

Apart from all this, however, there is the crucial fact that in the outward appearance it presents to the world of this and the coming generation The Times is now all yours. One of the things which most struck me when we had our long talk the other day was your saying that the title was the only remaining thing in the paper that was derivative. Now the odd man out has gone. Something really worthy has taken its place.

'The end crowns the work' is a proud saying, not to be lightly bandied about. But in this case it is true. And how typical of you, of P.H.S., and of our strange British true sense of values – which seems an inversion to the rest of the world – that the crown, so long delayed, should be the masthead.

Today you should feel great satisfaction and thereby, I hope, happiness. Few men can look on so complete an achievement. And Monday's book [*Printing The Times*] will be its herald.

Yours sincerely
W. J. Haley

But this handsome tribute was cold comfort to Morison. He was used to a more intimate relationship with the Editor, whose loss no compliment about his professional skill could assuage. He was, moreover, disappointed in the changes in the editorial policy of the paper. There was no broad statement of the policy, and the ideas behind it, which should stand for the West against the East. Instead, Morison saw a new trend, typified for him in the literary articles Haley wrote under the name of Oliver Edwards, towards Culture, for which (as an idea) he had only contempt and distrust. He recognized that it was a difference of principles, without personal animosity, but he had hoped for something different. For Morison, to be at a distance from the centre of activity was an irritation past bearing, the more so since he felt that it was his own judgement that was at fault.

Morison retreated to other work. He wrote a critique of the layout of *Life* for his old friend Daniel Longwell, now a power on the magazine. For the Newberry, he wrote *Byzantine Elements in Humanistic Script* (1952); for Cambridge, *A Tally of Types* (1953), in which he celebrated the fruitful link he had built up between the Press and Monotype; and, after long neglect, he bent his mind seriously to the task of analysing and describing the typographic achievement of Bishop Fell. Lord Beaverbrook stimulated him to tackle Calvin and the Geneva Bible, in a Special Supplement on the Bible for *The Times*, for which Morison arranged a special cover. His interest in Thomas More was reawakened by the acquisition, from Dr Ernst Weil, the learned bookseller, of a little miniature on vellum of More. From Samuel Gurney, Morison bought the last few copies of the fine Medici Society colour reproduction of one of the Holbein drawings of More at Windsor. He wrote to Mary Alexander in Chicago.

I hope one day to be able to proceed with my piece on the portraiture of Thomas More. I have been through & photographed (had photographed I shd say, as I have [not] done the pictures with my own camera) the typical specimens in London & Paris, & will sometime get to Basel, which may finish it . . . then I have to write up the pictures.*

'You evidently have a soft spot for Babylon-on-Lake-Michigan,' wrote Lowe.* In milder Princeton, wintering at Key West, he could not understand Morison's passion for Chicago, with its strenuous climate. It was a lure that drew him back every year, the more so now that he had become involved with the *Encyclopaedia Britannica*. In April 1947, Morison had entertained Robert Maynard Hutchins, Chancellor of Chicago University and trustee of the *Encyclopaedia Britannica*, and heard about William Benton, its publisher. The connection grew: he met Benton, who put him up in New York in 1949 at the University Club. It was Morison who then suggested that he might repay this gift with work.

An annual visit to New York is necessary for my mental and intellectual health. It would be an exaggeration to say that any small thing that I have accomplished has been due to my having brought off

successfully the great venture of twenty-five years ago but I soberly
believe that if I had not come then, and regularly since, to this country
I should never have developed the critical capacity, initiative and
energy which have stood me in good stead during the past twenty-
five years. I have not a few ideas of possible use to EB Inc. They are
radical ideas arising out of the present critical position in which the
English-speaking democracies, for which the EB is a standard and a
necessity, find themselves. . . .

The Anglo–American democracies need an Encyclopaedia superior
in point of reliability, exposition, completeness, illustration and typography to anything the Nazis, Fascists or Communists have ever put
out.*

In 1955, Benton sent Morison a complete set of the *Encyclopaedia Britannica*, to which he responded promising a memorandum setting out his ideas. At the same time, he was writing
a similar piece for *The Times*. He wrote to Barnes.

I have been in such a rush since I saw you that I have not had an
opportunity, being preoccupied on a Memo of great bulk on the
question of a Sunday edition of *The Times*, to write about myself or
even to thank you for your inspiring card, for which I was most
grateful.

The Hutchins–Morison discussion was inconclusive. While he is all
for my ideas, whatever they are in detail, to be imposed on the E.B.,
he asked me to write a memorandum.

My answer was that I could not say until the middle of September
whether I could or could not get the time in which to concentrate
upon the memorandum. I have not even now, the 23rd of the month,
been able to give my mind to the possibility of preparing a sensible
document on the reorganizing of the text of the E.B. so as to integrate
(blessed word) its present massive treatment of facts, figures and other
details with a descriptive and genealogical account of the cultural,
ideological and political events that have decided the present day
pattern in which we live and move and have our being.

'A Possible New Sunday Newspaper' was one of Morison's
most detailed and penetrating analyses of the post-war Press. It
was provoked by the feeling, current among the new men at
The Times, that P.H.S., so often asked to print the *Observer*, could
do as well on its own. His conclusion was unmistakable. Massing

arguments, from St Matthew, VI 24, to a breakdown of the photographic features in the *Sunday Times* and the *Observer*, he ended:

The decision whether P.H.S. can serve two masters, the old governing class which it understands, and the new lower middle class which it does not, is the paramount question.

The moral is that the authority of *The Times* can be maintained only by the arts that created it.*

Beaverbrook continued to amuse, delight and infuriate Morison. In 1952, in the spring and again in the summer, Morison stayed at his villa on Cap d'Ail. There he would have a room in a summer-house, apart from the main house and near the sea, where he could retire and write or think, if the company became too much for him. Morison enjoyed the mixture, politicians like Churchill and Bracken, tycoons, Onassis and Sir Patrick Hennessy, and a supporting cast of journalists, relations and society women; all these new faces and the Mediterranean sun warmed him. Sometimes, when he saw Churchill somnolent after dinner, Beaverbrook would tease Morison until, aroused, he would hit the table with his fist. 'God damn you, Morison,' said Churchill, jerked awake, 'don't do that again.' Or Bracken and Beaverbrook would conspire to mock all that Morison respected. But it was all stimulating.

5 September 1952

Dear M.B.,

Impossible to say how much I benefited, and still benefit, from that exhilarating week of sun, sea and rest on your glorious green and blue lawns, not to mention the company . . . besides your untaciturn self. . . .

I am sending you as promised the good folio edition of Calvin's Institutes got out by him in French in 1560. This followed on a Latin edition of 1559. I don't possess this or you should have it. But this French edition is a fine monument. . . .

Yours,

S.M.

457

'My dear Stanley,' Beaverbrook replied on 9 September, thanking him.

I shall not turn it on to the Province of New Brunswick at present. Perhaps later on the Library there will get it. And if so, the presentation will be made in your name, for it is a good thing to associate you as far as possible with the memory of that great, illustrious, pious John Calvin.

Calvin's splendour shines out through the years. And were it not for Knox, then the vision would be much brighter and the fame far greater.

Calvin led them on to many things. They both wanted a full biography of Knox, for example: 'Have you ever reflected that, but for Calvin and Knox, the *Daily Express* would be printed in black letter throughout?'* Reform and roman type came to Britain hand in hand: this suggested a new idea, a journal of Reformation Studies.

I would like to see your money used to the maximum advantage. We ought to know why, in terms of ideas, we are where we are in this Year of Grace 1954, and the Reformation remains one of the major sources of our ruling ideas. Many of them derive from Calvin, and he must, by every right, be accorded a principal position in the periodical.

I don't suppose we should disagree about this; but there may be occasions of disagreement, if the arrangement is not sufficiently clear in advance. If I took on work of this kind I should take it for granted that the contributors to the periodical were responsible to the editor, i.e. me.

But I should like to know to whose authority I should bow the knee. I could not be responsible to a Board consisting of Masters of Colleges or Deans of Faculties, assembled by Brendan Bracken or anybody else.

This is no attack on Brendan or any of his friends. If the Board were all nominated by me I should still feel such an arrangement impossible. You are an individualist – so am I.*

In 1952, after the gaieties of the summer, Morison was looking forward without relish to the winter. A life-time spent in ignoring minor ailments now left him more than normally prone to them. But on 4 November, the magician waved his wand: WILL YOU SPEND THE NEW YEAR WITH ME STOP THE CHURCH IS JUST AROUND THE CORNER. BEAVERBROOK. They had talked before of a visit to the house that he had at Nassau in the Bahamas: 'You must tell me where they are from London, Edom, Moab or Philistia?' Now Morison was delighted to accept, and on 29 November he set off for warmth, sea air, and a life of unfamiliar hedonism: 'This house is far from being a Trappist monastery,' he wrote to E. A. Lowe. He returned to it several times, sometimes distrustful, sometimes bored, but generally enjoying its unfamiliar, and sometimes simple, pleasures.

> *8 Feb.* A day fishing on the yacht. I caught 3 – the first time in my life to hold a rod. B sneezed.
> *9 Feb.* B kept his bed.
> *10 Feb.* B down & none the worse. More fishing; I caught 2.*

On this occasion, after Nassau he went to visit Lowe at Miami, from Miami to Chapel Hill in North Carolina where Professor B. L. Ullman entertained him, while demolishing some of Morison's arguments in his 1943 paper on Humanistic Script. From Chapel Hill, he went on to Chicago for a fortnight, and did not return to London till the middle of February, taking in another week at Nassau en route. His friendship with Beaverbrook prospered. He confided to him his problems with the proposed Sunday edition, his gradually increasing interest in Colonel House (with Northcliffe, the hero of the story of Anglo-American diplomacy between 1917 and 1922), and the new involvement with the *Encyclopaedia Britannica*.

It is more than curious that there should be an article on Predestination, running to a column and a quarter, and no article on Progress; also, the article on 'Reformation' is written by one of the most notorious anti-Catholics. The *Encyclopaedia* is evidently still run by the Presbyterians. They can go on running it, perhaps, if I really 'have my way' and establish a brand-new *Super-Encyclopaedia* of fifty volumes dealing only with Ideas and Doctrines, and their pedigree and history. . . . But can I get the first ten million dollars out of the Ford Foundation?*

In 1958, Morison was bound for Chicago to address 'The Supreme Soviet' of the *Encyclopaedia Britannica*, but had to cry off, because he was ill. In the autumn of 1960, however, he prepared another memorandum in the style he had developed for this form of document – with its short precise sentences, paragraphs numbered, sections carefully headed, it gave a formidable appearance of regimented power. Gradually, the West–East argument mounted, until in the concluding paragraph the editorial board were rhetorically confronted with 'the responsibility for THE GREATEST PRINTED INTELLECTUAL INSTRUMENT WHICH THE WEST HAS AT ITS DISPOSAL'.

At Chicago, uninhibited by any practical responsibilities, Morison could give his passion for ideas full scope. But he did not neglect the practical side of life. Although Morison officially gave up his advisory posts at Monotype in 1954 and then, at the end of 1959, at Cambridge (in both he was succeeded by John Dreyfus), he retained his interest. In 1956, van Krimpen's post-war irritations with Monotype, and his feeling that they were blindly neglecting the superior talent of the hand-punchcutter, came to a head in a sharp note in which (or so at least van Krimpen felt) he attacked by implication Morison's policy at Monotype for the last thirty years. Morison himself was not sure.

It may be that this is the real point at which you and I divide. When I, for better or worse, became interested in what is now called typography, the prevailing doctrine was firmly set, not by the typographers (for the simple reason that there were none) but by the calligraphers (of whom there were many), and these calligraphers were learned as well as expert. They dominated the situation in this country and, to a considerable extent in Germany, upon which country Britain depended for a good deal of its 'display' material. It was a world dominated by Johnston, Graily Hewitt, Percy Smith on the one hand, and St. John Hornby and the private presses on the other.

It is possible that where you and I differ, is in the relative assessment we give to the crafts of calligraphy and engraving. I have been at great pains to maintain the engraving craft in the service of typography; to graft from the old tree of the hand-engraver upon the young sapling of the machine punch-cutter. This, you will say, is the wrong way to graft. If the hand punch-cutters had been numerous enough to organize themselves so as to take command of the machine I doubt very much whether you or I would have much to debate; the difficulty would have been solved, and engravers would have used the machine in accordance with their own traditional capacity. As it was, the machine fell into the hands of engineers who knew nothing about letter design fifty years ago – and know nothing to this day.

The various expedients resorted to by me to get a punch-cutter from Frankfurt and so forth were unavailing.

My next effort was to seize upon Gill's Perpetua as a sculptured script. How far successful it is in type is not for us to say. At least it corresponded with my intentions. The Times type is an attempt to draw upon Bristol board an engraved-looking letter. It was, however, never engraved, – as in the case of Perpetua. Hence, The Times type only particularly realizes my intentions.

There are many things in your memorandum worth pondering; but I think you need not have brought such heavy guns to bear upon mock antique. I see nothing of the mock antique in our Bembo, or in Mardersteig's.

There are other points, however, on which I think you rather overstate our differences. I do not really believe that you mean that Monotype and foundry type are two essentially different things. I do not believe these differences are essential. I believe they are different but I question whether the difference is so great. However, this is merely a matter of verbal expression.

I am certainly all for your appreciation of the 'designer' and his 'intentions' – when he knows himself what he 'wants'. You appreciate quite rightly the importance of a 'designer' who understands his job. I am not sure, though, that this is the same thing as a designer who understands what the job is. I am all for the doctrine that 'the soul, so to say, of any design lies in the subtleties'. Certainly neither I nor anybody else attached to this Institution, wishes, or ever has wished, to eliminate hand punch-cutting. That elimination has been achieved by the typefounders.

In saying what you do say in behalf of the hand-cut punches, you have to wrestle with the problem created by the fact that the hand-cutting of punches is a defunct art. You may have one, and Peignot may have one, but these men are, in point of actual fact, without apprentices. I would lament this quite as fully as you do. I would agree that the 'best hand-cut punches are superior to any machine-cut ones.'

I hold, however, that, in the last thirty years or so, due to the calligraphical doctrine I mentioned earlier, typography has been made to bear the weight of all sorts of calligraphical experiments, many of which went far to break down the true (as I hold them to be) standards of type-cutting. Thus came in a flood of pseudo-calligraphic designs. These are fully as open to the philosophical objections that you bring against Poliphilo. . . .

Do you, or do you not stand with me in recognizing the fact that roman type from the end of the fifteenth century down to the twentieth century, was a casting from a mould made for the purpose of embodying a matrix struck from a hand-engraved punch? Secondly, do you stand with me in believing that four hundred years of such engraving creates in the image printed from these castings a second nature which is so strong as to be unchangeable? Thirdly, do you stand with me in believing that the imitation of the work of the hand-engraver by the hand-calligrapher is open to the same objection that you bring to Pierpont's pathetic self-satisfaction with his imitation of Poliphilo – with all warts? If you and I agree upon these three points, then we can agree upon everything.

I dictate this clean off the belly, on a fine, sunny morning. Pay no more attention to it than it deserves.*

Van Krimpen agreed, on the whole, although unable to acquit Bembo of archaistic features. His point was simple:

This was that there is a machine the action of which I have to accept since I am not able to improve it; that, in my opinion, what is being put on that machine can be greatly improved when both the real nature of the machine – which, being a machine, should be respected as such – and the historically grown Monotype unit system and casting methods are also accepted. And it has been my endeavour to give directions for achieving this. My purpose, therefore, was perfectly and solely practical. Only in order to make clear that I think this machine, and in fact no other machine, should be applied to producing things that are not of the machine I had to talk of copies and adaptations and of mock antique. Work done by hand and mechanical products are two fundamentally different things. We should never forget that and we should let them remain different: the one makes things; for the other designs have to be made.*

He continued to complain about the changes at Monotype, but his last letter, 2 July 1958, reverted to the peaceful topic of Gregory of Tours, and a prospect that tempted Morison.

During the second half of May I have been to the Benedictine Priory of Toumliline in the Middle Atlas Morocco. It might do you good to go there as it did me. The Monks will certainly give you as they did me, the episcopal suite of three rooms, one of which is a private bath room, & the genuine curfew – sometime between eight and ten the electric current is, after a warning sign, cut for the night – will not hinder you since as far as I know, you are not exactly a friend of late hours. . . . At Verona I have seen our friend Giovanni. He seems to be quite well – I hope you are too.

Yours

J.v.K.

In October 1958 he died, leaving Morison bereft of the man who had, next to Mardersteig, understood and shared his ideas and his passion to improve the form of printed letters. Only one other aspect of typography tempted him to write again, the intrusion of the 'artist' into typography. In 1961 the International Center for the Typographic Arts sent him a manifesto written by W. J. H. B. Sandberg. Morison read it, and found himself in sharp dissent.

I do not agree that typography is important because 'characters and pieces of newspaper enliven the early works of braque and picasso'. I do not agree that mallarme (*sic*) is any guide to 'new typography'; nor, indeed, do I concede that a 'new typography is necessary or desirable. A new alphabet devised by a competent scientist may be to the point, but this has yet to be proved. Tinkering with the alphabet by typographical playboys has the justification that it is enjoyed by fellow playboys. The Center may wish to condescend to this form of typographical diversion. A number of men (philologists) have designed new (i.e. phonetic) alphabets for the English language, and had these been successful what artists call a new style might have developed. We have not reached this point.

Mr. Sandberg dignifies his name with a capital, but reduces the name of his city by giving it a lower case 'a' (for Amsterdam). This may be justified in a coterie but not when applied to a message designed for 20,000 people. Is this the way to bring a 'quick message to the many'?

The constant fidgetting and constant striving after effect is natural to the species of mankind known as 'artists'. The world would be poorer without their fidgetting and striving. Certainly 'artists' are people, and are as entitled as any other people, to be dissatisfied with the status quo. This does not mean that the status quo ante has no meaning and need have no consequence. Precisely because history records the fidgetting and striving, and also the discipline and relaxing of men engaged in sculpture &c. the present generation of typographers would be well advised to attend to the reasons why and how the people of the past created capital letters, minuscule letters, small caps. and italic upper and lower-case. All these alphabetical forms have their historic pedigrees. Insofar as the Center's artists and philosophers ignore this fact, I am in opposition. My vote is in favour of artists being given proper instruction and due encouragement to obey . . . where obedience is appropriate.

And it is appropriate when and where the instructor has possessed himself of that wisdom, which may be learnt from experience; i.e. the experience, not of one man or one generation of sculptors, scribes, painters, engravers and printers, but of many generations of such. This accumulation of experience is the fruit of the intelligent study of history, of tradition and of continuity.

The application of this knowledge to the present typographical task is a highly responsible act. And the more so when we see, as we now do, new continents springing into literacy. The service of many millions of people is not to be confused with the entertainment of a few score. The task of designing the letter-forms and display conventions appropriate to what you call 'the typographic community of the world' is not a task to be handed over to egoists who obey only a personal impulse to innovate.*

The application of reason to lettering and typography could still draw him. He helped Reynolds Stone draft a protest about the poor lettering of the new motorway road-signs, and sent the Mint a tart report on the decline in the quality of the engraved letters on coin.* As his eyes grew weaker, he found it harder to judge the fine distinctions in small sizes of type, and for his work on the Fell types he was thankful to fall back on the expert help of Harry Carter, now archivist at the Oxford University Press.

Together they went to Antwerp, in July 1953. Morison sent a postcard to Beatrice. 'Exciting Garamond, Granjon & Le Bé I identifications made & new specimens discovered. Have persuaded the people here to lend their punches & mats &c to Oxford.'

In November 1956 Morison produced the first draft of his introductory matter, by now vastly enlarged beyond the essay originally intended. Predictably enough, Morison had become fascinated with the character of John Fell, a man who combined Authority and Faith (if the wrong one) with a passion for letters, and what letters could do. As in 1943, Morison was straying on to theologically mine-strewn ground, and the Secretary to the Delegates, C. H. Roberts, felt bound to get professional advice. He invited Morison to dinner at his college, St John's, founded and endowed with a library by Fell's admired predecessor, Laud.

It was an unforgettable evening, with the sun so amiably warm and bright, casting the most beautiful long shadows on your wonderful lawns. It was an admirably generous dinner, with most pleasant companionship and conversation. I thoroughly enjoyed the pilgrimage through the library and, of course, the visit to the President.

I greatly relished our quite extensive talk. It was superb to finish with that walk you took me round the cloisters and quads. I thought your lighting a wonderfully modest but excellent illumination. Altogether, an evening I shall ever remember.

As to the Fell book; nothing would give me greater pleasure than to have it looked at by Greenslade. I have complete confidence in his judgement, and from what I have read of his writing, I incline to the opinion that his views and mine agree in many respects.

I have no objection to anything being cut out that does not properly belong to the understanding of what Fell's effort was, and what it signified.*

As Morison grew older, the mass of correspondence which he maintained (on the whole pretty punctually) became too much for him. On 14 January 1957, an old New York friend, R. G. Wasson, wrote to announce the impending publication of 'our

forth-coming book – the long-delayed book on ethno-myco-
logy'. Long before, he had asked Morison's advice about a suitable
printer for it, now grown to two large and profusely illustrated
quarto volumes. 'I am grateful to you for having suggested
Mardersteig to me originally – he is splendid.' Months passed,
and no reply came. Wasson turned to Pargellis for help. Pargellis
wrote, and pricked Morison's already tender conscience. On
1 April he began:

My Dear Pargellis
   I was vastly flattered to receive a long autograph from you – an
astounding achievement for an American. Homo americanus can
write his name in what 'they' call 'BLOCK' letters but never goes so
far as to write letters except on the typewriter. Imagine my blush
when I read that the cause was not having written to Gordon Wasson
about his mushroom book. Certainly the book is no mushroom itself
& I don't want him to think I have neglected him for any such
'reason'. I am, as you generously speculate, busy on a mushroom of
my own. When I began that accursed series of lectures they were
about the action & reaction of Greek on Latin Script & vice versa.
When I had done all this (six lectures) on orthodox art-history,
culture-history, lines I suddenly awoke to the fact that our lettering
reflected the struggle for power between Byzantium and Rome. So
I put that in. Then I perceived that this wasn't sufficient so I had to
inject the struggle between Church & State. As I knew nothing about
these high matters I had to look into them in order to prove that the
Carolingian Minuscule & all that was a calligraphical symbol of
Charlemagne's determination to put himself forward as the Western
Augustus, a title that the true Emperor at Constantinople had kept
for himself. A wholesale reconstruction of the lectures was involved
& isn't yet finished. Here is April 1 & the lectures begin May 12.
Lantern slides to be made & all that agony. Not being a lecturer, as
you are, I am very nervous of making a gigantic muck of it in front
of a prime audience of Oxonian critics.

   In fact, Morison was not as unfamiliar with his audience as he
made out. On 17 November 1955, in the Bodleian Library, he
had addressed the Oxford University Bibliophiles on 'Venice
and the Arabesque Ornament', thus returning to one of his first
loves. On this occasion, he dwelt more on the influence of the

trade relations of Venice and Constantinople on the design of printer's flowers than on the flowers themselves. As was his custom now, he had a few copies set up and printed at the Private Printing Office of a text considerably longer than the lecture as delivered. As he spoke, the sight of the front row of chairs, entirely filled with Bodleian staff, from the Librarian downwards, was too much for his sense of mischief. He had been, he said, to consult a manuscript in Duke Humphrey's library, 'so far as I was able to observe it in the dim medieval twilight which pervades that institution'. A visible *frisson* passed along the front row.

He was not seriously alarmed, therefore, to return to Oxford, this time at the Ashmolean, on 12 May 1957, to give the first of the Lyell Lectures, under the magnificent title 'Aspects of Authority and Freedom in relation to Graeco-Latin script, inscription and type, sixth century B.C. to twentieth century A.D.'. Nor was the audience limited to 'Oxford critics'; friends and admirers came from Cambridge and London, and further afield. They were not disappointed. Morison was in his most impressive form, his matter ample but expressed with brevity and force, his delivery resonant but brisk, a rapid flow (he had a gift for cramming more syllables into a single vocal sound than anyone else could) punctuated with pregnant silences. A dazzling sequence of slides passed before their eyes, illustrating Morison's conviction that the major alterations in the form of the alphabet that passed from the Phoenicians to the Greeks and then to the Romans had been canonized by the authority of political or ecclesiastical power.

To the plain monoline inscriptions of the Athenian democracy, Alexander added the serif from Persia, and Augustus variation in the width of the stroke, the stress of the letter. In the fusion of cultures in north Africa, uncial appeared; the mixture of this with the European cursives was preserved in Ireland, whence it returned to Europe, to be mixed with the old Roman capitals (revived by Gregory I in 604) and the local cursives, a mixture from which sprang the Carolingian minuscule, canonized by

467

successive Holy Roman Emperors. Byzantine influence, never far distant, became stronger in the fifteenth century and the elegant new script (itself a reversion to earlier models) of humanistic scholarship was promoted by the Roman Pope to challenge the elegant script, classic knowledge and dangerous theology of the Orthodox contingent at the Council of Florence. This humanistic letter won the battle for primacy when the invention of printing converted script into type; it was a compound of Roman capitals and Carolingian minuscule, and as such had a diagonal stress. The change from diagonal to vertical stress was authorized by Louis XIV's Academy of Sciences in the *romain du roi*, thus producing the 'modern' face. Finally, the forces that upset the autocracies of the eighteenth century chose 'classic' lettering for their banner, the 'Sans Serif' type which the new democracy adopted for its own, through its mouthpiece the popular press – and here Morison repeated his *coup-de-théâtre* of 1932 with a slide of that very day's *Evening Standard*.

At twenty past six on 29 May, the audience walked out into the summer evening, holding the last of the six 'extended texts' that Morison had printed, part at *The Times* and part at Cambridge, with the articulated history of letter-forms before them that Morison had first conceived forty years or more ago. It could be faulted in detail and even in depth. Morison himself never ceased to ponder and adjust what he had written, but as a vision it is unsurpassed, an inspiration to the future as vivid as the Printing Supplement of *The Times* was to Morison in 1912.

Meanwhile, the letter to Pargellis remained unfinished. Two months later he drew a line at the foot of his uneasy reflections on the future of England after Suez.

The above was begun on April 1. The wings of time have stretched since. Here is July 8. Meanwhile I have worked over the lectures, got together 120 slides, printed the papers, delivered them & after a month of indolence at the office, recovered from the effort. This epistle is the first evidence of better health than I have been in for many months. The Lectures appear to have been a success and I am sending four sets, temporary though they are, reeking with misprints,

& having no pictures. . . . There is little else to report. I have to read a paper to the Thomas More Society here in October on the portraiture of T.M. I have done a good amount of preliminary investigation of the alleged Holbein paintings &c and have wanted to make a thorough study of the engravings. Imagine my condition of mind to discover after much search here that the great collection amassed by some amateurs in London is now in Chicago – Loyola to be precise. Of course I ought to fly over at once . . . and why not? Really it's too late for this year. I must make an 'interim' of the paper to the T.M. Soc. and revise it next year when I have solid hopes of coming to Chicago for more than three or four days.

The lecture to the Thomas More Society was given on 18 October. In the end, Morison was scribbling up to the last minute.

I performed, in a frantic rush, my T. More piece before two judges and a host of Q.C.'s and other eminent legal luminaries (and I forgot, a Bishop). All went well and I remained pretty prostrate over the weekend. Having now, for the first time for years, nothing on my list of promises, anything that I must perform by an unalterable date . . . I feel a man of freedom. For weeks I have been struggling with a pain in the back and other ailments probably due to nervous strain.*

But just after this tolerably cheerful moment, Morison suffered a dreadful blow. His favourite sister Edith, who had retired from a senior post in the Bank of England in 1949 and was living at Brighton, was taken ill and died suddenly. As she lived alone, her death (in obviously painful circumstances) was not discovered for some days. Morison was deeply upset by it, coming at the end of a wretched year in which Casey, Dwelly, James Wardrop, William Maxwell, Miss Olive Abbott who had for long done research work in Paris for him, and Edmund Hopkinson had also died. He tried to exorcise the thought of Edith's end by writing an account of what had happened, but he was in a low state at the funeral and was taken ill again. It was not till 10 February next year that he finally finished his letter to Pargellis.

After this blow I fell victim to the current influenza pest. Apparently I caught it extra-badly, and, by catching a relapse, was kept in bed and in doors for six weeks – and at their termination crawled back to work with the greatest reluctance. Arrears of correspondence, unkept promises, unread proofs, were ignored and nothing was done for ten weeks. This being so, and the prospect showing little sign of improvement, I decided to rest in the sun at Nassau – and arrived here on Sunday Feb 2 in a state of exhaustion and in a climate of icy wind. After a week of alternate cold wind and warm sun, pouring rain and dark cloud I have picked up enough energy to put pen or pencil to paper.

The voyage out had been fairly peaceful. He read Dante for the first time for more than thirty years (prompted by Kantorowicz's *Frederick II*).* But as soon as he arrived, Mathew had rung him up in New York to announce a major coup for *The Times*, the purchase of Anthony Eden's memoirs. Morison soon found himself deep in negotiations with Houghton Mifflin, *Life* and other publishers. He found time to go to the Frick Collection to see the original Holbein of More, and to discuss with the curator the report (based on X-ray photographs taken while it was being cleaned) which proved beyond doubt that it was authentic. At Nassau he settled down to revise the script of his November lecture accordingly, in the intervals of trying to negotiate the co-serialization of Eden's memoirs in *The Times* and the *Daily Express*. This was Morison's revenge for his defeat over the Lloyd George papers. 'The competition between *TT* and the D.E. for the Eden memoirs was keen; and when I arrived the Old Gentleman refused to speak to me on the subject. It has taken me a week to pull him round & make peace.' The position was the more difficult because of 'my connexion, or association (which everybody exaggerates) with my host – who is vigorously hated, not least, in P.H.S.'.*

The Eden coup and the success of the 'Top People Take The Times' publicity campaign were some comfort to Morison and Mathew during an uneasy period at *The Times*. Before the war, the paper had been strong enough for the proprietors to undertake the task of re-equipping its mechanical plant and rebuilding the premises. The first of these tasks was virtually complete by

1939, but further progress was brought to a halt by the war. Post-war shortages, especially of paper, had a further depressing effect, and by 1956, when newsprint came off the ration, the circulation of *The Times* had fallen from 270,000 in 1947 to about 220,000. From a commercial point of view, however, the situation was more cheerful: each year since 1947 had shown an adequate profit. Further, an agreement with Townsend Hook, manufacturers of the paper used by *The Times* for some time past, was concluded by Mathew (the negotiations had begun before he arrived); it was strengthened by investment in the company, which, with the expected boom in paper, looked promising. But more important than this was the slight shift in the balance of power caused by the beginning of a five-year programme in 1954 by which the Chief Proprietors, both old men now, proposed to transfer their controlling shares in The Times Publishing Company to their elder sons.

Suez, and its aftermath (the threat to oil-supplies had a marked effect on *The Times*'s advertising revenue) was a check. This and, on the other hand, the possibility of resuming the rebuilding plans, and of changing and expanding *The Times* and the business generally, suggested to some of the directors a re-examination of the way *The Times* was run, and the board therefore commissioned a report on the subject from Cooper Brothers, the chartered accountants. On 8 November 1957, they submitted a brief for their enquiry for approval, which was given on 14 November. Morison was doubtful of the wisdom of this course.

But the Terms indicated in the Cooper letter are certainly far-reaching and very optimistic. I don't know how many inquisitors will carry out the investigation but if their report is to be ready 'by the end of January' they will have to give up their weekends in the country.

The Terms are, indeed, so 'widely drawn' that they can include any subject that seems attractive. I do not see, however, that the investigation implies criticism . . . of our management but of our whole system beginning with the 'administrative structure'. In other words Cooper wishes to review the entire directorial and executive arrangements as well as our method of keeping accounts. . . .

In sum, the Cooper letter is as much a criticism of the board as

471

anything else. Indeed, that cannot be escaped. My own reflection is that the investigation will do little good; perhaps little harm.*

Soon after this, Morison fell ill, and then went off to New York and Nassau, whence he did not return until 7 March; he was in a depressed state and 'continued to be low for weeks'.* By this time, the Report was in, and had caused some alarm. It was very long. It treated The Times Publishing Company like any other commercial organization, anxious to improve and enlarge its product, to sell it to an increasing proportion of the market, and (so far as it could) to increase the size of the market itself. Considering these objectives, and weighing The Times against the more 'successful' national papers, the Report found it self-satisfied and unambitious to change. The Times hoped that circulation would increase to 300,000; if it set out to explore and exploit the market properly, 400,000 and even 600,000 could be achieved within measurable time. Looking round for the cause of this sluggishness, the Report felt the direct responsibility of Editor and Manager to the Chief Proprietors an anomaly; it reduced the board to an advisory body. The board should be strengthened by the addition of professionally qualified members, and encouraged to take a more active part in the running of the company; as a first step, a committee of the board should be set up to examine how best to put into operation the changes necessary to 'rescue' The Times. All this was buttressed with a wealth of detailed analysis and criticism, ranging from accounting procedures to advertising, the editorial and production departments and such minor matters as the presentation of photographs and the running of the jobbing department.

A special meeting of the board was convened in March 1958 to consider the Report. Some directors accepted its view, and felt that the management, and in particular Mathew, had failed in their task. To others, the Report, excellent though it was on detail, seemed (due, perhaps, to inadequate briefing) to have wholly missed the purpose of The Times, and the delicate relation of Editor, Manager and Chief Proprietors on which it depended;

consequently, its predictions were misleading and alarmist. At the meeting the Report was referred, as Cooper Brothers suggested, to a committee. This move relieved the tension, but Morison was distressed that no formal answer was made by those who disagreed with the Report. At the suggestion of Lord Astor and Mathew, he undertook the task and on 14 April produced a report of some 12,000 words.

It was a notable piece of work, even by Morison's standards. Concise and forceful, its style vivid yet without rhetoric, Morison went straight to the point, the 'contract' between Editor, Manager and Chief Proprietor and the function of the board in this structure of management. Agreeing that the articles of association of the company were open to the misconstruction Cooper Brothers had put on them, he set out to explain the real facts as he saw them. In 1922, the new Proprietorship began with the expressed conviction, unaltered since, 'that, as the historic character of *The Times* had not been created by money, money should not be the test of its success'. Lord Astor and Mr John Walter had not adopted this principle blindly or casually.

Since 1922, they had known that the prime responsibility of the Chief Proprietorship is to organize the office so that the tradition, authority and leadership of the paper are maintained in the present, and safeguarded for the future. The national interest clearly demands it. It is difficult for any outside critic to deny this. Obviously Great Britain cannot function without a strong, educated, efficient, informed, governing class. *The Times* is the organ of that class. It remains and, for all we can see to the contrary under a non-capitalist economy, must remain absolutely necessary to that class. As long as free political discussion is the necessary pre-requisite of legislation this is obvious. Secondly, the due discussion of the country's affairs cannot be adequately conducted in Parliament alone so long as it is elected quinquennially and sits only for a few months in the year. The existence of a competent governing class is rightly said to be *absolutely* dependent upon *The Times* because no other newspaper attempts to rival it in self-respect, impartiality, independence, range of significant news, capacity to reason upon the matter printed. No other newspaper possesses the space in which adequately to discuss in leading articles and letters to the Editor the topical and national problems of to-day and to-morrow.

This was true a hundred years ago and it is true today. A country like Great Britain depends for its administrative efficiency upon its politically intelligent and professional men; these in turn depend upon *The Times* for the material upon which to reflect and, ultimately, act.

Bearing this responsibility, it was not to be supposed that Astor and Walter would hand it over, especially on the authority of a firm of accountants who did not seem to understand its nature or even its existence.

The Chief Proprietors may not be enthusiastic over this disregard of their position and authority. Secondly, although *The Times* can exist and even flourish without the present Directors, it can do neither without its Manager and its Editor. . . . It is naïve to suppose that these men would relish the reduction of the authority of the Chief Proprietors; secondly, the bringing on to the Board of sundry individuals recruited from Fleet Street; and thirdly, the turning of *The Times* into an imitation *Telegraph*.

It was, in Morison's view, the duty of the directors to support, not diminish, the Chief Proprietor's authority. Without it, their own would be in danger.

It will be discovered, say by 1968, that the authority and prestige attached to *The Times* has vanished, and the intelligent Director would disappear with its decline in reputation. And, let it be marked, it will then be too late to advertise *The Times* as a newspaper for those who are 'top' people and those who wish to be 'top' people. By 1968, if Messrs Cooper have their way, there will be no 'top' newspaper. Instead, there will be two *Telegraphs* struggling for the same lower-middle class patronage.

Let the Report therefore be accepted gratefully as to its financial part; its 'criticisms and suggestions in these departments are abundantly worth examination': on the other hand, 'the constitutional recommendations' should be set aside. Finally, if the primrose path to higher circulation was to be avoided, so also

474

was the ivory tower, with the paper supported 'as a newspaper of culture'.

The Times thus scheduled as an ancient monument and a dignified relic of high Victorian journalistic propriety, will be preserved for posterity.

Far better for the relic to be taken out of its glass case and for it to follow the dignified example of the *Morning Post*, so long its elder brother, and accept absorption by the *Daily Telegraph*, whose powers of survival, it is said, exceed those of *The Times*. Printing House Square would be sold off and the rebuilding problem solved at last. A television 'feature' would dramatically record the end of a legend. The Chief Proprietors would sigh, the Manager would head a Printing Works elsewhere; the Editor would head the National Book League and the Historian would retire to a Monastery. Five volumes of the *History of 'The Times'* would remain as its obituary.*

Reality seldom provides a neat dramatic climax. In the autumn of 1958, *The Times* increased the productivity of its presses substantially by taking on the *Observer* and the European edition of the *Toronto Globe and Mail*. The increase in circulation from the 'Top People' publicity was beginning to be felt. (Morison had enlisted his old friend Bingy Saxon Mills, who had invented the slogan, and together with Mathew and Rodney Fraser, Ivor Fraser's son, they had planned the whole campaign.) At the end of the year, despite the Report's predictions, *The Times* showed a modest profit. Next year the City of London gave approval to the new building plans; the Eden memoirs were serialized and, if not directly profitable, added considerably to the prestige of the paper; and by December the circulation, 218,000 in January 1956, had risen to 262,000. Earlier, Lord Astor and John Walter had completed their withdrawal by resigning as Chairman and Vice-Chairman of *The Times* board, in favour of, respectively, Gavin and Hugh Astor.

Long before this, Morison had begun to have apprehensions about the effect of his memorandum on the Cooper Brothers Report. A view so trenchantly expressed could not be universally popular (it had not smoothed Mathew's path), and Morison, with this last duty done, began to consider his own imminent retirement, and 'my personal situation vis à vis those who, by reason of their youth, cannot know of my past (and even present) special activities, which are, in their nature, what the advertising boys would call "creative" and for once they would be right'.* He wanted to defer his retirement, due in May 1959, and was worried by the possible repercussions of what he had only intended for the Chief Proprietors.* Argument about the Report rumbled on until February 1959, when the sub-committee's report was finally 'accepted', although Mathew's view remained that it was more interesting than authoritative.

For the last time Morison found himself writing a note for the Chief Proprietors. Growing old, he became over-alarmed at the prospect of becoming poorer. His lifelong independence ('they don't employ me – I employ them') left him without formal pension rights, and (as he told Pargellis) he had not saved much; he was dependent on the generosity of his old friends, and he was determined that they should not underrate his services. The task of reminding them was none the less disagreeable. He sent Mathew a first draft:

Many of the world's greatest talkers are reticent about themselves. The present writer has at least three times refused offers from publishers for his autobiography. I cannot, therefore, be accused of exhibitionism.

The accompanying draft memorandum is not to be taken, therefore, as a piece of self-indulgence. I do not suppose a more nauseating job has befallen the present scribe.

It is superfluous, perhaps, to say this to you, who passed on the authoritative command, on the entirely false assumption that I 'liked writing memoranda'.

There is nothing more ruinous to the style of a writer, or more paralysing to his imagination than to be compelled to write semi-legal memoranda, such as I have been doing now for about two years, or more – beginning with the Sunday Paper idea.*

The memorandum was drafted and redrafted, and the final version was not ready until 1 July next year. Morison had celebrated his seventieth birthday en route between Geneva (he had been trying to unearth the details of Northcliffe's madness from the Evian doctors' reports) and Cap d'Ail; he had seen the Mathews, who were on holiday nearby, and 'engulfed a bottle of Dom Perignon 1934' at dinner with Beaverbrook.* He now submitted his estimate of all he had done for the paper. There was the change of type and of the title (now 'followed by every London daily newspaper except the Daily Mail' – Morison had tried to convert the *Mail*, with Stone's help, just after the war, but without success), and the writing that went with the change, the two Memoranda and *The Typography of 'The Times'*. He had written the major part of the *History*, and acted as unofficial adviser to successive editors. In this capacity he had attracted men who had proved their worth to the company. He himself had edited the *Literary Supplement*, doubling circulation and profits. To finish the *History*, he had had to sacrifice other and more attractive work. Since its publication, he had 'made himself variously useful to the Chief Proprietors and the Manager'. He had produced *Printing The Times*, the *magnum opus* of the Private Printing Office which he had transformed 'from a decadent cock-robin shop into a flourishing press'. He had contrived the 'Top People' campaign. He had, in short, done much to preserve and enlarge the paper's reputation among the influential or about-to-be influential. 'The prestige, prosperity and reputation of *The Times* are inseparable from the ability, impersonality and anonymity of those who are responsible for what appears in its columns.' Such men are rare: his own case 'is more than exceptional; indeed, in recent years (at least) unprecedented'.

What had started in earnest had ended in self-parody. Morison had no real fear that his old friends would neglect him. Cheerfully, he denied to Mathew that he was contemplating leaving P.H.S. for Peterborough Court and the *Daily Telegraph*.

If I were induced to enter into such a connection it would initiate from my old friend at the *Daily Express* a flow of Canadian invective that would burn up every blade of grass between Leatherhead and Guildford [where Beaverbrook and Mathew lived] – and so far east as Edenbridge. This is a state of affairs that I pray for us to be delivered from.*

Surrey remained unblasted. *The Times* was generous, and Morison finally received an *ex gratia* payment of £5000 with a pension of £3000 a year for life. He was obliged to scotch another *canard* for Mathew.

I do not understand how the idea got abroad that, having retired from The Times, I would occupy myself with the task of writing something in the nature of a volume of 'Memoirs', to be published relatively soon.

It might be appropriate, therefore, if I were to say that it is true that I have been asked by two or three publishers on several occasions, to write an Autobiography but have always replied in the negative. I have no inclination to write anything of the kind. The utmost I would ever consent to would be to turn out something philosophical, religious, or ideological.

I cannot imagine myself, whatever the 'advance', sitting down to describe Printing House Square 'from the inside', or anything of that kind of 'telling all'.

Perhaps I should add that, having worn out my eyesight on Claritas and other typographical inventions for the benefit of P.H.S. I am not likely to respond to any request to give typographical or any other assistance to any other newspaper office. In any event I should always apply to you for permission to continue conversations with any enquirer, however eminent.*

He had spent just over thirty years in the service of *The Times* on which he now looked back with mixed feelings. 'The best years were 1930 to 1939. The B.W. years were interesting, more interesting perhaps but less enjoyable. You can put this in my obit (if you write it).'* He went into the office for the last time on 31 March 1960. *The Times* was finally moving. As he moved out, the demolition gang moved into the old building which for thirty years had been *The Times* to him.

19

IN 1956, George Barnes resigned as Director of Television at the B.B.C. to become Vice-Chancellor of the new University of Keele. Morison and he necessarily saw each other less often, but in 1957 Morison went on holiday with the Barneses to France, to visit Solesmes, the centre for the study of Gregorian chant. It was a pilgrimage for Morison: plain chant had enraptured him for fifty years, and listening to his large collection of records of it was his one relaxation. In 1960 Barnes had an operation, to Morison's concern.

I am upset to read that you have been under the knife – & relieved to see from your script written in bed, too, that you are well on the way to recovery. . . . Now, my dear fellow, do buck up and get well & stay well. Perhaps, as in my case, the forced bed may be a benefit. I have been busy, in between times, writing a memoir of Talbot Baines Reed author of the Fifth Form at St Dominic's. This is virtually a history of the Boy's Own Paper and of all its predecessors including the penny dreadfuls & penny bloods – about 35 or more 1000 words for Crutchley for his next annual present.*

Morison had never found time for his edition of Reed's *History of the Old English Letter Foundries*, and it was A. F. Johnson who did the job in 1952. He had, however, always kept his interest in Reed, whose busy life, as typefounder, historian and author of stories for the *Boy's Own Paper*, had been too soon cut short at the age of forty-one in 1893. Morison could still work fast and demand fast work: *Talbot Baines Reed* – text, illustrations from contemporary magazines, Reed's crest (engraved by David Gentleman) – was the 1960 Cambridge Christmas book.

It was in 1925 that he started work on Reed. Even before that, he had heard of, and was anxious to publish, the fascinating papers left by the Le Bé family, punchcutters and typefounders

479

in the sixteenth and seventeenth centuries. This ambition was revived by André Jammes, a Parisian bookseller. Morison met Jammes and found him both learned and charming. He wrote an introduction for a catalogue on the Parisian royal printers, entitled *Typographia Regia*, in 1957, and next year *L'Inventaire de la Fonderie Le Bé* appeared as the first of Jammes' 'Documents Typographiques' series. Pollard, to whom Morison sent the text of his introduction, was 'most excited' to see this long-discussed document, of critical importance to the identification of type-faces, in print, and Morison himself thought it 'a very fair piece of work', complicated as it was by the need to reproduce the marks used by Le Bé to identify all his typographic material, although a little disappointed that a facsimile of part of the document was not possible.

All the rest appears to me to be very satisfactory, and I am very greatly obliged to you for all the trouble you took over those symbols. It now remains for the bibliographers to digest the information and ascription now, for the first time, placed in their hands.*

Morison turned next to the even more fascinating and complicated 'Memorandum' of the lives of his father and his colleagues, by the second Guillaume Le Bé (*c.*1565–*c.*1645), but was defeated by old age (it appeared after his death, edited by Harry Carter).

It was Jammes, too, who stimulated him to explore the life of Marcello Cervini, prefect of the Vatican library, promoter of Greek studies and printing, virtual founder of the Vatican learned press, patron of Palestrina, and pope (as Marcellus II) for a few too brief weeks in 1555. He had been the hero of Morison's last talk to the Double Crown Club 'On Learned Presses' held at King's College, Cambridge, on 23 June 1955. The text was printed at Cambridge, and Brooke Crutchley explained its surprising appearance at the dinner in a note at the end.

It is the business of a Learned Press to protect authors from the consequences of their own shortcomings; and so, in view of the closeness of the time and of S.M.'s well-known proclivity for rewriting his works in proof, we took the precaution of not sending him a proof of this paper.

Morison, with Jammes's help, discovered the papers on Cervini of Léon Dorez, a scholar who had earlier worked on the subject, and 'Marcello Cervini, Pope Marcellus II: Bibliography's Patron Saint' appeared in a presentation volume of essays for Mardersteig on his seventieth birthday.

He was especially drawn to Cervini, who, like him, was born on the day of St John *ante portam Latinam*; the patron saint of printing seemed to have set his mark on Cervini, too, and the desire to disseminate new texts and books was conspicuous in his life. Morison was also drawn by the life of another earlier pope, Damasus I, whose Roman inscriptions he had first described in the *Fleuron* and later in the Lyell lectures; he wrote a paper at the instigation of Ullman, in whose *festschrift* it later appeared in 1964. Morison was also interested in Damasus on account of his position in the critical manœuvres of Church and State in the fourth century, a topic on which he lectured in Cambridge in 1956, at the instigation of Simon Barrington-Ward, his old friend's son, now Chaplain of Magdalene College. In 'Kingship and Christianity' Morison set out the views, pondered for half a century and tempered hard in recent arguments with Beaverbrook. Athanasius and the successors of Constantine, Charlemagne, Alcuin and Hadrian II, Calvin and Knox – the ground was now familiar but its fascination unending.

Morison still returned to Cambridge. His official connection with the Press continued, although Lewis had left, eventually to retire to his native Somerset. He was given the C.B.E. in 1952, and modestly disclaimed Morison's congratulations.

No, S.M., the Press would not have done such good work without your guidance and no one knows that better than I do. My long association with you may not have made me a better man in the spiritual sense but you made me a better printer.*

In 1960 he died. Barnes, who knew what Morison must be feeling, wrote sympathetically: 'You had a wonderful partnership with him and it produced results which are part of the history of printing.' Morison replied.

He was a wonderful friend, – having made an act of faith in me at a time when it was not, so to speak, compulsory. It was he who imposed me upon the Monotype and also upon Cambridge, both of which yielded an abundance of opportunity – which was the all-important factor.
 I have known very few men so naturally good. No man could enjoy more than he did the thrust of competition, yet he never over-reached any man. He could 'tell the tale', but I never heard him tell a lie.
 It was most curious to see the vestiges of West Country Puritanism still manifest in his near total abstinence and his orderliness of mind, and knowledge of money.*

But Barnes himself, younger than either, was far from well after his operation and he, too, died in September. Morison, who had no expectation of out-living him, was deeply distressed.

I shall certainly miss him extremely because his mind was so curiously of a piece with orthodoxy for the *sake* of orthodoxy. There are many such people, of course, but few, as Barnes, made a principle of conformity with the 'best' opinion. Bless him.*

In 1956 Morison moved from Tufton Street to a larger flat at 2 Whitehall Court, that romantic pile between Whitehall and the river, next to Charing Cross station. Here the last eleven years of his life were spent. The black bookcases, chairs and tables (re-placed by Heal's after the war) were moved for the last time. The pictures, engravings by Dürer, portraits of More, Calvin, Sixtus V and other heroes, two icons, the cartoon by Laurence Irving of Morison struggling to resist the Mephistophelian blan-dishments of Lord Beaverbrook to write the history of the *Express*, the fine colour print of the Sutherland portrait of Beaverbrook that Morison had had printed, all hung on the walls. The mantelpiece, with its gallery of old friends and new from Mabillon to Lowe, reflected other pieties. All the rest, apart from a spartan bed, and the couch, on which he was forced to spend more time in the day, was books: on politics and printing, palaeography and the church, liturgies and facsimiles, always threatening to outgrow the available space (to make more, he sold most of his liturgical books to the Newberry Library). He was beginning to find it a strain to keep up the black suits, ties, socks and shoes, and the white shirts, and from time to time Arthur Crook, whom he had first employed on the *T.L.S.* and had now succeeded Pryce-Jones as Editor, would see that they were replaced.

The windows faced south, and through the plane trees in the Embankment garden the river could be seen. 'Here the sun is full and warm, the tide high, gay vessels, funnel lowered, passing the window, and me hard at work on the problems of Church and State under Theodosius.'* As Morison wrote his paper on Damasus, he watched the tugs lower their funnels to go under Hungerford Bridge. Along the bridge, the trains rumbled across the river, as they had when as a boy he went on family holidays to the Kent coast by the South Eastern and Chatham Railway.

Morison was an institution. His pungent sayings (of an Italian scholar of calligraphy, 'It interests me that he should have heard of any English effusions on the subject. My experience has been that the dago is more insular than the frog.'*) were treasured by his friends, and certain phrases, 'I want information', 'Foul', 'According to me', became proverbial. C. K. Ogden would begin his letters, 'Instructissime', and endorse them 'Dr U. Mentation'; Arnold Bank, who shared his enthusiasm for Italian writing-books, would begin (as Tagliente began his dedication) 'Magnifico mio'. His admiring friends conspired, with his rather grudging co-operation, to celebrate his achievements. John Carter produced *A Handlist of the Writings of Stanley Morison*, annotated by its subject, often with caustic remarks on the inadequacy of his earlier work. Steinberg and Hans Schmoller, the typographer of Penguin Books, wrote an article on Morison and his work for the German magazine *Druckspiegel*. Morison thought they could have spent their time better. Schmoller replied.

That may be so, but I shall never want to waste my time in a better cause.

A little hero worship now and again does no harm; and, looking backward, I can think of one or two occasions when you yourself have indulged in it. Why, then, should you not also be its victim for once, particularly in another language whose readers have not had the same opportunities of forming their own judgement of your many activities?*

His name was now (among all those connected with print) a household word, and, as so often, veneration was not always based on accurate knowledge. Schmoller set a question on Bodoni in the City and Guilds examination for compositors: 'Who was called "The prince of typographers and the typographer of princes"? In which country did he work, and what is his chief claim to fame?'

Perhaps I ought to have remembered, when setting the paper, the old saying about asking a silly question, because my prize reply is the following:

'Stanley Morris. He worked in England and invented the Golden Books.'*

In 1953, Morison, making a new will in view of his retirement, made an exceedingly odd discovery. He was considering the conversion of the covenant by which he paid his wife's allowance into an annuity, and wrote to her solicitors to enquire, among other things, her exact age. They replied that she was born on 11 November 1872. Morison was incredulous: 'I have always believed, and must still believe, that Mrs Morison would be 70 years of age last year, or this year; in other words, I would have put down her birthday as 11th November 1882'. The solicitors were firm: they had the information direct from Mrs Morison who had documents to support it. Morison was still bewildered, and he took out copies of her birth certificate and their marriage certificate from Somerset House. There the astonishing facts were: she *had* been born in 1872, and at the time of their marriage she had been not 33, as she then said, but 43.

He was not only astounded, but humiliated and angry. In his

484

view, this discovery put the events of 1924–6 in an entirely new light. Of the four people whose lives were completely altered at that time, he had felt that Mabel had suffered most, and that he had been more directly responsible for her suffering. But for ten, or was it fifteen, years she had lived under a lie, and had he known the truth – what might he not have done? He would at least have been spared much remorse and self-reproach. The sense of guilt he had felt for thirty years had been quite misplaced. So he may have concluded: at all events, his distinct if courteous misogyny, due to shyness and to fear of the strength of his own emotions, gradually became a thing of the past. He took a new pleasure in the company of the pretty girls he met, particularly Josephine Rosenberg, who sometimes visited or went on his travels with him. Reynolds Stone's wife Janet, hitherto rather in awe of an occasional and rather formidable guest, became his adored confidante.

In 1954 she had sent him a book on her father. He answered to Stone:

This gave me great pleasure, apart from the production. It is always heartening to read about good men. It is a job I seldom have. If I write about a man it is usually about a politician. These are not good in the sense in which the Bishop was.*

Now she felt emboldened to write to ask direct the question that had bothered van Krimpen and Mardersteig. Morison, who addressed his most intimate friends by their surnames, began 'Dear Janet' quite easily.

The question you ask is not easy to answer because the situation of typecomposing machines is not very settled at present. From my little knowledge I should say that the companies will not, for quite a time, cut any more founts for bookwork on the 'old' lines. By 'old' lines I mean the use of cast metal type. It seems pretty clear that for the time being and until things have settled down any new designs will be arranged for photographic composition and this stage hasn't yet been reached because the machines aren't yet advanced sufficiently. I can only say now, that if asked I would recommend that R.S. be approached for a design. But there are many awkward considerations that need to be taken into account before the right kind of photo-compn type can be excogitated – which is the stage preliminary to the making of the design.

As you might suspect I am not altogether ignorant of some of the conditions under which this new process will work – if it does work. Nobody knows what saving there will be, if any, between metal and film or whether, if film is used, the printing will be better done by offset or letterpress i.e. whether the contact with paper will be made by a lithographic plano plate or an etched, intaglio plate. The electronic etching machines are altering the situation. As you can see, an etched line is not the same thing as a drawn line – & thus the design is altered: slightly yet perceptibly.

Until the conditions are clearer, the excogitation of the *right* design will not be possible. Meanwhile what the British companies will do is to repeat the contemporary designs which are still in demand for the hot metal machines . . . & so it is.

Meanwhile my love to all

Stanley Morison*

Morison always had a warm heart for the future. He let his *Times* article on Calvin be used as a specimen for one of the earliest photo-composing machines, the Rotofoto invented by George Westover, who left Monotype in order to develop it. In 1959, his speculations on photocomposition were printed,* and his introduction to Burt's *The Psychology of Typography* is notably generous in its consideration of modern developments. Here he was looking at the subject from the point of view he knew best, the type designer's, and nothing in the years since has yet altered that verdict. But soon his correspondence with Janet spread to other subjects: the beautiful Madonna that Morison had got Stone to carve out of a piece of bog oak; his eyes, briefly strengthened by new spectacles from Zürich – '*perhaps*, less range and *perhaps*, less convenience, but *certainly*, less strain'; and his growing acquaintance with Eden over the publication of his memoirs.

Since the writing of the last volume of the History of *The Times*, Morison knew his way about the political history of Europe between the wars in detail. Eden, besides valuing his expert knowledge, liked Morison for himself: 'I had much regard for Stanley Morison and always enjoyed his company. We agreed on many things, including the course of international events before the war.'* Morison impressed on Eden his high estimate of *The Times*'s pre-war motives:

In 1937 the Germans and the Nazis had many friends in London. Dawson and Barrington-Ward both believed that the tendencies of Vansittart and others at the Foreign Office were wrong because they obstructed the only alternative to war which was direct negotiation.*

Perhaps mindful of his own experience, he told Eden not to allow undue consideration for friends and colleagues to sway his judgement.

You should ask yourself whether you are not over modest when you play down the inter-cabinet & inter-office 'politics'. Of course it occurs everywhere in business; but here it is operating in terms of war and peace – something a little more important than profit and loss.*

In the course of this work, he went to see Count Dino Grandi at Milan and Albaredo. Grandi used to go to Beaverbrook's villa at Cap d'Ail, and Josephine Rosenberg, who had come with Morison, watched the two old men chatting about the past, and reflected how improbable it would have seemed, at the time of the events they were discussing, that they should now be doing so.* In 1964, when the final volume of the *Memoirs* came out, Morison was able to view the work with a certain proprietary pride. He approved of Eden's style, which 'grows in authentic force from being devoid of spurious "dramatics" or "over-writing"', and admiring of the record of the stamina which Eden had shown in his last years in politics. Eden knew Morison well by now, and had already thought of the ideal present for him.

I owe you an apology, as well as thanks. Some weeks ago your wine merchant delivered, with your compliments and Lord Avon's advice that the wine should be rested for three or four weeks before tasting, a case of white wine from the Dordogne. It was from the Chateau de Panisseau, a kind of Blanc de Blancs. And it was bottled at the Chateau. I opened it on Easter Morning, drank your and Clarissa's health and read your manuscript with even greater enjoyment. It is softer than the Blanc de Blancs to which I am accustomed, but not less dry and I found – and find it – a true refreshment in the morning. It was a delicious surprise as a gift, and a novelty to me as a wine. I am correspondingly grateful to you for your thought to send it. The only lack was the sun which should have been shining on the glass.*

Now that Morison was old, he became restless. Other old men would have been thankful to be still: Morison, perhaps in compensation for the busy life he had had, went about the world, often when really too ill to travel. He went to Switzerland about his eyes, and to see his close friend André Tschan, the Monotype manager at Berne. Tschan shared Morison's fascination with the character of Calvin, and helped him with his continuing work on the Geneva Bible. During the quatercentenary celebrations of the foundation (by Calvin) of the present University of Geneva, Tschan and Morison visited the Bibliothèque et Musée de la Réformation.

We sat in front of the famous Mur des Réformateurs listening to and watching the spectacle 'Son et Lumière'. Everybody and everything was dead quiet when our friend, in a typically Morisonian way, suddenly got hold of my arm and exclaimed loudly: 'Listen, Tschan, what if Calvin had become THE Pope instead of a reformer. . . . The face of Europe, the face of the world would have been changed.'*

Together with Josephine Rosenberg, Morison had an unexpectedly agreeable holiday at Klosters, watching the skiers and breathing the Alpine air. He was apt to get painfully short of breath now, and the altitude did him good. His back, too, was better; the trouble had been diagnosed last winter as a permanent defect of the spine. 'This involved a lot of pain; or, perhaps, Mr. Dulles's word "agony" is more appropriate.'*

But the experience, pain and all, was not regrettable. At one time I was certain I should never walk again, and at another that if ever I again cld walk up the steps to the British Museum into the Reading Room I could never haul up the vols of the General Catalogue. Now I can do all these and even hasten or almost run to a bus.*

Strengthened, he went to Paris to visit Lowe, and said a fond farewell to M. Beck of the Louvois Hotel, where he had stayed when in Paris for over thirty years. He went to Italy to visit Mardersteig at Verona, and a new friend, Signora Carla Marzoli, who (like Jammes) enlisted Morison's help to write an introduction to an enterprising catalogue, this time of writing-books. This enabled Morison to put into print his findings (so far as he could) on the inscriptions that Sixtus V had put up as part of his grand scheme for beautifying and reconsecrating the city of Rome in 1586–90, and the engraved versions of their designer, Luca Horfei. This revived his interest in his long-planned history of Italian writing-books. First written between 1923 and 1924, partially set up in type in the early 1930s and again in April–May 1953, it had a long history. Morison now set to work again, enlisting Wells's help in the further drafting, the revising and redrafting of a text which, like *Fell* and the Lyell lectures, he could not bear to let go. In October 1959, the Newberry put on a Morison exhibition (with its subject's reluctant co-operation), which Wells recorded in the Library *Bulletin*.

The manuscripts of his books were not the only thing he found it difficult to relinquish. He missed the power he had had at *The Times*. But here, too, he found an answer in his travels. At the end of August 1960, he wrote to Pargellis.

Just now, 24 hrs since, I returned from a fortnight first at Bad Nauheim near Frankfurt & the second week at Leningrad. Two widely varying types of company: 1st E. A. Lowe, 2nd W. Benton. The first was slow, meditative discussion, on the MSS of the VIII century – which was the reason I joined Benton as he had a yacht bound for Leningrad – where there are VIII century MSS of Bede & others. These were the inducement. I don't like yachts, not even if they are sizeable like the Queen Lizzie. I had a full day on the Corbie scripts and spent the rest of the time in the Hermitage and saw the sights, the most impressive of which was the new Underground or Subway. A truly fine layout and noble use of material & space. Marble Halls, profuse

& good decoration & No advertising not even for the Communist Party of the USSR. The line, only nine stations, speaks for itself. And I've seen no reference to it in the Capitalist Press.

Much time was spent with the Senator arguing, disputing, agreeing about his plans, projects, ideas concerning books, films, reading clubs of which vast conception the most important was the new edition of the focal work: the *Encyclopaedia Britannica*. About this he reminded me that I had once upon a time stigmatised the present set as looking as if it had been got together in the Balkans somewhere. Well, now was the opportunity. . . . Much to the effect that I ought to take an interest in all this & not a merely typographical interest. 'You should be a consultant, &c.' As I have for years been preaching to Benton, Hutchins and others the absolute, urgent, need to reconstruct *au fond* the *EB* so that it may be, & look, worthy of the West; & that he Benton is [at] a point of destiny in his life, by the choice he now makes, to do far more for the Western World than ever he can in the Senate, as Assistant Scy of State or as Amer Amb. to the Court of St. James'; such admonition naturally gave him the opportunity to say 'What about yourself? Why don't you give a hand &c.'

Naturally I put off answering such questions but at the end of the journey I agreed that, provided when I returned to London I found no obstacles, I would come to Chicago in time to attend the editorial meeting at 10 am on Oct 10, and other consequent meetings.*

In October, he presented his memorandum on the *Encyclopaedia Britannica* at the Chicago meetings, and was invited in consequence to a great conference on the editorial future of the work, to be held at Santa Barbara in California next spring. Just after Easter 1961 he set off and arrived at the San Ysidro Ranch ('a *very* picturesque place') on 6 April. When the meeting opened, he spoke first on his often-stated theme of the need for 'convictions'. Rather to his surprise, Geoffrey Crowther agreed with him, but he sensed that, despite Benton's enthusiasm, the audience was not really interested. At the end of the day's session, Morison spoke again,

by way of gathering up the fragments of more or less agreed position. But the agreement (i.e. on our having convictions and not being ashamed to give them precise statements) is not very clearly expressed or, I think, deeply felt.*

After the meeting, Morison went to Mass 'at the old (1785) Mission Church here: an Indian built and decorated place – rather fine in a terrifying way'. From there he went on to Marquette University at Milwaukee, Wisconsin, to receive another honorary degree, to Chicago and Ann Arbor (to visit Eugene Power, an early subscriber to the *Fleuron* and generous friend, now a millionaire on microfilms and the Xerox copying-machine). He gave his lecture on Damasus to the Medieval Academy of America at Chapel Hill, and lunched with Benton. 'He is determined that since he can't get a visa I must go to China & see if the *Ency Brit* can open an office in Peking! A daunting assignment. All I agreed to was to meet & discuss the idea, in Constantinople in July.'* He returned to London, thinking about the *Encyclopaedia Britannica* and impressed more than ever by Senator Benton. Benton, like Beaverbrook and Astor before him, was impressed, too, by the scope and power of Morison's vision. On the leisurely trip round the Mediterranean in the 'Flying Clipper', he offered Morison membership of the Board of Directors. On his return, Morison was torn between this new opportunity and his scholarly work.

Why is it that sitting comfortably in slippers & dressing gown with a glass of wine should be so comfortable, so relaxing – until one reaches for a pen and starts to compile some sentences about an Encyclopaedia or a Newspaper.*

But next January found him flying back to face

the intensest cold and bitterest wind that the stalwart natives of Chicago have experienced since 75 years ago. I can't describe the strange physical reactions of this elderly carcase to the sub-zero temperature and the murderous wind. I have been here i.e. in Chicago (Edgewater Beach & Drake Hotel) since Friday night (5 Jan) and haven't walked so much as a total of 100 yards. Two Sundays have I missed mass, which is a life-time record. The snowfalls, 6 inches or more at a time, have made walking impossible. This would have been difficult in any case for the first three days of the Encyclopaedia conferences because, when Americans work, they work! and all our time was absorbed by the proper business of the Britannica.*

Half the board were delayed – Chicago airport was closed with the snow, and Morison spent the time discussing typographical improvements, in which he also took an interest. He promised to return. In 1962, his mind was taken up with another great project, the realization of the half-fulfilled dream of 1940. He was overloaded at the time with writing of all sorts, a familiar enough condition.

But to these have been added committee after committee and this is not familiar. I am not good at it and hate every moment. But it is all unavoidable. Also it is unexpected. I have to do it because it is the result of a suggestion I made on the spur of the moment to the chairman of a great International Printing Machinery Exhibition to be held in London, this month next year, 1963. To my astonishment this character agreed that the kind of historical annex I asked for was as practicable as it was desirable and at a subsequent meeting I was instructed to organize an exhibit to be entitled Printing and the Mind of Man. I am *bringing* you the manifesto. Naturally I thought I could get all the work done by others – & I have been fortunate; but hardly fortunate enough. So much is necessary in the way of guidance and I have found it necessary to write out the instructions to various committees in order to keep everything relevant and all of it consistent and logical.*

The sympathetic chairman of IPEX 1963 was Jack Matson, Managing Director of Monotype in succession to Silcock, under whom Morison's relations with the Corporation acquired a new warmth. With his ready help, all went well. 'Printing and the Mind of Man' was opened exactly a year later. It consisted of three parts: the first two forming the main display was at Olympia, the technical exhibition illustrating the progress of printing, and, mixed with it, the exhibition of the most important books popularized by the press; the third, the exhibition of fine printing was at the British Museum. Three committees, old friends, like Percy Muir, John Carter (who devised the exhibition's sonorous name) and S. H. Steinberg, and new, worked away in the intervening year, choosing books and other objects to show, and writing catalogue notes for such diverse pieces as the first editions of St Augustine and the first publication on nuclear fission, and equipment from original punches and matrices from Fell's bequest to the latest in photo-composing machines. Loans, uninhibited by war, poured in from all over the world. Morison inspired all his co-workers to work as never before, and, for a brief fortnight, a collection of the history of printing and its progeny, such as had never been gathered together before, were displayed at Olympia to fascinate visitors from all over the world. As for the 1940 Cambridge exhibition, Reynolds Stone did an engraving for the catalogue, an elegant title-piece in his best capitals. It was, altogether, a notable tribute to the vision and drive with which Morison pursued his ideal. The catalogue of the inspirational part of the exhibition, enlarged and illustrated, was afterwards published as a substantial folio, *Printing and the Mind of Man*, as a permanent testimony of the Exhibition.

The blocks for the exhibition catalogue provided Morison with yet another opportunity of admiring Stone's skill as an engraver and his feeling for capital letters. It was displayed again – never perhaps better – in *The Typographic Book* (1965), a revised version of *Four Centuries*, whose title-page is dominated by the Sixtine capitals developed for the Breviary. Stone was also called on to engrave a set of six glass goblets which Morison gave Beaverbrook as a birthday present, and for his even more exotic gift for Benton's sixty-fifth birthday in 1965. Each time Morison was delighted to find his own ideas matched and transformed by the imaginative sympathy of the engraver.

About this time, too, as his physical disabilities increased, Morison began to realize that he would not, now, have time to finish all the plans he had in his mind. In 1960, Pargellis had applied on his behalf for a grant from the Ford Foundation to complete them. He made a characteristically generous assessment of Morison's achievements, ending: 'A Morison is bred once in a generation. Specialised as many of the items on his list are, there are people everywhere who hang upon his written word.'* Of the twenty works on the list that Pargellis attached, only four were completed in Morison's lifetime. The essay on *Talbot*

Baines Reed was the first of these. *The Likeness of Thomas More*, the published version of his 1957 lecture, followed it; it had been previously issued as one of the most beautiful – and largest – of Morison's *beischriften*, each copy with a specimen of the Medici Society Print that Morison had bought; a copy, specially bound in white leather, was presented to the Pope, who bestowed an Apostolic Blessing on the author on 20 November 1963. *Type Specimen Facsimiles*, a joint pre-war idea of Morison and Pollard, finally came out in 1963, edited by John Dreyfus; to it Morison had contributed a highly original essay on the history of the study of typography, the prehistory of the science that he had himself done so much to advance. This piece, too, had taken a long time to prepare.

The accompanying proof came this morning. I do not know what the 'gentle reader' will make of it, but the sight of it terrifies me.

I see that I wrote the first draft in October/November 1958, at the time when my back was at its worst. In the Spring 1959 I re-wrote it and you saw the typescript then made, in April, and offered some useful amendments. Carter, also, had a go at it and I made a further revision and sent it up to Cambridge in July 1959, – and now we are in February 1960!*

Pollard made one or two observations, which Morison, unreasonably (but for his sense that time was short), found provoking.

Your demand for footnotes is impossible to satisfy. I put the thing forward as an Introduction and call it a 'sketch'. Had I given it all the benefit of foot-and-note disease it would have been more than half as long again. I expect to hear from Cambridge about my corrections & additions and the expense thereof.*

He gave up his study of Colonel House, a subject which he now knew to be beyond him, and agreed to the abandonment of an edition of his collected papers (this luckless work, blitzed in 1941, was laboriously re-created by Steinberg, only to disappear, in still mysterious circumstances, at Cambridge in 1951);* he passed

494

his work on Italian writing-books into other hands, and concentrated on the Lyell lectures and on Fell.

Here Morison (for once) was not the only defaulter. The Clarendon Press reader had made his criticisms, and two years later Roberts wrote to ask Morison's reaction to them. He replied:

I remember receiving your reader's comments on the introductory chapter; and thereafter making a number of excisions and revisions. I also tidied up all outstanding queries, and finally satisfied myself that I could make no further improvements in the material.

Coming to this conclusion, I tied up the bulky stuff with a healthy piece of string, and took it down to Oxford and personally delivered it. I think this would have been about the 21st June 1961. I omitted to obtain a receipt for the parcel. I expect, however, that it is either in the secretarial safe or, failing that, the printer's.*

Even now, the book could not be hurried. It was a Morisonian folio, entirely set by hand in Bishop Fell's types, and the business of composing, proofing and printing was necessarily a slow one. On 1 July 1964, Harry Carter reported that a proof of the first sheet was ready. A year later, Roberts wrote: 'We are now, in no indecent haste, beginning to consider such matters as title page and blurb.' This occupied another year or so, with sundry distractions – a collection of Lowe's papers, and the Lyell lectures.

The latter had by now grown to about three times their original size. The visit to Leningrad had required substantial revision to the part on Bede (Morison found his 1935 application slip still tucked into the manuscript twenty years later); long and frequent discussions with Lowe on the Maurdramnus Bible required eight separate revisions of that crucial passage between 1960 and 1966; new discoveries, Byzantine and numismatic, or on his favourite Sixtus V, required more work. Several times Morison declared that all was finished, the bulky parcel would be packed up and put into a taxi with him, bound for Paddington and Oxford. On each occasion, a day or two later the manuscript would reappear on the black table at Whitehall Court: perhaps, after all, the relation of Leutchar's Corbie script to that of Maurdramnus was not quite right; was the account of the origins of the insular

495

minuscule (that thorny subject) sufficiently balanced? Morison could not bear to part with it; the quest of nearly fifty years was never to be ended.

All these speculations and enquiries were pursued against a gradually increasing involvement with the *Encyclopaedia Britannica*. Benton, lost in admiration of Morison's courage, erudition and independence, could not do enough for him, and Morison never succeeded in plumbing the depths of his generosity. At the end of 1962, he enabled Morison to acquire the neighbouring flat at Whitehall Court, to provide space for his ever-increasing collection of books. Next summer, cruising again in the eastern Mediterranean, a means of making a return occurred to Morison. The absence of 'theme' in the *Encyclopaedia Britannica*'s current policy was indicative, to him, of the absence of a strong over-all editorial direction. Who could better provide for this lack than William Haley? Hutchins, he knew, would approve; he had discussed the possibility with him at San Ysidro in 1961. Crowther was doubtful, but Benton was sufficiently impressed by the idea to arrange a meeting on his way through London on 23 September. Morison wrote warmly to Haley who came and discussed the prospects with him at some length. 'I have never forgotten that day when you descended – I use the word advisedly – upon me at Broadcasting House,' he wrote to Morison. Nothing came of these discussions immediately, although, as Benton wrote to Morison 'I like to hope that the door may still be ajar'.

The cruises on Benton's yacht had come to take some of the part that the visits to Beaverbrook at Cap d'Ail and Nassau had once held in his life. In June 1963, Beaverbrook had married the widow of his old friend Sir James Dunn, and Morison to his distress found that he was no longer welcome at Cherkley and elsewhere. 'I am said', he remarked with some pique, 'to have spoken disrespectfully of the rich as a class.' Beaverbrook himself was often ill and irritable with gout. But all the old warmth returned when Morison sent him his two most recent books.

9th December, 1963

My dear Stanley,

What wonderful gifts you send me! First the beautiful volume on Thomas More and for this I have already expressed my great delight to you personally. By post today comes another magnificent achievement – a history of typography.

These are two tremendously important and valuable publications and they are wonderfully well produced. I am delighted to see that the latter is indexed!

I have asked the Evening Standard to review 'The Likeness of Thomas More'. I hope it will please you.

Once again my very warm thanks my dear Stanley, and with affectionate regards,

Yours ever,
Max

Nor did he forget his regular birthday present.

7 May 1964

My Dear Max

You are a true and faithful friend to remember my 'date' and send me the gift of Dom Perignon – with, what I value more, a birthday letter all in your own autograph.

Thank you, too, for the honourable mention in the E.S. Diary. Your scribe turned off the piece very elegantly.

Gratefully and affectionately

Stanley

A month later he died. Morison went to his memorial service at St Paul's, and after it A. J. P. Taylor (now director of the Beaverbrook Library of contemporary archives), walking away down Ludgate Hill, met Morison laboriously walking back up the hill so St Paul's. 'Why?' he asked. 'I must go back to be alone there.' His friendship with Beaverbrook had been like no other in his life, and in May 1967 when the Beaverbrook Library was officially opened Morison was there, almost blind and in a wheelchair; it was his last public appearance.

When, in the summer of 1963, Morison had suggested Haley's name to Benton as Editor-in-chief of the *Encyclopaedia Britannica*, it was his view that the move would also benefit *The Times*. He

497

had always had the highest opinion of Haley as managing editor, such as the *Encyclopaedia Britannica* required. On the other hand, he was convinced that *The Times* needed different editorial leadership if it was to surmount the problems involved in a period of rapid change. In 1961 came the Royal Commission on the Press, and Selwyn Lloyd's 'Little Budget', neither calculated to improve the morale and stability of the national newspapers; still, *The Times* began its main rebuilding (the whole scheme was estimated at £4,000,000), and acquired a majority holding in Townsend Hook. Despite all this, there was a profit of over £500,000 to show at the end of the year. Next year, Gavin Astor became the third Chief Proprietor, and Lord Astor was exiled by an ungrateful government to the south of France. The final stage of the rebuilding went ahead, but *The Times* like other businesses was affected by the generally poor trading position. In 1963, conditions were no better (Britain's application to join the Common Market was rejected). *The Times* moved into its new building, and it was a matter of pride that so far it had all been paid for out of profits.

But the future was not easy to predict. Reserves were low, and even setting aside the demands of reorganizing *The Times* it was clear that prospects were not encouraging. Proprietorial resources had been depleted by the purchase of the last Walter holding by the Astor family. Through Francis Mathew, Morison still kept very much in touch with the paper and he was well aware that Mathew's position was far from easy. The issues raised at the time of the Cooper Brothers Report were still not settled, and in the absence of Lord Astor's gentle but experienced control as Chief Proprietor a great deal of the burden of management fell on Mathew. The increase in circulation to 350,000, hoped for in 1958, had not taken place; it had remained what it was at the end of the 'Top People' campaign. Radical measures were called for; first the Financial Times Group and then the Thomson Organization were both sounded as possible sources of further finance.

In February 1964, Mathew and Morison had a series of meetings with Roy Thomson, whose success with the *Sunday Times* had been a conspicuous feature in the 'quality' press. Later in the year, however, the financial position was restored, though in a manner that Mathew regretted, by the sale of *The Times*'s holding in Townsend Hook to the *News of the World*. All outstanding liabilities were paid off, including the last stage of the building, and at the end of the year there was a profit of £334,000 instead of the predicted deficit. In November, Morison and Mathew went to Grasse to discuss the current situation and the future with Lord Astor. On 8 November, it was Mathew's fifty-seventh birthday and the fifteenth anniversary of his coming as manager, an occasion for modest celebration. At the end of February, they went again, and after further talks with Gavin Astor on their return were hopeful that a firm foundation for the future of *The Times* might be possible without the need to call on outside aid.

Morison was now involved in the hasty preparation of his magnificent present for Benton, a set of inscriptions commemorating the major incidents of his life, each decorated with a border and a device engraved by Stone, printed at great speed at Cambridge. Copies were flown out to New York; Morison came up from Princeton to arrange for the delivery of copy no.1 to Benton in Arizona on 29 March 1965. As he did so, the dreadful news came of Francis Mathew's sudden death from a heart attack.

It was a blow from which Morison never really recovered. It finally put an end to his hopes of restoring *The Times* to the place that Barrington-Ward and he had long ago hoped and planned for it. Mathew had been a person of such calm certainty, serious yet convivial, kind yet with a touch of the buccaneer, always unruffled and polite, no matter what trials and crises he had to face – while he was alive, nothing had seemed impossible. He died just as the policy for which he stood had seemed to be vindicated, and in the sudden shock all were united in praising him and the view he had represented. To Janet Stone Morison wrote: 'Am intending quiet reposeful month of May, pulling self together after such shocks as the death of Francis Mathew, my true friend (benefactor) even, thrombosis of Lawrence Irving (a friend since 40 years).'* As soon as he was able Irving wrote to comfort him. He had been delighted to read in the April issue of *The Times* House Journal a special message from Gavin Astor reiterating the Proprietors' determination to support the paper's traditional independence, and to see that the goals Mathew had set were achieved. 'We are now reaping the benefit of bold and imaginative planning,' he wrote. Gradually Morison began to recover, but not to interest himself, except as a bystander, in the future of *The Times*. Mathew's old friends came to talk to him: Lord Astor (Morison was now one of his oldest and closest friends connected with the paper) discussed the future with him. George Pope succeeded Mathew, and the new machinery that the building now accommodated came into action. Hugh Astor became alternate Chief Proprietor, and a joint Managerial–Editorial Committee was set up; plans were finally made, after years of discussion, to put the news on the front page. Early in 1966, Haley forecast to the board further demands for investment, repeating as Morison had fourteen years earlier: 'If nothing is done, *The Times* will wither.' In May, the great change took place, and for the first time the news appeared on the front page of *The Times*. The circulation began to rise steadily. But despite assurances of confidence in the future, the new generation was still uneasy. Negotiations were reopened with the *Financial Times* and Thomson: by October terms were agreed with the latter, and the Monopolies Commission approved the merger, which finally took place on 20 December 1966. But, before this, the door that Benton had left ajar began to open; on 7 November, Morison wrote to tell him that Haley was now willing to act in a consultative capacity for the *Encyclopaedia Britannica*. It was ironic that next year, when the proposal, defunct since 1963, of Haley as editor was revived, Morison was too ill to take any part in the discussions.

Benton's affection for Morison grew no less, now that his strength and vigour were almost gone. Thanking Morison for a letter as well as a present on his birthday he wrote: 'I don't deserve your letter. But I am profoundly grateful for it. May I again tell you how deep is my admiration and affection for you – and how rewarding I have found my association with you?' They were lunching together on 14 July 1965 with Adlai Stevenson only an hour before he died. It was as great a shock to Benton as Mathew's death to Morison, and in turn Morison did his best to comfort him.

Gradually, Morison's ailments grew worse. In October 1966, he went to Chicago for the last time. His back was now too painful to travel by air, and he went by sea both ways, reliving old memories: 'So long since I've come in by sea that I shall enjoy the Nantucket–New York part as I did when I first came in the Aquitania in 1924. No doubt the enforced rest is benefit. But I don't like rest.'*

In February 1967 appeared the last of his works to be published in his lifetime, a second edition of the often reprinted *First Principles of Typography*. To this Morison added a postscript: the text had remained unchanged for over thirty years, and he felt some explanation was necessary. This had first appeared in a German translation in 1962, to explain the distinction Morison felt between his view and the 'artistic' attitude' typified by the Bauhaus school. Typography, as he saw it, was not a field in which self-expression had any part. The 'art' of typography lay in giving rational typographic form to the text, within the wide framework of a tradition, which gave that familiarity on which the eye depended for legibility and comprehension.

Tradition itself is not well understood at the present day in some quarters. If it were a reflexion of the stagnation or prejudice of past ages of printers, little attention need be given to it by historians and none by practitioners of the arts and crafts. But tradition is more than the embalming of forms customary in states of society that have been long since cast aside. The sum of experience accumulated in more than one man's lifetime, and verified by succeeding generations, is not to be safely discarded.

Tradition, therefore, is another word for unanimity about fundamentals which has been brought into being by the trials, errors and corrections of many centuries. *Experientia docet.*

Janet Stone continued to bring warmth into his life, and presents of butter and new-laid eggs from the once-despised country. He could confide to her the petty discomforts and triumphs ('shaved standing for the first time for many months') of old age; on her visits to London, he would visibly brighten, the champagne would come out, and for the time he would be as lively as ever. But as he grew blinder it became harder to sustain an interest in the world. On 20 March 1967 there was a full-page advertisement in the *Daily Mirror* beginning 'The last of the big suspenders' in 144pt Gill Extra Bold. Morison tore it out and sent it to Beatrice: 'This is the design & size of the type wh. S.M. can now read. Mem. E.G. did this as a jeu d'esprit. It amused him that the Corp. cd produce it.' On 22 March, a bitterly cold day, he tried to make a last long-postponed pilgrimage to the grave of Thomas Barnes in Kensal cemetery. He went with Jack Lonsdale of *The Times* and a photographer. They searched, but Morison could no longer remember where, among so many, the grave was. Hunched up against the cold, he tried to look for it himself, but was forced to give up. A month later he wrote his last letter to Lowe then in Rome, eight pages all in his own hand, now shrunk to a pitiful scribble, with huge spaces between lines to avoid the risk of writing over what he had written.

Holy Saturday 1967

My Dear E.A.L.

You were so good to present me with such a fine copy of book on the new gates of S. Peter, made the more precious by the expressive good wishes of your generous hostess at No. 18 which I so well & happily remember. Also you sent me a lovely colour card of S. Maria in Cosmedin, my favourite Roman Church. The message on the card was not so heartening, for it said that, so far, you had not been able to get up to the Vatican. I sympathise for I have myself been very handicapped & unable to work. In fact I have been, and am, much depressed on this account; & this is the reason for S.M.'s apparent neglect of E.A.L. I have not been able to exert the necessary muscular strength to write or the requisite vigour of vocal cord to dictate. On top of the ultra-low blood-pressure came an ultra-common cold such as I have not suffered for 3 years that undid the improvement made, I thought, by 3 sessions with an osteopath who, at the time, seemed to be strengthening my arms and legs. Linked with all this is a daily deterioration of the eyesight which linked with the lassitude occasioned by the low blood-pressure, created a heavy depression unrelievable by the printed word which I, now, can no longer read. And this makes writing very hard since it is not possible to read what one has written. And, of course, I can't write much at a time. Altogether, the combination necessitates patience which I am happy to say is in sufficient supply; so with Christian philosophy & selections [from the] radio I manage to pass the leisure hours with some pleasure. I would not have you think I am without compensations & if I write about my infirmities it is because I don't want you to think me wilfully neglectful of you or forgetful of your own physical difficulties, which are certainly not less in degree than mine. From what I have said you will not be surprised to be told that I am not going to Chicago for the April meetings of the Ency Brit board of directors. I may or may not be able to travel in October. It's too far ahead to say. The onset of Spring is cheering & I hope that you, too, dear brother, will feel the benefit of the sun & warmth. I look to you to apprise me of your movements later in the year. No doubt Rome was very crowded for Easter: you will be glad when the pilgrims & tourists have returned to their several home-countries.

Wednesday *after* Easter. The weather here so fiendish I was again laid low & failed to pick up the pen or pencil over Easter. Today I am pulling myself together for the sun is out once more & I face the world with some cheerfulness – & expectation of a beneficial session with the osteopath. Once more I hope Rome is now cleaner & sweeter & that you are happily at work in your beloved Vatican Library. Would that I was there with you.

Ever yrs
S.M.

In April, he went into the Middlesex Hospital for an operation, and in the early part of the summer his condition improved. His voice, which had faded to a whisper, came back, and a stream of visitors came to see him; Wells came in from Chicago; Haley and Benton came and when the latter returned to America, Haley kept him regularly posted. Morison received them all lying on the day bed in the big sunny room, with the reflections from the Thames making patterns on the great row of folios beside it. When the visitors were gone, he would shut his eyes and listen to plain-chant on his radio or gramophone. To his great delight, Lord Astor wrote inviting him to stay and convalesce. But, as the autumn came on, he began to slip away. He had now no wish to stay; he was not in pain, but discomfort was permanent, and he bore it with resignation. Beatrice, and his old *Times* friend Winifred Lodge, were more and more often there.

There was just time for him to half-see, to feel and to smell *John Fell: the University Press and the 'Fell' Types*, which arrived in September. He had written to thank the Press Reader, Cyril D. Piper, who had worked so hard on the book. He got an answer which touched him.

I joined the O.U.P. as a Reading Boy at the age of 15 in 1908, and except for two periods of war service have now reached the age of 74 and still reading in Walton St. Reading Dept. Many famous volumes, including lovely Bibles, have passed through my hands over the years – I have been a Press Reader since 1925 – but I was particularly proud to be entrusted with your lovely 'Fell Book' because as an apprentice compositor before 1914 I was taught the love and skill of good setting mainly with the Fell types.*

The book was to be published on 12 October, but it soon became clear that he would not be able to come to the party and the exhibition which the Oxford University Press had laid on in the new offices in Ely House. He grew more impatient to be off. The last words I heard him say were: 'I feel so certain – why can't I go soon?'

At 11 p.m. on 11 October 1967, he died; Beatrice and his secretary Miss Gaskin were with him.

Next day at Ely House, all his friends were gathered together for the opening of the Fell Exhibition. It was a characteristic stroke of timing. Francis Meynell, with a gratulatory speech in his hand, improvised an elegy which compassed an acquaintance of fifty-five years.

This exhibition and this book are a monument to Bishop Fell: they become no less a monument to Stanley Morison. I will not, I could not, speak doleful words about him. He has lived his life. I must amend that conventional phrase – he has lived his lives. We must rejoice in him and his multitudinous works. We must be happily grateful for his devotion – his effective and affectionate devotion – to that combination of historical research and current practice which has been achieved by no one else, in any time, in any country.*

A week after his death, on 18 October, a Solemn Mass of Requiem was held at Westminster Cathedral. The planning of this service had taken a long time and some careful thought. It was after the blitz that Morison began to consider his funeral arrangements, and early in 1942 he went to see Mr Bernard Dunne of Burns & Oates who was to be responsible for them. Morison was anxious that the full Requiem should be used; for his own sake, so that the cause of correct liturgical practice should be served, and so that his many friends, of every religious persuasion or none, should fully understand the meaning and purpose of the Requiem Mass. The service sheet was printed at the Cambridge University Press, in the semi-bold version (first used for the Pitt Brevier bible of 1936) of his own Times type. The text was given in parallel columns, Latin and an English translation, and the parts said by the celebrant alone in English, so that everyone should understand exactly what was happening. The homily was preached by Canon F. J. Bartlett, who set out the themes of the Mass, concluding with a memorable quotation from Baron Hugel:

The intellectual virtues are no mere empty name. Candour, moral courage, intellectual honesty, scrupulous accuracy, chivalrous fairness, endless docility to facts, disinterested collaboration, unconquerable hopefulness and perseverance, renunciation of popularity and easy honours: these qualities bear upon them the impress of God and of his Christ.

After the Requiem, the coffin was taken to the City of Westminster cemetery at Mill Hill and buried in a plot which Morison had long before designated. At the head, there is a slate headstone carved by Reynolds Stone, the last job he ever did for Morison. After some discussion, a form of words was decided. When he went with Lord Beaverbrook to receive his honorary degree at St Thomas's University in New Brunswick, the memory of the apostle Thomas had been much in his mind, a man who needed to see before he could believe. 'It was not', he said, 'of my own choosing that I was born a rationalist, and a rationalist born is a rationalist for life. I see what I see and have seen less by the eye of faith than by the eye of reason.' So, beneath name and dates and the description 'Scholar and Typographer', all in the Sixtine capitals which were to Morison the sum of the Roman alphabet, Stone engraved the words

QVIA VIDI
CREDIDI

CONCLUSION

MANY of Stanley Morison's strongly held beliefs are unfashionable now. When everyone expects to see his own work fully and publicly acknowledged, the idea that the work may be greater than the man who does it, the reticence that Morison learnt from Gerard Meynell and later saw embodied in the tradition of *The Times* – all this does not commend itself in an age when the right of the individual to do what he wants, and to receive the credit for doing so, has never been more strongly asserted. When, too, the individual artist's success is measured by the individuality of his style, by its difference from the work of others, the study (let alone imitation) of the past becomes irrelevant. So it might be thought that Morison's concentration on the past, and his choice of models from it for the type designs he originated, were an indication of a lack of originality.

But you can never put back the clock. Morison had no use for pastiche anywhere but in its place. He could describe the fine edition of *The English Liturgy* printed in 1903 as 'a genuine piece of contemporary design made before "artistic" typography relapsed into the archaistic'.* His own typography was not imitative; if he had learnt from the past, its influence was dominated by his own strong rationalism. Equally, his adaptations of past designs were not mere imitations; his criticism of Poliphilus shows what he thought of servile copying. They were designed to bring out the qualities in the original design best suited to the demands of the time in which they were produced and to the means of producing them. Equally, you cannot turn your back on the past. Increasing knowledge of it is bound to come; those who ignore it or (like Goudy) use it only as a vehicle for their own individuality – these are the Luddites. When, in the last *Fleuron*,

A. J. A. Symons was trying to explain the current lack of interest in the fine printing of the Nineties, he wrote:

Such eclipses are natural, and perhaps desirable. A new medium in art requires attention and applause for its development; and the easiest way of gaining them is to supplant what is already admired, already developed. . . . We are the losers by these revolutions only while we forget that excellence in any medium is its own justification, with a permanent claim upon our minds.

Morison never forgot this, nor (and this is especially true in the modern typographic free-for-all) that while all letters except the merely dull have their purpose, for which they should be appropriately used, some are more beautiful than others. In all his typographic work – the design of books and advertisements, as well as types – he tried to bring out the best and most effective in what he had to dispose of, not to set his own mark on it. He was fortunate in linking himself with Monotype at a point when, having created Imprint and Plantin, they understood how to set about the adaptation of the designs he wanted. On the other hand, once arrived, he left nothing to chance; all his work was the result of long investigation, was pondered, tried and tested, before it was as carefully released. This quality has permeated all other kinds of typographic work; this is why it can be truly said that his influence can be seen, directly or indirectly, in the form of all the reading matter we now see.

Morison found typography without organized history or principles: he left it with both, and in addition a substantial body of work exemplifying them. The future is unlikely to dispute the size of this achievement: Morison's other work is more open to question. No one can argue about the magnitude, the breadth of view, of the *History of The Times*, but even such substantial works as *John Fell* or *Politics and Script* are so strongly tinged with Morison's original views of Church and State that his conclusions may have to be revised. Yet again no one would wish this originality away: it was so entirely characteristic of Morison that every issue and contingency found him with a considered opinion, as Brooke Crutchley noticed in the radio portrait of him:

When he did his thinking, it was very difficult to know, but he always seemed to have his mind made up on anything. It was very difficult to fault him. You might not like it sometimes, but you couldn't dispute the rational approach to any opinion that he formed.

In this, he was (it has been truly said) like Samuel Johnson. Like Johnson, he had a gift for friendship with an extraordinary diversity of people; was at ease in all the different circles he moved in, without ever adapting himself in any way to fit in. Like Johnson, too, he was clubbable; at the Garrick, the Athenaeum, the Burgundians, he was thoroughly at home, and in each he had a group of admiring friends who drew from him those trenchant and pregnant turns of phrase (alas, unlike Johnson, he had no Boswell). But his acquaintance was not limited to the members of clubs. As well as press-lords and scholars, Morison had a special affinity with every taxi-driver, waiter and so on that he met. All his friendships had a confidentiality, almost secrecy, that made people talk of Morison keeping his life in compartments. What they forgot was that the secrecy often covered a generous charity, both moral and practical, to which he set no limit. When the most charming of the waitresses at the Garrick married a member, both staff and members were astonished (yet not altogether surprised) to find that Morison had been closest in their confidence.

But despite this he was essentially a lonely man. The spiritual progress that brought him to the Catholic Faith in his youth was an internal one. He lived a solitary life; there was nowhere to which he 'belonged'. Towards the end of his life, in 1961, he was asked to take part in a radio portrait of Gill, and the questions he was asked led him to think aloud about their differences. Both were 'committed' men, in every sense; but Gill had so much more at stake.

509

And this is where the mind comes in, this exactitude that I mentioned to you in his line, you see. A cut line is a very different thing from a drawn line. You can muck about with a drawn line a lot with a piece of rubber or a piece of indian ink or chinese white, or anything of that kind. He didn't do that when he was cutting. He cut. He committed himself. He wasn't afraid of committing himself.

There's no evasion in the thing at all. He believed in certain things – what? The fundamental basic things. The man, the woman, the child, the family, all that which he bore out. It's a very different thing for me. No wife, no child, no family, my golly, I mean I can see at once, without any further argument, I mean, how remote I am from the realities he faced and did. There's no doubt about it. I've felt it continually – continually. He not only saw it all, but did it – all these things. And he didn't shrink from committing his family as well.

Equally, Morison felt his own isolation continually. He seemed to draw a sort of warmth (certainly he became warmer himself) from family life, especially families like the Mathews with a large number of children. Certainly, he was never drawn to the monastic life. It was his individuality, his inability to merge his personality and opinions in a community, that made this impossible. Here again, there was a parallel with Gill.

We have been surfeited for so long with scepticism, with so many people who think it is better to discuss than to decide – one more aspect of the 'it is better to travel hopefully than to arrive'. Gill liked to arrive. And when he was carving these statues there is no doubt whatever that he struggled to arrive at the end of a certain notion of behaviour and conduct which in the view of some (I suppose) reasonably decent observers of the human race would have marked him as quite a special sort of character. It wasn't that he was merely a bigot as I might be said to be, he was more tolerant than I am ever disposed to be, he was genial which I'm not very good at, and although he and I agreed about so many things, there were a great many things we didn't agree about. We did have a fundamental basis of agreement in a detestation of vulgarity, particularly that created by the capitalist system by which they made their profit. So that you can still find, and you will find for a long time I fear, so many people rich in the West End and some petty fogging investors in Surbiton, all profiting by things about which they know nothing and never really will – but there's a profit there. Now this sort of thing was abhorrent to Gill: the word profit in his nostrils stank and it should stink in the nostrils of any decent man, he thought – and so do I, and did.*

In saying that he was not genial, Morison was hardly fair to himself, even if he lacked the instinctive cheerfulness that never deserted Gill. But he liked to think himself a bigot. If he had a special feeling for the people he met in his far-ranging historical researches, it was for those popes and bishops in whom faith and the capacity to suffer for it were allied with the strength of mind and political sense to get things done in the world. This was no Corvine dream; but Morison had no hesitation in asking himself what he would have done, if he had been Athanasius, Damasus I or Marcello Cervini.

That Athanasius was a character, had adventures we all love to read about, and finally won, does not alter the fact that from the statesman's standpoint, he was a narrow-minded combination of bigot, pedant and rebel; a crank who incessantly questioned whether unity should be at the expense of what he was pleased to call the truth as defined at Nicea; a malcontent always asking whether communion with some people was to be achieved at too high a price.*

He had no use for the unbelieving Gibbon's prim condemnation of Damasus, who tried to keep the Church on a straight course between conscience and expediency.

Damasus understood that art of so 'adapting' himself as to attach power to his office and maintain it. Had Damasus been a conscientious prig like Gibbon, or nothing but a shifty opportunist, we should never have heard of him. He would have remained a satisfactory deacon, and no doubt a competent archivist, like his father. But his character, far from being 'very ambiguous', was firm, and his policy was consistent. The essential factor in the situation which he faced all his life lay clearly before him. It was a question of the reality of power. In the mind of Damasus the nature of power is such that it has to be seized or served. He seized power and used it to secure the independence of the Church of Rome and the leadership of the Catholic Church.*

But it was Pope Marcellus II to whom Morison felt most closely drawn. His preoccupation with the early Fathers, with libraries and the liturgy and printing, formed a bond, which was strengthened by the realization of what he might have done. If he had not died at fifty-five, after a papacy of only six weeks, might he, a saint of powerful intellect, strong ideals and equal administrative ability, outstanding among the corrupt, self-seeking, ineffective men who preceded and succeeded him – might he, not Calvin, have become the dominant ecclesiastical figure of the later sixteenth century? Might not the Council of Trent have become, as he intended, the great reconciliation of Christian Europe? To Morison, as to Marcellus, unity was the key: unity of typographic expression and letter-design, unity of the history of politics and religion, unity of the Church, unity with Christ. Like Marcellus, he was magnanimous, and like Marcellus he would have wished no other place in history than his own strict sense of justice should demand: 'lassaro, quanto a me, che la Justitia habbia il loco suo, come soglio far sempre'.

1 *a*   Alice Louisa Morison

1 *b*   Arthur Morison

1 *c*   Morison as a schoolboy

1 *d*   Morison aged sixteen

2 Morison, about 1912

for refusing the duties ordered

Today sentenced to two months hard labour; to be served at H.M. Prison, Winchester, which will be my address for this 'stretch'. Hope all well. Will write again when able.
Stan.

3 a   Postcard from Morison to his mother, 9 July 1916

3 b   Letter-card to Fr Thurston, 18 May 1918

3 c   Programme for Fanny's First Play, 7 and 8 February 1918

HAMPSTEAD TRINITY SUNDAY. 1918
N.W.   Wm. Smith to you 'em.
I look to get one in on the T.S.!
I should dearly love a few days off the tomatoes in which to do a bit of research: I should love

The Revd Herbert Thurston, S.J.,
31 Farm Street   W 1
London

FANNY'S FIRST PLAY:

An easy play for a little theatre by Bernard Shaw

PLAYED without preface, prejudice or epilogue to the Wakefield Work Centre on Thursday and Friday, 7th and 8th February, in the Fifth Year of the Great War.

THE CAST

Mrs. Gilbey	John Cairns
Mr. Gilbey	R. Webly
Juggins	Ariel Ezill
Darling Dora	Walter Holmes
Mrs. Knox	Arthur Cooper
Mr. Knox	Stanley Morison
Margaret Knox	Drury Channell
Lieutenant Duvallet	Page Arnot
Bobby Gilbey	Hugh Plummer

¶ The first and third scenes are laid in the Gilbeys' house, the second in the Knox'. The performance begins at 7.15 p.m.
¶ Produced by George Smith at the New Theatre, Wakefield.
¶ Secretary: H. McCall. Stage Manager: D. McInnes. Stewards: E. Hopwood and J. Ring.

At the PELICAN PRESS, Gough Square, E.C.

No. 11 Hollyberry Lane, Hampstead
London, N.W.3

Dear Mr. Bullen: I am writing to suggest next Friday for your coming here for a talk. I hope it will be possible for Mrs. Bullen to come also. If another day would be more convenient please tell me - my phone number is Victoria 3860.

Here is where the rogues live:

It isn't so easy to find & it might perhaps be best if we met at say outside Times Book Club at 3 or 3.15?

Yours
Stanley Morison

22 January 1923

4*a*   Letter from Morison to H. L. Bullen, 22 January 1924

4*b*   Letter from Beatrice Warde to Morison, 22 March 1925

Dear Morison:

That article for the 'Recorder' is so completely without distinction that I am convinced that it is an unconscious plagiarism from some third-rate author. I hide my head and submit it herewith.

Sincerely yours

BL Warde

March 22, 1925

5   Beatrice Warde – drawing made by Eric Gill in 1929

6 Morison at work, c. 1930

THE FLEURON
A JOURNAL OF TYPOGRAPHY
from the Editor
27 FITZROY SQUARE, W.
LONDON

12th July, 1928.

Dear Gill,

I think you will be interested to see the enlarged photograph of the alphabet from Cleverdon's book, which I asked the Monotype Company to send you yesterday. You will remember that I had the notion that it would make a very good fount. I still think so. We agreed to experiment with the design: I was to have the enlargement made; have it worked over; and submit to you for criticism. I am now a little nervous about the serifs. I like them very much indeed, and would propose having entirely flat, unbracketed terminations, very much in the style of the accompanying proof of series 135; but as far as the ascenders are concerned, I think a simple, and not a double serif would be best. Subject to your approval, I should make the fount of a definitely light, blonde colour; the kind of letter which should look exceedingly well with Intaglio plates.

Please do not trouble to write at length about the matter. You can scribble in shorthand in the margin of this letter, which is left purposely wide.

I am attending to the question of the new lower case y with a straight stroke for the book-face, and a new capital Y for the 30 point capitals.

Yours,

S M

P.T.O.

[handwritten left margin:] Is it your wish that I work on these photos at all? I don't think there is much to do. Shall I do a few typical letters & then send it to you to do the rest. Then you can't you agree, send it back for my scrutiny. I think a very nice face can be made on this model. Eg

[handwritten right margin:] yes. V. much so. / I agree / yes, but not quite certainly.

[handwritten:] or this. / this:

7   Morison to Gill, 12 July 1928

8 *a*   Eric Gill and William Burch on the Monotype stand at the Printing Exhibition at Olympia, April 1929

8 *b*   Morison, in a characteristic pose, arguing with Ernest Ingham. Cartoon by Wiktorya Gorynska, 1928

9 No. 2566 *Ladas* at King's Cross on 16 July 1929

N T E R plurima diuinæ ſapientiæ, bonitatis, & potentiæ ſigna, eaq́; euidentiſſima, haudquaquam poſtremas ſibi vendicat Imperiorum Monarchiarumq́; ordo, & conſeruatio. In quam ſi attentius animorum aciem direxerimus, depræhendemus, inter admiranda diuinæ Maieſtatis & Sapientiæ opera, nihil ea, in hac mortalium vita, vel prius eſſe vel auguſtius: quippe quæ ſocietatis humanæ ſit vinculum, iuſtitiæ, omniumq́; virtutum, in quibus vitæ huius cultus præcipuè conſiſtit, conſeruatrix, adeoq́ue pietatis, & religionis aſſertrix. Hoc opus diuinæ bonitatis & ſapientiæ ideo accuratius intueri & mente complecti nos decet,

10a   The original of 'The Times' New Roman: Granjon's 'Gros Cicero', from Philippus Lonicerus, *Chronica Turcica* (Frankfurt, 1578)

N T E R plurima diuinæ ſapientiæ, bonitatis, & potentiæ ſigna, eaq́; euidentiſſima, haudquaquam poſtremas ſibi vendicat Imperiorum Monarchiarumq́; ordo, & conſeruatio. In quam ſi attentius animorum aciem direxerimus, depræhendemus, inter admiranda diuinæ Maieſtatis & Sapientiæ opera, nihil ea, in hac mortalium vita, vel prius eſſe vel auguſtius: quippe quæ ſocietatis humanæ ſit vinculum, iuſtitiæ, omniumq́; virtutum, in quibus vitæ huius cultus præcipuè conſiſtit, conſeruatrix, adeoq́ue pietatis, & religionis aſſertrix. Hoc opus diuinæ bonitatis & ſapientiæ ideo accuratius intueri & mente complecti nos decet,

10b   The same passage set in Monotype Times

11*a*   Starting *The Times* on the night of 2 October 1932

11*b*   An editorial meeting at *The Times* in 1938

12a Walter Lewis – a photograph taken about 1930

12b The Patrick Stirling single arrives at Cambridge, 24 August 1938

12c A drawing by Jan van Krimpen to illustrate the problems of combining his Romulus and Cancelleresca Bastarda, with the last letter added by Morison, about 1934

lachis. Ascendit quoque cu ommisit
de eglon inhebron· & pugnauit con
tra eam· coepitq; & pcussit in ore
gladii. Regem quoque eius & omnia
oppida regionis illius· uniuersasq;
animas que in ea fuerant comora
te· non reliquit in ea ullas reliqui
as, sicut fecerat eglon· sic fecit &
hebron· cuncta que in ea reppe
rit· consumens gladio, Inde re
uersus in dabira coepit eam atq;
uastauit. Regem quoque eius· &
omnia que in circuitu erant oppi
da pcussit in ore gladii nondimi
sit in ea ullas reliquias, Sicut fece
rat hebron & lebna· & regib; earu
sic fecit dabir & regi illius, Percus
sit itaque iosue omne terra mon
tana· & meridiana atq; cam pes
trein· & ase doth· cu regibus suis·

`abcdefghilmNNopqrsstuxrz`

a|b

13   A page from the Maurdramnus Bible, with a complete
alphabet of the script as reconstructed by Arnold Bank

14*a*   Morison looking at Karl Marx's grave

Wednesday 8.50 pm

My Dear Beaverckffe
Oh! Oh!! What a
show !!! And how
perfect you were...
John Walker and all
here praised you to the
skies... & even
forgave S. M. all

his sins of cooperating
with personal publicity
and all that. By
universal consent you have
now started a new career
for yourself. And how
jealous the Tories will
be.
    Above all, how N
would have loved & approved
you ; as I do.
        Yrs
            Stanley Morison

14*b*   Letter from Morison to Lord Beaverbrook, 14 May 1952

15a Morison and Beatrice Warde on board the *Queen Mary* in the 1960s

15b Morison with Mrs Francis Mathew

16 Morison in 1964

APPENDIX A

THE records of the tribunals appointed to deal with conscientious objectors under the Military Service (No. 2) Act were ordered to be destroyed in 1920. The Middlesex County Tribunal did not, seeing their historical importance. The documents on Morison's case (MH 47/139) show not only the course but the nature of his objection. The file, officially deposited in the Public Record Office, is still under an embargo by the Department of Health and Social Security, owing to its confidential nature. I am most grateful to the Department for permission to print the extracts which follow.

1. 21 February 1916. *Form R.41. Military Service Act, 1916. Application as to Exemption. Addressed to Hendon Local Tribunal. No. 52.*
    Name: Stanley Arthur Morison
    Age: 27
    Address: 14 Woodville Road, Golders Green
    Occupation: Publisher's Reader (the reading of MSS submitted for publication, seeing through the Press etc and subsidiary duties too numerous to mention but all literary).
    Ground of application: Conscientious Objection
    Nature of application: Total exemption
    Reasons in support (should be fully stated):
        The very nature of conscience forms the chief difficulty in giving 'fully stated reasons'. Conscience is a ratiocinative faculty but not at all dependent upon reason from which it is distinct. I have a conscientious objection to killing and nothing can induce me to accept [service] in which the taking of life will be my duty. Nor for the same reasons can I undertake work in RAMC or similar regiments. All I can say about my conscience is that I have it, that it is opposed to military service and that to prove my sincerity I shall embrace the penalties whatever they are for non compliance with the Tribunal's order if it is unfavourable to this my petition.

Decision of Local Tribunal:
> Application refused. The Tribunal are not satisfied that there is any real ground for conscientious objection

16 March 1916

J. Henry Sturgess
Chairman

2. 13 March 1916. *Statement by Fr I. O'Leary, in support of Morison's application.*

I have known Stanley A. Morison for many years, and I can honestly say that his conscientious objection to war, in any shape or form, is based upon *bona fide* convictions which he has firmly held for some considerable time.

16 March 1916. *Decision of Local Tribunal (see above).*

3. 20 March 1916. *Form R.43. Notice of Appeal. No. of Case 343, endorsed M[iddx] 377.*

> *Name*: Stanley Arthur Morison
> *Address*: 9 Golden Square, Hampstead (lately 14 Woodville Road, Golders Green)
> *Occupation*: Publisher's Reader
> *Whether attested or not*: not attested
> *Grounds*:
>> That the Tribunal was badly conducted by its chairman.
>> That it was unjust and biased.
>> That my evidence was for the most part ill-considered and for the rest it was refused admittance.
>> That in my resenting irrelevant questions I was referred to by the Chairman as the worst case that had come before the Tribunal.
>> And that prejudice was thereby created
>> In short I claim that the decision is unjust and quite against the evidence I brought.
>
> *Reasons for decision of Local Tribunal*:
>> The Tribunal are not satisfied that there is any real ground for conscientious objection therefore refused.

J. Henry Sturgess   20 March 1916

> *Decision of Appeal Tribunal*:
>> Exemption from combatant service
>> Leave to appeal refused

William Register   5 April 1916

4. 31 March 1916. *Notice of Hearing before Appeal Tribunal, County of Middlesex, Guildhall, Westminster. Wednesday 5 April at 2.30 p.m.*
5 April 1916. *Decision of Appeal Tribunal.*

5. 7 April 1916. *Forms R.57 and 58. Notice of Decision of Appeal Tribunal.*

    Grants: exemption from combatant service only.

    Ground: that conscientious objection to combatant service has been established.

6. 9 April 1916. *Letter from Morison to the Clerk, Middlesex Appeal Tribunal, Guildhall, Westminster.*

9 Golden Square, Hampstead

Sir:

    Thank you for sending me form M.377 informing me of the Middlesex Appeal Tribunal's decision in my regard.

    I beg however to say that the decision does not meet the case. At the hearing, the Chairman admitted that I had made out a very good case and yet I am awarded 'non-combatant service' though I made it clear that this was quite as objectionable to me as ordinary military service. I shall be only too pleased to undertake Ambulance or other work in a civil capacity at the discretion of the Tribunal but I cannot possibly accept the N.C.C. service. I am genuinely anxious to serve my country. I am not a conscientious objector to National Service but only to Military Service. I beg you therefore to represent this to the Tribunal and to request them to allot me work in which I can take an enthusiastic interest. I cannot undertake Military Service even in the N.C.C. and feel that I can be much more use otherwise.

    Please therefore, forward me a form for further appeal.

Yours faithfully
Stanley A. Morison

endorsed in blue pencil: Leave to appeal refused at hearing.

7. 10 April 1916. *Duplicated form letter to Morison from the Clerk of the Appeal Tribunal.*

Referring to your application for leave to appeal to the Central Tribunal, I beg to inform you that this application was made at the hearing, and refused.

APPENDIX B

DURING its existence the Guild of the Pope's Peace produced a substantial number of pamphlets. These are exceedingly uncommon, and the list which follows cannot hope to be complete. It may, however, lead to the discovery of other copies.

1. *Preliminary Notice of the Guild of the Pope's Peace.* [1916] 11¼ × 8¾ 4pp. Possibly never issued. F (proof).
2. *Preliminary Notice* . . . [1916], 8 × 5½, 4pp. A shortened version of 1, with Meynell's name instead of John F. L. Bray as secretary. F.
3. '*We invite all the friends of peace in the world to help us in hastening the end of the war.*' [1916], 8½ × 5½, 2pp. F.
4. *Prayer for Peace by Pope Benedict XV.* [1916, 1917], 5¼ × 3⅜, 4pp. There were at least two printings with different flower borders, the first with 'PRAYER FOR PEACE' and the second 'Prayer for Peace'; in the second the head-piece block is slightly damaged. It was designed 'for insertion in prayer books'. 'Single copies gratis, price per thousand on application.' F.
5. *The Pope's Easter Message.* 1916, 6⅝ × 4⅛, 4pp (first only printed). F.
6. *A Little Book of Prayers for Peace*, compiled by E. I. Watkin. This was the book printed in the Fell types. 'Price 6d.'
7. *The Pope and the War.* 1917, 'Finely printed at the Pelican Press. Price 2d.'
8. 'Two Small posters . . . with extracts from the Pope's pronouncements'. [1917], 15 × 10. 'Printed in two colours at the Pelican Press. Price 3d. for the two.'
9. *The Pope's Plan for the Destruction of Militarism.* 1917, 7 × 4, 4pp. 'Printed at the Pelican Press . . . in November 1917.' F.
10. *The Popes & Peace.* 1917, 6¾ × 4, [4] + 28pp. Printed at the Pelican Press; the Nihil Obstat is dated 29 October. F.

Note: There was also a letter-heading, 10 × 8, sometimes converted into a notice by the addition of the Guild's aims and rules. Quotations are from the list of publications in no. 10. 'F' indicates that Sir Francis Meynell has a copy.

APPENDIX C

ALTHOUGH Morison and Edward Johnston knew and respected each other for a long time, there is little tangible evidence of their acquaintance. It is the greatest pity that the 'pattern book' to which the following letters refer never came to fruition. Planned by one of the greatest authorities on lettering in this century for execution by the other, it would have been a notable monument. As it is, only these four letters survive to commemorate their friendship.

THE IMPRINT
11 Henrietta Street, W.C.
1 May 1913

Dear Sir,

Mr Meynell, who is in Newcastle for a day or two, asks me to request you to be kind enough to send your article for the May IMPRINT as *soon as possible*.

Yours faithfully,
Stanley A Morison

12 December 1923

Dear Morison

It's absurd for you who can write so well to be seeking my assistance. I *have* an impression there is a letter & a pattern book of yours buried somewhere on my desk. I hope it will not pain you to know that they will probably not be answered until – or, rather, before – next January (if then). But it will be best really to avoid having to answer, by fixing a meeting for some day next year. I should be both pleased & proud to meet you & a Mr. J(Jenkinson?) [at lunch some Monday] a better writer & a better palaeographer than Yrs faith – I mean sincerely

E.J.

St. Stephen's House
Westminster, S.W.1.
26 March 1924

Dear Johnston,

There goes to you by this post a small collection of facsimiles of the kind of writing in which you know I am interested. I hope to find you one other specimen before long of what appears to me to be an upright hand of English origin, but the present will indicate the lines of my thought.

My suggestion is that you write plain and flourished varieties of (a) upright and (b) a sloping hand, the upright to be a rather rounder and more formal hand and the sloping somewhat of a current hand.

I send for your use the dummy which I made up a little time ago and which I hope makes my plan clear. If you should any time desire to see me with reference to it I need not say that I shall be delighted to meet you at Victoria or South Kensington.

I understand that Gerard is acting as agent for you in the matter of the payments for this work. I will address myself to him in his matter without delay.

Yours sincerely,
Stanley Morison

101 Great Russell Street
W.C.1.
13 July 1924

Dear Johnston

Last week I was in Cambridge for a few hours and took the opportunity of visiting the Fitzwilliam & seeing the Cockerell. We spoke of calligraphy and inevitably of you then of your promise to write the plates for my copy-book. It appears that this is particularly interesting to S.C.C. and he gave me a word of advice without which he said I should probably never succeed in getting the plates from you. His suggestion was that I should annex to the contract, not a sum of money but a catalogue of penalties, viz, that if the plates be not delivered by the right time you be boiled in oil until your ligatures melt & you suffer the loss of your majuscules. This seems a very serious sentence but perhaps you will not drive the court to consider it! I must have the plates though. There are other birds beside the Cockerell dying to see these plates & I do beseech you to put your hand to them. It will be so easy and quick once you have the work started. There are six plates and I will pay you £5 for each or if you give them to me by August 10th, I will pay £50 for the set.

Yours
Stanley Morison.

NOTES

CHAPTER I

PAGE

23   *printers:* Register of Births, no. 447, 4 Oct 1889, Leyton Sub-district, West Ham, Essex.

London: Wanstead rate-books (Lady Day 1889 to Lady Day 1893). Essex County Record Office, Chelmsford; *Kelly's Directory of Walthamstow...*, 1889–93, under Snaresbrook.

24   *Kent Villa:* Marriage and birth registers; *Kelly's Post-Office Directory of London*, 1880–8.

25   *gone:* Register of Electors for Great Malvern, Worcestershire Record Office; *Pigott's Commercial Directory*, 1835 and 1842; *Slater's Directory*, 1851 and 1863; *Post-Office Directory of Worcestershire*, 1854 and 1860; *Billings's Directory...of Worcestershire*, 1855 and 1858; birth certificate of Arthur Andrew Morison.

26 *Hackney:* Information from Douglas Cole.
   early in 1897: Kelly's Hornsey and Crouch End Directory, 1897.
   routes: C. H. Grinling, *The History of the Great Northern Railway 1845–1922,* 3rd ed. (1966) pp. 385–8.

27 *neighbourhood: Arts et Métiers Graphiques,* no. 23 (mai 1931) pp. 225–9.

28 *grown up:* SM, *'Black-Letter' Text* (1942) p. 3.

29 *nephew: Who's Who in the Theatre,* 7th ed. (1926), s.vv. Cole and Kelly; Annual Report of the Liverpool and Birkenhead Branch of National Canine Defence League for 1918.
   inconvenience: G. and W. Grossmith, *The Diary of a Nobody,* 9th ed. (1934) p. 15.

30 *Wightman Road:* Edith Morison's birth certificate, dated 16 Oct 1899; *Kelly's Hornsey and Crouch End Directory,* 1897–1900 (William Cole had been at 14 Stapleton Hall Road, not far off, since 1897).
   only: Kelly's Hornsey and Crouch End Directory, 1905.
   syndicate': Barrington-Ward diaries, 2 Apr 1941.

31 *did:* Speech of thanks for the award of the Bibliographical Society's Gold Medal, 16 Mar 1948.
   libraries': In James M. Wells, 'The Work of Stanley Morison', *Newberry Library Bulletin,* vol. v, no. 5 (Aug 1960) p. 221.

32 *buy: Anton Zwemmer: Tributes from Some of his Friends on the Occasion of his Seventieth Birthday* (1962) p. 22.
   to £39: Minutes of the London City Mission Committee.

33 *Hornsey:* It has not proved possible to identify the shop exactly. There were tobacconists at 4A and 10, and a confectioner at 6 Brecknock Road. No Morison is listed there in the directories for the period, although all three shops changed hands more than once between 1900 and 1912. Perhaps 4A is the most likely; it only opened in 1902 and it closed in 1912, when Mrs Morison left Harringay.

35 *after life:* The first verse of Psalm 42 begins 'Quemadmodum desiderat cervus ad fontes aquarum' in the Vulgate. 'Sicut cervus' is the form used in the tracts for the prophecies in the office for Holy Saturday, of which SM was particularly fond (see p. 178).
   action': In James M. Wells, 'The Work of Stanley Morison', p. 160.
   of port': Moran, p. 7.

36 *mind:* J. H. Crehan, *Father Thurston* (1952).
   Arthur: Liber Baptizatorum in Ecclesiae S. Mariae in Caelum Assumptae apud Warwick Street (1 Apr 1881–7 Apr 1909) f. 302. His godfather was Peter Judge, whom I have not been able to identify.

37 *error: Arts et Métiers Graphiques*, loc. cit.
  books: Crehan, *Father Thurston*, bibliography, nos. 99, 107 and 122.
38 *production:* Gold Medal Speech.

CHAPTER 2

46 *year:* Minutes of the London City Mission Committee.
49 *Imprint':* P. Johnston, *Edward Johnston* (1959) pp. 191–3.
  people: John Mason's notebook, quoted in the *Monotype Newsletter 71* (Oct 1963).
50 *abandoned:* Since the basis of the design was the original founders' version of Caslon, the Monotype Company had first planned to make the *Imprint* face part of the existing series 20, a poor imitation of Caslon first introduced in 1903–6, and finally withdrawn in 1937. The new series number 101 was not given to Imprint until February 1913.
  days': All the text of the first number was set in one size of roman type: there were as yet neither italic nor small capitals. The point was first raised at the end of December, and the order sent in January, with a copy of the magazine by way of encouragement. The italic was ready on 5 February, and appeared in the third number (17 March 1913).
51 *yours':* P. M. Handover, preface to SM, *On Type Designs*, new ed. (1962).

CHAPTER 3

52 *far':* So he told Mrs Robert Hunter Middleton.
53 *together:* Viola Meynell, *Francis Thompson and Wilfred Meynell* (1952) pp. 192–3.
  week: SM to Francis Meynell, 3 Nov 1948.
  accomplishments': Ibid.
54 *time':* MR, vol. XXI, no. 192 (1922) p. 15. Meynell's patronage of Eric Gill's younger brother Max, who did the 'Wonderground' Map, also deserves to be remembered.
55 *clear:* Letters from Gerard Meynell to Johnston in the library of the University of Texas, Austin; from Mason, Deval and Muir Catalogue 10, no. 346.
56 *others':* 'Mr Morison as "Typographer"', p. 10.
  be': Joseph Thorp, *B. H. Newdigate: scholar-printer, 1869–1944* (1950) p. 6.
  monks': F. Meynell and SM, 'Printers' Flowers and Arabesques', *Fleuron 1* (1923) p. 37.

57   *activity*': 'Mr Morison as "Typographer"', p. 12.

    letter: Since this was written, an earlier letter to Edward Johnston has come to light (see Appendix C). The remark on SM's correspondence with Bishop is in his letter to Graham Pollard, 5 Jan 1939.

58   *Stanley A. Morison:* This requires some further explanation. The 'Catholic Library' was a series published by the Manresa Press. 'Goodier' is Fr Alban Goodier, S.J., later Archbishop of Hierapolis and a prolific author. E. I. Watkin was later to become a friend of Morison. Fr G. H. Joyce was the author of *Miracles.* The 'F.T. business' presumably refers to Francis Thompson.

59   *TUERI:* This much-used block contained two errors, one heraldic (three martlets instead of three Cornish choughs) and the other in Latinity (it should be NE CESSEAS).

60   *orchards*"': SM to Francis Meynell, 11 Oct 1951; Francis Meynell to SM, 15 Oct 1951.

    movement: SM to Francis Meynell, 3 Nov 1948.

    Tablet': SM to D. B. Updike, 30 Oct 1923.

    Catholic: 'It was a merry society trying its very hardest to "ginger" the Bishop of London who in order to secure tolerance for "Catholic practices" gave encouragement to every other party also' (SM to Updike, 10 Dec 1923).

    subjects: All these reviews and notices were unsigned.

62   *military:* The history of conscription and conscientious objection to it has been told from the Quaker, Socialist and Government points of view by John W. Graham, *Conscription and Conscience: a history 1916–1919* (1922); David Boulton, *Objection Overruled* (1967); and John Rae, *Conscience and Politics: the British Government and the Conscientious Objector to Military Service 1916–1919* (1970). The last gives the most reliable and unbiased account.

63   *plea*': Letter from E. I. Watkin, 30 July 1968.

65   *ecclesiologist:* (1853–1931). It is easy to see how Morison might have come in touch with him. In 1896 he had represented his church at the commission set up by Leo XIII to investigate the validity of Anglican orders, and had almost been successful, though finally frustrated by Cardinal Vaughan and the English Catholic Clergy. Like most ecclesiastical frontiersmen he must have been used to enquiries like this.

66   *in 1914:* She was baptised at St Peter-in-Chains by Fr Isidore O'Leary on 12 September 1914.

    authors: On Fortescue, see John G. Vance and J. W. Fortescue, *Adrian Fortescue: a memoir* (1924).

67   *Fortescue*': Mgr Vance, quoted by Moran, p. 9.

68   *slowly:* Adam Roberts, 'Draft Dodgers' (a review of Rae's *Conscience and Politics*), *New Statesman*, 20 Nov 1970, p. 686.

     Central Tribunal: See Appendix A. The account of Morison's statement at the appeal hearing is taken from MM Fragments, although Mrs Morison had clearly become confused about the order of events and put this after Morison's later arrest.

69   *arrived':* MM Fragments.

CHAPTER 4

70   *eat:* MM Fragments.

     Cheltenham Bold': Philip James, 'The Pelican Press, 1916–1923', in *Signature 12* (July 1939).

73   *prison:* Rae, *Conscience and Politics*, pp. 88–93, 164–80; Boulton, *Objection Overruled*, pp. 185–90, 195–7, 211–12.

74   *before:* Letter from A. W. Griffith.

76   *time:* Francis Meynell, *My Lives* (1971) p. 90.

77   *pamphlets:* Information from Mr Page Arnot and Mr A. V. Austin.

80   *Jesuits:* Crehan, *Father Thurston*, pp. 125–32.

81   *seen:* The publisher's device, too, appears to be derived from Burns & Oates', although the three martlets or choughs look more like ducks.

82   *is':* Letter to SM, 27 Apr 1919. H. T. Brandreth, *Episcopi Vagantes and the Anglican Church* (1947) gives the further history of these bizarre clerics.

83   *composition':* N. Pevsner, *London: except the Cities of London and Westminster*, Buildings of England (1952) pp. 195, 187.

     Lettering: Letter to Mrs Bridges, [5] Nov 1923; 'Mr Morison as "Typographer"', p. 14, and *Tally*, p. 43 (Johnston's fig. 180).

     it: Letter to E. A. Lowe, ?Apr 1948.

84   *printers:* 'Mr Morison as "Typographer"', p. 13.

     ordered: James, 'The Pelican Press', p. 24.

     June: Meynell, *My Lives*, pp. 137–8.

88   *Marble Arch:* Information from J. S. Maywood.

93   *considerable:* Morison paid generous tribute to the influence of T. L. De Vinne, in 'Mr Morison as "Typographer"', *Handlist* and *Type Specimen Facsimiles*. The illustrations of *The Craft of Printing*, letter-forms of all sorts from Roman inscriptions to Bodoni, show that Morison already knew Sir Edward Maunde-Thompson's *Introduction to Greek and Latin Palaeography* (1912), the bible of all who were interested in the history of lettering, and Lietzmann's *Tabulae in usum Scholarum* series. Two volumes in this series –

F. Ehrle and J. P. Liebaert, *Specimina Codicum Latinorum*, and E. Diehl, *Inscriptiones Latinae* – Morison took with him wherever he went. Bindings worn, pages covered in notes, plates cut about to provide examples for books from *The Craft of Printing* to his Lyell lectures, his copies still survive, and show the hard use to which they were put. It is interesting also to note that the illustration on page 4, some lines in a fine fifteenth-century *textus quadratus*, are 'from a MS. breviary in the author's possession'. Morison had begun to be a book-collector.

94 *practicable' : SM, an Original Member of the Double Crown Club* (1968) p. 15.

CHAPTER 5

96 *Club: Two Men*, pp. 2–4.
   Updike: SM, 'Recollections and Perspectives' in *Updike: American Printer* (1947) p. 61.

97 *respect:* The design was started in 1917, and issued to the trade in 1919. See P. Beaujon, *The Type Specimen of Jean Jannon* (1927) pp. 11–12.

98 *thankfully:* ALM diary. The Pelican Press provided a pretty 'change of address' card, in Cochin and Fournier-le-jeune types, dated 1 June 1921.

100 *managers:* MM Fragments.
   papers' : Moran, p. 11.

101 *Menut's Garamond:* This is a reference to the first modern adaptation of the Imprimerie Nationale 'Garamond' (the *Caractères des l'université*), first cut by the Peignot type foundry in 1912. Menut, with whom Morison must have been in correspondence, was temporarily in charge of the business, before Charles Peignot, son of Georges Peignot who had had the design cut, returned from military service.

103 *opinions:* O. Simon, *Printer and Playground* (1956) p. 2.

104 *force:* SM's speech at the Double Crown Club dinner in memory of Oliver Simon, 26 April 1956.
   off-accent' : Radio Portrait, p. 12.

106 *printing:* An expanded text of the Supplement was reprinted as *A Brief Survey of Printing History and Practice* in 1923.

108 *typography:* Simon, *Printer and Playground*, p. 24.

112 *printers:* MM Fragments.

114 *Pentecost:* SM to D. B. Updike, 10 Dec 1923.

115 *situation:* Fortescue to SM, 22 July 1920.

CHAPTER 6

colour': F. C. Avis, *Edward Philip Prince, Type Punchcutter* (1967) pp. 24–5.

117 *history'*: Moran, p. 7.

museum: M. Sabbe, *Plantin, the Moretus and their Work* (1926) pp. 112–13.

dead: M. Parker and K. Melis, *Inventory of the Plantin–Moretus Museum Punches and Matrices* (1959) p. 36 (no. 53 A).

live: MR, vol. XXIII, no. 203 (1924), pp. 1–2.

job': MR, vol. XXV, no. 205 (1925) p. 2; vol. XXXVI, no. 3 (1937) p. 17 and insert.

᾿118 *idea*: MR, vol. XXXVI, no. 1 (1937) pp. 13–16.

120 *Garamond*: SM would take any opportunity of publishing what seemed to him useful information; later in the year his 'A Note on Rococo Printing', a study of eighteenth-century printers' flowers, appeared in Jonathan Cape's house journal *Now & Then*.

pleased: SM to Updike, 25 July 1923. Monotype in fact began work in January 1922, not 1921, and Morison had known about Goudy's version for the American company at least as early as the previous September (see p. 101 above). But in January 1921 Morison's head was full of the new types for the Cloister Press, and he may have begun to put pressure on English manufacturers to produce a 'Garamond' then.

121 *characters*: Type Drawing Office file.

Corporation: Moran, p. 11.

month: TDO, series 156, p. 4. Apart from SM's copy of the 1642 *Imitatio Christi*, the books – all Imprimerie Nationale brochures – supplied for copying were Anatole France's *Ce qui disent nos morts* (1916), *France Amérique* (1918), *President Wilson's message to the French people on the declaration of war by the United States, with the reply*, and *Histoire de Charles VI* [*sic* for Prosper Mérimée's *Chronique du règne de Charles IX*, printed at the Imprimerie Nationale for Édouard Pelletan in 1913]. Both the last two seemed to have been used, but *France Amérique* is the official source (MSR 156–14).

122 *today*: Quoted in MR, vol. XXI, no. 192 (1922) p. 16.

123 *successful'*: Tally, pp. 10, 11, 46, 56–7.

early part of 1923: Probably in January or February; compare SM's letters to Updike of 14 January ('ligatures wh. at my requisition are now to be had on the Monotype (English Corp^n) for use with their Garamond') and 23 February ('You might care to possess some of the special ligatures and ornaments; I shall be very happy to arrange that you get any of these that you may like').

123 *knowledge'*: 'Mr Morison as "Typographer"', p. 15.

124 *May 1923:* S. C. Roberts, *MR*, vol. XXII, no. 199 (1924) p. 14; *Adventures with Authors* (1966) p. 65.

specimen: TDO, series 169, p. 1. The 1798 Caslon *Specimen* included a number of sizes of a new transitional design (first shown in 1796), which has no obvious affinity (except in some of the figures) to Baskerville's original types. But the 1798 Fry *Specimen* showed their famous plagiary, first cut in 1766; the italic is a little bolder than the Baskerville design, which may have been considered an improvement.

125 *Jenson's:* Tally, p. 30.

126 *volume:* TDO, series 170, p. 1.

127 *success':* Tally, pp. 38, 43–4.

available: Tally, p. 11.

129 *construction:* 'Mr Morison as "Typographer"', pp. 14–15.

modestly: Interview for *Radio Portrait*.

136 *y'day':* SM to Simon, 25 June 1923. The blocks were not described in the *Fleuron*.

Rome: SM to Bullen, 26 July 1923.

138 *accumulation':* SM to Updike, 25 July 1923.

CHAPTER 7

146 *since':* SM, *John Fell: the University Press and the Fell Types* (1967) p. 205.

beings': SM to Bridges, 28 Dec 1923.

writing-books: SM to Mrs Bridges, 5 Nov 1923 (Cambridge University Library Add. MS 4251 (B) 984).

147 *Updike:* SM to Updike, 19 Nov 1923.

148 *others:* On Type Faces, p. 58.

151 *printers':* Stevens Lewis Watts, *Henry Lewis Bullen and his Work* (1966) p. 13.

152 *forward:* SM to Updike, 30 Jan 1924.

153 *printing:* SM to Updike, 13 Feb 1924.

154 *Yciar:* The famous sixteenth-century Spanish calligrapher – Updike's hand was notoriously bad.

hesitated: Updike to SM, 21 Mar 1924.

156 *family:* Cartier was dead and Morison hoped to complete and publish the book. For a variety of reasons he was unable to do this, and it was Marius Audin who eventually brought it out in 1937, with prints of the original blocks that Morison had discovered in 1923.

Paris: SM to Updike, 22 May 1924.

157   *start:* He startled Maggs by leaving out the full stops at the end of paragraphs (*A Catalogue of Maggs Catalogues, 1918 to 1968* (1969) p. 12).

magazines': A. Havinden, 'Prologue' in Michael Frostick, *Advertising and the Motor-Car* (1970) pp. 12-15.

Cochin: Moran, p. 10.

158   *membership:* Information from R. Page Arnot and Walter Holmes.

159   *job:* Beatrice Warde, 'Some Notes on the British Typographic Reformation, 1919-39', in *Printing Review,* 1946; reprinted in *The Crystal Goblet,* ed. H. Jacob (1955). Bullen needed an assistant while he supervised the great 1923 A.T.F. Specimen Book (Watts, *Henry Lewis Bullen and his Work,* p. 13).

is: Updike to SM, 13 Nov 1923.

161   *tendencies':* SM to Updike, 15 July 1923.

162   *encountered: Sunday Times,* 15 Oct 1967.

Winship: Updike to SM, 9 Sept 1923.

163   *go:* SM to Updike, 20 Oct 1923.

CHAPTER 8

164   *unstable:* SM to Updike, 10 Oct 1923. *Of God and his Creatures,* a translation of the 'Summa contra Gentiles', was published in 1905.

165   *headquarters: Tally,* p. 10.

167   *return:* Roberts, *Adventures with Authors,* p. 66.

them: Tally, p. 3: *Two Men,* passim.

168   *delivery:* Simon, *Printer and Playground,* p. 36; Frank Sidgwick, 'The Double Crown Club' in *Signature 2* (1936).

editor: Simon, *Printer and Playground,* p. 31.

169   *Tagliente:* 'Mr Morison as "Typographer"', pp. 13-14.

171   *did):* MM Fragments.

well: Information from Mrs Reynolds Stone.

London University): Information from Fr Gervase Mathew.

helpful: Dr Kiel to SM, 30 Oct 1924.

174   *spent':* SM to Mardersteig, 3 Feb 1925; information from Dr Mardersteig: the carpet from Montagnola is now at Verona.

176   *Pantheon-Verlag:* SM to Mardersteig, 2 and 9 Mar 1925, with Mardersteig's reply, 24 Mar.

May 1788: SM to Updike, 2 Feb 1925.

time: Updike to Warde, 15 Apr 1925 (in the Ransom collection of documents on Warde, Newberry Library, Chicago).

177   *Bibliothèque Nationale:* Long after, SM thought that he had written the article (*Handlist* 31). He was clearly puzzled by the contents,

which he dismissed as 'valueless except for a small point, not well made, about *ct* and *st*'.

size: TDO, series 178 and 185; MSR, series 185, 14pt and 18pt.

178 *finished':* BW home, 28 Mar 1925.

180 *Jakob Hegner:* H. Kiel 'Tendencies in German Fine Printing since the War', *Fleuron 4* (1925); H. Schmoller, 'Carl Ernst Poeschel', *Signature,* new series, *11* (1950); G. K. Schauer, *Deutsche Buchkunst* (1963) pp. 236–9.

Rüdesheim: SM to Simon, 18 May 1925, is written on the card of the hotel.

CHAPTER 9

185 *work"':* SM, *John Fell: the University Press and the Fell Types* (1967) p. vi.

guess': Bridges to SM, 15 July 1925.

186 *quantités:* Warde to Plumet, and to Ribadeau Dumas, 4 July 1925.

187 *volume':* Bridges to SM, 13 Aug 1925.

189 *ignored':* Bridges to SM, 20 Oct 1925.

190 *binder's:* Warde to H. W. Kent, 16 Nov 1925.

191 *hand):* Information from Ernest Ingham.

192 *too':* BW home, 27 Sept 1925.

193 *him:* SM to Updike and Mardersteig, *c.* Nov 1925.

195 *case:* Ibid.

Fleuron: 7 Oct 1925.

196 *J. van Krimpen:* Morison passed this letter on to Robert Bridges for his Society for Pure English tract.

of an artist: SM to Jan van Krimpen, 22 Mar 1926.

country': *The Life and Works of Eric Gill* (1968) p. 16.

Pepler: BW home, 16 Nov 1925; SM to Gill, 15 Jan 1926.

197 *this:* Warde to Kent, 16 Nov 1925, 18 Jan and 22 May 1926.

Empire: BW home, *c.* mid-Jan 1926.

198 *best':* SM to Bridges, 19 Jan 1926; selfconsciousness was too much for him, and Bridges had to use a piece of his letter of 28 Dec 1923.

letters: SM to Bridges, 8 Feb; Bridges to SM, 9 Feb 1926.

199 *storm: Is Zat So,* by James Gleason and Richard Taber, opened in London on 15 February.

Suggestions: BW home, 19 Feb–*c.*10 Mar (only two of seven letters are dated, but she was back by 5 Mar); Warde to Kittredge, 6 Feb 1926.

200 *really:* BW home, after 5 Apr 1926 (incomplete).

201 *telegram:* Bridges to SM, 3 and 6 Apr 1926; for the part played by Edward Thompson in this, see his *Robert Bridges, 1844–1930* (1944) p. 73.

202 *Fournier:* Warde to H. W. Kent, 22 May 1926.
wisest': BW home, *c.* 28 Mar and *c.* end Mar 1926.
legible: Malin to SM, 13 May 1926.

203 *on':* Warde to H. W. Kent, 22 May 1926.
type: SM to Gill, 18 May; Gill to SM, 25 May 1926.
years: Penrose Annual, vol. 63 (1970) p. 74.

204 *satisfactory:* SM to Gill, 27 July 1926.
&c.: Malin to SM, 14 Sept 1926.
type': Gill to SM, 16 Sept 1926.
asked: Gill to SM, 14 Sept 1926.

205 *easily':* Gill to Desmond Chute, 23 May 1925 (*Letters of Eric Gill,*
ed. W. Shewring (1947) p. 188).

206 *equal:* BW, 'Eric Gill', *MR,* vol. XLI, no. 3 (1958) p. 10.
indifferent': MM Fragments.
miles: BW home, *c.* end Mar 1926.

207 *gossip:* Ingham, visiting Germany during the strike, found Poeschel
puzzled and curious after SM's visit the previous summer.
kampfen: Undated, but *c.* Aug–Sept 1926.

208 *sleeping:* Malin to SM, 1 Oct 1926.
Florence': Mardersteig to SM, 24 Sept 1926.
London: BW home, 21 Oct 1926.

209 *him:* Updike to SM, 22 Nov 1926.
success: BW to SM, 26 Nov 1926.

210 *history:* Pollard to SM, 5 and 11 Nov 1926.
be': BW to SM, *c.* Christmas 1926.

CHAPTER 10

211 *Ribadeau Dumas:* The first Monotype trial is dated 14 Jan 1927.

212 *it:* SM to Cleverdon, 11 Jan 1927.

213 *age:* Simon Nowell-Smith, 'A Poet in Walton Street', in *Essays
Mainly on the Nineteenth Century Presented to Humphrey Milford*
(1957) pp. 58–71.
Hanna Kiel: SM to Mardersteig, second half Mar 1927.

217 *Stanley Morison:* SM to Mrs Bridges, 10 Mar 1927.

218 *character:* BW, 'Eric Gill', *MR,* vol. XLI, no. 3 (1958) p. 15.

219 *advertising:* Moran, p. 18.
slug': BW to SM, *c.* Christmas 1926, and 28 Feb 1927.

220 *home:* SM to Updike, 2 June 1927.
types': TDO, series 231, p. 1.

221 *drawings:* TDO, series 231, p. 3.
Seasons: SM to Meynell, 25 July 1927.

221   *departments'*: SM to Updike, 6 Oct 1926.

      underwear': BW home, 19 Nov 1927.

224   *rested: Proceedings of the British Academy*, vol. XL (1955) pp. 241–51.

226   *situation'*: SM to Pollard, 23 Jan 1928.

      better: TDO, series 239, p. 1.

      E.G.: Gill to SM, 31 Jan 1928.

227   *modifications:* TDO, series 270, p. 1.

228   *time:* SM to Updike, 28 Feb 1928.

      months': SM to Gill, 2 Mar 1928.

229   *grindstone:* SM to Cleverdon, 5 Mar 1928.

230   *available:* TDO, series 231, pp. 4; MSR, series 231 – 24 pt.

      Officina Bodoni: SM to Mardersteig, 26 Mar 1928.

      article': SM to Symons, 26 Apr (Bodleian, M.S. Walpole a.10).

232   *end: British Federation of Master Printers' Members Circular* (June 1928) pp. 182–6.

      Institute: Moran, p. 13.

      preserve: BW in *The Crystal Goblet*, ed. Jacob, pp. 198–9.

      know: Gill to Desmond Chute, 10 June 1928 (*Letters of Eric Gill*, ed. Shewring, p. 232).

235   *Preference':* Gill to SM, 22 July 1928.

236   *job':* BW, 'Eric Gill', *MR*, vol. XLI, no. 3 (1958) p. 1.

237   *originality: Fleuron 6* (1928) pp. 96–7.

      documented: Ibid. p. 206.

238   *experience':* 'Mr Morison as "Typographer"', p. 16.

242   *smoother':* MSR, series 270 – 16pt.

      again: TDO, series 270, pp. 4–5.

243   *use':* Tally, p. 36.

      type: Mardersteig to SM, 20 Dec 1928.

244   *Mardersteig:* TDO, series 270, pp. 7–8.

      "watersheds"': Tally, pp. 33–4.

246   *him':* BW home, 13 Dec 1927.

      Corp^n.: Gill to BW, 21–2 Jan 1929.

247   *back:* BW to Gill, 1 Feb 1929 (William Andrews Clark Library).

248   *pages:* SM to Cleverdon, 30 Aug 1928.

      on': SM to Cleverdon, 15 Dec 1928.

CHAPTER II

255   *success:* See review in the *Progressive Printer*, Apr 1929 (quoted in *MR*, vol XXVIII, no. 230 (1929) p. 6).

256   *prison: The Testament of Beauty*, IV 433 ff.

257   *monarchies:* Ibid. IV 270 ff.

259 *available*: Matrices were available by July (*MSR*, series 270 – 13pt).

261 *world*': The original of this letter seems to be lost. It is here quoted from P. M. Handover 'Stanley Morison at P.H.S.', in *The Times House Journal*, new series, vol. XI, no. 6 (May 1960) p. 100.

266 *matter*: BW, 'Eric Gill', *MR*, vol. XLI, no. 3 (1958) pp. 16–17.

267 *S.M.*: SM to BW, 29 Jan 1929. Mr and Mrs Rossi owned the Étoile.
comforters: SM to Holbrook Jackson, 3 Dec 1928 (William Andrews Clark Library, Los Angeles).

268 *elsewhere*: BW to Gill, 25 May 1929.
word': SM to Mrs Morison, 29 May 1929.
John Bell': SM to Pollard, 19 July 1929.
Arts et Métiers Graphiques: no. 23 (1931) pp. 225–9.

269 *newspapers*: Pollard to SM, 12 Mar 1929.

270 *himself*: In *The Times* Archives. (Morison must have written it soon after his arrival, because the Monotype recutting of Cloister, completed in August 1929, is mentioned in a marginal postscript note.)

271 *Chief Proprietor*: Morison privately kept another for himself: no limited-edition statement should ever be taken at its word.
in 1702: Morison had bought a copy in 1923, and illustrated it in *Four Centuries* and 'The French National Printing Office'.

274 *recutting*: SM to Updike, 30 Oct 1929.
classes: SM to Cleverdon, 3 Jan 1930.

276 *maniac*: Van Krimpen to SM, 24 Feb 1930.
qualities: SM to van Krimpen, 3 Mar 1930.

277 *&c.*: SM to BW [end June 1930].
November: Mrs Alexander to Updike, 28 Nov 1930.

282 *down*': Gill to BW, 13 May 1930.
won: Morison's own views were given at length to 'a Newspaper World representative' (BW) in an interview printed in the *Newspaper World*, 20 December 1930, pp. 25-6.

CHAPTER 12

285 *manner*': *Printing The Times since 1785* (1953) p. 60. For changes in *The Times* from 1908, see *The History of The Times*, vol. III and vol. IV, pt I, and *Printing The Times*, pp. 55–60.
vulgar: *Printing The Times*, p. 64.
Ionic: Ibid. pp. 165 ff.
itself: Ibid. p. 167.

286 *publishers*': *Memorandum on a Proposal to Revise the Typography of The Times* (1930) p. 3.

289 *design*: Ibid. p. 31.

290 *was*: Ibid. pp. 6, 23 and 35.

290 *favoured:* ' *The Times* New Roman: Cutting and Designing the New Type', in *The Times House Journal* (1932).

Perpetua: In this respect, Morison put Bell and Perpetua together; see above, p. 205, and also *Tally,* p. 75.

Urgent': TDO, series 239, p. 12.

291 *use: Printing The Times,* p. 167.

types: Minutes of meeting, 28 Jan 1931.

292 *Perpetua: Printing The Times,* p. 168.

line: Tally, p. 89.

Lardent: Cited by Moran, p. 22.

on: Parker and Melis, *Inventory of the Plantin–Moretus Museum Punches and Matrices,* p. 36; *Type Specimen Facsimiles,* ed. J. Dreyfus (1963) p. 9; A. F. Johnson in the *Library,* 4th ser., vol. XVIII (1937–8) pp. 201–11; and *The Type Specimen of Delacolonge,* ed. H. Carter (1969) pp. 50–1.

293 *ready:* TDO, series 327, pp. 1–2.

diary: 4 June 1931.

296 *mind':* Barrington-Ward diary, 29 July 1931.

problem: Printing The Times, p. 68.

staff: Board minutes.

297 *here':* Postcard to Pollard, early Nov 1931.

nearly £2000: F. G. Easto to W. I. Burch, 7 July 1931.

298 *dilemma:* He wrote to both on 24 June.

299 *printed:* Easto to Lints Smith, 27 Sept 1932.

changed: Mechanical Department Report, *c.* 26 Sept 1932.

300 *over:* Barrington-Ward diary, 1 Oct 1932.

Mardersteig: SM to Simon, 8 Oct 1932; Mardersteig to SM, 20 Oct 1932.

301 *himself:* Menu; Barrington-Ward diary, 29 Oct 1932.

cost £3000: Easto to Lints Smith, 14 Dec 1934.

2 April: Easto and SM to Lints Smith, 2 Apr 1936.

CHAPTER 13

303 *terms:* Pollard to SM, 16 July, and SM to Pollard, 19 July 1929; SM to Pollard, 10 Feb 1930.

304 *edition:* SM to Pollard, 4 Mar 1930.

years: Moran, p. 24. The original wood block was seen by Mr Allen Hutt at the *Daily Worker*'s printers *c.* 1933–4, but it was probably destroyed soon after.

Well of Truth: BW to Gill, 28 Jan 1930.

sensation': The menu for the Double Crown dinner was a pastiche of

Dawks's *News-Letter* style by S. C. Roberts, relating to current typographic events and persons, set in Dawks's own types (rediscovered by Blake at Sheffield).

305 *revelation'*: Pollard to SM, 6 June 1930.
Morison: BW home, 17 Apr 1931.

306 *H[ewitt]*: SM to Heal, 15 Aug 1931.

307 *notice*: SM to Heal, 16 Aug 1931.
him: SM to Pollard, 24 Dec 1930.

309 *Newspaper Room*: SM to Horton, 9 May 1931.
Ichabod Dawks: Pollard to SM, 21 Mar 1932. He bequeathed his books, including those given to him by Morison, to the London Library.
design: Updike to Morison, 28 Oct 1929; MSR, series 341 – 14pt and 12pt, and TDO, series 341, p. 1.

311 *Dec 31*: SM to J. Mills Whitham, 18 Dec 1932.

312 *lot*: SM to BW, 11 Jan 1933. The Ludlow typesetting machine cannot letter-space as finely as the Monotype.
today's: SM to BW, 9 Jan 1933.
moving: SM, Memorandum to the Chief Proprietors, 1 July 1959.

313 *places*: Barrington-Ward diary, 2 Jan 1934.
Private Printing Office: Ibid. 13 Apr 1934.

314 *form'*: Ibid. 25 May 1934.
view': Temperley to Barrington-Ward, 30 Oct 1934 (in Birrell & Garnett file of SM's correspondence).
London University: Pollard to SM, 28 Aug 1934; SM to Pollard, 29 Aug.

315 *cabled'*: SM to Pollard, 9 Jan 1933.
was sent: John Carter in *SM, an Original Member of the Double Crown Club* (1968) pp. 21–2.

316 *so*: SM to Blake, 29 Mar 1933.

318 *Libraries*: R. Ettinghausen, *Rare Books and Royal Collectors* (1966) pp. 178–81.
Morison): Barrington-Ward diary, 12 Apr 1934.
Sidney Squires: Notes towards a Specimen of the Ancient Typographical Materials principally collected and bequeathed to the University of Oxford by Dr John Fell d. 1686, vol. 1 (1953) p. 3.
in 1566': Handlist, p. 21.

319 *Mori'*: SM to van Krimpen, 11 Oct 1930.

320 *lands*: SM to van Krimpen, 13 Mar 1933.

321 *Macy)*: Mardersteig to SM, 7 May 1932.
bastarda: SM to van Krimpen, 3 Aug 1932.

322 *forty*: SM to van Krimpen, 13 Sept 1934.

322 *concerned*: BW to Gill, ? first half of 1932.

323 *fine*: BW home, after Christmas 1931.

324 *peace'*: BW home, *c*. Sept 1934.

war: P. M. Handover, 'Stanley Morison at P.H.S.', *The Times House Journal*, new series, vol. XI, no. 6 (May 1960) p. 101.

Highgate: He died on 13 October 1932, aged seventy-six (death certificate).

experience': Information from Miss Lodge.

CHAPTER 14

333 *down*: Lewis to SM, 10 Jan 1935.

Monday: SM to Lewis, 11 Jan 1935. James MacLehose had shared apprenticeship with the first Daniel Macmillan at a bookseller's in Glasgow, where James later set up as a printer. His sons Norman and James married Daniel's brother Alexander's daughters Olive and Mary in 1886 and 1896, respectively. (C. L. Graves, *Life and Letters of Alexander Macmillan* (1910) p. 373.)

334 *job*: Roberts, *Adventures with Authors* (1966) p. 67.

himself: *Two Men*, pp. 15–16.

336 *thing*: SM to Lewis, 25 July 1934.

out: SM to Lewis, 30 July 1934.

337 *Curwenpressish'*: SM to Lewis, 16 Apr 1935.

advantage: SM to Lewis, 20 May 1935.

338 *off'*: Lewis to SM, 14 June 1935.

Vichy: SM to BW, 4 Sept 1935.

339 *Stanley Morison*: SM to Barrington-Ward, [8] Sept 1935.

340 *Philistines*: SM to BW, from Leningrad, mid-Sept 1935.

city': SM to BW, 16 Sept 1935.

well: SM to Lewis, *c*. 10 Oct 1935.

bode well: Van Krimpen to SM, 2 July 1935.

341 *John Holroyd-Reece*: SM to van Krimpen, 19 Nov 1935.

liability: Mardersteig to SM, 25 Nov; SM to Mardersteig, 30 Nov 1935.

342 *company*: SM to van Krimpen, 19 Dec 1935.

founts': SM to BW, 9 July 1931.

343 *drawings*: SM to van Krimpen, 16 June 1933.

Romein': Van Krimpen to SM, 22 July 1933, and 17 Sept 1934.

year: *MR*, vol. XXXV, no. 4 (1936–7), and vol. XXXVI, no. 4 (1938).

344 *proof*: SM to van Krimpen, 5 Mar 1932.

detail: Van Krimpen to SM, 26 July 1932; SM to van Krimpen, 4 Mar 1933.

344   *types:* SM to van Krimpen, 28 Nov; van Krimpen to SM, 2 Dec; SM to van Krimpen, 13 Dec 1935.

      conclusive: Van Krimpen to SM, 16 Dec 1935.

345   *"pub crawling"':* SM to van Krimpen, 19 Dec 1935.

      remains: SM to van Krimpen, 30 Dec 1935.

347   *November 1937:* TDO, series 453, p. 2; MSR, series 453 – 14pt.

      till 1957: H. Carter and G. Buday, 'Nicolas Kis and the Janson Types', in *Gutenberg Jahrbuch* (1957) pp. 207–12.

      out: SM to Simon, 15 Nov 1935.

349   *Press:* SM to Updike, 15 Sept 1937.

      egoism: SM to Updike, 23 Mar 1937.

350   *happened:* SM to Blake, 3 May 1936.

CHAPTER 15

351   *G.P.O.:* F. Marcus Arman, 'The Issued Stamps of King Edward VIII', in *Philatelic Bulletin,* vol. 6, no. 4 (1968) pp. 8–10.

352   *but £36-ers:* SM to Pollard, 29 Aug 1936.

      about: SM to Gill, 22 Feb 1935.

      them: SM to Gill, 20 Feb 1935.

353   *in:* SM to Gill, 22 May 1936.

355   *Jesus Christ:* SM to Gill, 22 and 25 Aug 1936.

      done: SM to Gill, 27 Aug 1936.

355   *wages:* SM to Gill, 7 Sept 1936.

358   *tables:* SM to Gill, before 16 Sept 1936.

359   *exceedingly:* Gill to SM, 16 Sept 1936.

360   *sin:* SM to Gill, 26 Sept 1936.

      &c.: SM to BW, 3 Feb 1936.

361   *trowel:* SM to Barrington-Ward, 6 Feb 1936.

      opinion': D. McLachlan, *In the Chair* (1971) p. 118.

363   *things':* Barrington-Ward diary, 31 Oct 1935.

      year: SM to Pollard, 17 Apr 1936.

      material: SM to Porter Garnett, 17 Mar 1936.

      'in charge': SM to Pollard, after 11 June 1937.

365   *thing:* SM to Barrington-Ward, 4 Feb 1938.

      me: Lewis to SM, 16 Feb 1939.

366   *triumph:* SM to Lewis, 17 Feb 1939.

367   *Pope:* Proc. Brit. Acad., vol. XL (1955) pp. 247–51.

      subject: SM to Lewis, 19 Apr 1937.

368   *him):* Crutchley to SM, 2 Sept 1938.

      bad: Gill to BW, 22 Dec 1937. The engravings of Beatrice are nos. 1, 2, 3, 5–8, 10–17, 19–22, 24 and 25.

369 *thank-offering*: SM to Lewis, 7 Dec 1938.
suggested: *History of The Times*, vol. IV, pp. 929–31.
people': Ibid. p. 939; compare McLachlan, *In the Chair*, pp. 146–8.

370 *Barnes-worthy*: SM to Barrington-Ward, 24 Sept 1938.
afternoon': *Two Men*, p. 38.
all: SM to Pollard, 28 Sept 1938.
influence: SM to Gill, 6 Apr 1938.

371 *paper*: H. Wickham Steed, *The Press* (1938) pp. 74–80, 249–50;
Barrington-Ward diary, 10 Nov 1938.
Beatrice: SM to Barrington-Ward, 27 Mar; to B.W., 9 Mar 1939.
Updike: SM to Updike, 2 May 1939.

372 *Street*: SM to Updike, 24 Aug 1939.
work: SM to Mrs Alexander, 13 Sept 1939.

373 *The Times*: SM to Wickham Steed, 8 Sept 1939.
something: SM to Howe, 8 Sept 1939.
elsewhere': SM to Barnes, 16 Sept 1939.

374 *come*': SM to Pollard, 8 Aug 1939.
properly: SM to Pollard, 4 Oct 1939.

375 *business*: SM to Howe, 1 Dec 1939.
days: Ibid.

376 *Politicians*: SM to Mrs Alexander, 15 Feb [1940].

379 *amenity*: Barrington-Ward diary.

380 *to 1690*: SM to Pollard, 9 Jan 1941.

381 *trades*': SM to Mrs Alexander, 13 Jan 1941.
Haut-Brion: SM to Barrington-Ward, 19 Feb 1941.
Italy: C. Webster and N. Frankland, *The Strategic Air Offensive in Europe, 1939–45*, vol. 1 (1961) pp. 157, 215, 463.

382 *bombing*: SM to C. E. Carrington, 23 Apr 1941.

CHAPTER 16

388 *sleep*: BW home, *c.* mid-May 1941.
itself': SM to Howe, *c.* 19 July; 29 July 1941.
loss: SM to Howe, 22 Aug 1941.

389 *perished*': Updike to SM, 2 July 1941.
rooms: SM to Updike, 20 Aug 1941.
suspected': Updike to SM, 30 Sept 1941.

390 *editorship*: Barrington-Ward diary, 3 Oct 1941.
Morison: See especially McLachlan, *In the Chair*, p. 264.

392 *answer*: Barrington-Ward diary, 1 Apr 1941.
it: Ibid. 2 Apr 1941.
well-timed: Ibid. 5 May 1941.

392   *September:* J. E. Wrench, *Geoffrey Dawson and Our Times* (1955) p. 440.
husband: Barrington-Ward diary, 11 June 1941 (SM's account is, perhaps, overstated).

393   *Thurs.:* SM to Mrs Carr, 28 July 1941.
indifference: SM thought him intensely reluctant to go; see McLachlan, *In the Chair* p. 180.
see: Dawson diary, 1 Oct 1941 (quoted in Wrench, *Geoffrey Dawson*, p. 446).
died': Barrington-Ward diary, 26 Sept 1941.
'*The World*': To Rupert Hart-Davis, about to commission a 'fox' device for his firm.

394   DELIGHTED: SM to Stone, 22 and 24 Dec 1943.
him: Stone to SM, 10 Dec 1944; SM to Stone, 12 Dec 1944.
service': SM, *English Prayer Books*, 3rd ed. (1949) p. 179.
world: SM to Howe, 29 July 1941.

395   '*aspect*': SM to Updike, 9 Dec 1941.
treated: SM to Nash, 11 Mar 1942.
association: In *Updike: American Printer*, pp. 56–66.

396   *mother:* SM to Mrs Becker, 28 Jan 1942.
across: SM to BW, 19–27 Feb 1942.
Imprint: Dwelly to SM, 1 Jan 1942.

397   *exuberance:* SM to Dwelly, 14 Jan 1942.
week: SM to Dwelly, 16 June 1942.
20 years: SM to Dwelly, 19 Oct 1942.

398   *end:* SM to Gurney, 30 Dec 1942.

400   *regime:* SM to BW, 10 Apr 1942.
Perpetua: SM to BW, 24 July 1942.

401   *century':* SM to Steinberg, 13 May 1942.
careless: Rand to SM, 12 Sept 1942 (copy sent to Steinberg).
master: Lowe to SM, 17 Aug 1942.

402   *position:* SM to BW, 9 Sept 1942.

403   *hands:* SM to BW, 21–3 May 1943.
faithfully': SM to BW, 30 Sept 1943.
boards'): SM to Howe, end July 1941.
gain': SM to Meynell, 19 Feb 1942.
Literary Supplement: Barrington-Ward diary, 4 July 1942; SM to BW, 1 July 1942.
work': Barrington-Ward diary, 29 Sept 1943.
1939: Ibid. 17 Jan 1944.

404   *The Times:* McLachlan, *In the Chair*, pp. 237–8.
working: Barrington-Ward diary, 21 Mar–17 May passim; Carr-Morison correspondence, 21 Mar–3 May 1944.

404   *Barrington-Ward:* Barrington-Ward diary, 10 Oct 1943.

405   *noted:* Ibid. 16 Nov 1944.

406   *Press:* SM, memorandum to Barrington-Ward, 30 Nov 1944.

407   *book:* SM to Mrs Carr, 9 Mar 1945.
     help: Information from Col. Ivor Fraser; SM to Stone, 18 May–17 June 1944.

408   *loyalties:* Jerrold to SM, 20 Mar; SM to Jerrold, 28 Apr; Jerrold to SM, 16 May 1944.
     Morison: 1 Sept 1944.
     editor: Mrs Law to SM, 4 Apr 1944.
     whole': SM to Mrs Law, 28 June 1944.
     me': Lewis to SM, 20 Oct 1944.
     night: SM to Lewis, 6 June 1944.

409   *well:* SM to Dreyfus, 14 June 1945.
     output: Van Krimpen to SM, 3 Aug 1945.
     problems: SM to van Krimpen, 28 Dec 1945.

410   *circles:* SM to van Krimpen, 17 Apr 1946.
     superfluous: SM to van Krimpen, 18 Sept 1946.
     improved: Barrington-Ward diary, 28 May 1945.
     Barrington-Ward: Ibid. 11 July 1945.
     England': Derek Hudson, *Writing Between the Lines* (1965) p. 163.

411   *Juifs:* SM to Mme Margot Zehrer, 25 Jan 1943.
     Church: *Times Literary Supplement,* 6 Oct 1945.
     feeling: Barrington-Ward diary, 8 Oct 1945.

412   *wonderful:* Goudy to SM, 3 June 1946.

413   *on:* Barrington-Ward diary, 24 June 1946.
     maintain"': Ibid. 29 July 1946. The quotation is from the end of Marvell's 'Horatian Ode on Cromwell's Return from Ireland'.
     1948: Ibid. 7 Mar 1946.
     there: Ibid. 28 Apr 1947.
     asked: Memo to Barrington-Ward, 17 June 1947.

414   *him:* SM to Astor, 2 Sept 1947.

415   *The History:* SM to C. S. Kent, 13 Oct 1947.

416   *now':* Barrington-Ward diary, 15 Oct 1947.
     inevitable': *The History of The Times,* vol. IV, p. 989.

CHAPTER 17

417   *Century:* SM to Pargellis, 8 July 1946.

419   *Wing Foundation:* Pargellis to SM, 8 Dec 1947.
     me: SM to Pargellis, 30 Dec 1947.

420 *History:* SM to Wickham Steed, 5 Oct 1950.
live': On 25 Oct; see Wrench, *Geoffrey Dawson,* p. 66.

421 *fact:* SM to BW, 8 May 1948.

424 *home:* BW home, *c.* end July 1946.

425 *good:* SM to Stone, 17 Dec 1946.

426 *judges:* SM to Stone, 24 Feb 1949.

428 *Maurdramnus:* SM to Steinberg, 28 Nov 1946.
reign': Latin *Script,* p. 10.

429 *contrived:* SM to Lowe, 30 May 1947.

430 *in:* SM to van Krimpen, 14 Sept 1948.
mood': SM to van Krimpen, 9 Feb 1948.

431 *Press:* SM to van Krimpen, 8 Sept 1950.

432 *patience:* SM to Mardersteig, 9 Aug 1951.
Kent: Barrington-Ward diary, 21 May 1947.
bit: Ibid. 28 May 1947.

434 *faced:* Memorandum written in 1949, pp. 3–4, 9–10.

435 *Editorial Manager:* SM to Wickham Steed, 5 Oct 1950.

436 *interesting':* Beaverbrook to SM, 20 Sept 1949.
time: SM to Beaverbrook, 20 July 1951.
peace: Beaverbrook to SM, 6 June 1950.
indeed': Beaverbrook to SM, 30 Apr 1951.

437 *supply:* Ibid.

438 *cannot:* SM to Barnes, 6 Aug 1951.

439 *they:* SM to Beaverbrook, 13 Feb 1952.

442 *desirable:* SM to Barnes, 18 Mar 1949.
Universal Church: SM to Barnes, 6 Aug 1951.

443 *say:* Lowe to SM, 15 May 1951.

444 *tried:* SM to Lowe, 8 June 1951.

446 *stamp':* SM to van Krimpen, 5 Dec 1952.
test it again: SM to Pargellis, 12 July 1948.

447 *elsewhere:* SM to Wells, 8 Apr 1953.

448 *for:* SM to Wells, 10 Apr 1953.
studies: SM to Pargellis, 27 Aug 1953.

CHAPTER 18

452 *arguments:* SM to Pargellis, 27 Aug 1953.
desire: SM to Silcock, 16 Dec 1953.

453 *years:* SM to Mathew, 24 June 1952.

455 *pictures:* SM to Mary Alexander, 1 July 1953.
Lowe: Lowe to SM, 22 May 1954.

456 *out:* SM to Benton, 25 July 1949.

457 *it*: Memorandum, 12 Sept 1955. Barrington-Ward must have lodged the quotation from Marvell in his mind (see above, p. 414).

458 *throughout'*: SM to Beaverbrook, 19 Sept 1952.
so am I: SM to Beaverbrook, 29 Sept 1954.

459 *I caught 2*: SM diary 1955.

460 *Ford Foundation*: SM to Beaverbrook, 31 Aug 1955.

462 *deserves*: SM to van Krimpen, 5 Mar 1956.
made: Van Krimpen to SM, 12 Mar 1956.

464 *innovate*: SM to Aaron Burns, 2 Aug 1961.
coin: Memorandum, 29 Nov 1962.

465 *signified*: SM to Roberts, 8 Aug 1957.

469 *strain*: SM to BW, 21 Nov 1957.

470 *Frederick II)*: SM to BW, 26 Jan 1958.
P.H.S.: SM to BW, before 11 Feb and 11 Feb 1958.

472 *harm*: SM to Mathew, mid-Nov 1957.
weeks': SM diary, 8 Mar 1958.

475 *obituary*: Memorandum, 12 Apr 1958.

476 *right'*: SM to Mathew, mid-1958.
Chief Proprietors: SM to Mathew, 11 June and 10 Dec 1958.
idea: SM to Mathew, 25 Sept 1958.

477 *Beaverbrook*: SM diary, 6 May 1959.

478 *from*: SM to Mathew, 23 June 1959.
eminent: SM to Mathew, 4 Nov 1960.
write it)': SM to Roger Fulford, 13 Aug 1959.

CHAPTER 19

479 *present*: SM to Barnes, *c*. Apr 1960.

480 *hands*: SM to Jammes, 19 Mar 1958.

481 *printer*: *Two Men*, p. 46.

482 *money*: Barnes to Morison, 17 May; Morison to Barnes, 24 May 1960.
Bless him: SM to Janet Stone, 1 Oct 1960.

483 *Theodosius*: SM to Janet Stone, 5 Mar 1961.
than the frog': SM to James Wardrop, 6 Sept 1954.

484 *activities*: Schmoller to SM, 29 June 1959.
Golden Books': Schmoller to SM, 7 July 1957.

485 *was*: SM to Stone, 6 Dec 1954.

486 *Stanley Morison*: SM to Janet Stone, 4 Dec 1957.
printed: SM's address on the subject, originally delivered to the Art Worker's Guild in 1958, was printed by Harold Seeger and Albert Sperisen at the Black Vine Press, San Francisco, and published by the Book Club of California in 1959.

487   *war'*: Letters from Lord Avon, 28 May 1968.
    negotiation: SM to Eden, 16 Aug 1961.
    loss: SM to Eden, 10 Nov 1961.
    so: SM diary, 20 Oct–3 Nov 1961.
488   *glass*: SM to Lord Avon, 1 Apr 1964.
    changed': Moran, p. 29.
    appropriate': SM to Wells, 19 Nov 1958.
489   *bus*: SM to Barnes, summer 1959.
490   *meetings*: SM to Pargellis, 31 Aug 1960.
    felt: SM to BW, 8 Apr 1961.
491   *July'*: SM to Lowe, 1 May 1961.
    Newspaper: SM to Lowe, 4 Sept 1961.
    Britannica: SM to Lowe, 16 Jan 1961.
492   *logical*: SM to Lowe, 13 July 1962.
493   *word'*: Pargellis to W. McNeill Lowry, 4 Feb 1960.
494   *February 1960*: SM to Pollard, 5 Feb 1960.
    thereof: SM to Pollard, 15 Mar 1960.
    in 1951: Steinberg to SM, 11 May 1963.
495   *printer's*: SM to Roberts, 13 Mar 1962.
500   *years)'*: SM to Janet Stone, 21 Apr 1965.
501   *rest'*: SM to BW, 1 Oct 1962.
504   *types*: Piper to SM, 25 Aug 1967.
505   *country*: *Periodical*, vol. XXXVII, no. 299 (1967–8) p. 165.

CONCLUSION

507   *archaistic'*: SM, *English Prayer Books*, 3rd ed. (1949) p. 163.
511   *so do I, and did*: *Radio Portrait*, pp. 30–1, 36, 25–6.
    high a price: SM, 'Kingship and Christianity' (1956) p. 5.
    Catholic Church: SM, 'An Unacknowledged Hero of the Fourth Century, Damasus I 366–384' (1964) pp. 262–3.

INDEX

CO = conscientious objector; *EB = Encyclopaedia Britannica*;
SM = Stanley Morison; *TT = The Times*

Haut-Brion, Chateau 381

Havinden, Ashley (b. 1903), artist and advertising agent 157

Hazell, W. Howard (1870–1929), printer with Hazell, Watson & Viney 46, 232

Heal, (later Sir) Ambrose (1872–1959), of Heal & Son, amateur of writing-masters and other trades 217, 283, 305

Heal & Son, furnishers 85, 217, 222, 282, 283, 482

Hegner, Jakob (1882–1962), publisher and printer 180, 196, 213

Heinemann, William, publishers 150, 194, 199, 443

Hennessy, Sir Patrick (b. 1898), Chairman, Ford Motor Co. of Great Britain 457

Herald 70, 83

Herald League 61, 64

Heriot Watt College 402

Hewitt, Graily (1864–1946), calligrapher 40, 279, 306, 460

Hill, Sir George (1867–1948), numismatist, Director of the British Museum 223

Hiller, Wendy 423

Hobson, Charles (1887–1968), advertising agent 96, 99–101, 105, 106, 119, 123, 165–6, 173, 175, 178, 180, 202, 266, 270

Hofer, Philip (b. 1898), librarian and collector 417

Holbein, Hans 148, 455, 469, 470

Holborn restaurant 156, 167

Holmes, Sherlock 30, 52, 330, 334

Holmes, Walter (b. 1890), Communist writer and journalist 77, 157, 303

Holz, Heinrich 277

Hooper, Horace (1859–1922), publisher and promoter 284

Hopkins, Gerard Manley (1844–89), poet and Jesuit 144, 255–6

Hopkinson, Edmund (1870–1947), Advertising Manager of *TT* 268–9, 324, 469

Horfei, Luca (*fl. c.* 1585–90), calligrapher, 489

Hornby, C. H. St John (1867–1946), partner in W. H. Smith, founder of Ashendene Press 140, 152, 296, 300, 460

Horne, Herbert 44

Horsman, Dorothy, production manager, Victor Gollancz 238

Horton, Ronald 294, 307–8

Houghton Mifflin, publishers 470

House, Col. E. M. (1858–1938), statesman 459, 494

Howard, G. Wren (1893–1968), publisher with Jonathan Cape 151, 167

Howe, Ellic (b. 1910), historian of printing and the irrational 373, 388, 394

Hugel, Baron Friedrich von 505

Humphries, Eric (1894–1968), printer, Lund Humphries 109, 121

Hutchins, Robert Maynard (b. 1899), Chancellor of Chicago University 455, 456, 496

Hutchinson, Francis Ernest (1871–1947), Canon of Worcester 411

Huxley, T. H. 34

Hypnerotomachia Poliphili (1499) 125–6

Imprimerie Nationale (earlier Royale), Paris 97, 120–1, 130, 199, 203, 227, 245

Imprint, The 21, 44–55, 103, 234

Independent Labour Party 61, 62

Ingham, Ernest (b. 1894), Director of the Fanfare and later of London Press Exchange 178, 191, 222, 238

Insel Verlag 40, 93, 179

International Center for the Typographic Arts 463–4

Irving, Laurence (b. 1897), artist and writer, Director of *TT* 443, 482, 500

Ivins, William M. (1881–1961), curator of prints, Metropolitan Museum, New York 162, 200, 280

Jackley, George (1885–1950), comedian 322

Jackson, F. Ernest (d. 1945), lithographer and artist 44–5, 46, 48, 49

Jackson, Holbrook (1874–1948), critic, editor and author of books on printing and other good things of life 106, 108, 134, 166, 167, 181, 267

Jacobi, Charles T. (1854–1933), printer with Chiswick Press 56, 140

Jacobs, W. W. 52

Jammes, André 480–1, 489

Jannon, Jean (1580–1658), punchcutter and printer 203, 221

Ludlow typesetting machine 312, 337
Lund Humphries Ltd, printers 109, 450
Lyell Lectures 307, 427, 466–9, 489, 495
Lyttelton, George 76

Mabillon, P. Jean (1632–1707), Benedictine scholar and palaeographer 483
Macaulay, Rose (1881–1958), novelist and scholarly writer 279
MacDonald, Ramsay (1866–1937), Prime Minister 318, 325, 331
Mackenzie, William Andrew (1870–1942), journalist and philanthropist 76, 86
MacLehose, Robert, & Co., printers at Glasgow 333
Macmillan & Co., publishers 333, 371
McMurtrie, Douglas (1888–1944), printer and writer on printing 155, 371
Macy, George (1900–56), publisher, founder of the Limited Edition Club 320, 371
Maggs Brothers, antiquarian booksellers 140, 141, 157, 221, 318, 334–5
Maillol, Aristide 40
Malin, Charles (1883–1957), punchcutter and engraver 197, 202, 204, 207, 211, 221, 278
Manoel II (1889–1932), King of Portugal and book-collector 334–5, 408
Manze's fish shop 33
Manzoni, Giacomo (1816–89), Italian patriot, book-collector and writer on bibliography 156, 239
Marcellus II, Pope, see Cervini, Marcello
Marcolini, Francesce (fl. 1527–59), printer at Venice 240
Mardersteig, Hans (later Giovanni, b. 1892), of the Officina Bodoni, first at Montagnola then at Verona, writer on lettering and typography 145, 150, 171–2, 173–4, 176, 183, 186, 193–4, 198, 208, 211, 215, 228, 230, 239–44, 245, 274, 279, 300, 321, 342, 430–2, 461, 463, 485, 489
Maritain, Jacques 411
Marquette University 491
Marrot, H. V. 449
Martindale, Fr C. C., S.J. (1879–1963), theologian and writer 59

Marx, Karl 64, 257, 352, 353–4, 391, 439–41
Mary, Queen of Scots 198
Marzoli, Carla 489
Mason, J. H. (1875–1951), typographer and designer; started printing classes at London County Council Central School of Arts and Crafts 44–9, 54, 55
Mathew, Arnold (1852–1919), bogus bishop 79–82
Mathew, Francis (1907–65), Manager of TT 433, 435, 443, 452–3, 470–8, 498–500
Mathews, Elkin, antiquarian booksellers 140, 222
Matson, Jack, Managing Director of Monotype Corporation 492
Maurdramnus, abbot of Corbie (fl. 765–81) 428–9, 443, 495
Maxwell, William (1873–1957), printer, of R. & R. Clark, Edinburgh 332–3, 402, 422–4, 469
Medici Society 39–40, 125–6, 133, 143, 455, 494
Meier-Graefe, Julius (1867–1935), writer on art 136, 147, 152
Meinhardt, Isolde 379
Mencken, H. L. 160, 162
Mende, Dieter 380
Mercator, Gerard (1512–94), Dutch scribe and cartographer 177, 274
Mergenthaler, Ottmar (1854–99), inventor of the Linotype machine 22
Merrymount Press, see Updike, D. B.
Meynell, Alice (1847–1922), essayist and poet 52, 58, 61
Meynell, Everard (1882–1926), writer and antiquarian bookseller 46, 58, 59, 85
Meynell, Francis (b. 1891), designer of books and advertisements, publisher and poet 56–61, 153, 157, 237, 267–8, 345, 404, 450, 504; at Burns & Oates 53, 56–61, 87; Romney Street Press 61; women's suffrage and conscientious objection 61–4, 76; bails SM 70; at Pelican Press 70–1, 76, 83–5, 96, 116; Assistant Editor of Daily Herald 83; 'Russian diamonds' 92; farewell dinner 98; Fleuron Society 108; and imprint 112; contributes to Fleuron 1 129, 131; Nonesuch Press 129, 221, 324

554

Meynell, Gerard T. (1877–1942), printer at Westminster Press and joint editor of *Imprint* 44–56, 116, 150, 167, 170, 196, 220–1, 234, 507, 518

Meynell, Hilda (*née* Saxe) 73

Meynell, Wilfrid (1852–1948), Catholic publisher, editor and writer 47, 56, 58–60, 86, 92

Middleton, R. Hunter 371

Milford, (later Sir) Humphrey (1877–1952), Publisher of Oxford University Press 184–5, 187–90, 200–1, 216–17, 252, 258–9

Miller & Richard, typefounders 118

Mills, G. H. Saxon ('Bingy', 1902–58), advertising agent 104–5, 113, 157, 475

Mills, W. Haslam (1874–1930), journalist and writer 100, 180

Monotype Corporation (up to 1931 Lanston Monotype Corporation, *q.v.* for U.S.A. Company) 106, 132, 146, 194, 216, 246–7, 253, 254–5, 375–6, 401–2, 409–10, 430–2, 502, 508

early history 116–18; produce type for *Imprint* 49–50

works at Salford 117–18, 121–2, 124–5, 165, 177, 211, 220–1, 235, 241–4, 295, 368, 372, 375, 388

Monotype Recorder 118–20, 121, 125, 127–8, 147, 150–1, 176–7, 192, 198–9, 209, 212, 221, 245, 246, 347–8, 368

SM's first connection 118–28; his programme pursued 164–5, 177–8, 196–7; subsequent relations 266–7, 342–8, 401–2, 409–10, 452, 492

and Cambridge University Press 127, 166–7, 454–5

Gill joins 232, 235–6, 255

and *TT* 270, 284; advertisement in 1912 Printing Supplement 43, and in 1929 Supplement 268–9

during War 372, 375–6, 380–1

post-war changes 409–10, 422, 430–2, 463

SM justifies his policy 460–2

Moore, A. R. 217, 283

Moore, George (1852–1933), novelist 181, 276–7

More, Thomas 148, 300, 455, 469, 482, 494, 497

Morel, Fédéric (1523–78), Parisian printer 120, 321

Mores, Edward Rowe (1730–78), antiquary and actuary; his *Dissertation upon English Typographical Founders and Founderies* (1778) 153, 182

Morgan, Charles (1894–1958), novelist 405

Mori, Gustav (1872–1950), historian of German type foundries 156, 319, 345

Morison, Alice Louisa (1863–1951), SM's mother 24–6, 29–30, 64, 69, 76, 77–9, 82, 92, 98, 247, 268, 436, 448

Morison, Arthur Andrew (1856–1932), SM's father 24–6, 29–30, 69, 324

Morison, Edith Marmorice (1899–1957), SM's sister 29, 64, 76, 82, 98, 448, 469

Morison, Jessie Emma (1888–1966), SM's sister 25, 76, 98, 448

Morison, Mabel (1872–1961), SM's wife 65–6, 67, 68–9, 70, 73–4, 76–8, 83, 92, 98, 103, 104, 150, 164, 170–3, 181, 206, 210, 484–5

Morison, Stanley (1889–1967)

LIFE

Born 23; childhood 26–8; first job 30, and visit to the British Museum 31; with London City Mission 32–3; conversion 35–6, and vocation, considered and rejected 56, 152; reads *TT* Printing Supplement (1912) 39; employed on *Imprint* 47, 50–6; at Burns & Oates 56–61, 76–90; conscientious objection 62–4, 68–73, 79, 513–15; marriage (1916) 68–9; imprisonment 73–9; at Pelican Press 70–1, 82–95; changes handwriting 83; moves to Cloister Press (1921) 96–110; foundation of *Fleuron* 110–13; first visit to Germany 111–13.

First contact with Monotype 116, 118–28; the *Fleuron* under way 129–35; abroad again 135–7; publishing plans 137–43, and writing 144–56; moves office 156–7; first visit to America (1924) 158–63; typographical adviser at Cambridge 166–7; editor of *Fleuron* 168; first visit to Mardersteig 171–4; with Wardes, and abroad again 174–83; *The Tapestry*

555

Morison, Stanley (*cont.*)

and Arrighi type 184–92; Gill and *Fleuron* 192–204; in America 200–2, 208–9, 218–19; break with Wardes, and separation 205–10; in Germany 213–15; moves to Fitzroy Square 217, 222, 225; Gill's type-designs 226–30, 232–6; controversy at the British Federation of Master Printers' Congress at Blackpool (1928) 230–2; *Fleuron 6* 236–8; Bembo cut 239–44; Bridges and *The Testament of Beauty* 252–6; adviser to *TT* 268–71; end of *Fleuron* (1930) 272–82.

Redesigning *TT* 283–302; writing 1929–31, 303–11; begins *History of TT* 312–14; Wise forgeries and Codex Sinaiticus 315–18; Reece and van Krimpen 319–22; pastimes 322–4; at Tangier 325–31; life at Cambridge 332–6; ill (1935), convalescent at Vichy and in Russia 336–40; van Krimpen and type-design 342–8; disputation with Gill 352–60; *TT*, *History* and *Literary Supplement* 360–6, 369–71; last pre-war works 367–9, 371–4; the War 374–83; flat, books and work destroyed (1941) 384–7.

Barrington-Ward editor of *TT*, and SM's new role 389–93; Dwelly and *English Prayer Books* 394–9; changes at Monotype 401–2, 409–10, 430–2; editor of *T.L.S.* (1945–8) 404–7, 410–12, 414–15; death of Barrington-Ward 413–16; Chicago 417–21; farewell to print 422–5; Bibliographical Society's Gold Medal and new work 426–9; Lord Beaverbrook and end of *History of TT* 429–30, 435–41; the future of *TT* 432–5, 441–5; refuses knighthood 446; revisits Johnston's house 447–8; old age 449–53.

Work for *EB* 455–6, 460; with Beaverbrook 457–60; van Krimpen and the theory of letter-design 461–4; *Fell* and Lyell lectures 465–8; illness 469–70; Cooper Brothers' Report, and retirement from *TT* 471–8; last works 479–81, 493–6; and friends 482–9; Russia again, and *EB* 489–92, 497–8; last of *TT* 498–500; last letter 502–3;

last illness and death 503–4; requiem and burial 505–6.

WORKS

Numbers refer to John Carter, *A Handlist of the Writings of SM* (1950), and P. M. Handover, 'A Second Handlist' (1959).

'Adoption of Latin Uncial' 1946 (137) 427–8

'American Penmanship' 1934 (102) 316

Andres Brun Calligrapher of Saragossa 1929 (57) 223, 239–40, 275, 320

Art of Carving (Trusler) 1931 (88) 310

Art of Printing 1938 (112) 369

'Black letter: its History and Current Use' 1937 (111) 347–8, 368

'*Black Letter*' *Text* 1942 (126) 384, 386, 388, 427

Brief Survey of Printing History and Practice 1923 (8) 106, 108, 138, 143, 147, 192

Byzantine Elements in Humanistic Script 1952 (149) 454–5

Calligraphic Models of Ludovico degli Arrighi 1926 (34) 195, 199, 202

Captain Edward Topham (89) and *Edward Topham, 1751–1820* 1933 (98) 310, 408

Catalogue of Specimens of Printing Types (Berry and Johnson) 1935 (105) 317

'Chancery Types of France and Italy' 1924 (22) 165, 166, 177

Cloister Press specimens 1921–2 (4) 100–1, 106, 147

Craft of Printing 1921 (3) 92–4, 132, 192, 427

'Decorated Types' 1928 (50) 183, 236–7

'Early Humanistic Script and the First Roman Type' 1943 (131) 384, 427, 459

English Newspaper 1932 (90) 279, 298, 307–9

English Prayer Books 1943 (129) 394–9, 402, 427, 438

English Writing Masters (Heal) 1931 (84) 283, 305–7

Eustachio Celebrino da Udene 1929 (56) 239–41

556

Morison, Stanley (cont.)

WORKS (cont.)

Works on SM: *Handlist* 483; *Druck-spiegel* article by Schmoller and Steinberg 483

Projected Works: sixteenth-century Italian writing-books 130, 132, 139, 489; 'Grammar of Fine Printing' 138–9, 173, 176; 'Use and Abuse of Italic' 183; 'Introduction to Modern Fine Printing' 193; revision of Reed's *Old English Letter Foundries* 245, 266–7, 274, 479; 'History of English Post Office' 311; 'Collected Papers' 373, 378, 384, 387; on God 381; biography of Knox and 'Journal of Reformation Studies' 458

love of London 23, 28, 79, 96, 105, 223, 336–7, 357, 449

interests: railways 26–7, 266, 268, 295, 334, 368–9; pantomimes 28, 64, 322–3; music 36, 222, 323–4; stamps 36–7, 297, 311, 326, 337, 351, 446; newspapers 40; cricket 43, 137, 277; book-collecting 131–2, 140–1; wine 180, 381, 398, 417, 487–8; Christmas 248, 322–3

early reading 31–2, 54

early political and rationalist opinions 34–5

religious views 35–6, 72, 79–82, 88, 114–15, 142, 354–60, 398

appearance 52, 103–4, 162, 429–30, 483

habitations 69, 83, 102, 206, 217, 222, 224–5, 273–4, 336–7, 375, 378–9, 380, 445, 449, 482–3

on Catholic Church 114–15, 142, 311, 354–7; and papacy 91–2, 114–15, 354–5

on typographic style 128–9, 335–6, 349–50, 463–4, 507

political views 158, 311, 325, 326, 331, 352–60, 390–1

on literature 161, 315, 406

reading: typographic 169; theological 194, 197

unmanned by death of parrot 225

on human relationship 249–51, 509–10

bad eyesight 265, 486

on capitalist system 305–6, 510

dislike of honours 318, 337, 446

attitude to Germany 360–2, 373, 380; Munich 369–71

'Vital Democracy' 390–1, and future of *TT* 433–4

on liturgy 396–7

on history of ideas 458, 459–60

on type-design 460–2, 485–6, 508

on old age and retirement 448, 451–3

value of tradition 501

Morley, Christopher (1890–1957) 412

Morning Post 475

Morrah, Dermot (b. 1896), leader-writer for *TT* (1934–61) 313, 364

Morris, William (1834–96), Socialist, poet, painter, calligrapher and founder of Kelmscott Press (1891) 20, 23, 40, 41, 44, 93, 125, 141, 156, 335, 336

Morrison, Emma (*née* Mason), SM's grandmother 25

Morrison, William, SM's grandfather 25

Moxon, Joseph (1627–1700), printer, punchcutter and map-maker, author of first comprehensive book on printing 84, 169, 191, 342

Moyllus, Damianus (*fl. c.* 1477–83), printer of first book on letter-construction 173, 215, 239, 312

Muir, P. H. (b. 1894), antiquarian bookseller 492

Munich 361, 369–71

Munzer, Egbert 380

Murray, D. L. (1886–1962), novelist, on staff of *TT* 365, 404–5

Murton, Reginald (1892–1965), SM's secretary, later with Charles Hobson 207, 225, 322, 424

Mynors, (later Sir) Roger (b. 1903), classical scholar 376

Namier, Sir Lewis B. (1888–1960), historian 410

Nash, John Henry (1871–1947), printer in San Francisco 28, 129, 142

Nash, Ray (b. 1905), writer on letter-design and calligraphy 316, 395

Nevins, Allan (b. 1890), historian 419

New Statesman 260

New York Herald-Tribune 285

559

Rogers, Bruce (*cont.*)
    suffers from bad hair-spacing 312
    to design SM's Collected Works 384
Rollins, Carl Purington (1880–1960), typographer with Yale University Press 142
romain du roi 19, 209, 245, 468
Rooses, Max (1839–1914), first director of the Plantin–Moretus Museum 117, 129
Rosenberg, Josephine 485, 487, 488
Rosetta Stone 31
Rothenstein, Sir William (1872–1945), painter and President of Royal College of Art 134, 451
Rothermere, Harold Harmsworth, Viscount (1868–1940), newspaper-owner, brother of Lord Northcliffe 268
Rowe, Mrs A. E. (d. 1965) 375, 384–6, 445, 450
Roxburghe Club 376
Royal Mint, decline of lettering at 464
Royen, J. F. van 276
Ruano, Ferdinando (*fl.* 1541–56), Spanish scribe working at Rome 156, 171
Rudge, William E. (1876–1951), printer at the Mount Vernon Press 159, 219
Ruppel, Dr Alois 367
Rupprecht Press 113
Russia, SM visits 339–40, 489–90
Rustic capitals 17
Rutherston, Albert (1881–1952), artist and illustrator 109, 166
Ruzicka, Rudolph (b. 1883), freelance artist and engraver 135–6, 139, 160

Sabon, Jacques (*fl.* 1557–80), punchcutter, manager of the Egenolff typefoundry 129
Sackville-West, V. (1892–1962), poet and novelist 248
St André, Bruges, abbey 36
St Bride Foundation Institute and Printing Library 33, 42, 131
St John, Christopher 63
Sandars Lectures 269, 307–9, 312, 326
Sandberg, W. J. H. B. 463
sans serif letters and type 17, 19, 55, 204–5, 226, 230, 231–2, 234, 266, 270, 467, 468
Santa Maria in Cosmedin, Rome 91, 502
Sassoon, Siegfried (1868–1967), poet 76, 166

Saturday Review of Literature 210
Schmoller, Hans (b. 1916), typographer and Director of Penguin Books 483–4
Scholderer, Victor (1880–1971), incunabulist, Deputy Keeper of Printed Books at British Museum 238, 279
Scholfield, A. F. (1884–1969), Librarian, Cambridge University Library 336
Schramm, P. E. 131
Schwabe, Randolph (1885–1948), artist and engraver 166
Scott, J. A. 166
Selfridge, Gordon (1858–1947), department-store owner 300
Servidori, Abate Domingo (*c.* 1724–90), author of *Reflexiones sobre la verdadera arte de escribir* (1789) 111, 171, 224
Shanks & Sons, P. M., typefounders 116–17
Shaw, G. Bernard (1856–1950), playwright and journalist 77, 98, 181, 257, 422–4
Shewring, Walter 235
Sidgwick, Frank (1879–1939), publisher 99, 167
Signature 347, 445, 449
Silcock, E. (b. 1888), Managing Director of Monotype Corporation 430, 492
Simon, Herbert (b. 1898), printer, Curwen Press 110, 450–1
Simon, Louis 168
Simon, Oliver (1895–1956), of Curwen Press, printer and editor of *Fleuron* and *Signature* 103–4, 108–13, 129, 132, 134, 136–7, 161, 163, 166, 167–8, 174–5, 180–1, 215, 282, 300, 321, 347, 445, 449–51
Simon, Ruth 168
Simons, Anna (1871–1951), calligrapher 40, 169
Sinibaldi, Antonio (1443–*c.* 1500), Florentine scribe 147
Sixtus V (1521–90), Pope 482, 489, 493, 495, 506
Smith, George (1879–1955), Glasgow City councillor and M.P. 77
Smith, Percy (1882–1948), designer of lettering 134, 449, 467
Smith, W. H., & Son, booksellers and stationers 39, 140, 295

Verini, Giovambattista (*fl. c.* 1525–40), author of books on writing and other subjects 417

Victoria and Albert Museum 54, 131, 148

Victoria House Printing Co. 70

Vox, Maximilien (b. 1894), typographer and designer 337

Wagstaffe, Christine 397

Wakefield, CO work-centre at 77–9, 303

Waldorf Hotel 379

Walker, (later Sir) Emery (1851–1933), pioneer of process-engraving, authority on typography, friend and partner of William Morris and T. J. Cobden-Sanderson 20, 45, 140, 141–2, 143, 178, 181

Walter, Catherine 338

Walter, John I (1739–1812), founder of *TT* 288, 338

Walter, John II (1776–1847), Chief Proprietor of *TT* 314

Walter, John III (1818–94), Chief Proprietor of *TT* 284, 365, 379, 440

Walter, John V (1873–1968), Joint Chief Proprietor of *TT* 284–5, 297–8, 381, 439, 440–1

Walter, Ralph (1871–1937), Director of *TT* 298, 338

Wanstead 23, 25

Warde, Beatrice (*née* Becker, 1900–69), Publicity Manager of Monotype Corporation, writer and lecturer 122, 169–70, 184, 202, 206–10, 246–7, 282, 294–6, 326–31, 502, 503
first meets SM 150–60, 161–3
comes to Europe 174–83
in London 174–5, 192–3, 197–200
'Musicae Typographia' 178, 192
and *Traité...de la musique* 192, 198
on eighteenth-century French typography and Fournier *le jeune* 198–9, 209
'Paul Beaujon' 200, 210
discovers Jannon 203
portrait by Gill 204, 266
goes back to U.S.A. 209–10
returns to live in London 221–3, 225, 228

Publicity Manager of Monotype 221, 266–7, 348, 402–3; on redesign of *TT* 294–6, 300
Fleuron 6 236, 238
SM's letter 248–50
Double Crown Club 267–8
on Gill 278, 304
on SM 318
SM stays with 379, 388
war-time visit to U.S.A. 396
at party for 'Shaw Million' 422–4

Warde, Frederic (1894–1939), typographer 143, 169, 173, 180, 184, 225, 236, 251; first meeting with SM 159–60, 163; comes to Europe 174–83; *Tapestry* 186, 191; article on Rogers 181, 199, 200; in London 174–5, 192–3; at Montagnola 186, 193–4, 197; modifies Arrighi type (Vicentino) 197, 198; returns to England 202–3; break with SM 206–9; and Pegasus Press 215; revisits England for cutting of Arrighi 228, 247–8

Wardrop, James (1905–1957), of Victoria and Albert Museum, writer on calligraphy 418–19, 451, 469

'War Economy' book production 399, 403

Warner, Sylvia Townsend (b. 1893), novelist 238

Warwick, CO work-centre at 74–5

Wasson, R. G. (b. 1898), banker and mycologist 465–6

Waterlow & Sons, printers 449

Watkin, E. I. (b. 1888), Catholic writer 57, 63

Wedgwood, James Ingall (1883–1951), clerical charlatan 79–80

Weeks, Sir Ronald (later Lord, 1890–1960), industrialist 432

Weil, Ernst (1891–1965), antiquarian bookseller 455

Weiss, Emil Rudolf (1875–1942), type-designer 136, 152, 169, 237, 238

Wellington, Irene 448

Wells, H. G. 76

Wells, James M. 446–7, 489, 503

Westminster Press 47, 49, 50, 55, 121

Westover, George (1886–1959) of Monotype Corporation, pioneer of film-setting 376, 431, 486